OSSIUM CARNES MULTAE

II

OSSIUM CARNES MULTAE

E

MARCI TULLII CICERONIS EPISTULIS

THE BONES' MEATS ABUNDANT

FROM THE
EPISTLES OF MARCUS TULLIUS CICERO

Reginaldus Thomas Foster and
Daniel Patricius McCarthy

fully cross-referenced together with
Daniel Vowles

THE CATHOLIC UNIVERSITY OF AMERICA PRESS
Washington, D.C.

The paper used in this publication meets the minimum
requirements of American National Standards for
Information Science—Permanence of Paper for Printed
Library Materials, ANSI z39.48-1984.

∞

Library of Congress Cataloging-in-Publication Data
Foster, Reginaldus Thomas, 1939– author.
Ossium Carnes Multae e Marci Tullii Ciceronis epistulis /
The bones' meats abundant from the epistles of
Marcus Tullius Cicero / Reginaldus Thomas Foster
and Daniel Patricius McCarthy.
pages cm
Includes bibliographical references and indexes.
ISBN 978-0-8132-3297-3 (pbk. : alk. paper) 1. Latin language—
Textbooks. I. McCarthy, Daniel P. (Daniel Patrick), author.
II. Title. III. Title: The bones' meats abundant from the
epistles of Marcus Tullius Cicero.
PA 2087.5F67 2015
478.2421—dc23
2015023750
· · ·
Neumagen School Relief, photograph courtesy of
Rheinisches Landesmuseum, Trier, second century A.D.
http://www.landesmuseum-trier.de/en/home/

"LATINITATIS CORPUS"

REGINALDO PROCURATORE
ADIUTORE DANIELE

QUINQUE IN VOLUMINIBUS

⌒

"LATIN'S BODY"

REGINALD BEING THE OVERSEER
DANIEL THE ASSISTANT

IN FIVE VOLUMES

Latinitatis Corpus: The "Body of Latin" is a way of speaking about an appreciation of the Latin language and through it an engagement with Latin writers and speakers throughout the history of western civilization. Through personal interaction with authors of every era and branch of knowledge and type of human experience, our own knowledge of western religions, sciences, and arts has increased, and the full range of human experience is made available.

As an appreciation of Latinity has grown within, the mingling with Latinity grows without. It includes decades of teaching the Latin language in our present day to anyone interested in learning, from the first session-class-meeting to the most fully developed association with authors of every age.

Teaching Latin during the academic term has given an opportunity to develop and test a proper method of drawing others into and guiding them in their dealing with the language. This method of teaching has been recorded in volume I, *Ossa Latinitatis Sola: The Mere Bones of Latin*, which presents the mere bones or skeletal structure of the language through one hundred and five encounters over three academic years. The reading sheets included in that volume consist of a collection of real Latin texts taken from sources of every age who become our guide and textbook. They contain innumerable examples to illustrate every aspect of the Latin language. In those Latin texts teachers are encouraged to seek and find examples in order to illustrate each aspect of the language and eventually to compose their own fresh collections of reading sheets annually.

To help teachers with this task of finding examples, you have here volume II, entitled, *Ossium Carnes Multae: The Bones' Meats Abundant*, which provides some fifty-one letters written by Cicero in their beautiful, functional fullness along with our commentary on nearly every phrase in which we illustrate specific examples of Latin usage present in these letters and cross-referenced to their corresponding encounters in the *Ossa* teaching book. To accompany these examples, we have also recorded recitations of the letters of Cicero, and we have composed our own school conversations to indicate how a teacher may use Cicero's texts from the first day. We call that collection volume III: *Os Praesens Ciceronis Epistularis: The Immediate Mouth of Cicero in His Letters.*

Another offering we are making is a collection of worksheets or exercises that direct the student in the learning of the language. We call these projects *ludi domestici* or "home games." The production of new *ludi* yearly for classes taught in Rome over several decades means that all we need to do now is collect them and arrange them according to their corresponding encounters of the Five Experiences. That volume IV of *Ludi* we call: *Ossibus Ludi Exercendis: Games for Exercising the Bones.*

The school work at Rome for decades provided the opportunity of visiting geographical and historical places, where the events of western history unfolded, while we were using original Latin texts as our guide. These texts have been collected, and we provide them in volume V under the title: *Ossibus Revisenda Migrantibus: Things—Places—Events to be Revisited, As Bones Roam About.*

We hope these our own five volumes of *Latinitatis Corpus: The Body of Latin* may appeal both to an academic community and more broadly to all those who are engaged in study, research, and teaching Latin, and may inspire them to produce similar works.

Besides these volumes, teaching Latin during the *Schola Latinitatis Aestiva*, "Summer School of Latin," is intended for more advanced study. The long summer evenings give particular opportunity to sit in a garden *sub arboribus*, "under the trees," to experience without end, *sine fine*, how the language was and is spoken.

Libraries will gain invaluable tools, and Latin teachers will find in this series the resources needed to fulfill their mission of drawing others into the documentation of human realities of western civilization expressed in Latin.

Varietas et ubertas Tulliani sermonis ipsa optima dux et magistra adhibeatur oportet ad usum linguae Latinae quam expeditissime comparandum. Nova quaedam ratio tradendae linguae Latinae exemplis illuminatur.

THE DIVERSITY AND THE RICHNESS OF CICERO'S SPEECH OUGHT TO BE USED AS ITSELF THE BEST LEADER AND TEACHER FOR ACQUIRING AS READILY AS POSSIBLE THE USE OF THE LATIN LANGUAGE. A CERTAIN NEW SYSTEM OF TEACHING THE LATIN LANGUAGE IS ILLUSTRATED WITH EXAMPLES.

CONTINENTUR

contents

IMAGINES | *illustrations* XV

EXORDIUM | *foreword* XVII
Antonio Salvi

PROLOGIUM | *prologue* XXIII
Shane Butler

PRAEFATIO | *preface* XXV
Sally Davis

LOCUTIONIS INDOLES AC NATURA CICERONIS IN EPISTULIS XXVII
the character and nature of speech in Cicero's letters

QUOMODO SIT HIC LIBER USURPANDUS XXXIX
in what manner this book is to be used

VOCABULORUM COMPENDIA LIII
abbreviations of words

∾

PARS PRIMA
EPISTVLARVM SVMMATIM
DELECTVS

1

part I: a choice of letters together

(contents continues)

PARS SECVNDA   177
EPISTVLARVM MINVTATIM
TRACTATVS
INTERPRETATIONE ADDITIS NECNON
COMMENTATIONE

part II: the treatment of the letters in detail
the translation added and also the commentary

Ossium letter N°	Reference	HEADING	T-P n°	part I page	part II page
1.	Q. Fr. II, 9 [11]	MARCUS QUINTO FRATRI SALUTEM	132	3	179
2.	Att. I, 5	CICERO ATTICO SAL.	1	5	186
3.	Fam. XVI, 4	TULLIUS TIRONI SUO S. P. D. ET CICERO ET Q. FRATER ET Q. F.	288	9	197
4.	Att. I, 6	CICERO ATTICO SAL.	2	13	211
5.	Fam. XIV, 12	TULLIUS TERENTIAE SUAE S. D.	415	15	215
6.	Att. I, 7	CICERO ATTICO SAL.	3	17	219
7.	Fam. VII, 10	M. CICERO S. D. TREBATIO	161	19	223
8.	Fam. I, 10	M. CICERO S. D. L. VALERIO IURIS CONSULTO	162	23	234
9.	Fam. XIII, 49	CICERO CURIO PROCOS.	163	25	238
10.	Fam. VII, 11	CICERO TREBATIO	167	27	241
11.	Att. I, 3	CICERO ATTICO SAL.	8	31	247
12.	Fam. XIII, 60	M. CICERO C. MUNATIO C. F. S.	164	33	254
13.	Att. I, 11	CICERO ATTICO SAL.	7	35	258
14.	Fam. XIV, 8	TULLIUS TERENTIAE SUAE S.	410	39	272
15.	Att. XI, 3	CICERO ATTICO SAL.	411	41	275
16.	Fam. XIV, 16	TULLIUS TERENTIAE SUAE S. D.	424	45	284
17.	Att. XI, 4	CICERO ATTICO SAL.	413b	47	288
18.	Fam. XIV, 6	SUIS S. D.	414	49	292
19.	Fam. II, 3	M. CICERO S. D. C. CURIONI	169	51	296
20.	Att. IV, 10	CICERO ATTICO SAL.	121	55	305
21.	Q. Fr. II, 7 [9]	MARCUS QUINTO FRATRI SALUTEM	120	57	311
22.	Fam. IX, 5	CICERO VARRONI	463	63	321
23.	Att. VII, 15	CICERO ATTICO SAL.	311	65	326

Ossium letter N°	*Reference*	Heading	T-P n°	part I page	part II page
24.	*Att.* VII, 20	Cicero Attico sal.	318	69	338
25.	*Fam.* XIV, 7	Tullius Terentiae suae s. p.	405	73	346
26.	*Q. Fr.* II, 6	Marcus Quinto fratri salutem	117	77	354
27.	*Att.* IX, 11A	Cicero imp. s. d. Caesari imp.	366	79	360
28.	*Att.* IV, 4b	Cicero Attico sal.	107	83	370
29.	*Fam.* II, 5	M. Cicero s. d. C. Curioni	176	85	374
30.	*Att.* XIV, 13b	Cicero Antonio cos. s. d.	717	87	381
31.	*Fam.* XIV, 18	Tullius Terentiae suae et pater suavissimae filiae, Cicero matri et sorori s. p. d.	306	93	396
32.	*Fam.* I, 3	M. Cicero s. d. P. Lentulo procos.	97	97	403
33.	*Q. Fr.* III, 3	Marcus Quinto fratri salutem	151	99	406
34.	*Att.* V, 6	Cicero Attico sal.	189	107	417
35.	*Att.* VI, 8	Cicero Attico sal.	281	109	424
36.	*Fam.* XV, 10	M. Cicero imp. s. d. C. Marcello C. f. cos.	239	113	433
37.	*Brut.* II, 2	Cicero Bruto sal.	839	117	442
38.	*Att.* III, 14	Cicero Attico sal.	70	119	450
39.	*Fam.* I, 6	M. Cicero s. d. P. Lentulo procos.	104	121	457
40.	*Att.* VII, 22	Cicero Attico sal.	320	123	462
41.	*Q. Fr.* I, 4	Marcus Quinto fratri salutem	72	125	470
42.	*Att.* II, 15	Cicero Attico sal.	42	133	484
43.	*Fam.* XV, 7	M. Cicero procos. s. d. C. Marcello cos. desig.	214	137	493
44.	*Att.* I, 2	Cicero Attico sal.	11	139	498
45.	*Fam.* VII, 5	Cicero Caesari imp. s. d.	134	141	503
46.	*Att.* VIII, 13	Cicero Attico sal.	348	149	515
47.	*Att.* X, 3a	Cicero Attico sal.	381	151	522
48.	*Fam.* V, 7	M. Tullius M. f. Cicero s. d. Cn. Pompeio Cn. f. Magno imperatori	15	153	528
49.	*Brut.* I, 14	Cicero Bruto sal.	913	157	536
50.	*Fam.* II, 1	M. Cicero s. d. C. Curioni	166	161	546
51.	*Att.* XVI, 5	Cicero Attico sal.	770	167	555

PARS TERTIA   575
QVINGENTA INSTAR EXEMPLORVM
INCISA SEV BREVILOQVIA
CICERONIS EPISTVLARIS

part III: five hundred clauses or tweets of Cicero in his letters
in the manner of examples

ADDITAMENTVM   605
ROMANORVM DE KALENDARIO

an addition
about the Roman calendar

APPENDICES   609

BIBLIOGRAPHIA | *bibliography*   611

INDICES   615

INDICES VNAS AD EPISTVLAS
indices for the letters alone

INDEX EPISTOLARVM HODIERNO MODO MEMORATARVM
index of letters mentioned by modern-day reference   617

INDEX EARVMDEM EX TEMPORIS RATIONE AB TYRRELL ET   619
PVRSER VSVRPATA
index of the same according to chronology employed by
Tyrrell and Purser

INDEX IPSAS SECVNDVM EXCIPIENTES   621
index according to the ones receiving them

INDEX VOCVM GRAECARVM | *index of Greek expressions*   623

INDICES NOSTRAM AD EARVM TRACTATIONEM SPECTANTES
indices referring to our treatment of them

KALENDARIA AD NOSTRAM COMPOSITA VTILITATEM   627
calendars composed for our own use

INDEX STRVCTVRARVM | *index of the structures*   628

INDEX EXEMPLORVM E LEXICO LEWIS ET SHORT HVC ADLATORVM   631
index of examples quoted here from the
Lewis and Short dictionary

Contents

INDEX DOCTRINARVM GRAMMATICO E LIBRO   640
GILDERSLEEVE ET LODGE DEPROMPTARVM
*index of the teachings taken from the grammar book of
Gildersleeve and Lodge*

INDICES INTER SE AD VOLVMINA "OSSA" ET "OSSIVM" RELATI
indices mutually referred back to the volumes "Ossa" and "Ossium"

ARGVMENTA: INDICIA PRIORIS HVIVSQVE VOLVMINIS RERVM   653
*subject matters: indicators of the material of the previous
and this volume*

TRANSVERSA RERVM CONSOCIATIO INTER VOLVMINA   662
"OSSA" ET "OSSIVM"
*cross-index of items between the volumes "Ossa"
and "Ossium"*

**INDICES MATERIAM TANGENTES QVINGENTORVM INCISORVM SEV
BREVILOQVIORVM CICERONIS EPISTVLARIS**
***indices touching on the content of five hundred clauses or tweets
of Cicero in his letters***

INDEX SVMMATIM SVMPTVS QVINGENTORVM INCISORVM SEV   720
BREVILOQVIORVM CICERONIS EPISTVLARIS ORDINE ALPHABETICO
*index of the 500 clauses or tweets of Cicero in his letters
taken together in alphabetic order*

INDEX FONTIVM QVINGENTORVM BREVILOQVIORVM   731
ATQVE IIS RESPONDENTIVM CICERONIS EPISTVLARVM
A NOBIS INVESTIGATARVM
*index of the sources of the 500 tweets of Cicero and
corresponding to them of Cicero's letters chosen by us*

INDEX NOMINVM RECENTIORVM | *index of modern names*   741

DE SCRIPTORIBVS | *about the authors*   743

ADIVTORES | *helpers*   745

AGNOSCENDA MERITA | *acknowledgments*   747

IMAGINES

illustrations

Our immense gratitude is expressed to the Biblioteca Medicea Laurenziana, Florence, Italy, for generously providing the digital images of the manuscripts of the letters which enrich the present volume. We readily acknowledge their conservation of these manuscripts over recent centuries and the care with which they have produced these beautiful digital images of each folio, along with their largesse in providing them for the benefit of our readers and all interested in the immortal words of Cicero.

The reference for each image, as requested, follows in Latin and Italian:

Firenze, Biblioteca Medicea Laurenziana, Ms. Plut. [A], f. [B]
Su concessione del MiBAC.
E' vietata ogni ulteriore riproduzione con qualsiasi mezzo.

Each image's Plutei manuscript shelf number (A) and folio (B) is as follows:

Letter	Image	Manuscript Shelf n° (Ms. Plut.)	Folio	Letter	Image	Manuscript Shelf n° (Ms. Plut.)	Folio
1.		49.18	33v	8.		49.09	18r
2.	1	49.18	50v	9.	1	49.09	228v
	2	49.18	51r		2	49.09	229r
3.	1	49.09	262v	10.	1	49.09	107r
	2	49.09	263r		2	49.09	107v
4.		49.18	51r	11.		49.18	50r
5.	1	49.09	244r	12.		49.09	232r
	2	49.09	244v	13.	1	49.18	52r
6.	1	49.18	51r		2	49.18	52v
	2	49.18	51v	14.	1	49.09	243v
7.	1	49.09	106v		2	49.09	244r
	2	49.09	107r	15.	1	49.18	156v

Letter	Image	Manuscript Shelf n° (Ms. Plut.)	Folio	Letter	Image	Manuscript Shelf n° (Ms. Plut.)	Folio
	2	49.18	157r		2	49.18	110v
16.		49.09	245r	36.	1	49.09	254v
17.		49.18	157r		2	49.09	255r
18.	1	49.09	243r	37.		49.09	174r
	2	49.09	243v	38.		49.18	75r
19.	1	49.09	19v	39.		49.09	5r
	2	49.09	20r	40.		49.18	123r
20.		49.18	84r	41.	1	49.18	26v
21.	1	49.18	32r		2	49.18	27r
	2 & 3	49.18	32v		3 & 4	49.18	27v
22.	1	49.09	136r	42.	1	49.18	65r
	2	49.09	136v		2	49.18	65v
23.	1 & 2	49.18	120v	43.	1	49.09	254r
24.	1	49.18	122r		2	49.09	254v
	2	49.18	122v	44.		49.18	50r
25.	1 & 2	49.09	243v	45.	1	49.09	104v
26		49.18	32r		2 & 3	49.09	105r
27.	1	49.18	142v		4	49.09	105v
	2	49.18	143r	46.		49.18	133r
28.		49.18	82v	47.	1	49.18	147r
29.		49.09	20v		2	49.18	147v
30.	1	49.18	198r	48.	1	49.09	69r
	2 & 3	49.18	198v		2	49.09	69v
31.	1	49.09	245r	49.	1	49.18	7r
	2	49.09	245v		2	49.18	7v
32.		49.09	3r	50.	1	49.09	19r
33.	1	49.18	41v		2 & 3	49.09	19v
	2 & 3	49.18	42r	51.	1	49.18	218v
	4	49.18	42v		2 & 3	49.18	219r
34.		49.18	90v		4 & 5	49.18	219v
35.	1	49.18	110r		6	49.18	220r

EXORDIUM

foreword

ANTONIUS SALVI

Cum primum volumen venerit ad finem, proximus liber sumit exordium, quo lingua Latina felicior evadat, utque legentibus animus constituatur paratior.

Saepenumero mens refertur ad praeteriti temporis spatium, cum iucunda quaedam agebantur. Commemorare liceat mihi pristina itinera quae florentibus annis suscepimus. Ego et Reginaldus quaedam loca invisere solebamus, quae antiquitate resipere videbantur, prae omnibus Formiam. Etenim libello aliquo instructi, ex sententiis Tullianarum epistularum collectis comparato, quae ad illud oppidum attinebant, lustrare solebamus urbana loca, parvum museum, maritimam oram, portum ipsum, ubi sedentes, quod de se narrabat scribebatque Cicero, legere consuevimus.

Ad sepulcrum tandem veniebatur ipsius Tullii, fictum quidem, in memoriam tamen illius nominis sempiternam redibamus. Accedebant interea nonnulli, qui de otii nostri et collocutionum insolentia mirabantur atque eadem opera de amissa sermonis Latini institutione conquerebantur.

Animum memoria offundit tot annorum, quibus una operati sumus, quibus ceteris cum sociis iucundissime sumus locuti, ipsius Urbis decora usurpantes et pristina verba. Novissime socius a nobis et comes quasi distractus Reginaldus in patriam remigravit, sed arta coniunctio numquam est intermissa.

Quid de scholis aestivis, ad quas undique gentium complures confluere solebant discipuli? Maxima autem cum iucunditate, absque illa molestia quae plerumque discipulos Latinam linguam discentes invadit, agebatur ludus, usque dum eidem in ipsa Horati villa imponebatur finis, ubi Bandusiae fons celebrabatur.

Quem locum obtineant Ciceronis epistulae

Noscitur epistulas Tullianas a Tirone collectas esse aliisque doctoribus, utpote cum pulcherrimas easdem haberent. Varia in ipsis reperiuntur argumenta—quod nostra quoque aetate usu venire solet—, quoniam quasi unum erat illius aetatis communicationis instrumentum. Hodie hanc ferme consuetudinem amississe nobis videmur, quandoquidem recentissima instrumenta ad celeritatem scribendi nos compulerunt. Cum multis in rebus tum maxime in scriptis exarandis neglegentia ac nimia festinatione plectimur.

Probe memini Reginaldum quosdam confecisse libellos, in quos omnes cuiusdam loci mentiones conferret, quae in epistulis Tullianis reperirentur. In iis—quod recordor—de Formiis, Caieta, Pompeiis argumenta et indicia sunt collecta. Quisque idem facere potest. Si sententias enim quasdam scrutamur, ad loca haec attinentes, easdemque enodare studemus, in ipsis locis residentes, certe maiorem haurimus vim ad illas intellegendas. Quocirca iucundior evadit inquisitio. Ut exemplum quoddam supponam, sic scribit Tullius in Formiano: "Ita dies et noctes tamquam avis illa mare prospecto, evolare cupio" (*Att.* IX, X, II). Sententia haec liquidius patet eandem legentibus et mare inibi prospectantibus.

Ceterum omnia cotidiana in epistulis narrantur, omnia quae illis et nostris temporibus hominibus accidere possunt. Procul dubio, aliae nunc sunt condiciones atque illis aetatibus. Tamen humanae res semper eaedem perstiterunt, hominum animi, sensus, affectiones. Sicut quisque pater, de Terentia et Tullia maximopere sollicitatur Cicero, dolet vehementer de amissa filia, gaudet visis amicis necessariisque. Sicut quisque patriae amator de reipublicae interitu maerore afficitur.

Peritiores Germani magistri quodammodo exterminare volunt Tullianas litteras, quippe quae non pertineant ad optimam Latinitatem. Quibus cogitationibus Reginaldus succensere solet, et merito quidem, quia nihil elegantius, nihil politius, nihil venustius illis operibus inveniri potest. Praeiudicata haec opinio ad nostram usque aetatem valuit. Exemplar quoddam sine iudicio est ab illis fictum alicuius perfectionis, quo constituto, singula pensantur.

Quae ratio potior epistularum intellegendarum habeatur

Abbas eximius Carolus Egger, recolendae memoriae, Operis Fundati "Latinitas" olim praeses, certamine quodam Vaticano interveniente, hanc docendi rationem audientibus demonstrabat: ante omnia simpliciores sunt adhibendae sententiae, quo discipuli eas facilius accipiant, quemadmodum illi magistri qui pueris tradere solent "omnis tenuissimas particulas atque omnia minima mansa ut nutrices infantibus in os inserunt" (*De Or.* II, XXXIX). Tum solidiora ministrantur id est difficiliores sententiae. Sed in antecessum—ita asseverabat Abbas—declinationes et coniugationes et ita porro sunt docendae, quod est a doctrina Reginaldi omnino alienum.

Haec revera est consuetudo institutionis impertiendae, grammaticae inculcandae, quod plerumque taedium gignit et iuvenes ab hac lingua arcent.

Aggredienda idcirco sunt scripta ipsa Latina, nominatim Tullianae epistulae, ad Reginaldi mentem, ut statim gustari liquida voluptate sermo possit. Sic pedetemptim ipsius linguae acquiritur cognitio.

Itaque interfecto Marco, epistulae manent, a viro illo eloquentissimo exaratae. Easdem prae manibus potissimum iuvat habere, ut aliquid sapidi gustare possimus.

Congruae tandem laudes sint tribuendae et Reginaldo Foster et Danieli McCarthy, qui veluti Tiro ille operam dant ut in volumen hoc, duce magistro, cum docendi tum discendi rationes congruenter transferantur.

P. Antonius Salvi, O.F.M.Cap.
Minutante
Capo Ufficio
Prima Sezione–Affari Generali
Segreteria di Stato
Città del Vaticano

IDEM EXORDIUM
the same foreword

Since the first volume has come to an end, the next book takes up its beginning, by which the Latin language may turn out more prosperous, and that a more prepared mind may be given for those who are reading.

Often times the mind is taken back to the space of past time, when certain pleasant things were being done. Let it be permitted to me to mention the first outings which we undertook as our years were blossoming. Reginald and I were accustomed to visit certain places which seemed to taste of antiquity, first of all Formia. For, having been equipped with a small book put together from the collected sentences of Cicero's letters, which pertain to that city, we were accustomed to survey city places, a small museum, the seashore, the harbor itself, where sitting we were accustomed to read that which Cicero was telling and writing about himself.

Finally arrival was being made at the tomb of Cicero himself, artificial indeed, nevertheless we were returning into the eternal memory of that name. In the meanwhile some people were approaching who were surprised at the extraordinary nature of our leisure and conversations and at the same time were complaining about the lost education in the Latin tongue.

The memory of so many years floods the spirit, in which we worked together, in which we spoke most pleasantly with other comrades, frequenting the beauties of Rome itself and ancient words. Most recently our buddy and companion Reginald, as it were having been dragged away from us, returned to his fatherland, but our close connection has never been interrupted.

What should I say about the summer schools, to which from everywhere in the world quite a few students were accustomed to gather together? But with the greatest pleasure, without that annoyance which most of the time takes over students learning the Latin language, the class was being carried out until on the same summer course an end was being put in the very villa of Horace, where the spring of Bandusia would be celebrated.

What place Cicero's letters hold

It is a known fact that the letters of Cicero were gathered together by Tiro and other teachers, indeed because they were considering the same letters as most beautiful. Various subjects are found in them—something which is accustomed to happen also in our age—because there was as it were one means of communication of that age. Today we seem to ourselves almost to have lost that habit, because most recent machines have driven us to a swiftness of writing. While in many areas then, most especially in writing out documents, we are punished by carelessness and excessive speed.

I well remember that Reginald put together certain small books into which he would insert all the mentions of a certain place, which were being found in Cicero's letters. Among those—as far as I remember—subject matters and references were collected about Formia, Gaieta, Pompeii. Everyone is able to do the same thing. For if we investigate certain statements pertaining to these places and we strive to unfold them, sitting down in the places themselves, certainly we draw a greater force for understanding those statements. For this reason the investigation turns out more pleasant. That I may add a certain example, Cicero writes in this way in his villa at Formia: "So I in this way am observing the sea days and nights as that famous bird of antiquity, I desire to fly away" (*Att.* IX, 10, 2). This statement becomes more clearly evident to people reading it and in the same place looking at the sea.

Furthermore all daily things are reported in the letters, all the things which in those times and in our times are able to happen to people. Without a doubt conditions now are otherwise than they were in those times. Nevertheless human affairs have remained always the same, the sentiments of people, the feelings, the affections. Just as every father, Cicero is very worried about Terentia and Tullia, he grieves sorely about his daughter having died, he rejoices once friends and relatives have been seen. Just as every lover of the fatherland (patriot) he is moved by grief over the collapse of the republic.

Rather expert German teachers in a certain way wish to marginalize Cicero's letters, in as much as which epistles do not allegedly belong to the best Latinity. At which thoughts Reginald is accustomed to be angry, and deservedly indeed, because nothing can be found more elegant, nothing more polished, nothing more attractive than those works. This prejudged opinion has remained strong all the way up to our present age. A certain model of some perfection has been created by them without discrimination according to which model, once established, all things are weighed.

What method is considered better for understanding the letters

The outstanding Abbot Carolus Egger, of memory to be celebrated, once upon a time the president of the Foundation Work "Latinitas," when a certain Vatican contest was taking place, was demonstrating this method of teaching to the ones listening: before all things simple sentences must be used so that the students may grasp them more easily, just as those famous teachers who are accustomed to hand down to children "all the slightest particles and all the smallest morsels as nurses insert them into the mouth of infants" (*De Or.* II, 39). Then more solid things are provided, that is to say more difficult sentences. But previously—so the abbot was asserting—declensions and conjugations and so forth must be taught, something which is totally distant from the teaching of Reginald.

This indeed is a habit of imparting instruction, of inculcating grammar, which most of the time generates disgust and keeps young people away from this language. Therefore, Latin writings themselves must be undertaken, namely the letters of Cicero, according to Reginald's mind, so that the language may be able to be tasted immediately with clear pleasure. Thus, little by little the knowledge of the language itself is acquired.

Thus, although Marcus has been killed, the letters remain having been written out by that most eloquent man. It is a pleasure especially to have the same letters in our hands so that we may be able to taste something delicious.

Finally, suitable praises must be given to both Reginald Foster and Daniel McCarthy, who, just as that famous Tiro, are making an effort that into this volume, the teacher being the leader, the methods of both teaching and learning may suitably be transferred.

P. Antonio Salvi, O.F.M.Cap.
Minutante
Capo Ufficio
Prima Sezione–Affari Generali
Segreteria di Stato
Città del Vaticano

PROLOGIUM

prologue

SHANE BUTLER

The covering slab of the tomb of the Venerable Bede († A.D. 735), in the majestic cathedral of Durham, is inscribed with a single line of self-rhyming "leonine" verse:

Hāc sunt in fossā Baedae venerabilis ossa.

In this pit are the bones of the Venerable Bede.

According to legend, a "dunce monk" charged with inscribing something on the slab when the bones were moved here left the space for *venerabilis* blank, at a loss for how to complete his own brief composition; an angel finished his work in the night, incidentally lending Bede the epithet that would come to be part of his ordinary proper name. This childlike epitaph seems a good way to introduce the present volume, a sequel to *Ossa Latinitatis Sola*, the authors of which are monks, but anything but dunces. A great writer like Bede leaves us not just his "bones" but his living, breathing voice, crudely but charmingly conjured in Durham by the struggling poet's singsong rhyme, by the dactyls and spondees of his meter, and even by his long vowels, dutifully marked with schoolroom macrons. The sound of Bede's own Latin is, of course, far more sophisticated than this, *sed caveat lector*: every author's signature voice begins in the flesh and blood we all share. Such voices, high and low, are the *carnes* promised by the present volume's title.

Consider an example from Cicero, whose letters are the heart of what's to come. His Latin style is the pinnacle to which countless later writers would aspire. But on headlong flight into exile, he was not above writing this:

Inimici mei mea mihi, non me ipsum ademerunt.

My enemies have taken my possessions from me, but not my very self.

Plenty of bones here, including a near-complete declension of the pronoun *ego*. But in the Latin's relentless alliteration of *m*, we hear Cicero crying "me, me, me!" (and just maybe, "mamma!") against the threat of erasure. That's the meat of the matter here, a Ciceronian *vox clamantis in deserto*, "the voice of one crying in the desert," with only his friend and correspondent Atticus to hear. Atticus—and us. For an indecipherable miracle has preserved this and hundreds of other private letters by Cicero from endless opportunities for destruction. Together they add up to a warts-and-all portrait of a man one either loves or hates or both. One way or another, it is in Cicero's letters—and in the letters of the alphabet that he assembles into sometimes jarring, more often euphonious Latin—that we finally encounter an ancient Roman fully in the flesh. Not surprisingly, these remarkable texts have been the Latin reader's delight since Petrarch rediscovered most of them in a dusty library in Verona in 1348. Petrarch himself, having read the letters straight through, was moved to write Cicero a reply, pretending to reproach him for the fickleness and inconstancy they betray, but really only accusing him of being human.

Audivi multa te dicentem, Petrarch tells Cicero, "I have listened to you as you said many things." And so will you, gentle reader of the letters collected in the following book, if you stick close to the advice of your wise and witty guides. It has been nearly a quarter century since I myself first heard Reginald Foster thunder out a threat to write a Latin textbook based on Cicero's letters. I could not be more pleased that this great teacher and humanist, who already has brought the past to life for so many, including me, finally has made good on that threat. Students not lucky enough to know *Reginaldus ipse* in the (ruddy) flesh now have, in these new textbooks, a genuine next best thing.

Shane Butler
Nancy H. and Robert E. Hall
Professor in the Humanities
Professor and Chair of Classics
Johns Hopkins University

PRAEFATIO

preface

SALLY DAVIS

My suggestions are offered chiefly for teaching high school students (roughly ages 15–18), since I am most familiar with teaching on this level.

Using the 500 sentences gleaned from Cicero's letters

How much better for young students to start with 500 short, Latin sentences than with complex political orations, or long epic poems with obscure allusions, because such brief quotes represent the language that the Romans spoke when they talked to their friends and reassured their families. We can take students to more difficult types of expression later.

I would start out each class period with five or ten of these, then twenty, more week by week. Read them quickly, perhaps invent colloquial or even slangy translations. After a few months of this, perhaps read the same aloud with no need for translation.

They are personal, charming, funny. We see Cicero happy, upset, in a hurry, chiding, teasing. He appears most human! I only wish there were more than these 500.

As for the language, vocabulary, and syntax, "it's all there, folks!" You can use these to teach everything about Latin—but really, there is no need to belabor the simplicity, elegance, and vividness of these sentences. I say just read quickly for about five or ten minutes, at the beginning of each class, and enjoy. This is learning Latin the easy way, seeing deep structures without elaboration and dissection. Let students get involved in the emotions that Cicero is expressing.

Transformations for fun: nouns, singular to plural; adjectives, plurals, comparatives; verbs, changing person, number, tense, mood. These can be done quickly, almost like a game.

Using the *Ossium Carnes Multae*

I would start with several of the shorter letters. At the outset, I would provide short background information for the letter we would be reading: place
written and places mentioned, names of addressee and others mentioned,
time of writing, and Cicero's current situation. Then students would want
to know what Cicero is going to say about these things. We would read the
letter aloud, definitely more than once by the time we have finished study-
ing it. With help from dictionary, teacher, and each other, we would create a
rough translation. Than we would go to Reginald's notes and make sure we
understand the Latin structures, then read his translation. Our next activity
would be to take a new letter, preferably related in some way to the first.
Students would be required to provide:

> background information
> rough translation
> commentary (a là Reginald)
> transformation exercises.

Lastly, we would compare our efforts at translation and commentary to those
of Reginald.

Some further questions and activities may be suggested outside the Latin
text itself:

Questions:

> What prompted the writing?
> What does Cicero hope to accomplish/gain by writing?
> What is Cicero's mood as he writes?
> How do you think the recipient felt when he received the letter?

Activities:

> Construct a reply to the letter (probably in English).
> Write what was the most difficult part of the letter and why.
> Memorize one sentence of the letter and recite it.
> Change all (or some) verbs from active to passive with necessary
>   changes to the rest of sentence.
> Change all (or some) sentences to/from indirect statement.

Sally Davis

LOCUTIONIS INDOLES AC NATURA
CICERONIS IN EPISTULIS

*the character and nature of speech
in Cicero's letters*

As has been announced and emphasized in volume 1, *Ossa Latinitatis Sola: The Mere Bones of Latin*, our intention here in volume 2 is to help teachers and students in this quest for patterns which illustrate the subject matter in the previous volume. There the reader was advised and directed to find proper examples in the accompanying reading sheets. Here as a help or guide we are already providing absolutely first-class illustrations of the *Ossa* taken from a bottomless source of super Latin which is sorely and tragically neglected by most teachers, commentators, manualists, namely, the large body of approximately 930 letters—Cicero's extant correspondence. The reason for this choice of study aides will now be explained in detail for the simple reason that many people simply do not know what kind of fantastic Latin is found in these letters. The quantity of his letters is indicated by the fact that the Oxford edition of Cicero's letters fills four separate bound volumes which are waiting to be understood, enjoyed, studied, imitated.

Tyrrell and Purser

The first idea here is to make clear to everyone what kind of superb Latinity we find in those letters. So, we shall quote our basic font, the seven volumes of *The Correspondence of M. Tullius Cicero*, edited by Robert Yelverton Tyrrell and Louis Claude Purser (Dublin–London 1904–1933, repr. Georg Olms 1969), and what these people have to say by way of introduction about the nature of Cicero's epistolary Latin.

> We have in the letters of Cicero an almost unique literary monument. The history of one of the most interesting epochs in the annals of the world is unfolded to us in a series of cabinet pictures by a master-hand.   (I, p. 74)

> But the quality in Cicero's letters which makes them most valuable is that they were not (like the letters of Pliny, and Seneca, and Madame de Sévigné) written to be published.   (I, pp. 75–76)

As a motto for the whole correspondence may be taken his own words in which he exalts the letter of Atticus over the oral description of Curio. He should be a good talker who could surpass the vivacity of Cicero's letters. But it is a serious error to ascribe carelessness to them. His style is colloquial, but thoroughly accurate. Cicero is the most precise of writers.   (I, p. 76)

We should, therefore, never admit the theory of carelessness in the writer to influence our opinion about the soundness of a phrase or construction.   (I, pp. 76–77)

There is a very remarkable characteristic of the style of these letters which is deserving of modest careful consideration—a very close parallelism between their diction and the diction of the comic drama. It is, indeed, to be expected *a priori* that the language of familiar letter-writing would closely resemble the language of familiar dialogue. In both cases the language may be expected to be largely tinged with the idiom of the *sermo vulgaris*, or *colloquialism*. Cicero, in an important passage, recognizes the *colloquial* character of his letters, referring, no doubt, especially to those which we have spoken of as his more private letters, namely, those to Atticus, Trebatius, Caelius, and his brother Quintus.   (I, pp. 77–78)

In the criticism of Cicero's letters we may go further, and say that to quote an analogous usage in Plautus or Terence is far more relevant than to quote an analogous usage from the Oratory or Philosophy of Cicero himself. [Note: We have seen that the dialogues, as might be expected, have far greater affinities with the letters, as regards the diction, than have the speeches and rhetorical essays of Cicero.] (I, p. 83)

From these serious and competent evaluations of Tyrrell and Purser, we can derive a first conclusion that of all the works of the "Father of Latinity" his letters are going to bring us the closest to his daily Latin speech, as they are not phony or constructed or artificial but spontaneous outpourings of his mind and heart in incomparable Latin.

Today we could say that Cicero's letters are the absolutely closest we can come to his telephone conversations, to his e-mail, to his tweets, texts, and video conferences. There are some people who falsely say we don't know how the Romans spoke Latin, but the fact is that from Cicero's letters we know almost exactly how they spoke Latin. And these same letters will soon provide all the "meats" we want for our Latin "bones."

Cicero ipse

If there are people not convinced by the previously quoted judgments, we shall now introduce Cicero himself defining, indicating, and suggesting the nature of his speech and consequently his mother Latin tongue in his letters. In each citation below we have disregarded the italics that appear in the text of Tyrrell and Purser. Rather, the formatting is our own, and we indicate our reason for selecting each instance with italics, and what prompted Cicero's expression is underlined.

(A) *Epistularum proprietas linguae*:
The special nature of the language of the letters

Complexus iuvenem dimisi, properans ad <u>epistulas</u>. Ubi sunt qui aiunt
ζώσης φωνῆς? Quanto magis vidi ex tuis <u>litteris</u> quam ex illius <u>sermone</u>
quid ageretur!   (*Att.* II, 12, 1)

Having given a hug I dismissed the young man, hastening to the <u>letters</u>.
Where are those people who say *the living voice*? How much more did I see
from your <u>letters</u> than from his <u>conversation</u> what was going on!

*Iocer*ne tecum per <u>litteras</u>? Civem mehercule non puto esse qui temporibus
his ridere possit.   (*Fam.* II, 4, 1 [175])

Should I joke with you by <u>letter</u>? By Hercules I don't think there is a citizen
who is able to laugh in these times.

Sed iam cupio tecum <u>coram</u> *iocari*.   (*Fam.* I, 10 [162])

But already now I long *to joke* with you <u>face to face</u>.

Verum tamen quid tibi ego videor in <u>epistulis</u>? nonne *plebeio sermone*
agere tecum? nec enim semper eodem modo. Quid enim simile habet
<u>epistula</u> aut iudicio aut contioni? … <u>epistulas</u> vero *cotidianis verbis* texere
solemus.   (*Fam.* IX, 21, 1 [497])

But still what do I seem to you [to be doing] in <u>letters</u>? Isn't it true to be
dealing with you *in common talk*? Nor indeed always in the same way. For
what does a <u>letter</u> have similar to either a court case or an assembly address?
… however we are accustomed to weave <u>letters</u> with *daily words*.

… brevior haec ipsa <u>epistula</u> est, quod, cum incertus essem ubi esses,
nolebam illum nostrum *familiarem sermonem* in alienas manus
devenire.   (*Att.* I, 9, 1 [5])

This very <u>letter</u> is more brief, because, since I was unsure where you were, I
did not want that *familiar talk* of ours to come into other peoples' hands.

(B) *Epistulae sermocinationum instar*:
Letters in the likeness-appearance of conversations

Quid est aliud tollere ex vita vitae societatem, tollere amicorum *colloquia
absentium*? Quam multa ioca solent esse in <u>epistulis</u> quae, prolata si sint,
inepta videantur …   (*Oratio Philippica* II, 4, 7)

What else is it to take togetherness of life out of life, [than] to take away the
conversations of absent friends? How many jokes are accustomed to exist in
<u>letters</u> which, if they have been published, seem stupid …

… crede mihi—requiesco paullum in his miseriis cum quasi tecum *loquor*; cum vero tuas <u>epistulas</u> lego, multo etiam magis.   (*Att.* VIII, 14, 1 [349])

… believe me—I take rest a little bit in these miseries when *I* as it were *speak* with you; however when I read your <u>letters</u>, even much more so.

Sed, ut supra dixi, tecum perlibenter *loquor* … Ego tecum tamquam mecum *loquor* …   (*Att.* VIII, 14, 2 [349])

But, as I said above, *I* most willingly *talk* with you … *I am speaking* with you as with myself …

… cum tua lego, te audire, et … ad te <u>scribo</u>, tecum *loqui* videor …
(*Q. Fr.* I, 1, 16 § 45 [30])

… when I read your stuff, I seem to hear you, and … when <u>I write</u> to you, I seem *to be conversing* with you …

… tamen adlevor, cum *loquor* tecum absens, multo etiam magis, cum tuas <u>litteras</u> lego.   (*Att.* XII, 39, 2 [583])

… nevertheless I am relieved, when absent *I am talking* with you, even much more so, when I read your <u>letters</u>.

Nam habeo ne me quidem ipsum quicum tam audacter *communicem* quam te.   (*Att.* XII, 36, 1 [578])

For I have not even my very self with whom *I may communicate* so boldly as with you.

… quoniam intervallo locorum et temporum diiuncti sumus, per <u>litteras</u> tecum quam saepissime *colloquar*.   (*Fam.* I, 7, 1 [114])

… because we have been separated by a space of places and times, *I shall converse* with you as often as possible by <u>letter</u>.

(C) *Epistulis incommoda adiuncta*:
Circumstances inconvenient for letters

In this section the circumstances are italicized, the composition is underlined.

Hoc *inter cenam* Tironi <u>dictavi</u>, ne mirere alia manu esse.
    (*Q. Fr.* III, 1, 6 § 19 [148])

<u>I have dictated</u> this to Tiro *in the midst of dinner*, lest you be surprised that it is by another hand.

Haec scripsi seu <u>dictavi</u> *apposita secunda mensa* apud Vestorium.
(*Att.* XIV, 21, 4 [728])

<u>I</u> wrote these things or rather <u>dictated</u> at the house of Vestorius *after the dessert table had been brought in.*

Accubueram hora nona, cum ad te <u>harum</u> exemplum in codicillis <u>exaravi</u>. Dices, ubi? apud Volumnium Eutrapelum ...   (*Fam.* IX, 26, 1 [479])

I had reclined at table at 3:00 P.M., when <u>I wrote out</u> to you a copy <u>of this letter</u> on little tablets. You will say, where? at the house of Volumnius Eutrapelus ...

Plura otiosus: haec, cum essem *in senatu*, <u>exaravi</u>.   (*Fam.* XII, 20 [930])

More things [I shall write] at leisure: <u>I wrote out</u> these things when I was *in the senate.*

Haec <u>scripsi</u> *navigans*, cum ad Pompeianum accederem, XIIII Kal.
(*Att.* XVI, 7, 8 [783])

<u>I wrote</u> these things *sailing*, when I was approaching to my Pompeian villa, on the 14th day before the Kalends.

Navem spero nos valde bonam habere: in *eam* simul atque conscendi haec <u>scripsi</u>.   (*Fam.* XIV, 7, 2 [405])

I hope we have a very good *boat*: as soon as I embarked on *it* <u>I wrote</u> these things.

... conscendens ab hortis Cluvianis *in phaeselum* epicopum has dedi <u>litteras</u> ...   (*Att.* XIV, 16, 1 [721])

I mounting *onto a small boat* fitted out with oars from the Cluvian gardens sent this <u>letter</u> ...

Hanc epistulam <u>dictavi</u> sedens *in raeda*, cum in castra proficiscerer ...   (*Att.* V, 17, 1 [209])

<u>I dictated</u> this letter sitting *in a chariot*, when I was setting out for the camp ...

Haec *festinans* <u>scripsi</u> in *itinere* atque *agmine*.   (*Att.* VI, 4, 1 [268])

In a hurry <u>I have written</u> these things on the *road* and *march.*

Habes <u>epistulam</u> plenam *festinationis* et *pulveris*.   (*Att.* V, 14, 3 [204])

You have <u>a letter</u> full *of haste* and *dust.*

… in ipso *itinere* et *via* discedebant publicanorum tabellarii et eramus in cursu … Itaque <u>subsedi</u> in ipsa *via*, dum haec, quae longiorem desiderant orationem, summatim tibi <u>perscriberem</u>.   (*Att.* V, 16, 1 [208])

… on the very *march* and *road* the letter carriers of the tax collectors were departing and we were on the run … Therefore <u>I sat down</u> on the *road* itself, until <u>I might write out</u> in brief to you these things, which are looking for a longer discourse.

… hoc litterularum <u>exaravi</u> *egrediens* e villa *ante lucem* …
(*Att.* XII, 1, 1 [505])

… this bit of a short letter <u>I have written out</u> *exiting* from the villa *before sunrise* …

Hanc <u>scripsi</u> *ante lucem* ad lychnuchum ligneolum …   (*Fam.* III, 7, 2 [156])

<u>I have written</u> this letter *before sunrise* at the light of a little wooden lamp …

Tantum tamen scito, Idibus Maiis nos Venusia *mane proficiscentis* has <u>dedisse</u>.   (*Att.* V, 5, 1 [188])

Still know this alone, that we <u>have sent</u> this letter *setting out in the morning* on May 15 from Venusia.

… cum leviter *lippirem*, has <u>litteras</u> dedi.   (*Att.* VII, 14, 1 [310])

… when *I* lightly *had running eyes*, I sent this <u>letter</u>.

(D) *Epistulas excipiunt librarii*:
Secretaries jot down letters

… neque semper *mea manu* <u>litteras</u> exspectabis.   (*Att.* V, 14, 1 [204])

… you shall not always expect <u>letters</u> *in my own hand*.

… <u>epistula</u> *librari manu* est.   (*Att.* IV, 16, 1 [144])

… the <u>letter</u> is *by the hand of my secretary*.

<u>Haec</u> ad te *mea manu*.   (*Att.* XII, 31, 3 [568])

<u>These things</u> [I wrote] to you *in my own hand*.

<u>Hoc</u> *manu mea*.   (*Att.* XIII, 28, 3 [604])

<u>This</u> *in my own hand*.

Lippitudinis meae signum tibi sit *librari manus* et eadem causa brevitatis, etsi nunc quidem quod <u>scriberem</u> nihil erat.   (*Att.* VIII, 13, 1 [384])

Let *the hand of my secretary* be a sign to you of my dripping eyes and the same, the reason for its brevity, although now indeed there was nothing that <u>I might write</u>.

Cum a me <u>litteras</u> *librari manu* acceperis, ne paullum quidem me oti habuisse iudicato, cum autem *mea*, paullum.   (*Q. Fr.* II, 15 (16), 1 [147])

When you will have received a <u>letter</u> from me *by the hand of the secretary*, you must realize that I had not even a little bit of free time, when however in *my hand*, then a little.

Itaque et consilium mutavi et ad te statim *mea manu* <u>scriptas</u> litteras misi …   (*Fam.* III, 6, 2 [213])

Thus I both changed the plan and I sent a letter to you immediately <u>written</u> *in my hand* …

Obsignaram iam <u>epistulam</u> eam, quam puto te modo perlegisse, scriptam *mea manu*, in qua omnia continentur …   (*Att.* V, 19, 1 [220])

I had already sealed that <u>letter</u>, which I believe you have just read through, written *in my hand*, in which all things are contained …

Hoc inter cenam Tironi *dictavi*, ne mirere *alia manu* esse. (*Q. Fr.* III, 1, 6 § 19 [148])

I have dictated this to Tiro in the midst of dinner, lest you be surprised that it is *by another hand*.

Haec <u>scripsi</u> seu *dictavi* apposita secunda mensa apud Vestorium. (*Att.* XIV, 21, 4 [728])

<u>I wrote</u> these things or rather *dictated* at the house of Vestorius after the dessert table had been brought in.

Hanc <u>epistulam</u> *dictavi* sedens in raeda, cum in castra proficiscerer …   (*Att.* V, 17, 1 [209])

I dictated this <u>letter</u> sitting in a chariot, when I was setting out for the camp …

Numquam ante arbitror te epistulam meam legisse nisi *mea manu* scriptam.… haec <u>dictavi</u> ambulans.   (*Att.* II, 23, 1 [50])

I think you have never previously read a letter of mine if not written *in my hand*.… these things <u>I have dictated</u> walking around.

(E) *Epistulis condimenta per clamores*:
Spices for the letters by means of interjections

Hui, totiensne me litteras dedisse Romam, cum ad te nullas darem?
(*Att.* V, 11, 1 [200])

Ho, that I have sent letters so often to Rome, although I was sending
none to you?

Hui, quam diu de nugis! (*Att.* XIII, 21, 5 [632])

Ho, how long about nonsense!

… nec tibi integrum est: *hui*, si scias quanto periculo tuo!
(*Att.* XIII, 35, 2 [643])

… nor is it in your power: *oh*, if you should only know with what great risk
for you!

Hem, mea lux, meum desiderium, unde omnes opem petere
solebant! (*Fam.* XIV, 2, 2 [79])

Oh for grief, my light, my longing, from whom all people used to seek help!

⁓

As a final attempt to inflame your enthusiasm and sharpen your appreciation of Cicero's letters, we would like to propose one single sentence as a
gold mine of Latinity. We want to point out all the elements of Latin which
are contained in this full sentence. You will be astonished to see how much
Latin can be understood and appreciated and taught from a few real lines
of Cicero and that from one of his letters. This sentence is arranged on the
page as will the fifty-one letters hereafter, and so gives an opportunity to
introduce a model of the method of presentation in this book. The quote is
followed by our English rendering:

Volo enim te scire, mi Paete, initium mihi suspicionis et cautionis et diligentiae fuisse litteras tuas, quibus litteris congruentes fuerunt aliae postea
multorum: nam et Aquini et Fabrateriae consilia sunt inita de me quae te
video inaudisse et, quasi divinarent quam iis molestus essem futurus, nihil
aliud egerunt nisi me ut opprimerent. (*Fam.* IX, 24, 1 [820])

My dear Paetus, I want you to know that for me the beginning of suspicion
and caution and care was your letter, to which letter afterwards other ones
of many people were in agreement: for decisions were made at both Aquinum and Fabrateria about me which I see you overheard and, as though
they were guessing how annoying I was going to be for them, they did nothing else except that they might squash me.

Following the quote and an English rendering in its entirety, the text's various Latin usages will be pointed out. In each case the Latin as it appears in the text is followed by the rendering as it appears in this our English translation. These are followed by brief statements that explain the usage of the expression according to our terminology for newcomers to our system; other outlawed terms used traditionally elsewhere may be added here lest we alienate anyone from the rest of Latin studies and therefore cause confusion where it should not exist. Following each explanation, an arrow directs the reader to references in other books: the corresponding *encounter* in the *Ossa* book so that the reader may review the matter there and its application here in Cicero's letters; perhaps the dictionary, signaled by "dict."; and perhaps to other reference works, listed in the abbreviations, found further below.

In this sentence all the forms of nouns-adjectives are used:

suspicionis ... cautionis, diligentiae, multorum, "of suspicion, of ... caution, of ... care, of many people": of-possession forms (so-called genitive; gen.).
> → **1** function: of-possession, 20.

mi Paete, "My dear Paetus": direct address forms (so-called vocative; voc.).
> → **2** function: direct address, 38.3.

congruentes ... aliae, consilia, "others ... in agreement, decisions": subject forms (so-called nominative; nom.) expressed clearly.
> → **3** function: subject, 2, 15.

Aquini ... Fabrateriae, "at Aquinum ... Fabrateria": place forms (so-called locative).
> → **4** function: place at which, names of cities and small islands, singular, *Aquini, Fabrateriae*, 69.3.2.

de me, "about me": in this prepositional phrase *me* is the form by-with-from-in (so-called ablative; abl.).
> → **5** function: by-with-from-in, 27.

nihil aliud, and the second *me*, "nothing else" and the second "me": object form used as an object (so-called accusative; acc.).
> → **6** function: object, 2, 15.

te scire, "you to know": object form used as a subject of an indirect statement (so-called accusative; acc.).
> → **7** OO, 71–73.

initium ... fuisse litteras tuas, "the beginning ... was your letter": object form used as a subject of an indirect statement.
> → **8** OO, 71–73.

te video inaudisse, "I see you overheard": object form used as a subject of an indirect statement.

→ **9** OO, 71–73.

mihi, quibus litteris, iis, "for me, to which letter, for them": to-for-from form (so-called dative; dat.).

→ **10** function: to-for-from, 33.

Verb times used are:

volo, "I want" T.1i.

→ **11** T.1i: 3, 12.

fuerunt, "[other ones] were" T.4bi.

→ **12** verb T.4a, T.4b: 8.

sunt inita, "[decisions] were made" T.4bi passive.

→ **13** T.4b pass., 26.

video, "I see" T.1i.

→ **14** T.1i: 2, 12.

divinarent, "they were guessing" T.2s.

→ **15** T.2s: 44.

essem futurus, "I was going to be" T.2s.

→ **16** T.2s: 44.

egerunt, "they did" T.4bi.

→ **17** verb T.4a, T.4b: 8.

opprimerent, "they might squash" T.2s.

→ **18** T.2s: 44.

No deponent verbal forms were used.

Three expressions of indirect discourse (*Oratio Obliqua,* OO) were used, each depending on a verb of Mind and Mouth (M & M):

Volo ... te scire, "I want you to know": *te scire* is OO depending on M & M verb *Volo.*

→ **19** M & M, 60, 71, GL nº 527, remarks 1–2; OO, 71–73.

scire ... initium ... fuisse litteras, "to know that ... the beginning ... was your letter": *initium fuisse litteras* is OO depending on M & M verb *scire.*

→ **20** M & M, 60, 71, GL nº 527, remarks 1–2; OO, 71–73.

te video inaudisse, "I see you overheard": *te inaudisse* is OO sandwiching the M & M verb on which they depend, *video*.

> → **21** M & M, 60, 71, GL n° 527, remarks 1–2; OO, 71–73.

In these expressions of OO, a contemporaneous infinitive appears, *scire*, and two antecedent infinitives, *fuisse, inaudisse*.

Other usages include:

quam … molestus essem futurus, "how annoying I was going to be": Indirect Question (IQ) depending on the verb of M & M, *divinarent*, "they were guessing."

> → **22** M & M, 60, 71, GL n° 527, remarks 1–2; IQ, 60;
> *consecutio*, 47–48;
> *consecutio*: futurity formula in the subjunctive, 61.3.

me ut opprimerent, "that they might squash me": final or purpose clause depending on *egerunt*, "they did."

> → **23** subjunctive use: purpose clause, 58.1.

quasi divinarent, "as though they were guessing": a conditional sentence of comparison equivalent to "as if they were guessing."

> → **24** conditional sentence of comparison, GL 602.

quibus litteris congruentes, "to which letter … [many people] were in agreement": *quibus litteris* are dat. because *congruentes* is either a compound verb or one of the 65 which take the dative—sometimes you can argue about which.

> → **25** dat. with compound verbs, 33.7.3, GL n° 347;
> 65 verbs with dat., 33.7.2, GL n° 346.

divinarent … essem futurus … opprimerent, "they were guessing … I was going to be … they might squash": all three are T2s and depend on T4b *egerunt*, "they did," establishing Track II in the sequence of tenses.

> → **26** verb T.4a, T.4b: 8; verb T.2s: 44; *consecutio*, 47–48.

essem futurus, "I was going to be": futurity formula of the verb *esse*, "to be," which could be translated in at least 4 ways: "I was going to be," "I was about to be," "I was fixing to be," "I would be" …

> → **27** *consecutio*: futurity formula in the subjunctive, 61.3.

There is sufficient Latin material here for about three calendar course years, but this is just to whet your appetite for an infinity of beautiful things to come from Cicero's letters.

Reginaldus Thomas Foster and Daniel Patricius McCarthy

QUOMODO SIT HIC
LIBER USURPANDUS

in what manner this book is to be used

Readers may be interested to know that the authors of the present volume, steeped in classical traditions, thought of no one less than Quintus Horatius Flaccus as they began this endeavor years ago, which years have slipped by so quickly—*senescentibus nobis* "as we were growing old." In fact this work, inspired by a certain projected leisure in our life, turned into a time- and energy-consuming undertaking, which has already spread over the course of practically nine years, but we were supported and encouraged by the above-mentioned Horatius, who in his immortal *Ars poetica*, amid numberless golden rules for writing, composing, speaking, proclaiming, said that your work, anything you write, should be put away in a cedarwood chest— to keep the bugs and worms away—and not be touched for nine years. In fact, his words are these:

> ... *nonumque prematur in annum*
> *membranis intus positis...* (Hor., *Ars poetica*, 388–89)

> ... and may it be pressed away unto the ninth year,
> once sheets have been put inside [the cedar box] ...

To keep us very humble along with all authors who think their works will change the world, not only will our works be unacceptable to us after nine years, but also what we think are great works are going to end up under this panorama of Horace:

> *parturient montes, nascetur riduculus mus* (Hor., *A.P.* 139)

> the mountains will be giving birth, a ridiculous little mouse
>   will be born

The origins of this book, however, extend well before the nine years taken to produce the text in your hands. About a month before the Roman Catholic Church opened the Second Vatican Ecumenical Council (October 11, 1962– December 1965), Br. Reginald Foster arrived in Rome to begin his licentiate studies in theology at the Teresianum. During those heady days at the start of the council, many participants wished to be able to speak in Latin on the council floor. They would gather for lessons held for two years at the Brazilian College using the volume *Latine loquor*, and so began Reginald's teaching career in Rome. After completing the licentiate and after ordination, Fr. Reginald was in his first year of studies at the recently established Salesian Pontifical University for higher studies in the Latin language, conducted naturally in Latin.

The last person to hold the title *Ab epistulis Latinis* was Card. Antonius Bacci and the title *Ab epistulis ad principes* was Msgr. Hamletus Tondini. Paul VI and his chief of staff, the Under-Secretary of State Giovanni Benelli, later card. abp. of Florence, said upon the sickness of Hamletus that they needed help in the office. So, Abbas Carolus Egger, who was the heavyweight Latinist in the Office of Latin Letters of the Vatican Secretariat of State, was also teaching at the Salesianum, when in April of 1969 he came into the classroom to ask:

> *Visne, Reginalde, pontifici scriptor esse Latinitatis?*
> Reginald, would you like to be the writer of Latin for the Pope?

Catching his breath, Reginald responded:

> *Certissime!*
> Most certainly!

Once freed by his Carmelite superiors to work in the Vatican, Reginald boxed up the typescript of his unfinished doctoral thesis, already extending to seven hundred pages and written in Latin, and took it with him to his new office in the Vatican. This thesis included an initial treatment on the language of Cicero's letters, which can be found in this volume under the title *Locutionis indoles ac natura Ciceronis in epistulis*, "The character and nature of speech in Cicero's letters," along with a review of the use of Cicero's letters as a teaching tool in the Renaissance.

Immediately after the council young seminarians were waiting, even hoping for remedial courses to learn some Latin fast as they began their studies; so at the request of the Vatican they gathered at the nearby Augustinianum, where Reginald would write a sentence on the board, and they would always begin with an authentic Latin text. Once this method was established, he has never looked back. These courses proved so successful that around 1972 they were transferred from so far out of town—near the Vatican—to a more central location at the Angelicum near Piazza Venezia.

An extraordinary, humble Jesuit named Emilio Springhetti in the 1930s established a Latin school at the Jesuit-run Gregorian University, where he taught the history and people of the Italo-Latin Renaissance of the fifteenth and sixteenth centuries and established a corresponding Latin library on pontifical authority. Upon his passing, the Scottish Jesuit Clarence

Gallagher was put in charge and invited Reginald to offer his courses there, before the Jesuits eventually dissolved the Springhetti Latin school and disbursed the library. He worked in the Vatican office every morning, and continued to teach at the Gregorian on most afternoons including Saturdays for over thirty years. He was able to excuse himself from afternoon duties at the Vatican because by lunchtime his desk was always clear of work.

After about nine years in the office, Reginald consulted with a colleague, a Claretian from Spain who honestly said, "Foster, you are never going to finish the doctoral thesis." Reginald pulled the typescript out of its box, opened it up and read a page, only to say, "This thing stinks! How could I write such trash nine years ago?" So he took the box out through the Vatican Gate of Sant'Anna and down the street to a line of dumpsters. He opened one and tipped in all 700 pages of Latin composition, and he never looked back. The whole thing would need to be redone, now that Reginald had the benefit of nine years of experience in the Vatican office.

After a career spanning forty years in the Vatican office, all the while teaching Latin during the academic term and in the now-famous summer school, due to poor health Reginald was delivered from Rome on a stretcher to his native Milwaukee. While in recovery, friends gathered and held a colloquium as part of the project *Liturgiam aestimare: Appreciating the Liturgy,* during which Daniel McCarthy asked if he could return in July to begin writing with Reginald his method of teaching the Latin language. As these pages are being reviewed for a final time, on this day, 8 June 2020, Reginald begins once again to hold his summer Latin program from his residence in Milwaukee but for the first time online using FaceTime. Reginald continued his original love of Cicero's letters and asked that this volume along with its audio component be included in what would eventually become the five volumes of this series. In a sense this has happened with the help of colleagues, without forcing anything, but *magna non sine difficultate,* "not without great difficulty."

This is a roundabout way of retelling the events in human lives of the realization of Horace's admonition to set a written work aside for nine years and then reassessing it before it is ever published.

༄

The original intent for this second volume, with the title of *Ossium Carnes Multae: The Bones' Meats Abundant,* was to excerpt a few words here and there from the letters of Cicero as examples to illustrate each of the 105 encounters of our previous book, *Ossa Latinitatis Sola: The Mere Bones of Latin.* Immediately we realized, however, that such a method would cut up the language and human thought as if it were a dead frog to be dissected, which Latin is not. Thus, consistent with the first book, this second one is not a presentation of grammar; rather it is an active, living introduction to a body of Latin literature where each passage must be understood in light of the fuller expression of Cicero.

We suggest that this book be used in conjunction with the *Ossa* book. That first volume of the series provides the bones or the structure for teaching the Latin language. However, we realize that some people may criticize the *Ossa* book for giving theory without much practical application. Extensive reading sheets are provided in the *Ossa* book without explanations of the Latin texts or their historical contexts, which are confidently left up to the teacher. This second volume is intended to put some flesh on the bones, taken from the letters of Cicero, as an example of how to teach from one monument of Latinity.

Repository of the letters

The stream of thoughts rushing through Cicero's mind as he wrote them on a wax tablet were copied nearly a millennium later and preserved in manuscripts written by anonymous scribes. These manuscripts containing the *Epistulae ad Atticum* were rediscovered in a library in Verona in 1345 by Petrarch (1304–1374), considered the father of the Italian Renaissance. As a point of reference, Thomas Aquinas had died less than a century earlier, in 1274. Hearing about this find, Coluccio Salutati (1331–1406), chancellor of Florence, requested a copy be sent to him from Milan. Upon receiving it around 1389 he realized that purely by accident he had received an independent collection of Cicero's letters, these the *Epistulae ad Familiares*. At about this same time the Medici family was rising to prominence in Florence and their private library eventually became the foundation of what is now the Bibliotheca Medicea Laurenziana, where a collection of these same letters is housed. Their manuscript of the letters *ad Atticum* dates to the ninth or tenth century, while their manuscript of the letters *ad familiares* was copied around 1391 from an older manuscript.

As a witness to the revolutionary effect of these letters let us look to the words of Petrarch, Salutati, and their near-contemporary Guarinus. In his collection *Letters to Family and Friends* Petrarch says:

> Haec et similia cum saepe … dixissem, forte accidit, ut in <u>epistolas Ciceronis</u> inciderem … et delectatus sum me dixisse quod tanto ante magnus ille vir dixerat. (Franciscus Petrarca, *Epistularum Familiarium* xviii, 8, 15).

> After I had said these and similar things often, it happened by chance that I came upon <u>letters of Cicero</u> … and I was so delighted that I had said that which that great man had said so long before.

Colluccius Salutati says in his *Letter to Pasquinus de Capellis*:

> Tu me, quod summis semper desideriis concupivi, fecisti <u>Tullianis epistolis</u> locupletem, amplitudine muneris faciens quod reddar ad gratias pauperrimus et egenus … O me felicem tali tantoque dono, Pasquine. (Colvccius Salutati, *Epistula ad Pasquinus de Capellis*).

That which I desired always with the greatest longings, you made me rich
with Tullian letters, bringing it about by the greatness of your gift that for
thanks I am rendered very poor and needy.... O happy me by such and so
great a gift, dear Pasquinus.

Their near-contemporary Guarinus of Verona (1374–1460) was born in the
year Petrarch died. In his *Oration for Beginning the Letters of Cicero*, Guarinus says:

> Ad prima studiorum delibamenta his annis propinanda non difficillimas
> orationes, non asperos artificii locos, sed facile quoddam et planissimum di-
> cendi genus delegi, quod suavissimo verborum ordine et leni sententiarum
> pondere lectorem alliciens prosit atque iuvet. Nonnullas enim decerpsi Cice-
> ronis epistulas, in quibus ille puri et facetissimi sermonis stilus exprimi-
> tur.   (GUARINUS VERONENSIS, *Oratio Pro Ciceronis Epistulis Incohandis*).

> For the first sips of studies in these years I have chosen to be offered to drink
> not very difficult orations, not rough instances of invention, but a certain
> easy and most clear type of speaking, which is useful and helps me enticing
> the reader by a most sweet order of words and a smooth weight of content.
> For, I have plucked out some letters of Cicero in which that style of pure and
> most humorous speech is expressed.

Their sentiments at the time of the Italian Renaissance echo the value placed
on these letters by people who were steeped in them, such as Quintilian and
his student Plinius and their near-contemporary Tacitus, all three writing
during the silver age of Latinity, and then in the post-classical period by
Fronto and his student, later emperor, Marcus Aurelius. Representing early
Christian literature are Lactantius and Jerome and Augustine.

Marcus Fabius Quintilianus (c. 35–c. 95) writes in his work *Institutio Or-
atoria*, on "Oratorical Training," that there is no dispute regarding the supe-
riority of Cicero's letters over those of Demosthenes.

> In epistulis quidem, quamquam sunt utriusque [Demosthenis et Ciceronis]
> dialogisve, quibus nihil ille, nulla contentio est.
> (MARCUS FABIUS QUINTILIANUS, *Institutio Oratoria* X, 1, 107–108)

> In his [Cicero's] letters indeed, although there are letters of each man
> [Demosthenes and Cicero] or dialogues, to which that man [Demosthenes]
> added nothing, there is no dispute.

In the same work Quintilian equates the name of Cicero with eloquence
itself.

> Est, apud posteros vero id consecutus, ut Cicero iam non hominis nomen,
> sed eloquentiae habeatur. Hunc igitur spectemus, hoc propositum nobis sit
> exemplum. Ille se profecisse sciat, cui Cicero valde placebit.
> (MARCUS FABIUS QUINTILIANUS, *Institutio Oratoria* X, 1, 112)

But among posterity Cicero has attained this: that "Cicero" is not held any longer as the name of a person, but of eloquence. Let us look to this man, that this example be set up for us. That person to whom Cicero will be very pleasing should know that he / she has advanced.

Quintilian in the same work dedicates a chapter on Cicero, who among all authors has to be read first.

> [QUI PRIMI LEGENDI] … Cicero, ut mihi quidem videtur, et iucundus incipientibus quoque et apertus est satis, nec prodesse tantum, sed etiam amari potest: tum, quem ad modum Livius praecipit, ut quisque erit Ciceroni simillimus. (Marcus Fabius Quintilianus, *Institutio Oratoria* II, 5, 20)

> [WHO TO BE READ FIRST] … Cicero, as he appears indeed to me, is pleasant for those also beginning and is clear enough, nor is he able not only to be profitable but also to be loved: then, as everyone will be most like Cicero, just as Livy orders.

Quintilian finally says that it is sufficient for him to imitate Cicero alone.

> sed non qui maxime imitandus, et solus imitandus est. Quid ergo? Non est satis omnia sic dicere, quo modo M. Tullius dixit? Mihi quidem satis esset, si omnia consequi possem. (Marcus Fabius Quintilianus, *Institutio Oratoria* X, 2, 24–25)

> But not he who must be imitated mostly, also is to be imitated solely. What therefore? Is it not sufficient to say all things, in which way M. Tullius spoke? It would be enough for me, if I would be able to attain all things.

Quintilian's student was Gaius Plinius Caecilius Secundus (c. 61–c. 112), who writes twice in his *Epistula I*, "Letter One," about the quality of Cicero's use of the Latin language.

> Est enim, inquam, mihi cum Cicerone aemulatio, nec sum contentus eloquentia saeculi nostri; nam stultissimum credo ad imitandum non optima quaeque proponere. (Gaius Plinius Caecilius Secundus, *Epistula* I, 5, 12–13)

> For there exists for me, I say, a rivalry with Cicero, nor am I content with the eloquence of our century; for I believe it is most foolish not to set up for imitation all the best things.

> In primis M. Tullium oppono, cuius oratio optima fertur esse quae maxima. (Gaius Plinius Caecilius Secundus, *Epistula* I, 20, 4)

> Among the first, I oppose M. Tullius, whose speech is said to be the best as the greatest.

Near contemporary to both Quintilian and Pliny was Cornelius Tacitus (c. 56–c. 118), whose work *Dialogus de Oratoribus*, "Conversations about Orators," says the following about Cicero's speech, choice of words, and composition.

Ad Ciceronem venio ... primus enim excoluit orationem, primus et verbis delectum adhibuit et compositioni artem.   (CORNELIUS TACITUS, *Dialogus de Oratoribus* 22, 2).

I come to Cicero ... as first he cultivated speech, as first also he applied a selection to words and art to composition.

Among the statements of Marcus Cornelius Fronto (c. 95–c. 166) we find two letters written by Marcus Aurelius (121–180) to Fronto his teacher.

Vale, mi iucundissime magister. Ciceronis epistulas, si forte electas totas vel dimidiatas habes, impertias; vel mone quas potissimum legendas mihi censeas ad facultatem sermonis fovendam.   (*Epistula Marci Aurelii ad Frontonem* II, 4)

Hail my most pleasant teacher. May you give me Cicero's letters if by chance you have whole ones chosen or halved ones; or advise which letters most especially you think must be read by me for promoting the ability of speaking.

Memini me excerpsisse ex Ciceronis epistulis ea dumtaxat quibus inesset aliqua de eloquentia vel philosophia vel de rep. disputatio; praeterea si quid eleganti aut verbo notabili dictum videretur, excerpsi. Quae in usu meo ad manum erant excerpta, misi tibi. Tres libros, duos ad Brutum, unum ad Axium, describi iubebis, si quid rei esse videbitur, et remittes mihi; nam exemplares eorum excerptorum nullos feci. Omnes autem Ciceronis epistulas legendas censeo mea sententia, vel magis quam omnes eius orationes. Epistulis Ciceronis nihil est perfectius.   (*Epistula Frontonis ad Marcum Aurelium* II, 5)

I remember that I picked out from the letters of Cicero only those things in which there was some discussion about eloquence or philosophy or the state; furthermore if some thing seemed to have been said with an elegant or notable word, I took it out. Those things at hand which had been chosen for my use I sent to you. Three books, two to Brutus, one to Axius, you will command to be copied if there will seem to be something of substance, and you will send back to me; for I made no copies of those selected passages. However, I believe in my opinion that all the letters of Cicero must be read, even more so than all his orations. There is nothing more perfect than the letters of Cicero.

The following two statements were made by Fronto to Marcus Aurelius:

Hic tu fortasse iamdudum requiras quo in numero locem M. Tullium, qui caput atque fons romanae facundiae cluet. Eum ego arbitror usquequaque verbis pulcherrimis elocutum et ante omnes alios oratores ad ea, quae ostentare vellet, ornanda magnificum fuisse.   (*Epistula Frontonis ad Marcum Aurelium* IIII, 3)

Here one perhaps already for a long time would be asking on what scale I locate M. Tullius, who stands out as the head and source of Roman eloquence. I judge that he in every possible way spoke with most beautiful words and before all other orators was superb for beautifying those things which he wanted to show off.

M. Tullius summum supremumque os romanae linguae fuit.   (*Epistula Frontonis ad Verum Imperatorem* I)

M. Tullius was the highest and most exalted voice of the Roman language.

Among our early Christians writers, Lucius Caelius Firmianus, commonly called Lactantius (c. 240–c. 320), said the following of Cicero's writing:

Ille ipse romanae linguae summus auctor.   (Caelius Lactantius Firmianus, *Institutiones Divinae* III, 13)

That man himself the greatest author of the Roman language.

Second of our early Christians writers is Eusebius Sophronius Hieronymus (c. 347–420), who wrote of Cicero and several of the above-cited authors who look to Cicero's example.

Me in disciplinam dedi, ut post Quintiliani acumina, Ciceronis fluvios, gravitatemque Frontonis et lenitatem Plinii, alphabetum discerem.   (Eusebius Sophronius Hieronymus, *Epistula* CXXV, 12)

I committed myself to a rigorous schedule so that, after the subtleties of Quintilian, the floods of Cicero, and the seriousness of Fronto and the smoothness of Pliny, I might learn the alphabet.

Finally Aurelius Augustinus (354–430) said the following of our beloved Cicero:

Cicero—vir eloquentissimus et verborum vigilantissimus appensor et mensor.   (Aurelius Augustinus, *contra Adversarium legis et prophetarum* XXIV, 52)

Cicero—a most eloquent man and a most scrupulous weigher and measurer of words.

Now it is up to us to follow their example and continue the Ciceronian renaissance. For the enjoyment and encouragement, for the education and edification of the readers of this our second volume the corresponding digital image or images selected from those Florentine manuscripts have been inserted on the page facing the typescript of each letter, inasmuch as this whole book has as its object the letters of Cicero: our presentation of the letters, commentary, sentences, and dialogues so that students and teachers may enter into this world, this conversation, this personal encounter, for this is as close as we can get to Cicero's writings on wax tablets, his quasi-phone calls in his letters of over two thousand years ago, and we are totally friendly with the copyist and Cicero himself.

We present our selection of the fifty-one letters of Cicero twice in this volume, but in different ways. In both cases the typescript text is taken directly from the edition produced by Tyrrell and Purser. This is most evident in Part II of this volume, where these letters are presented along with our rendition of them and commentary. The same text of each letter is also presented in Part I of this volume with one or more images from a manuscript from the Medicean library that carries the text. In this case, however, the line breaks of the typescript edition follow the layout of the text on the manuscript page so that the reader may have an easier time seeing the correspondence and divergence between the edition by Tyrrell and Purser and the manuscripts housed in Florence. We have added the initial capital letters for visual resemblance to the manuscript. We have kept the capitalization of the greeting of each letter as it appears in the edition of Tyrrell and Purser, although these appear in different ways in the manuscripts or are lacking there. We have introduced line-break hyphens where words are divided in the manuscript. The Arabic numeration of the parts of the letter follows that of Tyrrell and Purser, except that we have omitted the numeral 1 in each instance because it is not only obvious, but would interfere with the capital letter at the beginning of many of the epistles. At the end of a letter, if the page permits, more of the beautiful manuscript image is provided, and the reader is informed of this by our note following the typescript text: *alia tuam ad oblectationem,* "the other things for your own pleasure." We hope that once you begin to appreciate these letters you will continue your own study of them with these remaining texts and others you may find on your own.

Part I: Cicero's letters as our guide

The body of this volume is divided into three parts. The first part presents 51 randomly chosen letters that Cicero wrote mostly to family and close friends, and these letters are our guide. The letters are presented in two ways on facing pages, both the images of the letter taken from the manuscripts mentioned above and the print edition by Tyrrell and Purser. All readers are encouraged to pick up and read these letters and to discuss Cicero's Latin expression with colleagues or students or oneself.

At the top of each letter in typescript is our number from 1 to 51, giving the letter's otherwise random sequence in this book. The reader will note that the letters are presented neither in chronological order nor in order of addressee, nor in any presumed order of difficulty, but naturally, capriciously. Our number for each letter is followed by another, from the Tyrrell and Purser, or T-P, numbering system, which organizes the letters in chronological order. Next, the standard reference for each letter is given in full form. For example, the first letter is addressed "AD QUINTUM FRATREM, II, 9 (11)," that is, "TO BROTHER QUINTUS." This letter is part of the collection of letters addressed to Quintus. In that collection, this letter is found in book 2, given as the Roman numeral II, and is letter number 9 (or number 11 in some editions). The greeting of the letter is then reproduced followed by the letter itself as it appears in Tyrrell and Purser as far as possible, because in a few instances an ellipsis in square brackets, "[…]," indicates that for a solid reason we have omitted some part of the text given in Tyrrell and Purser. Otherwise, we have followed Tyrrell and Purser's hypothetical reconstruction of the original, including their orthography, italics, symbols, Greek words, punctuation, word spaces, capitalization, subnumbering, ellipsis, and in a few cases words in square brackets. We depart from Tyrrell and Purser by adding a few ellipses of our own distinguished by square brackets. This will allow students to read against a medieval manuscript, and to notice changes in orthography, word spacing, and other features that differ from this edition of Tyrrell and Purser.

Part II: Our commentaries on Cicero's Letters

The second part of this book replicates the same letters of Cicero, but in piecemeal, each one divided into smaller sections that follow Tyrrell and Purser's subnumbering of each letter, presented one section at a time. To be realistic and honest with our readers, we yield to the necessity of adding our own English version of each letter's section in such a way that translations of our own creation are always distinguished from Cicero's Latin text.

After each translation, we offer a linguistic commentary that indicates how Cicero is using the Latin language. Our purpose is to teach the uses of the Latin language immediately, forcing the reader *in medias res*, "into the middle of things," as we listen to Tully talking today on the phone. We have limited each comment to only a few of Cicero's Latin words, which we present in italic script at the beginning of most of our entries or commentaries. Next, their corresponding English words from our translation are given in quotation marks. After a colon appears our explanation of Cicero's Latin talk. We have tried to limit each entry to one or at most a few elements of the Latin language. The more common elements are indicated briefly by abbreviations, explained at pp. LIII–LVII.

Following each brief commentary is a reference arrow "→" followed by a system of cross-references developed with much care and toil by Daniel Vowels, who has taught Latin from the draft copies of the *Ossa* and this book for several years in London, England. The element of the Latin language under consideration is given, followed by a number that directs the reader to one of the numbered encounters of the *Ossa* book, where a patient and focused explanation of each element is available. For the sake of clarity the encounters in the *Ossa* book are numbered from 1 to 105 in these references.

For example, our commentary for the first line of the second letter appears in this book as follows:

> *quantum … acceperim*, "what … I got": IQ depending on M & M verb
> *existimare*, "to judge." This and the next IQ are on Track I, established by
> *existimare potes*, "you are able to judge."
>
> → **36** M & M, 60, 71, GL nº 527, remarks 1–2;
>   IQ, 60; *consecutio*, 47–48.

At the end of this commentary is an arrow indicating the references to each topic in the *Ossa* book. The abbreviation M & M refers to verbs of mind and mouth, which are considered in the *Ossa* book in encounter 60 (Third Experience, encounter 25). The abbreviation IQ refers to indirect questions, which are also covered in encounter 60 of the *Ossa* book. The term *consecutio* refers to the sequence of tenses, which is considered in encounters 47–48 of the *Ossa* volume (Second Experience, encounters 12, 13).

Some references direct the reader to a good dictionary, abbreviated "dict." For consistency, a specific meaning of the word is indicated using the system of numerals and letters found in the Lewis and Short dictionary, adjusting the latter's italics or punctuation for consistency with this our volume. Our references to dictionary entries may be presumed to be direct citations from the dictionary although we have dropped quotation marks whenever possible, out of concern for the clarity of our text.

A few other references direct the reader to the reference work by Gildersleeve and Lodge, abbreviated as "GL," followed by the paragraph number, and only by exception to the page number.

In a few instances the references direct the reader to another part of this book, such as the Roman Calendar located at the end of this volume as an addendum, or to a particular work listed in the bibliography.

Part III: The 500 sentences

The third part of this book is a special gift and help for our users. It consists of 500 sentences compiled by us the authors, going through Cicero's letters almost at random to find complete, whole, unadulterated sentences of typically three or four words, like talking with Cicero on the phone. There are 200 declaratory sentences, 100 questions, 100 exclamations, and 100 commands. These were originally presented at a conference held in Malta around the year 1973, and more recently at the annual conference of the Classical Association of Minnesota held at St. Catherine University in St. Paul, in 2013. Duplications found there have been replaced by additional sentences here.

Using this volume

This book may also be used in a certain reverse order by anyone looking for examples to illustrate one of the encounters in the *Ossa* book. Any teacher or self-learner may turn to the back of this book, where a Cross-Index enumerates all 105 encounters of the *Ossa* book. For example, if you are teaching from encounter number 78 (experience 4, encounter 8) of the *Ossa* book, and presenting the five verbs that take their complement in the ablative, and you quickly want to find some example sentences in these letters of Cicero which demonstrate this use of the language, you may turn to the cross-index on page 653 at the end of this volume and look under encounter 78. In the Subject Matters index on page 653 you will find listed the reference numbers associated with the arrows following each of our commentaries on this usage in the specific letters of Cicero treated in this book, although innumerable other examples can and must be found by any individual. Our commentary will lead the reader to the specific text of the letter, and to the whole letter presented in Part I of this volume. In this way, some of the more difficult to find expressions can more easily be located, in their natural occurrences. Other indices are also provided to help the reader locate a letter by its standard reference or by its T-P number or according to its addressee.

What this book is not

Some people may seek in this volume an historical introduction to the letters of Cicero, for which the interested reader may consult numerous commentaries in the library including the volumes by Tyrrell and Purser from which we have drawn these letters, or the excellent translations provided by Shackleton Bailey which capture the feeling and spirit of the letters in modern English. Our intent here is to provide something which historical, contextual studies often do not provide, namely, direct access to the very Latin expression of Cicero. In doing so, however, this volume is not intended to be a classroom textbook or a workbook or a program that teachers follow. Rather, this is envisioned as a preparatory text for classroom teaching or a model for learning by which we hope to inspire Latin teachers and self-learners to apply this method to their own preferred authors. We seek an encounter with the full corpus of Latin literature, giving Cicero as a model here.

Companion volume III: *Os praesens Cieronis:*
The Immediate Mouth of Cicero

According to our method, which is different from most traditional methods, from the very first encounter students meet authentic Latin authors, Cicero among them, without adaptation of their texts. In addition to the initial description of our method of teaching and learning the Latin language presented in this *Ossa* book, we now wish to show how our method may be used to introduce students to any genre of Latin literature from the very first encounter, using Cicero's letters as our guide.

An appreciation of the beauty of Latin may take hold right away and inspire students as they absorb and digest the letters of Cicero presented in this volume. They may wish to assimilate and learn to speak with *viva illa vox*, "that living voice"; this is humanly possible and totally rewarding. For this purpose we provide a companion volume III, the third in this series, titled *Os praesens Ciceronis epistularis: The Immediate Mouth of Cicero in His Letters*. It provides an audio reading of the same 51 letters of Cicero discussed in this volume. The listener may read along with these audio recordings, so the full text of each of the 51 letters is once again presented there, this time with the complete text of our translation of each letter on the facing page to encourage an immediate understanding of the Latin text in the hearing.

In the audio volume we also provide a help and guide to the teacher of Latin at every level and to the self-learner. This guide shows how the authentic expression of Cicero may be presented during the first four encounters with the language for each of the five Latin Experiences, as can be done for any other body of Latin literature.

Thus, we begin with the first four encounters of the First Experience and show how the letters of Cicero and the five-hundred sentences may be incorporated into the learning experience from the very beginning. Immediately we shall give eight specific examples lettered from A to H for each of these encounters so that we may head off certain initial difficulties experienced by teachers and beginners. Examples of how his writings may be used in the first four encounters of the second, third, fourth, and fifth experiences then follow for a total of 160 dialogues.

These conversations are given in the form of brief exchanges between an instructor and learners. They are based on the actual experience of teaching from authentic texts from every Latin author over the course of a career and from the experience of learning Latin through such a dialogical method. In each dialogue we begin with a genuine Latin sentence from epistolary Cicero and begin to work with it and gradually develop the capacity to create our own sentences based on those authentic Latin examples. People may consider sentences from these 51 of our letters and from the 500 sentences and then begin to work with them by reversing the singular and plural, flipping the active and passive, changing the verb times and persons, constructing new phrases and sentences based on the material offered by the literature, from the First Encounter with authors of the Latin Language all the way through the Fifth Experience with the fullness of Latin possibilities.

Admonitio–adhortatio: **Advice–encouragment**

This contribution is intended to provide nothing other than a guided introduction to one body of literature, one of many types included in any packet of reading sheets, such as the many authors chosen almost at random and included in the reading sheets appended to each experience of the *Ossa* book. The reading sheets remain the standard because they contain excerpts from every kind of Latin literature by many authors from Plautus writing before 184 B.C.E. until the most recent Latin papal pronouncements. We have repeatedly emphasized in the *Ossa* book that the reading sheets in their totality are the ultimate source of all the teaching in the *Ossa* book.

We hope that other teachers and self-learners will do the same with other forms of literature and other authors. For example, a similar book could illustrate the entire Latin language from the Book of Psalms in the Vulgate Bible, another from the writings of Boethius, whose Latin is out of this world, or from Augustine of Hippo, Leo the Great, Renaissance literature, Erasmus, Thomas More's *Utopia*, Spinoza, Galileo, Catholic councils: Trent, Vatican I, Vatican II; or any Latin text you want. We encourage other people to create volumes from other authors or collections like this one; the goal is not to limit ourselves to one author, but to open up the whole Latin world to every learner.

> *Bene vobis cedat!*
> May it turn out well for you!

Or we may say with dear Plautus:

> *di bene vertant*!
> may the heavens turn it out well!

VOCABVLORVM COMPENDIA

abbreviations of words

* *	*locus desperatus*, "despaired-of text," that is, a defective text that would be hopeless to try to restore
†	*locus desperatus*, "despaired-of text" (see above)
§	paragraph
A	*Aulus*
AA	Ablative Absolute
abbrev.	abbreviated, abbreviation
abl. abs.	ablative absolute
abl.	ablative, form or function by-with-from-in
abp.	archbishop
acc.	object, object form or function
a. d.	*ante diem*
adj.	adjective, adjectives
adv.	adverb
A.M.	ante meridiem
A.P.	Horatius, *Ars poetica*
Att.	*Ad Atticum*
B.	v.: S. T. E. Q. V. B. E.; S. V. B. E. V.
BCE, B.C.E.	before the Common Era
Bk.I	noun and adjective Block 1
Bk.II	noun and adjective Block 2
Br.	Brother
Brut.	*Ad Brutum*
C.	*Caius, Caii, Gaio, Gaium*
c.	common gender *or* century
C., Cn., CN.	Gnaeus, GNAEUS
Card., card.	cardinal
CE, C.E.	of the Common Era

cf.	*confer,* "compare"
char. result	characteristic result clause
class.	classic, classically
Cn.	*Gnaeum*
colloq.	colloquial
comm.	common gender
Comment.	Commentatio, Commentary
comp.	comparative
cond.	conditional
conj.	conjunction
consecutio	*consecutio temporum,* "sequence of tenses"
Constr.	Constructed
corresp.	corresponding
COS.	CONSULI
D.	v.: S. D. P.; S. D., data, dabam
d.	*diem, data, dabam*
dat.	dative, form or function to-for-from
De Or.	Cicero, *De Oratore*
demonstr.	demonstrative
dep.	*deponens,* deponent
DESIG.	DESIGNATO
Dict., dict.	dictionary: Lewis-Short, *A Latin Dictionary*
dim.	diminutive
E.	v.: S. T. E. Q. V. B. E.; S. V. B. E. V.
e.g.	*exempli gratia,* "for the sake of an example"
eccl.	ecclesiastical Latin
Ep.	Epistula
epist.	epistolary, letter-writing
Epist.	Epistula, Epistle
et al.	*et alii, et alia,* "and the others," "other"
etc.	*et cetera,* "and the rest"
f.	feminine gender
F.	Filius, Filio
F.	*Frater*
Fam.	*Ad Familiares*
Febr.	Februarias
fn.	footnote
Fr.	*Ad Fratrem*
freq.	frequently

fut.	future, futurity
gen.	genitive, form or function of-possession
GL, G&L	Gildersleeve and Lodge
Gp.I	verb Group 1
Gp.II	verb Group 2
Gp.III	verb Group 3
Gp.IV	verb Group 4
Hor.	Horatius
HS	sestertius, ii, m. "a sesterce," a small Roman coin
Ian.	Ianuarias
Id.	*Idibus, Idus*
i.e.	*id est*, "that is"
IMP.	IMPERATOR, IMPERATORI
impers.	impersonal
ind.	indicative
indecl.	indeclinable
indef.	indefinite
inf.	infinitive
in gen.	in general
init.	*in* or *ad initium;* at the beginning
interrog.	interrogative
IQ	Indirect Question
irreg.	irregular
Iun.	Iunias
Jr.	*Iunior,* junior
Kal.	Kalendas
L	fifty
L.	Luci, Lucius
L&S	Lewis and Short
lang.	language
loc.	locative, form or function of place where
m.	masculine gender
M.	Marcus
M & M	[expression(s) of] Mind and Mouth. See *Ossa* 60.
MA	Modal Attraction
Msgr.	Monsignor
n.	neuter gender
N.B., n.b.:	Nota Bene, nota bene
n°	number

nom.	nominative, subject form or function
Non.	Nonas
nostri*	special use of *nostri*. See *Ossa* 24.6
Nov., Novembr.	Novembras
num.	numeral
O.F.M.Cap.	*Ordo Fratrum Minorum Capuccinorum* (Capuchin)
obj.	object, objective
OCD	*Ordo Carmelitarum Discalceatorum*, Order of Discalced Carmelites (Carmelite)
Octobr.	Octobras
OO	Oratio Obliqua, indirect discourse
orig.	originally
OSB	*Ordo Sancti Benedicti*, Order of Saint Benedict (Benedictine)
Ossa	*Ossa Latinitatis Sola*
Ossium	*Ossium Carnes Multae*
p.	page
P.	*Publius, Publio*. See also S. P. D.
p. a.	participal adjective
parenth.	parenthetical [statement]
part.	participle
pass.	passive
perf.	perfect
pers.	personal
pl.	*plebis*
plur.	plural
P.M.	post meridiem
poss.	possessive
pp.	pages
prep.	preposition
prid.	pridie
PROCOS.	PROCONSUL, PROCONSULI
pron.	pronoun, pronouns
Q. Fr.	*Ad Quintum Fratrem*
Q.	Quinto, Quinti, Quintus, Quintum. See also S. T. E. Q. V. B. E.
Q.	*Quintus*
Quinct.	Quintilis
rel.	relative
repr.	reprinted

rhetor.	rhetorical
S.	v.: S. D. P.; S. D.; S. T. E. Q. V. B. E.; S. V. B. E. V.
S. D.	*salutem dicit*: he says a greeting
S. D. P.	*salutem dicit plurimam*, "he says a big greeting"
S. T. E. Q. V. B. E.	*Si tu exercitusque valetis, bene est*, "If you and the army thrive, it is well"
S. V. B. E. V.	*Si vales bene est, ego valeo*, "If you thrive, it is well, I too thrive"
SAL.	SALUTEM
Sex.	*Sexti*
Sext.	Sexti *or* Sextiles
sing.	singular
so c.	so called
St.	Saint
subj.	subject, subject form or function (subjunctive is spelled out)
subst.	substantive, –ly
sup.	superlative, supine
superl.	superlative
T.	See S. T. E. Q. V. B. E.
T.1, T.1i	Time 1 indicative
T.1s	Time 1 subjunctive
T.2, T.2i	Time 2 indicative
T.2s	Time 2 subjunctive
T.3, T.3i	Time 3 indicative
T.3s	Time 3 subjunctive
T.4	Time 4a or Time 4b indicative
T.4a, T.4ai	Time 4a indicative
T.4b, T.4bi	Time 4b indicative
T.4s	Time 4 subjunctive
T.5, T.5i	Time 5 indicative
T.6, T.6i	Time 6 indicative
T-P	Tyrrell-Purser
Track I	Primary sequence of tenses
Track II	Secondary (historical) sequence of tenses
V.	See S. T. E. Q. V. B. E.; S. V. B. E. V.
v.	verb
v. irreg.	irregular verb
v. n.	neuter verb, intransitive
vestri*	special use of *vestri*. See *Ossa* 24.6
voc.	vocative, form or function of direct address

EPISTVLARVM SVMMATIM DELECTVS

∾

*part I: a choice of
letters together*

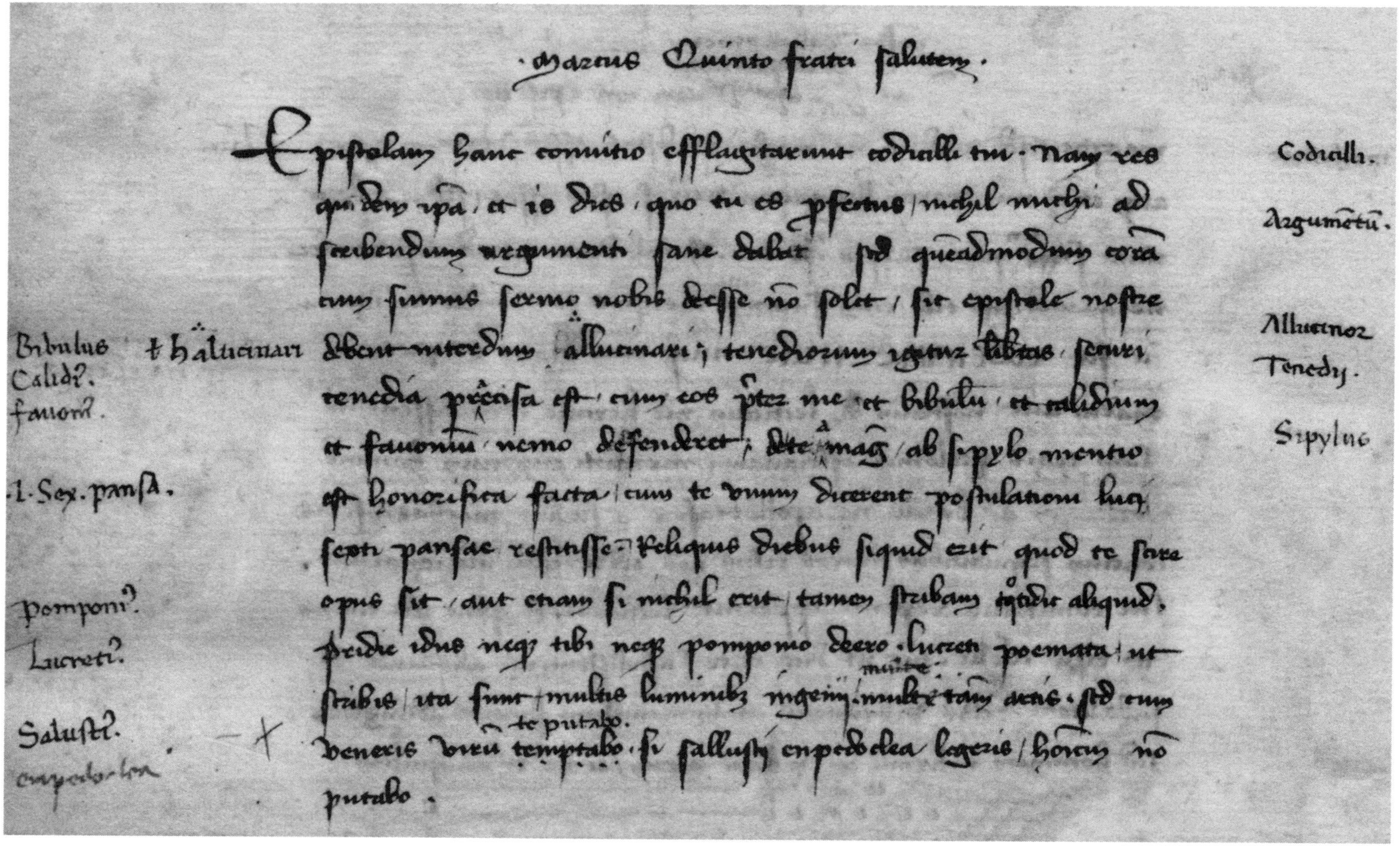

·Marcus Quinto fratri salutem·

Epistolam hanc convitio efflagitarunt codicilli tui. Nam res
quidem ipsa, et is dies, quo tu es profectus, nichil michi ad
scribendum argumenti sane dabat. Sed quemadmodum coram
cum sumus, sermo nobis deesse non solet, sic epistole nostre
debent interdum alluci(n)ari; tenediorum igitur libertas securi
tenedia precisa est, cum eos preter me et bibulum et calidium
et favonium nemo defenderet; de te a magnetibus ab sipylo mentio
est honorifica facta, cum te unum dicerent postulationi lucii
sexti pansae restitisse. Reliquis diebus siquid erit quod te scire
opus sit, aut etiam si nichil erit, tamen scribam cotidie aliquid.
Pridie idus neque tibi neque pomponio deero. Lucreti poemata, ut
scribis, ita sunt, multis luminibus ingenii, multe tamen artis. Sed cum
veneris, virum te putabo, si sallustii enpedoclea legeris, hominem non
putabo.

Bibulus · Calidius. · Favonius. · l. halucinari · L. Sex. pansa. · Pomponius. · Lucretius. · Salustius. · enpedoclea

Codicilli. · Argumentu. · Allucinor · Tenedii. · Sipylus

1

EPISTULA 132 T-P
AD QUINTUM FRATREM II, 9 (11)

MARCUS QUINTO FRATRI SALUTEM.

Epistulam hanc convicio efflagitarunt codicilli tui. Nam res quidem ipsa et is dies quo tu es profectus nihil mihi ad scribendum argumenti sane dabat. Sed quem ad modum, coram cum sumus, sermo nobis deesse non solet, sic epistulae nostrae debent interdum alucinari. 2. Tenediorum igitur libertas securi Tenedia praecisa est, cum eos praeter me et Bibulum et Calidium et Favonium nemo defenderet. 3. De te a Magnetibus ab Sipylo mentio est honorifica facta, cum te unum dicerent postulationi L. Sesti Pansae restitisse. Reliquis diebus si quid erit quod te scire opus sit, aut etiam si nihil erit, tamen scribam cotidie aliquid. Pridie Id. neque tibi neque Pomponio deero. 4. Lucreti poëmata ut scribis ita sunt, multis luminibus ingeni, multae tamen artis. Sed cum veneris .... Virum te putabo, si Sallusti "Empedoclea" legeris, hominem non putabo.

CICERO ATTICO SALUTEM

Quantum dolorem acceperim et quanto fructu sim privatus et forensi et domestico Luci fratris nostri morte, in primis pro nostra consuetudine tu existimare potes. Nam mihi omnia quae iucunda ex humanitate alterius et moribus homini accidere possunt ex illo accidebant. Qua re non dubito quin tibi quoque id molestum sit, cum et meo dolore moveare et ipse omni virtute officioque ornatissimum tuique et sua sponte et meo sermone amantem affinem amicumque amiseris.

Quod ad me scribis de sorore tua, testis erit tibi ipsi quantae mihi curae fuerit ut Quinti fratris animus in eam esset is qui esse deberet. Quem cum esse offensiorem arbitrarer, eas litteras ad eum misi quibus et placarem ut fratrem et monerem ut minorem et obiurgarem ut errantem. Itaque ex iis quae postea et saepe ab eo ad me scripta sunt confido ita esse omnia ut et oporteat et velimus.

De litterarum missione sine causa abs te accusor. Numquam enim a Pomponia nostra certior sum factus esse cui dare litteras possem, porro autem neque mihi accidit ut haberem qui in Epirum proficisceretur, neque dum te Athenis esse audiebamus.

De Acutiliano autem negotio quod mihi mandaras, ut primum a tuo digressu Romam veni, confeceram; sed accidit ut et contentione nihil opus esset et ut ego, qui in te satis consili statuerim esse, mallem Peducaeum tibi consilium per litteras quam me dare. Etenim cum multos dies aures meas Acutilio dedissem, cuius sermonis genus tibi notum esse arbitror, non mihi grave duxi scribere ad te de illius querimoniis, cum eas

(marginal notes)
humanitas
oportet
curiliano
Luci? f.
Quinti
pomponia
Athenis
peduce

2

EPISTULA 1 T-P
AD ATTICUM I, 5

CICERO ATTICO SAL.

Quantum dolorem acceperim et quanto fructu sim privatus et forensi et domestico Luci fratris nostri morte in primis pro nostra consuetudine tu existimare potes. Nam mihi omnia quae iucunda ex humanitate alterius et moribus homini accidere possunt ex illo accidebant. Qua re non dubito quin tibi quoque id molestum sit, cum et meo dolore moveare et ipse omni virtute officioque ornatissimum tuique et sua sponte et meo sermone amantem, adfinem, amicumque amiseris. 2. Quod ad me scribis de sorore tua, testis erit tibi ipsa quantae mihi curae fuerit, ut Quinti fratris animus in eam esset is qui esse deberet. Quem cum esse offensiorem arbitrarer, eas litteras ad eum misi quibus et placarem ut fratrem et monerem ut minorem et obiurgarem ut errantem. Itaque ex iis quae postea saepe ab eo ad me scripta sunt confido ita esse omnia ut et oporteat et velimus. 3. De litterarum missione sine causa abs te accusor. Numquam enim a Pomponia nostra certior sum factus esse cui dare litteras possem, porro autem neque mihi accidit ut haberem qui in Epirum proficisceretur nequedum te Athenis esse audiebamus. 4. De Acutiliano autem negotio quod mihi mandaras, ut primum a tuo digressu Romam veni, confeceram; sed accidit ut et contentione nihil opus esset et ut ego, qui in te satis consili statuerim esse, mallem Peducaeum tibi consilium per litteras quam me dare. Etenim cum multos dies auris meas Acutilio dedissem, cuius sermonis genus tibi notum esse arbitror, [...]

Subodiosum .

audire quod erat subodiosum leue putassem / ß abste ipo qui me accusas /
vnas michi scito inde redditas esse / cum et ocs ad faciendum plus / et
facultatem dandi maiorem / haieris / quod fieri era si cuius anus iniecerit offensior
esse me recolligi oportere quod dicas necg id neglegi / ß et mieo quodd
modo affectus . Ego aut que dicenda fuerunt de te non preterey / quid
aut contendendum esset / et tua prudentia uoluntate fruiture oportere qui
si ad me pscripsisio intelligeres me / necg diligentise esse noluisse / ß tu
esse necg negligentione face / ß tu nehis . De rabuna te meni radius
locutus est te uia scripfisse nichil esse uia qd laboraret / qri predinis
usurapta et ad inuedeamur te ignorance / de tutela legitima in qua dint
esse puella nichil ussicepisse . Epistona emprione gaudeo tibi placuisse que
tibi mandaui . et que tu intelligeres conueniat uos usurulumo velim ut faciens
auos quod fructuolosa tua fuisse poteris . nam nos ex ois molestys . ß et
laboribus / uno illo in loco conquiescemus que fratre quonde expectamus
Terentia magnos annulos dolores habet . et te et sorore tuã et
matre magni diligit . salute ß tibi plurima . faciit . et tulliola debue
uie . Cura ut ualeas / et nos ames . et tibi pscuadeas te a me faciem
amati .

† usu capi posse

Terentia
Tulliola .

audire, quod erat subodiosum, leve putassem. Sed abs te ipso qui me accusas unas mihi scito litteras redditas esse, cum et oti ad scribendum plus et facultatem dandi maiorem habueris. [...]

Alia tuam ad oblectationem.

Tulliuf tironi fuo fal. plur. die. Sic ero &q. fraer & q. f. uale tefum ad
fettaf tuif littterif ualde prior pagnaf pauf binaf paulum altera prore
amf quaxe nunc quidem nondu brio quin quod plane ualeafte neque
nauigationi neque uiae commttaf flauf tie maxure uideyf fi plane confir
matum uidero domedico & tu bene exiftamari foribif & ego fic audio fed
plane curatione eiuf non probo tuf enim dandum tibi nonfuit qum.
ka koc tomaxoc. etter federamen & ad illum foriphi accurate Radif
fonem ad curium uero flauuiffimum hominem & fummi offici fummne
que humanitatt multa foriphi mbir&iam ut firibi uideretur te adfe
tuf fero te ipfo enim nofter uereor ne negligentior fit primum quia
omnef graeci deinde quod cum ame litteraf accepiffe mibi nullaf
remifit fed eum tu laudaf aut gratur quod faciendumfit iudicabif illud
mitto te trogo fi tampau neparof ulla inne quod ad ualeudinem opuf

3

EPISTULA 288 T-P
AD FAMILIARES XVI, 4

Tullius Tironi suo s. p. d. et Cicero et Q. frater et Q. f. varie sum adfectus tuis litteris: valde priore pagina perturbatus, paullum altera recreatus. Qua re nunc quidem non dubito quin, quoad plane valeas, te neque navigationi neque viae committas. Satis te mature videro si plane confirmatum videro. De medico et tu bene existimari scribis et ego sic audio; sed plane curationes eius non probo; ius enim dandum tibi non fuit, quom κακοστόμαχος esses. Sed tamen et ad illum scripsi accurate et ad Lysonem. 2. Ad Curium vero, suavissimum hominem et summi offici summaeque humanitatis, multa scripsi: in his etiam ut, si tibi videretur, te ad se traferret. Lyso enim noster vereor ne neglegentior sit; primum quia omnes Graeci, deinde quod, cum a me litteras accepisset, mihi nullas remisit; sed eum tu laudas: tu igitur quid faciendum sit iudicabis. Illud, mi Tiro, te rogo sumptu ne parcas ulla in re quod ad valetudinem opus [...]

fit scripsi ad curium quod dixisset dare & medico ipsi puto aliquid dandum ee
quo sit studiosior innumerabilia quae sunt in me officia domestica forensia
urbana prouincialia in re priuata in publica in studiis in litteris nostris
omnia uiceris si ut spero te ualidum uidero ego puto te bellissime sirroce
erit cum quaestore me samo decursurum non inhumanius est teque uenuit
uisus es diligit & cum ualetudini tuae diligentissime consulueris tum mihi
consulto nauigationi nulla in re iam te festinare uolo nihil laboro nisi ut
saluus sis sic habeto mi tiro neminem ee qui me am & qui dem te amet quin
sima maxime intersit te ualere cum multis est cura ad huc dum mihi nulla
loco deserueris numquam te confirmasse potueris nunc te nihil impedit
omnia depone corpori seruire corpori serui quam cui diligentiam in uale
tudinem tuam contuleris tam me eius me ueuidicabo uale mi tiro uale
uale & salue tepta mihi salutem dicit & omne uale uii id nou locade

sit. Scripsi ad Curium quod dixisses daret: medico ipsi puto aliquid dandum esse quo sit studiosior. 3. Innumerabilia tua sunt in me officia, domestica, forensia, urbana, provincialia: in re privata, in publica, in studiis, in litteris nostris. Omnia viceris, si, ut spero, te validum videro. Ego puto te bellissime, si recte erit, cum quaestore Mescinio decursurum. Non inhumanus est teque, ut mihi visus est, diligit: et, cum valetudini tuae diligentissime consulueris, tum, mi Tiro, consulito navigationi. Nulla in re iam te festinare volo. Nihil laboro nisi ut salvus sis. 4. Sic habeto, mi Tiro, neminem esse qui me amet quin idem te amet, et cum tua et mea maxime interest te valere tum multis est curae. Adhuc, dum mihi nullo loco deesse vis, numquam te confirmare potuisti. Nunc te nihil impedit: omnia depone, corpori servi. Quantam diligentiam in valetudinem tuam contuleris, tanti me fieri a te iudicabo. Vale, mi Tiro, vale, vale et salve. Lepta tibi salutem dicit et omnes. Vale. VII. Idus, Novembr. Leucade.

.M. fonti.
.Q. Cicer.
Pompeia.

Cicero Attico salutem.

Non committam posthac ut me accusare de epistolarum neglegentia
possis. tu modo videro in tanto otio, ut par mihi sis,
domum rabirianam neapoli quam tu iam ementem et exedificantem
me habebas .M. fonteius emit. illud cellam rem r rerū, id te scire volui.
si quid forte ea res ad cogitationes tuas pomovet. q. fratr ut
mihi videtur, quo volumus eo est. in pomponiam, et cum ea nunc
in expensilibus predius erat. et secum habebat tōtam hōiam cum ipso
mathei bureanium. parva nobis deesse ad iij . kl. sextiles. hic
habebam forec que te fore vellem, tu velim si qua ornamenta
gymnasij describere poteris que loci sint eius, quam tu non ignoras,
ne preteritione nos tusculano ita delectamur, ut nobis nosipse
tum demum cum illo venerimus, placeamus. quid agas omnibus de rebus
et quid denique sis, fac ut sepe dilgentissime certiores, apud matrem
recte est. ea que nobis cura est.

.Cl . anno ī S rpā c̄ō . c̄ō . confirmi me curaturū idibz sextz. tu velim
ea que nobis emisti et parasti, scribis eos operam / ut q̄ primum
habeamus. et velim cogites id quod multum pollicitus es / quēadmodū
bibliothecā nobis conficeres. posse. omnem spem delectationis nre quā

Nota obitū patris Cicerōnis

4

EPISTULA 2 T-P
AD ATTICUM I, 6

CICERO ATTICO SAL.

Non committam posthac ut me accusare de epistularum neglegentia possis. Tu modo videto in tanto otio ut par in hoc mihi sis [...]

[...] Id te scire volui, si quid forte ea res ad cogitationes tuas pertineret. 2. [...]

[...] Tu velim, si qua ornamenta γυμνασιώδη reperire poteris quae loci sint eius quem tu non ignoras, ne praetermittas. Nos Tusculano ita delectamur ut nobismet ipsis tum denique cum illo venimus placeamus. Quid agas omnibus de rebus et quid acturus sis fac nos quam diligentissime certiores.

Alia tuam ad oblectationem.

Tullius terentiae suae · s · d · quod nos in italia saluos uenisse gaudes
perpetuo gaudeas uelim sed perturbati dolore animi magnisque iniu
riis metuo id consilii ceperimus quod non facile explicare possimus
qua re quantum potes adiuua quid autem possimus in mentem non

uenit... tuum quod credas hoc tempore nihil esse & longum est · et non
tuam & non uideo quid pro de ... si uenerit · uale · d · pr · non
nov · brundisio ·

Tullius · s · d · terentiae suae · quod scripsisti te pro uenisse ... ui ... de
nummo remittendo quae scripsisti uir hoc tempore si qua est conatio
mittuntur igitur si mecum dur ... aut est quircer aut mehabilis ..
for ... te ... coram iudicabit quidem & quod in mittere tmus rebus
minime mirum ... pitabris id faciet uale · vi · id · quintabr ·

5

EPISTULA 415 T-P
AD FAMILIARES XIV, 12

TULLIUS TERENTIAE SUAE S. D. Quod nos in Italiam salvos venisse gaudes, perpetuo gaudeas velim. Sed perturbati dolore animi magnisque iniuriis metuo ne id consili ceperimus quod non facile explicare possimus. Quae re [*sic*] quantum potes adiuva. Quid autem possis mihi in mentem non venit. In viam quod te des hoc tempore nihil est: et longum est iter et non tutum, et non video quid prodesse possis si veneris. Vale. D. prid. Non. Nov. Brundisio.

Alia tuam ad oblectationem.

et qd dicturus sis, scire uolo. nam ego diligenter simphonie censores. apud matrē

·Cī· anoon·H·S· xx·d· confirmui me curaturū uibz. febz. tu uelim
ea que nobis emisti. et parasti sordis des operam. ut ꝑ mmus
habeamus. et uelim egeras. id qd michi pollicitus es. q̄admodum
bibliotheca nobis conficere possis. omnē spem delectatois nr̄e. qm̄

.a.f.
Acutus?

cum in ocul uenerimus hr̄e nolumus. in tua humanitate posita bonus + habeamus
·Cicero Attico salutem·

A pud te est. ut ut nolumus/mater tua/et soror/a/me/quinto q̄ fr̄e diligtur.
cum acutho sum locutus. Ia tibi negat ia. suo procuratore/quicquam
scriptum esse/et mirature. istam controuersiam fuisse. qd ille renunciaret.
satis dari amplius abfe nō peti. quod te de tabulano negocio scripsisse
scribis. id esse ratio et gratum esse intelligo. z magnope rocundum.
Ille nr amicus ue me hercule optimus z michi amicissimus fane tibi
iratus est. hoc si quante tu extimes scirem/tum quid michi elaborandi
sit scire possim. ·I· num·H·S· ccls. ccc·. etc·. pro signo megalum
ut tu ad me scripseras. curaui. hec michi pontelicum capitibus aeneis
de quibus ad me scripsisti. iam nuc me admodum delectant./

Tullius.

6

EPISTULA 3 T-P
AD ATTICUM I, 7

CICERO ATTICO SAL.

Apud matrem recte est eaque nobis curae est. L. Cincio HS xxcd constitui me curaturum Idibus Februariis. Tu velim ea quae nobis emisse te et parasse scribis des operam ut quam primum habeamus, et velim cogites, id quod mihi pollicitus es, quem ad modum bibliothecam nobis conficere possis. Omnem spem delectationis nostrae, quam cum in otium venerimus habere volumus, in tua humanitate positam habemus.

Alia tuam ad oblectationem.

M· cicones̄ s· r· d· crebario· legi tuas litteras ex quibus intellexi te
ceſariniō ualde tuye confulaturum dori eſt· quod gaudeaſtee
inſula loca uenifſe· ubi aliquid aſpere uidere·quod ſii n̄ bri
tanniam quoque profecaif eſſet·profecto nemo milla tanta
inſula potuior æ fuifſk· uerum tanon rideamuſ·licſ̄ fuum
enim aut mutatur· fub i mundeo tibi ultro ēiam accerſitum
abeo adquem eſſen nonpropter ſuperbiam eus ſed propter
occupationem adſpuiye· nonpoſſunt· ſedau miſſa epiſtula
nihil mihi ſcripſiſta detur rebuſ que morcule mihi nonnn
noti cumerſunt quam meae ualde metuo ne frigeaſ inhibernſ
quam obyem camino luculento uerendum cenſeo idem mucio
ſmaniho placebat·py̆arfeyſam quiſagiſ nonabundareſ quam
quamuif nunciſfic ſanſ calere audio·quoquidem nuntio
ualde morcule de te timueram ſedau in ye miltayſ multo et
cuncior quam in adiocacaonibus· qui neque moceano natare
uoluerin ſtudioſiſſimuf homo natandi· neque ſpectaſt

7

EPISTULA 161 T-P
AD FAMILIARES VII, 10

M. CICERO S. D. TREBATIO. Legi tuas litteras ex quibus intellexi te Caesari nostro valde iure consultum videri. Est quod gaudeas te in ista loca venisse ubi aliquid sapere viderere. Quod si in Britanniam quoque profectus esses, profecto nemo in illa tanta insula peritior te fuisset. Verum tamen—rideamus licet: sum enim a te invitatus—subinvideo tibi ultro te etiam arcessitum ab eo ad quem ceteri non propter superbiam eius sed propter occupationem aspirare non possunt. 2. Sed tu in ista epistula nihil mihi scripsisti de tuis rebus quae mehercule mihi non minori curae sunt quam meae. Valde metuo ne frigeas in hibernis: quam ob rem camino luculento utendum censeo: idem Mucio et Manilio placebat, praesertim qui sagis non abundares. Quamquam vos nunc istic satis calere audio: quo quidem nuntio valde mehercule de te timueram. Sed tu in re militari multo es cautior quam in advocationibus, qui neque in Oceano natare volueris, studiosissimus homo natandi, neque spectare [...]

ēē darior quam antea ne andabatam quidem defraudare potteramus·
Sed iam facti iocti fumus ego dete adcautssem quamdiligenter scrip
serim tutetefur quam saepe ego sedmercule iam intermiseram ne
uiderer liberalissimi hominis mei que amantissimi uoluntati
ergame diffidere sed tamen hislitteris quas proxime dedi
putaui ēē hominem commonendum idfeci quid profecerim·
faciasme uelim certiorem· et simul detoto stasio consiliis que
omnibus scire enim cupio quidagas quid expectes quamlon
gum istum tuum discessum anobis futurum putes· ac emmabi
persuadeas uelim unumihi ēē solacium quare facilius possem
parite ēē sine nobis fioibi ēē idemolumento sciam sin autem
id noneft nihil duobus nobis eft stultius me quire non romam
actrabam· aequi non huc aduoles; una merculenia uel sauera
uel iocosa congremo plurisserit quam nonmodo hoster sed
etiam fratrenn hae du quare omnibus derebur fac urquam
primum sciam autconsolando autcontristre·

essedarios, quem antea ne andabata quidem defraudare poteramus. Sed iam satis iocati sumus. 3. Ego de te ad Caesarem quam diligenter scripserim, tute scis: quam saepe, ego. Sed mehercule iam intermiseram, ne viderer liberalissimi hominis meique amantissimi voluntati erga me diffidere. Sed tamen iis litteris quas proxime dedi putavi esse hominem commonendum. Id feci. Quid profecerim facias me velim certiorem et simul de toto statu tuo consiliisque omnibus. Scire enim cupio quid agas, quid exspectes, quam longum istum tuum discessum a nobis futurum putes. 4. Sic enim tibi persuadeas velim, unum mihi esse solacium qua re facilius possim pati te esse sine nobis, si tibi esse id emolumento sciam: sin autem id non est, nihil duobus nobis est stultius: me, qui te non Romam attraham, te, qui non huc advoles. Una mehercule nostra vel severa vel iocosa congressio pluris erit quam non modo hostes sed etiam fratres nostri Haedui. qua re omnibus de rebus fac ut quam primum sciam: 'aut consolando aut consilio aut re iuvero.'

M arcus cicero salutem dicit lentulo valerio iurisconsulto cur enim tibi
hoc non graphicor Nescio praeterea cum his temporibus audacia pro
sapientia liceat uti lentulo nostro ego per litteras tuo nomine gratias
diligenter egi sed aliud est de finas tam nostrus litteris uni & nos aliquando
reuisse & se tibi maluisse ubi aliquo numero sit quam sit cui sit solus sa
per euide arequam quid en quiis tam nunc ueniunt par ante e super bumes
se dicunt quod mihi respondeas par cum contumelio sum quod male
respondeas sed iam cupio te cum coram iocari quare fac ut quam pri
mum uenias Neque ut ipulam tuam accedas ut opossimus saluum uenit
se gaudere Nam illo siue neris ut ut ipulum ex cognosce se tuorum meminem

MARCI TULLII CICERONIS

EPISTOLARUM AD PUBLIO LENTULUM

8

EPISTULA 162 T-P
AD FAMILIARES I, 10

M. CICERO S. D. L. VALERIO IURIS CONSULTO; cur enim tibi hoc non gratificer nescio, praesertim cum his temporibus audacia pro sapientia liceat uti. Lentulo nostro egi per litteras tuo nomine gratias diligenter. Sed tu velim desinas iam nostris litteris uti et nos aliquando revisas et tibi malis esse ubi aliquo numero sis quam istic ubi solus sapere videare. Quamquam qui istinc veniunt, partim te superbum esse dicunt quod nihil respondeas, partim contumeliosum, quod male respondeas. Sed iam cupio tecum coram iocari. Qua re fac ut quam primum venias neque in Apuliam tuam accedas, ut possimus salvum venisse gaudere; nam illo si veneris, tu, ut Ulixes, cognosces tuorum neminem.

Alia tuam ad oblectationem.

Cicero curio procos. q. pompeius sex. f. multis &uariis causis
necessitudinis mihi coniunctus est cum antea meis commendatio
nibus &rem &gratiam ... te prouinciam &auctoritatem suam tueri confuerit nunc
profecto te prouinciam optinente meas litteras adsequi debet
ut nemini se intellegat commendatiorem umquam fuisse quam
obrem a te maiorem inmodum peto ut cum omnis meos atque
actuos obseruare pro necessitudine nra debeas hunc inprimis

ta. Intuam fidem recipias ut ipse intellegat nullam rem sibi meo
... usui au... ornamento quam meam commendationem te potuisse fuale
Cicero caelio aed. curul. m. fabio uiro optimo &homine docto sum
mo familiarissime utor mirifice q. eam diligo cum propter sum
mum ingenium eius summamque doctrinam tum propter singu
larem modestiam eius negotium sicutum suscipias &efficere res

9

EPISTULA 163 T-P
AD FAMILIARES XIII, 49

CICERO CURIO PROCOS. Q. Pompeius Sext. F. multis et veteribus causis necessitudinis mihi coniunctus est. Is, cum antea meis commendationibus et rem et gratiam et auctoritatem suam tueri consuerit, nunc profecto te provinciam obtinente meis litteris adsequi debet, ut nemini se intellegat commendatiorem umquam fuisse. Quam ob rem a te maiorem in modum peto, ut, cum omnis meos aeque ac tuos observare pro necessitudine nostra debeas, hunc in primis ita in tuam fidem recipias ut ipse intellegat nullam rem sibi maiori usui aut ornamento quam meam commendationem esse potuisse. Vale.

Alia tuam ad oblectationem.

Primum sciam aut consolando aut consilio auctore uere .

Cicero Trebatio. nisi aut eroma profectus ee nunc eam certe
relinqueres quis enim tot interrogatur iure consultum desiderat
ego omnibus unde petitur hoc consili, dederim ut a singulis
interrogibus binas aduocationes postulem. satis nec tibi uideor
abste suscriule didici sie sed heus tu quid agis haec quid sit
uideo enim te iam iocas per litteras haec signa meliora sunt
quam inmeo tusculano sed quid sit sarecupio consuli quidem

10

EPISTULA 167 T-P
AD FAMILIARES VII, 11

CICERO TREBATIO. Nisi ante Roma profectus esses, nunc eam certe relinqueres. Quis enim tot interregnis iure consultum desiderat? Ego omnibus unde petitur hoc consili dederim ut a singulis interregibus binas advocationes postulent. Satisne tibi videor abs te ius civile didicisse? 2. Sed heus tu, quid agis? ecquid fit? Video enim te iam iocari per litteras. Haec signa meliora sunt quam in meo Tusculano. Sed quid sit scire cupio. Consuli quidem […]

te acuefaciar scribir sedego tibi abillo consuli mallem quodsi aut
sit aut futurum puras perfer ista in militiam & permane. ego enim
desiderium tui spe tuorum commodoq; consolabor. sin autem ista
sunt maiora recipite ad nos nam aut erit hic aliquid aliquando
aut si minus una mecule conlocatio nra plurisert quam omnes
amurobrunce. denique scitote recaulens sermo nullus erit fiduras
frustra afuers nonmodo laborum sed &iam sodalem nrm ualerui
pertimesco. mira enim persona induci potest briannici iure consul
ti hac ego non video quamuis turrideas sed de reseuerissima tecum
ursoleo locor remoto loco tibi hoc amicissimo animo prexio ut si
ista mea commendacione tuam dignitatem optinebis perforas
nostri desiderium honestatem & facultatestuas augeas sin
autem ista frigebunt recipiaste ad nos omnia tamen quae eus
&tua uirtute profecto. &nostro summo ergate studio consequuts
icero trebatio mirabur quod nar quando nrm humanitatem

te a Caesare scribis, sed ego tibi ab illo consuli mallem. Quod si aut fit aut futurum putas, perfer istam militiam et permane: ego enim desiderium tui spe tuorum commodorum consolabor: sin autem ista sunt inaniora, recipe te ad nos. Nam aut erit hic aliquid aliquando aut, si minus, una mehercule collocutio nostra pluris erit quam omnes Samarobrivae. Denique, si cito te rettuleris, sermo nullus erit: si diutius frustra afueris, non modo Laberium sed etiam sodalem nostrum Valerium pertimesco. Mira enim persona induci potest Britannici consul-ti. 3. Haec ego non rideo, quamvis tu rideas, sed de re severissima tecum, ut soleo, iocor. Remoto ioco tibi hoc amicissimo animo praecipio, ut, si istic mea commendatione tuam dignitatem obtinebis, perferas nostri desiderium, honestatem et facultates tuas augeas: sin autem ista frigebunt, recipias te ad nos. Omnia tamen quae vis et tua virtute profecto et nostro summo erga te studio consequere.

conciliandam, maximo te mihi usui fore uideo, quare ianuario mense
ut conspicuus, cura ut Rome sis. Duum tuum fore desidero, uel
mortuam esse et simul qd nouith sit me latine in officio nō numerae
et in montem albanum hostias non adducerer. Suō rei obligatonem
ad te .i. finscium mittierum esse arbitror, uos hic te ad mensem
ianuarii expectamus, eo quodam rumore, an ex litteris tuis ad alios
missis, nam ad me de eo nihil a faucio scripsi. signa que nobis curasti
ea sunt ad Caietam exposita, uos ea non uidimus neqz enim
grandi roma potis nobis fuit. eosmus qui pro nostrix soluerez
te multum amamus qz ea abs te diligenter parueqz curata sunt. Sed
ad me sepe scripsisti de nro amico placando fez et excepit suis oia.
si maiandum in modum est ab abdicato, quibus de suspicionibus
etsi audisses, arbitror tam, sqme cum nescio cognosces Salluhni.
pritom restituen in suo uetere scacam nō potui, hoc ad te scripsi,
quod id me aliqua abs te solebat in se expente et illum qz manile
exorabilem menm fudu tibi nec desuisse. Tulliolam. C. psomi.
f. frugi despondimus.

A. Faustus ~ faustium
S. Aristi.
Tulliola. C. pisonis

CICERO ATICO SALUTEM.

Cetera expectatione nobis tui comoues. Tuaqz quidem cum iam
te aduentare arbitraremur repente abste in menses quintile revexit

11

EPISTULA 8 T-P
AD ATTICUM I, 3

CICERO ATTICO SAL.

Aviam tuam scito desiderio tui mortuam esse et simul quod verita sit ne Latinae in officio non manerent et in montem Albanum hostias non adducerent. Eius rei consolationem ad te L. Saufeium missurum esse arbitror. 2. Nos hic te ad mensem Ianuarium exspectamus ex quodam rumore an ex litteris tuis ad alios missis: nam ad me de eo nihil scripsisti. Signa quae nobis curasti, ea sunt ad Caietam exposita. Nos ea non vidimus: neque enim exeundi Roma potestas nobis fuit: misimus qui pro vectura solveret. Te multum amamus quod ea abs te diligenter parvoque curata sunt. 3. Quod ad me saepe scripsisti de nostro amico placando, feci et expertus sum omnia, sed mirandum in modum est animo abalienato: quibus de suspicionibus, etsi audisse te arbitror, tamen ex me cum veneris cognosces. Sallustium praesentem restituere in eius veterem gratiam non potui. Hoc ad te scripsi, quod is me accusare de te solebat: *at* in se expertus est illum esse minus exorabilem, meum studium nec *sibi nec* tibi defuisse. Tulliolam C. Pisoni L. F. Frugi despondimus.

Alia tuam ad oblectationem.

...eteram apud te hocte uehementer etiam atqz etiam rogo.

M· cicero · c · munacio · c · f · fal · L· liuineius tryphio est omnino
l· regis familiarissimi mei liberius cuius calamitas etiam
officiosiorem me facit in illum nam beniuolentior quam semper
fui et nunc possum sed ego liberum eius p se ipsum diligo
summa enim eius erga me officia extiterunt hif nostris tcm
poribus quibus facillime bonam beniuolentiam hominum et
fidem perspicere potui eum tibi ita commendo ut homines grā
et memores bene meritos de se commendari debent perstudiam
mihi feceris si ille intellexerit se quod pro salute mea multa
pericula adierit saepe hieme summa nauigarit prostudio erga me
beniuolentia gratum etiam tibi fecisse.

M· cicero · f · d · p · filio · pro pr · t · pinnio familiarissime meusum ee
faire te arbitror quod quidem ille testamento declarauit
qui me cum maiorem tum etiam secundum heredem instituerit

12

Epistula 164 T-P
Ad Familiares XIII, 60

M. CICERO C. MUNATIO C. F. S. L. Livineius Trypho est omnino L. Reguli familiarissimi mei libertus: cuius calamitas etiam officiosiorem me facit in illum: nam benevolentior quam semper fui esse non possum. Sed ego libertum eius per se ipsum diligo: summa enim eius erga me offica exstiterunt iis nostris temporibus quibus facillime [bonam] benevolentiam hominum et fidem perspicere potui. 2. Eum tibi ita commendo ut homines grati et memores bene meritos de se commendare debent. Pergratum mihi feceris, si ille intellexerit se, quod pro salute mea multa pericula adierit, saepe hieme summa navigarit, pro tua erga me benevolentia gratum etiam tibi fecisse.

Alia tuam ad oblectationem.

. Cicero Attico Salutem .

Et mea sponte faciebam antea, et post dubias epistolas tuas diligenter
In eandem rationem scripsi, magnopere sum commotus. Eo accedebat
hortator assiduus Sallustius, ut agerem diligentissime cum Lucceio, no modo
de uxa ueteri gratia reconcilianda, si cum omnia fecissem, no modo
ea voluntate eius que fuerat erga te recipere non potui. Verum
ne causam quidem dicere immutate voluntatis. tam si nactus ille
quidem, illud sui arbitrui, et ea que tam tum cum aderas, offendicet
tui animo intelligebam, tamq; sic quiddam profecto quod magis in animo
eius insidet, quod mea epistole tue neq; mei legatio, tam pot facile
delere, sed tu pme, no modo oratione, si tuo uultu illo familiari tolles.
si modo tanti putaras id, qd si me dubies, et si hesitamur ne grace
soles, te requirebis recte putabis, ar ne illius miece, me cum ego

Lucci?

13

EPISTULA 7 T-P
AD ATTICUM I, 11

CICERO ATTICO SAL.

Et mea sponte faciebam antea et post duabus epistulis tuis perdiligenter in eamdem rationem scriptis magno opere sum commotus. Eo accedebat hortator adsiduus Sallustius ut agerem quam diligentissime cum Lucceio de vestra vetere gratia reconcilianda. Sed, cum omnia fecissem, non modo eam voluntatem eius quae fuerat erga te recuperare non potui, verum ne causam quidem elicere immutatae voluntatis. Tametsi iactat ille quidem illud suum arbitrium et ea quae iam tum cum aderas offendere eius animum intellegebam, tamen habet quiddam profecto quod magis in animo eius insederit, quod neque epistulae tuae neque nostra *adlegatio* tam potest facile delere quam tu praesens non modo oratione sed tuo vultu illo familiari tolles, si modo tanti putaris, id quod, si me audies et si humanitati tuae constare voles, certe putabis. Ac ne illud mirere cur, cum ego [...]

antea significarem tibi, & leuis/me speraturo illu in ęm mea potare forte/nunc
eidem uideare difficile. Incredibile est/quantum mihi uideatur illius uoluntas
obstinatior. et in hac secunda affirmatio2. Et hęc aut fundunt cum
uehenie/aut & molesta eunt. in uero culpa est. Quod in epła mea
scripsi erat/me ea arbitrari disiquum esse/scio/nihil tam excentu cę
nuc fome/& candidatos sibus in equitatibus. nec quido fueras sunt
comitia fact. Vez hec audies de phyladelpho tu uidez quę achadmui
mę gauisti. & primu mitas opus quę illius lor/no modo usus/ß cuą
especturis deletate. libros no suos cane cuiquã tradas/nobis eos que-

_ me eo2

_ admonui scribs conscua summu/incredi fridie tenet: sicut odium tam
cetcrap reui quas tu incredible est. ß breui tpe/quato domnores
offensunculis quas uelophis uenerio/illi leniu sine negoni neg Cornelius configebant
ad te eę post eą/redit/opino. Do consent aquisdunum configebant
est. nam ea cerlio propinqui minore eetcesimę minum monee
no possunt. Et ut penui illa redeam, mihi ego illa imprudentius
africus. lentulus. Vir libertu. omte tuo mundam scripsi atcz inabile
ß nescio an ΤΑΤΟΜΑΤΟΝ ΉΜΩΝ

Nam mihi pompeiam prudeomi numquam apte pompeam actui
Antonio suorem oportet. eodem ß tpe aget pretex db populum /
Sed eiusmon est/ut ego/nos ß bonum/nec applacem exstimationem ę per
honeste possim boiem defendere. nec mihi libeat/qd uel maximi sit. t ia lubeat
etenu cadit hoc. quod rou ruusinol frt. mandat tibi ut perspicias/
librum ego sue/sane neqia hoiemplatem dico ratiocinatoe. et cliente
tui. de eo mihi ualcrius interpres mandat thyrlius ß te audisse.
scribit hec. et hoiem cu Antonio Brumuum ueroe in cotidie retidus

antea significarim tibi per litteras me sperare illum in nostra potestate fore, nunc idem videar diffidere, incredibile est quanto mihi videatur illius voluntas obstinatior et in hac iracundia obfirmatior: sed haec aut sanabuntur cum veneris aut ei molesta erunt in utro culpa erit. 2. Quod in epistula tua scriptum erat, me iam arbitrari designatum esse, scito nihil tam exercitum esse nunc Romae quam candidatos omnibus iniquitatibus, nec quando futura sint comitia sciri. Verum haec audies de Philadelpho. 3. Tu velim quae Academiae nostrae parasti quam primum mittas. Mire quam illius loci non modo usus sed etiam cogitatio delectat. Libros vero tuos cave cuiquam tradas. Nobis eos, quem ad modum scribis, conserva. Summum me eorum studium tenet, sicut odium iam ceterarum rerum: quas tu incredibile est quam brevi tempore quanto deteriores offensurus sis quam reliquisti.

Alia tuam ad oblectationem.

Tullius terentiae suae sal. si uales bene est ego ualeo uale audi nem tuam
uelim cura diligrastime nam mihi & scriptum & nu[n]tiaum est

el infebrim subito in aciste quod celeriorem fecist & decesaris licenti
ceterorem fecitam hi gratiam tam pote hac siquid opure te siquid acci
dentem on faciet uc siam cura ucua lac uale · d · IIII · NON · IUN ·

T ullius terentiae suae sal. plurimam ad ceteras meas miserat accessit
dolore dolabelle ualetudine & deiusillae omnino deomnibusredur
necquid consili capiam necquid faciam eo tamel moram & tullia uale
audinem curer uale.

T ullius s.c.d. terentiae suae quid fieri placere scripsi ad pompinium se
mus quam oportaare cum eo siloca erit intelleges quid fien uelim aper
cius scribi quo ad illum scripteram necence non fuit decere & deceeerir
rebur quam primum uelim nobis lumeas miceas uale & uale sic nem tuam cum
diligentem uale · uii · idus · quintiles.

14

EPISTULA 410 T-P
AD FAMILIARES XIV, 8

TULLIUS TERENTIAE SUAE S. Si vales bene est, ego valeo. Valetudinem tuam velim cures diligentissime. Nam mihi et scriptum et nuntiatum et te in febrim subito incidisse. Quod celeriter me fecisti de Caesaris litteris certiorem, fecisti mihi gratum. Item posthac, si quid opus erit, si quid acciderit novi, facies ut sciam. Cura ut valeas. Vale. D. IIII. Nonas Iun.

Alia tuam ad oblectationem.

15

EPISTULA 411 T-P
AD ATTICUM XI, 3

CICERO ATTICO SAL.

Quid hic agatur scire poteris ex eo qui litteras attulit: quem diutius tenui, quia cotidie aliquid novi exspectabamus, neque nunc mittendi tamen ulla causa fuit praeter eam de qua tibi rescribi voluisti, quod ad Kal. Quinct. pertinet quid vellem. Utrumque grave est, et tam gravi tempore periculum tantae pecuniae et dubio rerum exitu ista quam scribis abruptio. Qua re, ut alia, sic hoc vel maxime tuae *curae* benevolentiaeque permitto et illius consilio et voluntati, cui miserae consuluissem melius, si tecum olim coram potius quam per litteras de salute nostra fortunisque deliberavissem. 2. Quod negas praecipuum mihi ullum *in communibus* incommodis impendere, etsi ista res *non* nihil habet consolationis, tamen etiam praecipua multa sunt quae tu profecto vides et gravissima esse et me facillime vitare potuisse: ea tamen erunt minora, si, *ut* adhuc factum est, administratione, diligentia tua levabuntur. 3. Pecunia apud Egnatium est; sit a me, ut est. Neque enim hoc quod agitur videtur diuturnum esse posse, ut scire iam possim quid maxime opus sit: etsi egeo rebus omnibus, quod is quoque in angustiis est quicum sumus; quoi magnam dedimus pecuniam mutuam opinantes nobis constitutis rebus eam rem etiam honori fore. Tu, ut antea fecisti, velim, si qui erunt ad quos aliquid scribendum a me existimes, ipse [...]

Jason?

Brutus.

Pollex

— Cicero Attico salutem.

— Cicero Attico salutem.

— Cicero Attico salutem.

conficias. Tuis salutem dic. Cura ut valeas. In primis id quod scribis omnibus rebus cura et provide ne quid ei desit de qua scis me miserrimum esse. Idibus Iuniis ex castris.

Alia tuam ad oblectationem.

diligenter uale · xii · k · quinCbLes ·

Tullius terentiae suae · f · d · u · b · e · u · & si eiusmodi temporanrafun
te mihi st habeam quid sit ut ad te litteraruin gesp̄ectum adscrib adte scribam
tamen nescio quomodo & p̄ts urar litteras exp̄ecto & si renibe adnos cum
habeo quisferit uobismnia debuit hicte officiosior esse quam fuit & id
ipsam quod facere uobismnia debite diligentiur facere & catmur quam quam illa
sint quae magstraremur m̄ag tq̄· dolamur quaemeta conficiunt
ita enioltterutnc quimedemea setnenta deorusorunt curratt uileas ·

p̄ · non · Ian ·

Tullius terentiae suae · f · d · r · u · b · e · u · si quid st haberem quod illite
scriberem facerem id & pluribus uerbir & sapiur nunc quaedamene
gonainder ego autem quomodo sim adficiaus ex lepta & robetio potest
cognoscere uisfac uraniam & cuillia e uulsiudinem curer uale ·

Tullius terentiae suae & p̄ater suauissime filiae ciceroman & soron · f · d ·
plur · Considerandu uobis etiam ac q̄ · & iam animemtae diligenter ·

16

EPISTULA 424 T-P
AD FAMILIARES XIV, 16

T ULLIUS TERENTIAE SUAE S. D. S. V. B. E. V. Etsi eius modi tempora nostra sunt ut nihil habeam quod aut a te litterarum exspectem aut ipse ad te scribam, tamen nescio quo modo et ipse vestras litteras exspecto et scribo ad vos cum habeo qui ferat. Volumnia debuit in te officiosior esse quam fuit et id ipsum quod fecit potuit diligentius facere et cautius. Quamquam alia sunt quae magis curemus magisque doleamus: quae me ita conficiunt ut ii voluerunt qui me de mea sententia detruserunt. Cura ut valeas. Pridie Non. Ian.

Alia tuam ad oblectationem.

Cicero Attico salutem

Isidore?
Brutus
Pollex

17

EPISTULA 413*b* T-P
AD ATTICUM XI, 4

CICERO ATTICO SAL.

Accepi ab Isidoro litteras et postea datas binas. Ex proximis cognovi praedia non venisse. Videbis ergo ut sustentetur per te. De Frusinati, si modo fruituri sumus, erit mihi res opportuna. Meas litteras quod requiris impedior inopia rerum quas nullas habeo litteris dignas, quippe cui nec quae accidunt nec quae aguntur ullo modo probentur. Utinam coram tecum olim potius quam per epistulas! Hic tua, ut possum, tueor apud hos. Cetera Celer. Ipse fugi adhuc omne munus, eo magis quod ita nihil poterat agi ut mihi et meis rebus aptum esset.

Alia tuam ad oblectationem.

cognoui praedium nullum uenisse potuisse quare eundem uelim quomodo
facias flacca causis formenas fieri uelle quod dnica bi gratias age id ego non
miror tamen uirta obi mercanno gratias agere posse pollacem fiad buc
non est profectus quam primum fac grauida curari uerulas · id ib · quincc ·
T ullius terentiae suae · n.l · plurimam omnis molegas & sollicitudines qui
bus & te miserrimam habeam · d quod mihi molestissimum est uallolam
quae mobis rñ uita dulcior est depofui · & ea ea quid causae autem fu
erit post pridue ! molles i quart · auobis durcessi · ΧΟΝΗΝΑΚΡΑΤΟΝ ·
noctu execifacim trasim leuauar ut mihi dura aliqui s medignam fe
cisse uidetur cui quidem ui do quemadmodum fol & pie & caste fiat
facit i def e apollum & aesculapio nauem spe onor ualde bonam habe
re in tam firnal aeq · confcendi · haec scripsi deinde consenbam ad nos

S uiis · q · d · nec supe ese cui tra era ardemur n exerem habemus nullam
quam feribo e uelimus facaui tuorum quas proximen ce ep i ·

18

EPISTULA 414 T-P
AD FAMILIARES XIV, 6

Suis s. d. Nec saepe est cui litteras demus nec rem habemus ullam quam scribere velimus. Ex tuis litteris quas proxime accepi cognovi praedium nullum venire potuisse. Qua re videatis velim quo modo satis fiat ei cui scitis me satis fieri velle. Quod nostra tibi gratias agit, id ego non miror te mereri ut ea tibi merito tuo gratias agere possit. Pollicem, si adhuc non est profectus, quam primum fac extrudas. Cura ut valeas. Idibus Quinctilibus.

Alia tuam ad oblectationem.

Marcuscicero saluedicit c̄ · · · currioni m̄ · p̄ ē · Studium vonde
furt declarandorum munerum tuonomine sednecmihiplacuit neccui
quam tuorum quicquame absentefien quodaboiadnuemiffer Nomer
ſozlmee grumequidem ſentiam tuτforibam idco poſſetplurbuſAuτ
neadeummedicere · Inparatum τeoffendam coτamique contrauſtāratio
nemmedicam utauτe tuctmeumſentenτiam Adducam ductcet τe
coſſatum Apudanimumτuuum relinquam quidτenſerim Uſiquando
quodnolim diſplucerē inbrauum conſilium copperτe poſſirmeum recorda
τe · breutτamen ſichabeτo Ineum ſtaτum τemporumτuuumrediτumin
cidere utchirbonir qiuaeqbinatura ſtudio forτunadctaſunt facil
uſomniα quaeſunτ ampliſſimailInrepublica conſequipoſſiτ quammu
neτbur quorumneque faculτatem quiſquam Admiratur eſτenim
copiαrum Nonurτurunſ · Nequequiſquam eſt quinfacilkloe lande

19

EPISTULA 169 T-P
AD FAMILIARES II, 3

M. CICERO S. D. C. CURIONI Rupae studium non de-
fuit declarandorum munerum tuo nomine, sed nec mihi placuit nec cuiquam tuorum quidquam te absente fieri quod tibi, cum venisses, non esset integrum. Meam quidem sententiam aut scribam ad te postea pluribus aut,
ne ad eam meditere, imparatum te offendam coramque contra istam rationem meam dicam, ut aut te ad meam sententiam adducam aut certe testatum apud animum tuum relinquam quid senserim, ut, si quando
—quod nolim—displicere tibi tuum consilium coeperit, possis meum recordari. Brevi tamen sic habeto, in eum statum temporum tuum reditum incidere ut iis bonis quae tibi natura, studio, fortuna data sunt, facilius omnia quae sunt amplissima in re publica consequi possis quam muneribus, quorum neque facultatem quisquam admiratur—est enim
copiarum, non virtutis—neque quisquam est quin satietate iam de- [...]

fersiursis sedaliter aequeostendorum facio facio quiingrediar adex
plicandam rationem sententiaetmeae quareomnem hancdisputationem
induierumtuum differosumma sicco Inexpectatione esse eaquetace ex
specari quaeqummaturre summoq; Ingenio expectandasium adque
fiesusdebes paratur quodtra esseconfido plurimemaximisquemunem
bus Sinosamicos &cituituos uniuersos &rempublicam adficier
Illudcognoscer profuctomihi aenequaeaturorem nequeiucundiorem
essequemquam

Cicerosalutemdicit

... cusmoni epistularum generamultae
Te nonignoras: sedunum illudcertissimum causicausa Inuenirer
ipsaest uttestoris faceremus abienris siquoderset quodeorsore
aumostra surripsorum Interesset Inhuius generis litteras amepro
fecto nomexpectas domer acarum enim uarum animrerum domesp
carum haber &scimprores &nunzior Inmeraurem rebusnihilest
sanenourreliquasium epistolarum generaduo quememagnopere
dolecant unumfam...

fessus sit. 2. Sed aliter atque ostenderam facio qui ingrediar ad explicandam rationem sententiae meae. Qua re omnem hanc disputationem in adventum tuum differo. Summa scito te in exspectatione esse eaque a te exspectari quae a summa virtute summoque ingenio exspectanda sunt: ad quae si es, ut debes, paratus—quod ita esse confido—plurimis maximisque muneribus et nos amicos et civis tuos universos et rem publicam adficies. Illud cognosces profecto, mihi te neque cariorem neque iucundiorem esse quemquam.

Alia tuam ad oblectationem.

CICERO

ante di. v. kt.

amano moni, aure diem. v. kal. mai. eo die man...
ante die. iiij. kal. mai. ... icip̃ t pompeiani, bene mane, hr̃ sc̃ipsi. puteoli6
magnus ē rumor, et ptolemei ee t̃ regno, sed hꝰ coen̄ uolui fuire. Ego
hic pascoz Bybliotecha faust. forecasse in puteolis, hꝰ uob3 putrofaiū et
lucinacp̃b3. ne ista gdez desit. sz me faxule a cetis obsechoib3 retroz, et
noluptari ff uep̃. sic iterauis suspitai reeceeoz. malo ꝙ que illa tua
redicula qua habes sub magie auerforelib ꝛedue, ꝙ t̃ ifioze fella
cicut. Tcaiꝗ apud re ambulare ꝙ cꝰ eo/quo tu uado ee ambulandu.
Sz ꝙ illa ambulatiu fores inde, aut si quisꝗ t̃ mouet ꝛeis , meaz ambulatocz,
et Laconi eam quob3 cicea fut— uoliu quo poteist— minisꝙ uergras
philormii ut opperiet, ut possmi ꝛibi abꝙ t̃ eo genere respuieze. poper?
t cumani paiulb3. uenit, nisit. Dme futa ꝗ plurit mutauet. ad cu
pofferbe mane uadebam, tu her scipsi.

CICER. AT. Sat.

Eleceariut me eple tue , quas accepi uno tpe. Duas ante die qñi kal. pose?
reliqua gefho fuie. ista ora eta. Sed cuiusmodi sit ueliu, scipseras. pores
a demecio. Scipsi mihi— pompei? — eade miumia t̃ albano expectari ante die
iiij. kal. Je tu uenifut, fomia, et si fuit uentuieos/int. uaruos emai
publicaiū putauet , ꝗ resiui , glabacoib3 ne respondit— ante ꝙ induxiseut.
Sed cuiusmodi fit— iuic suc sisfires aut eu is fuia uenem. ad me muttas
uelru. nos sic uocam, litteras eū ipic mirifico.ita me baxule founo
Dionysio qui ribi. onē que nos ΠΛΗΝ ΤΟΥ ΣΕΝΤΛΥΚΤΕΡΟΝ ΗΠΑ

locus.
Ptoleme?
faustus.
il Lucernensibz.
Aristoteles.

Laconicu eagenach.
philotim?
pompei?

dematici?
popai?
Erasini?

Dionysius.

20

EPISTULA 121 T-P
AD ATTICUM IV, 10

CICERO ATTICO SAL.

Puteolis

magnus est rumor Ptolomaeum esse in regno. Si quid habes certius, velim scire. Ego hic pascor bibliotheca Fausti. Fortasse tu putabas his rebus Puteolanis et Lucrinensibus. Ne ista quidem desunt. Sed mehercule *ut* a ceteris oblectationibus deseror voluptatum propter rem publicam, sic litteris sustentor et recreor maloque in illa tua sedecula quam habes sub imagine Aristotelis sedere quam in istorum sella curuli tecumque apud te ambulare quam cum eo quocum video esse ambulandum. Sed de illa ambulatione fors viderit aut si qui est qui curet deus. 2. Nostram ambulationem et Laconicum eaque quae Cyrea sint velim quod poterit invisas et urgeas Philotimum ut properet, ut possim tibi aliquid in eo genere respondere. Pompeius in Cumanum Parilibus venit: misit ad me statim qui salutem nuntiaret. Ad eum postridie mane vadebam, cum haec scripsi.

Alia tuam ad oblectationem.

Suspicor.

Marcus Quinto fri suo plurim.

librū meū
Gratum tibi esse librū meū . ẽ . n . suspicabar : tam valde placuisse
ꝗ scribis, valde gaudeo . Suadesq̄ gaudio . ꝙ me admones & no
cūcunctat / suadesq̄ ut meminerim tuos oratones / que
est in optimo ille libro . Ego vero memini / et illa ora

21

EPISTULA 120 T-P

Ad Quintum Fratrem II, 7 (9)

MARCUS QUINTO FRATRI SALUTEM.

Placiturum tibi esse librum meum suspicabar: tam valde placuisse quam scribis valde gaudeo. Quod me admones de nostra Urania suadesque ut meminerim Iovis orationem quae est in extremo illo libro, ego vero memini et illa omnia [...]

multa nocte.

Crassus.

Clod.

uellem

.p. Crassus.

.. byzantiu~

Belantes
Brogite.

Afrini?

mihi magis scripsi quam ceteris. 2. Sed tamen postridie quam tu es profectus, multa nocte cum Vibullio veni ad Pompeium, cumque ego egissem de istis operibus atque inscriptionibus, per mihi benigne respondit: magnam spem attulit: cum Crasso se dixit loqui velle mihique ut idem facerem suasit. Crassum consulem ex senatu domum reduxi. Suscepit rem dixitque esse quod Clodius hoc tempore cuperet per se et per Pompeium consequi: putare se, si ego eum non impedirem, posse me adipisci sine contentione quod vellem. Totum ei negotium permisi meque in eius potestate dixi fore. Interfuit huic sermoni P. Crassus adulescens, nostri, ut scis, studiosissimus. Illud autem quod cupit Clodius est legatio aliqua—si minus per senatum, per populum—libera aut Byzantium aut *ad* Brogitarum aut utrumque. Plena res nummorum. Quod ego non nimium laboro, etiam si minus adsequor quod volo. Pompeius tamen cum Crasso locutus est. Videntur negotium suscepisse. Si perficiunt, optime: si minus, ad nostrum Iovem revertamur. 3. A. d. iii. Id. Febr. senatus consultum est factum de ambitu in Afrani sententiam, quam ego dixeram cum tu adesses.
Sed magno cum gemitu senatus consules non sunt persecuti [...]

core sententias / quas Afranio in scenis adscripsit / addiderunt / & adtexuerunt
re pretores ita reiecerunt / ut Deos sexaginta prinain
essent; Et sic Catonem plane respubuerunt / quod multa .~
tenent omnia; Idque ita omnes intelligere volunt .~/

Oratio .C. filii Tabiae.

Tu metuis ne me interpelles. primū f in ipso effeceris in
facio quod fac interpellare. Ante a te id me hexenla mea
Error noster infinae generis immortalem / qua quidem ego
nihil totō abste. Tu vero ut me et appelles, et interpelles /

o

eorum sententias qui, Afranio cum essent adsensi, addiderunt ut praetores ita crearentur ut dies sexaginta privati essent. Eo die Catonem plane repudiarunt. Quid multa? tenent omnia idque ita omnis intellegere volunt.

Alia tuam ad oblectationem.

haberedeemt nihil.

Cicero uchodni mihi uero adhonas bemematurum uidetur foreneq. folum propterre p. fed &tum propteranni tempuf quaue iftum diem probonaq. eundem ipfe fequicaur confilium nifi eofquidem quidfecur nonfunt nonpraenter & nobif praemtendum putare. locuaenim fumuf nonfpem fed officium. reliquumuf autem nonofficium fed efperanonem. trauet eundiore ffumuf quaquife domo non commouerunt fumor tfquaf quam iffi fifopib. domi non reuertorunt fed nihil immiffor fquaftin trattam

ato folum & quo quomodo feret habere magiftllo ueror quin bello occider uti quam hoscuro quibuf nonfanf fucamas quia uiuimuf mihi fifpanumfuore Imufculanum ante nonuf uentendi ficae uidebofinmi pfequiar incum anti & Iantetater vertfaci i inlauacio parcaifn.

Cicero uaqroni caninuf nr mezuf uerbf admonute urfenbremadeeff quideet quodputare tefcire oporme efigiuur aduenauf caifaorffeilick inexpectaaone neque tundignoraffed tamen cumille fenbriff &incopinor fe malfienfe uenarurum. fenberernu adeum fir nen d fucereE. mulfofeima leftor fore ipfiumque mulufoperue uidem commodiuf eum effet poffe. idego nom intelligebam quid maee et fedaonen birrnuf mihdifuer &fe adeum & balbum Roppium fenbriff uirtas fucere hominef urcof

22

EPISTULA 463 T-P
AD FAMILIARES IX, 5

CICERO VARRONI. Mihi vero ad Nonas bene maturum videtur fore, neque solum propter rei publicae sed etiam propter anni tempus. Qua re istum diem probo: itaque eundem ipse sequar. 2. Consili nostri, ne si eos quidem qui id secuti non sunt non paeniteret, nobis paenitendum putarem. Secuti enim sumus non spem sed officium: reliquimus autem non officium sed desperationem. Ita verecundiores fuimus quam qui se domo non commoverunt, saniores quam qui amissis opibus domum non reverterunt. Sed nihil minus fero quam severitatem otiosorum et, quoquo modo se res habet, magis illos vereor qui in bello occiderunt quam hos curo quibus non satis facimus quia vivimus. 3. Mihi si spatium fuerit in Tusculanum ante Nonas veniendi, istic te videbo: si minus, persequar in Cumanum et ante te certiorem faciam, ut lavatio parata sit.

Alia tuam ad oblectationem.

pacem hortari non desino / que uel iniusta utilior est et q̄ iustissimum bellum armis ...

Sed hec / ut fors tulerit . **CICERO ATTICO SALUTEM** .

de pace .

A te adhuc discessi / nullum adhuc intermisi diem / quin aliquid ad te literarum darem . Non quo haberem magnopere quid scriberem / sed ut loquerer tecum absens / quo mihi cum coram id non licet . Nichil est iocundius . Capuam cum uenissem ad reg̅ . b. pridie quam has literas dedi . Consules coueni / multos q̄ ñ ordinis . Omnes cupiebant Cesarem / abductis presidijs stare conditionib̅ ijs quas tulisset . Uni friuonio leges ab illo nobis imponi nõ placebat . Sed is auditus in cõsilio . Cato enim ipse iam seruire q̄ pugnare mauult . Sed tamen ait / in senatu se adesse uelle / cum de conditionibus agatur / si Cesar adductus sit / ut presidia deducat . Ita q̄ maxime opus est profecturam ñ curat / quod mihi ne obsit in senatu esse uult . Postumus autem de quo nominatim senatus decreuit ut statim in siciliam iret / Furfano q̄ succederet / negat se sine Catone iturum / et fidem in senatu opera q̄ periuolat ... nealeq̄ q̄m magna existimat . Ita res ad farnum precepitis / cum inicio in siculas permittitur . In disputationibus nisi summa ueritas est / plena q̄ negant Cesarem in condicione mansurum / postulata q̄ hec abeo interposita esse / quo minus quod opus esset / ad bellum / a nobis pararetur . Ego aut eum puto facturum / ut presidia deducat . Uicent enim si cõs factus erit ... et minore scelere uicerit / q̄ quo ingressus est . Sed accipienda plaga e .

Cesar.

fauoni?

de Catone .

postum?

fufan?

23

EPISTULA 311 T-P
AD ATTICUM VII, 15

CICERO ATTICO SAL.

Ut ab urbe discessi, nullum adhuc intermisi diem quin aliquid ad te litterarum darem, non quo haberem magno opere quod scriberem sed ut loquerer tecum absens, quo mihi, cum coram id non licet, nihil est iucundius. 2. Capuam cum venissem a. d. VI Kal., pridie quam has litteras dedi, consules conveni multosque nostri ordinis. Omnes cupiebant Caesarem abductis praesidiis stare condicionibus iis quas tulisset. Uni Favonio leges ab illo nobis imponi non placebat, sed is *haud* auditus in consilio. Cato enim ipse iam servire quam pugnare mavult. Sed tamen ait in senatu se adesse velle, cum de condicionibus agatur, si Caesar adductus sit ut praesidia deducat. Ita, quod maxime opus est, in Siciliam ire non curat; quod metuo ne obsit, in senatu esse vult. Postumius autem, de quo nominatim senatus decrevit ut statim in Siciliam iret Furfanioque succederet, negat se sine Catone iturum et suam in senatu operam aucto-ritatemque quam magni aestimat. Ita res ad Fannium pervenit. Is cum imperio in Siciliam praemittitur. 3. In disputationibus nostris summa varietas est. Plerique negant Caesarem in condicione mansurum postulataque haec ab eo interposita esse quo minus quod opus esset ad bellum a nobis pararetur. Ego autem eum puto facturum ut praesidia deducat. Vicerit enim si consul factus erit, et minore scelere vicerit quam quo ingressus est. Sed accipienda plaga est. [...]

eius puto facturum, ut presidia reducat · vicere enim; si populus qui ·
a minore solvere viceret; q[uod] a quo ingressus est · Et accipienda pugna ·
Sumus eni[m] flagra[n]t[e] t[er]printhi, cu[m] ius a penima · D. i[n]u[s]   Augustore ·
quidens omne[n]s no[n] m[od]o privatam, que in urbe est; si et[iam] publicam, q
t[er]e[n]no est; t illi reliquerunt · Donga u[n]s ad legiones Arianas e[ss]e p[er]fenus ·
Tabuenus, s[er]ia[m], se habet · Ego tuas opiniones de his reb[us] exp[ec]to ·
f[or]mius me odtino recipe cogitabam · Cicero Attico Salute[m] ·
Omnis arbitror michi tuas literas reddi[tas] esse; si primas t[er]prestare;/
Reliquas, ordine; que sunt misse per Terentiam de mandatis Cesaris

Sumus enim flagitiose imparati cum a militibus tum a pecunia, quam quidem omnem non modo privatam, quae in urbe est, sed etiam publicam, quae in aerario est, illi reliquimus. Pompeius ad legiones Appianas est profectus: Labienum secum habet. Ego tuas opiniones de his rebus exspecto. Formias me continuo recipere cogitabam.

Alia tuam ad oblectationem.

quid agam non habeo . Capuam mihi

fiatur de pompei rebus cognoscerem . Cicero Attico .

Reliquentem cum me tempus fiat . fricem em deficeret . Bellum
nostri nullam administrant . Caue enim putes quicq; esse minoris
bus consiliabus, quorum ego sp audiendi aliquid et cognoscendi nostri
apprime . magno imbri Capuam, tam pridie nonas . ut eum iii sue .

24

EPISTULA 318 T-P
AD ATTICUM VII, 20

CICERO ATTICO SAL.

Breviloquentem iam me tempus ipsum facit. Pacem enim desperavi, bellum nostri nullum administrant. Cave enim putes quidquam esse minoris his consulibus: quorum ergo spe audiendi aliquid et cognoscendi nostri apparatus maximo imbri Capuam veni pridie Nonas, ut eram iussus. [...]

Illi aut nondum veniunt, sed erant venturi, marius imperiali. CN. autem
lucere dicebatur. CN. autem

At illum micae nuntiat, sed adhuc reboris legionii invenire, no firmissimag.

Fut fugam interdidat. Ego aut in italia, KAICERNAПOEAHEIN, no te
ad consule, fine extra, quid ago ad me nondum hiems litteres improvidi
et negligentes duos ad fugam, hortatur amicia. CN. causa bonoru tprudo
coniungendi cum tyranno. Dum quidem incertius est philatim ne an
philistratum sit imitatius. Hac itelim explices, et me siuos consilio,12
sire tps ista iam calere puto, sed tamen quantu potens. Ego si quid
hic hodie novi cognovo, fit ita eu adeunt edisilce ad suas novno
tuas quotidie litteras expectabo. Ad hac aut cum potero rescribo, ordi
cies et Ciceronem in firmiano relqui. CICERO ATTICO Salute.

Et malis tuis ni fauis audes, sp ego. Istuas eu emas. Boni aut hic
quid expectes, nichil e. Veni Capuam, ad nonas Febr. ita ut iusserunt
cos. Eo eni die ego lentulus venit fero. Alter cos. oio no venerat vor. idus.
Eo eni die ego Capua discesi, et mansi statis. Inde hac litteras,
postridie ante lucem dedi. Hoc apud dum, fu cognovi, nichil in con
fidibus, nullum usp dilectuos, nec eni coniquisitores, BAINONTOCu
ne in audent, cum ille, ad faventiu, quem, nostre dire rusp sit, michil
agit, nec nomina dant. Sciut eni no uoluntas fp spes. CN aute
noster. Diresp miserum et incredibilem, ut tibis uset, no auis est,
no consilii, no copie, no diligentia, mittam illa fugam, ad urbe trepip.

Marginal notes:

.CN.

Al simul mori lv.
Kalouдaгто Saгgi

phularis.
prefectratus

Lentulus.

apparere.
фaироттооσɯттal

.CN.

Illi autem nondum venerant, sed erant venturi inanes, imparati. Gnaeus autem Luceriae dicebatur esse et adire cohortes legionum Appianarum, non firmissimarum. At illum ruere nuntiant et iam iamque adesse, non ut manum conserat—quicum enim?— sed ut fugam intercludat. 2. Ego autem in Italia κἂν ἀποθανεῖν nec te id consulo—sin extra, quid ago?—Ad manendum hiems, lictores, improvidi et neglegentes duces; ad fugam hortatur amicitia Gnaei, causa bonorum, turpitudo coniungendi cum tyranno: qui quidem incertum est Phalarimne an Pisistratum sit imitaturus. Haec velim explices et me iuves consilio, et- si te ipsum istic iam calere puto. Sed tamen quantum poteris. Ego si quid hic hodie novi cognoro, scies. Iam enim aderunt consules ad suas Nonas. Tuas cotidie litteras exspectabo. Ad has autem cum poteris rescribes. Muli- eres et Cicerones in Formiano reliqui.

Alia tuam ad oblectationem.

nomen... quam primum fac & cura ut ualeas · idib · quinct ·

Tulliuf tereneae suae · sal · plurimam omnif moleftiur & follicitudinef qui-
bur & te miferrimam habui : & quod mihi moleftiffimum eft · tulliolam
quae nobif uita noftra dulcior eft · deposui : & eiec quidem cauſae autem fuerit poft pridie l mellei quam · auo bif dixceri · ΧΟΛΗ ΝΑΚΡΑΤΩΝ ·
noctu eiiecit eadem tratium leatatur ut mihi detur aliquif medicinam fecit me uidetatur eum quidem medicum do quemadmodum fole ut pie & cafte facit
facit : ideft apollini & aefculapio nauem ſ̃ p̃ pono f uel debonam habere : In tantum fimul atq. confcendi haec ſcripſi : deinde confortabam ad nof
erof familiaref multaſ aep · fiulif quibuf te & tulliolam ram diligen-
tiffime commendabo cohortaturoſ i quod animo foraiore eſſer in
fiuof formaref cognofcem quam quam uiſ rum & tamen eiuſmo
diſpero negoua effe uoʃ uoſ fac commodiffime fieuerem effe & mea li-
quando cum fimilibuf noftri ram p · defenfaroſ uiprimum ualendine
ram uidemcuref · deinde ftabiut debriur uilliſiuf uere qua do longiſ
mie aberunt amitabuf fundo arpinaui bene poteruſ ira cum familia

25

EPISTULA 405 T-P
AD FAMILIARES XIV, 7

TULLIUS TERENTIAE SUAE S. P. Omnis molestias et sollicitudines, quibus et te miserrimam habui, id quod mihi molestissimum est, *et* Tulliolam, quae nobis nostra vita dulcior est, deposui et eieci. Quid causae autem fuerit postridie intellexi quam a vobis discessi. Χολὴν ἄκρατον noctu eieci: statim ita sum levatus ut mihi deus aliquis medicinam fecisse videatur. Cui quidem tu deo, quem ad modum soles, pie et caste satis facies [id est Apollini et Aesculapio]. 2. Navem spero nos valde bonam habere: in eam simul atque conscendi haec scripsi. Deinde conscribam ad nostros familiaris multas epistulas quibus te et Tulliolam nostram diligentissime commendabo. Cohortarer vos quo animo fortiores essetis nisi vos fortiores cognossem quam quemquam virum. Et tamen eius modi spero negotia esse ut et vos istic commodissime sperem esse et me aliquando cum similibus nostri rem publicam defensuros. 3. Tu primum valetudinem tuam velim cures: deinde, si tibi videbitur, villis iis utere quae longissi- [...]

mae aberunt amitabusfundo aspinaa bene pocentiusira cumfamilia
urbana fiantnona carior fuerit acerro bellissimus abualicem plurima
dicet atiam atq. Oxiamuale . d . VII . idus . IIN .

Tulliur Tereniae suae sal. siualerbeneest egqualeo ualeaudinemtuam
uelim euit diligentissime namimihi clempeum Knutaaaumest

me aberunt a militibus. Fundo Arpinati bene poteris uti cum familia urbana si annona carior fuerit. Cicero bellissimus tibi salutem plurimam dicit. Etiam atque etiam vale. D. VII. Id. Iun.

Alia tuam ad oblectationem.

· M · Q · f · salutem ·

O litteras mihi tuas iucundissimas / expectatas / ac primo quidem
cum desiderio / me vero etiam cum timore / atque hoc faro litteras
me solas accepisse / post illas / quas tuus nauta occuli / nulli
datas / sed cura ut facile presens sermoni refacientem & bo-
tumque no quo differre / dabas metas / senatus frequens dixim'
fruit in supplicatione gubernio denegandis / dilutat proclus hor-
nemini condisse / forte valde plausibile medi / cum sua sponte
modesam / tum iucundus quod
iudicium sine oppugnatione / sine gratia mea : etiam ante quod
dabus ut possidere fieret dictum & agro campano iactum rei ,
no est actum / in hac causa mihi / a / qua passet / sed plura
cui confirmarem coram esset / vale mi optime et optatissime
frater / et adiuola / idem te precor mei rogamus illud felicet salicet /
cenabis / cum venexis .

Gabriel?
Proculi?

Vita.

· Marcus Quirto filio salutem ·

Placituram tibi esse · P · u · suspicabar : tam valde placuisti
sed probis valde ipsum gaudio. quod me admones de no
librum meum

Suscripsi.

26

EPISTULA 117 T-P
AD QUINTUM FRATREM II, 6

MARCUS QUINTO FRATRI SALUTEM.

O litteras mihi tuas iucundissimas exspectatas, ac primo quidem cum desiderio, nunc vero etiam cum timore! Atque has scito litteras me solas accepisse post illas, quas tuus nauta attulit Ulbia datas. Sed cetera, ut scribis, praesenti sermoni reserventur. Hoc tamen non queo differre. Id. Maiis senatus frequens divinus fuit in supplicatione Gabinio deneganda. Adiurat Procilius hoc nemini accidisse. Foris valde plauditur. Mihi cum sua sponte iucundum tum iucundius quod me absente. Etenim εἰλικρινὲς iudicium sine oppugnatione, sine gratia nostra erat. 2. Ante quod Idibus et postridie fuerat dictum de agro Campano actum iri, non est actum. In hac causa mihi aqua haeret. Sed plura quam constitueram: coram enim. Vale, mi optime et optatissime frater, et advola; idem te pueri nostri rogant. Illud scilicet: cenabis, cum veneris.

Alia tuam ad oblectationem.

finis.

142

27

EPISTULA 366 T-P
AD ATTICUM IX, 11A

CICERO IMP. S. D. CAESARI IMP. Ut legi tuas litteras quas a Furnio nostro acceperam, quibus mecum agebas ut ad urbem essem, te velle uti 'consilio et dignitate mea' minus sum admiratus: de 'gratia' et de 'ope' quid significares mecum ipse quaerebam, spe tamen deducebar ad eam cogitationem ut te pro tua admirabili ac singulari sapientia de otio, de pace, de concordia civium agi velle arbitrarer, et ad eam rationem existimabam satis aptam esse et naturam et personam meam. 2. Quod si ita est et si qua de Pompeio nostro tuendo et tibi ac rei publicae reconciliando cura te attingit, magis idoneum quam ego sum ad eam causam profecto reperies neminem; qui et illi semper et senatui, cum primum potui, pacis auctor fui, nec sumptis armis belli ullam partem attigi, iudicavique eo bello te violari contra cuius honorem populi Romani beneficio concessum inimici atque invidi niterentur. Sed ut eo tempore non modo ipse fautor dignitatis tuae fui verum etiam ceteris auctor ad te adiuvandum, sic me nunc Pompei dignitas vehementer movet. Aliquot enim. […]

at dïoś

q̃ dïoś

... sïnt aïa cũ̃ tuoś duoś dclaȝ, q̃ p̃cipue colatos, r̃ quibus essent fir-
ut sũȝ amicissimê. Quãmobr̃ a te peto uel potius omnibus et p̃e-
cibus, oro et obtestor ut in tuos maximis aïs aliquid in p̃titus tempore huic quoq̃ cogitationi, ut tuo beneficio bonus uir grauis plus
deniq̃ essẽ maxime benefici memoria possim, q̃ si mãuirü ad me
tuȝ p̃tinerent sequerem me a te trauis imp̃tirarum, sed ut arbitror, sed ad tuam fidem et ad rem publicam ptinent me r̃ pure et
... r̃ iustrus et ad nutum concordiã p̃ te q̃ accõcdã stnuas
... r̃ cõuellctä. Ego uim ante tibi de Lentulo, gratias egissem, uũȝ ei felu-
ti qui mihi fuerat fuisses, tãȝ locus eius litteris quius ad me genti-
simo animo de tua liberalitate, beneficio q̃ mīsti, eademȝ me sãliutem
ille
a te accepisse quam, uj, i que si me medilugio fe[e] te gnuum, uir obsau.
bam.
... ut etiam, i tempora esse p̃ssinȝ sequerã tuos litteris uerum derentum.
Ik. cum mich epla affectue a Iepm curuiuallatuȝ esse tempenuuȝ
ratibus etiam, cuius potuo teneri no medull fïnus q̃ lacunis possem
reliqua, nec cogame uir fuñare, mihi ad te exemplum, uistuos uos,
... ... aut n̄ auto r̃ iu-.
hanc eadem quibus mentueuno obuiȝ cesaris rebelluir torquuer?
felix, ut uiu, ille mereuuuȝ gottuuȝ exoptuȝ, ad quam honestũ ad qua
expedut, tua cõfilia q̃uaȝ cũ̃ uul[t] a tuo aunumonibus, qua tuueris
qua nauigationis qua congressus fuonis, q̃ue cũ̃ Cesareona cuȝ
honestūnuȝ cauteuaȝ, eptuuȝ uicut uuicauto q̃ fuauus q̃ librduus q̃ firl-
na.. De Dionisio situs admiuetis, qui aprid me henoratioe fuit, q̃
apud Siguonem flauenus, r̃ quo uis fueris n̄ mehr hec uia fortuná

Lentulus. + cõseruaj cõuellctä.

Lepta /
pompeȝ?

Mati. /
Trebat?

Epta.)

Dionis? /
Siccio? /
Panet?

Cred epla ut ex /
epla Atticã

sunt anni cum vos duo delegi quos praecipue colerem et quibus essem, sicut sum, amicissimus. 3. Quam ob rem a te peto vel potius omnibus te precibus oro et obtestor ut in tuis maximis curis aliquid impertias temporis huic quoque cogitationi ut tuo beneficio bonus vir, gratus, pius denique esse in maximi benefici memoria possim. Quae si tantum ad me ipsum pertinerent, sperarem me a te tamen impetraturum, sed, ut arbitror, et ad tuam fidem et ad rem publicam pertinet me, et pacis et utriusque vestrum *amicum, ad vestram* et ad civium concordiam per te quam accommodatissimum conservari. Ego, cum antea tibi de Lentulo gratias egissem cum ei saluti qui mihi fuerat fuisses, tamen lectis eius litteris quas ad me gratissimo animo de tua liberalitate beneficioque misit, eandem me salutem a te accepisse *putavi* quam ille: in quem si me intellegis esse gratum, cura, obsecro, ut etiam in Pompeium esse possim.

Alia tuam ad oblectationem.

... cū tuus apud me sit · / perbelle feceris si ad nos veneris · offendes
resignatione tyrcanione mirificam / libroru meorū bibliotheca ·
quos reliqua multo meliores sūt q̄ putarā, et nollem meh̄ mittas
de tuis librariolis duos aliquos q̄z tyrcanio utat glutinatoreb;

ad cetera adminifices · is que imperes ut sumat membranulam
ex qua indices fiat quos vos greci ut opinor sillabos appellatis ·

Sz hr̄ si ut erit comodi · Ipe vero utg̃ fac venias / Si
potes ī his locis adherescere et philā adducere · ita enim
et equū e, et rupit tilha / medius fidius ne tu errasti

emisti

loci p̄claru · Gladiatores audio pugnare mirifice · si locare
voluistes duobz his muneribz liberasses · Sz hec posterii · Tu
fac venias · et de librarijs si me amas diligent;

· CICERO ATTICO SAL· ·

gratē ·

Plin tu an me existimas ab ullo malle me ad lege probari
afferre, aue igr̄ cū qua misi · pius · inegrebat ab eo ad quem
misi; et nō habebam exemplar? quid erā dudū eis revirteb
quod renovarēn e subtripenda is viadat in PALINΩDIA ·
si uideat recta vera honesta consilia · Nō est credibile que sit psidia

si inho principibz, ut rolūt ee / et ut cent si quoq̃ broent fidi? pugnam X
vocans/ induceus / reflectius / pratens abhic · anne hoc erat ī no
ut cū his ī ī is p· consentirē · idem erat et fuerat · vro aliquando
te auctore vos api indices ea tenuisse prafuse j fecerat / no etiam

ut p̄tbarem · ecs̄ mehercule multi necessitate nobis tponere huius

28

EPISTULA 107 T-P
AD ATTICUM IV, 4b

CICERO ATTICO SAL.

Perbelle feceris, si ad nos veneris. Offendes designationem Tyrannionis mirificam in librorum meorum bibliotheca, quorum reliquiae multo meliores sunt quam putaram. Et velim mihi mittas de tuis librariolis duos aliquos quibus Tyrannio utatur glutinatoribus, ad cetera administris, iisque imperes ut sumant membranulam ex qua indices fiant, quos vos Graeci, ut opinor, σιττύβας appellatis. 2. Sed haec, si tibi erit commodum. Ipse vero utique fac venias, si potes in his locis adhaerescere et Piliam adducere. Ita enim et aequum est et cupit Tullia. Medius fidius ne tu emisti λόγον praeclarum: gladiatores audio pugnare mirifice. Si locare voluisses, duobus his muneribus liber esses. Sed haec posterius. Tu fac venias, et de librariis, si me amas, diligenter.

Alia tuam ad oblectationem.

Cicero salutem dicit c......... curioni hactenegotia quomodo se habeant
neopistole quidem narrare audeo tibi &siubicumque est uttempsiadte
Amelneademorinauram quodhabergracilor uelquianonuidet
eaquenosuelquodexcelso &inlustriloco sitast laureua Inpluri
morum &sociorum &cuuum conspectu quae adhoc necabeuro net
uario sermone fabridurussima &una &una omnium uiocesserim
unum illud nescio gracoler neabi amoream quod mirabilis est expa
caziorediraxrui nonquouequeat in nezuauraruoprmoni hominu
et
non respondeas fedmercule necumuener nonhabear tamquodu
refizasiunt ommadebilivaza sumprope excundu fedhaecipsaneseto
rectanonsint licterus commissa quareckena cognoceer exalur tu
tamen fructhaberaliquamspemderepublica siuedeportataparta
modhasrecogrraquaseesse Inbocuuacuurodebent quisitrempub
licam adfluicram &oppressam misenis remporibus &ependira
moribus Inuecterem dignicatem &libertatem uindicaturuste

29

EPISTULA 176 T-P
AD FAMILIARES II, 5

M. CICERO S. D. C. CURIONI. Haec negotia quo modo se habeant ne epistula quidem narrare audeo. Tibi, etsi, ubicumque es, ut scripsi ad te ante, in eadem es navi, tamen quod abes gratulor, vel quia non vides ea quae nos, vel quod excelso et illustri loco sita est laus tua in plurimorum et sociorum et civium conspectu: quae ad nos nec obscuro nec vario sermone sed et clarissima et una omnium voce perfertur. 2. Unum illud nescio, gratulerne tibi an timeam, quod mirabilis est exspectatio reditus tui, non quo verear ne tua virtus opinioni hominum non respondeat, sed mehercule ne, cum veneris, non habeas iam quod cures: ita sunt omnia debilitata *et* iam prope exstincta. Sed haec ipsa nescio rectene sint litteris commissa. Qua re cetera cognosces ex aliis. Tu tamen, sive habes aliquam spem de re publica sive desperas, ea para, meditare, cogita quae esse in eo civi ac viro debent qui sit rem publicam adflictam et oppressam miseris temporibus ac perditis moribus in veterem dignitatem et libertatem vindicaturus.

affixo

. Ciuo Antonio . Cos . Fabitem Sta .

30

EPISTULA 717 T-P
AD ATTICUM XIV, 13b

CICERO ANTONIO COS. S. D.

Quod mecum per litteras agis, unam ob causam mallem coram egisses. Non enim solum ex oratione, sed etiam ex vultu et oculis et fronte, ut aiunt, meum erga te amorem perspicere potuisses. Nam cum te semper amavi, primum tuo studio, post etiam beneficio provocatus, tum his temporibus res publica te mihi ita commendavit ut cariorem habeam neminem. 2. Litterae vero tuae cum amantissime tum honorificentissime scriptae sic me adfecerunt ut non dare tibi beneficium viderer, sed accipere a te ita petente ut inimicum meum, necessarium tuum, me invito servare nolles, cum id nullo negotio facere posses. 3. Ego vero tibi istuc, mi Antoni, remitto atque ita ut me a te, cum his verbis scripseris, liberalissime atque honorificentissime tractatum existimem, idque cum totum, quoquo modo se res haberet, tibi dandum putarem, tum do etiam humanitati et naturae meae. Nihil [...]

Cledi?

Claudius.

p. Clodi?

enim umquam non modo acerbum in me fuit, sed ne paullo quidem tristius aut severius quam necessitas rei publicae postulavit. Accedit ut ne in ipsum quidem Clodium meum insigne odium fuerit umquam, semperque ita statui, non esse insectandos inimicorum amicos, praesertim humiliores, nec his praesidiis nosmet ipsos esse spoliandos. 4. Nam de puero Clodio tuas partis esse arbitror ut eius animum tenerum, quem ad modum scribis, iis opinionibus imbuas ut ne quas inimicitias residere in familiis nostris arbitretur. Contendi cum P. Clodio, cum ego publicam causam, ille suam defenderet. Nostras concertationes res publica diiudicavit. Si viveret, mihi cum illo nulla contentio iam maneret. 5. Qua re quoniam hoc a me sic petis ut, quae tua potestas est, ea neges te me invito [...]

...rerum, puto, quoq3 hoc a me dabis, si tibi ordinue, no quo aut etas mea, ab illius etate, quiq3 debeat perirūi suspicari, aut dignitas mea vllam contentionem extimescerat, s3 ut nos incipi iure nos coniunctiores simus q̃ adhuc fuimus. Interpellantibz enim hystrionis? rius, animo tuus magis patuit, q̃ sermo, s3 sic hac tenus. Illud exteenuan, cap, q̃ te vellet, quoq3 ad te ptinecet, arbitrabor, semp sue vlla subitratione, sermo studio farias, hoc ochin tibi penitus psuadeas.

Cicero Attico Salutē dicit.

Iterum eadem ista mihi ororantue quinctius ne penulibz, puralibz sabe ne et si alibe samany, quod venirer equidem, s3 hec cupio qui fuerunt aby, q̃ sarō, Sciō mihi mybinu nettinem. Explanabis igitur hoc— Siligentius. Ego autem cui cum illa domum ad te bocus roj. K. sarē multis verbis terbz fere horas, post, arcpi rido, et magn quidem psidaus sug, iterg tota tua plena facratum, et boces, reclāana, et phisoum more pincolano inssisse me sarē, et mihi necesse vesabscas. πoλετιτ̃ K.
ωτεpλ.. illa videanus in Brutos Cassinuq3 effenso, quasi cos ego resposdan, quod satis laudaxe nō postun. Firmi, ego ......
s3 illos quum tirauno, tiranna, manere vero...

usurum, puero quoque hoc a me dabis, si tibi videbitur, non quo aut aetas nostra ab illius aetate quidquam debeat periculi suspicari aut dignitas mea ullam contentionem extimescat, sed ut nosmet ipsi inter nos coniunctiores simus quam adhuc fuimus; interpellantibus enim his inimicitiis animus tuus *mihi* magis patuit quam domus. Sed haec hactenus. Illud extremum: ego quae te velle quaeque ad te pertinere arbitrabor semper sine ulla dubitatione summo studio faciam. Hoc velim tibi penitus persuadeas.

Alia tuam ad oblectationem.

cognoscere cuisac uouam & tulliae ualeludinem curae uale

Tullius cerenuae suae & pater suauissimus filiae ciceromis & cronis .f. d.

plur. Considerandi uobis & iam accep. etiam amem mtae diligenter

31

Epistula 306 T-P
Ad Familiares XIV, 18

Tullius Terentiae suae et pater suavissimae filiae, Cicero matri et sorori s. p. d.

Considerandum vobis etiam atque etiam, animae meae, diligenter […]

pro eo quod facturas romae nefaras iamecum In aliquo circulo co id non solum
meum consilium esse sed etiam uirium mihi uenirute Inmentem haec romae
uos ee circo posse perdola bella netiam quaeren posse nobis adiumento esse
si quae iura uroque rapine fiere coeperint sed rursus illud memoui
quod ui deo omnis bonos ab ee romi eeos mulieres suas secum habere
haec autem regio In qua ego sum uirorum ee quum oppidorum eam dixi
praediorum proximul cum esse mecum ee cum ibi erat commode ee In
uirus esse ponitar mihi plane non satis constat adhuc uerum sic melius
uos uidere qui dali uae facuere iseo loco feminae ee ne cum uelras esse re
non licere id uelim diligenter ee iam ateque etiam uobis cum ee cum a
mias confiderear domus uu propugnacula ee praedium habeae phi tramo
dicceas ee uelim tabellu nor In traulare certor uero ad hie aliquus a uobis
scteras accipiam miss me uutam date operam ucuulearas finos uultar
ualere · VIIII · k · formas

puto quid faciatis, Romaene sitis an mecum an aliquo tuto loco. Id non solum meum consilium est sed etiam vestrum. Mihi veniunt in mentem haec: Romae vos esse tuto posse per Dolabellam, eamque rem posse nobis adiumento esse, si quae vis aut si quae rapinae fieri coeperint. Sed rursus illud me movet, quod video omnis bonos abesse Roma et eos mulieres suas secum habere. Haec autem regio in qua ego sum nostrorum est cum oppidorum tum etiam praediorum, ut et multum esse mecum et, cum abieritis, commode in nostris esse possitis. 2. Mihi plane non satis constat adhuc utrum sit melius. Vos videte quid aliae faciant isto loco feminae et ne cum velitis exire non liceat. Id velim diligenter etiam atque etiam vobiscum et cum a-micis consideretis. Domus ut propugnacula et praesidium habeat Philotimo dicetis. Et velim tabellarios instituatis certos, ut cottidie aliquas a vobis litteras accipiam. Maxime autem date operam ut valeatis, si nos vultis valere. VIIII Kal. Formiis.

diligentia gratia prouidebo. A. trebonio qui tuo in prouincia magna
negotia & ampla & expedita habet. multos annos uiros ualde fa
miliariter. his cum amantia semper. & suo splendore & nostra cae
rorumq amicorum commendatione gratissimus h prouincia fuit
Tum hoc tempore propter tuum inmemorem. nostramq neceffitu
dinem uehementer confidit. ifment hac uirtuf & apud te gratiosam
fore. quae neq ipse um fallax uehementer rogote commendoq
tibi eius omnia negotia. libero procuratoref familiam imprimis
que ut quae tam pius. de eius re decreuit ea comprobet. omnibusq
rebus eum tra tracter ut ih collegat meam commendationem non
uulgarem fuisse.

ADXVI KLFEB. CUMINSENATU PULCHERRIMAE STAREMUS. 4
quodiam illum sententiam bibuli de tribur legacur pridie eius dies
fregeramus. unumqi ces tamen esse relicum sententia uolcacii.

32

EPISTULA 97 T-P
AD FAMILIARES I, 3

M. CICERO S. D. P. LENTULO PROCOS.

A. Trebonio, qui in tua provincia magna negotia et ampla et expedita habet, multos annos utor valde familiariter. Is cum antea semper et suo splendore et nostra ceterorumque amicorum commendatione gratiosissimus in provincia fuit tum hoc tempore propter tuum in me amorem nostramque necessitudinem vehementer confidit his meis litteris se apud te gratiosum fore. 2. Quae ne spes eum fallat vehementer rogo te, commendoque tibi eius omnia negotia, libertos, procuratores, familiam, in primisque ut quae T. Ampius de eius re decrevit ea comprobes omnibusque rebus eum ita tractes ut intellegat meam commendationem non vulgarem fuisse.

Alia tuam ad oblectationem.

33

EPISTULA 151 T-P
AD QUINTUM FRATREM III, 3

MARCUS QUINTO FRATRI SALUTEM.

Occupationum mearum tibi signum sit librari manus. Diem scito esse nullum, quo die non dicam pro reo. Ita, quidquid conficio aut cogito, in ambulationis tempus fere confero. Negotia se nostra sic habent, domestica vero, ut volumus. Valent pueri, studiose discunt, diligenter docentur, et nos et inter se amant. Expolitiones utriusque nostrum sunt in manibus: sed tua ad perfectum iam res rustica Arcani et Lateri. Praeterea de aqua, de via nihil praetermisi quadam epistula quin enucleate ad te perscriberem. Sed me illa cura sollicitat angitque vehementer, quod [...]

Messala.
Gabini?

Commi?corall?
P. Sylla.
L. Torquat?

dierum iam amplius L intervallo nihil a te, nihil a Caesare, nihil ex istis locis non modo litterarum sed ne rumoris quidem adfluxit. Me autem iam et mare istuc et terra sollicitat, neque desino, ut fit in amore, ea quae minime volo cogitare. Qua re non equidem iam te rogo ut ad me de te, de rebus istis scribas—numquam enim, cum potes, praetermittis—sed hoc te scire volo, nihil fere umquam me sic exspectasse ut, cum haec scribebam, tuas litteras. 2. Nunc cognosce ea quae sunt in re publica. Comitiorum cotidie singuli dies tolluntur obnuntiationibus, magna voluntate bonorum omnium: tanta invidia sunt consules propter suspicionem pactorum a candidatis praemiorum. Candidati consulares quattuor omnes rei: causae sunt difficiles, sed enitemur ut Messalla noster salvus sit, quod est etiam cum reliquorum salute coniunctum. Gabinium de ambitu reum fecit P. Sulla, subscribente privigno Memmio, fratre Caecilio, Sulla filio. Contra dixit L. Torquatus omnibusque libentibus non obtinuit. [...]

Dices quid fat. & quibus? nomin & maiestate tribuo /
quo quidem in iudicio odio premitur omnis generis.
magnis rebus editus: Iustifacioibus frugaliss͂io
virtute: cõfidentia vacuum, quo satis gratis et firmis
altius pompeius/vehemens in iudicibus cogentibus . quid
futuerus sit nostris . totum tamen illum in Cicerone non
vido /animum probo d'illius permitiem moderans /
ad tectum exemptu beniss͂imi . Bibo fere & omnibus
rebus /bonum illud adducam /Cicero huius nostra ppt /
fimo fridio et /promis/iustifacioᵗᵒzᵗᵒ hominis opinor
balla creatura . et bona . ed nostram infirmis genus
esse/ paulo exactius/et ΟϹΤΙΚΩΤΕΡΟΝ non ignoras./
quare nempe quo impudem viventis sex /atque illam

3. Quaeris quid fiat de Gabinio? Sciemus de maiestate triduo: quo quidem in iudicio odio premitur omnium generum, maxime testibus caeditur: accusatoribus frigidissimis utitur: consilium varium, quaesitor gravis et firmus, Alfius, Pompeius vehemens in iudicibus rogandis. Quid futurum sit nescio, locum tamen illi in civitate non video. Animum praebeo ad illius perniciem moderatum, ad rerum eventum lenissimum. 4. Habes fere de omnibus rebus. Unum illud addam: Cicero tuus nosterque summe studiosus est Paeoni sui rhetoris, hominis, opinor, valde exercitati et boni. Sed nostrum instituendi genus esse paullo eruditius et Θετικώτερον non ignoras. Qua re neque ego impediri Ciceronis iter atque illam [...]

disciplinam volo. Et ipse puer magis illo declamatorio genere
duci et delectari videtur. In quo quoniam ipsi quoque fuimus,
patiamur illum ire nostris itineribus. eodem enim perventurum
esse confidimus; sed tamen si nobiscum eum rus aliquo
eduxerimus, in hanc nostram rationem, consuetudinemque
inducemus. magna enim nobis a te proposita merces
est, quam certe nostra culpa numquam minus assequemur
quibus in locis et qua spe hiematurus sis, ad me
quam diligentissime scribas velim.

Marcus. Quinto fratri salutem.

Gabini.
Lentulus

pompei.

Gabinius absolutus est. omnino nichil accusatore Lentulo
subscriptoribusque eius infantius, nichil illo consilio
sordidius; sed tamen nisi incredibilis contentio, preces
pompei, dictature, etiam rumor, plenus timoris fuisset,
ipsi Lentulo non respondisset, qui tum illo accusatore
illoque consilio sententiis condemnatus sit .xxxii. cum lxx.
tulissent. Est omnino tam gravi fama hoc iudicium ut

disciplinam volo, et ipse puer magis illo declamatorio genere duci et delectari videtur—in quo quoniam ipsi quoque fuimus, patiamur illum ire nostris itineribus (eodem enim perventurum esse confidimus), sed tamen, si nobiscum eum rus aliquo eduxerimus, in hanc nostram rationem consuetudinemque inducemus. Magna enim nobis a te proposita merces est quam certe nostra culpa numquam minus adsequemur. Quibus in locis et qua spe hiematurus sis ad me quam diligentissime scribas velim.

Alia tuam ad oblectationem.

Tricenni veni ad xv · k · iunias / q̃ pontiū statuerā expectare / comodʒ-
sim̄ dixi expectare dies eos quos dʒ ille veniret / cū Ponipeio ⸓fuisse .
eoqʒ magis qʒ ei gratii esse dʒ dictabā · quīq̃ eta a me petiuit ut ⸓-
cū et · apud se / essem quotidie / quod conceʃ libenr · andros eiꝯ eius
preclaros dʒ r · p · ſmones accipiam̄ / iṅfirmꝰ eta consiliꝯ adueris
ad hoc meum negotm · Eʒ ad te breuior iā r̃ ſcribend inƿ̃o ſeri /
dubitās / ⁊ome ne sis / an iā ⁊ effet / quod tame quod ignorabo ſuba
aliquis potuis qʒ comitium / ut tib̃ eū possut · uddi / a me litere ńo
reddant · Nec tame iā babio quid aut mandem tib̃ , aut ſcriuerem · exbaurio .
madaui omiā / que quidem tu ut · pollicers exhauneris · Naurabo ñ
aliquid habebo noui · illud tame no reſtinam ɘuū abesse pintabo dʒ
cesaris noie rogare / ut confiteri reſinquas · Auid expecto tuas lras
et · maxume ut noui trꝯ iᵽnonꝰ trie · CIC · AT · SAT ·

Comende uel potius iṅ meos ſingulos / breuiorio litaras dʒ te mitto · Condic
enim magis ſuspicor / te epirum iā iſſeti · ſed tame ut mandam
lras me excuſasse / quod aut dʒ ⁊⸓imperuus qui nos prefectos
⸓latuit nouos vacatones iṅſoueris caufiū / ego cum teſtium
ꝓfirebar bciṅbrinū / insllig inſedim gnida / ego cum teſtiū
iṅ ſomp · ⁊ ordind iṅ · v · hal · iunias · iunias / bal iunias · lux ꝓ
⁊ / ⸓⸓imꝯ cuṅg̃ egregiā uillā habuerā · auaṁ iam / ſ ꝑ

34

EPISTULA 189 T-P
AD ATTICUM V 6

CICERO ATTICO SAL.

Tarentum veni a. d. XV Kal. Iunias. Quod Pomptinum statueram exspectare, commodissimum duxi dies eos, quoad ille veniret, cum Pompeio consumere, eoque magis quod ei gratum esse id videbam, qui etiam a me petierit ut secum et apud se essem cotidie: quod concessi libenter. Multos enim eius praeclaros de re publica sermones accipiam, instruar etiam consiliis idoneis ad hoc nostrum negotium. 2. Sed ad te brevior iam in scribendo incipio fieri, dubitans Romaene sis an iam profectus. Quod tamen quoad ignorabo, scribam aliquid potius quam committam ut tibi, cum possint reddi a me litterae, non reddantur. Nec tamen iam habeo quod aut mandem tibi aut narrem. Mandavi omnia, quae quidem tu, ut polliceris, exhauries: narrabo, cum aliquid habebo novi. Illud tamen non desinam, dum adesse *te* putabo, de Caesaris nomine rogare, ut confectum relinquas. Avide exspecto tuas litteras et maxime ut norim tempus profectionis tuae.

Alia tuam ad oblectationem.

Cum intrassem ad te pridie, calamūsque sumpsisse /Batonis/ etiam
certus ad me vēr domū ephes / et eplam tua reddidit pridie
.k. oct. Letanus sum filiolae navigationis tue opportunitas
filiē etiam benevole smone eius̄ de coniugio tullie mee. Batoni?
aut meos tenores adstulit me cesareae nos. Cū lepta etiam
phisie lorunus e. speco falsa / sz vere horribilia. Exercitū mille
modo dimissus. Cū illo Pretores designatis Cassius pr. pl.
Lentullu consulē favere. Pompeio t aio ētē vrbem relinquere.
Sz hercle, tu inquid molestates fres, et illo, quī se plet auxefere
paterno / Precoris tue filio. ut a quibz victus. Ez ad rem spes
et estae vehementissime tardarent. detraxit xxx. ipse tres
etiam appetenes predi / .k. oct. ephis consentires huc eplam
quae oō i peregrinis simul e poram expedierim sī expedirim
requirio. l. quinxe yssimum
remittam. annotaturi examo. qanto Pr. us. q
quā annotaturi putaremo trahit putaruamo tracri. Unde magiś Rex romanus erat
grandios inquā sur.
quand non pot
tall laus de
grandior urgent et ergou quid gesq. Unde
quand usurparum obirut et reunt

35

EPISTULA 281 T-P
AD ATTICUM VI, 8

CICERO ATTICO SAL.

Cum instituissem ad te scribere calamumque sumpsissem, Batonius e navi recta ad me venit domum Ephesi et epistulam tuam reddidit pridie Kal. Octobris. Laetatus sum felicitate navigationis tuae, opportunitate Piliae, etiam hercule sermone eiusdem de coniugio Tulliae meae. 2. Batonius autem meros terrores ad me attulit Caesarianos, cum Lepta etiam plura locutus est, spero falsa, sed certe horribilia, exercitum nullo modo dimissurum, cum illo praetores designatos, Cassium tribunum pl., Lentulum consulem facere, Pompeio in animo esse urbem reliquere. 3. Sed heus tu, num quid moleste fers de illo, qui se solet anteferre patruo sororis tuae fili? At a quibus victus! Sed ad rem. 4. Nos etesiae vehementissime tardarunt. Detraxit XX ipsos dies etiam aphractus Rhodiorum. Kal. Octobr. Epheso conscendentes hanc epistulam dedimus L. Tarquitio, simul e portu egredienti sed expeditius naviganti. Nos Rhodiorum aphractis ceterisque longis navibus tranquili- tates aucupaturi eramus: ita tamen properabamus ut non posset magis. 5. De raudusculo Puteolano gratum. Nunc velim dispicias res Romanas, videas quid nobis de triumpho cogitandum putes, [. . .]

Bibulus.

ad qᵐ anni meᵗ vacant. Ego niſ Bibuluſ, qui dᵘ onᵘ hoſpeſ ĩ Syria
fuit, pedem porta nõ pluſ extulit, ſ δomo ſua. aδmiſcet & tempᵽ, equo aᵗⁱᵒ
eaⁱⁱ. Nũc uero ΛΙΣΧΡΟΝΣΙΩΠΠΔΗ, ᵖ̃ explorare totã æquo δie congreſſi
ᵖ̃mᵘ conſiliⁱ cape poſſmⁱ. Ut multa qui et apᵖeraᵖ̃, et ei liᵇᵒeraᵇ δaᵗⁱ,
qui aut meoⁱ, aut paulo ante uenerⁱⁱ eſſet. Ciⁱazo tⁱbi plurimam
ſaluⁱ δicit. In δiⁱⁱⁱ uⁱⁱcⁱⁱ nᵘ uⁱⁱcⁱⁱ, et pile tue et flue.

turpe tacere αἰσχρὸν σιωπᾶν

Cicero Attiⁱ ſal̃.

Impreſſa ĩ egᵒ ſſᵇ̃, ᵖⁱ. 18 oct. accep aⁱ καſͭᵒ ᵖzuo meo, fraⁱ tuaⁱ ſiaſ.
Quaⁱ quiⁱⁱ m ⁱⁱⁱⁱⁱ ᵇ̃ⁱ iⁱⁱ Diⁱ, aⁱmiⁱanᵒ ſuⁱ. et ᵖⁱⁱⁱ obſiⁱⁱⁱⁱⁱ
epⁱⁱola breuitate eiⁱ, et apᵖeⁱⁱ uerſⁱⁱ ΣΙΗΤΥΣΙΝ literaⁱⁱⁱⁱ que
poſⁱⁱ tue compoſiⁱⁱⁱ et clariſiⁱⁱ eⁱⁱ. Ac ne multa cognoⁱⁱ ᵖⁱ eo
ſ iⁱⁱ meſſiaⁱⁱ, te ſoⁱⁱa uⁱⁱⁱⁱⁱ. ᵖⁱ ΣΙΙΙ. k oct. ei fibi pⁱⁱⁱⁱⁱⁱ
uⁱⁱⁱⁱⁱⁱ. Nec magiſ ſ ſaⁱⁱ fraⁱ queⁱo, eⁱ ⁱⁱ acaſⁱⁱ, ſlle ⁱ tⁱ, et ⁱ
uⁱⁱⁱⁱⁱⁱ, et ⁱⁱⁱ δⁱⁱⁱ exⁱⁱⁱ auⁱⁱⁱ, ut ⁱⁱⁱⁱ eⁱ ⁱⁱⁱⁱ. δ
uⁱⁱⁱⁱ, et ⁱⁱⁱ δⁱⁱⁱ exⁱⁱⁱ auⁱⁱⁱ, ut ⁱⁱⁱⁱ eⁱ ⁱⁱⁱⁱ. δ
uⁱⁱⁱⁱⁱ apⁱⁱⁱⁱⁱ, quoⁱⁱ exⁱⁱⁱ ⁱ epⁱⁱⁱⁱⁱⁱ, ſiⁱⁱⁱⁱⁱ ⁱⁱⁱ ⁱ ⁱⁱⁱⁱⁱ ᵖⁱⁱⁱⁱⁱ.
ſⁱ ſⁱⁱⁱ uⁱⁱⁱ, aⁱmiⁱⁱⁱⁱ ſ ſuⁱⁱ ſ ⁱⁱⁱⁱ ᵖ̃ ⁱⁱⁱⁱⁱⁱⁱ ſⁱ me tuⁱ manⁱⁱ.
ſⁱⁱⁱⁱⁱⁱⁱ. Suaⁱⁱ & hoc ᵖⁱⁱ. Speⁱo eⁱⁱ queⁱⁱⁱ peⁱⁱⁱⁱⁱ ⁱ teⁱⁱⁱⁱⁱⁱ
ⁱ, ᵇⁱⁱⁱⁱⁱⁱ ut me iubeⁱ, aⁱⁱⁱⁱⁱ/oⁱⁱⁱ te ⁱⁱ ut ⁱⁱⁱⁱⁱ uⁱⁱⁱⁱ. ⁱ ⁱⁱⁱⁱ
ⁱ tuⁱⁱⁱⁱⁱ te auⁱⁱⁱⁱⁱ meⁱⁱ ⁱⁱⁱⁱ gauⁱⁱⁱ ΠΑΡΑΦΜΙΖΟΗ. ſi me amaⁱ
ΤΗΝΤΟΥΦΡΡΑΤΟΥ ΦΙΛΟΤΕΙΜΙΑΗΑΥΤΟΤΑΤΑ. ᵇⁱⁱⁱ ⁱ me ᵇⁱⁱⁱⁱⁱ ᵖⁱⁱⁱⁱⁱⁱ
ⁱⁱ uⁱⁱⁱⁱ δⁱⁱⁱ ⁱ iⁱⁱⁱⁱ eⁱⁱ ⁱⁱⁱⁱ ᵖⁱⁱ ⁱⁱⁱⁱⁱ gⁱⁱⁱⁱⁱⁱ ⁱ. pⁱⁱⁱ ⁱⁱ

Cicero fi.

filia.
Tullia.

Att.

confuſione σύγχυσιν

obſcura παραφυλάξω ... τῶ συγχυσω φιλοτ...
uⁱⁱⁱⁱⁱ

Turiâm.

ad quem amici me vocant. Ego, nisi Bibulus qui, dum unus hostis in Syria fuit, pedem porta non plus extulit quam *domi* domo sua, adniteretur de triumpho, aequo animo essem. Nunc vero αἰσχρὸν σιωπᾶν. Sed explora rem totum, ut quo die congressi erimus consilium capere possimus. Sat multa, qui et properarem et ei litteras darem qui aut mecum aut paullo ante venturus esset. Cicero tibi plurimam salutem dicit. Tu dices utriusque nostrum verbis et Piliae tuae et filiae.

Alia tuam ad oblectationem.

...minusque atque agendas.

M cicero Imp. ral. o. c. marcello. c.f. cor. quo id accidit quod mihi maxime fuit optatum ut communium marcellorum marcellinorum etiam mirifica rerum
generis actio minui rum fuit ergo me temperaninur quo ergo ita accidit urcom-
mium urin studio tuur consului latur facui face eponit. Inquem mea rei gere-
tatuq. & honore eorum potissimum incider & pecore id quod facillimum fac
turt nomus pernante ut confido senatu utquam honorum ficerur revenatum com-
ftaum locus mea recacar facundum aurea simih reccum minur & quu
ee cumtaur omnibus adlegorem ad tello aquibur im dllegus me praecipue
diligi patur fau beneficia li me fuu ir amplissima neq. enim Alua meae neque
honor amicor quisquam dica pot ee fraceretur quaurame faciat semper
que fecate. ee homnem qui ignorat arbitror nemnem domus tua deniq
tocum semper omnibus fumur officiis probatae ee neq. uo roru in me

36

EPISTULA 239 T-P

AD FAMILIARES XV, 10

M. CICERO IMP. S. D. C. MARCELLO C. F. COS. Quoniam id accidit, quod mihi maxime fuit optatum, ut omnium Marcellorum, Marcellinorum etiam—mirificus enim generis ac nominis vestri fuit erga me semper animus—quoniam ergo ita accidit ut omnium vestrum studio tuus consulatus satis facere posset, in quem meae res gestae lausque et honos earum potissimum incideret, peto a te id, quod facillimum factu est non aspernante, ut confido, senatu, ut quam honorificentissime senatus consultum litteris meis recitatis faciundum cures. 2. Si mihi tecum minus esset quam est cum tuis omnibus, adlegarem ad te illos a quibus intellegis me praecipue diligi. Patris tui beneficia in me sunt amplissima neque enim saluti meae neque honori amicior quisquam dici potest; frater tuus quanti me faciat semperque fecerit esse hominem qui ignoret arbitror neminem; domus tua denique tota me semper omnibus summis officiis prosecuta est: neque vero tu in me [...]

diligendo cumquam conofficiorum quare cupio humidorem modum umeq
ce quinormaltiffimum adfee meaniq. & infupplicatione decernenda adhucse
urrebus cuibmanonem dacrabi.ce commendam puter

M cicero Imp. S. D. C. Marcello cos quante cura cabimeur honofuerit &quumide
estinte confulhme ornando ciomplificando qui fueras semper comparens
buntur &iumpacaono &inreprialoquebatur cogioutamen eumeorum om
raum fomenv lagmhil eteaum quodegonomeua cuia debeam faccurusque
fun cum fuacdiofe idibenter nammagnifacere cuidebas debeceumem nemunt
mala quarrah cumeaum fudla communiabenefica praesena eusque liam asme
son inmeram eum deceda meaquidem senemma maximum uunciulam quodtra
rem p. generurizq. gerena quamhicurur nihiler ueqquamurerb omnerbom
debaure quomina ramiundem eguunur debeam nomeeufen quamobreneabi
uelumusfore scuus quofmeren &quuosfore confidoegofime ruagaao nommora
brour quaelmeaordaer impore eserar propadiame uofperouidebo.

M cicero Imp. S. D. L. paullo cordefig. &inmihinumquam furedtiumquinte
populus.r. proaumfummi.inuem q. meacum

diligendo cuiquam concessisti tuorum. Qua re a te peto in maiorem modum ut me per te quam ornatissimum velis esse meamque et in supplicatione decernenda et in ceteris rebus existimationem satis tibi esse commendatam putes.

Alia tuam ad oblectationem.

M. TVLLI CICERONIS EPISTVLARVM

ADPLANCVM EXPLI. Hocerat alma parens

INCI EIVSDEM ADM. BRVTVM.

EI CETEROS FELICITER SEPTIBA imphili

siquis sciaf uenietbibe
Sinte paruulos adme uenirprealiijimesterii
Pone super cilui fite cognoscis amicus/regnuc

Nouerit roma
norum industria

37

EPISTULA 839 T-P
AD BRUTUM II, 2

CICERO BRUTO SAL.

Planci animum in rem publicam egregium, legiones, auxilia, copias ex litteris eius, quarum exemplum tibi missum arbitror, perspicere potuisti. Lepidi, tui necessarii, qui secundum fratem adfinis habet quos oderit proximos, levitatem et inconstantiam animumque semper inimicum rei publicae iam credo tibi ex tuorum litteris esse perspectum. 2. Nos exspectatio sollicitat, quae est omnis iam in extremum adducta discrimen. Est enim spes omnis in Bruto expediendo, de quo vehementer timebamus. 3. Ego hic cum homine furioso satis habeo negotii, Servilio, quem tuli diutius quam dignitas mea patiebatur, sed tuli rei publicae causa, ne darem perditis civibus hominem, parum sanum illum quidem sed tamen nobilem, quo concurrerent, quod faciunt nihilio minus; sed eum alienandum a re publica non putabam. Finem feci eius ferendi. Coeperat enim esse tanta insolentia ut neminem liberum duceret. In Planci vero causa exarsit incredibili dolore, mecumque per biduum ita contendit et a me ita fractus est ut eum in perpetuum modestiorem sperem fore. Atque in hac contentione ipsa, cum maxime res ageretur, a. d. V. Idus Aprilis litterae mihi in senatu redditae sunt a Lentulo nostro de Cassio, de legionibus de Syria: quas statim cum recitavissem, cecidit Servilius, complures praeterea—sunt enim insignes aliquot qui improbissime sentiunt—, sed acerbissime tulit Servilius adsensum esse mihi de Planco. Magnum illud monstrum in re publica est [...]

Note: This letter is not found in the two Medicean Laurentianan manuscripts presented in this volume. The 1958 Oxford edition of Cicero's letters to Brutus indicates that their first five letters, including this their second letter, do not exist in any extant manuscript. See the Oxford edition, 3:104, 149.

Cicero Attico salutem.

Extimo litteras plenius sum expectatione de Pompeio quidni de nobis dedit
aut offendat. Cumina enim credo ee habita, quibus absolutis scribe. Ille plaruiss[?]
agr de nobis, si tibi stulaus ee videor, qui speron, fano tuo nsa, et sto te male
epistola potuis z mica spac, solitum ee tremoiae. Nuc uelim mich plane p
phatbus quid uideas, sto nos nisi simul multis peiratis in hanc exunmis mrduse.
ea si quid casus aliquo eo pare coniigouentaimum molestie feramus, nos uxst[?]
z adhuc nuie. Ego propter mie relebritate, z oidiana expectatione, exium
non ap, non comoni mic adhuc thesalonica. Sed tam gtudmur non a plurio,
nam io quidem retinet, meus ab ipo loco, mmime apposuo ad tolezandl in tanto
luctu calamitatem. Sp eprum ideo ut frugferam non q p subit mich inuisi
nunty nenecant, et litage, quare nichl effe nocesse q proprie fratum ee.
hunc si aliquid a comnyo audierimus, noi um Num conueterinus neq adhuc
fibit quo perstiuius, sed fuet. Data. xv. leg fortleo. thesalonicae.

Cicero Attico salutem.

Accep idbue scriptibus quatuor epistulas, a te missis, unas quia me
obmngas, ut sun frmior, alterun, qua Capt liberlmy aisi sub se miet

38

EPISTULA 70 T-P
AD ATTICUM III, 14

CICERO ATTICO SAL.

Ex tuis litteris plenus sum exspectatione de Pompeio quidnam de nobis velit aut ostendat. Comitia enim credo esse habita: quibus absolutis scribis illi placuisse agi de nobis. Si tibi stultus esse videor qui sperem, facio tuo iussu, et scio te me iis epistulis potius et meas spes solitum esse remorari. Nunc velim mihi plane perscribas quid videas. Scio nos nostris multis peccatis in hanc aerumnam incidisse. Ea si qui casus aliqua ex parte correxerit, minus moleste feremus nos vixisse et adhuc vivere. 2. Ego propter viae celebritatem et cotidianam exspectationem rerum novarum non commovi me adhuc Thessalonica. Sed iam extrudimur, non a Plancio —nam is quidem retinet—verum ab ipso loco minime apposito ad tolerandam in tanto luctu calamitatem. In Epirum ideo, ut scripseram, non ii, quod subito mihi universi nuntii venerant et litterae qua re nihil esset necesse quam proxime Italiam esse. Hinc si aliquid a comitiis audierimus, nos in Asiam convertemus neque adhuc stabat quo potissimum, sed scies. Data XII Kal. Sext. Thessalonicae.

Alia tuam ad oblectationem.

QUI LEGERANTUR ACCIPIES IN TOLLIONE QUI OMNIBUS·

negotiis nominibus fuit solum sed praefuit me insummo dolore
quem laetarusrebuscapio maximefelicet consolaturspes.
Scconfilius tuarumamicorum &ipsadie quaedebilitat cogita
tiones &inimicorum &prodcorumtuorumfucilesecundoloco
mecomsolaturrecordationetemporum.quorum imag
nem uideohrebustuis? Nam&siminore insreuuolistruetua
digmitas quammea adfluctusizamenest tantasimilitudo ut
frementeemihiignoscere.fieanontimuerim quaetuaequidē
umquam emendadixisti? sedpraestatrerum quimihi are
nenir utgnecidicunt unguiculus es cognituhluftrabimhi
ma Incestudioofficie quotexpectanonfallum opinionemeuā?
credeuam amplitudinem hominum huium arameomniasum

LEGITIUAS LITTERAS QUIBUSADMESCRIBIS GRATUMTIST
esseq000...

39

EPISTULA 104 T-P
AD FAMILIARES I, 6

M. CICERO S. D. P. LENTULO PROCOS.

Quae gerantur accipies ex Pollione, qui omnibus negotiis non interfuit solum sed praefuit. Me in summo dolore, quem in tuis rebus capio, maxime scilicet consolatur spes, quod valde suspicor fore ut infringatur hominum improbitas et consiliis tuorum amicorum et ipsa die, quae debilitat cogitationes et inimicorum et proditorum tuorum. 2. Facile secundo loco me consolatur recordatio meorum temporum, quorum imaginem video in rebus tuis. Nam etsi minore in re violatur tua dignitas quam mea adflicta est, tamen est tanta similitudo ut sperem te mihi ignoscere, si ea non timuerim, quae ne tu quidem umquam timenda duxisti. Sed praesta te eum qui mihi a teneris, ut Graeci dicunt, unguiculis es cognitus. Illustrabit, mihi crede, tuam amplitudinem hominum iniuria. A me omnia summa in te studia officiaque exspecta: non fallam opinionem tuam.

prouide, nichil habeo, tanta rerum prauitate quas firbun? Tuas litteras
expecto. ·Cicero·Attico·Sal·

Petam in italia iudeo nullam esse, qui no istius potestate sit · de Pompeio
sino nichil, cum q̄ nisi in nauim se contulerit, excepturus in tuto · Q̄ celeritate
incredibilem · huius aut nostri, sed no possum, sine dolore attissare eum,
de quo angor et crucior · Ut credas no sine causa times no quominus
quam Cesar expectat ad diuinnitatem uittorie, et dttarionis, sz uideo, quare
attirio sit arturio, recere sit, censso redenedum de oppido ip̄o. ego consilij,
quod optimu fieri uidntur fides · Cum philotimo loquere, atq̄ adē rē re -
na habebis distius. Ego quod agam? qui, aut retia, aut mari persequar?
enim, qui ubi sit nescio, sz si terra quidem, qui possum? mari quo tradam?
Igitur ipa me fir posse tuo, oculu era hortantur, suae et trans bonestare, iratto
modo quidem, ex petiui confilu, ut foleo, explentur res no pot et mari fiḡb
in mentem uenit, iudisn firbun, et ip̄e quid fic arturus ·

·cicero·attico·Sal·litt·

Si dans sibi uesperis philotinu literas accepi, somam extra firma, hic
cohortes expecteri, lentulo et dterino ducenda, in comun exatu couentuis
esse, Cesarem intercludi posse, eiiq̄ de timere, bononi iduo reuacatio,
Hinc finphibos qui geiscos · Hec merito quidem, ne sint somnia · sz
tamen · M. lepidus · L. torquatus · C. cassius · C. attinus etppl. Hi cū sint

40

EPISTULA 320 T-P
AD ATTICUM VII, 22

CICERO ATTICO SAL.

Pedem in Italia video nullum esse qui non in istius potestate sit. De Pompeio scio nihil, eumque, nisi in navim se contulerit, exceptum iri puto. O celeritatem incredibilem! huius autem nostri—sed non possum sine dolore accusare eum de quo angor et crucior. Tu caedem non sine causa times, non quo minus quidquam Caesari expediat ad diuturnitatem victoriae et dominationis, sed video quorum arbitrio sit acturus. Recte sit; *sed* censeo cedendum. 2. De Oppiis egeo consili. Quod optimum factu videbitur facies. Cum Philotimo loquere, atque adeo Terentiam habebis Idibus. Ego quid agam? qua aut terra aut mari persequar eum qui ubi sit nescio? Etsi terra quidem qui possum? mari quo? Tradam igitur isti me? Fac posse tuto—multi enim hortantur—num etiam honeste? Nullo modo quidem. A te petam consilium, ut soleo? Explicari res non potest. Sed tamen si quid in mentem venit velim scribas et ipse quid sis acturus.

Alia tuam ad oblectationem.

Amabo te mi frater / nisi Nono meo facto, et tu in omē meā
euenustis longiorā, et polez meo potuis ē imprudēre
infirmagāres adsiqueto: mulli et cingyti oraltos
redi: a, quibz o putnatō ess coarpind oxbu Bigas
onā zuaē sbyg ni Spr! in langezō inter p go
euā zuaē, elle eti

Gazenō quinto frō faliuces

41

EPISTULA 72 T-P
AD QUINTUM FRATREM I, 4

MARCUS QUINTO FRATRI SALUTEM.

Amabo te, mi frater, ne, si uno meo facto et tu et omnes mei corruistis, improbitati et sceleri meo potius quam imprudentiae miseriaeque adsignes. Nullum est meum peccatum nisi quod iis credidi a quibus nefas putaram esse me decipi, aut etiam [...]

quibus ne id expedire quidem arbitrabar. Intimus, proximus, familiarissimus quisque aut sibi pertimuit aut mihi invidit: ita mihi nihil misero praeter fidem amicorum, cautum meum consilium *defuit*. 2. Quod si te satis innocentia tua et misericordia hominum vindicat hoc tempore a molestia, perspicis profecto ecquaenam nobis spes salutis relinquatur. Nam me Pomponius et Sestius et Piso noster adhuc Thessalonicae retinuerunt, cum longius discedere propter nescio quos motus vetarent. Verum ego magis exitum illorum litteris quam spe certa exspectabam. Nam quid sperem potentissimo inimico, dominatione obtrectatorum, infidelibus amicis, plurimis invidis? 3. De novis autem tribunis plebis est ille quidem in me officiosissimus Sestius et, spero, Curius, Milo, Fadius, Fabricius, sed valde adversante Clodio, qui etiam privatus eadem manu poterit contiones concitare, deinde etiam intercessor parabitur. 4. Haec mihi proficiscenti non proponebantur, [...]

sed saepe triduo summa cum gloria dicebar esse rediturus. Quid
tu igitur? inquies. Quid? multa convenerunt quae mentem
exturbarent meam: subita defectio Pompei, alienatio consulum,
etiam praetorum, timor publicanorum, arma. Lacrimae meorum me ad
mortem ire prohibuerunt, quod certe et ad honestatem et ad
effugiendos intolerabilis dolores fuit aptissimum. Sed de hoc
scripsi ad te in ea epistula quam Phaëthonti dedi. Nunc tu, quoniam
in tantum luctum laboremque detrusus es quantum nemo umquam,
si levare potest communem casum misericordia hominum, scilicet
incredibile quiddam adsequeris: sin plane occidimus—me
miserum!—ego omnibus meis exitio fuero quibus ante dedecori
non eram. 5. Sed tu, ut ante ad te scripsi, perspice rem et pertempta
et ad me, ut tempora nostra non ut amor tuus fert, vere
perscribe. Ego vitam, quoad putabo tua interesse aut ad
spem servandam esse, retinebo. Tu nobis amicissimum Sestium
cognosces: credo tua causa velle Lentulum, qui erit consul. [...]

fed non

fugere?

Equidem fateaz fatuam verbis Sufficiora. Tu et quod opus
fuit, et quod fit uidebis dio. Si tuam plandine communemq;
calamitatem nemo supperet, aut p re aliquid confici aut
nullo modo poterit? Sin te quoq; inimin; oppone expedirent
ne ceffariis, nos cum gladiys meam; sed liberis agitectur.
Dein her absint rebus, sic oro ut ad me, et omnib; respub e,
ut in me an porius aut confilij mimus preso esse, sp; ante;
amoris voco, et offici no minus.

M.T. acc epistula ad quinu frate .11. incipit
liber.

Agaruus. Q. fratri falutem.

Epistulam quam legi, mane Rebraz, sed font humanitaz licium;
quod ad me misso fenatu bestis venir ur signd esse actu;
ad te si mihi uidictus perhiberem? fuatis fuit pignora;
sp putabamur esse posse? imp dcembri; sed dies pp: complano
nos frung; sed duo confulo designati. p fuilus, magno lucullus.
leg. fecundus magno lucullus legendis mulatura efabero

humanit.

Quamquam sunt facta verbis difficiliora. Tu et quid opus sit et quid sit videbis. Omnino, si tuam solitudinem communemque calamitatem nemo dispexerit, aut per te aliquid confici aut nullo modo poterit: sin te quoque inimici vexare coeperint, ne cessaris: non enim gladiis tecum sed litibus agetur. Verum haec absint velim. Te oro ut ad me de omnibus *rebus* rescribas et in me animi aut potius consili minus putes esse quam antea, amoris vero et offici non minus.

Alia tuam ad oblectationem.

Quod scribis ita video, non minus mecum mea te quam me ipsum ex epistola tua, nec tamen ipsa me nascitur fumum opionum et delectat longe et iudere esse, cum tuas litteras lego, et, ut fit in tantis rebus, modo hoc modo illud audire. Illud in explorare non possum, quidnam miserie possit nulle reuisones ad fanilitate agunda. Bibuli aut ipsa magnitudo diem in commotu dilatione, quod habet nisi quia iudicii sine ulla concessione rei publica in manu in publico fore est. Fiat fiat, tu pl. finibil aliud, ut co estius, in ex opito venerare, nam ut illa tu carere non video posse fieri.

Illectum si me tum aliquid udet disputare, si id quidem ne subiit es, quo si quid erit eiusmodi, sic adiolabimus. Prouenit hoc non sit tamen rem publica, iudiciorum spectaculi michi propono, modo te

Bibulus publ?

† sine exitu
ferunt

42

EPISTULA 42 T-P
AD ATTICUM II, 15

CICERO ATTICO SAL.

Ut scribis, ita video non minus incerta in re publica quam in epistula tua, sed tamen ista ipsa me varietas sermonum opinionumque delectat. Romae enim videor esse cum tuas litteras lego et, ut fit in tantis rebus, modo hoc, modo illud audire. Illud tamen explicare non possum, quidnam inveniri possit nullo recusante ad facultatem agrariam. 2. Bibuli autem ista magnitudo animi in comitiorum dilatione quid habet nisi ipsius iudicium sine ulla correctione rei publicae? Nimirum in Publio spes est. Fiat, fiat tribunus pl., si nihil aliud, ut eo citius tu ex Epiro revertare. Nam ut illo tu careas non video posse fieri, praesertim si mecum aliquid volet disputare. Sed id quidem non dubium est quin, si quid erit eius modi, sis advolaturus. Verum ut hoc non sit, tamen sive ruet sive eriget rem publicam, praeclarum spectaculum mihi propono, modo te [...]

confessore spectare liceat. Cum hec maxime scriberem, cum
nondum plane ingenuicam, salue inquit Atticus, hoc est Roma credere,
quos ego bonos effugi, cum in hoc mod, ego non in mone patrios
et ad mirabula nostra pergam, denique si salus non potuero, cum in
illud facile, ut formiano tibi stolex ita tamen quoniam tu cum in
mil facile, ut formiano tibi stolex ita tamen quoniam tu cum in

Terentiae epistola et affectus sua et diligencia in gerouersia
muliumand presertim crios ex eog cum defendere eorum qui agros publi
eos possocant, si tu in aliquid publicamos pendre. haec etiam
renasat ea obligatione et KIKEP ω NΑPICTOKPΑTIKω
TΑTOC NΑIC salue dicit.
Cicero Attico salutem

Censeo michi etiam dormienti pridie k. maias epistola et illa reddita
in qua de agro campano scabis quod quereis primis ita me purpugit
ut sompnii michi abemeat si id cogitatione magis si molestia.
Cogitaben aut haec face sumurcebant primi ex eo quo superiorib
libis compiceras ex familiaritate illius audisse prolustius aliquid
quod uerus intrigebant manus aliquid amuicam hoc michi zussmor
non uidebatur. Deinde ut me ego consolec ono expectato largitionis
agrarie magram campani imdetii esse desmeta qui agros ut dena
ingera sint non amplius homo numquemilla por susbuere reliqua ono
mihitudo ab illis abalienetur necesse et si revoca si illa res et que
bonoru animos quos nunc uideo ex ornotos uehementias possit incende
her ante et et eo magis quo portonne stalle sublans agro campano in
mihi quod uidebali suurt donnilliorn pretex iur sima que michi uidetur

consessore spectare liceat. 3. Cum haec maxime scriberem, ecce tibi Sebosus! Nondum plane ingemueram, 'Salve,' inquit Arrius. Hoc est Roma decedere! Quos ego homines effugi, cum in hos incidi? Ego vero in montis patrios et ad incunabula nostra pergam. Denique, si solus non potuero, cum rusticis potius quam cum his perurbanis, ita tamen ut, quoniam tu certi nihil scribis, in Formiano tibi praestoler usque ad *a. d.* III. Nonas Maias.

4. Terentiae pergrata est adsiduitas tua et diligentia in controversia Mulviana. Nescit omnino te communem causam defendere eorum qui agros publicos possideant. Sed tamen tu aliquid publicanis pendis: haec etiam id recusat. Ea tibi igitur et Κικέρων ἀριστοκρατικώτατος παῖς, salutem dicunt.

Alia tuam ad oblectationem.

M acero procos · f·o· M·marcello cos· desig · magnam sum laetitia adfectus cum
audiui consule mee factum ee · eum quae honore tibi decor foras are uoloatq ·
ace prouia pararatq cui dignitate administrari nam cum te semper amaui dilexi
que cum metam antiquissimam cognoui Inomni uita et reteram mearum cum
parusaui pluribus beneficiis uel defensus cui criaabur temporibus uel ornauit Reum
dir et iamcoai retter et ee debeo cum praeteream maximitate grauissimae

atq. optime feminae maiora ergo salutem dignitateq. meam studia quam
erant amuliere postulanda perspexerim quapropter accepto Inmalorem
modum uene ab eorum diliges atq. defendar .
M acero procos. f·o· c· marcello colleque marcellum cor. factumque

43

EPISTULA 214 T-P
AD FAMILIARES XV, 7

M. CICERO PROCOS. S. D. C. MARCELLO COS. DESIG. Maxima sum laetitia adfectus cum audivi consulem te factum esse, eumque honorem tibi deos fortunare volo atque a te pro tua parentisque tui dignitate administrari. Nam cum te semper amavi dilexique tum mei amantissimum cognovi in omni varietate rerum mearum, tum patris tui pluribus beneficiis vel defensus tristibus temporibus vel ornatus secundis et sum totus vester et esse debeo, cum praesertim matris tuae, gravissimae atque optimae feminae, maiora erga salutem dignitatemque meam studia quam erant a muliere postulanda perspexerim. Quapropter a te peto in maiorem modum ut me absentem diligas atque defendas.

quide certe nectuatipeni hn haue me laude me betuue et puplia uel laude qui me
totum signauum ... termahanc̄
Julio cesare ... C. mario sigillo consulib̃ coſ ... effe iudicetur, multum te amamus. l.
trevienta, abſce eua diu nihil litterare. Ego de meis detractionib̃
scripsi ante diligenter, hoc tpē Catilinam spectore meum defendere
cogitamus, iudices hēmus quod uolumus, firma amicatorie uolutate.
Spero si absolutus exit, conuniatorem illum nobis fore in ratione
petitionis, si aliter acciderit, humaniter feremus, tuo aduentu nobis
opus est maturo, nam prorsus summa hominum est, opio tuos familiarēs
nobiles hões, aduersarios honori meo fore, ad eos uoluntatem mihi
conciliandam, maximo te usui fore uideo, quare januario mense
ut constituis̃, cura ut Rome sis, Diuum tuam suo desiderio tui
mortuam esse, et simul quod uorth sit ne latine in offino nõ maneret
et in monitem albanum hostias nõ adducerent, eus rei obolatonem
ad te. l. faustrum misstrum esse arbitror, uos hic te ad mensem
januarii expectamus, ex quodam rumore, an ex litteris tuis ad alios
misse, nam ad me de eo nihil scribis scripsi, signa que nobis curaſſ
ea sunt ad caietam exposita, uos ea non uidimus, neq enim
exeundi Roma potie nobis fuit, gusimus qui pro mortuis soluzzet
te multum amamus, et ea abste diligent pariiuſce curata sunt, et
ad me sepe scripsis si de meo amio placando, feci et expertus sum om̃a.
si mirandum in modum est, est do abalienato, quibus de supionibus
etsi auditet, arbitror te aii, ex me, cum uenero cognoscere Salluſbi
patris uestanthiae in suo uetere sẽratam nõ potui, hoc ad te scripſi,
quod is me aimchar de te solebat in se exprue et illum et mimis
excorabilem, meum studii tibi nec defuisse, tulliolam, C. pisoni l.
f. frusi respondimus.

44

EPISTULA 11 T-P
AD ATTICUM I, 2

CICERO ATTICO SAL.

L.

Iulio Caesare C. Marcio Figulo consulibus filiolo me auctum scito salva Terentia. Abs te tam diu nihil litterarum? Ego de meis ad te rationibus scripsi antea diligenter. Hoc tempore Catilinam, competitorem nostrum, defendere cogitamus. Iudices habemus quos voluimus, summa accusatoris voluntate. Spero, si absolutus erit, coniunctiorem illum nobis fore in ratione petitionis: sin aliter acciderit, humaniter feremus. 2. Tuo adventu nobis opus est maturo: nam prorsus summa hominum est opinio tuos familiaris, nobilis homines, adversarios honori nostro fore. Ad eorum voluntatem mihi conciliandam maximo te mihi usui fore video. Qua re Ianuario mense, ut constituisti, cura ut Romae sis.

Alia tuam ad oblectationem.

C icero cuetari imp · f · d · uide quammihi perfuaferim te me et
alterum non modo in hif rebuf quae ad me ipfum. fed etiam
in hif quae ad meof pertinent. c.t. rebuf num cogitaram quo
cumque exirem mecum ducere. ut cum meof omnibuf faudif
beneficiif quam ornatiffimum domum reducerem. fed poftea

45

EPISTULA 134 T-P
AD FAMILIARES VII, 5

CICERO CAESARI IMP. S. D. Vide quam mihi persuaserim te me esse alterum non modo in iis rebus quae ad me ipsum sed etiam in iis quae ad meos pertinent. C. Trebatium cogitaram quocumque exirem mecum ducere, ut eum meis omnibus studiis, cumque exirem mecum ducere, ut eum meis omnibus studiis, beneficiis quam ornatissimum domum reducerem. Sed postea [...]

quam et pompei commotio diuturniore · quam putaram · et mea

quaedam tibi non ignota dubitatio · ut impedire profectionem meam

uidebatur · aut certe tardiore · uide quid mihi sumpserim · coepi uelle

expectarium expectare · ate quae speras · sed iam me neque mercule mnuf

et prolixe de ea uoluntate promisi · quam eram ex mea pollice

ri casus ueis minificus quidam me ... uenit · quae siue ea est opinionis

meae · uel sponsor humanitatis ... uiae · nam cum de hoc ipso crebatio cum

balbo nro loquerer accuratius domi meae · ... mihi datur ...

quibus in ex ... scripta menta · m · refuuunque m mihi commendas

uel regem galliae faciam uel hunc leprae delega fiurs ad meallium

mitte quemornem · sustulimus manus et ego et balbus · ... fuit oppor

tunitas · ut illud nescio quod non fortuitum sed diuinum uideretur ·

mitto igitur adte crebatium ... ut in ito mea sponte

post autem in uita cacio mittendum dyxerim · hunc mi caesar sic uelim

omni tua comia te complectare · ...

quam et Pompei commoratio diuturnior erat quam putaram et mea quaedam tibi non ignota dubitatio aut impedire profectionem meam videbatur aut certe tardare, vide quid mihi sumpserim. Coepi velle ea Trebatium exspectare a te quae sperasset a me, neque mehercule minus ei prolixe de tua voluntate promisi quam eram solitus de mea polliceri. 2. Casus vero mirificus quidam intervenit quasi vel testis opinionis meae vel sponsor humanitatis tuae. Nam cum de hoc ipso Trebatio cum Balbo nostro loquerer accuratius domi meae, litterae mihi dantur a te quibus in extremis scriptum erat "M. † itfuium quem mihi commendas vel regem Galliae faciam, vel hunc Leptae delega, si vis. Tu ad me alium mitte quem ornem." Sustulimus manus et ego et Balbus: tanta fuit opportunitas ut illud nescio quid non fortuitum sed divinum videretur. [. . .]

...nam ut illud nescio quod non fortuitum sed diuinum uideretur,

mitto igitur ad te debatium ad quietam tuo ut initio mea sponte

post autem inuitatu tuo mittendum dixit in hunc mi ca cesar sic ut dum

omnia tua comitat ad complectare. ut omnia quae per me possis adduci:

ut in meos conferre uelis num num hunc conferas de quo tibi homines haec

spondeo non illo uerbo re uerbo meo quod cum ad te demit lone scripsisse

iure lusisti. sed mox te romano quomodo homines nomine nepi locamur:

probiorem hominem meliore murum pudentiorem et nemine accedit

etiam quod fili tua familia induci iniure ciuili singulis memoria summa

scientia. huic ego neque tribuna cum neque pro fec tu tam neque

ullius benefici certum nomen p etc. beniuolentia continuum et liberali

atem peto neque impedio quo minus si tibi ita placuerit etiam hisce eu

Mitto igitur ad te Trebatium atque ita mitto ut initio mea sponte, post autem invitatu tuo mittendum duxerim. 3. Hunc, mi Caesar, sic velim omni tua comitate complectare ut omnia quae per me possis adduci ut in meos conferre velis in unum hunc conferas. De quo tibi homine haec spondeo non illo vetere verbo meo quod, cum ad te de Milone scripsissem, iure lusisti, sed more Romano quo modo homines non inepti loquuntur, probiorem hominem, meliorem virum, pudentiorem esse neminem. Accedit etiam, quod familiam ducit in iure civili, singulari memoria, summa scientia. Huic ego neque tribunatum neque praefecturam neque ullius benefici certum nomen peto, benevolentiam tuam et liberalitatem peto, neque impedio quo minus, si tibi ita placuerit, etiam hisce eum [...]

ornet gloriolae insignibus. Tuum denique hominem ubi ita trado dema
nu ut aiunt. Inmanum ducun tam & tuccona & fide praestantem. simus
enim putidiusculi quam perte ut licet. tuerum ut uideo licebit curaut
ualeas & me ut amas f. amat.

Cicero s. f. d. treba[tio]. Inomnibus meis epistolis quas ad caesarem aut ad bal
bum mitto legitimam aquaedam est accessio commendationis tuae. nex
ea uulgaris. sed cum aliquo insigni iudicio meae ergate beneuolenciae.
tumodo ineptias istas & desideria urbis & urbanitatis depone. & quo
confilio profectus es id assiduitate & uirtute consequere. hoctibi
tam ignoscemus nos amici. quam ignouerunt me deae quae corinthum
arcem matam habebant. matronae opulentae opamatef quibus illa ma
nibus cum ptissimis perfuasit. ne sibi uirtio illae uortere I quod abeet
a patria. nam multa suam rem bonegessere & publicam. patria procul
multa quidom in aetatem agerent propterea sunt improbata. quo in
numero tu certe fuisses. nissite occurissemus Galdium sumus

ornes gloriolae insignibus: totum denique hominem tibi ita trado, de manu, ut aiunt, in manum tuam istam et victoria et fide praestantem. Simus enim putidiusculi quamquam per te vix licet, verum, ut video, licebit. Cura ut valeas et me, ut amas, ama.

Alia tuam ad oblectationem.

CICERO · ATTICO · SALUTEM.

L...

46

EPISTULA 348 T-P
AD ATTICUM VIII, 13

CICERO ATTICO SAL.

Lippitudinis meae signum tibi sit librari manus et eadem causa brevitatis, etsi nunc quidem quod scriberem nihil erat. Omnis exspectatio nostra erat in nuntiis Brundisinis. Si nactus hic esset Gnaeum nostrum, spes dubia pacis; sin ille ante tramisisset, exitiosi belli metus. Sed videsne in quem hominem inciderit res publica? quam acutum, quam vigilantem, quam paratum? Si mehercule neminem occiderit nec cuiquam quidquam ademerit, ab iis qui eum maxime timuerant maxime diligetur. 2. Multum mecum municipales homines loquuntur, multum rusticani. Nihil prorsus aliud curant nisi agros, nisi villulas, nisi nummulos suos. Et vide quam conversa res sit; illum quo antea confidebant metuunt, hunc amant quem timebant. Id quantis nostris peccatis vitiisque evenerit non possum sine molestia cogitare. Quae autem impendere putarem scripseram ad te et iam tuas litteras exspectabam.

Alia tuam ad oblectationem.

ut commode michique gratum, si me de his rebus ...
opus sit feceris certiore. Ego in Arcano opperior, dum ista cognosco. a.d. VI.
idus. Alterum tibi eodem die hanc epistulam dictavi et pridie dederam
mea manu longiorem. Visum te aiunt in regia, nec reprehendo, quippe,

cum ipse istam reprehensionem non fugerim. Sed expecto tuas litteras, neque iam sane
video quid expectem; sed tamen, etiam si nichil erit, id ipsum ad me velim scribas.
Cesar michi ignoscit per litteras quod non venerim, seseque in optimam partem
id accipere dicit. Facile patior quod scribit secum Tullum et Servium questos
esse quia non idem sibi quod michi remisisset. Homines ridiculos, qui cum filios misissent ad Cn. Pompeium circumsedendum, ipsi in senatum venire dubitarent.
Sed tamen exemplum misi ad te Cesaris litterarum. CICERO. ATTICO. SAL.
Multas a te accepi epistulas eodem die, omnes diligenter scriptas, eam vero que
voluminis instar erat, sepe legendam sicuti facio, in qua non frustra laborem
suscepisti; michi quidem pergratum fecisti. Quare, ut id quoad licebit, id est,
quoad scies ubi simus, quam sepissime facias te vehementer rogo. Ac deplorandi
quidem, quod quotidie facimus, sit iam nobis aut finis omnino, si potest, aut mode-
ratio quedam, quod profecto non potest. Non enim tam dignitatem, quos honores,
quem vite statum amiserim cogito, sed quid consecutus sim, quid prestiterim, qua
in laude vixerim. His denique in malis, quid intersit inter me et istos, quos propter
omnia amisimus. Hi sunt, qui nisi me civitate expulissent, obtinere se non
posse putaverunt licentiam cupiditatum suarum, quorum societatis et scelerate con-
sensionis fides, quo eruperit vides; alter ardet furore et scelere, nec remittit
aliquid, sed in dies ingravescit; modo Italia expulit, nunc alia ex parte persequi,
ex alia provincia expoliare conatur, nec iam recusat, sed quodammodo postulat,

Epistula

Cesar.
Tull.
Servi.
Cn. Pompei.

inter

t amisimus

47

EPISTULA 381 T-P
AD ATTICUM X, 3A

CICERO ATTICO SAL.

A. d. VII

Id. alteram tibi eodem die hanc epistulam dictavi, et pridie dederam
mea manu longiorem. Visum te aiunt in regia nec reprehendo, quippe
cum ipse istam reprehensionem non fugerim. Sed exspecto tuas litteras, neque iam sane
video quid exspectem, sed tamen, etiam si nihil erit, id ipsum ad me velim scribas.
2. Caesar mihi ignoscit per litteras quod non venerim seseque in optimam partem
id accipere dicit. Facile patior, quod scribit, secum Tullum et Servium questos
esse quia non idem sibi quod mihi remisisset. Homines ridiculos! qui cum filios misissent ad Cn. Pompeium circumsedendum, ipsi in senatum venire dubitarint.
Sed tamen exemplum misi ad te Caesaris litterarum.

Alia tuam ad oblectationem.

litteras crebrius mittas .7

M. tullius. m. f. cicero s.d. gn. pompeio gn. f. magno imperatori

s.t.t.e.q.u.b.e. ex litteris tuis quas publice misisti
cepi una cum omnibus incredibilem uoluptatem tantam
enim spem otii ostendisti quam ego semper omnibus te uno
fretus pollicebar sed hoc scito tuos ueteris hostis nouos
amicos uehementer litteris perculsos atque ex magna spe
deturbatos iacere ad me autem litteras quas misisti qua
quam exiguam significationem tuae erga me uoluntatis
habebant tamen mihi scito iucundas fuisse nulla enim re
tam laetari soleo quam meorum officiorum conscientia
quibus si quando non mutuae respondeant apud me plus
officii residere facillime patior illud non dubito quin
si te mea summa erga te studia parum mihi adiunxerint
res p. nos inter nos conciliatura coniuncturaque sit
ac ne ignores quid ego in tuis litteris desiderarim
scribam aperte sicut & mea natura & nra amicitia
postulat res eas gessi quarum aliquam in tuis litteris

48

EPISTULA 15 T-P
AD FAMILIARES V, 7

M. TULLIUS M. F. CICERO S. D. CN. POMPEIO CN. F. MAGNO IMPERA-
TORI. S. T. E. Q. V. B. E. Ex litteris tuis quas publice misisti
cepi una cum omnibus incredibilem voluptatem: tantam
enim spem oti ostendisti quantam ego semper omnibus te uno
fretus pollicebar. Sed hoc scito, tuos veteres hostis, novos
amicos, vehementer litteris his perculsos atque ex magna spe
deturbatos iacere. 2. Ad me autem litteras quas misisti, quamquam exiguam significationem tuae erga me voluntatis
habebant, tamen mihi scito iucundas fuisse: nulla enim re
tam laetari soleo quam meorum officiorum conscientia,
quibus si quando non mutue respondetur, apud me plus
offici residere facillime patior. Illud non dubito quin,
si te mea summa erga te studia parum mihi adiunxerint,
res publica nos inter nos conciliatura coniuncturaque sit.
3. Ac ne ignores quid ego in tuis litteris desiderarim,
scribam aperte, sicut et mea natura et nostra amicitia
postulat. Res eas gessi quarum aliquam in tuis litteris [. . .]

&intimae necessitudinis &reip· causa gratulationem ex
spectari quam ego abste praeter missam ee arbitror
quoduenire necuiuf animum offenderes sedscito exque
nos prosalute patri uegessimus orbisreipu iudicio acresti
monio comprobari quaecum uenerisrauto consilio tanaq;
animi magnitudine ame gesta ee cognosces utrtibi multo
maciore quam afrianusfurt ame nonmulto minore quam
laelium fucile &inrep· &inamicitia adiunctum esse patiar.

M · cicep8·m· liamop·f· crasso· quartum admeum studium
exstiterit dignrarifaue uel uendae uel &liamaugende
nondubito quin adreomnesui scripserint nonenim furt
autmediocre autobscurum aut eiusmodi; quodsilentio
posset praeterin nam&cumconsulibus &cummultis
consularibus tanta contentione decertari quanta num
quam anteaulla incausa fuscepiquennibi perpe&uam pro
pugnationem proomnibusornamentusudiss...

et nostrae necessitudinis et rei publicae causa gratulationem exspectavi: quam ego abs te praetermissam esse arbitror quod vererere ne cuius animum offenderes. Sed scito ea quae nos pro salute patriae gessimus orbis terrae iudicio ac testimonio comprobari. Quae, cum veneris, tanto consilio tantaque animi magnitudine a me gesta esse cognosces ut tibi multo maiori quam Africanus fuit iam me non multo minorem quam Laelium facile et in re publica et in amicitia adiunctum esse patiare.

Alia tuam ad oblectationem.

· Cicero Bruto salutem ·

Breues litere tue, breues dico, immo nulle · tribus ne versiculis · B₁₆
temporibus breuis ad me tamen ad scripsissem potuisse, et
requirens meas; que vi[sa] ad te tuorum; sine meis venit, que
aut epistola no̅ reddidit habuit, que si ad te pedate no̅ su̅t
ne domesticus quidem tuas plerus̅ arbitror ; Ciceroni sa̅lis
te longiores saluieus epistolam; recte ad quidem, ff̅ ha-
quoq̅ debut esse plenior; plenior; Ego au̅r eius ad me!
& ciceronis abste defessu scripsisses; fratrem epistolā tabellarius
breuissi; ad Ciceronem, ut eram si in verilam remissū; ad te
reddict; nihil eius reddendus; nihil illā bonestius; fff̅ ff̅
aliquatens ea scripserans satisdatum reuera; mea fuimt
contentione in; alterius anim esse sciem; quod ego vim eratione
confabulaborans; tum domini; catonis; consuli· B. Bibulo; quod
ad te eram scripseram; sed videlicet eius illam puellam

                                        extructi·

Cicero·

Cicero·
Domus?·
Cato·
Consilius·
tribuli

49

EPISTULA 913 T-P
AD BRUTUM I, 14

CICERO BRUTO SAL.

Breves litterae tuae, breves dico? immo nullae: tribusne versiculis his temporibus Brutus ad me? nihil scripsissem potius. Et requiris meas! Quis umquam ad te tuorum sine meis venit? Quae autem epistula non pondus habuit? quae si ad te perlatae non sunt, ne domesticas quidem tuas perlatas arbitror. Ciceroni scribis te longiorem daturum epistulam: recte id quidem, sed haec quoque debuit esse plenior. Ego autem, cum ad me de Ciceronis abs te discessu scripsisses, statim extrusi tabellarios litterasque ad Ciceronem, ut, etiamsi in Italiam venisset, ad te rediret; nihil enim mihi iucundius, nihil illi honestius. Quamquam aliquoties ei scripseram sacerdotum comitia mea summa contentione in alterum annum esse reiecta—quod ego cum Ciceronis causa elaboravi, tum Domiti, Catonis, Lentuli, Bibulorum; quod ad te etiam scripseram—: sed videlicet, cum illam pusillam [...]

epistolam tuam, ad me dabas, nondum erat tibi ɔ noꞇ[us],
quare omni fiduc̄ia, te mi Brute conteñdꝰ, ut communem
meum ne ɗmittas, tenuimꝗ. ꝺɗuꞇus ꝗ ɠ iꝓꝝ f̄ coꝝ p̄ au
Eufoꝛpius es, uestpue, tibi, iam, iamꝗ frucenduꝛ est Romani
cum bellum eꞇ ꝺꝗꝗ no paruo ꝶllere ꞇepiɗ, s ɗꝓꝶus aut
ceſaꞇus, qui erat optimus, no modo nobil pꝺꝝ pɗ eꞇiam
uoꝗ querelu tui ꝭllaꝗꞇiuɜ qui f̄, uedeam attigent, cert
ciuꝰ nemo ꝗ ꝗue ꝗuiɗꝛ cuaꞇy appellar fut̄ ꝗ f̄ non
iu tua cauꞇa confecit et f̄, bonum preclaꝛ cu Planco
cōmunitum ɠabemus s ꝺno ꞇgnotas s̄ sunt meus, aium
bonum, et uiſen̄ paientibus et cauno preɗeoꝗ, ꝗ cauny fut
ꞅpro nouiſimus, tuos magna gꞇudinoe tui uouꝶꝗ/tuaꝗꞇ
auctoritas, eo ɗꝓꝺabu, Gubiuni iꞅe ꝗ ɗue ꝺꝗꝗ Ƒꞇꝶꝛini
tibꝗ ꝑſnale, no te ꝺꝰnus maceꝛy, ꝗuibꝰ Bꝛuꞇumeꞇo, a tuo
ciuiBus appulꞇꝝ, ꝗ꜀e ꝓſuiſꞇe paꞇꝛic, ſꞇꝗ f̄ matuur uocaus
ꝓſcꞇuerim ꝝ ꝺue ꝗuerbus. 2

· Cicero Bruto saluter.

- Meſſalam, Babo, ꝗuiBus ꞇgꞇur lꞇꞇeris tuus accurate ſcꝛiptis ɗ ꞇ affe
qui poſſiꞇꝗ, ꝓbabulus, ut cepficiꞇy ꝗue gꞇcaꞇur, ꝗueꝗ ſuꞇ
ꞇ ꝶ publicam, ſꝗ ꞇbi f̄ ꝓponiꞇ qui eꞇ opꞇme omiu nouꞇ.

epistulam tuam ad me dabas, nondum erat tibi id notum.

2. Quare omni studio a te, mi Brute, contendo ut Ciceronem meum ne dimittas tecumque deducas, quod ipsum, si rem publicam, cui susceptus es, respicis, tibi iam iamque faciendum est. Renatum enim bellum est, idque non parvum scelere Lepidi; exercitus autem Caesaris, qui erat optimus, non modo nihil prodest, sed etiam cogit exercitum tuum flagitari; qui si Italiam attigerit, erit civis nemo, quem quidem civem appellari fas sit, qui se non in tua castra conferat. Etsi Brutum praeclare cum Planco coniunctum habemus, sed non ignoras quam sint incerti et animi hominum infecti partibus et exitus proeliorum. Quin etiam si, ut spero, vicerimus, tamen magnam gubernationem tui consilii tuaeque auctoritatis res desiderabit: subveni igitur, per deos, idque quam primum, tibique persuade non te Idibus Martiis, quibus servitutem a tuis civibus depulisti, plus profuisse patriae quam, si mature veneris, profuturum. II. Idus Quintilis.

Alia tuam ad oblectationem.

MARCUS CICERO SALUTEM DICIT CURIONI· QUAMQUAM ME NON

NE NEGLEGENTIAE SUSCIPTUM TIBI ESSE DOLIO TAM EN NON TAM MIHI

molestum fuit accusari abs te officium meum quam iucundum requiri tpr̄e

fer am quam inquo accusabar culpa uacarem Inquo iure m desideraui eefig

nificabas me a litteras praece ferret pompeo cum mihi quidem felica

men dulcem & optat cum amor m tuum: equidem nemmem praec m mi

quem quidem ad te peruenerent m puta rem cu litteras non dederim

& enim qui s est t cam scribendo Impiger quam & gozac uero bis cam t fu

mum & eas per breuis accepi quare si m iquis es t i m me iudex commenda

bo eadem ego ce crimine t Immond facere noles ca mihi atquum praebere

debebis· sed del t c c enit hac c enus Nonenim ut e or ne non scribendo

t e expleam praesertim si m e non egere f t ud tum meum nonas permabere

egot es t f ut i ger tam diu a nobis & dolui quod c aru f ructu iucundis sime

consuetudinis & la f lor quod absens t om ma cum maxim a digni tace

es con f am a f

50

EPISTULA 166 T-P
AD FAMILIARES II, 1

M. CICERO S. D. C. CURIONI. Quamquam me neglegentiae nomine suspectum tibi esse doleo, tamen non tam mihi molestum fuit accusari abs te officium meum quam iucundum requiri, praesertim quom in quo accusabar culpa vacarem, in quo autem desiderare te significabas meas litteras prae te ferres perspectum mihi quidem, sed tamen dulcem et optatum amorem tuum. Equidem neminem praetermisi, quem quidem ad te perventurum putarem, cui litteras non dederim. Etenim quis est tam in scribendo impiger quam ego? A te vero bis terve summum et eas perbrevis accepi. Qua re si iniquus es in me iudex, condemnabo eodem ego te crimine: sin me id facere noles, te mihi aequum praebere debebis. Sed de litteris hactenus: non enim vereor ne non scribendo te expleam, praesertim si in eo genere studium meum non aspernabere. [...]

coexpleam praeferum fineonegere fraudium meum nonaspernabere
egote afuiffe tandiuanobis &dolui quodcarus fructu iucundiffime
confueuadinis &laetior quodabfentomnia cummaximadignitate
etconfecutuf quodque nominibufautrebufmeritopacif forta
nareffondis breueeft quodmetibi praefperem e ur increditi
lur Inceamoricogit Tantaeft expectatio uelarim uelingeniti
ucegote opferuare oprefariq nondubitam ficadnofconformatuf
reuerfione itaquam expectationem uiconciraft hancfuftinere
acauertporfir & quoniam meamtuorum ergamemericorum
memoriaitlu umquamdelebit obliuioteroge utomemmerifiquum
taecumq: abiaccessioneffient &fortung &dignitaatseafenom

2. Ego te afuisse tam diu a nobis et dolui quod carui fructu iucundissimae consuetudinis, et laetor quod absens omnia cum maxima dignitate es consecutus quodque in omnibus tuis rebus meis optatis fortuna respondit. Breve est quod me tibi praecipere meus incredibilis in te amor cogit. Tanta est exspectatio vel animi vel ingeni tui ut ego te obsecrare obtestarique non dubitem, sic ad nos conformatus revertare ut, quam exspectationem tui concitasti, hanc sustinere ac tueri possis. Et quoniam meam tuorum erga me meritorum memoriam nulla umquam delebit oblivio, te rogo ut memineris, quantaecumque tibi accessiones fient et fortunae et dignitatis, eas te non [...]

potuisse consequi quae suo puer olim fidelissimis atque amantissimis consiliis

paruisset. quare hoc animo in nos te esse debebis ut ab illa nostra lamingua

uescens in amore. Atque ad ualescentia tua conquiescat

Marcus Cicero salutem dicit scipioni.   Gaiute priuatus sum

amoris summis erga me propter tuo durissimo uiro quicquam fuerit lui

dibus tum uero te filio superasset omnium fortunam fieri contigisset

ut te ante uideret quam agnasit ut ad discederet. sed spero non ostium amicitiam

nion egere te stibus tibi patrimonium dari fortunem me te te habebit cum

dicatur us aequae fit & iucundus actus stipem.

Marcus Cicero salutem dicit cu   curioni m.... et studium uonde

fuit declarandorum munerum tuo nomine sed nec mihi placuit nec cui

quam tuorum quicquam te absente fieri quod dabis cum uenisset nomes

sed me grum aequidem sententiam tues oribus tuis oribus ideo posset plumbus uit

ne ad eum me dicere. In paratum te offendam coramque contra is faracio

nem me dicam ut uult te lucium eam sententiam adducam lucces te potuisse consequi, nisi meis puer olim fidelissimis atque amantissimis consiliis paruisses. Qua re hoc animo in nos esse debebis ut aetas nostra iam ingravescens in amore atque in adulescentia tua conquiescat.

Alia tuam ad oblectationem.

...profficientius exploratores reddunt, et rebus eternis, trahi

...litera venturus expectabat. Cui quidam ego non respondi

51

EPISTULA 770 T-P
AD ATTICUM XVI, 5

CICERO ATTICO SAL.

Tuas iam litteras Brutus exspectabat: cui quidem ego [non] novum [...]

+ attulerunt

+ attulerunt & rica~ an ille ~xutam putabat. Et tamen rumoris nescio
quid adplancat comissione gregorium frequentauit no fuisset; pater quidem
me numine fefellit. Seo enim quid ego & grece lude expositionem
nunc sub ...phrasie est ... q omnia. D ... fuit mecum suo expresse
et si ego expressi ille ... plene fuisse. Et q tum fuit ... et
f me m omni genere delectatur. in cogit magorum in quo numine satis
faciebat. Quia enim comitatus est tuus. et proprie meis quibusdam
que in manib habebam. et ... oratione et proprie. et tali.
animo in x. D. quod nos habuimus finiens fuit. hoc cum multi
no confirmasset. f etiam persuasisse est mecum amicare multum
Ibis/tibi respondeam/fe suprum. et te et nobis futurum/nec
fe postulare ... satim res deo/f cum ipse ... mutationem hoc quod
et fe amaueo quod nisi fidem mihi fuisset mutationem hoc quod
Dico firmum esse/et fecissem so quod facturus sum. Quare enim
... dissentem as ...cutum fuit et ... patrum est ... quod ad te nobis

attuleram de "Tereo" Acci. Ille "Brutum" putabat. Sed tamen rumoris nescio quid adflaverat commissione Graecorum frequentiam non fuisse, quod quidem me minime fefellit. Scis enim quid ego de Graecis ludis existimem.

2. Nunc audi quod pluris est quam omnia. Quintus fuit mecum dies compluris, et si ego cuperem, ille vel pluris fuisset, sed, quantum fuit, incredibile est quam me in omni genere delectarit, in eoque maxime in quo minime satis faciebat. Sic enim commutatus est totus et scriptis meis quibusdam quae in manibus habebam et adsiduitate orationis et praeceptis, ut tali animo in rem publicam quali nos volumus futurus sit. Hoc cum mihi non modo confirmasset sed etiam persuasisset, egit mecum accurate multis verbis tibi ut sponderem se dignum et te et nobis futurum, neque se postulare ut statim crederes, sed, cum ipse perspexisses, tum ut se amares. Quod nisi fidem mihi fecisset iudicassemque hoc quod [...]

ΜΕΤΕΩΠΟΤΕΠΟΝ

ΟΜΟΛΟΓΙΑΙ

μετεωρόπον

ὁμολογίαι

dico firmum fore, non fecissem id quod dicturus sum. Duxi enim mecum adulescentem ad Brutum. Sic ei probatum est quod ad te scribo ut ipsi crediderit, me sponsorem accipere noluerit eumque laudans amicissime mentionem tui fecerit, complexus osculatusque dimiserit. Quam ob rem etsi magis est quod gratuler tibi quam quod te rogem, tamen etiam rogo ut, si quae minus antea propter infirmitatem aetatis constanter ab eo fieri videbantur, ea iudices illum abiecisse mihique credas multum adlaturam vel plurimum potius ad illius iudicium confirmandum auctoritatem tuam. 3. Bruto cum saepe iniecissem de ὁμοπλοίᾳ, non perinde atque ego putaram adripere visus est. Existimabam μετεωρότερον esse, et hercule erat et maxime de ludis. At mihi, cum ad villam redissem, Cn. Lucceius, qui multum utitur Bruto, narravit illum valde morari, non tergiversantem sed exspectantem si qui forte casus. Itaque dubito an Venusiam [...]

tendam et ibi exspectem de legionibus: si aberunt, ut quidam arbitrantur, Hydruntem: si neutrum erit ἀσφαλές, eodem revertar. ⋆⋆

[...]

Nota bene: Tyrrell and Purser explain the missing text here as the insertion of letter Att. XII, 3. See their note in volume 5, page 378.

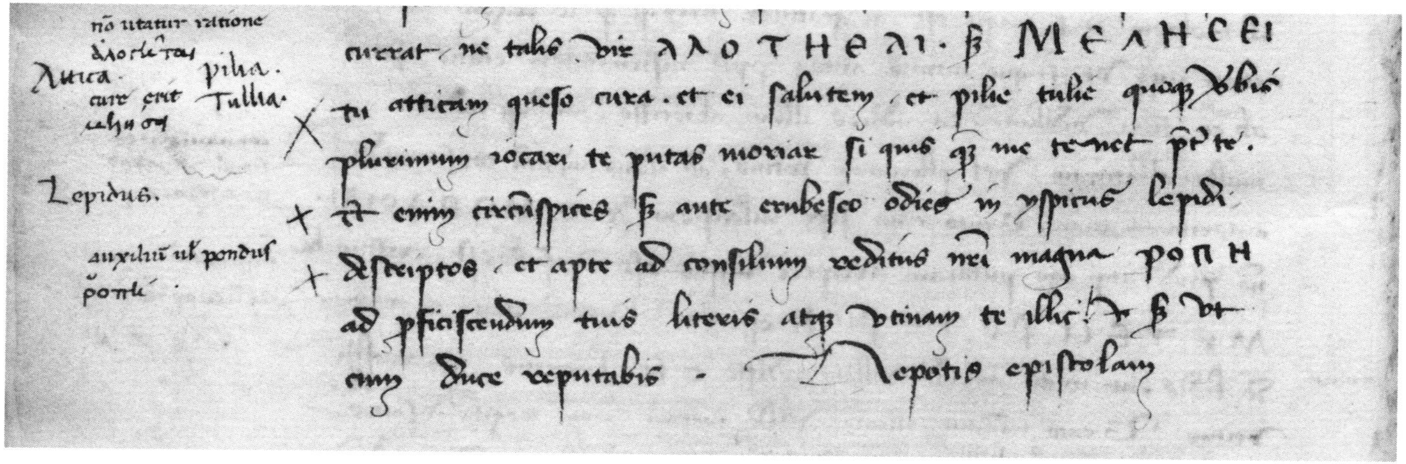
nō utatur ratione
ἀδολέσχας
Attica. pilia.
cure erit Tullia.
Lepidus.
auxiliū uł pondus
poⁿtt.
curat ne talis vir ΑΛΟΤΗΕΛΙ. sed ΜΕΛΗΣΕΙ
te atticam queso cura. et ei salutem et pilie tulie quoque verbis
plurimum rogari te putas moriar si quis quam me tenet preter te.
et enim circumspices sed ante erubesco odices in ypsirus lepidi
descriptos. et apte ad consilium reditus nei magna ΡΟΠΗ
ad proficiscendum tuis litteris atque utinam te illic! sed ut
enim duce reputabis. Nepotis epistolam
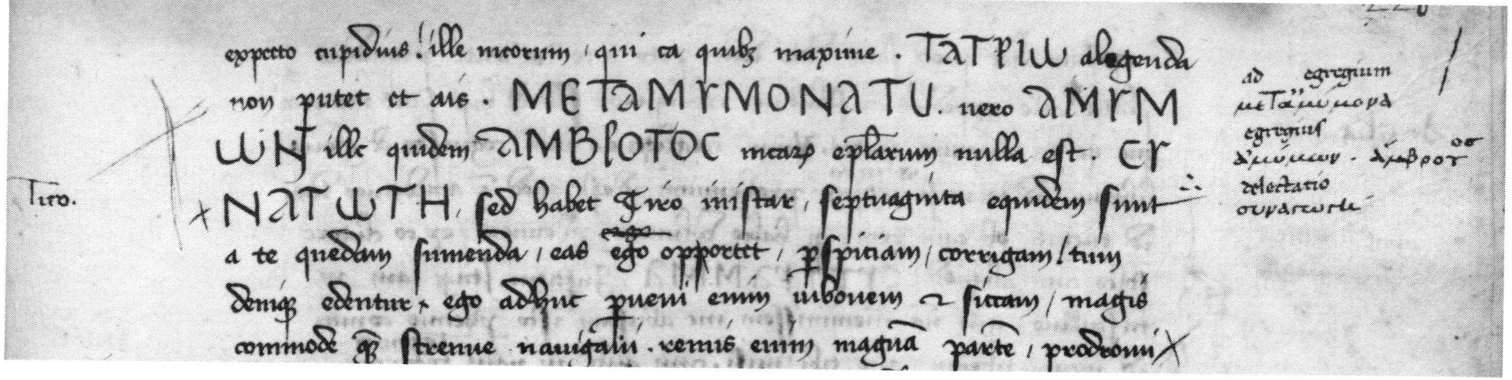
Tiro.
ad egregium
egregius
delectatio
expecto cupidius! ille meorum qui ea quibus maxime ΤΑΤΡΙΩ a legenda
non putet et ais. ΜΕΤΑΜΥΜΟΝΑΤU. vero ΑΜΥΜ
ΩΝ ille quidem ΑΜΒΙΟΤΟΣ mearum exemplarium nulla est. ΣΥ
ΝΑΓΩΓΗ sed habet tuos instar septuaginta equidem sunt
a te quedam sumenda eas ergo opportet perspiciam corrigam tum
demum edentur. ego adhuc puerum enim [illegible] magis
commode quam strenue navigavi. remis enim magna parte prodromi

[...] Iocari me putas? Moriar si quisquam me tenet praeter te. Etenim † circumspice, sed ante quam erubesco † 4. O dies in auspiciis Lepidi *lepide* descriptos et apte ad consilium reditus nostri! Magna ῥοπή ad proficiscendum *in* tuis litteris. Atque utinam te illic! Sed ut conducere putabis. 5. Nepotis epistulam exspecto. Cupidus ille meorum? Qui ea quibus maxime γαυριῶ legenda non putet? Et ais μετ᾽ ἀμύμονα. Tu vero ἀμύμ- ων: ille quidem ἄμβροτος. Mearum epistularum nulla est συ- ναγωγή, sed habet Tiro instar septuaginta. Et quidem sunt a te quaedam sumendae: eas ego oportet perspiciam, corrigam; tum denique edentur.

PARS SECVNDA

EPISTVLARVM MINVTATIM TRACTATVS

INTERPRETATIONE ADDITIS

NECNON COMMENTATIONE

❧

*part II: the treatment of
the letters in detail*

the translation added and
also the commentary

LETTER 132 T-P
AD QUINTUM FRATREM II, 9 (11)

MARCUS QUINTO FRATRI SALUTEM.

Epistulam hanc convicio efflagitarunt codicilli tui. Nam res quidem ipsa et is dies quo tu es profectus nihil mihi ad scribendum argumenti sane dabat. Sed quem ad modum, coram cum sumus, sermo nobis deesse non solet, sic epistulae nostrae debent interdum alucinari.   (*Q. Fr.* II, 9 [11], 1)

MARCUS A GREETING TO BROTHER QUINTUS.

Your little writing tablets demanded this letter with a violent reproach. For the matter itself indeed and that day on which you set out of course was giving me no bit of subject matter for writing. But just as, when we are face to face, a conversation is not accustomed to be lacking to us, thus our letters off and on should digress freely.

efflagitarunt, "[writing tablets] demanded": the full form in T.4b is *efflagitaverunt*.
→ **1** contractions: verbs, 39.2, GL n° 131.

is dies quo tu es profectus, "that day on which you set out": *quo*, "on which," is an abl. expressing time at which. The verb *es profectus*, "you set out," is T.4b of the deponent verb *proficiscor, fectus*, 3, so its form is passive but its meaning active, and its word order is reversed from that which appears in Latin manuals, because that is how Cicero expressed himself.
→ **2** abl.: time at which, 70.1; verb: deponent, 29; sentence structure, 1.

ad scribendum, "for writing": a gerund.
→ **3** gerund, 77.1.

nihil ... argumenti, "no bit of subject matter": *argumenti*, "of subject matter," is the gen. of part, and typically is separated here by three words from the word on which it depends *nihil*, "no bit."
→ **4** gen. of part, 99.

mihi … dabat, "was giving me": *dabat*, "was giving," is T.2i and *mihi*, "to me," is the natural function to-for-from. Note the word order.

> → **5** verb T.2i: 12.2.1; natural dat., 33.7.1; sentence structure, 1.

quem ad modum … sic, "just as … thus": *quem ad modum*, literally, "according to what manner," may also be written as one word *quemadmodum*; as a whole it functions as an adv. and here corresponds to the *sic*, "thus," further down the sentence.

> → **6** dict., *quemadmodum*, adv., II., B., 1. corresp. with *sic*;
>   comparative correlative sentences, 90.5, GL n° 642.

cum sumus, "when we are": a mere time clause, therefore in the indicative T.1.

> → **7** *cum* + indicative = "when": temporal sentences, 66.3.

sermo nobis deesse non solet, "a conversation is not accustomed to be lacking to us": *deesse*, "to be failing, missing, lacking," is an inf. that completes the idea expressed in the main verb of this sentence *non solet*, "[a conversation] is not accustomed."

> → **8** verb: complementary infinitive, 77.

nobis deesse, "to be failing us": the natural meaning of *nobis* in the function to-for-from includes its use here with *deesse*, "to be absent from [us]," "to be wanting to [us]," "to fail to obtain for [us]."

> → **9** dict., *desum, fui, esse*, v. irreg., I., (β) with dat. so most frequent;
>   natural dat., 33.7.1.

interdum, "off and on": according to the first meaning in the dictionary, "occasionally," "off and on," "at times," but many people understand this adv. as "in the meanwhile," a meaning which really is expressed by *interim* and *interea*, and only later was attributed to *interdum*.

> → **10** dict., *interdum*, adv.

debent … alucinari, "should digress freely": the deponent verb *alucinor, atus*, 1, produces this inf., which is passive in form but active in meaning; *alucinari*, "digress freely," also means "to talk idly," "to follow no definite train of thought." It complements the action of *debent*, "[letters] should," in T.1i.

> → **11** verb: deponent, 29; verb: complementary infinitive, 77.

❧

Tenediorum igitur libertas securi Tenedia praecisa est, cum eos praeter me et Bibulum et Calidium et Favonium nemo defenderet.   (*Q. Fr.* II, 9 [11], 2)

The freedom therefore of the people of Tenedos was cut down by the sword of Tenes, when no one was defending them besides me and Bibulus and Calidius and Favonius.

securi Tenedia, "by the sword of Tenes": the noun *securis, is*, f. "a sword," produces here *securi*, "by the sword." *Tenedia*, "of Tenes," is also in the function by-with-from-in and means "by a Tenedian [sword]," referring to the people and island of Tenedos in the Aegean Sea. King Tenes was a strict administer of justice.

→ **12** Block II nouns, 15; abl.: instrument, 28.5.3–4, 89.2, GL n° 401.

praecisa est, "[freedom] was cut down": T.4b in the passive, also means "was lopped off."

→ **13** verb T.4b passive, 26.

cum eos … nemo defenderet, "when no one was defending them": *praecisa est*, "[freedom] was cut down," is in T.4b and establishes Track II. The English rendering above understands *cum … defenderet*, "when [no one] was defending [them]," in T.2s as a temporal clause in the subjunctive to indicate the circumstance for *praecisa est*. It could also give the reason for the action of *praecisa est*, as a causal clause meaning "because [no one] was defending [them]."

→ **14** subjunctive use: temporal circumstance *cum* = "when," 66.3.2;
subjunctive use: causal *cum* = "because, since," 59.1;
consecutio, 47–48.

praeter me et Bibulum et Calidium et Favonium, "besides me and Bibulus and Calidius and Favonius": the preposition *praeter*, "besides," takes the objects given here in succession joined with *et … et … et …* , "and … and … and…."

→ **15** prep. with obj., 6; conjunction: *et …* , *et …* , 3.2.

❧

De te a Magnetibus ab Sipylo mentio est honorifica facta, cum te unum dicerent postulationi L. Sesti Pansae restitisse. Reliquis diebus si quid erit quod te scire opus sit, aut etiam si nihil erit, tamen scribam cotidie aliquid. Pridie Id. neque tibi neque Pomponio deero.   (*Q. Fr.* II, 9 [11], 3)

An honorary mention was made about you by the Magnesians from Sipylum, when they were saying that you alone had resisted the request of Lucius Sestius Pansa. On the remaining days, if there will be anything which is necessary that you know, or even if there will be nothing, still I shall write something every day. On the day before the Ides [12 February] I shall fail neither you nor Pomponius [Atticus].

mentio est honorifica facta, "An honorary mention was made": note the word order where *honorifica*, "honorary," describes *mentio*, "a mention"; the verb is *est … facta*, "was made" in T.4b in the passive.

→ **16** verb T.4b passive, 26.

Magnetibus, "the Magnesians": see under the entry for *Magnesia, ae*, f.

→ **17** dict., *Magnesia, ae*, f.

cum ... dicerent, "when they were saying": depending on *est ... facta*, "was made," in T.4b establishing Track II, this clause is in T.2s and gives the circumstance for the mention made. If Cicero had used the indicative, *cum ... dicebant*, "when they were saying," he would have indicated a mere temporal coincidence, as for example at 10:30 in the morning.

→ **18** subjunctive use: temporal circumstance *cum* = "when," 66.3.2;
     cum + historical times of indicative = "when": temporal coincidence, 66.3.1;
     consecutio, 47–48.

te unum ... restitisse, "that you alone had resisted": the content of what "they were saying" *dicerent*, is given in OO, where the acc. subject is *te unum* and the inf. *restitisse* describes a previous action; this can be rendered as above, or without the initial word "that" as in "[they were saying] you alone had resisted" or keeping the acc. and inf. in English as "[they were saying] you alone to have resisted."

→ **19** OO, 71–73.

restitisse, "[you] had resisted": *restitisse* is from *resisto, resistere*, "to oppose, resist," not from *resto, restare*, "to remain, be left over"; the third part is the same for both verbs.

→ **20** dict., *resisto, resistere, stiti*, 3; dict., *resto, restare, stiti*, 1.

te ... postulationi ... restitisse, "you ... had resisted the request ...": the verb *restitisse* is one of the 65 verbs whose object is given in the to-for-from function, here *postulationi*, which can be heard in English if we say "you had been resistant to the request," but this dat. object is often difficult to hear in English as here, "you ... had resisted the request."

→ **21** 65 verbs with dat., 33.7.2, GL n° 346.

L. Sesti Pansae, "of Lucius Sestius Pansa": the full text here is *Lucii Sesti Pansae*, where all three words are masculine and agree in the of-possession form.

→ **22** function: of-possession, 20.

Reliquis diebus, "On the remaining days": the *abl.* of time at which indicates successive moments of time, "during the following days"; had Cicero said *Reliquos dies*, "for the remaining days," he would have indicated extent of time.

→ **23** abl.: time at which, 70.1.

si quid erit, "if there will be anything": a factual condition where *erit*, "there will be," is T.3i. After the word *si*, "if," the word *aliquid* is often written as *quid*, still meaning "anything" or "something" as an indefinite pronoun, not interrogative.

> → **24** pronouns: indefinite, 42.4; after *si* the *ali*-s fly away, 42.5;
>   conditionals: factual, 86.1.

quod … opus sit, "which is necessary": the antecedent of *quod*, "which," is *quid*, "anything [which]." The reason for the subjunctive *sit*, in T.1s, is that the relative clause *quod … opus sit*, describes the character of that *quid*, "anything." Thus the *quod* stands for *tale ut id*, "such that it," as in *si quid erit tale ut id opus sit*, "if there will be anything such that it is necessary [that you know]."

> → **25** subjunctive use: characteristic result, 68.2; *opus est*, 75.3.

te scire, "that you know": depending on the expression *opus sit*, "[which] is necessary," the subject of *sit* is the whole expression given in OO *te scire*, as in the English rendering, "if there will be anything which you knowing is necessary." In this OO, the infinitive *scire* has its own subject given in the object form *te*, which may be rendered as above or without the initial "that" as in "[which is necessary] you know," or less effective here one could keep the acc. and inf. in English and say "you to know."

> → **26** OO, 71–73.

aut etiam si nihil erit, "or even if there will be nothing": before giving the consequence, Cicero gives a second factual condition again in T.3i, *erit*, "there will be."

> → **27** conditionals: factual, 86.1.

tamen scribam cotidie aliquid, "still I shall write something every day": the consequence of the factual conditional sentence is also in T.3i, *scribam*, "I shall write."

> → **28** conditionals: factual, 86.1.

Pridie Id., "On the day before the Ides [12 February]": the adv. *pridie*, "on the day before," is used with the object form, as if to say *pridie ante idus* "on the previous day before the Ides." Here *Idus*, "the Ides," abbreviated as *Id.*, which in February are on the thirteenth day.

> → **29** about the Roman calendar, pp. 605–608;
>   GL Appendix, Roman Calendar, pp. 491–92.

neque tibi neque Pomponio deero, "neither shall I fail you nor Pomponius": *tibi … Pomponio*, with the natural meaning of the function to-for-from: "for you … for Pomponius." The two dat. objects are coordinated by *neque … neque … ,* "neither … nor.…"

> → **30** natural dat., 33.7.1;
>   conjunction: *neque … , neque … ,* 3.2, GL n° 445.

Lucreti poëmata ut scribis ita sunt, multis luminibus ingeni, multae tamen
artis. Sed cum veneris.... Virum te putabo, si Sallusti "Empedoclea" legeris,
hominem non putabo.   (Q. *Fr.* II, 9 [11], 4)

The poems of Lucretius, as you write, are so: of many flashes of intelligence,
but of great artistry. But when you will have come.... I will consider you a
[tough] man, if you will have read the "Empedoclea" [poem] of Sallustius, I
will not consider you a human being.

> *ut scribis,* "as you write": *ut* with the indicative, *scribis,* "you write," here
> means "as."
>
> → **31** dict., *ut,* I., B. meaning "as."

> *multis luminibus ingeni, multae tamen artis,* "of many flashes of intelligence,
> but of great artistry": Cicero uses two different ways to describe the poems
> of Lucretius. First he uses the abl. of description, *multis luminibus,* "with
> many flashes," which he describes further with the gen. as *ingeni,* "[flashes]
> of intelligence." Next he continues with the gen. of description and says
> *multae ... artis,* "of great artistry." He praises the work in two ways distinct
> also in their Latin expression.
>
> Note: this text has been disputed for centuries, because of the adversa-
> tive *tamen,* "still," "however," "yet," which would almost deny the first part,
> namely that art does not go with intelligence. You would expect here *atque*
> to join beautiful content with great artistry. We might render this text as:
> "Brilliant content, but still great artistry," which Cicero expects should not
> go together. Until the first century c.e. the of-possession form *ingénii,* "of
> intelligence," was written and heard *ingéni.*
>
> → **32** quality in gen., 96.1; quality in abl., 96.2;
>   early gen. ending in –*i,* GL n° 33, remark 1.

> *cum veneris,* "when you will have come": a temporal clause where *veneris,*
> "you will have come" is in T.6i. The sentence is incomplete, so you can add
> anything you want to complete it, perhaps *cum veneris disputabimus,* or ...
> *edisseremus,* both of which can just about mean, "we shall discourse about
> these things when you get back here."
>
> → **33** *cum* + indicative = "when": temporal sentences, 66.3.

> *si Sallusti "Empedoclea" legeris,* "if you will have read the 'Empedoclea'
> [poem] of Sallustius": another factual condition in T.6i, *legeris,* "you will
> have written." Tyrrell and Purser indicate that this work is not extant and it
> is not clear that this refers to the well-known historian Sallustius.
>
> → **34** conditionals: factual, 86.1.

> *Virum te putabo ... hominem non putabo,* "I will consider you a [tough] man
> ... I will not consider you a human being": in this one sentence Cicero uses
> both *Virum,* "a man," "a male" in contrast to *hominem,* "a human being,"

"a human person." The idea is that he will be considered as strong as an ox, able to plough through the poem, but not a real human person, with more refined tastes. The main verb, *putabo*, "I will consider," in T.3i is repeated. If we presume that the infinitive *esse*, "to be," is missing, then his thought is expressed in OO. In this case, the one subject in the object form *te* applies to both statements possibly in OO. The predicate of the first is *Virum*, "a [tough] man," and in contrast *hominem*, "a human being." However, if we take *putabo* to mean, "I will consider you a man" or "I will judge you a man," then you simply have a double accusative without the need of an implied verb or OO.

> → **35** M & M, 60, 71, GL n° 527, remarks 1–2; OO, 71–73;
> dict., *puto, avi, atum*, 1., II., B., 2., c.—with two acc.

LETTER 1 T-P
AD ATTICUM I, 5

CICERO ATTICO SAL.

Quantum dolorem acceperim et quanto fructu sim privatus et forensi et domestico Luci fratris nostri morte in primis pro nostra consuetudine tu existimare potes. Nam mihi omnia quae iucunda ex humanitate alterius et moribus homini accidere possunt ex illo accidebant. Qua re non dubito quin tibi quoque id molestum sit, cum et meo dolore moveare et ipse omni virtute officioque ornatissimum tuique et sua sponte et meo sermone amantem, adfinem, amicumque amiseris.   (*Att.* I, 5, 1)

CICERO A GREETING TO ATTICUS

First of all in keeping with our closeness you are able to judge what great sorrow I got and of what great benefit both public and private I was deprived at the death of Lucius our brother. For all the pleasant things which are able to happen to a person out of the kindness and behavior of another were happening to me from him. For which reason I do not doubt that this is also troublesome for you, since both you are moved by my sorrow, and you yourself have lost a relative and friend most decorated with every virtue and dutifulness and fond of you both on his own accord and by my conversation.

CICERO ATTICO SAL.: *Cicero Attico salutem*

quantum ... acceperim, "what ... I got": IQ depending on M & M verb *existimare*, "to judge." This and the next IQ are on Track I, established by *existimare potes*, "you are able to judge."

→ **36** M & M, 60, 71, GL nº 527, remarks 1–2;
   IQ, 60; *consecutio*, 47–48.

quanto ... sim privatus, "of what ... I was deprived": IQ depending on M & M verb *existimare*, "to judge."

→ **37** M & M, 60, 71, GL nº 527, remarks 1–2;
   IQ, 60; *consecutio*, 47–48.

quanto fructu, "of what great benefit": the abl. of separation is used with the verb *sim privatus*, literally, "I was deprived *from* what great benefit," whereas the English idiom is to be deprived "*of* what great benefit."

→ **38** abl.: separation, 27.

mihi ... accidebant, "to me ... [things] were happening": Sentence structure: the second word in the sentence *mihi* connects with the final word *accidebant*.

→ **39** sentence structure, 1.

alterius here does not mean strictly "of the second person" nor "of the other person," but "of any other person" for the simple reason that the of-possession form of *alius, alia, aliud* "any other person" should be *alíus*, with an accent on the í, but is practically nonexistent and so substituted by *alterius*.

→ **40** dict., *alius, alia, aliud*, adj. and subst.—*alīus* is rare for which *alterius* is common;
famous nine, 42.6.

homini accidere, "to happen to a person": the natural use of the dat. in *homini*.

→ **41** natural dat., 33.7.1.

non dubito quin ... sit, "I do not doubt that this is": after a negative, here *non dubito, quin* means "that," and is followed by the subjunctive, sounding indicative in English.

→ **42** negative *dubitare* + *quin* + subjunctive, 93.4, 101.2, GL n° 555.2.

moveare, "you are moved": one of Cicero's favorite variations, here of *movearis*, T.1s.

→ **43** variation: *–ris*, 39.3.

cum et ... moveare et ... amiseris, "since both you are moved ... and you ... have lost": *cum* begins a causal sentence on Track I depending on *dubito*, "I doubt" in T.1i establishing the sentence on Track I, followed by T.1s giving contemporaneous time and T.3s giving antecedent time.

→ **44** subjunctive use: causal *cum* = "because, since," 59.1;
consecutio, 47–48.

ipse ... amiseris, "you yourself have lost": the pronoun *ipse* agrees with the subject *tu* of *amiseris* with fifteen words between them.

→ **45** sentence structure, 1; three cousins: *iste–ille–ipse*, 41.3.

A note on the abundant use of "and": in the first sentence, the first *et* joins *acceperim* with *sim privatus*, but the second two *et ... et ...*, "both ... and ...," join *forensi* with *domestico*. In the third sentence, the first two *et ... et ...*, "both ... and ...," join *moveare* with *amiseris*; the *que* on *officioque* joins *virtute* with *officio*; the *que* on *tuique* joins *ornatissimum* with *aman-*

tem; the next *et ... , et ...* , "both ... , and ... ," joins *sponte* with *sermone*; the *que* on *amicumque* joins *adfinem* with *amicum*. A note on style is that the *que* joins closer things, the *et* joins larger or more separated elements, and *et ... , et ...* , has the special meaning "both ... , and...."

→ **46** conjunction: *et ... , et ...* , 3.2.

The third sentence has the following boxes:

Qua re non dubito	main sentence T.1i
(quin tibi quoque id molestum sit	result T.1s
{ cum et meo dolore moveare	causal 1 T.1s pass
et ipse ...	causal 2 begins
[omni virtute officioque	
ornatissimum]	adj. direct object 1
[tuique et sua sponte et	
meo sermone amantem,]	direct object 2
[adfinem, amicumque]	direct object 3, 4
amiseris. })	causal 2 concludes T.3s

→ **47** structure of Latin sentences, 103 p. 587, *Ossa* Readings: 1-D, 1-I, 3-D, 3-I, 4-D, 4-I.

tui, "of you": here a pronoun of-possession depending on *amantem*, meaning "fond of you," not an adjective of-possession meaning "yours," which would not make sense here. To test this, the plural of *tui* here is *vestri* not *tuorum*.

→ **48** personal pronouns: function of-possession, 24.3; adj.: possessive, 24.3, 100.2.

∿

Quod ad me scribis de sorore tua, testis erit tibi ipsa quantae mihi curae fuerit, ut Quinti fratris animus in eam esset is qui esse deberet. Quem cum esse offensiorem arbitrarer, eas litteras ad eum misi quibus et placarem ut fratrem et monerem ut minorem et obiurgarem ut errantem. Itaque ex iis quae postea saepe ab eo ad me scripta sunt confido ita esse omnia ut et oporteat et velimus.   (*Att.* I, 5, 2)

The fact that you write to me about your sister, she herself will be a witness to you for what a great concern it was to me: that the attitude of brother Quintus might be toward her such which it was supposed to be. Whom because I knew to be somewhat upset, I sent to him such letters by which I might both calm him down as a brother and advise him as someone younger and scold him as someone making a mistake. Therefore, from those things which later on were often written by him to me I trust that all things are in such a state as both is fitting and we desire.

Quod ... scribis, "The fact that you write": with this *quod* he starts a new subject, but it is also semi-independent from the main verb *erit*, "she will be"; it just hangs a bit and it is almost explanatory.

→ **49** *quod* = "the fact that" as a new subject, GL n° 525.2.

quantae ... fuerit, "how much ... it was": an IQ in the subjunctive depending on the M & M expression, *testis erit*, "she ... will be a witness"; English in the indicative.

→ **50** M & M, 60, 71, GL n° 527, remarks 1–2; IQ, 60.

quantae mihi curae fuerit, "for what a great concern it was to me": double dat. of person concerned *mihi*, and of finality or result *curae*.

→ **51** double dat., 91.2.

fuerit, "it was": the subject of *fuerit* is the entire phrase *ut Quinti fratris animus in eam esset is qui esse deberet*, "that the attitude of brother Quintus might be toward her such which it was supposed to be." The expression *ut ... esset* is a purpose clause describing *curae*, "for a concern that [his attitude] might be." The whole purpose clause serves as the subject of *fuerit*, as in the example, "That you might be healthy was a concern to me," or more simply, "Your health was a concern to me." The heroic task here is to get as close to the Latin as English can manage, which is made difficult by the lengthy subject, so in our rendering we have added the word "it [was]" as a placeholder that stands for the entire subject given after a colon. It is as if you were saying, "she will be a witness for what a great care your health was for me," but instead of saying "your health," Cicero gives a much more developed subject consisting of eleven words.

→ **52** subjunctive use: purpose clause, 58.1.

in eam, "toward her": one of the four prepositions in the box which take the object form to indicate geographical motion or as in this case moral motion toward her, or even against.

→ **53** prep. with obj., 6.

is qui esse deberet, "such which it was supposed to be": the use of the subjunctive here, T.2s on Track II, is due either to characteristic result, where *is* means "such" and *qui* means *ut is*, thus, *is ut is*, "such that it"; or depending on *esset* it is in the subjunctive due to modal attraction and stands for *debebat*, "it was supposed to be" as in "[the attitude] might be such which it was supposed to be."

→ **54** subjunctive use: characteristic result, 68.2;
     subjunctive use: modal attraction, 83; *consecutio*, 47–48.

eas litteras, "such letters": here *eas* is a pronominal adj. meaning "those, these, such"; *eas* does not mean here "them women."

→ **55** demonstrative pron.: *is, ea, id*, 3.1, 40.2.

quibus ... placarem ... monerem ... obiurgarem, "by which I might calm ...
advise ... scold": relative sentence of purpose in which *quibus ... = ut iis ...*,
"so that by them ..."; the verb *placarem* is from *placare*, "to calm," not from
placere, "to be pleasing."

> → **56** subjunctive use: relative clause of purpose, 58.2;
>   dict., *placeo, cui* and *citus, citum*, 2., "to be pleasing";
>   dict., *placo, avi, atum*, 1, "to assuage, appease,"
>   Reggie says: "to calm down."

esse omnia, "that all things are": OO depending on M & M verb *confido*,
meaning "I trust all things to be" or "I trust that all things are."

> → **57** M & M, 60, 71, GL n° 527, remarks 1–2; OO, 71–73.

ut ... oporteat et velimus, "as ... is fitting and we desire": here *ut* does not
indicate result or purpose, but simply "as" followed by two subjunctives in
modal attraction depending on *esse omnia* in OO.

> → **58** dict., *ut*, I., B. meaning "as";
>   OO, 71–73; subjunctive use: modal attraction, 83.

∽

De litterarum missione sine causa abs te accusor. Numquam enim a Pomponia nostra certior sum factus esse cui dare litteras possem, porro autem
neque mihi accidit ut haberem qui in Epirum proficisceretur nequedum te
Athenis esse audiebamus.   (*Att.* I, 5, 3)

I am being accused without reason by you about the sending of letters. For
I was never informed by our Pomponia that there was [someone] such to
whom I was able to entrust a letter, furthermore however, neither did it happen to me that I had someone such who was heading out for Epirus nor were
we yet hearing that you were in Athens.

abs te ... a Pomponia, "by you ... by ... Pomponia": preposition with the abl.
Note: the preposition may appear as *a, ab,* or *abs*, the last of which was used
by Cicero in his earlier letters and then practically abandoned. This is his
earliest extant letter, written when he was 38 years old; within about a de-
cade he gave up the use of *abs* but here he uses *abs* and *a* with no difference
in meaning. Caution: some people may confuse *abs*, "from," with *absque*,
"without." Thus, people may confuse *abs dubio*, literally, "far from a doubt,"
as meaning "without doubt."

> → **59** prep. with abl., 28.4.

certior sum factus, "I was ... informed": an idiom that does not mean, "I was
made more certain." In T.4b, the sentence is on Track II.

> → **60** *consecutio*, 47–48.

esse, "that there was": OO depending on *certior sum factus*, "I was … informed"; the subject of *esse* is the implied antecedent of *cui*, "*someone* such to whom."

→ **61** OO, 71–73.

cui … dare … possem, "someone such to whom I was able to entrust": a relative sentence of characteristic result where *cui* followed by T.2s implies *eum talem ut ei dare possem*, "someone such that I was able to entrust to him"; result sentences sound indicative in English.

→ **62** subjunctive use: characteristic result, 68.2.

neque … nequedum, "and … not … and … not yet": negative correlatives meaning "neither … nor…." All alone, *neque* means "and not," rather than simply "not," and *nequedum* means "and not yet," as the equivalent of *et nondum*. Furthermore, *et nondum* does not correlate with *neque*, "neither … and not," but *nequedum* does.

→ **63** conjunction: *neque … , nequedum … , 3.2;*
dict., *neque*, adv. and conj.; dict., *nondum*, adv.;
neque … , neque … , GL nº 445.

qui … proficisceretur, "someone such who was heading out": a relative sentence of characteristic result where *qui* followed by T.2s implies *eum talem ut is proficisceretur*, "someone such that he was heading out," again sounding indicative in English.

→ **64** subjunctive use: characteristic result, 68.2.

Note: in the above two sentences of characteristic result, the distinction between result and purpose may be only a matter of perspective. If these are understood as expressing an intention, then *cui* stands for *ut ei*, "so that to him," and *qui* stands for *ut is*, "so that he," and they may be rendered in English as: *ut ei dare possem* "in order that I might be able to entrust to him"; *ut is proficisceretur* "in order that he might depart." This distinction is most essential; although it is given in GL in the smallest print, it should be presented in bold letters.

→ **65** difference between purpose and result is perspective, GL nº 543, note 2.

in Epirum, "for Epirus": Atticus had a villa in Epirus, in today's Albania. Here the preposition *in* followed by the object *Epirum* expresses geographical motion toward the city Epirus.

→ **66** prep. with obj., 6.

Athenis, "in Athens": place function instead of the locative; being a noun only in the plural number *Athenis* does not have a locative function and therefore the abl. is used instead, which confutes those who insist that the

loc. is the same as the gen., which would be *Athenarum*; just as books published in Paris say *Parisiis*.

> → **67** function: place at which, names of cities and small islands, plural, *Parisiis*,
> 69.3.2;
> function: place at which, names of cities and small islands, plural, *Athenis*,
> 69.3.2.

te … esse, "that you were": OO because of M & M *audiebamus*.

> → **68** M & M, 60, 71, GL n° 527, remarks 1–2; OO, 71–73.

❧

De Acutiliano autem negotio quod mihi mandaras, ut primum a tuo digressu Romam veni, confeceram; sed accidit ut et contentione nihil opus
esset et ut ego, qui in te satis consili statuerim esse, mallem Peducaeum tibi
consilium per litteras quam me dare. Etenim cum multos dies auris meas
Acutilio dedissem, cuius sermonis genus tibi notum esse arbitror, non mihi
grave duxi scribere ad te de illius querimoniis, cum eas audire, quod erat
subodiosum, leve putassem. Sed abs te ipso qui me accusas unas mihi scito
litteras redditas esse, cum et oti ad scribendum plus et facultatem dandi
maiorem habueris. […]   (*Att.* I, 5, 4)

However, concerning the business of Acutilius, what you had assigned to
me I had carried out as soon as I came to Rome after your departure; but it
happened that both there was in no way need of haste, and that I, because
I have decided that there is enough good sense in you, preferred that Peducaeus give you advice by letter rather than I. For, after I had devoted my ears
to Acutilius for many days, the type of whose talk I believe is well known to
you, I did not think it was important for me to write to you about his complaints, since I had thought it a light matter to hear them, something which
was somewhat odious. But you must know that one letter has been delivered
to me from you yourself, who are accusing me, although you have had both
more of leisure for writing and a greater opportunity of sending.

quod mihi mandaras, "what you had assigned to me": *mandaras* is the
contracted form of *mandaveras*, T.5i. The antecedent of the relative *quod* is
an unexpressed *id*, the object of *confeceram*.

> → **69** contractions: verbs, 39.2, GL n° 131;
> rel. pron.: subject or object, 10;
> rel. pron.: omission of the antecedent, 11.2.

ut primum "as soon as": a conjunction also expressible by *cum primum* and
ubi primum and *simul ac* and others, all meaning "as soon as."

> → **70** dict., *primus, a, um*, adj. II., B. *primum*, 3. with *cum*, (α) *cum primum*.

Romam, "to Rome": this form gives the place to where, the end of a journey.

> → **71** function: place to where, *Romam*, 69.1.2.

accidit ut et ... nihil opus esset et ut ego ... mallem, "it happened that both
there was in no way need ... and that I ... preferred": *accidit* in T.4b establishes Track II and produces a result clause *ut ... esset*, "that ... there was,"
in T.2s, and *ut ego ... mallem*, "that I ... preferred," in T.2s.

> → **72** subjunctive use: complementary result (consecutive), 68.1;
>   *consecutio*, 47–48.

contentione nihil opus esset, "there was in no way need of haste": the expression *opus esset* is complemented by *contentione* in the abl., although it can
also be used with the form of-possession as in *contentionis nihil opus esset* or
with the subject form as in *contentio nihil opus esset*, all meaning "exertion
was not necessary." We took our rendering of *contentione* as "haste" from
the dict. meaning for *contendere*, "to journey hastily."

> → **73** *opus est*, 75.3; dict., *opus, eris*, n., III., A. *opus est*, "it is needful" ... , the
>   person needing in the dat., the thing needed in nom., abl., rarely gen.;
>   dict., *nihil*, n., indecl., I., B. adv. "in no respect, not at all";
>   dict., *contendo, di, tum*, 3, II., B., 1., "to journey hastily."

qui ... statuerim esse, "because I have decided that there is ...": the sequence
of tenses here is by conservative reckoning somewhat violated or incorrect,
but it is quite human and natural. The narration is on Track II, and then
Cicero uses *statuerim* in T.3s on Track I. His Latin usage is intelligible on a
psychological basis, because the *accidit ut esset et mallem* in T.4b and T.2s
and T.2s are past things which Cicero had taken care of previously. But *ego
qui statuerim* is referring to Cicero, who is writing at the moment, and that
is why *statuerim* does not really pertain to that business of a few days or a
week ago. Paraphrasing Cicero we might say, "because I have decided and
am still convinced." The expression *qui statuerim* depends on the *ego*, the
person writing as Cicero looks at himself in the mirror, which means we are
on Track I, and *statuerim* in T.3s expresses antecedent action touching on
the present. Here the *qui* followed by the subj. stands for *cum ego*, meaning
"inasmuch as I" or "because I," in the phrase *ego cum ego statuerim*, "I,
inasmuch as I have decided." Next he continues on Track II with *mallem*, "I
preferred."

> → **74** *consecutio*, 47–48.

satis consili statuerim esse, "I have decided that there is enough good sense":
the M & M verb *statuerim*, "I have decided" in T.3s produces an OO whose
subject is the indeclinable noun *satis*, "enough," and verb is the contemporaneous inf. *esse*, "there is."

> → **75** M & M, 60, 71, GL n° 527, remarks 1–2; OO, 71–73;
>   *consecutio*, 47–48.

satis consili, "enough good sense": until the first century C.E the gen. form
was written *consili* with only one *–i* at the end. Later and until today it
would more commonly be written *consilii* without a change of accent. It

functions here as a gen. of part meaning directly, "there was enough of good sense."

→ **76** early gen. ending in *–i*, GL n° 33, remark 1;
gen. of part, 99.

Peducaeum … dare, "that Peducaeus give": OO depending on the M & M verb *mallem*, "I preferred." This could be rendered in English as "I preferred him to give" or "I preferred that he give" or "I preferred he give."

→ **77** M & M, 60, 71, GL n° 527, remarks 1–2;
OO, 71–73; *consecutio*, 47–48.

quam me, "than I": *me* is parallel to *Peducaeum*, and both are in the object form as subjects of the inf. *dare* in OO, all depending on the M & M verb *mallem*, "I preferred."

→ **78** *quam*, 43; M & M, 60, 71, GL n° 527, remarks 1–2;
OO, 71–73; *consecutio*, 47–48.

cum … dedissem, "after I had devoted": *cum* with T.4s means "when, after" and describes the historical circumstance. The sentence is on Track II depending on *duxi*, "I did … think" T.4b.

→ **79** subjunctive use: temporal circumstance *cum* = "when," 66.3.2;
consecutio, 47–48.

multos dies, "for many days": object form without a preposition expressing the extent of time.

→ **80** acc.: time during which, 70.2.

auris meas, "my ears": = *aures meas*; here the ending *–īs* = *–es*, the object or acc. ending in the plural. The subject plural remains *–es*, and does not change to *–īs*, whereas the gen. singular ends in *–ĭs*, with a short vowel, as correct Latin verse will show.

→ **81** Block II nouns: *–is* = *–es*, 38, GL n° 56.

cuius sermonis genus notum esse, "the type of whose talk": the rendering requires a certain ability in English in that what looks like, "whose of talk the type" means "the type of whose talk" or "whose type of talk." Remember, do not begin with the first word!

→ **82** *ossium gluten*, the bones' glue, 1.7; sentence structure, 1.

cuius … arbitror, "whose … I believe": the larger sentence depending on *dedissem … duxi*, "I had devoted … I did … think" is on Track II, but *arbitror*, "I believe," is T.1i and the whole relative clause is set almost parenthetically into the larger sentence. The antecedent of *cuius* is *Acutilio*.

→ **83** relative clauses, 10–11; *consecutio*, 47–48.

notum esse, "is well known [to you]": OO depending on M & M *arbitror*, "I believe."

> → **84** M & M, 60, 71, GL nº 527, remarks 1–2; OO, 71–73.

non mihi grave duxi scribere, "I did not think that writing … was important for me": OO where *duxi* is an M & M verb producing *scribere esse* in OO where the verb *esse* is understood and its subject is the gerund *scribere*, which is described by the neuter adj. *grave*.

> → **85** gerund, 77.1;
> M & M, 60, 71, GL nº 527, remarks 1–2; OO, 71–73.

cum … putassem, "since I had thought": *putassem* is a contraction for *putavissem* in T.4s and is antecedent to the *duxi* in T.4b establishing Track II. Note that *cum* followed by the subjunctive can always mean "because" as here, or "although." In a present or future sentence, *cum* followed by the ind. means "when." However, in an historical or past sentence, *cum* followed by the ind. means "when," as in the pure coincidence of time, but *cum* followed by the subjunctive means "when," as an expression of circumstance almost with the force of cause and effect.

> → **86** contractions: verbs, 39.2, GL nº 131; *consecutio*, 47–48;
> subjunctive use: causal *cum* = "because, since," 59.1;
> subjunctive use: concessive *cum* = "although," 64;
> *cum* + historical times of indicative = "when": temporal coincidence, 66.3.1;
> subjunctive use: temporal circumstance *cum* = "when," 66.3.2.

quod erat subodiosum, "something which was somewhat odious": *quod* here is "something which." The antecedent of the *quod* is the whole idea of listening to this man's complaints, *eas audire*, "to listen to those [complaints]." Cicero made dozens of adjectives like this; from *odiosum*, "hateful," *subodiosum* is tempered a bit, "on the verge of hateful," "on the edge of hateful" or "a little bit hateful."

> → **87** rel. pron.: subject or object, 10; dict., *subodiosus, a, um*, adj.;
> *quod* referring to previous sentence: GL nº 614, remark 2.

unas … litteras redditas esse, "that one letter has been delivered": OO depending on the M & M verb *scito*, "you must know." The infinitive *redditas esse* is equivalent to a T.4a passive and maintains Track I.

> → **88** M & M, 60, 71, GL nº 527, remarks 1–2; OO, 71–73;
> *consecutio*, 47–48.

scito, "you must know,": also rendered as "thou shalt know". This is the comic, legal, second imperative command form, whose plural is *scitote*. To be honest the form *scito* is also called by some the future imperative, but Plautus uses both imperative forms in the same line. Some manuals wrongly assert that this form hardly exists, but it is often used in colloquial speech, as commonly in Plautus and Terentius, even in the Latin Vulgate Bible, Erasmus *et al.*

> → **89** commands: first, second, 17.

mihi scito litteras redditas esse, cum ... habueris, "you must know that one
letter has been delivered to me although you have had": the command form
scito sets this sentence on Track I thus producing *habueris,* T.3s "you have
had," describing antecedent action in the subjunctive. The command *scito*
also produces the statement in OO, whose subject in the object form is *litteras,* "one letter," and whose verb is the antecedent inf. *redditas esse,* "[one
letter] has been delivered." Both forms *habueris* and *redditas esse* maintain
Track I and sound the same time in English, practically the equivalent of
T.4a, "has been delivered to me" and "you have had."

> → **90** commands: first, second, 17;
>   M & M, 60, 71, GL n° 527, remarks 1–2;
>   OO, 71–73; *consecutio,* 47–48.

cum ... habueris, "although you have had": *cum* with T.3s means "although"
and gives a concession. The action of *habueris,* T.3s, is antecedent to both
scito, "you must know" and to *accusas,* "[who] are accusing," T.1i both establishing Track I.

> → **91** subjunctive use: concessive *cum* = "although," 64;
>   *consecutio,* 47–48.

Note: in just a few lines of this first letter we have seen *cum* meaning
"when," "since," and "although."

> → **92** subjunctive use: causal *cum* = "because, since," 59.1;
>   subjunctive use: concessive *cum* = "although," 64;
>   *cum* + historical times of indicative = "when": temporal coincidence, 66.3.1;
>   subjunctive use: temporal circumstance *cum* = "when," 66.3.2.

oti ... plus, "more of leisure": *oti* is a partitive gen. which is separated from
the word on which it depends, *plus,* and is placed out front.

> → **93** gen. of part, 99.

ad scribendum, "for writing"; the preposition *ad* followed by an acc. gerund.

> → **94** gerund, 77.1.

dandi, "of sending": a gerund in the gen.

> → **95** gerund, 77.1.

LETTER 288 T-P
AD FAMILIARES XVI, 4

TULLIUS TIRONI SUO S. P. D. ET CICERO
ET Q. FRATER ET Q. F.

Varie sum adfectus tuis litteris: valde priore pagina perturbatus, paullum altera recreatus. Qua re nunc quidem non dubito quin, quoad plane valeas, te neque navigationi neque viae committas. Satis te mature videro si plane confirmatum videro. De medico et tu bene existimari scribis et ego sic audio; sed plane curationes eius non probo; ius enim dandum tibi non fuit, quom κακοστόμαχος esses. Sed tamen et ad illum scripsi accurate et ad Lysonem.   (*Fam.* XVI, 4, 1)

TULLIUS TO HIS TIRO SAYS A BIG GREETING
AND CICERO AND BROTHER QUINTUS
AND THE SON OF QUINTUS

I was moved by your letters in different ways: I was much disturbed by the first page, relieved a little bit by the second. For which reason now indeed I do not doubt that, until you are totally well, you are committing yourself neither to sailing nor to the road. I shall have seen you soon enough, if I shall have seen [you] fully strengthened. Both you write that there is a good reputation about the doctor, and I hear so; but I absolutely do not approve his treatments; for broth should not have been given to you, since you were *someone having a weak stomach*. But nevertheless I wrote both to him carefully and to Lyso.

TULLIUS TIRONI SUO S. P. D. ET CICERO ET Q. FRATER ET Q. F.: *Tullius Tironi suo salutem plurimam dicit et Cicero et Quintus frater et Quinti filius*

Note: There are two named Cicero: senior and junior. There are two named Quintus: Cicero's brother is Quintus whose son is also Quintus.

valde ... paullum, "much ... a little bit": contrasting adverbs.

> → **96** adv., 37; dict., *validus, a, um*, adj.; dict., *paulus, a, um*, adj.

priore pagina ... altera, "by the first page ... by the second": also, "by the former page ... by the latter."

> → **97** abl.: instrument, 28.5.3–4, 89.2, GL nº 401.

qua re ... non dubito quin ... committas, "For which reason ... I do not doubt that ... you are not committing": the negative expression *non dubito*, "I do not doubt," produces a result clause where *quin*, which normally means "that not," here after the negative doubt means simply "that." This is followed by the subjunctive *committas*, in T.1s, which, as a result clause, is typically rendered into the indicative in English such as "you are committing," but it may also be rendered here in the future, "you will surrender," because futurity is included in T.1s. It may also be rendered as "you may commit," in the subjunctive, if there is a potential subjunctive underlying *committas*. These are about the limits of what English will allow.

> → **98** dict., *quare* or *qua re*, adv.: II., B. "for which reason";
> negative *dubitare* + *quin* + subjunctive, 93.4, 101.2, GL nº 555.2;
> *consecutio*: futurity in the subjunctive, 61.1;
> subjunctive use: underlying potential of the present or future, 94.3,
> GL nº 257.

quoad ... valeas, "until you be ... well": this temporal expression in Latin is used usually with the ind., but here the subjunctive indicates Cicero's uncertainty about Tiro's recovery. Cicero did not foresee any definite time when this was going to happen, and the sentiment of this letter suggests he feared for Tiro's well-being. In Latin the ind. is used in such cases if it refers to a concrete fact, such as "until you have enough money," *quoad satis habes pecuniae*, where *habes*, "you have" is T.1i.

> → **99** *quoad* with an uncertain outcome, 65.2.2.

videro ... videro ..., "I shall have seen ... I shall have seen ...": both verbs are in T.6i, indicating that Cicero considered them as two certain completed actions, finished and for sure.

> → **100** T.6i and T.6i paired: GL nº 244, remark 4.

bene existimari, "that there is a good reputation": both verbs of M & M in T.1i, *scribis*, "you write," and *audio*, "I hear," give rise to a statement in OO where there is no subject for *existimari*, which is thus passive and used impersonally so that its subject is contained in the verb itself. The dictionary gives several examples in which this verb is both passive and impersonal.

The desire to supply a presumed subject referring to the doctor such as *illum bene existimari*, "that he is well esteemed," adds something neither there nor necessary to Cicero's expression.

The positive degree of the adverb *bene*, "well," whose irregular comparative degree is *melius*, "better," and superlative degree *optime*, "best," we might render as "it is being well thought."

> → **101** dict., *existimo, avi, atum,* 1, *ter*;
> passive verb used impersonally, GL n° 208;
> impersonal gerund, GL n° 528.2;
> M & M, 60, 71, GL n° 527, remarks 1–2; OO, 71–73;
> adv.: irregular comp. and superl., 37.3, GL n° 93.

ius ... dandum tibi non fuit, "broth should not have been given to you": the formula of passive necessity is composed of the finite verb *fuit*, "it was," in T.4b combined with the participle of passive necessity *dandum*, "needing to be given," "having to be given," "owing to be given," or "[not] to be given." Their combination within the limits of English produces the expression set in the past, "should not have been given."

The Latin has an ambiguity because *tibi* can mean either "to you," as the natural dat. after a verb of giving, or it can mean "by you" as the dat. of agent as is typical after the passive necessity formula. The entire letter makes the idea clear here, but this may not be so on another occasion. English has difficulty expressing the necessity, "ought," in the past, because you cannot say, "soup oughted not to be given to you," so we have to say "soup ought not to have been given to you," where the "ought" is still present and "not to have been given" is past. Other possible expressions are, "that soup was not supposed to be given to you," "that soup was not to be given to you."

> → **102** participle of passive necessity, 50, 51.1.4;
> passive necessity formula, 53.4;
> natural dat., 33.7.1; dat. of agent, 53.5.

quom κακοστόμαχος *esses*, "since you were *someone having a weak stomach*": *quom* is another form for *quum* and *cum*, meaning variously, "when," "because," "although." The Latin equivalent for the Greek text is: *esses imbecilium stomachum habens seu ventriculum habens*, "you were someone having poor digestion or having a weak stomach." The passive necessity formula *dandum fuit*, "[broth] should not have been given," is T.4b establishing Track II, producing *esses*, "you were," in T.2s.

> → **103** Bibliography: *Onomasticon Tullianum*;
> Greek expressions, pp. 623–626;
> subjunctive use: temporal circumstance *cum* = "when," 66.3.2;
> *consecutio*, 47–48;
> subjunctive use: causal *cum* = "because, since," 59.1;
> subjunctive use: concessive *cum* = "although," 64;
> participle of passive necessity, 50, 51.1.4; passive necessity formula, 53.4.

accurate, "carefully": *accuratius*, "too exactly," *accuratissime*, "very precisely," "most carefully."

> → **104** adv.: positive, comp., superl., 37.

Ad Curium vero, suavissimum hominem et summi offici summaeque humanitatis, multa scripsi: in his etiam ut, si tibi videretur, te ad se traferret.
Lyso enim noster vereor ne neglegentior sit; primum quia omnes Graeci,
deinde quod, cum a me litteras accepisset, mihi nullas remisit; sed eum tu
laudas: tu igitur quid faciendum sit iudicabis. Illud, mi Tiro, te rogo sumptu ne parcas ulla in re quod ad valetudinem opus sit. Scripsi ad Curium
quod dixisses daret: medico ipsi puto aliquid dandum esse quo sit studiosi-
or.   (*Fam.* XVI, 4, 2)

I wrote many things to Curius, however, a most gentle man and of the
greatest dutifulness and the greatest humaneness: among these things even
[I wrote] that he should transfer you to himself if it would seem good to
you. For I fear that our Lyso is too careless; first of all because [they are] all
Greeks, then because he sent no letters back to me, although he had received
letters from me; but you do praise him: you therefore will judge what must
be done. I ask you this, my dear Tiro, that you not spare expense in any matter whatever is necessary for your health. I wrote to Curius that he should
give what you would have said: I think something has to be given to the
doctor himself, so that he may be all the more zealous.

> *vero*, "however": while it looks like it means "truly," here it means "but,"
> "however," as the dictionary indicates.
>
> → **105** dict., *verus, a, um*, adj., II., adv., B. *vero*, "truly," 2. "but" (always placed
>   after a word).

> *suavissimum hominem et summi offici summaeque humanitatis*, "a most
> gentle man and of the greatest dutifulness and the greatest humaneness":
> Cicero describes Curius in two ways, first with an adjective and noun set
> alongside in apposition, *suavissimum hominem*, "a most gentle man," and
> then with the gen. of quality *summi offici summaeque humanitatis*, "of the
> greatest dutifulness and the greatest humaneness." Until the second century
> C.E. the gen. form was written *offici*, because it sounded the same as the
> subsequent spelling *officii*.
>
> → **106** apposition, GL n° 320–21;
>   quality in gen., 96.1; early gen. ending in –*i*, GL n° 33, remark 1.

> *multa scripsi … ut … te ad se traferret*, "I wrote many things … [I wrote]
> that he should transfer you to himself": the main verb *scripsi*, "I wrote," in
> T.4b establishes Track II and produces a purpose clause. The full form of
> *traferret* is *transferret*, written without the "n," because it was not heard, just
> as the abbreviation for *consul* on the facade of the Pantheon is *cos* rather
> than *cons*. The purpose clause is *ut … te ad se traferret*, "that he would
> transfer you to himself," that is to say, "that he should take you into his
> house," where *traferret* is in T.2s in Latin and sounds subjunctive in English.
>
> → **107** subjunctive use: purpose clause, 58.1; *consecutio*, 47–48.

si tibi videretur, "if it would seem good to you": this is not as a contrary to fact conditional, because when we test it, the result does not make sense here: "if it would seem good to you, but it does not." Rather the verb *videretur,* "it would seem" is T.2s by MA. The idea of futurity is included in T.2s, as if to say here, "if some day it would seem good to you in the future." The verb *videretur* in the passive includes the meaning of "good, proper, useful, suitable, decent," as in most Romance languages today.

> → **108** subjunctive use: modal attraction, 83;
>   *consecutio:* futurity in the subjunctive, 61.1;
>   conditionals: contrary to fact, 86.3.

vereor ne ... sit, "I fear that [Lyso] is": one of the verbs of fearing that take *ne* meaning "that" followed by the subjunctive.

> → **109** verbs of fearing with *ne,* 95.

neglegentior, "too careless": the comparative degree has a number of different interpretations: "more negligent," "rather negligent," "somewhat negligent." We don't forget that the comparative degree does not mean "very negligent," which is the superlative.

> → **110** adj.: comp. and superl., 36.

primum quia ... deinde quod ... remisit, "first of all because [they are] ... then because he had sent": even when writing to his secretary Cicero is conscious of his style and varies the word for "because" from *quia* to *quod.*

> → **111** causal: *quod, quia, quoniam,* "because, since", 59.2.

In writing to his personal secretary, Cicero leaves out the verb that goes with *quia,* such as *sunt,* as is done in good prose when it is obvious.

> → **112** ellipsis—omission of the verb, GL nº 209.

quod, cum a me litteras accepisset, mihi nullas remisit, "because he had sent no letters back to me, although he had received letters from me": the main verb *vereor,* "I fear," in T.1i establishes Track I and produces *sit,* in T.1s. The causal clause is formed by *quod ... remisit,* "because he had sent [no letters] back," where *remisit* is T.4b thereby establishing Track II for the clause *cum ... accepisset,* "although he had received," in which *accepisset* is in T.4s, describing an action antecedent to *remisit.* Other possible meanings for *cum accepisset* are, "when he had received," "because he had received."

> → **113** *consecutio,* 47–48;
>   causal: *quod,* "because, since," + indicative, one's own reason, 59.2;
>   subjunctive use: concessive *cum* = "although," 64;
>   subjunctive use: temporal circumstance *cum* = "when," 66.3.2;
>   subjunctive use: causal *cum* = "because, since," 59.1.

quid faciendum sit iudicabis, "you ... will judge what must be done": here *iudicabis,* "you will judge," in T.3i is a verb of M & M giving rise to an IQ where the asking word is *quid,* "what," and the verb is the passive necessity formula combining *sit*, in T.1s and the passive necessity participle *faciendum*, "what is needing to be done," "what has to be done," "what is to be done."

> → **114** M & M, 60, 71, GL n° 527, remarks 1–2; IQ, 60;
> participle of passive necessity, 50, 51.1.4;
> passive necessity formula, 53.4.

illud ... te rogo, "I ask you that": *rogo*, "I ask," is one of six or seven words that take a double object, here both *illud*, "that," and *te*, "you," in the object form.

> → **115** double acc., GL n° 339;
> dict., *rogo, avi, atum,* 1., I., A.... *aliquem aliquid*.

Illud ... te rogo sumptu ne parcas, "I ask you this ... that you not spare expense": the main verb *rogo*, "I ask," is one of a handful of verbs that take a double object, here *Illud ... te*, "[I ask] you this." Again, *rogo*, "I ask," in T.1i establishes Track I producing a purpose clause that expands the content of *illud*, "this." In this case, the purpose clause is negative *ne parcas*, "that you not spare," in T.1s and one of the 65 verbs which take a complement in the dat. Some people will be disturbed about *sumptu*, which we learn as abl. but a nice handbook will show also an early dat. form, later written as *sumptui*; note this is put out in front of *ne parcas*.

> → **116** double acc., GL n° 339; dict., *rogo, avi, atum,* 1., I., A.... *aliquem aliquid*;
> subjunctive use: purpose clause, 58.1;
> 65 verbs with dat., 33.7.2, GL n° 346;
> dat.: *sumptu*, GL n° 61, note 2.

mi Tiro, "my dear Tiro": both words are in direct address, also called the vocative. The voc. of *meus* is *mi*. This form of direct address is more familiar, more intimate, warmer than may be first apparent. This is reflected in the dictionary under *meus, a, um*, where the vocative *mi* is said to mean "*my dear! my beloved!*"

> → **117** dict., *meus, a, um*, adj., –voc.; function: direct address, 38.3.

ulla in re quod ... opus sit, "in any matter whatever is necessary": also, "whatever is a necessity." This clause may be in the subjunctive due to MA, because the rel. clause depends on another subjunctive *ne parcas*, "that you not spare." The indefinite relative *quod*, "whatever," can take the subjunctive.

The antecedent of the relative *quod* is *opus*, contained in the relative clause itself. Thus, *quod* goes with *opus*, rather than with *re*. In place of *quod*, Cicero could have said *quae*, meaning "in any matter, which is a necessity for your health," but instead he said *quod*, meaning "in any matter, whatever necessity exists for your health."

> → **118** incorporation of rel. antecedent, GL n° 616;
> *opus est*, 75.3; subjunctive use: modal attraction, 83.

Scripsi ... daret, "I wrote [to Curius] that he should give": the main verb, *Scripsi*, "I wrote," in T.4b establishing Track II, is complemented by a purpose clause giving the intention for his writing, *daret*, "that he would give," in T.2s without the typical *ut*, thereby expressing the strong force of the command in the *scripsi*, "I wrote." We have seen this frequently when Cicero uses *velim*, "I would like," in T.1s complemented by the subjunctive without the typical *ut*, to express the force of the original wish, *velim*, "I would <u>really</u> like." In English we might speak in this same way, for example, "I would like they come on time for once!," expressing the force of the wish.

> → **119** subjunctive use: purpose clause without *ut*, 58, GL n° 546, remark 2;
>   commands: other expressions, *velim*, 85.1.7.

quod dixisses, "what you would have said": the reason *dixisses* "you would have said," is in the subjunctive, T.4s, may be by MA, because it is dependent upon and antecedent to that of *daret*, "that he would give," in T.2s. Again, the indefinite relative *quod*, rendered as "whatever," can take the subjunctive.

Tracing the tracks is helpful here. The main verb, *Scripsi*, "I wrote," in T.4b establishes Track II. It produces a purpose clause and its verb *daret*, "that he would give," in T.2s expressing futurity on Track II. In order to express an action that occurs in the meanwhile between the other two actions, an action completed before the time of *daret*, an action that anticipates the action of *daret*, and in fact expresses the so-called future perfect time in the subjunctive, there is only one option on Track II: T.4s, here *dixisses*, "you would have said," for which reason we do not call T.4s by the misleading, error-producing, unhelpful, and obfuscating jargon "pluperfect," which will lead you astray.

> → **120** subjunctive use: modal attraction, 83;
>   *consecutio*: futurity in the subjunctive, 61.1;
>   *consecutio*, 47–48.

medico ipsi puto aliquid dandum esse, "I think something has to be given to the doctor himself": the main verb *puto*, "I think," a verb of M & M in T.1i, produces a statement in OO where the subject in the object form is *aliquid*, "something," and the inf. is the passive necessity formula whereby the contemporaneous inf. *esse*, "to be," is joined with the participle of passive necessity *dandum*, "[something] has to be given," "needs to be given," "ought to be given," "is to be given." The same bivalence we saw above with *ius . . . dandum tibi non fuit*, "broth should not have been given to you," occurs here as well, where *medico ipsi*, may be the natural dat. after a verb of giving, as in our translation, "something has to be given to the doctor himself," or it could possibly be the dat. of agent that naturally occurs with the participle of passive necessity, meaning "something has to be given by the doctor himself." We take it as the former, suggesting a payment or bribe, rather than the latter because of the following purpose clause.

> → **121** M & M, 60, 71, GL n° 527, remarks 1–2; OO, 71–73;
>   participle of passive necessity, 50, 51.1.4;
>   passive necessity formula, 53.4;
>   natural dat., 33.7.1; dat. of agent, 53.5.

quo sit studiosior, "so that he may be all the more zealous": the intention for
giving something to the doctor is expressed in the purpose clause where *quo*
stands for *ut eo*, "so that by that much more," followed by the comparative
degree *studiosior*, "[so that by that much more he may be] more zealous."

> → **122** subjunctive use: relative clause of purpose, *quo* = *ut eo*, 58.2, GL n° 545.2
> *quō* = *ut eō*;
> adj.: comp., 36.

◦᷍ᴗ

Innumerabilia tua sunt in me officia, domestica, forensia, urbana, provincialia: in re privata, in publica, in studiis, in litteris nostris. Omnia viceris, si, ut spero, te validum videro. Ego puto te bellissime, si recte erit, cum
quaestore Mescinio decursurum. Non inhumanus est teque, ut mihi visus
est, diligit: et, cum valetudini tuae diligentissime consulueris, tum, mi Tiro,
consulito navigationi. Nulla in re iam te festinare volo. Nihil laboro nisi ut
salvus sis.   (*Fam.* XVI, 4, 3)

Numberless are your kindnesses toward me, at home, in the forum, in the
city, in the province: in the private, in the public sector, in our interests, in
our studies. You will have surpassed all (kindnesses), if, as I hope, I shall
have seen you strong. If it will be all right, I think that you will be voyaging
most delightfully with Mescinius the quaestor. He is not discourteous, and
he appreciates you as he has appeared to me: and, when you will have looked
out for your health most carefully, then, my dear Tiro, you must look out for
the sailing. I want you to hurry up now in no matter. I am concerned about
nothing except that you be safe and sound.

> *in me*, "toward me": the expression *in* followed here by *me* in the object form
> indicates motion toward a place either geographical or, as here, moral. This
> expression is synonymous with *erga me*, *adversus me*, "toward me."
>
> → **123** *in* with object, 6.3.

> *Omnia viceris, si ... videro*, "You will have surpassed all (kindnesses), if ...
> I shall have seen [you strong]": both *viceris*, "You will have surpassed" and
> *videro*, "I shall have seen," are T.6i. As here, most of the conditionals in Lat-
> in are in the ind., and many people would want to put that *videro* in some
> subjunctive form to indicate that he does not know whether he is going to
> see Tiro or not. But, that is not the point. The multiplication of the subjunc-
> tive in cond. sentences especially the foggy future, for example where both
> verbs are in T.1s, is a sign of failing Latin or the abuse of the subjunctive.
> That sloppy Latin is evident, for example, in the 1983 *Codex Iuris Canonici*,
> the *Code of Canon Law*, in which perhaps under the influence of Italian
> nearly every conditional is put into the subjunctive. In contrast, when the
> code of canon law was written for the oriental churches and published in
> 1990, it was reviewed by a skilled Latinist, a Jesuit, who put most of the very

same canons in the indicative and who gave a consistency of vocabulary and style of expression to the entire code, something woefully lacking to the 1983 code.

> → **124** conditionals: factual, 86.1; conditionals: foggy future, 86.2;
> T.6i and T.6i paired: GL nº 244, remark 4.

ut spero, "as I hope": the indicative *spero*, "I hope" in T.1i, indicates that this is not a purpose clause. Rather, *ut* here means "as." We might add that its first definition in the dictionary is "how," as in *ut vales*?, "How are you doing?" Here *ut* does not mean "in order that," something which too many students take as a dogma, producing only purpose sentences. For example, "Ut vales?" means "how are you doing?," according to the first definition of *ut* in the dictionary.

> → **125** dict., *ut*, I., B. meaning "as."

puto te . . . , si recte erit, . . . decursurum, "If it will be all right, I think that you will be voyaging": the main verb *puto*, "I think," in T.1i, is a verb of M & M producing a statement in OO where the subject in the object form is *te* complemented by the infinitive whose full implied form is *decursurum esse*, meaning all alone, "to be about to sail," "to be fixing to sail," "to be going to sail," "to be on the point of voyaging." This futurity formula is equivalent to T.3i. This statement in OO is the consequence of a condition that appears in the middle of the sentence, *si recte erit*, "If it will be all right," also in T.3i. Because the condition depends on the statement in OO, many people would place the condition in the subjunctive by MA, such as *si recte sit*, "If it will be all right," or *si recte fuerit*, "If it will have been all right," the latter expressing completed futurity in T.3s, here the subjunctive equivalent of T.6i, to coordinate with *erit*, in T.3i. Cicero typically does not succumb to the later temptation to put the condition into the subjunctive by MA, unless there is a good reason for it. Rather, he treats the conditionals according to their own distinct nature. As a side note, Cicero rarely ever uses the foggy future.

> → **126** M & M, 60, 71, GL nº 527, remarks 1–2; OO, 71–73;
> futurity participle, 50, 51.1.3;
> *consecutio*: futurity formula in the subjunctive, 61.3;
> conditionals: factual, 86.1; conditionals: foggy future, 86.2;
> subjunctive use: modal attraction, 83.

ut mihi visus est, "as he has appeared to me": here *ut* means "as," because it is followed by the ind., *visus est*, "he has appeared," in T.4a passive; this is not a purpose or result clause, just like we saw above, *ut spero*, "as I hope." Here *mihi* may be taken as a dat. of agent meaning "[he was seen] by me," or as a natural dative meaning "[he appeared] to me," as in the translation.

> → **127** dict., *ut*, I., B. meaning "as"; natural dat., 33.7.1; dat. of agent, 53.5.

cum valetudini tuae ... consulueris, "when you will have looked out for your health": the verb *consulo, consulere, consului, consultum* 3, here does not mean "to consult," which would take a simple object form as its complement, but rather "to look out for," "to provide for," "to consult the interests of," and is one of the 65 verbs that takes its complement in the dat., here *valetudini tuae*, "for your health." We have taken the form *consulueris*, "you will have looked out," as T.6i as a temporal sentence in the ind., but the same form could also be T.3s and the presence of the subjunctive changes the meaning of the *cum* to "because you have looked out for your health." The idea expressed in the letter, however, leaves the question of Tiro's health open, suggesting T.6i.

> → **128** 65 verbs with dat., 33.7.2, GL n° 346;
> *cum* + indicative = "when": temporal sentences, 66.3;
> subjunctive use: causal *cum* = "because, since," 59.1.

tum ... consulito navigationi, "then ... you must look out for the sailing": the same verb as in the previous entry with its complement in the dat., here *navigationi*, "for the sailing." The form *consulito*, "you must look out," is the second command form, sometimes called the future imperative. It may be preferable to translate *consulito* in the archaic form, "thou shalt look out," to distinguish it in English from T.3i "you will look out," but the difficulty can also be avoided by rendering it as "you must look out." This and the phrase in the previous entry are coordinated by the correlatives *cum ... tum ...*, "when ... then ...".

> → **129** commands: first, second, 17;
> correlative comparative sentences, 90.5, GL n° 642;
> dict., *tum*, adv. demonstr., I, C, 1–3; GL n° 588.

mi Tiro, "my dear Tiro": see commentary above in this letter, section 2.

> → **130** dict., *meus, a, um*, adj., –voc.;
> function: direct address, 38.3.

te festinare volo, "I want you to hurry up": *volo* is an M & M verb producing a statement in OO where *te* is the subject in the object form and the verb is *festinare*, a contemporaneous infinitive. This may be rendered in English using the equivalent of the acc. and inf. as we have done here "you to hurry up," or with the connecting word "that" and the subject and a finite verb, "I want that you hurry up." A third way would conceivably be to take this latter phrase with the subject and finite verb but drop the connecting word "that," "I want you hurry up," which in this case is hardly possible in English. Knowing these three ways is helpful to teachers and learners in establishing the range of possibilities, which are then subject to the limits of English expression.

> → **131** M & M, 60, 71, GL n° 527, remarks 1–2; OO, 71–73.

nihil laboro, "I am concerned about nothing": the verb *laboro*, "I exert myself," "I take pains," "I am concerned," here is complemented by *nihil*, which has adverbial meaning "in no way," "not at all." Here *nihil* is not the object. The expression does not mean "I am not working," but "I am bothered in no way," as described in the dict.

→ **132** dict., *laboro, avi, atum*, 1, I, B, 2.

ut salvus sis, "that you be safe and sound": the particle *ut* means about 50 things in the Latin language, at least! Here it is followed by *sis*, "you be safe and sound," in T.1s, as a purpose clause expressing the intention of the verb *laboro*, "I am concerned [that you may be safe and sound]."

→ **133** subjunctive use: purpose clause, 58.1.

Sic habeto, mi Tiro, neminem esse qui me amet quin idem te amet, et cum tua et mea maxime interest te valere tum multis est curae. Adhuc, dum mihi nullo loco deesse vis, numquam te confirmare potuisti. Nunc te nihil impedit: omnia depone, corpori servi. Quantam diligentiam in valetudi-nem tuam contuleris, tanti me fieri a te iudicabo. Vale, mi Tiro, vale, vale et salve. Lepta tibi salutem dicit et omnes. Vale. VII. Idus, Novembr. Leu-cade.   (*Fam.* XVI, 4, 4)

Thus, know for sure, my dear Tiro, there is no one who loves me who the same one does not love you, and while you being well concerns you and me to the greatest extent, then it is for a concern to many. Up to this point, while you want to fail me in no instance, you have not ever been able to strengthen yourself. Now nothing is stopping you: put all things aside; do a service to the body. How much diligence you will have applied to your health, I shall judge myself to be rated of so much value by you. Goodbye, my dear Tiro, goodbye, goodbye and fair thee well. Lepta says a greeting to you, as all do. Goodbye. On the seventh day before the November Ides [7 November]. From Leucadia.

Sic, habeto, "Thus, know for sure": this exact expression is found in the dict. meaning "Be persuaded," "Believe," "Know." This common expression often appears with an object clause, as here. The form, *habeto*, is the second com-mand form, also called the future imperative.

→ **134** dict., *habeo, ui, itum*, 2, II., D.; commands: first, second, 17.

habeto … neminem esse, "know for sure … there is no one": the main verb *habeto*, "know for sure" is used in this expression as a verb of M & M. Thus it produces a statement in OO where *neminem* is the subject in the object form and the inf. is *esse*, "there is no one." When *habeo, habere*, means, for example, "to have [money]" it does not produce a statement in OO as here.

→ **135** M & M, 60, 71, GL n° 527, remarks 1–2; OO, 71–73.

mi Tiro, "my dear Tiro": see section 2 in this letter, above. This occurs again in the present letter, where Cicero says, *Vale, mi Tiro,* "Good bye, my dear Tiro." This is true also of the feminine, *mea Terentia,* "O my dear Terentia." Cicero calls his beloved wife and children, *meae animae,* "my darlings."

qui me amet quin idem te amet, "who loves me who the same one does not love you": the subjunctive *amet* appears twice here in T.1s, and for different reasons. Its first appearance is perhaps due to MA because the relative clause *qui me amet,* "who loves me," depends on and is closely connected with the statement in OO, *neminem esse,* "there is no one." The second appearance is an expression of characteristic result in which *quin* stands for *qui non,* which is more fully expressed here as *talem ut idem non te amet,* "such that the same one does not love you."

> → **136** OO, 71–73; subjunctive use: modal attraction, 83;
>   negative characteristic result: *quin* (= *talis ut is non*) + subjunctive, 101.2,
>   GL n° 632;
>   subjunctive use: characteristic result, 68.2; relative clauses, 10–11.

cum … tum …, "while … then …": correlatives.

> → **137** correlative comparative sentences, 90.5, GL n° 642;
>   dict., *tum,* adv. demonstr., I., C., 1–3; GL n° 588.

cum tua et mea maxime interest te valere, "while you being well concerns you and me to the greatest extent": the verb *interest* is complemented by *tua … mea,* whose use here was borrowed from their use with the verb *rē-fert,* where *tua* and *mea* agree with the *re* on *rē-fert.* Thus, here they do not mean "yours and mine," but "you and me." This merits a lengthy detailed exposition as given in the dictionary under the two entry-words *intersum* and *rē-fert* as explained in the *Ossa* book.

> → **138** dict., *intersum, fui, esse,* v. irreg.;
>   dict., *rē-fert, rē-tuli, rē-latum, rē-ferre,* v. irreg.;
>   *interest* and *refert,* 102.

The subject of *interest* is the statement in OO, where *te* is the subject in the object form and its inf. *valere* is contemporaneous, also expressed as "that you are in good health interests you and me." It might be helpful to render it as "you being in good health interests you and me."

> → **139** OO, 71–73.

multis est curae, "it is for a concern to many": the double dative with the verb *est,* "it is," where the dat. of the person affected is *multis,* "to many people" and the dat. of a goal is *curae,* "for a cure."

> → **140** double dat., 91.2.

dum … numquam, "while … never": these particles help to correlate the two statements.

> → **141** dict., *dum,* conj.; dict., *numquam,* adv.

dum mihi ... deesse vis, "while you want to fail me ...": the M & M verb *vis*, "you want," is complemented by the gerund functioning as an object *deesse*, "[you want] failing," "[you want] to fail"; *deesse* is one of the 65 verbs that takes its complement in the dat., here *mihi ... deesse*, "to fail me," "to be absent for me," "to be absent as far as I am concerned." The problem with these verbs is that the dat. is often difficult to hear in English and so not seen in Latin. Incidentally, *vis*, "you want," is an irregular verb from *volo*, not the noun meaning "power," "strength."

> → **142** M & M, 60, 71, GL n° 527, remarks 1–2; gerund, 77.1;
>   pronoun forms to-for-from, 33.3–5;
>   65 verbs with dat., 33.7.2, GL n° 346; irregular verbs: *volo*, 82.

numquam te confirmare potuisti, "you have not ever been able to strengthen yourself": while this may look like OO, the complement of *potuisti*, "you have been able," is the gerund functioning as an object *confirmare*, "[you have been able] to strengthen," and its object in turn is *te*, "to strengthen yourself," here reflexive because it refers back to the subject of *confirmare* and *potuisti*.

> → **143** gerund, 77.1; reflexive pron.: first and second person, 30.

corpori servi, "do a service to the body": test your understanding of these two words by reversing each, making it plural, and you end up with *corporibus servite*, "do you-all a service to bodies."

> → **144** commands: first, second, 17; natural dat., 33.7.1.

quantam diligentiam ... tanti, "How much diligence ... of so much value": *tanti* is the gen. of evaluation, "of such value," "of such worth."

> → **145** gen. of indefinite price, 75.2;
>   correlative comparative sentences, 90.5, GL n° 642.

quantam diligentiam ... contuleris ... iudicabo, "How much diligence you will have applied ... I shall judge": the main verb *iudicabo*, "I shall judge," is T.3i, which corresponds to *contuleris*, "you will have applied," in T.6i, as completed futurity prepares for futurity. We shall see many examples of this in the letters and in all classical literature.

> → **146** times-tenses of the indicative mode and their vernacular meaning, 7;
>   T.3i and T.6i paired: 7, Time 6, and GL n° 244, remark 2.

tanti me fieri ... iudicabo, "I shall judge myself to be rated of so much value": the main verb *iudicabo*, "I shall judge" in T.3i is a verb of M & M and produces a statement in OO where the subject in the object form is *me*, here referring back to the subject of *iudicabo*, "I shall judge ... myself," thus with reflexive meaning, and the inf. is *fieri*, which is the passive form of *facere*, "to reckon," "to mark someone up" or with verbs of rating "to make of such value." Thus, "I will judge that I am being reckoned of such a great value."

> → **147** M & M, 60, 71, GL n° 527, remarks 1–2; OO, 71–73;
>   reflexive pron.: first and second person, 30;
>   dict., *facio, feci, factum*, 3: I. *pass.: fio, factus, fieri*.

tanti me fieri a te, "to be rated of so much value by you": the passive verb *fieri,* "to be rated," is accompanied by the preposition *a* with the abl., *te,* where *a te,* "by you" are an expression of the personal agent doing the rating.

→ **148** abl.: personal agent, 28.5.3–4, 89.2.

Vale … vale, vale … Vale, "Goodbye … goodbye, goodbye … goodbye": there is human poignancy when Cicero says goodbye four times, then fair thee well.

et omnes, "and all people": the personal name *Lepta,* "Lepta," is the subject of the verb *dicit,* as in "Lepta says," in T.1i, but then Cicero adds another subject *et omnes,* "and all people," and this plural subject is added to the singular verb as an additional subject.

→ **149** GL n° 211, remark 1.

Leucade, "from Leucadia": from the name of the town Leucas, this form is the natural abl. of separation.

→ **150** function: place from where, names of cities and small islands, *Leucadia,*
        69.2.2;
        abl. separation from place, 27.

VII. Idus, Novembr., "On the seventh day before the November Ides": the full form is, *septimo [ante] Idus Novembres,* where *ante,* "before," is implied to produce the object form *Idus,* that is, 7 November.

→ **151** about the Roman calendar, pp. 605–608;
        GL Appendix, Roman Calendar, pp. 491–92.

LETTER 2 T-P
AD ATTICUM I, 6

CICERO ATTICO SAL.

Non committam posthac ut me accusare de epistularum neglegentia possis.
Tu modo videto in tanto otio ut par in hoc mihi sis [...] Id te scire volui, si
quid forte ea res ad cogitationes tuas pertineret.   (*Att.* I, 6, 1)

CICERO A GREETING TO ATTICUS

I shall not allow in the future that you are able to accuse me about
carelessness of correspondence. You must just see to it that in so much
leisure you be equal to me in this respect ... I wanted you to know this, if
perhaps that matter pertained in any way to your own thoughts.

CICERO ATTICO SAL.: *Cicero Attico salutem*

committam ... ut ... possis, "I shall [not] allow ... that ... you are able":
committam is a verb of effecting that produces a complementary result
clause *ut ... possis,* which in English sounds indicative.
→ **152** subjunctive use: complementary result (consecutive), 68.1.

videto, "you must [just] see to it": second command form, also "you shalt see
to it".
→ **153** commands: first, second, 17.

videto ... ut ... sis, "you must see to it ... that ... you be": *videto* is a verb
of resolving producing a complementary purpose clause *ut ... sis,* which
sounds subjunctive in English.
→ **154** subjunctive use: purpose clause, 58.1.

te scire, "you to know": OO depending on M & M verb *volui,* "I wanted."
→ **155** M & M, 60, 71, GL nº 527, remarks 1–2; OO, 71–73.

si ... pertineret, "if ... [that matter] pertained": attraction of mode depending on the OO *te scire*, and so should sound indicative.

　　→ **156** subjunctive use: modal attraction, 83; OO, 71–73.

quid, "in any way": there are two entries for *quis, quid* in the dictionary: one is interrogative, "who?," "what?," the other is indefinite "someone," "something," "anything." Because the subject is *ea res*, "this matter," and since the verb *pertineret* does not take an object, the *quid* is adverbial; here, *si quid* does not mean "if anything," or "if something," but *si quid ... pertineret* means "if this matter pertained in any way." This adverbial use of *quid* surprisingly is not emphasized by L&S, but is illustrated in L&S under the compound *aliquid*, found in the entry for *aliquis, aliquid*.

　　→ **157** dict., *aliquis, aliquid*, indef. subst. pron. II., G.,—adv., A. *aliquid*.

☙

[...] Tu velim, si qua ornamenta γυμνασιώδη reperire poteris quae loci sint eius quem tu non ignoras, ne praetermittas.　　(*Att.* I, 6, 2)

You, I would like, that [you] not leave out, if you will be able to find any ornaments *suitable for a discussion hall*, such which belong to that place of which you are not ignorant.

Tu ... praetermittas, "You, ... that [you] ... not leave out": sentence structure, the first person Cicero thinks of is Atticus, and so begins his sentence with *Tu velim*, "You, I would like." The first word of the sentence, *Tu*, is the subject of the last word of the sentence, *praetermittas*. To ease the English rendering, we felt a need to give the subj. once again but in square brackets.

　　→ **158** sentence structure, 1.

velim ... ne praetermittas, "I would like that you not skip over": here *velim* T.1s is a verb of wishing that gives rise to a negative purpose clause in T.1s, so we have a subjunctive depending on a subjunctive on Track I.

　　→ **159** subjunctive use: purpose clause, 58.1;
　　　　　consecutio: subjunctive depending on a subjunctive, 62.1.

qua, "any": here *qua* is the indefinite pronoun in neuter plural standing in for *aliqua*. It is not to be confused with *quā*, the fem. abl. sing. meaning "by which." By the way, the neuter plural is not *aliquae*, it is *aliqua*.

　　→ **160** pronouns: indefinite, 42.4; after *si* the *ali*-s fly away, 42.5.

γυμνασιώδη, "*suitable for a gymnasium*": which refers not to athletics, but to a classroom, lecture hall.

　　→ **161** Bibliography: *Onomasticon Tullianum*;
　　　　　Greek expressions, pp. 623–626.

quae ... sint, "such which belong": a relative sentence of characteristic result
where the *quae* implies *talia ut ea sint*, "such that they belong."

> → **162** subjunctive use: characteristic result, 68.2.

loci sint eius, "they belong to that place": the verb *sint* with the form of-possession indicates possession or belonging, meaning "they are of that place,"
or "they are proper to that place."

> → **163** dict., *sum, fui, esse*, v. irreg. with the gen., II, B, 1.

quem ... ignoras, "[of] which you are [not] ignorant": a simple relative
sentence. The Latin expression is "which you do not know," whereas English
idiom given here is "to be ignorant *of* something."

> → **164** rel. pron.: subject or object, 10.

◌

Nos Tusculano ita delectamur ut nobismet ipsis tum denique cum illo venimus placeamus. Quid agas omnibus de rebus et quid acturus sis fac nos
quam diligentissime certiores.   (*Att.* I, 6, 2 *cont.*)

We are so delighted by the Tusculan villa that we please our very selves then
finally when we have come to that place. Inform us as diligently as possible
what you are doing with regard to all matters and what you will be doing.

> *ita ... ut ... placeamus*, "so ... that we are pleasing": a pure result clause
> depending on *delectamur*, "we are delighted." It sounds indicative in
> English.
>
> > → **165** subjunctive use: pure result (consecutive), 67.1–2, GL nº 552.
>
> *tum ... cum ...* , "then ... when": coordinating particles.
>
> > → **166** dict., *tum*, adv. demonstr., II., A. with temporal clause introduced by *cum*,
> > GL nº 588.

cum ... venimus, "when we have come" or "when we do come": *cum* followed
by the indicative *venimus* indicates simple time "when" and does not indicate any past circumstance, which in an historical time frame would be
expressed in T.2s or T.4s; the form *venímus* is T.1i but *vénimus* is T.4i; this
distinction is demonstrable in poetic meter, but not in prose.

> → **167** *cum* + indicative = "when": temporal sentences, 66.3;
> *cum* + historical times of indicative = "when": temporal coincidence,
> 66.3.1;
> dict., *venio, veni, ventum*, 4.

illo, "to that place" or "thither": an adv. Sad to say *cum illo* may look like
"with him" but here it means literally "when ... to that place." Sorry, but this
is Latin: consult the dictionary!

> → **168** dict., *ille, a, ud*, pron. demonstr., II., B., d.,—hence adv. 2. *illō* to that place,
> thither.

quid agas ... et quid acturus sis, "what you are doing ... and what you will be doing": two statements of IQ depending on the M & M expression *fac nos certiores*, "inform us." Any teacher may ask how to say here, "what you did," and the students would say, *quid egeris*, and add that it also means "what you have been doing," "what you have done," "what you had done," "what you were doing"; and you have all the possible time frames in the subjunctive.

→ **169** M & M, 60, 71, GL n° 527, remarks 1–2;
         IQ, 60; *consecutio*, 47–48.

quid acturus sis, "what you will be doing": this formula is necessary to express futurity in the subjunctive, which has no special future form in Latin. Other English expressions of this futurity include: "... what you will do," "... what you are about to do," "... what you are fixing to do," "... what you are going to do," "... on the verge of doing." The Romans don't really like this formula much, and so used other adverbial combinations to express this futurity.

→ **170** *consecutio*: futurity formula in the subjunctive, 61.3.

fac nos ... certiores, "make us informed" or simply "inform us": *fac* is one of four famous command forms, *dic, duc, fac, fer*, without a final –*e*, although in Plautus and Terentius we do find the forms *dice, duce, face*, where the final –*e*, is still on the imperatives. This is an extremely common idiom in all ages of Latin sadly misunderstood in superficial reading.

→ **171** commands: famous four, 39.4;
         dict., *certus, a, um*, adj., II., B., 2., *certiorem facere aliquem*, "to inform, appraise one of a thing."

quam diligentissime, "as diligently as possible": special meaning of *quam* followed by the superlative.

→ **172** *quam* with the superlative, 43.3; adv.: positive, comp., superl., 37.

LETTER 415 T-P
AD FAMILIARES XIV, 12

TULLIUS TERENTIAE SUAE S. D.

Quod nos in Italiam salvos venisse gaudes, perpetuo gaudeas velim. Sed perturbati dolore animi magnisque iniuriis metuo ne id consili ceperimus quod non facile explicare possimus. Quae re [*sic*] quantum potes adiuva. Quid autem possis mihi in mentem non venit. In viam quod te des hoc tempore nihil est: et longum est iter et non tutum, et non video quid prodesse possis si veneris. Vale. D. prid. Non. Nov. Brundisio.   (*Fam.* XIV, 12)

TULLIUS SAYS A GREETING TO TERENTIA

The fact that you are happy we have arrived safe and sound in Italy, I would like that you rejoice forever. But I am afraid that we, totally disturbed by grief of spirit and great injustices, have taken that kind of decision which we are not able easily to settle. For which reason help as much as you can. However, it does not come into my mind what you are able [to do]. There is no reason that you put yourself on the road at this time; it is both a long journey and not safe and I do not see what you are able to profit if you will have come. Take care. I am sending this on the day before the November Nones [4 November] from Brindisi.

TULLIUS TERENTIAE SUAE S. D.: *Tullius Terentiae suae salutem dicit*

Quod nos in Italiam salvos venisse gaudes, "The fact that you are happy we have arrived safe and sound in Italy": the main verb *gaudes,* "you are happy," in T.1i, is a verb of emotion, which can function as a verb of M & M producing OO, here *nos … venisse.* The happiness is elaborated in OO where the object form *nos* functions as the subject of the infinitive verb *venisse* describing antecedent action, "we have arrived," "we arrived," "we were arriving."

> → **173** verbs of emotion + OO, GL n° 533;
> M & M, 60, 71, GL n° 527, remarks 1–2; OO, 71–73.

This usage of *Quod*, "The fact that," is really not a relative, but a neuter substantive clause introducing a new subject, as in "as to the fact that … ," usually with the indicative.

→ **174** *quod* = "the fact that" as a new subject, GL nº 525.2.

gaudeas velim, "I would like that you rejoice": the polite request where *velim*, "I would like," is T.1s and is preceded by the subjunctive *gaudeas*, "that you rejoice," in T.1s and given without an *ut*. This formula, *velim* with the subjunctive, is extremely common and found all over Cicero's correspondence.

→ **175** commands: other expressions, *velim*, 85.1.7;
        subjunctive use: purpose clause without *ut*, 58, GL nº 546, remark 2.

metuo ne id consili ceperimus, "I am afraid that we … have taken that kind of decision": the verb of fearing *metuo*, "I am afraid," in T.1i establishing Track I, is followed by *ne* with positive force, "that," whereas *metuo ut*, means "I am afraid that not." It takes some explanation, given in the *Ossa* book. *ceperimus* is T.3s and so describes any time of antecedent action, "we have taken," "we took," "we used to take," "we did take," "we were taking." In this short sentence the neuter *id* is followed immediately by the genitive of part *consili*, an older form of *consilii*, which together can mean, "that bit of decision," "that type of decision"; these two words are typically separated from one another by one or more words.

→ **176** verbs of fearing with *ne*, 95; *consecutio*, 47–48; gen. of part, 99.

metuo ne id consili ceperimus quod non facile explicare possimus, "I am afraid that we … have taken that kind of decision which we are not able easily to settle": first, the sequence of tenses begins with the main verb *metuo*, "I am afraid" in T.1i establishing Track I. Next, *ne ceperimus* in T.3s describes antecedent action on Track I, whereas *quod possimus* in T.1s returns to the present ongoing action, the same time as *metuo*. Had he wanted to describe an action contemporaneous with *ceperimus*, he would have had to switch to Track II and say *quod … possemus*, "which we were not [easily] able [to settle]."

The result of the decision they have taken is characterized in the clause *quod … possimus*, where the subjunctive *possimus* in T.1s is rendered in the indicative in English, "we are [not] able" according to the nature of a characteristic result clause. The full meaning of *quod* is "such which … ," and the *quod* stands for *tale ut id*, "such that [we are not able easily to settle] it." The infinitive *explicare*, "to settle," complements the action of *possimus*, "we are able."

→ **177** verbs of fearing with *ne*, 95;
        subjunctive use: characteristic result, 68.2; *consecutio*, 47–48;
        verb: complementary infinitive, 77.

Quae re: note that this must definitely be a printing or copyist mistake and should read *Qua re*, as it does in other editions, which is rendered in the English as "For which reason."

→ **178** dict., *quare* or *qua re*, adv., II., B. "for which reason."

Quid autem possis mihi in mentem non venit, "However, it does not come into my mind what you are able [to do]": *Quid possis*, "what you are able," is an IQ depending on the mental operation of "coming into mind" in the expression *mihi in mentem non venit*, "it does not come into mind for me." The *mihi* here is sometimes called an ethical dative and means, "for me," "what concerns me," or a dative that makes reference "to me," as in "it does not come into mind for me." The dat. of reference, or the so-called ethical dative, is implied in the example *Magno mihi est honori vos salutare*, "It is for a great honor to me to greet you all," presented in *Ossa* 91.2.

→ **179** M & M, 60, 71, GL n° 527, remarks 1–2; IQ, 60;
dat. of reference, 91.2, GL n° 352; ethical dat., see 91.2, GL n° 351.

In viam quod te des hoc tempore nihil est, "There is no reason that you put yourself on the road at this time": the main sentence is *nihil est*, which means "there is nothing" or "nothing exists." It is followed by *quod ... des*, "[there is no reason] that you put," which is a causal clause expressing a possible motive expressed in English in the indicative, but the clause here functions almost like an IQ meaning "There is no reason why you put yourself on the road." That being said, the English is ambiguous because the expression "that you put" can be either indicative or subjunctive.

→ **180** dict., *nihil*, n., indecl., I (λ) (μ), (ν) *Nihil est*; GL n° 631.2 *nihil est quod*;
dict., *do, dedi, datum, dare*, II., D. "to put."

et non video quid prodesse possis si veneris, "I do not see what you are able to profit if you will have come": the main verb *video*, "I do [not] see," is a verb of M & M in T.1i establishing Track I. The content of this mental operation is given as an IQ where *quid prodesse possis*, "what you are able to profit," could be rendered in the subjunctive, "what you should be able to profit," if as happens 10% of the time the underlying question is a natural subjunctive as discussed above. The IQ also serves as the consequence of a factual conditional given as *si veneris*, "if you will have come," where *veneris* is either T.6i or T.3s by MA, both describing future completed action according to the natural time frame of both times.

→ **181** M & M, 60, 71, GL n° 527, remarks 1–2;
IQ, 60; *consecutio*, 47–48;
conditionals: factual, 86.1; subjunctive use: modal attraction, 83.

D. prid. Non. Nov., "I am sending this on the day before the November Nones [4 November]": the abbreviation *D.* stands for either *data*, "sent," from which we get the English word "date"; or *dabam*, "I was sending" in the epistolary tense with the meaning "I am sending." The rest of the text is, *pridie Nonas Novembres.*

> → **182** about the Roman calendar, pp. 605–608;
>   GL Appendix, Roman Calendar, pp. 491–92.

Brundisio, "from Brindisi": the natural meaning of the by-with-from-in function is here "from."

> → **183** function: place from where, names of cities and small islands, *Brundisio*, 27, 69.2.2;
>   abl. separation from place, 27.

LETTER 3 T-P
AD ATTICUM I, 7

CICERO ATTICO SAL.

Apud matrem recte est eaque nobis curae est. L. Cincio HS xxcd constitui
me curaturum Idibus Februariis. Tu velim ea quae nobis emisse te et parasse
scribis des operam ut quam primum habeamus, et velim cogites, id quod
mihi pollicitus es, quem ad modum bibliothecam nobis conficere possis.
Omnem spem delectationis nostrae, quam cum in otium venerimus habere
volumus, in tua humanitate positam habemus.   (*Att.* I, 7)

CICERO A GREETING TO ATTICUS

With your mother things are OK and she is for a care to us. I have decided
that I shall procure 20,400 sesterces for Lucius Cicinius on the February
Ides [13 February]. I would like that you make an effort that we have as soon
as possible those things [statues] which you write you have purchased and
prepared for us, and I would like you to consider that which you promised
me, in what way you are able to fix up the library for us. We have [as] placed
in your kindness all the hope of our enjoyment, which we wish to have when
we shall have come into retirement.

CICERO ATTICO SAL.: *Cicero Attico salutem*

nobis curae est, "[she] is for a care to us": the double dative, one is the person
concerned, *nobis*, the other is the result, *curae*.
> → **184** double dat., 91.2.

HS: in capital letters this is the sign for the monetary unit *sestertius*, v. L&S.
> → **185** dict., *sestertius, a, um,* num. adj. contr. from *semis-tertius.*

xxcd: there should be a line over xx to mean 20,000; cd = 400; *vigenti mil-
lia quadringenta sestertium*, "20,400 of sesterces." With money designations
in Latin you will go crazy.
> → **186** GL p. 493.

me curaturum, "that I shall procure": OO depending on the M & M verb *constitui*, "I have decided"; the futurity infinitive is *curaturum esse*, where *esse* is implied, as is very frequently done by all Latin authors.

→ **187** M & M, 60, 71, GL n° 527, remarks 1–2; OO, 71–73;
    futurity participle, 50, 51.1.3;
    verb: subsequent active infinitive, 72.1.

When *constitui* means "I have reached a conclusion" as a mental operation, it is followed by OO as here. But when it means "I have decided" as by decree to do an outside, concrete action, it is followed by *ut* and the subjunctive, as in *constitui ut curem Idibus*, "I have decided that I take care of this on the Ides." Note the difference with *constitui me curaturum Idibus*, "I have reached a conclusion that I shall take care of this on the Ides."

→ **188** dict., *constituo, ui, utum*, 3;
    M & M, 60, 71, GL n° 527, remarks 1–2; OO, 71–73;
    subjunctive use: purpose clause, 58.1.

Idibus Februariis, "on the February Ides [13 February]": the abl. of time at which, in which, when; properly without a preposition. Literally *Idibus Februariis* means "on the February Ides," following standard Latin where the names of the months are adjectives. In ecclesiastical Latin the months are nouns such as *Idibus Februarii*, "on the Ides of February."

→ **189** abl.: time at which, 70.1.

Tu velim … des operam, "I would like that you make an effort": sentence structure, the first two words present two different subjects, *Tu*, "you," and *ego*, "I," implied in *velim*, "I would like," but *Tu* is the subject of *des* further along. Cicero is thinking of Atticus, but he has to write in his own name, thus he begins the sentence with *Tu*, "you" referring to Atticus, and must continue with *velim*, "I would like."

→ **190** sentence structure, 1.

quae nobis emisse te et parasse scribis, "which you write you have purchased and prepared for us": The M & M verb *scribis* gives rise to two antecedent statements in OO, *emisse* and *parasse* with the common subject, *te*; while *nobis* may be the complement of *scribis*, "you write to us," it is taken here as the dat. of interest, "for us; on our behalf." The object of both infinitives is *quae*, meaning in turn, "which you have purchased" and "which you prepared for us."

→ **191** M & M, 60, 71, GL n° 527, remarks 1–2; OO, 71–73;
    natural dat., 33.7.1; relative clauses, 10–11.

parasse, "to have prepared": contraction for *paravisse*.

→ **192** contractions: verbs, 39.2, GL n° 131.

ut ... habeamus, "that we have": an expression of purpose depending on *des operam*, "you make an effort." As an expression of purpose, the English "we have" is in the subjunctive, but you can't see it.

→ **193** subjunctive use: purpose clause, 58.1;
consecutio: subjunctive depending on a subjunctive, 62.1.

quam primum, "as soon as possible": special meaning of *quam* followed by the superlative.

→ **194** *quam* with the superlative, 43.3.

velim cogites, "I would like that you consider": in both this and the expressions that opened this sentence, the verb of wishing *velim* is followed by another subjunctive *des* or *cogites* but the *ut* is left out, which is the usage when the verb of wishing is very strong. Almost a command is felt.

→ **195** commands: other expressions, *velim*, 85.1.7;
subjunctive use: purpose clause without *ut*, 58, GL n° 546, remark 2.

quem ad modum ... possis, "in what way you are able," "how you are able": IQ depending on the M & M verb *cogites* in T.1s, "you to consider"; the single word *quemadmodum*, as seen in the manuscript image in part I, is understood by its parts *ad quem modum*, "according to what manner," "how," written as *quem ad modum*.

→ **196** dict., *quemadmodum*, adv., I. Interrog.;
M & M, 60, 71, GL n° 527, remarks 1–2; IQ, 60;
consecutio: subjunctive depending on a subjunctive, 62.1.

omnem spem ... positam habemus, "all the hope ... we have [as] placed": Sentence structure, the first two words *omnem spem* are the object of the last word *habemus*, and the participle *positam* agrees with them.

The box effect of clauses, one within another, may be diagrammed:

Omnem spem delectationis nostrae,	main sentence begins
[quam	relative clause begins
(cum in otium venerimus)	temporal clause, *cum* = "when"
habere volumus],	relative clause concludes
in tua humanitate positam habemus.	main sentence concludes.

→ **197** structure of Latin sentences, 103 p. 587, *Ossa* Readings: 1-D, 1-I, 3-D, 3-I, 4-D, 4-I;
relative box, 11.4.

We rendered *spem ... positam habemus* by "the hope ... we have [as] placed," in which we added in brackets "[as]" in order to keep the participle *positam* separate from the verb *habemus*, in T.1i, because Cicero did this rather than use T.4a *spem posuimus*, "we have placed the hope." Another way to render this, while still keeping Cicero's use of the participle, is "we have the hope placed." To say, "we have placed the hope," is to make of these two verbal forms a single verbal expression in T.4a, as we speaking English and other modern languages can easily see and say. The differences in meaning between the two English renderings is very fine, but one takes *positam* as a participle, as Cicero did, and the other takes the two words *positam habemus* as a single verbal expression as we find in our modern languages. Such a Latin expression generated some of our modern talk.

→ **198** sentence structure, 1.

quam … habere volumus, "which we desire to have": the relative *quam* is the object of *habere*, "to have."

→ **199** rel. pron.: subject or object, 10.

cum … venerimus, "when we shall have come": *cum* followed by the indicative is purely temporal, "when."

→ **200** *cum* + indicative = "when": temporal sentences, 66.3.

LETTER 161 T-P
AD FAMILIARES VII, 10

M. CICERO S. D. TREBATIO.

Legi tuas litteras ex quibus intellexi te Caesari nostro valde iure consultum videri. Est quod gaudeas te in ista loca venisse ubi aliquid sapere viderere. Quod si in Britanniam quoque profectus esses, profecto nemo in illa tanta insula peritior te fuisset. Verum tamen—rideamus licet: sum enim a te invitatus—subinvideo tibi ultro te etiam arcessitum ab eo ad quem ceteri non propter superbiam eius sed propter occupationem aspirare non possunt.   (*Fam.* VII, 10, 1)

MARCUS CICERO SAYS A GREETING TO TREBATIUS

I read your letter from which I understood that you appeared to our Caesar as very versed in law. There is reason why you should rejoice that you came into those regions [in Gaul] where you seemed to have some good judgment. But if you had gone ahead into Britain also, for sure no one would have been more expert than you in that such great island. However still—it is OK that we laugh: for I have been provoked by you—I somewhat envy you the fact that you have even been summoned spontaneously by him to whom other people are not able to aspire not because of his haughtiness but because of his busy activity.

M. CICERO S. D. TREBATIO: *Marcus Cicero salutem dicit Trebatio*

intellexi te … videri, "I understood that you appeared": the M & M verb *intellexi* produces a sentence in OO with *te* its acc. subject and *videri* the passive infinitive verb, meaning "you to be seen" or "you seemed" or "you were appearing."

→ **201** M & M, 60, 71, GL n° 527, remarks 1–2;
OO, 71–73; verb: contemporaneous passive infinitive, 72.3.

Est quod gaudeas, "There is reason why you should rejoice": this usage of *quod*, "the fact that," is really not a relative, but a neuter substantive clause introducing a new subject, as in "as to the fact that . . . ," usually with the indicative. The use of the subjunctive here is somewhere between an object clause, "[there is a reason] that you are joyful," which turns out to be almost a causal clause where the *quod* means "because," and an IQ "[there is a reason] why you are joyful," where the *quod* almost means "why." You can't define it much more. In many instances in Latin you may never know for which reason the subjunctive was used, without asking the author. Indeed there are sentences where the reason for the subjunctive could be one of five or six.

→ **202** *quod* = "the fact that" as a new subject, GL n° 525.2;
object sentence: *quod* = "that," GL n° 524;
causal: *quod*, "because, since," 59.2; IQ, 60.

gaudeas te . . . venisse, "you should rejoice that you came": OO depending on the whole M & M expression *est quod*, "there is reason why [you should rejoice]."

→ **203** M & M, 60, 71, GL n° 527, remarks 1–2; OO, 71–73.

ubi viderere, "where you seemed": subjunctive by attraction depending on the sentence in OO, *te venisse*, "that you came," thus, in the indicative in English.

→ **204** OO, 71–73.

aliquid sapere, "some good taste": *aliquid* is an adverb, "to some extent" or "some," so the expression does not necessarily mean "to know something."

→ **205** dict., *aliquis, aliquid*, indef. subst. pron., II., G.,—adv., A. *aliquid*.

viderere, "you seem": a famous variation dear to Cicero for *videreris* in T.2 subjunctive.

→ **206** variation: *–ris*, 39.3.

Quod si, "But if": sometimes written as one word *quodsi*, as in the manuscript; it looks like "something if," "which if," or "the fact that if"; cf. the dictionary, which describes this combination as one used to start a new sentence meaning "But if," as here.

→ **207** dict., 2. *quis, quid*, pron. indef., I. As *subst.*, B. In connection with *si*.

si . . . profectus esses, . . . fuisset, "if you had gone ahead, . . . [no one] would have been": both verbs are T.4s, producing a contrary to fact condition at a point in the past, on Track II. It can be tested by adding: "if you had gone ahead—*but you didn't*—no one would have been . . .—*but maybe there was.*"

→ **208** conditionals: contrary to fact, 86.3.

peritior te, "more expert than you": *te* is an abl. of comparison.
> → **209** abl.: comparison, 90.2, GL n° 398.

rideamus licet, "it is OK that we laugh": *rideamus* T.1s depends on the verb
licet, here without the *ut*; the full expression is, *licet ut rideamus*, "it is permitted that we laugh."
> → **210** dict., *licet, licuit* and *citum est*, 2., I ... "with *ut* or (more freq.) with the
> simple *subj.*"

subinvideo, "I somewhat envy": Cicero liked to invent words beginning
with *sub–* meaning "somewhat," such as *subiratus*, "somewhat angry" and
submolestus, "somewhat annoying."
> → **211** dict., *subinvideo*, no perf., *subinvisum*, 2., "to envy a little";
> dict., *subirascor, atus*, 3., producing *subiratus, a, um*, P. a.;
> dict., *submolestus, a, um*, adj.

subinvideo tibi, "I somewhat envy you": *invideo* is one of the 65; what sounds
like the object in English, "you," in Latin is expressed by a complement,
completing the action of the verb, in the form to-for-from, *tibi*.
> → **212** 65 verbs with dat., 33.7.2, GL n° 346.

ultro, "spontaneously": not to be confused with the preposition *ultra*
meaning "beyond," "on the other side." One of the many meanings for *ultro*
besides the natural meaning "beyond," "further," is this meaning "spontaneously," "voluntarily." The dictionary gives a column of examples for this
meaning.
> → **213** dict., *ultro*, adv., II, C.;
> dict., *ultra*, adv., and prep., II. prep. with acc. "on the farther side of."

te ... arcessitum, "the fact that you have been summoned": OO depending on the M & M verb *subinvideo* "I somewhat envy" and expressing the
content of the envy; the full passive, antecedent infinitive is *arcessitum esse*,
with the *esse* understood.
> → **214** M & M, 60, 71, GL n° 527, remarks 1–2; OO, 71–73.

ab eo, "by him": preposition with the abl. Its contrary is the following.
> → **215** prep. with abl., 28.4.

ad quem, "to whom": preposition with object indicating motion to or toward.
> → **216** prep. with obj., 6.

❧

Sed tu in ista epistula nihil mihi scripsisti de tuis rebus quae mehercule
mihi non minori curae sunt quam meae. Valde metuo ne frigeas in hibernis:
quam ob rem camino luculento utendum censeo: idem Mucio et Manilio

placebat, praesertim qui sagis non abundares. Quamquam vos nunc istic satis calere audio: quo quidem nuntio valde mehercule de te timueram. Sed tu
in re militari multo es cautior quam in advocationibus, qui neque in Oceano natare volueris, studiosissimus homo natandi, neque spectare essedarios,
quem antea ne andabata quidem defraudare poteramus. Sed iam satis iocati
sumus.   (*Fam.* VII, 10, 2)

But you in that letter of yours wrote nothing to me about your own affairs
which, by george, are not for a lesser concern to me than my own. I am
sorely afraid that you may freeze in the winter quarters: for which reason
I believe use must be made of a blazing hearth: the same thing met the approval of Mucius and Manilius, especially because you were not abounding
in military cloaks. And yet I hear that you all there are now hot enough: by
which message indeed I had by george very much feared about you. But you
are much more cautious in military matters than in court appeals, because
neither did you want to swim in the Ocean, you a person with the greatest
love of swimming, nor to view charioteers, whom previously we were not
able to cheat out of even blindfold gladiatorial match. But we have already
joked around enough.

mihi non minori curae, "not for a lesser concern to me": double dat. of
person concerned *mihi,* and of finality or result *curae.* The comparative adj.
minori agrees with *curae.*

→ **217** double dat., 91.2; dict., *parvus, a, um,* adj., II. comp. *minor, us,* "less, lesser."

metuo ne frigeas, "I am ... afraid that you may freeze": as with all verbs of
fearing, *ne* here means "that," and *ut* means "that not."

→ **218** verbs of fearing with *ne,* 95.

camino luculento utendum censeo, "I believe use must be made of a blazing
hearth": the M & M verb *censeo* produces the sentence in OO *utendum esse,*
where *esse* is understood. In English we could say here, "I believe a blazing
hearth has to be used," but Latin does not permit this. The verb *utor,* rather,
is one of the five which take the abl. When *utor* is used with passive meaning, and the only time a deponent verb can be used with passive meaning
is in the passive necessity formula as here, its subject becomes impersonal,
as in "it must be used," or as in the passive necessity formula *utendum esse,*
"use must be made." Even in this use its complement must stay in the abl.,
which produces here *camino luculento.* This is the case for all verbs that
take the functions gen., dat., abl. (the oblique cases) where the verb is in the
passive voice and the object must remain oblique. In the English rendering
you can't hear the abl.

→ **219** M & M, 60, 71, GL n° 527, remarks 1–2;
        OO, 71–73; famous five verbs with the ablative, 78.1;
        participle of passive necessity, deponents, 50, 51.2.4;
        passive necessity formula, 53.4.

Mucio et Manilio placebat, "[it] met with the approval of Mucius and Manilius": *placebat* is one of the 65 with a dat. object. You can hear the dat. in English if you say, "it was pleasing to Mucius and Manilius."

→ **220** 65 verbs with dat., 33.7.2, GL n° 346.

qui … non abundares, "because you were not abounding": the relative causal clause where *qui* followed by T.2s stands for *cum tu … non abundares*, "because/since you were not abounding."

→ **221** subjunctive use: causal *qui, quae, quod* = "because, since," 59.4.

quamquam, "and yet": also meaning "however," but here *quamquam* does not mean "although."

→ **222** dict., *quamquam*, conj., II.

vos … calere audio, "I hear that you all … are … hot": the M & M verb *audio*, "I hear," in T.1i produces a statement in OO where the subject in the object form is *vos*, and the inf. *calere* describes contemporaneous action; here the "hot" wars of Caesar with the Gauls.

→ **223** M & M, 60, 71, GL n° 527, remarks 1–2; OO, 71–73.

multo es cautior quam, "you are much more cautious … than …": the comparative *cautior* "more cautious" is described by *multo*, "[more cautious] by much," and coordinates with *quam*, "than." The meaning of *multo*, "by much," is not heard in the smoother English rendering, "much more cautious."

→ **224** adj.: comp., 36.

qui neque … natare volueris … neque spectare, "because you wanted neither to swim … nor to view": the main verb *es*, "you are," is in T.1i and establishes Track I. The relative *qui*, followed by the subjunctive *volueris*, in T.3s, is a causal clause where the *qui* stands for *cum tu*, "because you." The verb *volueris*, variously meaning "[because] you wanted," "you have wanted," "you did want," "you were wanting" is complemented by two infinitives, *natare*, "to swim," and *spectare*, "to view"; both are correlated by *neque … neque …*, "neither … nor …" and function as gerund objects of *volueris*, "[because] you wanted."

→ **225** dict., *neque*, adv. and conj.; *neque …, neque …*, GL n° 445;
subjunctive use: causal *qui, quae, quod* = "because, since," 59.4;
consecutio, 47–48;
verb: complementary infinitive, 77; gerund, 77.1.

studiosissimus homo natandi, "you a person with the greatest love of swimming": the adj. *studiossissimus*, "most zealous," "very interested in," in the superlative degree takes its complement in the gen., here the gerund *natandi*, "of swimming."

→ **226** adj.: superlative, 36; gerund, 77.1.

andabata, "out of … blindfold gladiatorial match": the form is the abl., meaning "out of a …."

→ **227** abl.: separation, 27.

❧

Ego de te ad Caesarem quam diligenter scripserim, tute scis: quam saepe, ego. Sed mehercule iam intermiseram, ne viderer liberalissimi hominis meique amantissimi voluntati erga me diffidere. Sed tamen iis litteris quas proxime dedi putavi esse hominem commonendum. Id feci. Quid profecerim facias me velim certiorem et simul de toto statu tuo consiliisque omnibus. Scire enim cupio quid agas, quid exspectes, quam longum istum tuum discessum a nobis futurum putes.   (*Fam.* VII, 10, 3)

You yourself know how carefully I wrote to Caesar about you: how often, I [know]. But for heaven's sake I had already stopped, lest I might appear to distrust the goodwill toward me of a most generous person and most fond of me. But nevertheless I thought the man had to be reminded by those letters which I sent the last time. I did that. I would like you to inform me what I profited and at the same time [inform me] about your whole situation and all of your projects/decisions. For I desire to know what you are doing, what you are expecting, how long you think that your departure from us will be.

Ego de te ad Caesarem quam diligenter scripserim, "how carefully I wrote to Caesar about you": the question word *quam* is embedded within its own IQ. The expression *de te ad Caesarem* is placed in front of its own *quam*, "how," both of which go with *scripserim*, "I wrote," whose subject is the first word, *Ego*, "I." The entire IQ is placed in front of the main sentence *tute scis*, "You yourself know," which gives rise to the IQ.

→ **228** sentence structure, 1.

quam diligenter scripserim, tute scis, "You yourself know how carefully I wrote": the main verb *scis*, "you know," in T.1i is a verb of M & M producing an IQ where the question word is *quam*, "how," "in what manner," accompanied by *diligenter*, "carefully," in the comparative degree and the verb *scripserim*, "I wrote," in T.3s. Here *tute* does not mean "safely," the adverbial form being either the very rare *tute* or the more common *tuto*, rather *tu-te* is the emphatic form of *tu*, here used as an intensive pronoun, "You yourself."

→ **229** M & M, 60, 71, GL n° 527, remarks 1–2;
      IQ, 60; adv.: positive, comp., superl., 37;
      dict., *tu*, pers. pron., I., B. with emphatic *–te* or *–met* as in *tute*;
      dict., *tueor, tuitus*, 2., II., B.…—adv.: *tute* and *tuto*, "safely."

intermiseram, "I had … stopped": this verb means here "to interrupt," and its complement is *scribere*, "[I had stopped] writing," a gerund.

→ **230** verb: complementary infinitive, 77; gerund, 77.1.

intermiseram, ne viderer ... diffidere, "I had stopped, lest I seem to distrust": Cicero's intention when he stopped writing—*intermiseram*, "I had stopped," in T.5i establishing Track II—is given in a negative purpose clause where *viderer*, "I might appear," is in T.2s. The subject of *viderer*, used personally, is the nom. subject of the infinitive *diffidere*.

→ **231** subjunctive use: purpose clause, 58.1; *consecutio*, 47–48;
personal construction: *videor*, 73.3, GL n° 528.1 and remark 2 and note 1;
nom. with the inf., 73.3, GL n° 528.1.

liberalissimi hominis meique amantissimi voluntati, "of a most generous person and most fond of me": so many endings in –i require knowledge of vocabulary to distinguish the function of each. *voluntati* is the dat. complement of *diffidere*, "to distrust the goodwill." Depending on *voluntati* is *hominis*, "of a person," who is described both as *liberalissimi*, "most generous" and "amantissimi," "most fond." Depending on *amantissimi* is *mei*, "most fond of me." The *–que* joins the two adjectives *liberalissimi ... –que amantissimi*, "most generous ... and most fond." In the middle of this phrase are *hominis mei*, both genitives, yet they do not have anything to do with one another. The *mei* belongs to the second part of the equation and the *–que* is attached to the first word of the second part: that's the nature of *–que*. This becomes clear when the phrase is set in the plural, *liberalissimorum hominum nostrique amantissimorum voluntatibus*, where the plural of *mei* is not *meorum* but *nostri*, "of us." One must read the whole sentence, let the functions stand out, and then think!

→ **232** *ossium gluten*, the bones' glue, 1; adj.: comp. and superl., 36;
personal pronouns: function of-possession, 24.1; conjunction: *–que*, 3.2.

diffidere, "to distrust": the subject of *viderer*, used personally, is the nom. subject of the infinitive *diffidere*, "[lest I seem] distrusting," itself one of the 65 verbs whose complement is in the dat., here *voluntati*; but it is often difficult to hear the dat. in the English rendering, "to distrust the goodwill."

→ **233** personal construction: *videor*, 73.3, GL n° 528.1 and remark 2 and note 1;
nom. with the inf., 73.3, GL n° 528.1;
65 verbs with dat., 33.7.2, GL n° 346.

iis litteris ... putavi esse hominem commonendum, "I thought the man had to be reminded by those letters": the main verb *putavi*, "I thought," in T.4b is a verb of M & M producing a statement in OO where the subject in object form is *hominem* and the passive necessity formula consists of *esse*, a contemporaneous inf. and *commonendum*, a participle of passive necessity, "the man had to be reminded," "... to be admonished," which sounds in the past because it is contemporaneous to *putavi*, "I thought." The instrument for this last word and action is given in the two words placed up front, *iis litteris*, "by those letters."

→ **234** M & M, 60, 71, GL n° 527, remarks 1–2; OO, 71–73;
participle of passive necessity, 50, 51.1.4;
passive necessity formula, 53.4;
abl.: instrument, 28.5.3–4, 89.2, GL n° 401.

Quid profecerim facias me velim certiorem, "I would like you to inform me what I profited": three subjunctive verbs in a row require clear thinking. The main verb is *velim*, "I would like," in T.1s establishing Track I and complemented by an expression of intention or purpose, the idiom *facias me ... certiorem*, "that you inform me," where *facias* is T.1s and appears without *ut*, which expression itself functions as a verb of M & M producing an IQ where the question word is *Quid*, "What," and the verb *profecerim*, "I had profited," in T.3s, describes antecedent action.

→ **235** M & M, 60, 71, GL n° 527, remarks 1–2; IQ, 60;
subjunctive use: purpose clause without *ut*, 58, GL n° 546, remark 2;
commands: other expressions, *velim*, 85.1.7;
consecutio: subjunctive depending on a subjunctive, 62.1.

Scire ... cupio quid agas, quid exspectes, "I desire to know what you are doing, what you are expecting": the main verb *cupio*, "I desire," in T.1i establishing Track I, is complemented by a gerund object, *scire*, "to know," "I desire knowing," which is itself a verb of M & M giving rise to three IQs, the first being *quid agas*, "what you are doing"; the second, *quid exspectes*, "what you are awaiting," both in T.1s and in English sounding ind.

→ **236** M & M, 60, 71, GL n° 527, remarks 1–2; IQ, 60;
verb: complementary infinitive, 77; gerund, 77.1.

Scire ... quam longum istum tuum discessum ... futurum putes, "to know ... how long you think that your departure from us will be": the third IQ depending on *Scire*, "to know," is *quam ... putes*, where *putes*, "you think," is also T.1s and a verb of M & M giving rise to a statement in OO where the subject in object form is *istum tuum discessum*, "that your departure," "that lousy departure of yours," and the full form of the implied inf. is *futurum esse*, "to be about to be," "will be."

→ **237** verb: complementary infinitive, 77; gerund, 77.1;
M & M, 60, 71, GL n° 527, remarks 1–2; IQ, 60; OO, 71–73;
futurity participle, 50, 51.1.3; *futurum esse* (*fore*), 72.1;
futurity formula, active, 53.3;
three cousins: *iste–ille–ipse*, 41.3.

❧

Sic enim tibi persuadeas velim, unum mihi esse solacium qua re facilius possim pati te esse sine nobis, si tibi esse id emolumento sciam: sin autem id non est, nihil duobus nobis est stultius: me, qui te non Romam attraham, te, qui non huc advoles. Una mehercule nostra vel severa vel iocosa congressio pluris erit quam non modo hostes sed etiam fratres nostri Haedui. qua re omnibus de rebus fac ut quam primum sciam:

'aut consolando aut consilio aut re iuvero'. (*Fam.* VII, 10, 4)

For thus I would like you to convince yourself, that there is one consolation for me why I am able more easily to allow you to live without us, if I know that this is for a profit to you: if however that is not the case, nothing is more stupid than the both of us: than I, because I am not enticing you to Rome, than you, because you are not flying over to here. By george one meeting of ours, either serious or humorous, will be of greater value than not only the enemies but even our Haedui [a Gallic tribe] brothers, for which reason see to it that I know as soon as possible about all things:

"I shall have helped you either by consoling or by counsel or with resources."

tibi persuadeas velim, "I would like you to convince yourself": the main verb is *velim*, "I would like," in T.1s; its complement appears in the subjunctive without *ut* to convey the force of feeling, *persuadeas*, "that you convince," an M & M verb in T.1s and one of the 65 verbs whose complement is in the dat., here *tibi*, the reflexive pronoun, "yourself."

> → **238** subjunctive use: purpose clause without *ut*, 58, GL n° 546, remark 2;
> commands: other expressions, *velim*, 85.1.7;
> M & M, 60, 71, GL n° 527, remarks 1–2;
> 65 verbs with dat., 33.7.2, GL n° 346;
> reflexive pron.: first and second person, 30.

persuadeas ... unum mihi esse solacium, "convince [yourself] that there is one consolation for me": the content of which Trebatio is to convince himself, *persuadeas*, "that you convince," is given in an object sentence where the subject in the object function is *unum ... solacium*, "one consolation," and the inf. *esse* is contemporaneous, "there is one consolation," "one consolation exists."

> → **239** M & M, 60, 71, GL n° 527, remarks 1–2; OO, 71–73.

qua re facilius possim pati, "why I am able more easily to allow": the noun *solacium*, "consolation" expresses an idea of M & M which gives rise to an IQ beginning *qua re*, "why" or "for which reason," and its verb *possim*, "I am able," in T.1s but rendered in the English in the ind. The object of *possim*, "I am able," is *pati*, "to allow," "to suffer," the gerund of a deponent inf.

> → **240** M & M, 60, 71, GL n° 527, remarks 1–2;
> IQ, 60; verb: deponent, 29;
> verb: complementary infinitive, 77; gerund, 77.1.

pati te esse sine nobis, "to allow you to live without us": as a verb of M & M, *pati*, "to allow," produces a statement that gives the content of the suffering in OO where *te* is the subject in the object form and the inf. *esse* is contemporaneous, "you to exist." Upon first glance *possim pati te* may look like it means "I am able to suffer you," but here *pati* means "to allow," as in the biblical quotation, "suffer the little ones to come unto me."

> → **241** M & M, 60, 71, GL n° 527, remarks 1–2; OO, 71–73.

si tibi esse id emolumento sciam, "if I know that this is for a profit to you": a conditional sentence where *sciam*, "I know," is in T.1s either by MA depending on the statement in OO, *pati te esse*, "to allow you to live," rendered in English in the ind. as above, or some might call it a foggy, less-vivid future in T.1s, rendered in the English as "if I should know." And of course we do not forget that *sciam* can be T.3i, meaning "I shall know." This is an example of having three possible reasons for this one form.

→ **242** subjunctive use: modal attraction, 83;
    conditionals: foggy future, 86.2.

As a verb of M & M, *sciam*, "I know," produces a statement in OO that gives the content of the knowledge, where the subject in the object form is *id*, and the inf. *esse* is contemporaneous, "that this is." The verb *esse* has a double dative, first of the person affected, *tibi*, "to you," and second of the goal, *emolumento*, "for a profit."

→ **243** M & M, 60, 71, GL n° 527, remarks 1–2; OO, 71–73;
    double dat., 91.2.

nihil duobus nobis est stultius, "nothing is more stupid than the both of us": rather than *nemo*, "no one," Cicero here uses *nihil*, "nothing." Agreeing with *nihil*, in the neuter is the adj. *stultius*, in the comparative degree, "more stupid," which goes with *duobus nobis*, "than we both," "than we two," the ablative of comparison. The comparative adv. looks the same *stultius*, "somewhat stupidly."

→ **244** adj.: comp., 36; abl.: comparison, 90.2, GL n° 398;
    adv.: comp., 37.

me, qui te non Romam attraham, "than I, because I am not enticing you to Rome": the *me* is an abl. of comparison and agrees with *duobus nobis*, "than the both of us," in the previous line. The verb, *attraham*, "I am [not] enticing," is in T.1s because this is a causal sentence where *qui* stands for *cum ego*, "because I," the subject of *attraham*, "because I am [not] enticing."

→ **245** abl.: comparison, 90.2, GL n° 398;
    subjunctive use: causal *qui, quae, quod* = "because, since," 59.4.

te, qui non huc advoles, "[than] you, because you are not flying over to here": as above, the *te* is an abl. of comparison that agrees with *duobus nobis*, "than the both of us," eight words previous, which is explicit in the English text, "than I, … than you…." The verb *advoles*, "you are [not] flying over [to here]" is in T.1s because this is a causal sentence where *qui* stands for *cum tu*, "because you," the subject of *advoles*, "because you are [not] flying over."

→ **246** abl.: comparison, 90.2;
    subjunctive use: causal *qui, quae, quod* = "because, since," 59.4.

pluris erit quam, "will be of greater value than": here *pluris* is a gen. of evaluation or price, meaning also "of greater value." *quam* means "than" and compares the two ideas.

→ **247** gen. of indefinite price, 75.2; *quam* with the comp., 43.2.

fac ut quam primum sciam, "see to it that I know as soon as possible": the main verb is the command form *fac*, "see to it," one of several that has lost the final *–e*, as *dic, duc, fer*. As a verb of causing, it produces a result clause *ut sciam*, "that I know," in T.1s and rendered in English in the ind. Here *quam* followed by the superlative *primam* has the special meaning "as soon as possible," thus presented in the dictionary.

> → **248** commands: famous four, 39.4;
> subjunctive use: complementary result (consecutive), 68.1;
> *quam* with the superlative, 43.3; dict., *primus, a, um,* adj., II., adv.,
>   B., *primum,* 3., (α);
> *quam* with the superlative, 43.3.

aut consolando aut consilio aut re iuvero, "I shall have helped you either by consoling or by counsel or with resources": the quote is from Terentius, *Heauton timorumenos* 86. The verb is *iuvero*, "I shall have helped," in T.6i. It is complemented by three ablatives of instrumentality, *consilio*, "by counsel," the singular *re*, given in English in the plural as "with resources," and the third is a gerund *consolando*, "by consoling."

> → **249** abl.: instrument, 28.5.3–4, 89.2, GL n° 401; gerund, 77.1.

LETTER 162 T-P
AD FAMILIARES I, 10

M. CICERO S. D. L. VALERIO IURIS CONSULTO;

cur enim tibi hoc non gratificer nescio, praesertim cum his temporibus audacia pro sapientia liceat uti. Lentulo nostro egi per litteras tuo nomine gratias diligenter. Sed tu velim desinas iam nostris litteris uti et nos aliquando revisas et ibi malis esse ubi aliquo numero sis quam istic ubi solus sapere videare. Quamquam qui istinc veniunt, partim te superbum esse dicunt quod nihil respondeas, partim contumeliosum, quod male respondeas. Sed iam cupio tecum coram iocari. Qua re fac ut quam primum venias neque in Apuliam tuam accedas, ut possimus salvum venisse gaudere; nam illo si veneris, tu, ut Ulixes, cognosces tuorum neminem.   (*Fam.* I, 10)

MARCUS CICERO SAYS A GREETING TO
LUCIUS VALERIUS, SKILLED IN LAW;

indeed I do not know why I am not doing you a favor with this [above formal address], especially since at these times it is permitted to use boldness instead of good taste. I rendered thanks carefully to our Lentulus by letter in your name. But I would like that you cease now to use our correspondence and that you come to visit us again sometime and that you prefer to be there where you are in some esteem rather than out there [in Cilicia] where you alone seem to be smart. And yet people who are coming from your area in part say that you are proud because you answer nothing legal, in part offensive, because you answer poorly. But already now I long to joke with you face to face. For which reason make sure that you come as soon as possible and not approach to your own Apulia so that we may be able to rejoice that you have arrived safe and sound; for if you will have arrived there [to Apulia], you, just like Ulysses, will know no one of your people.

M. Cicero s. d. L. Valerio iuris consulto: *Marcus Cicero salutem dicit Lucio Valerio iuris consulto*

The address is given above the body of the letter, and the first sentence refers to it in the word *hoc*, "with this," referring to the solemn heading of the letter. The abbreviations S. D. are spelled out in the manuscript in Part 1: *salutem dicit*.

   → **250** sentence structure, 1.

cur ... gratificer nescio, "I do not know why I am ... doing ... a favor": the M & M verb *nescio* produces an IQ, given in the subjunctive in Latin but ind. in English.

   → **251** M & M, 60, 71, GL n° 527, remarks 1–2;
         IQ, 60; verb: deponent, 29.

tibi ... gratificer, "I am ... doing you a favor": the dep. *gratificer* is one of the 65 verbs whose object is in the form to-for-from, *tibi*, which can be heard in English as "I am ... doing a favor for you."

   → **252** 65 verbs with dat., 33.7.2, GL n° 346.

cum ... liceat uti, "since ... it is permitted to use": the gerund *uti* is the subject of *liceat*, "since using boldness is allowed."

   → **253** gerund, 77.1.

cum ... liceat, "since ... it is permitted": a causal sentence where *cum* means "because" or "since" and is followed by T.1s *liceat*.

   → **254** subjunctive use: causal *cum* = "because, since," 59.1.

his temporibus, "at these times": the form by-with-from-in without the preposition indicates time in which, at which. In contrast, the occasional phrase *in his temporibus* means "in these circumstances," not "at these times." In the Vulgate edition of the Bible, *In illo tempore* is not standard Latin, but is used to say, "At that time."

   → **255** abl.: time at which, 70.1.

audacia ... uti, "to use boldness": *uti* is one of the five deponent verbs whose English object is expressed in Latin through the function by-with-from-in, here, *audacia*, meaning together, "to procure usefulness by boldness," as an instrument, but you cannot hear the abl. in English.

   → **256** famous five verbs with the ablative, 78.1.

tu velim desinas ... et ... revisas et ... malis, "I would like that you cease ... and that you come ... and that you prefer": the verb of wishing, *velim*, is followed by three verbs in T.1s, the first being *desinas*, whose subject is *tu* placed out front; for all three the *ut* is left out, which is a very frequent usage when the verb of wishing is very strong.

   → **257** subjunctive use: purpose clause without *ut*, 58, GL n° 546, remark 2;
         commands: other expressions, *velim*, 85.1.7;
         conjunction: *et ... , et ... ,* 3.2.

ubi ... sis, "where you are": this expression looks like an IQ, but there is no M & M verb to produce an IQ. The use of *sis* in T.1s could naturally be an expression of characteristic result, where *ubi* stands for *ita ut ibi* [*sis*], "in such a way that there [you are]," as in the fuller expression, *ibi malis esse ita ut aliquo numero sis*, "that you prefer to be there [namely, here with us] in such a place that as a result you are in some esteem," and so be expressed in the ind. in English. Otherwise it could express purpose as in *ut ibi sis*, "so that you may be there," and so be expressed in the subjunctive in English. Or the least probable would be due to modal attraction depending on the previous subjunctive *malis*, "that you prefer" and thus rendered in the ind. in English.

→ **258** dict., *ubi*, adv., II., B., instead of the relative pronoun; IQ, 60; subjunctive use: characteristic result, 68.2; subjunctive use: relative clause of purpose, *ubi*, 58.1; *consecutio*, 47–48; subjunctive use: modal attraction, 83.

ubi ... videare, "where you alone seem": the same variety of reasons for the subjunctive exists here as above for *ubi sis*. The expression looks like IQ, but is not. As above, *videare* in T.1s could be an expression of characteristic result, where *ubi* stands for *ita ut ibi* [*videare*], "in such a way that there [you seem]," also in the ind. in English. Otherwise it could express purpose as in *ut ibi videaris*, "so that there you may seem" and so be expressed in the subjunctive in English. Or the least probable would be due to modal attraction depending on the complementary infinitive *esse*, "[you prefer] to be" and thus rendered in the ind. in English;

→ **259** dict., *ubi*, adv., II., B., instead of the relative pronoun; IQ, 60; subjunctive use: characteristic result, 68.2; subjunctive use: relative clause of purpose, *ubi*, 58.1; *consecutio*, 47–48; subjunctive use: modal attraction, 83.

videare, "you seem": Cicero's favorite variation for *videaris*, T.1s passive.

→ **260** variation: –*ris*, 39.3.

Quamquam ... dicunt, "And yet ... people ... say": here *quamquam* does not mean "although" because it does not produce a subordinate sentence; rather it starts an independent sentence and means "and yet; still."

→ **261** dict., *quamquam*, conj., II.

qui ... veniunt, "who are coming"; the antecedent of *qui* is *ii*, "those people," which is the implied subject of *dicunt*, "those people say," way down the line. Thus, (1) the relative is geographically out in front and (2) the antecedent of *qui* is not written.

→ **262** rel. pron.: omission of the antecedent, 11.2; sentence structure, 1.

quod ... respondeas ... quod ... respondeas, "because you answer ... because you answer": two reasons for the subjunctive are likely; perhaps by modal attraction depending on OO *te superbum esse*, "that you are proud," and *te*

... esse ... contumeliosum, "that you are ... offensive"; more probably an example of reported speech where *quod* followed by the subjunctive indicates the author is quoting someone else. On this basis one could say without hesitation: "people ... say that you are proud because, *as they say / allegedly*, you answer nothing ... offensive because, *as they say / allegedly*, you answer poorly."

> → **263** subjunctive use: modal attraction, 83; OO, 71–73;
>   causal: *quod*, "because, since," + subjunctive, reported reason, 59.2.

fac ut ... venias neque ... accedas, "make sure that you come ... and not approach": the verb of effecting *fac* produces two result clauses in T.1s; thus in the ind. in English.

> → **264** commands: famous four, 39.4;
>   subjunctive use: complementary result (consecutive), 68.1.

ut possimus, "so that we may be able": a purpose clause arising from the two result clauses mentioned above.

> → **265** subjunctive use: purpose clause, 58.1.

salvum venisse, "that you have arrived safe and sound": OO depending on the emotional idea contained in the verb *gaudere*, "to rejoice"; the subject *te* is understood. As a reminder, these verbs of emotion can take OO or *quod* with the ind. or subjunctive.

> → **266** verbs of emotion + OO, GL n° 533;
>   verbs of emotion + *quod*, GL n° 542;
>   M & M, 60, 71, GL n° 527, remarks 1–2; OO, 71–73;
>   verb: complementary infinitive, 77.

gaudere, "to rejoice": a complementary infinitive depending on *possimus*, "we may be able."

> → **267** verb: complementary infinitive, 77.

si veneris ... cognosces, "if you will have arrived ... , you ... will know": examples of the balance between T.6i *veneris* and T.3i *cognosces*. The Romans are much more precise and careful about this than users of English for sure. The timeline is clear if we hypothesize a calendar. Writing during the spring, he could say *si veneris*, "if you will have come," referring perhaps to 1 August, and *cognosces*, "you will know," referring perhaps to 3 August, which means that T.6i, the completed future *veneris* happens first, before T.6i the simple future *cognosces*.

> → **268** T.3i and T.6i paired: 7, Time 6, and GL n° 244, remark 2.

tuorum, "of your people": the possessive adjective is used as a noun meaning "of your men, people, family, guys."

> → **269** adj.: possessive, 24.3, 100.2; possessive adj.: used as nouns, 100.2.

LETTER 163 T-P
AD FAMILIARES XIII, 49

CICERO CURIO PROCOS.

Q. Pompeius Sext. F. multis et veteribus causis necessitudinis mihi coniunctus est. Is, cum antea meis commendationibus et rem et gratiam et auctoritatem suam tueri consuerit, nunc profecto te provinciam obtinente meis litteris adsequi debet, ut nemini se intellegat commendatiorem umquam fuisse. Quam ob rem a te maiorem in modum peto, ut, cum omnis meos aeque ac tuos observare pro necessitudine nostra debeas, hunc in primis ita in tuam fidem recipias ut ipse intellegat nullam rem sibi maiori usui aut ornamento quam meam commendationem esse potuisse. Vale.   (*Fam.* XIII, 49)

CICERO TO CURIUS, PROCONSUL

Quintus Pompeius the son of Sextus has been associated with me by many and old reasons of familiarity. Since before this time he was accustomed to look out for his both prosperity and political influence and authority by means of my recommendations, now for sure—as you are maintaining the province—he ought to obtain by my letters that he understands that to no one has he ever been more recommended. For which reason I ask of you in a stronger manner that, although you ought to respect all my people equally as your own in keeping with our relationship, first of all you take this man into your confidence in such a way that he himself understand that no thing was able to be for himself for greater usefulness or honor than my recommendation. Farewell.

CICERO CURIO PROCOS.: *Cicero Curio proconsuli*

Q. Pompeius Sext. F., "Quintus Pompeius the son of Sextus": the abbreviations stand for: "Quintus Pompeius Sexti Filius." You will find these abbreviations all around Rome. For example on the facade of the Pantheon the inscription begins: *M. Agrippa L. F.*, which stands for *Marcus Agrippa*

Lucii Filius, meaning "Marcus Agrippa the son of Lucius."

→ **270** dict., entries for the letters *S* and *F*; dict., *sextus* (abbrev. *Sex.*), *i*, m.

Is ... debet, "he ... ought": in the second sentence, the first word *Is* is the subject of *debet* much further down the sentence.

→ **271** sentence structure, 1.

cum ... consuerit, "Since ... he was accustomed": once again *cum* can mean "because," in a causal clause, or "although," as a concessive clause.

→ **272** subjunctive use: causal *cum* = "because, since," 59.1;
subjunctive use: concessive *cum* = "although," 64.

te provinciam obtinente, "—as you are maintaining the province—": AA with the force of "because" or "while" or "as long as." Where possible in English, we distinguish AA in the text with dashes, as here.

→ **273** ablative absolute, 54–55.

ut ... intellegat, "that he understands": result clause depending on *asequi debet*, "he ought to obtain"; thus in ind. in English.

→ **274** subjunctive use: complementary result (consecutive), 68.1.

se ... fuisse, "has he ... been": OO depending on M & M verb *ut ... intellegat*, "that he understands."

→ **275** M & M, 60, 71, GL n° 527, remarks 1–2; OO, 71–73.

maiorem in modum, "in a stronger manner": super Latin expression of the prep. *in* with the object or acc. *modum* meaning generally, "in the manner of," here "in a greater manner."

→ **276** prep. with obj., 6; adj.: comp., 36.

peto, ut ... recipias, "I ask ... that ... you take": an expression of purpose.

→ **277** subjunctive use: purpose clause, 58.1.

cum omnis meos aeque ac tuos ... debeas, "although you ought ... all my people equally as your own": two real possibilities; either causal, where *cum* means "because-since," or concessive, where *cum* means "although." The dict. entry for *aequus, a, um,* adj. gives the adverb *aeque* and then states that *aeque ac* means "equally as." Here *omnis* is an alternative form for *omnes*, which agrees with *meos* and *tuos*, all object plurals, "all my people [equally as] your own."

→ **278** subjunctive use: causal *cum* = "because, since," 59.1;
subjunctive use: concessive *cum* = "although," 64;
dict., *aequus, a, um,* adj., II., C., *aeque*, adv.... *aeque ac*;
Block II adj.: *–is* = *–es*, 38, GL n° 78.

ut ... intellegat, "that he ... understand": a purpose clause depending on *ita ... recipias*, "that you take ... in such a way"; thus, a purpose clause depending on a purpose clause. Yet, the distinction between a purpose and result

clause may be quite thin, consisting of a distinction of perspective (GL n°
543 note 2).

> → **279** subjunctive use: purpose clause, 58.1;
>   *consecutio*: subjunctive depending on a subjunctive, 62.1;
>   difference between purpose and result is perspective, GL n° 543, note 2.

nullam rem ... esse potuisse, "no thing was able to be": OO depending on M
& M verb *ut ... intellegat*, "that he ... understand."

> → **280** M & M, 60, 71, GL n° 527, remarks 1–2; OO, 71–73.

sibi ... usui aut ornamento, "for himself for ... usefulness or honor": double
dat. of person concerned *sibi*, and of finality or result both *usui*, "for ...
usefulness," and also *ornamento*, "for ... honor."

> → **281** double dat., 91.2.

sibi, "for himself": *sibi* is an indirect reflexive referring not to the subj. of its
own clause, *nullam rem*, "no thing," but to the subj. of the main sentence,
ipse, "he himself."

> → **282** reflexive pron.: third person, 31.

LETTER 167 T-P
AD FAMILIARES VII, 11

CICERO TREBATIO.

Nisi ante Roma profectus esses, nunc eam certe relinqueres. Quis enim tot interregnis iure consultum desiderat? Ego omnibus unde petitur hoc consili dederim ut a singulis interregibus binas advocationes postulent. Satisne tibi videor abs te ius civile didicisse? (*Fam.* VII, 11, 1)

CICERO TO TREBATIUS

If you had not departed from Rome before, now certainly you would abandon it. For who is looking for a legal expert at the time of so many legal interruptions? I would give this bit of advice to all people from whom it is being sought, that they demand two appeals from the individual temporary magistrates. Do I not seem to you to have learned civil law from you enough?

> *profectus esses ... relinqueres*, "you had departed ... you would abandon": contrary to fact condition where *profectus esses* is T.4s of the deponent verb *proficiscor* and *relinqueres* is T.2s. The shift from talking about a previous action *ante*, "before," in T.4s to speaking in the present moment *nunc*, "now," in T.2s is an example that contrary to fact conditionals are outside the sequence of tenses.
>
> → **283** conditionals: contrary to fact, 86.3;
> subjunctive use: 3% sequence of tenses, 94.1;
> verb: deponent, 29.

> *tot interregnis ... interregibus*, "at the time of so many legal interruptions ... from ... temporary magistrates": *tot* is a numerical adj., "so many." The abl. of time, *interregnis*, means "at the time of ... legal interruptions." The matter in discussion here involves technical terminology describing the *interrex* or *interregnum* and is available in any classical dictionary.
>
> → **284** dict., *tot*, num. adj. indecl.; abl.: time at which, 70.1.

unde petitur, "from whom it is sought": the dict. indicates that *unde* is an adv. meaning "whence," "from where," but the dict. also says it will stand for a relative pronoun "from whom," "by whom," "whence [it is sought]."

　　→ **285** dict., *unde*, adv., II., A., "from whom, from which."

hoc consili, "his bit of advice": gen. of part. These two words are usually separated by one or more other words.

　　→ **286** gen. of part, 99.

dederim, "I would give": T.3s expresses the potential of the present, which is often taken superficially and erroneously as "I would have given" or "I might have given" by people who have not been thoroughly trained.

　　→ **287** subjunctive use: potential of the present or future, *dederim* in T.3s, GL n° 257.2.

ut … postulent, "that they demand": purpose clause in T.1s therefore on Track I, depending on *dederim*, "I would give," T.3s. The idea which many people refuse to accept is that *dederim* is potential of the present, which establishes Track I producing a purpose clause in T.1s.

　　→ **288** subjunctive use: potential of the present or future, *dederim* in T.3s, GL n° 257.2;
　　　　subjunctive use: purpose clause, 58.1; *consecutio*, 47–48.

a singulis … abs te, "from the individual [magistrates] … from you": both forms *a* and *abs* are followed by the form by-with-from-in with no difference in meaning here, "from." The form *abs*, according to the usage in Cicero's letters, was practically abandoned by him in midlife.

　　→ **289** prep. with abl., 28.4.

videor, "I … seem": with the verb *videor* and about 4–5 others the Romans prefer the personal construction, not the impersonal construction. Whereas in English, Italian, and German we would say "it seems that I," the Latins say "I seem" especially with *videor*. Another example is, "it seems that the students are tired today." Instead of saying *videtur* followed by the acc. and the inf., *videtur discipulos esse fatigatos*, the Romans say *videntur discipuli fatigati esse* and make the whole thing personal.

　　This also occurs with the verb *existimor*. Instead of saying "it is thought that we are the best," *existimatur nos esse optimos*, the Romans say *existimamur esse optimi*, "We are thought to be the best." Another verb is *dicitur*. Rather than saying *dicitur simias ante nos factas esse*, "it is said that monkeys were created before us," the Romans prefer to say *simiae dicuntur ante nos esse factae*, "monkeys are said to have been created before us." There are a few other verbs with this usage.

　　The subject of *videor*, used personally, is the nom. subject of the infinitive *didicisse*.

　　→ **290** personal construction: *videor*, 73.3, GL n° 528.1 and remark 2 and note 1; nom. with the inf., 73.3, GL n° 528.1.

didicisse, "to have learned": an antecedent inf.

→ **291** verb: antecedent active infinitive, 72.1.

~

Sed heus tu, quid agis? ecquid fit? Video enim te iam iocari per litteras. Haec signa meliora sunt quam in meo Tusculano. Sed quid sit scire cupio. Consuli quidem te a Caesare scribis, sed ego tibi ab illo consuli mallem. Quod si aut fit aut futurum putas, perfer istam militiam et permane: ego enim desiderium tui spe tuorum commodorum consolabor: sin autem ista sunt inaniora, recipe te ad nos. Nam aut erit hic aliquid aliquando aut, si minus, una mehercule collocutio nostra pluris erit quam omnes Samarobrivae. Denique, si cito te rettuleris, sermo nullus erit: si diutius frustra afueris, non modo Laberium sed etiam sodalem nostrum Valerium pertimesco. Mira enim persona induci potest Britannici consulti.   (*Fam.* VII, 11, 2)

But hey you, what are you doing? Is anything happening? For I see that you are already joking by letter. These are better statues than in my Tusculan estate. But I desire to know what's up. Indeed you write that you are being consulted by Caesar, but I would prefer that your interests be consulted by him. But if either it is happening or you think it will be, suffer out that military service and stay: for I shall console my longing for you with the hope of your advantages: if however those are rather empty, get yourself back to us. For either there will be something here some day or, if not, by george one conversation of ours will be of greater value than all the people of Samarobriva. Finally, if you will have brought yourself back quickly, there will be no gossip/talk: if you will have been absent for a longer period of time uselessly, I deeply fear not only Laberius but even our buddy Valerius. For a marvelous personage of a British lawyer/barrister can be introduced.

quid agis?, "what are you doing": T.1i; you can easily run through all the times with this question: *quid ages*?, T.3i "what will you do?," *quid egisti*?, T.4a "what have you done?," T.4b "what did you do?"; *quid egeras*?, T.5i "what had you done?"; *quid agebas*?, T.2i "what were you doing?"

→ **292** verb T.4a, T.4b: 7 Time 4a, 7 Time 4b: 8.2; verb T.4, T.5, T.6: 8.2; verb T.1i, T.2i, T.3i: 12.

ecquid fit?, "is anything happening?," "is anything being done?": *fieri* is the passive form of *facere*; the form *facitur* is so rare as not to be existent or perhaps in some graffiti, or ridiculous for most observers.

→ **293** dict., *facio, feci, factum*, 3: I. *pass.: fio, factus, fieri.*

Note well, the verb *fio, fieri* is one of the famous four verbs whose simple form is active but meaning passive, thus the reverse of a deponent verb. The compound forms of this verb in Times 4, 5, 6 return to the passive form with passive meaning. The famous four are: *fio*, "I am made"; *veneo*, "I am for sale"; *pereo*, "I am lost"; *vapulo*, "I am being beaten." These verbs are not specifically treated in the *Ossa* book, but they are one of the discoveries to be made in encountering Latin literature, as is happening here.

→ **294** four reverse deponents: GL n° 169, remark 1; GL n° 214, remark 1.

te ... iocari, "you are joking": OO depending on M & M verb *video*, "I see."

→ **295** M & M, 60, 71, GL n° 527, remarks 1–2; OO, 71–73.

signa meliora, "statues ... better": there is a play on words here because *signa* can refer to "signs" as "indications" of the joking attitude of Trebatius or to the "statues" at Cicero's Tusculan estate. Let us remember the singular of *meliora* is *melius* and the positive is *bona*, the superlative *optima*.

→ **296** dict., *signum, i*, n.; adj.: irregular comp. and superl., 36.5, GL n° 90.

quid sit, "what's up": IQ in T.1s depending on M & M in the verbs *scire cupio*, "I desire to know," and sounding ind. in English. You can easily run through all the subjunctive times on Track I with this question; *quid fuerit*, T.3s "what was up"; *quid futurum sit*, expressing futurity "what will be." That is the verb to be in all its possibilities here.

→ **297** M & M, 60, 71, GL n° 527, remarks 1–2;
IQ, 60; *consecutio*, 47–48;
forms of the subjunctive, *esse*, 46;
consecutio: futurity formula in the subjunctive, 61.3.

Consuli ... te, ... consuli, "that you are being consulted, ... were being consulted": dictionary essential information reveals a play on words: *consulere* with the object form means "to consult something or someone," therefore *consuli te scribis*, "you write that you are being consulted [as an expert]," where *te* is the subject of the passive verb *consuli* in OO, but would be the object of the active form of the same verb. But as one of the 65, *consulere* with the form to-for-from, the dat., means "to look out for someone," "to consult the interests of someone" or "to provide for someone." The passive form maintains the dat. complement, and therefore the next phrase is *tibi consuli mallem*, "I would prefer that provision be made for your interests, for you" or "... that your interests be consulted"; thus: "you write that you *are being consulted* by Caesar, but I would prefer that *provision be made* for you," or "... that you be looked out for."

→ **298** dict., *consulo, lui, ltum*, 3;
verb: contemporaneous passive infinitive, 72.3; OO, 71–73;
65 verbs with dat., 33.7.2, GL n° 346.

mallem, "I would prefer": T.2s of *malo* used in a contrary to fact conditional indicating "I would prefer right now something that is not here/is impossible." Another time of the subjunctive is *malim*, T.1s indicating possibility, potential as in "I would prefer some day."

→ **299** conditionals: contrary to fact, 86.3; irregular verbs: *malo*, 82.

istam militiam ... ista sunt inaniora, "that military service ... those are rather empty": illustration of *istam* and *ista* referring to "*that* military service
of yours" or even "*those crummy* (*advantages*) *of yours* are rather empty/
meaningless."

> → **300** three cousins: *iste–ille–ipse,* 41.3.

desiderium tui, "my longing for you": *tui* is the personal pronoun "of you,"
not the adjective "yours" which would be *tuum*; how a person understands
tui becomes clear when asked to give its plural, which is *vestri* not *tuorum.*

> → **301** personal pronouns: function of-possession, 24.3; adj.: possessive,
>   24.3, 100.2.

pluris erit, "[conversation] will be of greater value": *pluris* is a gen. of
evaluation-price, literally, "[conversation] will be of greater value-price."

> → **302** gen. of indefinite price, 75.2.

rettuleris ... erit, "you will have brought ... back, there will be," the classic
Roman pair of times *retuleris* T.6i and *erit* T.3i. You will not hear this time
sequence at all in English if you say, "if you get yourself back fast, there will
be no talk."

> → **303** T.3i and T.6i paired: 7, Time 6, and GL nº 244, remark 2.

afueris ... permitesco, "you will have been absent ... I deeply fear": here the
time sequence is future, *afueris* in T.6i, but *permitesco* is T.1i because his fear
is already real.

> → **304** times-tenses of the indicative mode and their vernacular meaning, 7,
>   and you still have to think!

༄

Haec ego non rideo, quamvis tu rideas, sed de re severissima tecum, ut
soleo, iocor. Remoto ioco tibi hoc amicissimo animo praecipio, ut, si istic
mea commendatione tuam dignitatem obtinebis, perferas nostri desiderium, honestatem et facultates tuas augeas: sin autem ista frigebunt, recipias
te ad nos. Omnia tamen quae vis et tua virtute profecto et nostro summo
erga te studio consequere.   (*Fam.* VII, 11, 3)

I do not laugh at these things, although you are laughing, but as I am accustomed, I am joking with you about a very stern matter. Joking having been
left aside—I order you this thing with a most friendly spirit, that, if you will
hold on to your dignity up there [in Gaul] by my recommendation, you may
bear the longing for us, that you increase your nobility and your resources:
if however those there things will be cool, that you bring yourself back to us.
However you will attain all things which you wish both by your valor for
sure and by our greatest enthusiasm toward you.

Examples of Block I nouns with the dictionary entry and the reversed form of each might be presented in class, such as the following:

signa, from *signum*, *–i*, n., so here neuter plur.; its sing. is *signum*.
litteras, from *littera*, *–ae*, f., so here obj. plur.: its sing. is *litteram*.
militiam, from *militia*, *–ae*, f., so here obj. sing.; its plur. is *militias*.
nostrum Valerium, obj. sing. of *noster Valerius*; its plur.: *nostros Valerios*.
→ **305** Block I nouns, 2.1.

quamvis ... rideas, "although ... you are laughing": *quamvis* is one of many words that mean "although," used here with the subjunctive, T.1s, and sounding indicative in English.
→ **306** subjunctive use: concessive *quamvis* = "although," 64.

tecum, "with you": the preposition follows its own object as for about half a dozen others: *mecum*, *nobiscum*, *vobiscum*, *secum*, sometimes *quicum*.
→ **307** dict., *cum*, prep. with abl., II., D., a.

Remoto ioco, "Joking having been left aside—": AA, one of the more famous from antiquity.
→ **308** ablative absolute, 54–55.

tibi ... praecipio, "I order you": *praecipio* is one of the 65 verbs that take a dat. complement.
→ **309** 65 verbs with dat., 33.7.2, GL n° 346.

praecipio, ut ... perferas ... augeas ... recipias te, "I order ... that ... you bear ... that you increase ... that you bring yourself back": three purpose clauses depending on the verb *praecipio*.
→ **310** subjunctive use: purpose clause, 58.1.

nostri desiderium, "longing for us": *nostri* is the personal pronoun "of us," not the adjective "our" which would be *nostrum*; how a person understands *nostri* becomes clear when asked to give its reversed form, which is *mei* not *nostrorum*.
→ **311** personal pronouns: function of-possession, 24;
        adj.: possessive, 24.2; gen. of possession, 100.1.

consequere, "you will attain": variation of the deponent verb *consequor* in T.3i, *consequeris*, accented *consequére*. Given the other future verbs, *obtinebis ... frigebunt*, "you will hold on ... things will be cool" the future time is warranted here. Otherwise *conséquere* is a variation for T.1i *consequeris*, "you are attaining," or the deponent command form "attain!," neither of which fit the idea of the rest of the letter.
→ **312** verb: deponent, 29; commands: deponent, 34; variation: *–ris*, 39.3.

LETTER 8 T-P
AD ATTICUM I, 3

CICERO ATTICO SAL.

Aviam tuam scito desiderio tui mortuam esse et simul quod verita sit ne Latinae in officio non manerent et in montem Albanum hostias non adducerent. Eius rei consolationem ad te L. Saufeium missurum esse arbitror.   (*Att.* I, 3, 1)

CICERO A GREETING TO ATTICUS

You must know that your grandmother died out of longing for you and at the same time because she allegedly feared that the Latin [communities / festivals] would not abide in their duty and would not bring victims to Mons Albanus. I think that Lucius Saufeius is going to send to you a consolation of this fact.

CICERO ATTICO SAL.: *Cicero Attico salutem*

Aviam ... scito ... mortuam esse, "You must know that your grandmother died": the thought begins with the object form *Aviam*, which is in fact the subject of the antecedent dep. infinitive *mortuam esse*, meaning either "she has died" or "she died." In the middle of this OO is the M & M verb on which it depends, *scito*—here we go again, the action and challenge of the Latin language.

→ **313** M & M, 60, 71, GL n° 527, remarks 1–2; OO, 71–73;
verb: deponent, 29; verb: antecedent deponent infinitive, 72.3.

scito, "You must know": the second command, sometimes called the future command form, is used instead of the first or regular command form, *sci*, which the Romans did not like, although their comedians did.

→ **314** commands: first, second, 17.

scito ... verita sit ... manerent ... adducerent, "You must know ... she feared ... [that the Latin communities / festivals] would not persevere ... would not bring": Some students might be interested to know why or how Cicero begins with *scito*, in the future or present which produces *verita sit*, in T.3s and then *manerent* and *aducerent* in T.2s. The command form *scito* "You must know," in the present establishes the sequence of tenses on Track I, producing the antecedent action *verita sit* T.3s from the deponent verb *vereor*. Because *verita sit* is set in the historical past, it functions in itself like a verb in T.4b and sets its own clause on Track II, thus producing two verbs in T.2s, *manerent* and *adducerent*.

> → **315** commands: first, second, 17;
> *consecutio*, 47–48;
> *consecutio*: subjunctive depending on a subjunctive, 62.1.

quod verita sit, "because she feared": *verita sit* is T.3s from the dep. verb *vereor, vereri* 2, "to fear." The subjunctive is due either to modal attraction because of *mortuam esse*, "that [your grandmother] died," or preferably because Cicero is reporting the speech of another, in this case the grandmother, and so it would be fitting to say: "your grandmother died out of longing for you and … because *as she said* she was afraid.…"

> → **316** verb: deponent, 29; passive and deponent forms of T.3s, 44.3;
> subjunctive use: modal attraction, 83;
> causal: *quod*, "because, since," + subjunctive, reported reason, 59.2.

verita sit ne … non manerent, "she feared [that the Latin communities / festivals] would not abide": verbs of fearing are followed by *ne* meaning "that," or by *ut* meaning "that not" or as here by *ne … non* also meaning "that not."

> → **317** verbs of fearing with *ne*, 95.

Latinae, "the Latin [communities / festivals]": perhaps this is a reference to *Latinae civitates*, "the Latin cities," or to *Latinae feriae*, "the Latin festival days." Tyrrell and Purser dedicate half of a page to the consideration of the missing noun (see 1:140 and Shackleton Bailey 1:121, 287). Romulus and Remus are from Mons Albanus, and the Romans had an annual procession up the mountain, where they would sacrifice. Cicero reports that the grandmother said that she was afraid that the Latin communities / festivals would not bring sacrifices to the mountain and that this is what caused her to die.

Eius rei … arbitror, "I think … of this fact": the Latin sentence begins with the genitive *Eius rei* out front and ends with the main verb; the English sentence is just the opposite. We don't expect any English word order in the Latin text.

> → **318** sentence structure, 1.

L. Saufeium missurum esse, "that Lucius Saufeius is going to send": OO with the futurity infinitive *missurum esse*, depending on the M & M verb *arbitror*, "I think." The teacher may ask here for four other meanings of this sentence, and the student may answer: "Lucius Saufeius will send, will be sending, is about to send, is fixing to send." Then the teacher can ask how to say that he

"is sending"—answer *mittere*—and "has sent"—answer *misisse*—and you
have all the infinitives possible there.

> → **319** M & M, 60, 71, GL n° 527, remarks 1–2; OO, 71–73;
>   verb: deponent, 29; verb: subsequent active infinitive, 72.1.

ᕲ

Nos hic te ad mensem Ianuarium exspectamus ex quodam rumore an ex litteris tuis ad alios missis: nam ad me de eo nihil scripsisti. Signa quae nobis
curasti, ea sunt ad Caietam exposita. Nos ea non vidimus: neque enim exeundi Roma potestas nobis fuit: misimus qui pro vectura solveret. Te multum
amamus quod ea abs te diligenter parvoque curata sunt.   (*Att.* I, 3, 2)

Here we are expecting you by the month of January, according to a certain
rumor or according to those letters of yours sent to other people: for you
have written to me nothing about it [your return to Italy]. The statues which
you have procured for us, they have been unloaded at Gaieta [Formia]. We
have not seen them: for neither has there been for us a possibility of leaving
from Rome: we sent [someone] who would pay for the transport. We love
you very much that those statues were cared for by you diligently and for a
small price.

ad mensem Ianuarium, "by the January month," or "at the January month."

> → **320** about the Roman calendar, pp. 605–608;
>   GL Appendix, Roman Calendar, pp. 491–92.

ex quodam rumore an ex litteris, "according to a certain rumor or according
to … letters": here the preposition *ex* means "according to," not "out of"; this
is similar to the case where *ex lege* means "according to the law" although
it looks like it means "outside the law," and in fact the adj. *exlex* means
"lawless."

> → **321** prep. with abl., 28.4; dict., *ex*, prep. with abl., III., G.; dict., *exlex, egis*, adj.

Signa … ea, "The statues … they": *Signa* really does nothing in the sentence
but anticipate *ea*. If you wish to defend this redundancy, you could say in
English, "those statues," or in poor Latin and English you could say, "the
statues … they," but it really should not be repeated in either language.

> → **322** sentence structure, 1.

sunt … exposita.… curata sunt, "they have been unloaded.… [those statues]
were cared for": the word order of these verb forms of course does not
change the meaning.

> → **323** verb T.4b passive, 26; sentence structure, 1.

Nos ea, "We [have not seen] them": sentence structure begins with the subject and object, while the verb is down the line.

> → **324** sentence structure, 1.

exeundi ... potestas "a possibility of departing": *exeundi* is a gen. gerund.
→ **325** gerund, 77.1.

Roma, "from Rome": the name of a town in the abl. of separation with no
preposition prompted by the gerund *exeundi*, "of leaving." To see this, you
have to read the whole sentence.
→ **326** function: place from where, names of cities and small islands, *Roma*, 69.2.2;
gerund, 77.1.

misimus qui ... solveret, "we have sent [someone] who would pay": *qui* followed by T.2s subjunctive is a purpose clause depending on *misimus* in T.4b
establishing Track II. At first glance *misimus qui* may look like "we sent,
[we] who" but the verb *solveret*, "he would pay," does not permit this. The
antecedent of the *qui* is not expressed, nor is the object of *misimus*; what sat-
isfies both is an implied *eum*, "him, a man, someone," so the *qui ... solveret*
stands for *eum ut is ... solveret*, "someone so that he would pay," where the
eum is indefinite, meaning "a person, someone."
→ **327** subjunctive use: relative clause of purpose, 58.2.

quod ea ... curata sunt, "that those statues were cared for": a causal clause
where *quod* followed by the ind. verb *curata sunt* means that Cicero is not
reporting the speech of another, which would be *quod ea ... curata sint*,
meaning "that *as is said* those statues were cared for." Rather, Cicero is
stating his own idea, strengthening the contrast with the reported speech
earlier in the letter and demonstrating the two ways in which *quod, quia,
quoniam* are used in two ways, with the indicative to give one's own idea
and with the subjunctive to report the idea of another.
→ **328** causal: *quod*, "because, since," + indicative, one's own reason, 59.2;
causal: *quod*, "because, since," + subjunctive, reported reason, 59.2.

parvo, "for a small price": with mercantile terms this is the abl. of price.
→ **329** abl.: definite price, 75.

The personal endings of verbs and their times used are given and you can
reverse them for class exercise:

we: *exspectamus* T.1i, *vidimus* T.1i, *misimus* T.4b, *amamus* T.1i.
you*: *scripsisti* T.4a, *curasti*.
he/she/it: *fuit* T.4a, *solveret* T.2s; then give the "they" forms.
→ **330** personal endings of verbs, 1.

Quod ad me saepe scripsisti de nostro amico placando, feci et expertus sum
omnia, sed mirandum in modum est animo abalienato: quibus de suspicionibus, etsi audisse te arbitror, tamen ex me cum veneris cognosces. Sallustium praesentem restituere in eius veterem gratiam non potui. Hoc ad

te scripsi, quod is me accusare de te solebat: *at* in se expertus est illum esse minus exorabilem, meum studium nec *sibi nec* tibi defuisse. Tulliolam C. Pisoni L. F. Frugi despondimus.   (*Att.* I, 3, 3)

The fact that you have written to me often about calming our friend, I have done this and I have tried all things, but he is of an estranged attitude in an extraordinary way: about which suspicions, although I believe you have heard, still you will get to know from me when you will have come. I was not able to restore Sallustius in person into his old agreeableness. I have written this to you because he was accustomed to accuse me in reference to you: *but* he experienced in his own case that that man was less moveable by entreaty, my interest had not been lacking neither *to himself nor* to you. We have engaged Tulliola to Caius Piso, the Son of Lucius Frugi.

Quod ... scripsisti, "The fact that you have written": with this *quod* he starts a new subject, but it is also semi-independent from the main verb, *feci,* "I have done"; it just hangs a bit and it is mostly explanatory.
> → **331** *quod* = "the fact that" as a new subject, GL n° 525.2.

de nostro amico placando, "about calming our friend [Lucceius]": the gerundive *placando* is from *placo, placare* 1 "to calm down," not *placeo, placere* 2 "to be pleasing"; the expression is always susceptible to two interpretations, either as a gerundive, as above, or as an expression of passive necessity, "about our friend needing to be calmed down."
> → **332** dict., *placo, avi, atum,* 1, "to calm down, appease";
> dict., *placeo, cui* and *citus, citum,* 2, "to be pleasing";
> gerundive, 77.2; participle of passive necessity, 50, 51.1.4.

mirandum in modum, "in an extraordinary way," or "in a surprising way": consult your dictionary entry for *modum.*
> → **333** see: dict., *modum, i,* m. II., B., 2., *mirum in modum*;
> see: dict., *mirus, a, um,* adj. I. *mirum in modum.*

animo abalienato, "of an estranged attitude": taken here as an abl. of quality or description, literally, "with an estranged attitude," or an AA, "—his attitude having been alienated—."
> → **334** quality in abl., 96.2;
> ablative absolute, 54–55.

cum veneris cognosces, "you will get to know ... when you will have come": the Roman precision in defining future times more carefully, where *veneris* is T.6i and *cognosces* is T.3i.
> → **335** T.3i and T.6i paired: 7, Time 6, and GL n° 244, remark 2.

Sallustium restituere ... non potui, "I was not able to restore Sallustius": The sentence's beginning with the object form *Sallustium* might make one think that it is the subject of the infinitive that follows, *restituere,* but only with the final verb, *potui,* is it clear that *Sallustium* is the object of *restituere,* which is the object or complement of *potui.* Were the final verb one of M & M, such as *audivi,* "I heard," then *Sallustium restituere* would be in OO meaning "that Sallustius was restoring." You must read the entire sentence.

> → **336** sentence structure, 1; verb: complementary infinitive, 77;
> M & M, 60, 71, GL nº 527, remarks 1–2; OO, 71–73.

eius veterem gratiam, "his old agreeableness": the subject of the sentence is "I" from *non potui,* "I was not able," and the *eius* has to refer to someone other than the subject, so here it refers to "his."

> → **337** personal pronouns: function of-possession, 24.5.

quod . . . solebat, "because he was accustomed": causal clause giving one's own idea.

> → **338** subjunctive use: causal *qui, quae, quod* = "because, since," 59.4.

me accusare . . . solebat, "he was accustomed to accuse me": again the clause begins with the object form *me,* followed by an infinitive *accusare,* and only when you get to the finite verb *solebat* is it clear that *me* is the object of *accusare,* which is the object or complement of *solebat,* and that *me . . . accusare* is not OO meaning "that I accuse."

> → **339** verb: complementary infinitive, 77.

As a classroom experiment, the students might note that each verb ends in –*i* but their subjects are different:

scripsisti = you

feci = ego

potui = ego

scripsi = ego

Therefore, the –*i* tells me everything or nothing.

> → **340** personal endings of verbs, 1.

at in se expertus est illum . . . nec sibi nec tibi, "*but* he experienced in his own case . . . that man . . . neither *to himself nor* to you": the italicized text indicates difficulties with the manuscript, which are discussed by Tyrrell and Purser (see 1:141, 439). There is a special use of *in* with the abl. *in se,* meaning "in the case of himself" or "in his own case," as indicated in the dictionary. The *se* refers to the subject of *expertus est;* the *illum* refers to another person; the *sibi* refers again to the subject of *expertus est.*

> → **341** dict., *in,* prep. with abl. and acc., I., C.;
> personal pronoun: object form, 3;
> reflexive pron.: third person, 31; verb: deponent, 29.

expertus est illum esse, "he experienced . . . that that man was": the M & M verb *expertus est,* "he experienced" in T.4b produces two sentences in OO placed next to each other by asyndeton. The first is *illum esse* where the

object *illum* functions as the subject of the infinitive *esse*, "that man was."
Because *esse* is contemporaneous to *expertus est* in T.4b, it is rendered in
English as "was."

> → **342** M & M, 60, 71, GL n° 527, remarks 1–2; OO, 71–73;
>   asyndeton, GL n° 473, remark.

meum studium nec ... defuisse, "my interest had not been lacking": the
second sentence in OO depending on the M & M verb *expertus est*, "he experienced" in T.4b. The object form *studium* functions as the subject of the
antecedent inf. *defuisse*, "had not been lacking." Both statements in OO are
juxtaposed by asyndeton.

> → **343** M & M, 60, 71, GL n° 527, remarks 1–2; OO, 71–73;
>   asyndeton, GL n° 473, remark.

nec sibi ... defuisse, "[my interest] has not been lacking neither to himself":
the indirect reflexive pronoun *sibi* does not refer to the subject of the OO,
meum studium, "my interest," but to the subject of the controlling M & M
verb *expertus est*, "he experienced."

> → **344** reflexive pron.: third person, 31;
>   M & M, 60, 71, GL n° 527, remarks 1–2; OO, 71–73.

nec tibi defuisse, "has not been lacking to you": the combination of *expertus
est*, "he experienced" in T.4b with the antecedent infinitive *defuisse*, "had
been lacking," expresses the Latin preference for precise temporal rela-
tionships among verbs, more so than is often used in English, which again
shows the precision of Latin over English. The verb *defuisse* is on the border
between a compound verb and one of the 65.

> → **345** 65 verbs with dat., 33.7.2, GL n° 346;
>   dat. with compound verbs, 33.7.3, GL n° 347.

LETTER 164 T-P
AD FAMILIARES XIII, 60

M. CICERO C. MUNATIO C. F. S.

L. Livineius Trypho est omnino L. Reguli familiarissimi mei libertus: cuius calamitas etiam officiosiorem me facit in illum: nam benevolentior quam semper fui esse non possum. Sed ego libertum eius per se ipsum diligo: summa enim eius erga me offica exstiterunt iis nostris temporibus quibus facillime [bonam] benevolentiam hominum et fidem perspicere potui.   (*Fam.* XIII, 60, 1)

MARCUS CICERO GREETINGS TO
CAIUS MUNATIUS, SON OF CAIUS

Lucius Livineius Trypho is of course the freedman of my very close friend Lucius Regulus: whose tragedy makes me even more dutiful toward him: for I am not able to be more benevolent than I have always been. But I cherish his freedman on his own: for there existed his terrific kindnesses toward me at those our times in which I was able most easily to grasp the goodwill and trust of people.

M. CICERO C. MUNATIO C. F. S.: *Marcus Cicero Caio Munatio Caii filio salutem*

officiosiorem, "more dutiful": the comparative degree has several meanings, "more, rather, somewhat, quite dutiful."

→ **346** adj.: comp., 36.

benevolentior, "more benevolent": an irregular comparative degree. The basic or positive form is *benevolus, a, um*, but its comparative degree is not as you might expect, *benevolior*. Much better sounding is the irregular form *benevolentior*. Again, the superlative degree is not as you might expect, *benevolissimus, a, um*, but following the same irregular form it is *benevolentissimus, a, um*.

→ **347** adj.: peculiarities, GL n° 87, remark 4; dict., *benevolus, a, um*, adj., I.

benevolentior quam, "more benevolent than": *quam* with the comparative *benevolentior*.

> → **348** adj.: comp., 36; *quam* with the comp., 43.2.

fui esse non possum: it would be humorous to point out in class that taken by itself *fui esse non possum* means nothing in this world, because *fui* does not go with *esse non possum*. Here *fui* connects with *quam* and *esse* connects with *possum*. If you see that *quam semper fui*, "than I have always been," forms a box, then you can see the rest of the sentence around the box *benevelentior … esse non possum*, "more benevolent [than I have always been] I am not able to be."

> → **349** sentence structure, 1; relative clauses, 10–11; relative box, 11.4.

per se ipsum, "on his own": this is not a direct reflexive here, but an indirect reflexive referring to the logical subject of this clause, which is the *libertus*, "the freedman." The expression *seipsum* can be written as one word.

> → **350** reflexive pron.: third person, 31;
> dict., *ipse, a, um*, pron. demonstr., II., F., 2. "Ipse defines the subject of a reflexive pronoun."

summa … officia, "terrific kindnesses" or "supreme kindnesses": these two words naturally go together.

> → **351** sentence structure, 1.

summa, "terrific" or "top": the superlative degree of the normal or positive form of the adjective *superus, a, um* ; the comparative degree is *superior, ius*; another common superlative *supremus, a, um*. The English words "superior" and "supreme" come directly from these Latin forms.

> → **352** adj.: comp. and superl., 36; adj.: irregular comp. and superl., 36.5, GL nº 90.

iis nostris temporibus quibus, "at those our times in which" or "in those our circumstances in which": all ablatives of time at which or in which. If *quibus* is not seen as an abl. of time, but is taken to mean "by which" or "with which," this confusion will destroy the meaning.

> → **353** abl.: time at which, 70.1.

facillime, "most easily": the normal or positive form of the adjective is *facilis, e*, which is one of the famous 6 adjectives which form their superlative not with *–issimus, a, um*, but with *–llimus, a, um*; they are: *facilis, e; difficilis, e; similis, e; dissimilis, e; gracilis, e; humilis, e.*

> → **354** adj.: irregular comp. and superl., 36.5, GL nº 90.

benevolentiam … perspicere potui, "I was able … to grasp … goodwill": *benevolentiam* is the object of *perspicere*, which is the complement of the main verb, *potui*.

> → **355** sentence structure, 1; verb: complementary infinitive, 77.

Eum tibi ita commendo ut homines grati et memores bene meritos de se commendare debent. Pergratum mihi feceris, si ille intellexerit se, quod pro salute mea multa pericula adierit, saepe hieme summa navigarit, pro tua erga me benevolentia gratum etiam tibi fecisse.   (*Fam. XIII, 60, 2*)

I recommend him to you in such a way as people thankful and mindful ought to recommend people having merited well of themselves. You will have done me a great favor, if he will have understood that he has done a favor even for you according to your kindness toward me, because for my well-being he faced many dangers, he often sailed in the middle of winter.

> *ita commendo ut ... debent*, "I recommend him ... in such a way as ... [people] ought": upon seeing *ita ... ut ...* you might expect a result clause meaning "in such a way that as a result ... ," but the verb *debent* is T.1 indicative, so *ita ut* means "in such a way as"; here the *ut* indicates a simple comparison, not a result clause.
>
> → **356** correlative comparative sentences, 90.5, GL n° 642;
>   subjunctive use: pure result (consecutive), 67.1–2, GL n° 552.

> *bene meritos de se*, "people having merited well of themselves": the idiom is *meritos de aliquo*, "people having merited of someone [else]." The reflexive pronoun *se* follows the rule of a direct reflexive and refers to the subject of the verb *debent*, which is *homines*, "people." The English, unfortunately, has a problem with the reflexive because there are two different groups of people and it sounds like the second group of people have merited well of themselves, whereas the second group of people have merited well of the first group of people. Thus, the thankful and mindful people recommend other people who have merited well of the thankful and mindful people.
>
> → **357** dict., *mereo, ui, itum*, 2, and *mereor, itus*, 2 dep., II., D. *Mereri de aliquo*,
>   or *de aliqua*;
>   reflexive pron.: third person, 31.

> *feceris ... intellexerit*, "You will have done ... he will have understood": both T.6i to convey certainty and give greater closure than the combination of T.3i and T.6i as in *facies ... intellexerit*, "you will do ... he will have understood."
>
> → **358** T.6i and T.6i paired: GL n° 244, remark 4;
>   T.3i and T.6i paired: 7, Time 6, and GL n° 244, remark 2.

A teacher can point out that the personal endings of these verbs all look similar, but their times are deceptively different. The only way to clarity is to know the dictionary entry for each verb and the possibilities and then to use your intelligence:

feceris, "you will have done": T.6i of *facio, facere, feci, factum 3*.

intellexerit, "he will have understood": T.6i of *intellego, intellegere, intellexi, intellectum 3*.

adierit, "he faced": T.3s of *adeo, adire, adivi, aditum 4*.

navigarit, "He … sailed": a contraction of *navigaverit*, T.3s of *navigo, navigare, navigavi, navigatum*.

The top two are T.6i and so have a future completed time, but the bottom two are T.3s and have a completely past time.

> → **359** verb meaning T.6, 7; verb meaning T.6, 8.2;
> forms of the subjunctive, T.3s, 44.3;
> times-tenses of the indicative mode and their vernacular meaning, 7;
> contractions: verbs, 39.2, GL n° 131.

se … fecisse, "that he has done": OO depending on the M & M verb *intellexerit*, "he will have understood." The acc. subject is separated from its infinitive verb by many words.

> → **360** M & M, 60, 71, GL n° 527, remarks 1–2;
> OO, 71–73; sentence structure, 1.

quod … adierit, … navigarit, "because he faced … he often sailed": both causal clauses are in the subjunctive by modal attraction, not to indicate the quoted opinion of another; the two clauses are juxtaposed by asyndeton, a Greek term referring to the lack of a connective word such as "and" or "but," which we do with equal ease, effect, rhythm in English.

> → **361** subjunctive use: modal attraction, 83; asyndeton, GL n° 473, remark;
> causal: *quod*, "because, since," + indicative, one's own reason, 59.2;
> causal: *quod*, "because, since," + subjunctive, reported reason, 59.2.

pro salute mea … , pro tua … benevolentia, "according to your kindness … for my well-being": two different meanings of *pro*, "on behalf of; for" and "according to; in keeping with"; if you mix these up and say "for your benevolence," it makes no sense here; that is why *pro* is among the richest prepositions in the Latin language.

> → **362** prep. with abl., 28.4.

hieme summa, "in the middle of winter": the abl. of time at which or in which does not mean "the highest winter"; rather it means "in the *height* of winter," "at *the high point* of winter," or we might way "in the dead of winter."

> → **363** abl.: time at which, 70.1.

Note the difference between this *summa* and the *summa … officia*, "terrific kindnesses," in the previous sentence. Vocabulary is important: check your dictionary.

> → **364** dict., *superus, a, um*, adj., III., sup., C. *summus, a, um*, 2. Trop., b. "best, most distinguished" which we might call "terrific" in English, and with *hiems*, "the depth of winter."

LETTER 7 T-P
AD ATTICUM I, 11

CICERO ATTICO SAL.

Et mea sponte faciebam antea et post duabus epistulis tuis perdiligenter in eamdem rationem scriptis magno opere sum commotus. Eo accedebat hortator adsiduus Sallustius ut agerem quam diligentissime cum Lucceio de vestra vetere gratia reconcilianda. Sed, cum omnia fecissem, non modo eam voluntatem eius quae fuerat erga te recuperare non potui, verum ne causam quidem elicere immutatae voluntatis. Tametsi iactat ille quidem illud suum arbitrium et ea quae iam tum cum aderas offendere eius animum intellegebam, tamen habet quiddam profecto quod magis in animo eius insederit, quod neque epistulae tuae neque nostra *ad*legatio tam potest facile delere quam tu praesens non modo oratione sed tuo vultu illo familiari tolles, si modo tanti putaris, id quod, si me audies et si humanitati tuae constare voles, certe putabis. Ac ne illud mirere cur, cum ego antea significarim tibi per litteras me sperare illum in nostra potestate fore, nunc idem videar diffidere, incredibile est quanto mihi videatur illius voluntas obstinatior et in hac iracundia obfirmatior: sed haec aut sanabuntur cum veneris aut ei molesta erunt in utro culpa erit.   (*Att.* I, 11, 1)

CICERO A GREETING TO ATTICUS

Both beforehand I was acting on my own accord and afterward I was very much disturbed—two of your letters having been written very carefully in the same vein. Sallustius was coming besides as a continual instigator for this purpose that I might deal most carefully with Lucceius about patching up your old favor. But, after I had done all things, I was not only not able to recover that goodwill of his which had existed toward you, but not even to elicit a reason of his unchanged attitude. Although he is indeed talking up that judgment of his [in court] and those things which I was understanding were hurting his feelings already then when you were present, nevertheless he has indeed a certain something which has settled more in his spirit, which neither your letters nor our mission is able to eliminate so easily as you in person will take away not only with your talk but with that familiar face of yours, if only you will have thought it of such great value, something which you certainly will think, if you will be listening to me and if you will want to be consistent with your own humaneness. But lest you be surprised about this, why, although I made it clear to you before by letter that I was hoping that he would be in our control, now I seem to be doubting this, it is unbelievable how much more stubborn his disposition seems to me and more resolute in this anger: but these things either will be healed over when you will have come or they will be displeasing to him in whomever of the two the fault will reside.

CICERO ATTICO SAL.: *Cicero Attico salutem*

Et ... et, "Both ... and": Note the special meaning.
> → **365** conjunction: *et ... , et ... ,* 3.2.

antea ... post, "beforehand ... afterward": the temptation is to take *post duabus epistulis* to mean "after two letters," but *post* takes the object form, not the abl., so here it is an adv. meaning "afterward."
> → **366** dict., *post,* I. adv., B. "afterwards," II. prep. with acc., *behind;*
>   prep. with obj., 6.

duabus epistulis tuis ... scriptis, "—two of your letters having been written ...": taken here as an AA, but it is impossible to know whether this is preferably an instrumental abl. going with *post ... sum commotus,* "afterward I was disturbed by two of your letters having been written."
> → **367** ablative absolute, 54–55; abl.: instrument, 28.5.3–4, 89.2.

magno opere, "very much": looks like it means "with a great work" but the dictionary says it is often written as one word *magnopere,* "greatly," as it was in the manuscript in part I. In fact it serves as the adverb of *magnus, a, um,* "great," because the adverb *magne* does not exist; the adverb's comparative form is *magis,* "to a greater extent, more so, more," and its superlative form is *maxime,* "mostly, especially, in the first place."
> → **368** dict., *magnopere,* I. adv. *magnus-opus,* "with great labor; greatly";
>   adv.: irregular comp. and superl., 37.3, GL n° 93.

Eo, "for this purpose": this form has numberless meanings: "I go," "to there," "by that means" and with a comparative such as *eo celerius,* "by that much more quickly" or "so much more quickly."
> → **369** dict., *is, ea, id,* pron. demonstr., I., C., 2., (θ) *Eo,* adverbially with the comp.;
>   dict., *eo, ivi or ii, ire, itum,* "to go."

accedebat, "[Sallustius] was coming besides": in the dictionary with the idea of increase, "was being added"; here perhaps "besides, over and above."
> → **370** dict., *accedo, cessi, cessum,* 3., II., B., 2. With the accessory idea of increase, "to be added."

ut agerem, "that I might deal": a purpose clause depending on *accedebat* in T.2i, establishing Track II. The nature of most purpose clauses already suggests future meaning, and the expression of the future is contained in the regular subjunctive without the futurity formula. Thus, *agerem* in T.2s already has futurity meaning, as in "he was an instigator so that *some day* I might deal."

→ **371** subjunctive use: purpose clause, 58.1; *consecutio*, 47–48;
    consecutio: futurity in the subjunctive, 61.1;
    consecutio: futurity formula in the subjunctive, 61.3.

de vestra vetere gratia reconcilianda, "about patching up your old favor": taken as a gerundive, but its meaning is clearer if written in the following way, as St. Thomas Aquinas might have preferred, *de vestram veterem gratiam reconciliando* where the abl. complement of *de* is now the gerund *reconciliando*, and its object in turn is *vestram veterem gratiam*, with the same meaning. Of course it may also be taken as a participle of passive necessity meaning "about your old favor needing to be patched up."

→ **372** prep. with abl., 28.4; gerundive, 77.2;
    gerund, 77.1; participle of passive necessity, 50, 51.1.4.

non modo ... non potui, "I was not only not able";

non modo oratione, "not only with your talk";

si modo ... putaris, "if only you will have thought": three instances in this one section where *modo* is not the abl. of *modus, i*, m. which would be *mŏdō*, with a long final *ō*. Here, rather, it is an adv. *mŏdŏ* with two short *ŏ*'s meaning "only, just now." Each have their own entries in the dictionary.

→ **373** dict., *mŏdŏ* and *modus, i*, m.

verum, "but": could mean "truly," but the dictionary also gives "but" or "however"; *verum* is always placed first in the sentence.

→ **374** dict., *verus, a, um*, adj., II., adv., A. *verum*, 2., a. In gen., "but."

ne causam quidem elicere, "not even to elicit a reason": *ne* goes with *quidem*, and together they mean "not even"; they emphasize the word between them, *causam*, as in "not even a reason"; *causam* is in turn the object of *elicere*; if you begin translating with the first word, you might mistake *ne* as beginning a negative purpose clause, "in order that not," but it lacks a subjunctive verb.

→ **375** sentence structure, 1; dict., *quidem*, adv., I., C., 1. *ne ... quidem*, "not even."

immutatae, "unchanged": taken here as the adj. *immutatus, a, um*, "unchanged" from *in-mutatus*. It may also be taken as an antecedent participle from the verb *immuto, are, avi, atum*, 1, "to change" meaning more fully "having been changed." Beware Latin traps, tricks too!, something which we can say in clear and concise unambiguous Latin: *Laqueos cavetote Latinos dolosque!*

→ **376** dict., *immutatus, a, um*, adj.; *immuto, avi, atum*, 1;
     Block I adj., 4.2–3; antecedent participle, 50, 51.1.2.

The structure, glory, architecture of Latin in the fourth sentence is revealed in the following "boxes" arranged in lines to help visualize them; the main verb is underlined, connective words and their verbs are underlined with dots, the subject and verb of the one OO is underlined with a wavy line:

{ Tametsi iactat ille quidem illud suum arbitrium et ea	concessive
[quae iam tum	rel. 1 in OO
(cum aderas)	temporal clause
offendere eius animum	rel. 1 in OO continued
intellegebam,] }	M & M verb producing OO
tamen habet quiddam profecto	main sentence
[quod magis in animo eius insederit,]	characteristic result
{ [quod neque epistulae tuae neque nostra *ad*legatio	rel. 2
tam potest facile delere	
(quam tu praesens non modo oratione	correlative
sed tuo vultu illo familiari tolles,)]	
[si modo tanti putaris,]	factual cond. 1
[id quod,	rel. 3
(si me audies)	factual cond. 2
(et si humanitati tuae constare voles,)	factual cond. 3
certe putabis.] }	rel. 3 concluded

→ **377** structure of Latin sentences, 103 p. 587, *Ossa* Readings: 1-D, 1-I,
     3-D, 3-I, 4-D, 4-I;
     relative box, 11.4.

Maybe Atticus would have had to read Cicero's sentence a few times to catch all of these clauses. Here we are making it easier for you and him.

Tametsi iactat, "Although he is ... talking up": a concessive sentence where *tametsi* means "although," and its ending *–si*, "if," indicates a conditional; thus it follows the rules of the conditionals; here it is followed by the indicative, T.1i *iactat*.

→ **378** conditionals: factual, 86.1.

Tametsi ... tamen, "Although ... nevertheless": these words coordinate with one another.

→ **379** GL n° 604, remark 3.

iactat ... illud suum arbitrium et ea quae, "he is talking up that judgment of his [in court] and those things which": *iactat* has two objects. The first is *arbitrium*, "judgment," and the second is *ea*, "those things," the antecedent of *quae*, "which."

> → **380** function: object, 1.3, 2.2, 2.4, 2.6; conjunction: *et*, 3.2.

arbitrium et ea, "judgment ... and those things": sentence structure, the *et* joins the two objects of *iactat*. This may seem simple, but the tendency is to think that the *et* joins *iactat*, "he is ... talking up," with *intellegebam*, "I was understanding." However, *intellegebam* belongs in the relative sentence *quae ... intellegebam*, "which I was understanding."

> → **381** sentence structure, 1; conjunction: *et*, 3.2.

ea quae ... offendere eius animum intellegebam, "those things which I was understanding were hurting his feelings": the M & M verb *intellegebam*, "I was understanding," produces a sentence in OO where the subject is the acc. relative pronoun *quae*, "which [things]," whose verb is the contemporaneous inf. *offendere*, rendered as "were offending" because it is contemporaneous to *intellegebam* in T.2i. This is why we do not call *offendere* a present infinitive, but a contemporaneous one. In turn, the object of *offendere* is *animum*, "feelings," given in the plural in English. It is easy to think that *quae* is the object of *intellegebam*, but then an account must be given for *offendere*.

> → **382** M & M, 60, 71, GL n° 527, remarks 1–2; OO, 71–73;
> rel. pron.: subject or object, 10.

cum aderas, "when you were present": *cum*, "when," followed by *aderas*, "you were present," in T.2i expresses mere coincidence of time, not a circumstantial cause, which would be expressed in the subjunctive such as *adesses*, almost meaning "because you were present."

> → **383** *cum* + historical times of indicative = "when": temporal coincidence,
> 66.3.1.

habet quiddam ... quod ... insederit, "he has a certain something which has settled": the main verb *habet*, "he has," is T.1i and establishes Track I. The *quiddam*, "a certain something" prepares for the characteristic result where *quod*, followed by *insederit* in T.3s, substitutes for *tale ut id insederit*, "[some certain something] such that it has settled," and the English sounds indicative, as the equivalent of T.4a.

> → **384** *consecutio*, 47–48; subjunctive use: characteristic result, 68.2.

habet quiddam ... quod ... potest, "he has a certain something which ... [neither letters nor mission] is able": the second *quod*, followed by *potest* "which is able," in T.1i, is a simple relative clause expressing a declaration.

> → **385** rel. pron.: subject or object, 10; rel. pron. + ind.: review, 42.2, 79.2.

tam ... facile ... quam, "so easily as": *tam* and *quam* are correlatives, "so much ... as much," so here *quam* means "as," not "than."

> → **386** correlative comparative sentences, 90.5, GL n° 642.

tolles, si ... putaris, "you ... will take away ... , if ... you will have thought":
putaris will drive people crazy who think it is T.1i passive, but it is a contraction for *putaveris*, "you will have thought," in T.6i, and corresponds with *tolles*, "you will take away," in T.3i, as Romans are wont to do. Here, *si ... putaris*, "if you will have thought," is an example of a factual condition in T.6i.

→ **387** conditionals: factual, 86.1; contractions: verbs, 39.2, GL n° 131;
T.3i and T.6i paired: 7, Time 6, and GL n° 244, remark 2.

tanti putaris, "you will have thought it of such great value": *tanti* is a gen. of evaluation or value, also meaning "of such great importance," "of so great value."

→ **388** gen. of indefinite price, 75.2.

id quod, "something which": referring to the entire previous thought.

→ **389** dict., *is, ea, id*, pron. demonstr. I., D. "Sometimes placed before the relative *quod*."

si ... audies et si ... voles, "if you will be listening ... and if you will want":
two logical conditionals in T.3i, coordinating with *putabis*, "you will think," also in T.3i.

→ **390** conditionals: factual, 86.1.

Verbs in T.3i demonstrate both systems for future time:

tolles, "you will take away": from *tollo, tollere, sustuli, sublatum*, 3, where *–e–* is the sign of T.3i.
audies, "you will be listening": from *audio, ire, ivi* or *ii, itum*, 4, where *–e–* is the sign of T.3i.
voles, "you will want": from *volo, velle, volui*, an irregular verb of group 3 where *–e–* is the sign of T.3i.
putabis, "you will think": from *puto, are, avi, atum*, 1, where *–bi–* is the sign of T.3i.
Thus, the importance of knowing exactly a verb's dictionary entry and thus to which group a verb belongs.

→ **391** verb formation T.3 in groups I and II, 12.3.1;
verb formation T.3 in groups III and IV, 12.3.2.

The fifth sentence may be arranged according to the following similar box pattern:

Ac   main sentence
   { <u>ne</u> illud <u>mirere</u>   negative purpose clause
     [<u>cur</u>,   IQ
       (<u>cum</u> ego antea <u>significarim</u> tibi per litteras   concessive
          <u>me</u> <u>sperare</u>   OO 1
          <u>illum</u> in nostra potestate <u>fore</u>),   OO 2
       nunc idem <u>videar</u> <u>diffidere</u>] },   IQ continued

incredibile <u>est</u>   main sentence continued
    [<u>quanto</u> mihi <u>videatur</u> illius   IQ 3
       voluntas obstinatior
      et in hac iracundia obfirmatior]:
<u>sed</u> haec aut <u>sanabuntur</u>   main sentence continued
    [<u>cum veneris</u>]   temporal
<u>aut</u> ei molesta <u>erunt</u>   main sentence continued
    [in <u>utro</u> culpa <u>erit</u>].   indefinite relative

→ **392** structure of Latin sentences, 103 p. 587, *Ossa* Readings: 1-D, 1-I, 3-D, 3-I,
    4-D, 4-I

If we map the verb forms of this one sentence on a calendar, with the present moment occurring sometime in the month of May, we end up with something like the following magnificent construction:

February	May	June	July	December
	mirere			
significarim				
sperare				
	fore —————————————————————→			
	videar			
	incredibile est			
	videatur			
			sanabuntur	
		veneris		
			erunt	
			erit	

→ **393** calendars, 83 pp. 514–15, 103 pp. 586.

The times of this calendar are all pure logic and it makes perfect sense for someone thinking and analyzing and reasoning, something which Atticus was doing with his Latin brain naturally!

The verbs are presented in the above calendar from top to bottom in the order in which they appear in the sentence. In the following description, the verbs are presented in the order in which they produce further expressions, thus in the order of their dependency or subordination.

The sequence of tenses functions perfectly in this sentence. The main verb, *incredibile est*, "it is unbelievable," in T.1i sets the sentence on Track I, which produces *ne … mirere*, "lest you be surprised," in T.1s, which produces in turn *cur … videar*, "why … I seem," also in T.1s, which produces *cum … significarim*, "although I made it clear," in T.3s and so on Track I. But, because *significarim*, in T.3s, is set in the historical past, it functions like a T.4b and narrates the rest of the sentence from this moment in the past. This is why the OO *me sperare* with the infinitive *sperare* contemporaneous with *significarim*, is set in the past, "that I was hoping," and depending on *spe-*

rare, is the OO *illum … fore* with the futurity infinitive *fore* which indicates a time subsequent to a point in the past, "he would be," as indicated by the arrows in the above diagram. All this looks/sounds like nonsense, but for any experienced Latinist is absolutely natural and essential and delightful.

> → **394** *consecutio*, 47–48;
> *consecutio*: subjunctive depending on a subjunctive, 62.1;
> OO, 71–73; futurity participle, 50, 51.1.3;
> *futurum esse* (*fore*), 72.1;
> futurity formula, active, 53.3.

ne … mirere, "lest you be surprised": Cicero's favorite variation for *mireris*, T.1s from *miror, ari, atus*, 1 dep.

> → **395** variation: *–ris*, 39.3.

cur … videar, "why … I seem": IQ in T.1i depending on the verb of M & M *mirere*, "you be surprised," in T.1s, thus establishing Track I.

> → **396** M & M, 60, 71, GL n° 527, remarks 1–2;
> IQ, 60; *consecutio*, 47–48.

cur … nunc idem videar diffidere, "why … now I seem to be doubting this": the personal use of *videar*, "I seem," according to the preference of the Romans, whereas other languages use the impersonal followed by OO, as in *me videtur diffidere*, "it seems that I am doubting." Instead, *videar* is used personally, and its subject is the nom. subject of the infinitive *diffidere*, "I seem to doubt."

> → **397** personal construction: *videor*, 73.3, GL n° 528.1 and remark 2 and note 1;
> nom. with the inf., 73.3, GL n° 528.1;
> M & M, 60, 71, GL n° 527, remarks 1–2; OO, 71–73.

cum … significarim, "although I made it clear": a concessive clause meaning "although," while the causal is also possible here meaning "because." *significarim* is a contraction for *significaverim*, "I made it clear," in T.3s; note that with only one letter different *significarem* is T.2s. To see the difference one letter can make, we might say here, "You must be awake, if you are not awake!," *Vigiles oportet si non vigilas*! Now we can say further, *vigiles oportet vigilent si non vigilant*!, "police officers have to be awake, if they are not awake!"

> → **398** subjunctive use: concessive *cum* = "although," 64;
> subjunctive use: causal *cum* = "because, since," 59.1;
> contractions: verbs, 39.2, GL n° 131; forms of the subjunctive, T.2s, 44.2;
> forms of the subjunctive, T.3s, 44.3.

Depending on the IQ *cur videar*, "why I seem," in T.1s continuing Track I, this concessive clause expresses antecedent action in *significarim*, "I made it clear," in T.3s, here the equivalent of T.4b.

> → **399** *consecutio*: subjunctive depending on a subjunctive, 62.1; IQ, 60.

significarim ... me sperare illum ... fore, "I made it clear ... that I was hoping that he would be": the M & M verb *significarim*, "I made it clear," the equivalent of T.4b, produces OO where *me* is the acc. subject of the inf. *sperare*, contemporaneous with *significarim*, thus meaning "I made it clear that [at that time] I was hoping." In turn *sperare* is an M & M verb producing OO, where *illum* is the acc. subject of the inf. *fore*, an alternative form for the futurity inf. *futurum esse*, "to be about to be," rendered in English here as "would be." Some people may confuse the English here, "would be," with some sort of a subjunctive; it is, rather, an expression of futurity looking from some time in the past, as is evident by the other meanings possible here: "to be about to be," "going to be." The time frame for this last OO is futurity from the time in the past established by *significarim*, "I made it clear," in T.3s.

→ **400** M & M, 60, 71, GL n° 527, remarks 1–2; OO, 71–73;
    futurity participle, 50, 51.1.3;
    futurum esse (*fore*), 72.1; futurity formula, active, 53.3.

quanto ... obstinatior et ... obfirmatior, "how much more stubborn ... and more resolute": with the comparative degree *obstinatior*, "more stubborn," *quanto* is an abl. of degree, literally, "by how much [more ...]" but in English you cannot hear the abl. "by." Again, the comparative degree *obfirmatior* corresponds to *quanto*, "by how much ... more resolute."

→ **401** abl.: measure, 90.3, GL n° 403; adj.: comp., 36.

sanabuntur cum veneris, "[these things] will be healed over when you will have come": *sanabuntur*, "[things] will be healed over" is T.3i and corresponds with *veneris*, "you will have come" in T.6i in a temporal sentence describing a completed action in futurity.

→ **402** T.3i and T.6i paired: 7, Time 6, and GL n° 244, remark 2.

in utro, "in whomever of the two": as a pronoun *uter* is a question, "which of the two," but as an indefinite pronoun *in utro* means "in whichever of the two," or here referring to people, "in whomever of the two," as the dictionary tells you.

→ **403** dict., 3. *uter, utra, utrum*, pron., I. interrogatively; II. Transf., A. Indef. rel.

❧

Quod in epistula tua scriptum erat, me iam arbitrari designatum esse, scito nihil tam exercitum esse nunc Romae quam candidatos omnibus iniquitatibus, nec quando futura sint comitia sciri. Verum haec audies de Philadelpho.   (*Att.* I, 11, 2)

That which had been written in your letter, that I was already thinking [that some person] had been designated, you must know that nothing has been so well worked over now in Rome as political candidates by all evil doings, nor that it is known when the elections are going to be. But you will hear these things from Philadelphus.

Quod ... scriptum erat, me ... arbitrari, "That which had been written ... , that I was thinking": the antecedent of *Quod*, "That which," is the entire statement produced by the M & M verb *scriptum erat*, "[which] had been written," in T.5i pass., namely the OO statement *me ... arbitrari*, "that I was thinking," where *me* in the object form is the subject of the deponent inf. *arbitrari*, describing contemporaneous action.

> → **404** rel. pron.: subject or object, 10;
> rel. pron.: omission of the antecedent, 11.2;
> M & M, 60, 71, GL n° 527, remarks 1–2; OO, 71–73;
> verb: deponent, 29; verb: contemporaneous deponent infinitive, 72.3.

me ... arbitrari designatum esse, "that I was already thinking [that some person] had been designated": the M & M verb *arbitrari*, "[I] was thinking," produces a statement in OO whose subject appears to be missing, as suggested by Tyrrell. The antecedent and pass. inf. *designatum esse* describes an action previous to *arbitrari*, "I was thinking," which in turn is contemporaneous with *scriptum erat*, "[which] had been written," in T.5i.

> → **405** M & M, 60, 71, GL n° 527, remarks 1–2; OO, 71–73;
> verb: contemporaneous deponent infinitive, 72.3;
> verb: antecedent passive infinitive, 72.3.

scito nihil ... exercitum esse, "you must know that nothing has been ... worked over": the main verb of the sentence *scito*, "you must know," the second command form, is a verb of M & M producing two statements in OO. In the first, *nihil* is the indeclinable subject of the inf. *exercitum esse*, "nothing has been worked over." According to the dictionary *nihil* almost means "nobody," as we might say in English, "Nothing is more beautiful than these children," where it might be better to say, "Nobody is more beautiful than these children," as here "you must know that *nobody* has been so well worked over now in Rome as political candidates."

Note that *exercitum esse*, "[nothing] has been worked over," is the equivalent of T.4a touching on the present moment contained in the verb *scito*, "you must know," whereas *designatum esse*, "[some person] had been designated," describes an action that occurred before *scriptum erat*, "[which] had been written," in T.5i. Also, *arbitrari*, "I was thinking," is the equivalent of T.2i because it is contemporaneous with *scriptum erat*, "[which] had been written."

> → **406** commands: first, second, 17;
> M & M, 60, 71, GL n° 527, remarks 1–2; OO, 71–73.

scito ... nec quando futura sint comitia sciri, "you must know ... nor that it is known when the elections are going to be": the M & M verb *scito*, "you must know," produces a second statement in OO, where the verb is the passive inf. *sciri*, "it is [not] known," used impersonally here. As a verb of M & M, *sciri,* "it is [not] known," produces an IQ *quando futura sint comitia,* "when the elections are going to be," and the whole IQ serves as the subject of the passive inf. *sciri.* While T.1s contains futurity, here futurity is explicit with the addition of *futura,* "about to be."

> → **407** M & M, 60, 71, GL nº 527, remarks 1–2; OO, 71–73; IQ, 60;
> passive verb used impersonally, GL nº 208;
> impersonal gerund, GL nº 528.2;
> *consecutio:* futurity formula in the subjunctive, 61.3.

tam ... quam ... , "so well ... as ...": correlatives also meaning "so much ... as much...."

> → **408** correlative comparative sentences, 90.5, GL nº 642.

Romae, "in Rome": the original form of place where used to be *Romai,* where the final *–i* was the sign of the locative. But it sounded like and so became *Romae,* which people sadly have confused with the gen.

> → **409** function: place at which, names of cities and small islands, singular,
> *Romae,* 69.3.2.

omnibus iniquitatibus, "by all evil doings": the abl. of instrument.

> → **410** abl.: instrument, 28.5.3–4, 89.2, GL nº 401.

Verum, "But": this form always begins the sentence. It could also mean "truly," but here it means "but" or "however." The form *vero* is placed later in the sentence and also means "truly" or "but" or "however."

> → **411** dict., *verus, a, um,* adj., II., adv., A. *verum,* 2., a. In gen., "but";
> dict., *verus, a, um,* adj., II., adv., B. *vero,* "truly," 2. "but" (always placed
> after a word).

☙

Tu velim quae Academiae nostrae parasti quam primum mittas. Mire quam illius loci non modo usus sed etiam cogitatio delectat. Libros vero tuos cave cuiquam tradas. Nobis eos, quem ad modum scribis, conserva. Summum me eorum studium tenet, sicut odium iam ceterarum rerum: quas tu incredibile est quam brevi tempore quanto deteriores offensurus sis quam reliquisti.   (*Att.* I, 11, 3)

I would like you to send as soon as possible the things [statues] which you have prepared for our Academy. How wonderfully not only the employment of that place but even the thought is a delight. However beware lest you hand over your books to anyone. Keep them for us, as you write. The keenest interest in them binds me tight, just as already the hatred of other things: which it is unbelievable in how short a time how much worse you will discover than you left them.

Tu velim ... mittas, "I would like you to send": a common expression of Cicero is *velim,* "I would like," in T.1s followed by the subjunctive without *ut* to express strong desire. The first word *Tu*, "you," is the subject of the last word in the sentence, *mittas*, "[you] to send." Cicero's sentence begins with *Tu*, "you," and he placed that at the beginning of his expression, as it was first in his thought, but it took the whole sentence to complete the entire idea with its verb.

> → **412** subjunctive use: purpose clause without *ut*, 58, GL nᵒ 546, remark 2; commands: other expressions, *velim*, 85.1.7.

quae ... parasti ... mittas, "you to send ... the things [statues] which you have prepared": the object of *mittas*, "you to send" is *ea*, "the things [statues]" implied in the relative pronoun *quae*, "which," placed at the front of the sentence, well in front of its verb. Once again we see the explicitly omitted antecedent of the relative pronoun.

> → **413** rel. pron.: subject or object, 10; rel. pron.: omission of the antecedent, 11.2.

quam primum, "as soon as possible": this is the special meaning of *quam* followed by the superlative.

> → **414** *quam* with the superlative, 43.3.

Mire quam, "How wonderfully": an exclamation meaning directly, "wonderfully how much."

> → **415** dict., *mirus, a, um*, adj., I. ... *mirum quam*, or *quantum*, "it is wonderful how," "how much."

Libros vero tuos, "However ... your books": note the word order in Latin. Between *Libros* and *tuos*, "your books" is *vero*, "but" or "however." There is an up-down sing-song quality of the word order.

> → **416** dict., *verus, a, um*, adj., II., adv., B. *vero*, "truly," 2. "but" (always placed after a word).

cave ... tradas, "beware lest you hand over": *cave*, "beware," is a verb of preventing that can be used with *ne*, "that not," which is normally omitted. For example, we can say, *cave cadas*, "beware lest you fall," "watch your step."

> → **417** negative commands: other expressions, 85.2.7 to which we should add the following.

The verb *cavere*, "to be aware," "to be on watch," is used naturally with *ne*, where *cave ne credas*, means "be careful that you not believe." However, Latin literature and Cicero above shows us that with *cavere* the Romans preferred to leave out the *ne* because it was felt so strongly in the verb itself for example: *cave istud umquam dicas*, "be careful that you not say that ever."

Nobis eos ... conserva, "Keep them for us": these words that go together in English are separated and placed at opposite ends of the sentence, showing that English word order does not help understand the Latin word order.

> → **418** sentence structure, 1.

quem ad modum, "as": the word order *ad quem modum* can help you to see
the meaning "according to what manner." It may also be written as one
word *quemadmodum,* as in the manuscript, albeit with line-end hyphen-
ation. This term is not used with the subjunctive here because the expression is not an IQ.

→ **419** dict., *quemadmodum,* adv., I. Interrog., II. Rel.

eorum ... ceterarum rerum, "in them ... of other things": these genitives do
not express possession. Rather *ceterarum rerum* functions as a gen. object
of *odium,* "hatred of other things" or "hatred toward other things," and
eorum functions as the gen. object of *studium,* "interest of them" rendered
in English as "interest in them." This type of gen. is technically called the
"objective gen."

→ **420** objective genitive, 24.1, GL n° 364, note 2.

*quas tu incredibile est quam brevi tempore quanto deteriores offensurus
sis,* "which it is unbelievable in how short a time how much worse you will
discover": the expression *incredibile est,* "it is unbelievable," functions here
as a verb of M & M producing a double IQ, the first introduced by *quam,*
"how," the second by *quanto,* "how much," both followed by the one verb
offensurus sis, where *sis* is in T.1s and accompanied by *offensurus,* "[you]
about to discover" or "you are going to find," an expression of futurity in the
subjunctive rendered in English in the ind. as "you will discover"; its object
is the rel. placed out front, *quas,* "which" or "which things."

→ **421** M & M, 60, 71, GL n° 527, remarks 1–2; IQ, 60;
     consecutio: futurity formula in the subjunctive, 61.3;
     rel. pron.: subject or object, 10.

quas tu, "which ... you": Cicero places the rel. object of *offensurus sis* at the
beginning of the sentence and then immediately turns his mind to *tu,* "you,"
the subject of the same *offensurus sis,* "which things you will discover."

→ **422** sentence structure, 1.

quas ... quanto deteriores, "which how much worse": here *quanto* is the
degree of difference meaning "by how much [more worse]," and *deteriores*
agrees with *quas,* "which things ... more worse."

→ **423** abl.: measure, 90.3, GL n° 403; adj.: comp., 36.

quam brevi tempore ... deteriores ... quam reliquisti, "how short a time ...
much worse ... than you left them": two different uses of *quam.* The first
begins an indirect question where *quam brevi tempore* means "in how
brief a time," and the second accompanies the comparative *deteriores ...
quam,* "worse than," and gives a comparison, *quam reliquisti,* "than you left
[them]." The expression *brevi tempore* is in the abl. to designate time within

which, not "at which" or "for which," and the expression *quam brevi tempo-re* means "in how brief a time" or "within how brief a time."

> → **424** *quam* with the comp., 43.2; adj.: comp., 36;
> IQ, 60; abl.: time within which, 70.3.

The Latin is gorgeous how he writes, inspiring us to say:

Mirandam prorsus Tullius hic molitur Latinitatis struem.
"Here Tullius is constructing a marvelous heap of Latinity."

LETTER 410 T-P
AD FAMILIARES XIV, 8

TULLIUS TERENTIAE SUAE S.

Si vales bene est, ego valeo. Valetudinem tuam velim cures diligentissime. Nam mihi et scriptum et nuntiatum et te in febrim subito incidisse. Quod celeriter me fecisti de Caesaris litteris certiorem, fecisti mihi gratum. Item posthac, si quid opus erit, si quid acciderit novi, facies ut sciam. Cura ut valeas. Vale. D. IIII. Nonas Iun.   (*Fam.* XIV, 8)

TULLIUS A GREETING TO HIS TERENTIA

If you are well it is fine, I am well. I would like that you care for your health most carefully. For it has been both written and reported to me that you suddenly fell into a fever. That you informed me quickly about Caesar's letter, you did me a favor. Likewise in the future, if anything will be necessary, if anything of news will have happened, you will see to it that I know. Take care that you be in good health. Goodbye. Sent on the fourth day before the June Nones [2 June.]

TULLIUS TERENTIAE SUAE S.: *Tullius Terentiae suae salutem*

velim cures, "I would like that you care": a favorite expression of Cicero, *velim*, "I would like," in T.1s, without the *ut*, "that," followed by *cures*, "that you take care," in T.1s.

> → **425** subjunctive use: purpose clause without *ut*, 58, GL n° 546, remark 2; commands: other expressions, *velim*, 85.1.7.

diligentissime, "most carefully": the superlative of the adv. *diligenter*, "attentively," whose comparative is *diligentius*, "more diligently" or "rather carefully."

> → **426** adv.: positive, comp., superl., 37.

et scriptum et nuntiatum et, "it has been both written and reported": the Oxford edition has *nuntiatum est*, which is used in our translation.

→ **427** Oxford edition, *Fam.* XIV, 8.

te ... incidisse, "that you ... fell": this entire statement in OO serves as the subject of the two verbs in the neuter, *et scriptum et nuntiatum est*, "it has been both written and reported [to me]," in T.4a passive. The subject is in the object form *te* and the inf. *incidisse*, "that you fell," is antecedent to both *scriptum est* and *nuntiatum est*, and so the equivalent of T.4b. With no change to the Latin, the sentence could also mean, "it was both written and reported to me that you suddenly had fallen into a fever," in times 4b passive and T.5i respectively.

→ **428** OO, 71–73.

quod ... me fecisti ... certiorem, "that you informed me": this causal clause employs an idiom, *me fecisti certiorem*, which does not mean "you made me more certain," but "you informed me."

→ **429** dict., *certus, a, um*, adj., II., B., 2. ... *certiorem facere aliquem*, "to inform one of a thing."

celeriter, "quickly": this is the positive adv. whose comparative is *celerius* "more speedily" or "somewhat quickly" or "too quickly" and superlative is *celerrime*, "most quickly" or "very speedily"; the superlative form is not *celerissime*. This is like some other adjectives ending in *–er* such as *asper*.

→ **430** adv.: irregular comp. and superl., 37.3.

fecisti mihi gratum, "you did me a favor": this is the usual translation of what looks like "you did something pleasing to me."

→ **431** dict., *gratus, a, um*, adj., I., A. See last few example sentences, "you ... will do us all a favor."

si quid opus erit, "if anything will be necessary": the expression *opus erit* means "there will be need," not, "it will be work," where *opus* is the subject of *est*.

→ **432** dict., *opus, eris*, n. III., A. *opus est*, "there is need," (β) with abl., (γ) with gen., (δ) with acc.; *opus est*, 75.3.

si quid opus erit si quid ... novi, "if anything ... necessary ... if anything of news": after the conditional *si*, the indefinite *aliquid*, "anything," is short-ened to *quid*, "something." The form *novi* may look like the verb "I know," but here it is the partitive gen., meaning "of new," and it is separated from the *quid*, "something," on which it depends.

→ **433** pronouns: indefinite, 42.4; after *si* the *ali*-s fly away, 42.5; gen. of part, 99.

facies ut sciam, "you will see to it that I know": the verb *facies*, "you will see to it" in T.3i is used very often in the Bible to indicate a light command, or

as Tyrrell says a "polite future." Here *facies*, "you will see to it," produces the
clause *ut sciam*, "that I know," where *sciam* is in T.1s, but as a result clause it
is rendered in English in the ind., "I know."

→ **434** commands: T.3i, 85.1.6;
　　　 subjunctive use: complementary result (consecutive), 68.1.

D. IIII. Nonas Iun., "Sent on the fourth day before the June Nones": the full
formula is [*epistula*] *Data IIII Nonas Iunias* where *epistula*, "the letter," is
implied; *D.* is the abbreviation for *Data*, from which we get the English
word "[calendar] date." The June Nones are 5 June, so counting back four
days inclusive results in 2 June because both 2 June and 5 June are counted
among the four days.

→ **435** about the Roman calendar, pp. 605–608;
　　　 GL appendix: Roman Calendar, pp. 491–92.

LETTER 411 T-P
AD ATTICUM XI, 3

CICERO ATTICO SAL.

Quid hic agatur scire poteris ex eo qui litteras attulit: quem diutius tenui, quia cotidie aliquid novi exspectabamus, neque nunc mittendi tamen ulla causa fuit praeter eam de qua tibi rescribi voluisti, quod ad Kal. Quinct. pertinet quid vellem. Utrumque grave est, et tam gravi tempore periculum tantae pecuniae et dubio rerum exitu ista quam scribis abruptio. Qua re, ut alia, sic hoc vel maxime tuae *curae* benevolentiaeque permitto et illius consilio et voluntati, cui miserae consuluissem melius, si tecum olim coram potius quam per litteras de salute nostra fortunisque deliberavissem.   (*Att.* XI, 3, 1)

CICERO A GREETING TO ATTICUS

What is being done around here you will be able to know from him who has brought the letter: whom I have held back for a longer time, because we were daily waiting for something of news. Nor however was there any motive of sending [a letter] right now besides the one about which you wanted an answer to be sent back to you, what I wanted, as far as the July Kalends [1 July] is concerned. Each matter is serious, both the risk of so much money [dowry for daughter] at such a critical time and that breaking off of negotiations [for the divorce] which you write about—the outcome of things being doubtful. For which reason I entrust this, as other things, even in the greatest degree to your care and benevolence and to her suggestion and wish, for which miserable woman [daughter Tulliola] I would have provided in a better way, if I would have deliberated about our well-being and fortunes with you a long time ago face to face rather than by letter.

Cicero Attico sal.: *Cicero Attico salutem*

Note the different verbal forms ending in *–i* with essentially different meanings:

tenui, "I have held back": T.4b.

mittendi, "of sending": of-possession gerund, literally, "of sending."

rescribi, "an answer to be sent back": passive infinitive literally, "to be written back."

The forms to-for-from reveal many patterns:

curae, "to … care": Bk. I nouns ending in *a, ae*.

benevolentiae, "to … benevolence": Bk. I nouns ending in *a, ae*.

consilio, "to … suggestion": Bk. I nouns ending in *um, i*.

voluntati, "to … wish": Bk. II nouns with a crazy form and *is*.

cui, "for which": relative pronoun.

miserae, "for … miserable woman": Bk. I adj. ending in *us, a, um*.

But note:

gravi, "at … a critical [time]": this may be the form to-for-from, but here it is the form by-with-from-in and agrees with *tempore* the abl. of time at which, in which, when; see comments below.

→ **436** abl.: time at which, 70.1.

quid … agatur, "What is being done": IQ depending on the M & M verb *scire*, "to know."

→ **437** M & M, 60, 71, GL n° 527, remarks 1–2; IQ, 60.

diutius, "for a longer time": comparative adv., whose positive is *diu* and superlative *diutissime*.

→ **438** adj.: comp. and superl., 36.

novi, "of news": partitive gen.; from the noun *novum, i*, n. "news," or even from the adjective *novus, a, um*, meaning "of a new thing," but not the verb meaning "I knew." Reversing this form reveals much about how it is understood; its reverse is *novorum*, not *novimus* nor *novus*.

→ **439** gen. of part, 99; Block I nouns, 2.1;
         Block I adj., 4.2–3; adj.: used as nouns, 5.2.

rescribi, "an answer to be sent back": the meaning of this verb includes the idea of "replying in writing"; here it is used impersonally, "it to be answered; it to be written back," and its subject is the IQ at the end of the sentence, *quid vellem*, "what I wanted [to be written back]." The verb *rescribi* is an expression of M & M giving rise to the IQ, *quid vellem*, which functions as the subject of *rescribi*.

→ **440** M & M, 60, 71, GL n° 527, remarks 1–2;
         IQ, 60; verb: contemporaneous passive infinitive, 72.3.

quod ad … pertinet, "as far as [July 1st] is concerned": *quod pertinet ad* is
one of three synonymous expressions, *quod attinet ad, quod spectat ad*,
meaning variously "what pertains to; what looks to; as far as pertains; as
what concerns."

→ **441** dict., *pertineo, ui,* 2., II., B., 2.… *quod ad aliquem (aliquid) pertinet.*

Kal. Quinct., "the July Kalends [1 July]": the Kalendae is the first day of
the month, and the month of *Quintilis* was later renamed July after Julius
Caesar, just as *Sextilis* turned out to be August after Augustus Caesar. Nero
wanted to name *Aprilis* after himself as *Neroneus*, but the plan was canceled.
The numbering of these months indicates that the first month was March,
therefore December is the tenth month, after *decem* for "ten."

→ **442** about the Roman calendar, pp. 605–608;
GL Appendix, Roman Calendar, pp. 491–92.

quid vellem, "what I wanted": an IQ in T.2s. The controlling verb is *voluisti* in T.4b, which sets the sequence on Track II. The Track II sequence is
continued through *rescribi*, a contemporaneous infinitive. Here *rescribi*
functions as a verb of M & M, which gives rise to this IQ in T.2s.

→ **443** M & M, 60, 71, GL nº 527, remarks 1–2;
IQ, 60; *consecutio*, 47–48.

Utrumque grave … gravi tempore, "each matter [is] serious … at … a critical
time": the adj. is *gravis, e*; many people are aware that *gravi* is the dat., but
they immediately assume that *grave* is the abl., but here it is the neuter subject in the singular and goes with *Utrumque*; this is one of 80% of all Bk. II
adjectives whose singular abl. ends in *–i*, here *gravi*, and it goes with *tempore*, which is one of 80% of all Bk. II nouns whose abl. ends in *–e*; the different
endings cause difficulties and total misunderstanding and nonsense in one
not seeing these connections.

→ **444** abl.: meaning and forms, 27;
dat.: meaning and forms, 33; Block II adj. in three ways, 18.

dubio rerum exitu, "—the outcome of things being doubtful": AA where the
participle "being" is only implied but felt. Scholastic, Medieval Latinists will
develop a form for that participle *ente*, which did not exist for Cicero.

→ **445** ablative absolute, 54–55.

vel, "even": *vel* here does not mean "or"—a common trap for sleepy readers!

→ **446** dict., *vel*, conj., II. intensive particle.

maxime, "to the greatest degree": adv. in superlative degree meaning also
"most especially"; its comparative degree is *magis*, "more; more so; to a
greater extent"; and the positive is *magnopere* or *magno opere*, "to a great
degree."

→ **447** adv.: positive, comp., superl., 37.

que, "and": style, –*que* joins closely related words such as *curae benevolen-tiaeque*, "to your care and benevolence," and another set of words joined by –*que*, namely, *salute nostra fortunisque*, "our well-being and fortunes."

→ **448** conjunction: –*que*, 3.2.

illius … cui miserae, "her … which miserable woman": *illius* can be mascu-line, feminine, or neuter, meaning "of him/her/it," just as can *cui*, "to him/her/it"; the feminine gender is indicated only with the adj. *miserae*, which agrees with *cui*, whose antecedent *illius* is also feminine. If the teacher asks the student what the plural of *illius* is, the student's understanding will be revealed; if they don't say *illarum*, then they don't understand it.

→ **449** three cousins: *iste–ille–ipse*, 41.3;
pronoun forms to-for-from, 33.3–5.

consuluissem … , si … deliberavissem, "I would have provided … , if I would have deliberated": contrary to fact conditional set in the past; you can confirm this by adding: "I would have provided, but I did not … , if I would have deliberated, but I did not."

→ **450** conditionals: contrary to fact, 86.3.

❧

Quod negas praecipuum mihi ullum *in communibus* incommodis impende-re, etsi ista res *non* nihil habet consolationis, tamen etiam praecipua multa sunt quae tu profecto vides et gravissima esse et me facillime vitare potuisse: ea tamen erunt minora, si, *ut* adhuc factum est, administratione, diligentia tua levabuntur.   (*Att.* XI, 3, 2)

The fact that you deny that anything special is threatening me in common disasters, even though that fact has something of consolation, nevertheless even the special things are many which you for sure see both are very se-rious and I was able to avoid most easily: however they will be lesser, if, as has happened so far, they will be alleviated by your administration, your diligence.

quod negas, "The fact that you deny": he starts a new subject with this *quod* followed by the indicative, which is also semi-independent from the main verb, *sunt*, "[things] are"; it just hangs a bit and it is almost explanatory.

→ **451** *quod* = "the fact that" as a new subject, GL n° 525.2.

mihi … impendere, "is threatening me": the prefix of the compound verb *in-pendere* can be restored as a preposition to get, *pendere in me*, "is hanging over me," where *in* takes the object. The problem is that you cannot hear the dat. in English. The accent here is *impendére*, "to hang over," "to threaten," whereas a different verb whose accent is *impéndĕre* means "to weigh out," "to expend." You will find both verbs in your dictionary.

> → **452** dat. with compound verbs, 33.7.3, GL n° 347.

non nihil ... consolationis, "something of consolation": the double negative "not nothing of consolation" indicates "a certain amount of consolation"; *consolationis* is a partitive gen. The Romans preferred to separate these words by one or more words, as here where *nihil* and *consolationis* are separated by one word.

> → **453** gen. of part, 99.

quae ... vides, "which you ... see": a simple relative clause with T.1i.

> → **454** rel. pron.: subject or object, 10.

et ... et, "both ... and": joining two infinitives, one contemporaneous *esse*, "[which] are," and one antecedent *potuisse*, "[I] was able."

> → **455** conjunction: *et ... , et ...* , 3.2; verb: contemporaneous active infinitive, 72.1; verb: antecedent active infinitive, 72.1.

gravissima, "very serious": adj. in the superlative degree of the positive *gravis, e*, the comparative form is *gravior, ius*.

> → **456** adj.: comp. and superl., 36.

me ... vitare potuisse, "I was able to avoid": OO depending on M & M verb *vides*, "you ... see"; *vitare* is a complement of *potuisse* in that it completes the action of the verb.

> → **457** M & M, 60, 71, GL n° 527, remarks 1–2; OO, 71–73; verb: complementary infinitive, 77.

facillime, "most easily": adv. in the superlative degree of the positive in four forms: *facile, facul, faculter*, and *faciliter*, the comparative is *facilius*.

> → **458** adj.: irregular comp. and superl., 36.5, GL n° 90.

minora, "lesser": an irregular comparative from the adj. *parvus, a, um*, with the superlative *minimus, a, um*.

> → **459** adj.: irregular comp. and superl., 36.5, GL n° 90.

ut ... factum est, "as has happened": with the indicative, here *ut* means "as."

> → **460** dict., *ut*, I., B. meaning "as."

❧

Pecunia apud Egnatium est; sit a me, ut est. Neque enim hoc quod agitur videtur diuturnum esse posse, ut scire iam possim quid maxime opus sit: etsi egeo rebus omnibus, quod is quoque in angustiis est quicum sumus; quoi magnam dedimus pecuniam mutuam opinantes nobis constitutis rebus eam rem etiam honori fore. Tu, ut antea fecisti, velim, si qui erunt ad quos aliquid scribendum a me existimes, ipse conficias. Tuis salutem dic. Cura ut valeas. In primis id quod scribis omnibus rebus cura et provide ne quid ei desit de qua scis me miserrimum esse. Idibus Iuniis ex castris.   (*Att.* XI, 3, 3)

The money is with Egnatius; let it be on my part as it is. For this business which is being carried out does not seem to be able to be long lasting, so that already I am able to know what is most especially necessary: although I am in need of all things, because he is also in tight straits with whom we are living; to whom we gave a lot of money on loan considering that thing would be also for an honor to us—once things have been organized. As you did before, I would like that you conclude the business if there will be people to whom you think something must be written from me. Say a greeting to your family. Take care that you be well. First of all that which you write, take care with all resources and make sure that nothing be lacking to her [Tullia] about whom you know I am most miserable. On the June Ides [13 June] from the camp.

> *sit a me*, "let it be on my part": the dictionary says that the preposition *a* joins a verb and adjective with the specific meaning "with regard to, in respect to, on the part of." Tyrrell suggests that the meaning here is something like "let it stay there as far as I am concerned," but admits that the expression sounds strange and points to the suggestion that the text may be corrupt here.
>
> → **461** dict., *ab, a, abs*, prep. with abl., II., B., 2., k.

> *ut scire iam possim*, "so that already I am able to know": the expression *esse posse*, "to be able to be," gives rise to this expression. The distinction between a result and a purpose clause is very thin here, as always, almost depending on how you read or pronounce the sentence. We have taken *ut scire iam possim* to be a result clause meaning, "so that already I am able to know." Another way we could translate this expression as a purpose clause would be: "this business … does not seem to be able to be long lasting so that already I may be able to get to know now what is most especially necessary."
>
> → **462** subjunctive use: purpose clause, 58.1;
>   subjunctive use: pure result (consecutive), 67.1–2, GL n° 552.

> *quid … opus sit*, "what is … necessary": IQ in T.1s depending on the M & M verb *scire*, "to know."
>
> → **463** M & M, 60, 71, GL n° 527, remarks 1–2; IQ, 60.

> *maxime*, "most especially": adv. in superlative degree meaning also "to the greatest extent" as above in this letter. The positive is *magnopere*, the comparative, *magis*.
>
> → **464** adv.: irregular comp. and superl., 37.3, GL n° 93.

etsi egeo rebus omnibus, "although I am in need of all things": *etsi*, "although," begins a conditional sentence here, which, because of the *–si* follows the rules for conditionals. The verb *egeo*, literally, "I am in need of," in T.1i indicates a factual condition. The verb *egeo* is sometimes put with the famous 5 verbs, *utor, fruor, fungor, potior, vescor,* and some other verbs which take an abl. complement, here *rebus omnibus*, meaning "I am in need of all things." The verb *egeo* can also be used with the gen., meaning "to be in need of something."

> → **465** conditionals: factual, 86.1; dict., *egeo, ui,* 2;
> famous five verbs with the ablative, 78.1.

is … quicum sumus, "he … with whom we are living": Cicero prefers *quicum* where we would expect and prefer *quocum*. Many people may not know the old abl. *quī*. The preposition *cum*, "with," follows the rel. *quocum* or here *quīcum*, "with whom [we are living]."

> → **466** dict., *quī*, adv. interrog., rel. and indef. (old abl. of 1. *qui*);
> abl. in pronouns and relatives, 28.1–2.

quoi, "to whom": this is an older spelling for *cui*, "to whom."

> → **467** dict., *qui, quae, quod*, pron. (old forms: I. dat. *quoi*);
> dict., *cum*, prep. with abl., II., D., a.… *quocum (quīcum)*.

opinantes nobis … eam rem etiam honori fore, "considering that thing would be also for an honor to us": the independent verb *dedimus*, "we gave," is in T.4b, establishing Track II. Agreeing with *nos*, "we," the implied subject of *dedimus*, "we gave," the contemporaneous participle *opinantes*, "considering," is a verb of M & M producing OO on Track II, where *eam rem* is the subject in the object form and its infinitive verb is *fore*, a substitute for the futurity expression *futuram esse*, agreeing with its subject, *rem*, "that thing would be." As a form of *sum, esse*, "to be," *fore* takes the double dative, here the dat. of the person affected *nobis*, "to us," and the dat. of the goal *honori*, "for an honor."

> → **468** M & M, 60, 71, GL nº 527, remarks 1–2;
> OO, 71–73; *consecutio*, 47–48;
> futurity participle, 50, 51.1.3; *futurum esse (fore)*, 72.1;
> futurity formula, active, 53.3; double dat., 91.2.

constitutis rebus, "once things have been organized": an AA, whose time frame is logically futurity completed because its action is antecedent to that of the futurity infinitive *fore*, "[that thing] would be—after things will have been organized."

If you follow the word order without regard for the whole sentence, then you may see *nobis constitutis rebus* and think that they somehow go together. Only when you get to *honori fore*, can you see the double dative and then discern that *constitutis rebus*, "once things have been organized," is in the abl. as an AA set into the middle of the datives *nobis … honori*, "for an honor to us." After everything is said and done, you still have to think it out because on first reading the function of *constitutis* is not clear until you get to the end of the sentence.

→ **469** ablative absolute, 54–55; double dat., 91.2; sentence structure, 1.

Tu ... velim ... ipse conficias, "I would like that you conclude [the business]": the first word *Tu*, "You," is the subject of the last word *conficias*, "that you conclude." Cicero's thought began and ended with reference to Atticus. Cicero frequently uses *velim*, "I would like," in T.1s followed by the subjunctive without *ut*, here *conficias*, "that you conclude."

→ **470** subjunctive use: purpose clause without *ut*, 58, GL n° 546, remark 2; commands: other expressions, *velim*, 85.1.7.

ut antea fecisti, "As you did before": here *ut* is followed by *fecisti*, "you did," in T.4b, and so means "as."

→ **471** dict., *ut*, I., B. meaning "as."

si qui erunt, "if there will be people": the *qui* here is not the relative pronoun and so does not mean *who*. Rather, following *si*, "if," here *qui* stands for *aliqui*, "some people," and so the whole expression means fully, "if there will be some people."

→ **472** pronouns: indefinite, 42.4; after *si* the *ali*-s fly away, 42.5.

ad quos ... existimes, "to whom you think": the presence of *existimes*, "you think," in T.1s indicates that *ad quos* does not begin a simple relative clause, but is rather a result clause where *ad quos* stands for *tales ut ad eos*, "such that to them." While true, this simple explanation gives the impression that the verb going with *ad quos* is *existimes*, whereas it depends on *scribendum*, as we explain below.

→ **473** subjunctive use: characteristic result, 68.2.

ad quos aliquid scribendum a me existimes, "[if there will be people] to whom you think something must be written from me": the M & M verb *existimes*, "you think," in T.1s, produces OO where the subject in the object form is *aliquid*, "something," and the inf. verb of passive necessity whose full implied form is *scribendum esse*, "something must be written." We render the expression *a me*, as "from me," giving an abl. of source or separation. However, it could also be taken as one of the rarer usages of agency with the passive necessity formula, where most grammarians would demand *mihi*, "by me." Depending on the OO is the prepositional phrase with the relative *ad quos*, "to whom." Thus, a fuller way of expressing this would be: "if there will be some people such that to them you think something must be written from me."

→ **474** M & M, 60, 71, GL n° 527, remarks 1–2; OO, 71–73; participle of passive necessity, 50, 51.1.4; passive necessity formula, 53.4; abl.: personal agent, 28.5.3–4, 89.2; prep. with obj., 6; rel. pron.: subject or object, 10; *qui, quae, quod* and *quis, quid*: indefinite, 79.1.

dic, "Say": one of several imperative forms that have dropped the final *–e*.

→ **475** commands: famous four, 39.4.

cura ut valeas, "take care that you be well": *ut valeas* is a purpose clause, and so rendered in English in the subjunctive, "that you may be in good health." Contrast this with the use of *ut* above to mean "as," in the expression *ut antea fecisti*, "As you did before."

→ **476** subjunctive use: purpose clause, 58.1; dict., *ut*, I., B. meaning "as."

provide ne quid ei desit, "make sure that nothing be lacking to her [Tullia]": a negative purpose clause where *ne* negates the whole clause and combines with *quid*, short for *aliquid*, "something," so also so expressed here as "that not anything."

→ **477** subjunctive use: purpose clause, 58.1;
pronouns: indefinite, 42.4; after *si* the *ali*-s fly away, 42.5.

de qua scis me miserrimum esse, "about whom you know I am most miserable": the verb of M & M *scis*, "you know," in T.1i produces OO where the subject in the object form is *me*, and the contemporaneous inf. *esse*, meaning "me to be," "that I am" or simply "I am." The antecedent of *de qua*, "about whom," is *ei*, "to her [Tullia]," and in its own clause, the *de qua* does not go with *scis*, as if to mean, "about whom you know," but rather with *miserrimum esse*, to mean "about whom I am most miserable." This is one of about twenty adjectives ending in *–er*, where the superlative is not, for example, *miserissimus* but *miserrimum*.

→ **478** M & M, 60, 71, GL n° 527, remarks 1–2;
OO, 71–73; verb: contemporaneous active infinitive, 72.1;
adj.: irregular comp. and superl., 36.5, GL n° 90.

Idibus Iuniis, "On the June Ides [13 June]": the abl. of time at which.

→ **479** abl.: time at which, 70.1.

LETTER 424 T-P
AD FAMILIARES XIV, 16

TULLIUS TERENTIAE SUAE S. D.

S. V. B. E. V. Etsi eius modi tempora nostra sunt ut nihil habeam quod aut a te litterarum exspectem aut ipse ad te scribam, tamen nescio quo modo et ipse vestras litteras exspecto et scribo ad vos cum habeo qui ferat. Volumnia debuit in te officiosior esse quam fuit et id ipsum quod fecit potuit diligentius facere et cautius. Quamquam alia sunt quae magis curemus magisque doleamus: quae me ita conficiunt ut ii voluerunt qui me de mea sententia detruserunt. Cura ut valeas. Pridie Non. Ian.   (*Fam.* XIV, 16)

TULLIUS SAYS A GREETING
TO HIS TERENTIA

If you are well, it is fine, I am well. Although our circumstances are of such a nature that I have no bit of a letter which either I am expecting from you or I myself should write to you, nevertheless in some way or another both I myself am waiting for your letter and I write to you whenever I have someone who may carry [it]. Volumnia was supposed to be more courteous toward you than she was and was able to do more carefully and prudently that very thing which she did. And yet there are other matters which we should care about more and grieve over more: which are so eating me up as those people wanted who pushed me off from my intention. Take care that you be well. On the day before the January Nones [4 January].

TULLIUS TERENTIAE SUAE S. D.: *Tullius Terentiae suae salutem dicit*

S. V. B. E. V., "If you are well, it is fine, I am well": in our letter 14 (*Fam.* XIV, 8; T-P 410) Cicero says: *Si vales bene est, ego valeo* which suggests the meaning here.

eius modi, "of such a nature": *is, ea, id* means "he, she, it," and from there we have *eius*, meaning "his, her, its," and besides that *is, ea, id* also means "this, that, such"; the expression *eius modi tempora nostra* means variously, "our times are of such a nature, of such a kind, of such a sort, of that type, of this type, of his type, of her type, of its type"; sometimes written as one word *eiusmodi*, as given in the dictionary.

→ **480** dict., *is, ea, id*, pron. demonstr., III. such, of such a sort.

eius modi ... ut habeam, "of such a nature ... that I have": *ut habeam* is a result clause in T.1s because of *eius modi*, "of such a type that as a result I have," sounding indicative in English.

→ **481** subjunctive use: pure result (consecutive), 67.1–2, GL n° 552.

nihil habeam quod aut a te litterarum exspectem aut ipse ad te scribam, "I have no bit of a letter which either I am expecting from you or I myself should write to you": the *Adnotatio Critica* of Tyrrell and Purser, other commentaries, and manuscripts say that the *quod* should really be *quid*, an indefinite pronoun meaning "anything" and going with *litterarum*, "anything of a letter." If that were the case, then the *quod* would seem to be doing double duty here not only as the indefinite pronoun *quid* meaning "anything," but also as a relative *quod* giving rise to a characteristic result.

→ **482** Tyrrell and Purser, *Adnotatio Critica*, Ep. 424, 4:596.

Nevertheless, this reckoning by Tyrrell-Purser and others does not explain the *nihil* at the beginning of the clause, which is a substantive, a noun. We would prefer that *nihil* join with *litterarum* as the object of *exspectem* and *scribam*. Thus, *nihil ... litterarum* means either "nothing of a letter," "no bit of a letter," "no part of a letter," "no trace of a letter."

→ **483** gen. of part, 99.

The relative *quod* is the direct object of the two verbs of characteristic result, *exspectem* and *scribam*, both in T.1s. Here *quod* stands for *tale ut illud*, "of such a nature that [either I am expecting] it...." As clauses of characteristic result, they would both sound indicative in English, unless there is an underlying subjunctive. Thus, *scribam*, "[which] I am writing" is rendered here in the indicative, but *exspectem*, "[which] I should expect [from you]" is rendered in the subjunctive because of the underlying idea.

→ **484** subjunctive use: characteristic result, 68.2;
      subjunctive use: underlying potential of the present or future, 94.3,
      GL n° 257.

nescio quo modo, "in some way or another": *nescio* is not functioning as a verb here and does not mean "I don't know in what way." Rather it functions as an indefinite pronoun meaning "in some-I-do-not-know way," "in some way or another I-do-not-know." The expression indicates uncertainty with regard to something specific in the clause but does not have an effect on the rest of the sentence as a verb would, which would produce an IQ in the subjunctive. It is one thing to say *nescio quo modo fecerit*, with an IQ in T.3s meaning "I do not know in what way she/he/it did it," and *nescio quo modo fecit*, in T.4b, "he/she/it did it in some way or another I don't know." The dictionary specifies the combination *nescio quomodo* meaning "I know not how" and confirms this usage with several references to classical authors including our Cicero. GL also confirm this in two short sentences at n° 467, remark 1, and the following note says that *nescio quomodo* means "I know not how = strangely." Some editions will put the two words together as *nescioquis* or here as *nescioquo* followed by *modo* as another word. Here it is followed by the ind. *exspecto* and *scribo* because the expression is not an IQ.

> → **485** dict., *nescio, ivi* or *ii, itum*, 4., I., (γ);
>   GL n° 467, remark 1 and note;
>   *nescio quis*, GL n° 467, remark 1 and note; IQ, 60.

litteras, "a letter": the plural in Latin can have singular or plural meaning in English referring to one epistle or multiple epistles.

> → **486** dict., *littera, ae*, f., II., A. Sing., B. Usually plur.

cum habeo, "whenever I have": *cum* with the indicative as a temporal clause.

> → **487** *cum* + indicative = "when": temporal sentences, 66.3.

qui ferat, "who may carry [it]": the T.1s *ferat* indicates that this is a characteristic result clause which stands for *eum talem ut ferat*, normally sounding indicative in English but here sounding potential and so subjunctive, "[whenever I have] someone such who may bring it."

> → **488** subjunctive use: characteristic result, 68.2;
>   subjunctive use: underlying potential of the present or future, 94.3,
>   GL n° 257.

Volumnia … officiosior, "Volumnia … more courteous": as a comparative *officiosior* can be masculine or feminine, here obviously with *Volumnia* it is feminine, although it looks masculine

> → **489** adj.: comp., 36.

Quamquam, "And yet": many will initially take this *Quamquam* to mean "even if" or "although" or "granted that" as a subordinate concessive clause. But here it begins a sentence in the indicative, which we take according to the second usage in the dictionary "as a rhetor[ical] particle of transition, in objections made by the speaker himself," meaning "and still," "and yet," because it is a transition starting a new sentence.

> → **490** dict., *quamquam*, conj., II.

alia sunt quae … curemus … doleamus, "there are other matters which we should care about … grieve over": two verbs in T.1s *curemus … doleamus* indicate this is a characteristic result clause which stands for *talia ut ea … curemus … doleamus*, "there are other things such that we do care about … grieve over them," rendered in the ind. or to be honest by the natural subjunctive "should" which is felt underlying this statement.

> → **491** subjunctive use: characteristic result, 68.2;
>   subjunctive use: underlying potential of the present or future, 94.3,
>   GL n° 257.

quae magis curemus magisque doleamus: quae me ita conficiunt, "which we should care about more and grieve over more: which are so eating me up": the first relative *quae,* "which," is followed by *curemus ... doleamus,* "we should care about ... and grieve over," both in T.1s. and sounding subjunctive in English, as explained in the previous entry. The second relative *quae,* "which," is followed by *conficiunt,* "[which] are ... eating me up," in T.1i and sounding ind. in English. The difference in mentality between these two modes of speaking is significant. Both subjunctive verbs leave room for thought and speculation about how we should care and grieve, whereas the indicative *conficiunt* leaves very little room for speculation with its concrete fact that "they are killing me!"

> → **492** subjunctive use: characteristic result, 68.2;
>   times-tenses of the indicative mode and their vernacular meaning, 7.

quae me ita conficiunt, "which are eating me up": a simple relative pronoun with T.1i immediately following after these two characteristic result clauses on the same topic *alia,* "other matters."

> → **493** rel. pron.: subject or object, 10;
>   times-tenses of the indicative mode and their vernacular meaning, 7.

qui ... detruserunt, "who pushed [me] off": a simple relative expression whose verb is in T.4b.

> → **494** rel. pron.: subject or object, 10;
>   times-tenses of the indicative mode and their vernacular meaning, 7.

LETTER 413*b* T-P
AD ATTICUM XI, 4

CICERO ATTICO SAL.

Accepi ab Isidoro litteras et postea datas binas. Ex proximis cognovi praedia non venisse. Videbis ergo ut sustentetur per te. De Frusinati, si modo fruituri sumus, erit mihi res opportuna. Meas litteras quod requiris impedior inopia rerum quas nullas habeo litteris dignas, quippe cui nec quae accidunt nec quae aguntur ullo modo probentur. Utinam coram tecum olim potius quam per epistulas! Hic tua, ut possum, tueor apud hos. Cetera Celer. Ipse fugi adhuc omne munus, eo magis quod ita nihil poterat agi ut mihi et meis rebus aptum esset.   (*Att.* XI, 4)

CICERO A GREETING TO ATTICUS

I received a letter from Isidorus and two letters having been sent afterward. From the last one I found out that the properties had not been sold. You will see to it therefore that she [Tulliola] be maintained with your help. Concerning the estate at Frosinone, if only we are going to be enjoying it, it will be for me a very suitable thing. The fact that you feel the absence of my letters, I am being blocked by the lack of materials, none of which I find worthy of a letter, as a person namely to whom neither the things which are happening nor which are being done are being proven right in any way. I wish that face to face with you some day rather than by letter! Here I am protecting your things as I can among these people. The other things—Celer [is looking after]. I myself have escaped so far every responsibility, all the more so because nothing was able to be negotiated in such a way that it would be suitable for me and my concerns.

CICERO ATTICO SAL.: *Cicero Attico salutem*

litteras … binas. Ex proximis, "two letters. From the last one": the plural form *litteras,* "a letter," can refer to a single letter as here, then [*litteras*] *binas,* "two letters," clearly refers to two more epistles, but immediately following it is not clear whether *proximis* refers to the two latter epistles or uses the plural form to refer to one epistle, the last one.

→ **495** dict., *littera, ae,* f., II., A. Sing., B. Usually plur.

cognovi praedia non venisse, "I found out that the properties had not been sold": the M & M verb *cognovi,* "I understood," in T.4b produces a statement in OO where the subject in the object form is *praedia,* "the properties," and the inf. *venisse,* "to have been up for sale," "had [not] been sold," describes an antecedent action. Note well, there are two verbs, *vēneo, venire,* "to be on sale," and *vĕnio, venire,* "to come"; here the form *venisse* is the same for both verbs, but the length of the first *–e–* is different, something which the Romans heard.

→ **496** M & M, 60, 71, GL n° 527, remarks 1–2;
OO, 71–73; *consecutio,* 47–48;
dict., *vēnĕo, vēnīre, īvi* or *ii, ītum,* 4, "to be on sale";
dict., *vĕnio, vĕnīre, vēni, ventum,* 4, "to come";
four reverse deponents: GL n° 169, remark 1, n° 214, remark 1.

praedia, "the properties": from *praedium, i,* it functions as a subject, "the estates," in the neuter plural object form in OO and its verb is the inf. *venisse,* "the properties had not been sold."

→ **497** Block I nouns, 2; OO, 71–73.

Videbis … ut sustentetur, "You will see to it … that she [Tulliola] be maintained": the main verb *Videbis,* "You will see to it," in T.3i produces a purpose clause giving the intention, *ut sustentetur,* "that she be maintained," in T.1s and rendered in English in the subjunctive.

→ **498** subjunctive use: purpose clause, 58.1.

fruituri sumus, "we are going to be enjoying it": Tyrrell mentions that there is a problem with the reading of *fruituri,* "[we] about to enjoy." From *fruor, frui, fructus,* 3, one would expect the form *fructuri sumus,* but there are about three or four texts where we find *fruitus,* or here *fruituri.*

→ **499** dict., *fruor, fructus,* 3 (I.… part. fut. *fruiturus*).

Note the following three forms ending in *–a,* each with a different function, *praedia, opportuna, inopia,* as given in turn below.

→ **500** *ossium gluten,* the bones' glue, 1.

opportuna, "very suitable": from *opportunus, a, um,* the feminine singular adjective agrees with *res,* "thing," functioning as the subject. Thus, *res opportuna* means "a very suitable thing."

→ **501** Block I adj., 4.2–3; 20% of nouns: *res, rei,* f., 35.

impedior, "I am being blocked": from *impedio, ire, ivi (ii) itum,* 4; this normal verb is used in the passive here. Note the ending in *–or*; only through a knowledge of dictionary vocabulary can you distinguish its use here from *tueor*, below.

→ **502** passive Times 1, 2, 3 indicative, 21;
ossium gluten, the bones' glue, 1.

inopia, "by the lack": from *inopia, ae*, functions as a feminine abl. in the singular. Thus, *impedior inopia rerum*, means "I am being blocked by the lack of materials":

→ **503** abl.: meaning and forms, 27.

quippe cui nec … nec … probentur, "as a person namely to whom neither [the things] … nor … are being proven right": derived from *qui-pe*, the expression *quippe cui* is causal and its meanings include, "inasmuch as to whom," "since to me," "inasmuch as to me," "inasmuch as someone to whom." This expression begins a sentence with its verb *probentur*, "[neither the things … nor …] are being proven right," in T.1s and rendered in English in the ind. Equivalent both to *quippe cui* is *utpote cui* and *ut cui* with similar meaning. These are causal clauses reinforced by *quippe, utpote, ut*, meaning "inasmuch as," "seeing that."

→ **504** subjunctive use: causal *quippe qui*, 59.5; GL n° 633.

nec quae accidunt nec quae aguntur … probentur, "neither the things which are happening nor which are being done … are being proven right": the subject of *probentur* is an implied *ea*, "the things," the antecedent of both relative pronouns *quae … quae … ,* "neither the things which … nor which.…" These two clauses are placed within the causal clause between the *quippe cui* and its subjunctive verb *probentur*, "as a person namely to whom … are being proven right." Another way to express this sentence is, "I have no things worthy of a letter inasmuch as someone to whom those things neither which are happening nor are being done are being made acceptable."

→ **505** rel. pron.: subject or object, 10;
rel. pron.: omission of the antecedent, 11.2.

utinam, "I wish <u>that</u>": this expression is used as a natural, optative subjunctive expressing a wish. There is no verb here, but according to the sentence it would be in T.1s, for example *colloquar*, "O that I may speak with you face to face," "would that I may speak with you," "If only I may speak with you," "I hope that I may speak with you."

→ **506** subjunctive use: *utinam*, 88.

olim, "some day": everyone will take it as "once upon a time," but the dict. says that it also refers to sometime in the future.

→ **507** dict., *olim*, adv., II. Of the future.

potius quam, "rather than": also means "preferably than."

> → **508** *quam* with the comp., 43.2;
>> dict., *potis*, adj., III., B.—hence adv. only in the *comp.* and *sup.* A. Comp. *potius*, "preferably."

tueor, "I am protecting": from *tueor, tueri, tuitus* 2 also means "I'm looking out for …"; this verb is deponent, which is confirmed by the presence of an object *tua*, "[I'm protecting] your things," "… your affairs." Be careful because *tua tueor* can also mean, "I your woman am looking out," where *tua* is the subject "your woman"; which makes no sense here, but, nevertheless, Latin will drive you crazy because you have to know the whole language and then still think! Note the ending in *–or*; only through a knowledge of dictionary vocabulary can you distinguish its different uses here from *impedior*, above.

> → **509** verb: deponent, 29; *ossium gluten*, the bones' glue, 1.

Note the forms of the following two verbs, each ending in *–i*, each with a different function requiring that you know your vocabulary:

> → **510** *ossium gluten*, the bones' glue, 1.

Ipse fugi, "I myself have escaped": from *fugio, fugere, fugi, fugitum*, 3, this is T.4a. We can change one letter to say, *fuge*, "Flee, you!"

> → **511** verb T.4, T.5, T.6: 8; commands: first, second, 17.

agi, "to be done": from *ago, agere, egi, actum*, 3, this is the contemporaneous passive inf. We can change one letter to say, *age*, "You do it!"

> → **512** contemporaneous passive infinitive, 72.3; commands: first, second, 17.

18

LETTER 414 T-P
AD FAMILIARES XIV, 6

SUIS S. D.

Nec saepe est cui litteras demus nec rem habemus ullam quam scribere velimus. Ex tuis litteris quas proxime accepi cognovi praedium nullum venire
potuisse. Qua re videatis velim quo modo satis fiat ei cui scitis me satis fieri
velle. Quod nostra tibi gratias agit, id ego non miror te mereri ut ea tibi
merito tuo gratias agere possit. Pollicem, si adhuc non est profectus, quam
primum fac extrudas. Cura ut valeas. Idibus Quinctilibus.   (*Fam.* XIV, 6)

HE SAYS A GREETING TO HIS PEOPLE

Neither is there often anyone to whom we may entrust a letter nor do we
have anything which we would like to write. From your letter, which I received most recently, I understood that no estate property was able to be up
for sale. For which reason I would like that you-all see in what way satisfaction may be made to him to whom you know that I want satisfaction to be
made [repay the dowry in divorce]. The fact that our girl [Tulliola] renders
thanks to you, I am not surprised about the fact that you are deserving that
she is able to render thanks to you according to your merit. See to it that you
drive off Pollex [Mr. Thumb, the letter carrier] as soon as possible, if he has
not yet set out. Take care that you be well. The July Ides [15 July].

SUIS S. D.: *suis salutem dicit*

cui litteras demus, "to whom we may entrust a letter": depending on T.1i *est,*
"there is," the verb *demus* in T.1s indicates that this is a characteristic result
clause in which *cui* stands for *talis ut ei,* "such that to him." The subject of
est is also the antecedent of *cui,* perhaps *is,* "he," or *aliquis,* "someone," thus
producing *aliquis talis ut ei,* "someone such that to him." As a characteristic
result, the verb *demus* would in English normally sound indicative, but here
it sounds subjunctive because it is potential, meaning "[Neither is there]
someone such to whom we may entrust."

→ **513** subjunctive use: characteristic result, 68.2;
  subjunctive use: underlying potential of the present or future, 94.3,
  GL n° 257.

quam scribere velimus, "which we would like to write": depending on T.1i *habemus*, "we have," the T.1s *velimus* indicates that this is a characteristic result clause in which *quam* stands for *talem ut eam*, "such that it," where the antecedent of that *eam* and thus of the *quam* is *rem … ullam*, "any thing such that it." As a characteristic result, the verb *velimus* would in English normally sound indicative, but here it sounds subjunctive because it is potential, meaning "[nor do we have] any such thing which we would like to write."

> → **514** subjunctive use: characteristic result, 68.2;
> > subjunctive use: underlying potential of the present or future, 94.3,
> > > GL nº 257.

cognovi praedium nullum venire potuisse, "I understood that no estate property was able to be put up for sale": the M & M verb *cognovi*, "I understood," in T.4b produces a statement in OO where the subject in the object form is *praedium nullum*, "no estate property," and the inf. *potuisse*, "was able," describes an antecedent state.

> → **515** M & M, 60, 71, GL nº 527, remarks 1–2; OO, 71–73.

Note well, there are two verbs, *vĕnio, venire*, "to come" and *vēneo, venire*, "to be on sale." The latter is one of the famous four verbs whose form is active but meaning passive, thus the reverse of a deponent verb. The famous four are: *fio*, "I am made"; *veneo*, "I am for sale"; *pereo*, "I am lost"; *vapulo*, "I am being beaten." These verbs are not specifically treated in the *Ossa* book, but they are one of the discoveries to be made in encountering Latin literature.

> → **516** dict., *venio; fio* (see: *facio*, init.); dict., *veneo; pereo; vapulo*;
> > four reverse deponents: GL nº 169, remark 1, nº 214, remark 1.

videatis velim, "I would like that you all check": the T.1s *videatis* is an expression of purpose where the *ut*, "that," is omitted after the wish *velim*, "I would like," itself an independent subjunctive. This expression is used to indicate a strong wish.

> → **517** subjunctive use: purpose clause without *ut*, 58, GL nº 546, remark 2;
> > commands: other expressions, *velim*, 85.1.7.

quo modo satis fiat, "in what way satisfaction be made": the M & M verb *videatis*, "that you all check," produces an IQ where *quo modo*, also written *quomodo*, means "how," "in what way." As an IQ, the Latin subjunctive *fiat* would normally be given in totally acceptable English in the ind., as in "in what way satisfaction is made," but underlying the IQ there may be a statement of potential or possibility which comes through in the English as "may be made."

> → **518** M & M, 60, 71, GL nº 527, remarks 1–2; IQ, 60;
> > subjunctive use: underlying potential of the present or future, 94.3,
> > > GL nº 257.

cui scitis me satis fieri velle, "to whom you know that I want satisfaction to be made": the M & M verb *scitis*, "you know," in T.1i produces a statement in

OO in which the subject in the object form is *me* and the inf. verb *velle*, rendered in English as "me to want," "that I want," or "[you know] I want." All alone, the verb *fieri* comes from *fio, fieri, factum*, and means "to be made"; this verb is used as the passive of *facio, facere, feci, factum*, 1, "to make," whose T.1s appears above as *fiat*, "be made."

→ **519** M & M, 60, 71, GL n° 527, remarks 1–2; OO, 71–73;
    irregular verbs: *volo*, 82; dict., *venio; fio* (see: *facio*, init.).

Quod, "The fact that": explanatory *quod* introduces a new subject, as if to say, "By the way,...."

→ **520** *quod* = "the fact that" as a new subject, GL n° 525.2.

id ego non miror te mereri, "I am not surprised about the fact that you are meriting": the M & M verb *miror*, "I am [not] surprised," has two objects in apposition. The first is *id*, "it," "the fact," and the content of that fact is given in the second, the entire statement given in OO where the subject in the object form is *te* and the contemporaneous inf. *mereri*, comes from a dep. verb and so is passive in form but active in meaning "that you are meriting."

→ **521** M & M, 60, 71, GL n° 527, remarks 1–2; OO, 71–73;
    verb: deponent, 29; verb: contemporaneous deponent infinitive, 72.3;
    apposition, GL n° 320–21.

te mereri ... merito tuo, "that you are deserving ... according to your merit": Cicero is playing on words, the verb *mereri* and the noun *merito*. We might render the expression as "you are meriting by your good service."

→ **522** dict., *mereo, ui, itum*, 2 and *mereor, itus*, 2 dep., ... 3. *meritum, i*, n.

mereri ut ea ... gratias agere possit, "[you] are meriting that she is able to render thanks": a result clause where the subjunctive in Latin *ut ... possit*, is rendered in English in the ind., "that she is able."

→ **523** subjunctive use: complementary result (consecutive), 68.1.

si ... est profectus, ... fac extrudas, "See to it that you kick out ... , if he has [not yet] set out": a logical conditional and thus given in the ind. here *est profectus*, "he has ... set out," coordinating with the command form *fac*, "see to it," which is one of several command forms that have lost their final –*e*. As a verb of causing, *fac* produces a result clause given here without *ut*, but immediately by *extrudas*, "that you pack off," in T.1s, rendered in English in the ind.

→ **524** commands: famous four, 39.4; conditionals: factual, 86.1;
    subjunctive use: complementary result (consecutive), 68.1.

quam primum, "as soon as possible": the special meaning of *quam* when followed by the superlative.

→ **525** *quam* with the superlative, 43.3.

Pollicem ... extrudas, "that you pack off Pollex [Mr. Thumb, the letter carrier]": the first word of the sentence, *Pollicem,* "Pollex," is the object of the last word, *extrudas,* "that you pack off" or "that you kick out." This expression could mean "see to it that you stick out your thumb," but we take it to express the fuller idea, "see to it that you throw Pollex out of the house and onto the postal road." The proper name *Pollex* refers to one of Cicero's slaves, who was tasked here as a letter carrier.

→ **526** sentence structure, 1.

Idibus Quinctilibus, "The July Ides": abl. of definite time. Romulus is said to have started the year in March, after his father Mars, which makes July the fifth month and December *Decem* the tenth month. The second king of Rome, Numa, is said to have given names to January and February which had been without names because the farms were fallow and time without purpose. The senate decided to change the name of the fifth month from *Quinctilibus* to Julius Caesar's month, and that is how we get "July." Similarly, later the sixth month, which would produce *Idibus Sextilibus,* was changed in honor of Octavian the Emperor to his honorary name, *Augustus,* thus "August." Euge!

→ **527** abl.: time at which, 70.1;
about the Roman calendar, pp. 605–608;
GL Appendix, Roman Calendar, pp. 491–92.

LETTER 169 T-P
AD FAMILIARES II, 3

M. CICERO S. D. C. CURIONI

Rupae studium non defuit declarandorum munerum tuo nomine, sed nec mihi placuit nec cuiquam tuorum quidquam te absente fieri quod tibi, cum venisses, non esset integrum. Meam quidem sententiam aut scribam ad te postea pluribus aut, ne ad eam meditere, imparatum te offendam coramque contra istam rationem meam dicam, ut aut te ad meam sententiam adducam aut certe testatum apud animum tuum relinquam quid senserim, ut, si quando—quod nolim—displicere tibi tuum consilium coeperit, possis meum recordari. Brevi tamen sic habeto, in eum statum temporum tuum reditum incidere ut iis bonis quae tibi natura, studio, fortuna data sunt, facilius omnia quae sunt amplissima in re publica consequi possis quam muneribus, quorum neque facultatem quisquam admiratur—est enim copiarum, non virtutis—neque quisquam est quin satietate iam defessus sit.   (*Fam.* II, 3, 1)

MARCUS CICERO SAYS A GREETING
TO CAIUS CURIO

Rupa's enthusiasm of proclaiming public shows in your name was not missing, but neither was it pleasing to me nor to anyone of your people that anything be done—you being absent—which would not be an undecided matter for you when [eventually] you would have come back [to Rome]. Indeed either I shall write to you my opinion afterward with more words or, lest you prepare for it, I shall find you unprepared, and face to face I shall express my reasoning contrary to that reasoning so that either I may draw you over to my opinion or leave as certainly well testified in your own mind what I thought so that, if ever your plan will have begun to be displeasing to you—something which I would not want—you may be able to remember my own. However in a few words consider it this way: that your return is falling into such a state of circumstances that as a result you are able to attain all the things which are the most glorious in public life more easily by means of those good things which have been given to you by nature, by effort, by good luck, than by means of public spectacles, at the richness of which neither anyone is surprised—for it is a matter of resources, not of moral stature—nor is there anyone who has not already become exhausted with the over-abundance.

M. Cicero s. d. C. Curioni: *Marcus Cicero salutem dicit Caio Curioni*

Disregarding the time of composition of the letter, we can imagine for pedagogical reasons a calendar to indicate the time-relation of one verb to another:

July	September	October	November	December
placuit				
fieri ─────────────────────────────────────▶				
		venisses		
			esset─────────────────────▶	

→ **528** calendars, 83 pp. 514–15, 103 p. 586.

declarandorum munerum, "of proclaiming public shows": a gerundive, which as gerund would be *declarandi munera*, in which it is easier to see that *munera* is the object of *declarandi*. The gerund with the object is less accepted in classical literature but is common in later Latin, although it has no difference in meaning from the gerundive found here. The gerundive is in the gen. because it depends on *studium*, itself the subject of *defuit*, "enthusiasm of proclaiming public shows ... was not missing."

→ **529** gerundive, 77.2; gerund, 77.1;
   dict., *desum, fui, esse*, v. irreg., II., B. "to fall short of," "miss".

munerum ... muneribus, "of ... public shows ... by ... spectacles": the *munus* are public games, spectacles, shows held as a public gift to the people, a public spectacle on government expense, usually in honor of a deceased person, here the late father of Curius.

→ **530** dict., *munus, eris*, n., II., C., 2., a.... a show of gladiators.

quidquam ... fieri, "that anything be done": OO that serves as the subject of the M & M verb *placuit*, "[neither] was it pleasing." It means directly, "that anything be done—you being absent—was neither pleasing to me nor to anyone of your people." As a contemporaneous inf., *fieri* is open-ended, represented by an arrow in the diagram above.

→ **531** M & M, 60, 71, GL n° 527, remarks 1–2;
   OO, 71–73; verb: contemporaneous passive infinitive, 72.3.

te absente, "—you being absent—": AA can be smoothed out to say, "when/ while you were absent"; the contemporaneous participle *absente* sounds past in English because of the idea expressed in the rest of the sentence, which is on Track II, established by *placuit*, "[neither] was it pleasing" in T.4b.

→ **532** ablative absolute, 54–55; contemporaneous active participle, 50, 51.1.1.

quod ... esset, "which would [not] be": the relative expression stands for *ut id esset*, but the question remains what kind of *ut* it is. Here it is taken as a clause of characteristic result with futurity from a moment in past. The result clause may be rendered more fully as *tale ut tibi non esset integrum*, "[that anything be done] such that as a result it would not be an undecided matter for you." Sequence of tenses: the verb *placuit*, "[neither] was it pleasing," is T.4b and sets the sentence on Track II, which continues through the incomplete, even ongoing-action infinitive *fieri*, "[that anything] be done"; the full natural time frame of T.2s includes futurity from a perspective of a time in the past, that is here futurity with regard to *placuit*, and *fieri*; this futurity is expressed in English as "would be."

→ **533** subjunctive use: characteristic result, 68.2;
consecutio, 47–48; *consecutio*: futurity in the subjunctive, 61.1.

The other alternative is that this could always be considered a purpose clause that sounds subjunctive in English, "such that it might not be undecided when you would have come." A third possibility is that *esset* is subjunctive by MA, because this clause is an integral part of a whole subjunctive complex. If this were the case, the idea still could be rendered as "which would [not] be."

→ **534** subjunctive use: relative clause of purpose, 58.2;
qui, quae, quod and *quis, quid*: relative clause of purpose, 79.5;
qui, quae, quod and *quis, quid*: modal attraction, 79.10;
subjunctive use: modal attraction, 83.

integrum, "an undecided matter": we do not use vocabulary cards because a word is not fully understood until all of its meanings given in the dictionary are understood. The meaning of *integrum* here is not "whole," "entire," but "an undecided matter," as in "untouched," "undetermined," "in which nothing has yet been done."

→ **535** dict., *integer, tegra, tegrum*, adj., II., D.... undecided, undetermined.

cum venisses, "when [eventually] you would have come back [to Rome]": a temporal sentence in the subjunctive by MA based on the OO *quidquam fieri*. The sequence of tenses builds upon what was said in the above item; T.4s indicates a future completed action, that is, completed with regard to the expression of futurity *quod ... esset*, "which would [not] be." This confirms our own designation of *venisses* as T.4s, not as the so-called "pluperfect," because the time here is not "past-pluperfect," but completed futurity in the subjunctive. The traditional terminology "pluperfect" does not work and is totally misleading and inaccurate, which is why we use T.4s. We have added "[to Rome]" for clarity.

→ **536** *cum* + historical times of indicative = "when": temporal coincidence, 66.3.1;
OO, 71–73; subjunctive use: modal attraction, 83;
consecutio: completed futurity in the subjunctive, 61.1.

All the words below end in –*am*, and for different reasons, which may provide class material, sharpen Latin wits, suggest language exercises, such as reversing from singular to plural and from plural to singular, flipping from active to passive, substituting synonyms:

> *Meam*, "my": possessive adj. agreeing with *sententiam*.
>
> *sententiam*, "opinion": noun in object function.
>
> *scribam*, "I shall write": T.3i.
>
> *eam*, "it": pronoun agreeing with *sententiam*.
>
> *offendam*, "I shall find [you]": T.3i.
>
> *coram*, "face to face": adv.
>
> *istam*, "that": pronoun agreeing with *rationem*, "reasoning."
>
> *meam*, "my": possessive adj. agreeing with *rationem*, "reasoning."
>
> *dicam*, "I shall express": T.3i.
>
> *meam*, "my": possessive adj. agreeing with *sententiam*.
>
> *sententiam*, "opinion": noun in object function.
>
> *adducam*, "I may draw [you] over": T.1s.
>
> *relinquam*, "[I may . . .] leave": T.1s.

> → **537** *ossium gluten*, the bones' glue, 1.8.

Again we can establish a different imaginary calendar to map out the times of the verbs of the second sentence to show their time-relation to another. We have not attempted to combine these two calendars because the events in the above calendar and in this calendar did not necessarily occur in the same year according to Cicero's vision.

January	March	July	September	October	November	December
	scribam					
	meditere ——————→					
	offendam					
	dicam					
	adducam					
	scribam					
senserim						
	nolim					
			coeperit			
				possis ————————————————→		
				recordari ————————————————→		

> → **538** calendars, 83 pp. 514–15, 103 p. 586.

In this calendar, note that *senserim* and *coeperit* are both T.3s, but one is antecedent to *relinquam* and the other to *possis*.

> → **539** *consecutio*: completed futurity in the subjunctive, 61.1.

scribam … offendam … dicam, "I shall write … I shall find … I shall express": three verbs in T.3i; the last of these establishes its clause on Track I.

→ **540** verb formation T.3 in groups III and IV, 12.3.2; *consecutio*, 47–48.

pluribus, "with more words," also "with a number of words; at greater length."

→ **541** abl.: meaning and forms, 27; adj.: comp., 36.

ne ad eam meditere, "lest you prepare for it": a negative purpose clause depending on *offendam*, "I shall find."

→ **542** subjunctive use: purpose clause, 58.1.

meditere, "you prepare": variation for *mediteris* T.1s of *meditor* with the special meaning "to practice; exercise one's self."

→ **543** variation: –*ris*, 39.3.

offendam, "I shall find": many will take *offendam* to mean "to offend," but here it means "I shall meet up with someone; meet; find; come upon someone."

→ **544** dict., *offendo, di, sum*, 3, I., B.… to come upon, to meet with; II., B.… to offend.

ut aut … adducam aut … relinquam, "so that either I may draw [you over] … or leave": purpose clauses in T.1s depending on *dicam*, "I shall express" in T.3i, which sets the rest of the sentence on Track I. Here students could reverse all five of these above-mentioned verbs ending in –*am* from their singular to their plural forms, where *scribam* becomes *scribemus* and *offendam* becomes *offendemus*, and *dicam* becomes *dicemus*, all three in T.3i, but *adducam* becomes *adducamus* and *relinquam* becomes *relinquamus*, both in T.1s. When the student does this, the teacher knows immediately how the student is understanding the original forms.

→ **545** subjunctive use: purpose clause, 58.1; *consecutio*, 47–48;
verb formation Time 3 in groups III and IV, 12.3.2;
forms of the subjunctive, T.1s: 44.1.

testatum, "as … well testified": the dictionary entry *testor* indicates this is a deponent verb, and the unexpected passive use of the participle *testatus, a, um*, as here, means "having been confirmed; witnessed, authenticated." The dictionary entry *testor* indicates that this verb is deponent, and thus active in meaning; it should not be passive in meaning, however, reading a full dictionary entry reveals a subentry for an active collateral form *testo*, followed by a specific reference to the participle *testatus, a, um*. This active form, then, can have passive meaning, which is also indicated in the dict.

→ **546** dict., *testor, atus*, 1., II., 1., collateral form, 1 active *testo, are*, 1., 2 passive, *testatus, a, um*;
GL nº 167, note 2;
verb: deponent, 29;
antecedent participle, deponents, 50, 51.2.2.

quid senserim, "what I thought": IQ in T.3s depending on the M & M expression contained in the participle *testatum*, "testified," which is part of the purpose clause *dicam, ut ... testatum relinquam*, "I shall express ... so that ... I may ... leave ... testified"; *senserim* occurs at any time prior to *relinquam*, and so means variously, "I did think; have thought; have been thinking; was thinking; had thought; had been thinking."

→ **547** M & M, 60, 71, GL n° 527, remarks 1–2; IQ, 60;
      subjunctive use: purpose clause, 58.1.

ut ... possis, "so that ... you may be able": *dicam*, "I shall express" in T.3i sets the sentence on Track I and produces the purpose clause *ut aut ... adducam aut ... relinquam*, "so that either I may draw you over ... or leave" in T.1s, which in turn produces its own purpose clause *ut possis*, in T.1s; the full natural time frame of T.1s includes futurity as here with regard to *adducam* and *relinquam*.

→ **548** *consecutio*, 47–48;
      consecutio: subjunctive depending on a subjunctive, 62.1;
      consecutio: futurity in the subjunctive, 61.1;
      subjunctive use: purpose clause, 58.1.

si quando, "if ever": here *quando* does not mean "when" or "because"; it is rather the indefinite adverb *aliquando* which is abbreviated to *quando* following *si*; cf. dict.

→ **549** dict., *aliquando*, adv.;
      adv.: indefinite, see: 42.4; after *si* the *ali*-s fly away, 42.5.

si ... coeperit, "if [your plan] will have begun": a factual conditional sentence in T.3s due to MA based on the multiple clauses in the subjunctive. The sequence of tenses builds upon what was said in the above item; T.3s indicates a future completed action, that is, completed in regard to the expression of futurity *possis*, "you may be able," upon which it depends. This perfectly illustrates our whole system and our designation of *coeperit* as T.3s, which here is not "perfect," but completed futurity.

→ **550** conditionals: factual, 86.1;
      subjunctive use: modal attraction, 83;
      consecutio: completed futurity in the subjunctive, 61.1.

meum recordari, "to remember my own": this usage will disturb some conservatives who think that verbs of remembering and forgetting take only the form of-possession gen., but the dict. indicates that the verb *recordari* is used most frequently with the object form, as here with *meum*.

→ **551** dict., *recordor, atus*, 1., dep., I., (α). With acc. (so most freq.);
      verbs of remembering and forgetting, 74.

Brevi, "in a few words": *brevi* is an abl. used as an adv., with two meanings here, "within a short time; in a short discourse."

→ **552** dict., *brevis, e*, adj., II., B....—hence *brevi*, adv., briefly;
      Block II adj. in three ways, 18; adv., 37.

sic habeto, "consider it this way": this expression produces OO because of the implied idea of M & M such as "take it like this; understand this; be convinced; take it from me that...."

> → **553** M & M, 60, 71, 71, GL n° 527, remarks 1–2; OO, 71–73.

reditum incidere, "[your] return is falling": OO produced by the M & M expression *sic habeto*, "consider it this way."

> → **554** M & M, 60, 71, GL n° 527, remarks 1–2; OO, 71–73.

iis bonis, "by means of those good things": an abl. of instrument.

> → **555** abl.: instrument, 28.5.3–4, 89.2, GL n° 401.

quae ... natura, studio, fortuna data sunt, "which have been given ... by nature, by effort, by good luck": because of the passive *data sunt*, the ablatives *natura, studio, fortuna* are instruments, not personal agents such as "mother nature" or "lady fortune," which would suggest the preposition *a* or *ab* to indicate personal agency.

> → **556** passive Times 4, 5, 6 indicative, 26;
> abl.: instrument, 28.5.3–4, 89.2;
> abl.: personal agent, 28.5.3–4, 89.2.

facilius ... quam, "more easily ... than."

> → **557** *quam* with the comp., 43.2.

muneribus, "by means of public spectacles": an abl. of instrument.

> → **558** abl.: instrument, 28.5.3–4, 89.2, GL n° 401.

neque quisquam est quin ... defessus sit, "nor is there anyone who has not already become exhausted": *quin* stands for *qui non*, which stands for *talis ut is non*, "nor is there anyone such that he has not already become exhausted."

> → **559** negative characteristic result: *quin* (= *talis ut is non*) + subjunctive, 101.2,
> GL n° 632.

There is an immense number of instances of the sound *qu ...* , so pleasing to the Romans, all over in this text.

∽

Sed aliter atque ostenderam facio qui ingrediar ad explicandam rationem sententiae meae. Qua re omnem hanc disputationem in adventum tuum differo. Summa scito te in exspectatione esse eaque a te exspectari quae a summa virtute summoque ingenio exspectanda sunt: ad quae si es, ut debes, paratus—quod ita esse confido—plurimis maximisque muneribus et nos amicos et civis tuos universos et rem publicam adficies. Illud cognosces profecto, mihi te neque cariorem neque iucundiorem esse quemquam.   (*Fam.* II, 3, 2)

But I am acting now otherwise than I had said, because I am approaching to explain the motive of my own opinion. For which reason I put off this whole discussion for your arrival. You must know that you are found in the greatest expectation and that those things are being awaited from you which must be expected from the highest virtue and the greatest character: for which things, if you have been prepared as you must—which I am confident is so—you will grace both us your friends and all your citizens and the whole state with very many and very great shows. That fact for sure you will understand that neither is anyone dearer to me nor more pleasant than you yourself.

aliter atque, "otherwise than": few people will understand this unless they go to the dict., which says that *atque* goes with *alius* and its derivatives and here means not "and" but "than"; for example, *aliud atque* means "something other than," and *alio atque* means "to another place than." At the beginning of the letter he says he will not go into detail but wait for a face-to-face conversation; now he backtracks a bit.

→ **560** *alius, a, ud*, adj., I., B. In comparisons, with *atque*.

ostenderam, "I had said": a careful reading of the dictionary will reveal this meaning of the verb.

→ **561** dict., *ostendo, di, sum*, and *tum*, 3., II., B., 1. "to indicate [by speech], say."

qui ingrediar, "because I am approaching": a causal sentence where *qui ingrediar*, "inasmuch as who [I] am now coming in," stands for causal *cum ego ingrediar*, "because I am approaching."

→ **562** subjunctive use: causal *qui, quae, quod* = "because, since," 59.4;
verb: deponent, 29; GL n° 633.

Summa ... te in exspectatione esse, "that you are found in the greatest expectation": OO depending M & M verb *scito*, "You must know"; *te* is not the object of *scito*, but the acc. subject of the infinitive *esse*, and that whole statement is the complement of *scito* in that it gives the content of the knowledge.

→ **563** M & M, 60, 71, GL n° 527, remarks 1–2; OO, 71–73.

scito, "You must know": the second command form, which the Romans preferred to the first form *sci*, "know," contrary to the indication on the part of some that the second command form hardly exists.

→ **564** commands: first, second, 17.

eaque a te exspectari, "and that those things are being awaited from you": OO depending on M & M verb *scito*, "You must know"; the preposition *a* goes with the abl. pronoun *te* and means "from you."

→ **565** M & M, 60, 71, GL n° 527, remarks 1–2; OO, 71–73;
prep. with abl., 28.4.

mihi te neque cariorem neque iucundiorem esse quemquam, "neither is any-one dearer to me nor more pleasant than you yourself": *te* is abl. of compari-son meaning "than you," and is accompanied by two comparative adjectives *cariorem ... iucundiorem*, "dearer ... more pleasant."

→ **566** abl.: comparison, 90.2, GL n° 398; adj.: comp., 36.

LETTER 121 T-P
AD ATTICUM IV, 10

CICERO ATTICO SAL.

Puteolis magnus est rumor Ptolomaeum esse in regno. Si quid habes certius, velim scire. Ego hic pascor bibliotheca Fausti. Fortasse tu putabas his rebus Puteolanis et Lucrinensibus. Ne ista quidem desunt. Sed mehercule *ut* a ceteris oblectationibus deseror voluptatum propter rem publicam, sic litteris sustentor et recreor maloque in illa tua sedecula quam habes sub imagine Aristotelis sedere quam in istorum sella curuli tecumque apud te ambulare quam cum eo quocum video esse ambulandum. Sed de illa ambulatione fors viderit aut si qui est qui curet deus.   (*Att.* IV, 10, 1)

CICERO A GREETING TO ATTICUS

In Puzzuoli [Puteoli] there is a big rumor that Ptolomy is in royal authority. If you have anything more certain, I would like to know. Here I am being fed with the library of Faustus. Perhaps you were thinking [I was being fed] by these realities of Puzzuoli and Lake Lucrine. Not even those things are missing. But by george just as I am left by the other delights of pleasures because of the political situation, so I am being supported and refreshed with literature, and I prefer to sit on that little stool of yours which you have under the picture of Aristotle than in the official chair of those guys [Pompey and Crassus] and to walk with you at your house than with him [Caesar] with whom I see one has to walk. But let fortune see to it about that walking [with you] or if there is any god who cares.

CICERO ATTICO SAL.: *Cicero Attico salutem*

Puteolis, "In Puzzuoli [Puteoli]": because the name of the town is plural, instead of the function of place where, also called the locative, the by-with-from-in abl. is used, as, for example, the name of Athens, *Athenis,* "in Athens," *Syracusis,* "in Syracuse."

→ **567** function: place at which, names of cities and small islands, plural, *Puteolis,* 69.3.2;
function: place at which, names of cities and small islands, plural, *Athenis,* 69.3.2;
function: place at which, names of cities and small islands, plural, *Syracusis,* 69.3.2.

est rumor Ptolomaeum esse, "there is a ... rumor that Ptolomy is": the noun *rumor* combined here with the verb *est,* "there is a ... rumor," functions as an expression of M & M producing a statement in OO where *Ptolomaeum* is the subject in the object function and the verb *esse* is the contemporaneous inf.

→ **568** M & M, 60, 71, GL n° 527, remarks 1–2; OO, 71–73.

Si quid habes certius, velim scire, "If you have anything more certain, I would like to know": a logical conditional where the condition *si ... habes,* "If you have," is in T.1i and the consequence *velim,* "I would like," is in T.1s not because it is a foggy future, which others call the future less-vivid, but because this is a favorite expression of Cicero to convey the potential of the present. After the condition *Si,* "If," the word *aliquid* is shortened to *quid,* "something," and goes with *certius,* "[something] more certain," the comparative degree in the neuter, which, by the way, is the same form as the comparative adv. "more certainly." Here the object of *velim,* "I would like" is the gerund *scire,* "[I would like] knowing," "[I would like] to know."

→ **569** conditionals: factual, 86.1;
subjunctive use: potential of the present or future, *velim* in T.1s, GL n° 257.2;
pronouns: indefinite, 42.4; after *si* the *ali-*s fly away, 42.5;
adj.: comp., 36; adv.: comp., 37; gerund, 77.1.

pascor bibliotheca, "I am being fed with the library": the passive *pascor,* "I am being fed," is complemented by *bibliotheca,* "with the library," "by the library," expressing instrumentality.

→ **570** passive Times 1, 2, 3 indicative, 21; abl.: instrument, 28.5.3–4, 89.2.

Fortasse, "Perhaps": there are six forms of this word all meaning "perhaps." Four most of the time take the ind., sometimes the subjunctive, *fors, forte, fortasse, fortassis,* and two usually take the subjunctive because they involve an IQ, *forsitan, forsan.* Here, the verb *putabas,* "[Perhaps] you were thinking" is in T.2i.

→ **571** dict., *fors, fortis,* f., II. Adverb., A. *fors,* B. *forte;*
dict., *fortasse* (also *fortassis*), adv.; dict., *forsitan,* adv.;
dict., *forsan,* adv.

tu putabas his rebus Puteolanis et Lucrinensibus, "you were thinking [I was being fed] by these realities of Puzzuoli and Lake Lucrine": these two towns are at the Bay of Naples. The abl. of instrument continues the thought of the previous sentence. What is implied is that the verb of M & M *putabas*, "you were thinking," in T.2i produces a statement in OO, *me pasci*, "that I was being fed."

→ **572** M & M, 60, 71; GL n° 527, remarks 1–2; OO, 71–73;
abl.: instrument, 28.5.3–4, 89.2, GL n° 401.

ut ... deseror ... sic ... sustentor et recreor, "just as I am left by ... so I am being supported and refreshed": correlatives where *ut*, "just as," is followed by the ind. *deseror*, "I am abandoned," and *sic*, "so," is followed both by *sustentor*, "I am being deprived of ... ," in T.1i and by *recreor*, "[I am being] refreshed," in T.1i, joined by *et*, "and." All three verbs are in T.1i and in the passive.

→ **573** correlative comparative sentences, 90.5, GL n° 642;
passive Times 1, 2, 3 indicative, 21;
conjunction: *et ... , et ... ,* 3.2.

a ceteris oblectationibus deseror, "I am left by the other delights": if the word *a* is original to the text then strictly speaking Cicero is treating *oblectationibus* as a personal agent, thus the rendering above where he treats a thing, "delights," as if they were a person much as we may talk about an action done by the state, a government, a mouse. Language is not after all mathematics. If however, at some point during the past 2000 years the word *a* was added to the text, and thus was not original to Cicero's thought, then he did not consider *oblectationibus* a personal agent, but an instrument, as in our rendering above.

→ **574** functions: their indication and meanings, 6;
prep. + abl. of separation or agent, 28.5.2.

maloque ... sedere quam, "and I prefer to sit ... than": the *–que*, "and" joins a second larger element to the *sic*, "[just as ...] so ... and [I prefer]." The main verb *malo*, "I prefer," has as its object the gerund *sedere*, "to sit," "[I prefer] sitting." Cicero's preference turns on the adv. *quam*, "than," which distinguishes sitting on a little stool from sitting in the official chair. The first part of this comparison includes a relative clause *quam habes*, "which you have," where the antecedent of *quam* is *sedecula*, "little stool, which." A note for precise readers: *malo*, "I prefer," goes with the second *quam*, an adv. meaning "than," whereas the first *quam* is a relative pronoun going with *sedecula*, "little stool, which"!

→ **575** irregular verbs: *malo*, 82; gerund, 77.1;
rel. pron.: subject or object, 10; *quam*, 43; conjunction: *–que*, 3.2.

tecumque apud te ambulare quam cum eo quocum, "and to walk with you at your house than with him [Caesar] with whom": the *–que* joins a second gerund to *sedere*, "to sit," here *ambulare*, "and to walk," "and walking," the second object of *malo*, "I prefer." Again, Cicero's preference turns on a second adverbial *quam*, "than," which distinguishes *tecum*, "with you," with *cum eo,* "with him." Note the use of *cum,* in *tecum,* "with you," and *cum eo,* "with him," but not *eocum.* A third expression *quocum,* also written *quicum,* joins the preposition *cum,* "with," to the relative pronoun *quo,* "with whom"; Latin subtleties!

→ **576** dict., *cum,* prep. with abl., II., D., a.… *mecum, tecum, secum, nobiscum* etc.… *quocum (quīcum);*
conjunction: *–que,* 3.2.

quocum video esse ambulandum, "with whom I see one has to walk": the verb of M & M *video,* "I see," produces a statement in OO where the full form of the implied inf. is *ambulandum esse,* meaning strictly "walking has to be done," "walking must be done"; because the expression is impersonal, its indefinite subject is contained in the expression itself.

→ **577** M & M, 60, 71, GL nº 527, remarks 1–2; OO, 71–73;
participle of passive necessity, 50, 51.1.4;
passive necessity formula, 53.4;
passive of intransitive verbs used impersonally, GL nº 208.2.

fors viderit, "let fortune see to it": to the astonishment of many *viderit* is considered to be T.6i. Gildersleeve and Lodge explains that T.6i can be used to expresses a command somewhat lighter than T.3i does and that Cicero limits this expression to *videris,* "<u>may</u> you see," which also is a light command. This is one instance, however, where Cicero does not use the "you" form *videris,* but instead uses *viderit,* whose subject is *fors,* "good fortune" or "Lady Luck."

→ **578** commands: summary, 85, but T.6i, GL nº 245.

si qui est qui curet deus, "or if there is any god who cares": the first *qui* is not a relative pronoun, but means "any"; after the condition begins with *si,* "if," *qui* is the shortened form of *aliqui,* "[if] anyone." The second *qui* is a relative pronoun that introduces a characteristic result and so stands for *talis ut is,* "such that he," followed by *curet,* "[god] cares," in T.1s. The expression may be understood to mean "if there is any god such who cares," "if there is such a god that cares."

→ **579** pronouns: indefinite, 42.4; after *si* the *ali-*s fly away, 42.5;
rel. pron.: subject or object, 10;
conditionals: factual, 86.1; subjunctive use: characteristic result, 68.2.

❧

Nostram ambulationem et Laconicum eaque quae Cyrea sint velim quod poterit invisas et urgeas Philotimum ut properet, ut possim tibi aliquid in eo genere respondere. Pompeius in Cumanum Parilibus venit: misit ad me statim qui salutem nuntiaret. Ad eum postridie mane vadebam, cum haec scripsi.   (*Att.* IV, 10, 2)

I would like that you inspect our walkway and sauna bath and those things which are the responsibility of Cyrus, as much as will be possible, and that you press Philotimus that he hurry up so that I may be able to answer you something in that area. Pompey came to his Cumaean villa [near Puzzuoli] on the feast of Pales [21 April, the foundation of Rome]: he sent someone to me immediately who might announce a greeting. I was going to his place on the next day in the morning, when I wrote these things.

quae Cyrea sint, "which are the responsibility of Cyrus": Cyrus was an architect at the time. One possible explanation for the use of the subjunctive here is as a causal clause, where *quae* stands for *cum ea*, "because they [are the responsibility of Cyrus]." Cicero is asking Atticus to inspect the quality of the work done by Cyrus.

> → **580** subjunctive use: causal *qui, quae, quod* = "because, since," 59.4.

velim ... invisas, "I would like that you inspect": *velim* in T.1s is complemented by *invisas*, "that you inspect," in T.1s without an intervening *ut*, "that," to express the force of the wish.

> → **581** subjunctive use: purpose clause without *ut*, 58, GL n° 546, remark 2;
>   commands: other expressions, *velim*, 85.1.7.

quod poterit, "as much as will be possible": literally "what will be able" where *poterit*, "[what] will be able," is in T.3i. The meaning "to be possible" is found in the dict. where the examples there are given with *quantum*.

> → **582** dict., *possum, potui, posse*, v. irreg., I. In gen.... *quantum* or *ut potest*,
>   "as much or as far as possible."

et urgeas, "and that you press": *velim* has a second complement, *urgeas*, "that you press," in T.1s, again without the *ut*, "that."

> → **583** subjunctive use: purpose clause without *ut*, 58, GL n° 546, remark 2;
>   commands: other expressions, *velim*, 85.1.7.

ut properet, "that he hurry up": the intent in urging Philotimus is given in this purpose clause where *properet*, "he hurry up," in T.1s is rendered in English in the subjunctive. The form *properet* is not to be confused with T.2s, *properaret*.

> → **584** subjunctive use: purpose clause, 58.1;
>   forms of the subjunctive, T.1s, 44.1;
>   forms of the subjunctive, T.2s, 44.2;
>   *consecutio*: subjunctive depending on a subjunctive, 62.1.

ut possim, "so that I may be able": also rendered, "so that I be able." The intention for urging Philotimus to hurry up is so that Cicero in his turn may be able to answer Atticus, expressed in a purpose clause where *possim*, "I may be able," "I be able," is T.1s, rendered in English in the subjunctive.

> → **585** subjunctive use: purpose clause, 58.1;
>   *consecutio*: subjunctive depending on a subjunctive, 62.1.

Parilibus, "on the feast of Pales": the feast of Pales is called the Parilia. Here the abl. of time is used, "at the feast of Pares."

> → **586** abl.: time at which, 70.1.

misit ad me ... qui salutem nuntiaret, "he sent someone to me ... who might announce a greeting": the main verb is *misit*, "he sent," in T.4b establishing Track II and producing a purpose clause that gives the intention in sending, where the antecedent of *qui*, "who," is an implied *eum*, "him, such who," "him, someone who," and the *qui* stands for *eum ut is*, "him, so that he," and is followed by *nuntiaret*, "[he] might announce." Cicero's expression here sounds very colloquial. On the street today we likewise might say, "he sent someone to say hello."

> → **587** *consecutio*, 47–48;
>   subjunctive use: relative clause of purpose, 58.2.

Note the occurrence of six verbs in the subjunctive all in a row:

> *sint ... velim ... invisas ... urgeas ... properet ... possim.*
> *sint*, "[which] are": causal; or for no reason, perhaps scribal error
> *velim*, "I would like": potential expressing politeness
> *invisas, urgeas*, "that you inspect ... and press": two purpose clauses

depending on *velim* where the *ut* is understood but not explicit to give greater force to the wishing.

> *ut properet*, "so that he may hurry up": a purpose that depends on *urgeas*
> *ut possim*, "so that I may be able": a purpose clause that depends on

properet.

vadebam, "I was going": in T.2i, the epistolary tense. As he is writing he means *vado*, "I am going," but he writes it from the perspective of the person reading the letter some days later, and so he writes *vadebam*, "when I was writing."

> → **588** letter-writer tense, GL n° 252.

LETTER 120 T-P
AD QUINTUM FRATREM II, 7 (9)

MARCUS QUINTO FRATRI SALUTEM.

Placiturum tibi esse librum meum suspicabar: tam valde placuisse quam scribis valde gaudeo. Quod me admones de nostra Urania suadesque ut meminerim Iovis orationem quae est in extremo illo libro, ego vero memini et illa omnia mihi magis scripsi quam ceteris.   (*Q. Fr.* II, 7 [9], 1)

MARCUS A GREETING TO BROTHER QUINTUS.

I was suspecting that my book would be pleasing to you: I am very happy that it pleased you so very much as you write. The fact that you advise me about our Urania and that you suggest that I remember the speech of Jupiter which is at the end of that book, I indeed remember and I wrote all those things for myself more than for other people.

Placiturum tibi esse librum meum suspicabar, "I was suspecting that my book would be pleasing to you": the main verb is *suspicabar,* "I was suspecting," in T.2i, a deponent verb of M & M which produces a statement in OO where *librum* is the subject in the object form and the inf. *Placiturum esse,* is the futurity formula with the future active participle *Placiturum,* "about to be pleasing," "going to be pleasing," and taken together can be rendered in English in several ways, "my book was going to please you," "would please you," "was about to please you." Note that the two parts of the inf. are calmly separated by *tibi,* the complement of *Placiturum,* one of the 65 verbs that take the dat.

> → **589** verb: deponent, 29;
> M & M, 60, 71, GL n° 527, remarks 1–2; OO, 71–73;
> 65 verbs with dat., 33.7.2, GL n° 346;
> futurity participle, 50, 51.1.3;
> verb: subsequent active infinitive, 72.1;
> futurity formula, active, 53.3.

librum … placuisse … gaudeo, "I am … happy that it pleased you": the main
verb *gaudeo*, "I am happy," as a verb of emotion sometimes takes its complement in *quod* followed by the subjunctive or ind. and sometimes in OO, as
here, where the subject of *placuisse*, an antecedent inf., is *librum*, "that the
book was pleasing," which together with *tibi*, "to you," are both from the
first part of the sentence.

> → **590** dict., *gaudeo, gavisus*, 2, I.… usually constr. with an object clause, *quod …*,
> (α)., with acc. and inf.;
> verbs of emotion + OO, GL n° 533;
> M & M, 60, 71, GL n° 527, remarks 1–2;
> OO, 71–73; sentence structure, 1.

tam … quam …, "so … much as": these correlatives go together.

> → **591** correlative comparative sentences, 90.5, GL n° 642.

valde … valde, "very … very": Cicero balances the statement naturally,
instinctively with these two words placed second from each end of this part
of the sentence.

> → **592** sentence structure, 1.

Quod, "The fact that": this expression introduces a new subject.

> → **593** *quod* = "the fact that" as a new subject, GL n° 525.2.

suadesque ut meminerim Iovis orationem, "and [the fact that] you suggest
that I remember the speech of Jupiter": the verb *suades*, "you suggest," in T.1i
produces a purpose clause that gives the mental content of the suggestion,
ut meminerim, "that I remember," a defective verb that does not have a T.1s,
so T.3s is used here with present meaning, because that is the only way to say
this with *meminerim*. This verb of remembering is used here with the object
orationem, "the speech," rather than the gen., as in other instances, such as
orationis, "[I am mindful] of the speech." Conservative grammarians and
old-timers will be angry here with Cicero because he is not following their
Latin rules.

> → **594** subjunctive use: purpose clause, 58.1;
> verbs of remembering and forgetting, 74;
> defective verbs, 14.4, GL n° 175.5: *coepi, memini, odi.*

ego vero memini, "I indeed remember": the same defective verb is used
again, this time *memini*, "I … remember," is in T.4, with present meaning.
With this form we can say "they remember," *meminerunt*, "you remember,"
meministi. Another similar verb is *odi, odisse*, "to hate." Here *vero*, "indeed,"
reinforces the statement, but it can also mean "but, however"; it is placed
somewhere after the first word of the sentence, wheareas *verum*, "but," "indeed," is always the first word.

> → **595** dict., *verus, a, um*, adj., II., adv., B. *vero*, "truly," b., "indeed," 2. "but"
> (always placed after a word);
> defective verbs, 14.4, GL n° 175.5: *coepi, memini, odi.*

magis ... quam, "more than": here *quam* means "than," whereas above *tam
... quam,* means "so much as," and in the next paragraph immediately below this one *quam perfectus,* means "later than you set out."

→ **596** *quam* with the comp., 43.2; adv.: irregular comp., 37.3, GL n° 93.

᨞

Sed tamen postridie quam tu es profectus, multa nocte cum Vibullio veni ad
Pompeium, cumque ego egissem de istis operibus atque inscriptionibus, per
mihi benigne respondit: magnam spem attulit: cum Crasso se dixit loqui
velle mihique ut idem facerem suasit. Crassum consulem ex senatu domum
reduxi. Suscepit rem dixitque esse quod Clodius hoc tempore cuperet per se
et per Pompeium consequi: putare se, si ego eum non impedirem, posse me
adipisci sine contentione quod vellem. Totum ei negotium permisi meque in
eius potestate dixi fore. Interfuit huic sermoni P. Crassus adulescens, nostri,
ut scis, studiosissimus. Illud autem quod cupit Clodius est legatio aliqua—si
minus per senatum, per populum—libera aut Byzantium aut *ad* Brogitarum
aut utrumque. Plena res nummorum. Quod ego non nimium laboro, etiam
si minus adsequor quod volo. Pompeius tamen cum Crasso locutus est. Videntur negotium suscepisse. Si perficiunt, optime: si minus, ad nostrum Iovem revertamur.   (*Q. Fr.* II, 7 [9], 2)

But nevertheless on the day after you set out, far into the night I came with
Vibullius to Pompeius, and when I had treated about those works and dedi-
cations, he [Pompeius] answered me most graciously: he brought great hope:
he said he wanted to speak with Crassus and he suggested to me that I do
the same thing. I led Crassus the consul home from the senate. He [Crassus]
took up the matter and said there was [something] which Clodius at this
time desired to attain by himself and with the help of Pompey: he [Crassus]
was thinking that if I would not stop him I was able to attain what I was
continuing to desire without fighting. I left the whole business to him and
I said I would be under his control. Publius Crassus Jr. was present at this
conversation, very interested in us, as you know. That which Clodius longs
for is some embassy—if not through the senate, through the people—some
free embassy either to Byzantium [Constantinople] or to Brogitarus or to
both. The whole business is full of money; something which I am not exces-
sively disturbed about, even if I attain to a lesser extent that which I want.
Nevertheless Pompeius spoke with Crassus. They seem to have undertaken
the whole business. If they finish it off, wonderful; if not, let us return to our
Jupiter.

postridie quam tu es profectus, "on the day after you set out": *quam* here
means almost "than," as in "later than you set out," "on the day later than
you set out," "on the day after you set out."

→ **597** *quam,* 43.

multa nocte, "far into the night": *nocte* is the form by-with-from-in of time at which, time in which, time when, meaning "late at night," "in the late of night," "advanced night."

> → **598** abl.: time at which, 70.1.

cumque ego egissem, "and when I had treated": the *–que* joins *veni*, "I came" with *respondit*, "he answered"; the *–que* is placed on the end of the first word of the second element, so *cum … egissem*, "when I had treated," depends on *respondit*, "he answered," not on *veni*, "I came." Because *respondit*, "he answered," in T.4b, establishes an historical time, *cum* can mean "because" or "since" or can give the circumstance "when," because it is followed by the subjunctive, *egissem*, "I had treated," in T.4s. As a temporal circumstance, it approaches the expression of a cause and effect.

> → **599** subjunctive use: causal *cum* = "because, since," 59.1;
>   subjunctive use: temporal circumstance *cum* = "when," 66.3.2;
>   conjunction: *–que*, 3.2.

per mihi benigne respondit, "he answered me most graciously": the adverb *perbenigne*, "very kindly" is separated into two parts *per* and *benigne* for reasons of clever elegance, and between them is placed the dat. that goes with *respondit*, "he answered," one of the 65 verbs that takes its complement in the dat., as if to say, "he answered to me very kindly," "he answered very to me kindly"; Latin tricks!

> → **600** 65 verbs with dat., 33.7.2, GL n° 346;
>   conjunction: *–que*, 3.2.

se dixit loqui velle, "he said he wanted to speak": the main verb *dixit*, "he said," in T.4b, as a verb of M & M produces a sentence in OO where *se*, is the subject in the object form and as a reflexive pronoun refers to the subject of *dixit*, "[Pompey] said," and the contemporaneous inf. *velle* is complemented by its own object *loqui*, "to speak," the gerund, thus, "Pompey said that he was wanting to speak with Crassus."

> → **601** M & M, 60, 71, GL n° 527, remarks 1–2; OO, 71–73;
>   verb: complementary infinitive, 77; gerund, 77.1;
>   reflexive pron.: third person, 31.

mihique ut idem facerem suasit, "and he suggested to me that I do the same thing": the *–que* joins *dixit*, "he said," and *suasit*, "he suggested." The verb *suasit*, "he suggested," is one of the 65 that almost naturally take their complement in the dat., as in "he suggested to me." The verb *suasit*, "he suggested," in T.4b establishes Track II and produces a purpose clause that gives the intent of the persuading, *ut idem facerem*, "that I do the same thing," where *facerem*, "I do," is in T.2s and rendered in English in the subjunctive.

> → **602** conjunction: *–que*, 3.2; 65 verbs with dat., 33.7.2, GL n° 346;
>   *consecutio*, 47–48; subjunctive use: purpose clause, 58.1.

domum reduxi, "I led ... home": one of several isolated expressions of place to which; these include *domum*, "to home," *rus*, "to the countryside," *humum*, "onto the ground" and *foras*, "to the outside."

> → **603** function: place to where, *domum*, 69.1.3.

Two sentences in Latin full of indirect discourse in OO and MA:

Suscepit rem	main 1
dixitque	main 2
esse	OO 1
⎧quod Clodius hoc tempore cuperet	rel. MA depending on OO 1
⎩per se et per Pompeium consequi;	
putare se,	OO 2
si ego eum non impedirem,	⎧foggy-future or
	⎩logical condition in MA
posse me adipisci sine contention	consequence OO 3
quod vellem.	MA
Totum ei negotium permisi	main 3
meque in eius potestate	OO 4 depending on main 4
dixi	main 4
fore.	OO 4 continued

> → **604** structure of Latin sentences, 103 p. 587, *Ossa* Readings: 1-D, 1-I, 3-D, 3-I,
>   4-D, 4-I;
>   relative box, 11.4.

suscepit rem dixitque, "He undertook the matter and said": *–que* joins *suscepit*, "he undertook," and *dixit*, "he said," two finite verbs both in T.4b, establishing Track II.

> → **605** conjunction: *–que*, 3.2; *consecutio*, 47–48.

dixitque esse, "and said there was [something]": *dixit*, "he said," in T.4b establishing Track II is a verb of M & M and produces indirect discourse in OO where the contemporaneous inf. verb *esse* has an implied subject *id*, "something," itself the antecedent of *quod*, "[something] which."

> → **606** M & M, 60, 71, GL nº 527, remarks 1–2;
>   OO, 71–73; *consecutio*, 47–48;
>   rel. pron.: subject or object, 10.

dixit ... putare se, "[he] said ... he was thinking": *dixit*, "[Crassus] said," in T.4b is still felt further down the sentence as a verb of M & M and produces a second statement of indirect discourse in OO where *se* is the subject in the object form and a reflexive pronoun referring to the subject of *dixit*, "[Crassus] said," and the contemporaneous inf. *putare*, "he was thinking." This statement in OO is placed next to the previous one *esse*, "there was [some-thing]," by asyndeton, that is juxtaposed one next to the other.

> → **607** M & M, 60, 71, GL n° 527, remarks 1–2;
>   OO, 71–73; verb: contemporaneous active infinitive, 72.1;
>   reflexive pron.: third person, 31;
>   asyndeton: examples in *Ossa*, pp. 754, 755, 757, 766.

quod Clodius ... cuperet ... consequi, "which Clodius ... desired to attain": a relative clause whose verb *cuperet*, "[Claudius] desired," is in T.2s by MA, depending on [*id*] *esse*, "there was [something]" in OO. The object of *cuperet*, is *consequi*, "[Claudius was continuing to desire] to attain," or "[Claudius desired] attaining," as a gerund.

> → **608** relative clauses, 10–11; OO, 71–73;
>   subjunctive use: modal attraction, 83;
>   verb: complementary infinitive, 77; gerund, 77.1;
>   rel. pron.: subject or object, 10.

putare se ... posse me adipisci, "he was thinking that ... I was able to attain": the statement in OO *putare se*, "he was thinking," is an expression of M & M which in turn produces its own statement in OO where *me* is the subject in object form and *posse* the contemporaneous inf. with its own object, *adipisci*, a gerund, "to attain." This statement in OO is also the consequence of a conditional sentence whose condition is the following.

> → **609** M & M, 60, 71, GL n° 527, remarks 1–2; OO, 71–73;
>   verb: contemporaneous active infinitive, 72.1;
>   verb: contemporaneous deponent infinitive, 72.3;
>   verb: complementary infinitive, 77; gerund, 77.1.

si ego eum non impedirem, "if I would not stop him": a conditional sentence whose consequence is given in indirect discourse, *posse me adipisci*, "I was able to attain." Because this condition depends on the consequence and so is involved in the indirect discourse, the verb *impedirem*, "I would [not] stop," in T.2s, could be removed from indirect discourse and restored to direct discourse in several ways. It could stand for *impediebam*, "If I was not block-ing him," in T.2i as a logical conditional. It could stand for *impediam*, "If I should not block him," in T.1s as a foggy or less-vivid future. It could stand for *impedirem*, "If I were to block him," in T.2s as a contrary to fact condi-tional. All three of these placed into OO in this sentence would produce the same form, *impedirem*, and thus are possible interpretations. According to the thought of the letter, this is not a contrary to fact conditional, but it is almost a foggy less-vivid future or a logical conditional in MA because it depends on *putare se*, itself in OO. Latin's eternal traps, mysteries, challeng-es. A reminder of old stuff is that Latin has only four subjunctive times to express every human thought.

> → **610** conditionals: factual, 86.1; conditionals: foggy future, 86.2;
>   conditionals: contrary to fact, 86.3;
>   conditionals in OO, 103; subjunctive use: modal attraction, 83.

quod vellem, "what I was continuing to desire": a relative statement where *vellem* is T.2s by MA because it depends on *posse me adipisci*, "I was able to attain," in OO. If the statement were in direct discourse, it would be *volebam*, "what I was wanting." The antecedent of *quod*, "what," is an implied *id*, "that thing," itself the object of *adipisci*, as in "I was able to attain that thing <u>which</u> I wanted."

> → **611** relative clauses, 10–11; OO, 71–73;
>   subjunctive use: modal attraction, 83.

permisi meque in eius potestate dixi fore, "I left … and I said that I would be under his control": the *-que* joins two main verbs, *permisi*, "I left," in T.4b and also in T.4b *dixi*, "I said," itself a verb of M & M that gives rise to a statement in OO where the subject in the object form is *me* and the verb is the last word in the sentence, the inf. *fore*, which stands for *futurum esse* "that I would be," "that I was going to be."

> → **612** M & M, 60, 71, GL n° 527, remarks 1–2; OO, 71–73;
>   futurity participle, 50, 51.1.3;
>   *futurum esse* (*fore*), 72.1; futurity formula, active, 53.3;
>   conjunction: *-que*, 3.2; sentence structure, 1.

Interfuit huic sermoni, "[Crassus] was present at this conversation": the compound verb *interesse* is complemented by the dat., meaning "to be in the middle of something," "to be present at something," so here *interfuit*, "[Crassus] was present" in T.4b is accompanied by the dat. *huic sermoni*, "at this conversation." We can restore the prefix as a preposition by saying, *fuit inter hunc sermonem*, "[Crassus] was in the midst of this conversation."

> → **613** dat. with compound verbs, 33.7.3, GL n° 347.

nostri, ut scis, studiosissimus, "very interested in us, as you know": *nostri*, "of us," complements *studiossissimus*, "most interested," because the dict. says that *studiosus, a, um*, "interested in," "zealous about," goes with the gen., as in the English expression, "zealous about us" or "interested in us." Between these two words comes the phrase *ut scis*, where *scis*, "you know," is in T.1i and *ut* here means "as."

> → **614** dict., *studiosus, a, um*, adj. I. (α). with gen. (most frequent);
>   *ut* I., B. meaning "as";
>   personal pronouns: function of-possession, 24.2.

aut Byzantium aut ad Brogitarum aut utrumque, "either to Byzantium [Constantinople] or to Brogitarus or to both": three expressions of place to where are given here. First, *Byzantium*, stands all alone meaning "to Byzantium [Constantinople]," like *domum*, "to home," where the object form gives the extent of place or end of a journey. Second, Tyrrell correctly adds *ad* to the name of the people *Brogitarum*, because personal names, like the names of towns and small islands, do not have the special object form to express the same idea of extent of place or end of a journey. The third form here continues the *ad ... utrumque*, "to both," under the influence of the two previous expressions.

> → **615** function: place to where, *Byzantium*, 69.1.2;
> function: place to where, *ad Brogitarum*, 69.1.2;
> function: place to where, *domum*, 69.1.3.

Plena res nummorum, "The whole business [is] full of money": the adj. *plenus, a, um*, complemented by the of-possession form means "full of," as here, where *plena nummorum* means "[the whole matter is] full of money." It can also be used with the form by-with-from-in, to mean "full with," as in the greeting, *Ave Maria gratia plena*, where *plena* is complemented by *gratia* in the abl. of means or instrument "full with grace."

> → **616** dict., *plenus, a, um*, adj., I. A. in gen., with gen., ... with abl., *et alibi*;
> abl.: instrument, 28.5.3–4, ,89.2, GL n° 401.

laboro, "I am ... disturbed": here the verb does not mean "I labor" but, "I labor under" and thus, "I am troubled," "I am disturbed," according to your dict.

> → **617** dict., *laboro, avi, atum*, 1., I., B., 2., "to be concerned."

si minus adsequor ... si minus, "if I attain to a lesser extent ... if not": two different meanings for *si minus*. The first means "if ... to a lesser degree," the second is a softened negation, "if not at all," "by no means," "if not."

> → **618** dict., *parvus, a, um*, adj.,: III., B., *minus*, 2–3.

❧

A. d. III. Id. Febr. senatus consultum est factum de ambitu in Afrani sententiam, quam ego dixeram cum tu adesses. Sed magno cum gemitu senatus consules non sunt persecuti eorum sententias qui, Afranio cum essent adsensi, addiderunt ut praetores ita crearentur ut dies sexaginta privati essent. Eo die Catonem plane repudiarunt. Quid multa? tenent omnia idque ita omnis intellegere volunt.   (Q. Fr. II, 7 [9], 3)

On the third day before the February Ides [11 February] a decision was made of the Senate about canvassing in favor of the position of Afranius, which I had mentioned to you when you were here present. But with a great groan of the senate the consuls did not pursue the opinions of those who, after they had agreed with Afranius, added that the praetors be nominated in such a way that for sixty days they would be private citizens. On that day they outrightly rejected Cato. Why [should I say] many things? they hold on to all things and they want all people to understand this in this way.

A. d. III. Id. Febr., "On the third day before the February Ides [11 February]": the full form is *ante diem tertium Idus Februarias*, meaning "the third day before the February Ides." The word *ante* is placed first, and the whole expression is a set formula, but the expression feels like the word *ante* should be placed rather before *Idus*, as in *die tertio ante Idus Februarias* "on the third day before the February Ides."

> → **619** about the Roman calendar, pp. 605–608;
>   GL appendix: Roman Calendar, pp. 491–92.

cum tu adesses, "when you were here present": the verb *dixeram*, "I had mentioned," in T.5i establishes Track II. Here *cum* followed by *adesses* in T.2s, can mean either "because" or "although," but here may be taken to give the circumstance "when."

> → **620** *consecutio*, 47–48;
>   subjunctive use: temporal circumstance *cum* = "when," 66.3.2;
>   subjunctive use: causal *cum* = "because, since," 59.1;
>   subjunctive use: concessive *cum* = "although," 64.

Afranio cum essent adsensi, "after they had agreed with Afranius": the verb *sunt persecuti*, "did [not] pursue," in T.4b establishes Track II. Again, *cum*, followed by *essent adsensi* in T.4s, can mean "because" or "although," but here it is taken to give the circumstance "when," rendered "after" because of the antecedent time of the verb. The dep. *assentior*, "I give assent," is one of the 65 verbs that has its complement in the dat., here *Afranio*, but in English the dat. may not be heard easily unless you say, "after they had given assent to Afranius."

> → **621** *consecutio*, 47–48;
>   subjunctive use: temporal circumstance *cum* = "when," 66.3.2;
>   subjunctive use: causal *cum* = "because, since," 59.1;
>   subjunctive use: concessive *cum* = "although," 64;
>   verb: deponent, 29; 65 verbs with dat., 33.7.2, GL n° 346.

addiderunt ut praetores ita crearentur ut dies … essent, "they added that the praetors be nominated in such a way that for … days they would be": *addiderunt*, "they added," in T.4b, establishing Track II, produces a purpose clause that gives the content of their speech, *ut … crearentur*, "that [the praetors] be nominated," in T.2s, which in turn produces another purpose clause expressing the content of the nomination, *ut dies … essent*, "that for … days they would be," also in T.2s, and both rendered in English in the subjunctive.

> → **622** *consecutio*, 47–48; subjunctive use: purpose clause, 58.1;
>   *consecutio*: subjunctive depending on a subjunctive, 62.1.

Eo die, "On that day": abl. of time at which or in which.

> → **623** abl.: time at which, 70.1.

repudiarunt, "they … rejected": a contraction for *repudiaverunt*, "they rejected," in T.4b.

> → **624** contractions: verbs, 39.2, GL n° 131.

Quid multa?, "Why [should I say] many things": the idiom is in the dictionary. Where there is no verb, you can add one such as *dicam*, to say, "Why should I say many things," or *scribam*, "Why should I write many things?" In English we might say, "Why should I go into detail?" Sometimes the expression is *Quid plura*, "Why [should I say] more things?"

→ **625** dict., *multus, a, um,* adj., II., B., 2.: … also elliptically … like *quid multa?*

ita omnis intellegere volunt, "they want all people to understand this in this way": here *omnis* is an alternative form for *omnes*, the object plural, "all people."

→ **626** Block II adj.: *–is* = *–es*, 38, GL n° 78.

N.B.: This whole magnificent spontaneous letter of our Cicero to his beloved Quintus gives us an opportunity to hear him clearly talking on the phone—if the letter is read or recited aloud a few times in school or at home: irresistibly beautiful and supremely useful, functional for us all.

LETTER 463 T-P
AD FAMILIARES IX, 5

CICERO VARRONI.

Mihi vero ad Nonas bene maturum videtur fore, neque solum propter rei publicae sed etiam propter anni tempus. Qua re istum diem probo: itaque eundem ipse sequar.   (*Fam.* IX, 5, 1)

CICERO TO VARRO

To me, however, it seems that it will be soon enough by the Nones, and not only because of the situation of the state but also because of the time of the year. For which reason I approve of that day: and so I myself will follow the same.

bene maturum, "soon enough": a full use of your dictionary will save you from saying this expression looks like it means "well mature."
> → **627** dict., *maturus, a, um*, adj., II., A.... *bene maturum*, "just at the right time."

fore, "it will be": *fore* is an alternative of *futurum esse*, "to be about to be," and the entire expression *ad Nonas bene maturum ... fore* is OO and serves as the subject of *videtur*.
> → **628** OO, 71–73; futurity participle, 50, 51.1.3;
> *futurum esse* (*fore*), 72.1; futurity formula, active, 53.3.

propter ... propter ... tempus, "because of the situation ... because of the time": stylistically Cicero uses the preposition *propter* twice, with the same object, *tempus*, that appears only with the second occurrence. A more refined style might expect him to leave out the second occurrence of *propter*, but its duplication here is a good sign that these letters preserve the ready thought just as it comes out of his pen.
> → **629** prep. with obj., 6; sentence structure, 1.

tempus, "the situation ... the time [of the year]": the word *tempus* is used with two variant meanings. The expression *rei publicae ... tempus* refers to the "situation of the state," but *anni tempus* refers to "the time of the year"; the first a circumstance or condition and the other an astronomical time. Note: it is one thing to say *illo tempore*, "at that time," but Cicero will also say *in illo tempore*, "in that circumstance." This shifts in later Latin when Christian authors always say *in illo tempore*, "at that time."

→ **630** dict., *tempus, oris*, n., I.... *anni tempora*, "the seasons," B., 2., a, "the state of the times, circumstances"; abl.: time at which, 70.1; prep. with abl., 28.4.

~

Consili nostri, ne si eos quidem qui id secuti non sunt non paeniteret, nobis paenitendum putarem. Secuti enim sumus non spem sed officium: reliquimus autem non officium sed desperationem. Ita verecundiores fuimus quam qui se domo non commoverunt, saniores quam qui amissis opibus domum non reverterunt. Sed nihil minus fero quam severitatem otiosorum et, quoquo modo se res habet, magis illos vereor qui in bello occiderunt quam hos curo quibus non satis facimus quia vivimus.   (*Fam.* IX, 5, 2)

I would think that regret of our decision has to be felt by us even if it would not cause regret to those who did not follow it. For we pursued not hope but duty: however, we abandoned not duty but desperation. Thus, we were more bashful than those who did not move themselves from [their] home, more reasonable than those who, after their wealth had been lost, did not return to home. But I tolerate nothing to a lesser degree than the strictness of the lazy people, and in whatever manner the thing finds itself, I respect more those people who fell in war than I bother about these whom we are not satisfying because we are living.

consili, "of [our] decision": GL mentions that until about first century the of-possession function of consilium was *consili*, although now we learn it as *consilii*. Knowing this will prevent confusion with some imagined form of the function to-for-from, dat. For example, *consili* is "of counsel," *consuli* is "to, for the cousul."

→ **631** early gen. ending in *–i*, GL n° 33, remark 1.

consili nostri ... paenitendum, "regret of our decision": the verb *paeniteo, paenitere, paenitui* 2 is one of the famous five verbs of emotion that take the of-possession genitive of the object of regret, here *consili nostri*, which begins this sentence and is separated from this verb on which it depends. These are used impersonally, as the note in GL indicates.

→ **632** verbs of emotion + gen., GL n° 377 and remark 2; sentence structure, 1.

eos ... non paeniteret, "it would not cause regret to those": here the verb has only the direct object of the one affected, *eos*, whereas above it has only the of-possession genitive of the object of regret, *consili nostri*. These are used impersonally, as the note in GL indicates.

→ **633** dict., *paeniteo, ui*, 2;
   verbs of emotion + gen., GL n° 377 and remark 2.

paeniteret ... putarem, "I would think ... it would [not] cause regret": both verbs are T.2s to express contrary to fact conditions in the present. This can be tested by affirming the opposite in each case, "I would think, but I do not, ... it would not cause regret, but it does."

→ **634** conditionals: contrary to fact, 86.3.

nobis paenitendum, "that regret has to be felt by us": the full infinitive is *paenitendum esse*, an expression of the passive necessity formula in OO depending on the M & M verb *putarem*, "I would think." The *nobis*, "by us," is the usual dat. of agent with the expression of passive necessity.

→ **635** participle of passive necessity, 50, 51.1.4;
   passive necessity formula, 53.4;
   dat. of agent, 53.5;
   M & M, 60, 71, GL n° 527, remarks 1–2; OO, 71–73.

Note the perfect example of the box system in the first sentence:

{ Consili nostri,	OO begins
[ne si eos quidem	contrary to fact conditional begins
(qui id secuti non sunt)	relative
non paeniteret],	contrary to fact conditional concludes
nobis paenitendum }	OO concludes
putarem.	main

→ **636** structure of Latin sentences, 103 p. 587, *Ossa* Readings: 1-D, 1-I, 3-D,
   3-I, 4-D, 4-I;
   relative box, 11.4.

verecundiores ... quam ... saniores quam, "more bashful than ... more reasonable than": both comparative adjectives are followed by *quam*, "than."

→ **637** adj.: comp., 36; *quam* with the comp., 43.2.

domo ... domum, "from ... home ... to home": the same word is used to express separation from, *domo*, "from home"; movement to or toward, *domum*, "toward home"; and the teacher could complete the list by adding the place where, *domi*, "at home."

→ **638** function: place from where, *domo*, 69.2.3;
   function: place to where, *domum*, 69.1.3;
   function: place at which, *domi*, 69.3.3.

quam qui, "than those who": both times Cicero says *quam qui* he omits the second half of each comparison. In both cases the antecedent of the *qui* is *ii*, as in *fuimus quam ii qui … saniores quam ii qui*. This antecedent is supplied in the English "than *those* who … than *those* who."

→ **639** *quam*, 43; rel. pron.: omission of the antecedent, 11.2.

amissis opibus, "their wealth having been lost": ablative absolute with an antecedent, passive participle.

→ **640** ablative absolute, 54–55.

minus … quam … magis … quam, "to a lesser degree than … more … than": the other degrees of *minus* are [*paulum*] and *minime*. The brackets indicate a substitution for the nonexistent form *parve*, so *paulum*, "to a small degree" is used from *paulus, a, um*. The other degrees of *magis* are [*magnopere*] and *maxime*. Again, *magne* does not exist for "greatly," so a substitute is used: *magnopere*, from *magno opere*, "with great effort." Both forms *magnopere* and *magno opere* are given in the dict. Note how far the comparative adverbs are separated from the *quam* that goes with each, especially the distance between *magis* and seven words later *quam*.

→ **641** dict., *magnopere*, I. adv. *magnus-opus*, "with great labor; greatly"; adv.: irregular comp., 37.3, GL n° 93; sentence structure, 1.

☙

Mihi si spatium fuerit in Tusculanum ante Nonas veniendi, istic te videbo: si minus, persequar in Cumanum et ante te certiorem faciam, ut lavatio parata sit.   (*Fam.* IX, 5, 3)

If there will have been for me an opportunity of coming to the Tusculan villa before the Nones, I shall see you there: if not, I shall follow you to the Cumaean villa and I shall inform you beforehand so that a bath may be ready.

si … fuerit … videbo, "if there will have been … I shall see": Romans were precise about using this combination of T.6i and T.3i, which should be respected by all and imitated by Latinists. The Romans used precise verb times to say precise things for a good reason, no matter what modern languages have done with all the precision.

→ **642** T.3i and T.6i paired: 7, Time 6, and GL n° 244, remark 2.

spatium … veniendi, "opportunity of coming": all students and scholars note the style which separates *spatium* from *veniendi* by five words. The form *veniendi* is a gerund in the form of-possession, meaning "of coming."

→ **643** gerund, 77.1; sentence structure, 1.

spatium, "an opportunity": this noun indicates an interval of time and thus a space, breathing room, opportunity.

→ **644** dict., *spatium, ii*, n., II., A., 2., a. "space, time, leisure, opportunity."

Cumanum, "Cumaean villa": Cicero's Cumaean villa was on the west end of the Bay of Naples.

→ **645** dict., *Cumae, arum*, f., II. *Cumanus, a, um*, adj., "of Cumae, Cumaean."

ante te, "you beforehand": these two words look like *ante* is a preposition and its object is *te*, meaning "before you," but here *ante* is an adverb meaning "previously, beforehand," and *te* is the object of *faciam*, "I shall inform you beforehand, first."

→ **646** dict., *ante*, II., adv. of space and time, B., 1. "before, previously."

LETTER 311 T-P
AD ATTICUM VII, 15

CICERO ATTICO SAL.

Ut ab urbe discessi, nullum adhuc intermisi diem quin aliquid ad te litterarum darem, non quo haberem magno opere quod scriberem sed ut loquerer
tecum absens, quo mihi, cum coram id non licet, nihil est iucundius.   (*Att.*
VII, 15, 1)

CICERO A GREETING TO ATTICUS

Since I departed from the city, so far I skipped no day that I did not send
to you some bit of a letter, not because I especially had something which I
might write, but that I, absent, might converse with you, than which thing
nothing is more pleasant for me whenever it is not possible face to face.

CICERO ATTICO SAL.: *Cicero Attico salutem*

A map of the clauses will help us to see our way through this sentence:

(Ut ab urbe discessi,)	temporal T.4b
nullum adhuc intermisi diem	main sentence T.4b
{ quin aliquid ad te litterarum darem,	negative result T.2s
[non quo haberem magno opera	causal T.2s
(quod scriberem)]	characteristic result T.2s
[sed ut loquerer tecum absens,	purpose T.2s
(quo mihi,	relative
< cum coram id non licet, >	temporal T.1i
nihil est iucundius.)] }	relative continued

→ **647** structure of Latin sentences, 103 p. 587, *Ossa* Readings: 1-D, 1-I, 3-D, 3-I,
4-D, 4-I;
relative box, 11.4.

Note well that four verbs in a row are in T.2s, each for a different even contrary reason and sounding accordingly in English. Latin demands precision,
thinking, not sloppy guessing. Each of these is given below:

→ **648** principles of the subjunctive, 45.

darem, from *quin … darem*, "that I did not send": a negative result clause
sounding in English in the ind.

haberem from *non quo haberem*, "not because I … had": the speech of
others reported by Cicero, sounding in English in the ind.

scriberem, from *quod scriberem*, "which I might write": a characteristic
result clause that sounds in English in the subjunctive because of an underlying potential idea.

loquerer, from *sed ut loquerer*, "but that I … might converse": purpose
clause giving Cicero's intention and sounding in English in the subjunctive.

ut … discessi, "Since I departed": *ut* or *ubi* with T.4i, here *discessi*, is very
common for "when," "since," "after." This expression is deceptive, and
people will think of numerous other meanings for *ut*, but here *ut* does not
mean "that."

→ **649** dict., *ut* or *uti*, adv., II., B. introducing a temporal clause, 1.: d. rarely
coincidence of time; e. *ut* = *ex quo tempore*, "since."

quin … darem, "that I did not send": the verb *intermisi*, "I skipped," in T.4b,
establishes Track II, and gives rise to a good example of *quin* starting either
a result clause *ut non … darem*, "so that I did not give [a letter]," or a relative
clause of result, *quo non … darem*, "on which day I did not give," both in
T.2s. In English the result clause is expressed in the indicative. There is a
remark in GL n° 632 that says that *quin* was felt not as *qui non*, but as *ut non*.

→ **650** *consecutio*, 47–48;
subjunctive use: pure result (consecutive), 67.1–2, GL n° 552.3;
subjunctive use: relative clause of pure result (consecutive), 79.6.

aliquid … litterarum, "some bit of a letter": *litterarum* is a genitive of part
and is typically separated from the word on which it depends, here by two
other words.

→ **651** gen. of part, 99.

non quo haberem … quo, "not because I … had … than which": the two occurrences of *quo* here have nothing to do with each other. The first *quo* is an
adv., meaning "for the reason that," "because," and begins a causal clause.
Here *quo* is a variant of *quod, quia, quoniam*, all meaning "because." Its
verb, *haberem*, is in T.2s to indicate that the cause given is not Cicero's own,
but that he is quoting someone else's opinion or even hearsay, a reason Cicero negates. This reported reason is rejected by Cicero, as indicated by the
non before the *quo*. Thus, the clause means "not because [as one may think]

I had [something]" or "not because [as some may say] I had [something]."
The second occurrence of *quo* is given further below.

> → **652** dict., *quo*, adv., I., B., 2. "For the reason that," "because"; adv., 37;
> causal: *quod, quia, quoniam,* "because, since," + subjunctive, reported
> reason, 59.2;
> causal: rejected reason, *non quo*, GL n° 541, note 2; *consecutio*, 47–48.

non quo haberem … sed ut loquerer, "not because I … had … but that I …
might converse": two clauses are being compared, the first a causal clause,
non quo haberem, "not because I had," where *haberem,* "I had," in T.2s indicating that it is the reported speech of others, a reason negated by Cicero,
as presented above. The second is a purpose clause giving Cicero's own
intention in writing daily, *sed ut loquerer,* "but so that I might converse,"
where *loquerer,* "I might converse," is T.2s and rendered in English in the
subjunctive.

> → **653** *consecutio,* 47–48;
> subjunctive use: purpose clause, 58.1; verb: deponent, 29.

magno opere, "especially": these two words substitute for an imaginary
"*magne,*" a would-be adv. of the adj. *magnus,* "great." These are sometimes
written as one word *magnopere* meaning "greatly." The comparative degree
of the adv. is *magis,* "in a higher degree," "more completely," and the superlative degree is *maximopere* or *maximo opere,* or *maxime,* "in the greatest
degree." The temptation is not to see the comparative here but to take *magno
opere* to mean "with great labor," which it can mean elsewhere—to the
shame and desperation of many.

> → **654** dict., *magnopere,* I. adv. *magnus-opus,* "with great labor; greatly";
> adv.: irregular comp., 37.3, GL n° 93.

quod scriberem, "which I might write": a characteristic result where *quod*
stands for *tale ut id,* "such that [I might write] it," "such which I might
write," "that I was writing." The characteristic subjunctive is rendered into
English in the ind., which would be here, "there was nothing which I was
writing," but here there is an underlying potential subjunctive that comes
through in the English with the force of saying, "which I might write."

> → **655** subjunctive use: characteristic result, 68.2;
> subjunctive use: underlying potential of the past, 94.3, GL n° 258.

quo mihi … nihil est iucundius, "than which thing nothing is more pleasant
for me": this second *quo,* which is a comparison in the ablative meaning
"than which," has nothing to do with the first. It connects with *iucundius,*
"more pleasant," a neuter comparative adj. at the end of the sentence. The
antecedent of the *quo* is the first part of the sentence, *ut loquerer tecum
absens,* "so that I, absent, might converse with you."

> → **656** abl.: comparison, 90.2, GL n° 398.

cum coram id non licet, "whenever it is not possible face to face": *cum* with all times of the indicative means "when," as here with *licet*, "it is … possible," in T.1i. The subject of *licet*, "it is permitted," "it is possible," is the *id*, "it," which refers again to the larger sentence, *ut loquerer tecum absens*, "so that I, absent, might converse with you." Here *coram* is again not a preposition meaning "in front of someone," but an adv., meaning "in your presence," "face to face," and describes their conversation in person.

→ **657** *cum* + indicative = "when": temporal sentences, 66.3;
      dict., *licet*, *licuit* and *citum est*, 2., I. (ε) impersonal verb;
      dict., *coram*, adv. and prep. with abl.

ᴥ

Capuam cum venissem a. d. VI Kal., pridie quam has litteras dedi, consules conveni multosque nostri ordinis. Omnes cupiebant Caesarem abductis praesidiis stare condicionibus iis quas tulisset. Uni Favonio leges ab illo nobis imponi non placebat, sed is *haud* auditus in consilio. Cato enim ipse iam servire quam pugnare mavult. Sed tamen ait in senatu se adesse velle, cum de condicionibus agatur, si Caesar adductus sit ut praesidia deducat. Ita, quod maxime opus est, in Siciliam ire non curat; quod metuo ne obsit, in senatu esse vult. Postumius autem, de quo nominatim senatus decrevit ut statim in Siciliam iret Furfanioque succederet, negat se sine Catone iturum et suam in senatu operam auctoritatemque quam magni aestimat. Ita res ad Fannium pervenit. Is cum imperio in Siciliam praemittitur.   (*Att.* VII, 15, 2)

When I had arrived at Capua on the sixth day before the Kalends [27 January], on the day before I sent this letter, I met the consuls and many men of our [senatorial] rank. All people were wanting Caesar to abide by those conditions which he had made—garrisons having been withdrawn. To Favonius alone it was not agreeable that laws be imposed on us by him, but he was not listened to in the assembly. For Cato himself now prefers to serve than to fight. But nevertheless he says that he wishes to be present in the senate because the discussion is being made about the conditions, whether Caesar has been persuaded that he withdraw the garrisons. So, he does not care to go to Sicily, something which is most necessary; he wants to be in the senate, something which I am afraid may be an obstacle. But Postumius, about whom the senate decreed in name that he would go immediately to Sicily and succeed Furfanius, denies that he will go without Cato and his own effort and authority in the senate which he highly values. Thus the matter came down to Fannius. He is being sent ahead to Sicily with command.

Capuam cum venissem, "When I had arrived at Capua": *Capuam* is the function of place to where, the end of a journey. The *cum* followed by *venissem*, in T.4s, can mean either "because," "although," but here it gives the historical circumstance, "When."

→ **658** function: place to where, *Capuam,* 69.1.2;
subjunctive use: temporal circumstance *cum* = "when," 66.3.2;
subjunctive use: causal *cum* = "because, since," 59.1;
subjunctive use: concessive *cum* = "although," 64.

a. d. VI Kal., "on the sixth day before the Kalends": the full Latin is *ante diem sextum Kalendas,* that is, 27 January. Tyrrell and Purser as well as S. Bailey all say 26 January without explanation for their calculation. Both the *Kalendas Februarias,* the first of February, and the 27th of January are included in this counting, thus January 27, 28, 29, 30, 31, 1 February, for a total of six days.

→ **659** about the Roman calendar, pp. 605–608;
GL appendix: Roman Calendar, pp. 491–92.

pridie quam ... dedi, "on the day before I sent": *pridie* itself means "on the day before" and is constructed with *quam.* An explanation for this combination is found in the dict., which states that *pridie* comes from the words *prior* and *dies,* and from this one can see the combination of the comparative *prior* with *quam,* "sooner than," as in "on the day sooner than I sent."

→ **660** dict., *pridie,* adv.; *quam* with the comp., 43.2.

Omnes cupiebant Caesarem ... stare, "All people were wanting Caesar to abide": the main verb *cupiebant,* "[All] were wanting," in T.2i establishing Track II, is a verb of M & M that produces a statement in OO where *Caesarem* in object form functions as the subject of the inf. *stare,* "Caesar to abide."

→ **661** M & M, 60, 71, GL n° 527, remarks 1–2;
OO, 71–73; *consecutio,* 47–48.

Note: the modern legal term *stare decisis,* means "to stand by things having been decided," and here we have *stare condicionibus,* meaning "to stand by the conditions."

abductis praesidiis, "garrisons having been withdrawn": AA where the participle *abductis,* "having been withdrawn," is antecedent to *stare,* "to abide," and can refer to any time previous to or even touching upon the time of *stare.*

→ **662** ablative absolute, 54–55; antecedent participle, 50, 51.1.2.

quas tulisset, "which he made": the main verb *cupiebant,* "[All] were wanting," in T.2i establishes Track II, which is continued through the contemporaneous inf. *stare,* "to abide." The verb *tulisset,* in T.4s, is in the subjunctive by MA, because it depends on and is closely involved in the statement in OO, *Caesarem ... stare,* "Caesar to abide"; it expresses antecedent action, "he made," "he had made," "he did make," "he had been making," "he was making previously," any expression that is previous to *cupiebant*, "they were wanting" in T.2i.

> → **663** subjunctive use: modal attraction, 83;
>   OO, 71–73; consecutio, 47–48.

If you were to hear Caesar standing in the senate he would say, *Ego sto condicionibus quas tuli*, which, if we take *tuli* as T.4a, he means "I am abiding by the conditions which I have made," or if we take *tuli* as T.4b, he means "I am abiding by the conditions which I made." When this sentence is put into indirect discourse depending on *cupiebant*, "[All] were wanting," in T.2i, then *sto*, "I am abiding," in T.1i becomes *stare*, "to abide," a contemporaneous inf., and *tuli*, whether in T.4a, "I have made" or T.4b, "I made," is rendered into T.4s *tulisset*, "he made," by MA.

> → **664** OO, 71–73; subjunctive use: modal attraction, 83.

Uni Favonio leges ... imponi non placebat, "To Favonius alone ... it was not agreeable that laws be imposed": the main verb is the last word, *placebat*, "it was [not] agreeable," in T.2b; as one of the 65 words whose complement is in the dat., its complement is *Uni Favonio*, "To Favonius alone," the first two words of the sentence. In between them is the subject of *placebat*, which is given in OO produced by *placebat* itself, a verb of M & M. Here *leges* in the object form functions as the subject of the inf. *imponi*, both passive and contemporaneous, meaning "that laws be imposed [was not agreeable to Favonius alone]."

> → **665** M & M, 60, 71, GL n° 527, remarks 1–2; OO, 71–73;
>   65 verbs with dat., 33.7.2, GL n° 346; sentence structure, 1.

mavult, "[Cato] prefers": the verb *malo, malui, malle*, is derived from *magis-volo*, "to choose rather," "to prefer." The form *mavult* is T.1i. People will think the form for T.1i should be *malit*, but that is T.1s, whereas this is T.1i *mavult*.

> → **666** irregular verbs: *malo*, 82.

ait ... se adesse velle, "he says that he wishes to be present": the main verb *ait*, "he says," in T.1i is a verb of M & M and produces a statement in OO where *se*, the reflexive pronoun in the object form, functions as the subject of the contemporaneous inf. *velle*, whose object is *adesse*, the gerund; the whole OO means "that he wishes to be present."

> → **667** M & M, 60, 71, GL n° 527, remarks 1–2; OO, 71–73;
>   reflexive pron.: third person, 31;
>   verb: contemporaneous active infinitive, 72.1; gerund, 77.1.

cum ... agatur, "because the discussion is being made": the verb *agatur* is T.1s in the passive and impersonal, so it contains its own subject, which we might express as "discussion is made." Here, *cum* followed by *agatur* in T.1s may mean either "because" or "although," or, if the clause is in the subjunctive by MA it could even mean "when."

> → **668** passive verb used impersonally, GL nº 208;
>   subjunctive use: causal *cum* = "because, since," 59.1;
>   subjunctive use: concessive *cum* = "although," 64;
>   subjunctive use: modal attraction, 83;
>   *cum* + indicative = "when": temporal sentences, 66.3.

si Caesar adductus sit, "if Caesar has been persuaded": the main verb *ait*, "he says" in T.1i introduces a logical conditional, both parts of which are given as reported speech. The consequence is given in OO, *se adesse velle*, "[he says] that he wishes to be present." Because the condition, *si Caesar adductus sit*, "if Caesar has been persuaded," in T.3s in the passive, both depends upon and is closely associated with its consequence in OO, the condition is in the subjunctive by MA. The verb *adductus sit* expresses antecedent action, "he has been persuaded," "he was being persuaded," "he had been persuaded," any expression that is previous to *ait* and *adesse velle*, "he says that he wishes to be present."

> → **669** conditionals: factual, 86.1; conditionals in OO, 103;
>   OO, 71–73; *consecutio*, 47–48;
>   subjunctive use: modal attraction, 83.

If you were to hear Cato speaking on that occasion, it would sound like the following: *Ego in senatu me adesse volo, cum de condicionibus agatur, si Caesar adductus est ut praesidia deducat*, "I want myself to be present in the senate since the discussion is being made about the conditions, whether Caesar has been persuaded that he withdraw the garrisons." When this direct speech of Cato is put into indirect speech in Cicero's letter depending on the M & M verb *ait*, "he says," in T.1i establishing Track I, then *volo*, "I want," in T.1i becomes the contemporaneous inf. *velle*, "[he] wishes," and *adductus est*, "[Caesar] has been persuaded," in T.4a, becomes *adductus sit*, in T.3s by MA.

> → **670** conditionals: factual, 86.1; conditionals in OO, 103;
>   *consecutio*, 47–48; subjunctive use: modal attraction, 83.

ut praesidia deducat, "that he withdraw the garrisons": this purpose clause gives the intention in persuading Caesar. It depends on *adductus sit*, "[Caesar] has been persuaded," in T.3s establishing Track I, thus producing *deducat*, "he withdraw," in T.1s.

> → **671** subjunctive use: purpose clause, 58.1; *consecutio*, 47–48.

quod maxime opus est, "something which is most necessary": here *opus est*, means "it is necessary" not "it is work."

> → **672** dict., *opus, eris*, n. III., A. *opus est*, "there is need," (β) with abl., (γ) with
>   gen., (δ) with acc.;
>   *opus est*, 75.3.

quod metuo ne obsit, "something which I am afraid may be an obstacle": the verb *metuo*, "I am afraid," is in T.1i. As a verb of fearing it is complemented by a purpose clause composed of *ne* and *obsit* in T.1s, which has a positive force. In early Latin these would have been two completely separate sentences, first a negative wish such as *Ne obsit*, "May it not be an obstacle," and the second a verb of fearing such as *Metuo*, "I fear [that it will]." The later expression combined these two sentences into one such as *Ne obsit, metuo*, "May it not be an obstacle, I fear [that it will]," and finally "I fear that it may be an obstacle." Thus, the *ne* sounds positive.

→ **673** verbs of fearing with *ne*, 95.

de quo nominatim senatus decrevit ut ... iret Furfanioque succederet, "about whom the senate decreed in name that he would go ... and succeed Furfanius": the main verb, *negat*, "[Postumius] denies," in T.1i establishes Track I. The relative clause has as its verb *decrevit*, "[the senate] decreed," in T.4b, which gives an historical perspective to the rest of the clause on Track II. The senate's intention in decreeing is given in a double purpose clause where *ut* is followed by two verbs, first *iret*, "that he go," in T.2s, and the second also in T.2s, *succederet*, "[and] succeed," which is a compound verb consisting of *sub-cedo*. If we were to reconstruct the verb with a preposition it would be *cederet sub Furfanium*, "[that] he follow up behind Furfanio." When the preposition *sub* is attached to the verb, then *Furfanium* becomes *Furfanio* and the whole phrase means "[that] he succeed Furfanio," but in English the dat. cannot be heard. The adverb *nominatim*, "in name" means "by name," "individually," "specifically."

→ **674** relative clauses, 10–11; *consecutio*, 47–48;
      subjunctive use: purpose clause, 58.1;
      dat. with compound verbs, 33.7.3, GL n° 347; dict., *nominatim*, adv.

negat se ... iturum, "[Postumius] denies that he will go": the main verb *negat*, "[Postumius] denies," in T.1i is a verb of M & M and produces a statement in OO where the object form *se*, a reflexive pronoun referring to the subject of *negat*, Postumius, functions as the subject of the inf. whose full implied form is *iturum esse*, literally "to be about to go."

→ **675** M & M, 60, 71, GL n° 527, remarks 1–2;
      OO, 71–73; *consecutio*, 47–48;
      reflexive pron.: third person, 31;
      futurity participle, 50, 51.1.3; verb: subsequent active infinitive, 72.1.

negat ... suam ... operam auctoritatemque, "his own effort and authority": the verb *negat*, "he denies," produces the above statement in OO and it also has these two complements in the simple object form.

→ **676** function: object, 1.3, 2.2, 2.4, 2.6, 15; reflexive pron.: third person, 31.

quam magni aestimat, "which he highly values": The form *magni*, as genitive of valuing, means "of great value." The expression *quam magni* does not read so well. Some authors take *quam* as a relative pronoun, others take the *quam magni* to mean "how greatly," but neither makes sense. See the discussion about the text in Tyrrell and Purser.

→ **677** gen. of indefinite price, 75.2.

pervenit, "[the matter] came down": this form may be one of two times, depending on which vowel is stressed. If the length of the second vowel –ĕ– is short, then the stress moves back to the first –e– as in *pérvenit*, which means "it comes down," in T.1i. If the second vowel –ē– is long, then it is stressed, as in *pervénit*, which means "it has come down" in T.4a or "it came down" in T.4b. We translated it as "it came down" in T.4b, but because the next verb is in the past, perhaps this one is in T.1i. You just do not know.

→ **678** times-tenses of the indicative mode and their vernacular meaning, 7.

❧

In disputationibus nostris summa varietas est. Plerique negant Caesarem in condicione mansurum postulataque haec ab eo interposita esse quo minus quod opus esset ad bellum a nobis pararetur. Ego autem eum puto facturum ut praesidia deducat. Vicerit enim si consul factus erit, et minore scelere vicerit quam quo ingressus est. Sed accipienda plaga est. Sumus enim flagitiose imparati cum a militibus tum a pecunia, quam quidem omnem non modo privatam, quae in urbe est, sed etiam publicam, quae in aerario est, illi reliquimus. Pompeius ad legiones Appianas est profectus: Labienum secum habet. Ego tuas opiniones de his rebus exspecto. Formias me continuo recipere cogitabam.   (*Att.* VII, 15, 3)

In our discussions there is the greatest variance. Most people deny that Caesar will remain in his own agreement and [they say] that these demands were inserted by him so that, what would be necessary for war, not be prepared by us. I however think he is going to bring it about that he withdraw the garrisons. For he will have won if he will have been made consul, and he will have won with a lesser crime than with which he began. But the blow must be taken in. For we are criminally unprepared both on the side of soldiers and on the side of money, all of which indeed we have left for him not only private [money] which is in the city but even public which is in the treasury. Pompeius has set out for the Appian legions: he has Labienus with himself. I am awaiting your ideas about these things. I was planning on getting myself to Formia immediately.

Plerique negant Caesarem ... mansurum, "Most people deny that Caesar will remain": the main verb *negant*, "[people] deny," in T.1i, is a verb of M & M producing a statement in OO where *Caesarem* in object form functions as the subject of the inf., whose full implied form is *mansurum esse*, a futurity formula combining the contemporaneous inf. *esse* and the future active participle *mansurum*, "about to remain," "going to remain," producing an English rendering in the future, "that Caesar will remain."

> → **679** M & M, 60, 71, GL nº 527, remarks 1–2; OO, 71–73;
> futurity participle, 50, 51.1.3;
> verb: subsequent active infinitive, 72.1.

Plerique negant ... postulataque haec ... interposita esse, "Most people deny ... that these demands were inserted": the idea of talking "[they say]" contained in the M & M verb *negant*, "[people] deny," produces this time a positive statement in OO where *postulata*, taken here as the noun, "demands," in the object form functions as the subject of the inf. *interposita esse*, which is both antecedent and passive, "that these demands were inserted by him." Cicero wrote the *esse* only here, although it is implied in the previous statement in OO, the futurity formula *mansurum esse*, "to be about to remain."

> → **680** M & M, 60, 71, GL nº 527, remarks 1–2;
> OO, 71–73; verb: antecedent passive infinitive, 72.3.

quo minus, "so that ... not": also written as one word *quominus*, this expression stands for *ut eo minus*, "so that all the less," or simply, "so that not." It gives rise to a prohibitive sentence, one to keep someone from doing something, and can also be expressed by *quin* or *ne* followed by the subjunctive, as here *pararetur*, in T.2s, meaning "so that ... not be prepared."

> → **681** dict., *parvus, a, um*, adj., III., B., 3., b. *quo minus, quominus*, "that not," "from";
> subjunctive use: relative clause of purpose, *quo = ut eo*, 58.2; GL nº 545.2
> *quō = ut eō*.

quo minus ... pararetur, "so that ... not be prepared": the main verb *negant*, "[people] deny," in T.1i establishing Track I, is a verb of M & M producing two statements in OO, the second one being *postulata ... interposita esse*, "that these demands were inserted," in T.4b, which shifts the sentence to an historical perspective on Track II, producing *pararetur*, "[not] be prepared," in T.2s on Track II. Its subject is an implied *id*, "it," the antecedent of *quod*, "that which" or "what."

> → **682** M & M, 60, 71, GL nº 527, remarks 1–2;
> OO, 71–73; *consecutio*, 47–48;
> rel. pron.: subject or object, 10.

quod opus esset, "what would be necessary": the antecedent of *quod* is an implied *id*, "it," the subject of *pararetur*, "it not be prepared." The content of that *id* is given in this relative clause where *esset* is in the subj, T.2s, by MA because the clause depends upon *pararetur*, which in turn depends on the statement in OO, *postulata ... interposita esse*, "that these demands were inserted," the equivalent of T.4b producing Track II. The meaning of *opus* here is not "work" but "need," "necessity" and the expression *opus est* means "there is need of."

> → **683** OO, 71–73; *consecutio*, 47–48;
> rel. pron.: subject or object, 10;
> subjunctive use: modal attraction, 83; *opus est*, 75.3.

This is an easy sentence to arrange according to calendar dates to see the shift in perspective from the present to the past:

February	March	May

negant

mansurum esse ⟶

interposita esse

esset ⟶

pararetur ⟶

→ **684** calendars, 83 pp. 514–15, 103 p. 586.

eum puto facturum ut praesidia deducat, "I ... think he is going to bring it about that he withdraw the garrisons": the main verb, *puto*, "I think," in T.1i establishes Track I and is a verb of M & M producing a statement in OO where *eum* in the object form functions as the subject of the inf., whose full implied form is *facturum esse*, the futurity formula where the future active participle *facturum* all alone means "about to make," "going to do," "fixing to bring about." The inf. *facturum esse* is a verb of causing, which produces a statement of the result *ut ... deducat*, where *deducat*, "he withdraw," is T.1s.

→ **685** M & M, 60, 71, GL n° 527, remarks 1–2;
        OO, 71–73; *consecutio*, 47–48;
        futurity participle, 50, 51.1.3;
        verb: subsequent active infinitive, 72.1;
        subjunctive use: complementary result (consecutive), 68.1.

Vicerit ... factus erit ... vicerit ..., "he will have won ... he will have been made ... he will have won ...": rather than the typical combination of T.3i and T.6i, here Cicero uses two verbs in T.6i, completed futurity, to indicate his certainty of this action, and then he uses T.6i for the third verb.

→ **686** T.6i and T.6i paired: GL n° 244, remark 4;
        T.3i and T.6i paired: 7, Time 6, and GL n° 244, remark 2.

minore scelere ... quam quo, "with a lesser crime than with which": *minore scelere* is a natural abl. of means with *minore* in the comparative degree, meaning "with a lesser crime." The other degrees of *minore* are *parvo*, "by less" and *minimo*, "by the least." The *quo* also agrees with *scelere* on the other side of the *quam*, "than with which."

→ **687** abl.: measure, 90.3, GL n° 403; adj.: comp. and superl., 36.

accipienda plaga est, "the blow must be taken in": the necessity formula in T.1i consists of the verb *est* and the participle of passive necessity *accipienda*, "it must be taken in," "it has to be taken in," "it ought to be taken in."

→ **688** participle of passive necessity, 50, 51.1.4;
        passive necessity formula, 53.4.

Sumus ... imparati, "we are ... unprepared": there is no verb *imparo*, so what looks like T.4 passive here is really *Sumus*, "we are," in T.1i, accompanied by the adjective *imparati*, "unprepared."

→ **689** Block I adj., 4.2–3; dict., *imparatus, a, um*, adj.

cum a militibus tum a pecunia, "both on the side of soldiers and on the side of money": here the preposition *a* means "on the side of," like the term *ab epistolis* used to identify the papal Latinist as *secretarius ab epistolis*, "the secretary on the side of letters," "the secretary from letters," in distinction from accounts or other types of secretaries. Note the coordinating words *cum ... tum ...*, "both ... and...."

→ **690** prep. with abl., 28.4; correlative comparative sentences, 90.5, GL nº 642.

non modo, "not only": here *modo* is not the abl. of *modus*, that is, not *mŏdō* with a long final –*ō*–; rather this form has two short vowels, *mŏdŏ*, and means "only," "merely," "but."

→ **691** dict., *modus, i*, m.; dict., *mŏdŏ*, adv., orig. abl. of *modus, i*, m.

illi, "for him": the natural use of the dat. going with the verb *reliquimus*, "we have left."

→ **692** natural dat., 33.7.1.

Ego ... exspecto, "I am awaiting": the first and last words of the sentence go together, the first being the subject of the last.

→ **693** sentence structure, 1.

Formias me continuo recipere cogitabam, "I was planning on getting myself to Formia immediately": the main verb *cogitabam* in T.2i is an epistolary time: namely, as Cicero is writing he has in mind, *cogito*, "I am thinking [of getting myself to Formia]," but instead he imagines Atticus reading the letter a couple of days later, and so he writes from the perspective of Atticus, *cogitabam*, "[when I was writing this letter] I was thinking [of getting myself to Formia]." This time, typically used only once or twice, is not sustained in the letter. It is usually found in T.2i in place of that T.1i. Here, in the previous sentence Cicero says *exspecto*, "I am awaiting," but then in the next sentence he says *cogitabam*, "I was writing," when in reality they are the same time.

→ **694** letter-writer tense, GL nº 252.

Although *me recipere* may look like a statement in OO, here rather the main verb *cogitabam*, "I was planning," in T.2i is complemented by the inf. *recipere*, "to get back" or "[I was planning] getting back," which is a gerund functioning as the object of the main verb, which has its own object *me*, "myself," the reflexive referring to the subject of *cogitabam*, "I was planning." The adv. *continuo*, from the adj. *continuus, a, um*, means "in continual suggestion," namely "immediately." The form *Formias* is the plural object indicating motion toward the end of a journey, "to Formia."

→ **695** gerund, 77.1; reflexive pron.: first and second person, 30;
      dict., *continuus, a, um*, adj.; function: place to where, *Formias*, 69.1.2.

LETTER 318 T-P
AD ATTICUM VII, 20

CICERO ATTICO SAL.

Breviloquentem iam me tempus ipsum facit. Pacem enim desperavi, bellum nostri nullum administrant. Cave enim putes quidquam esse minoris his consulibus: quorum ergo spe audiendi aliquid et cognoscendi nostri apparatus maximo imbri Capuam veni pridie Nonas, ut eram iussus. Illi autem nondum venerant, sed erant venturi inanes, imparati. Gnaeus autem Luceriae dicebatur esse et adire cohortes legionum Appianarum, non firmissimarum. At illum ruere nuntiant et iam iamque adesse, non ut manum conserat—quicum enim?—sed ut fugam intercludat.   (*Att.* VII, 20, 1)

CICERO A GREETING TO ATTICUS

Already now the circumstance itself makes me short-talking [tweeting]. For I have given up on peace; our men are directing zero war. For be careful lest you think that there is anything of lesser value than these consuls: of whom, therefore, in the hope of hearing something, and of getting to know our preparation, I came to Capua as I had been commanded on the day before the Nones [4 February]—there being a tremendous rain shower. They, however, had not yet arrived, but they were set to arrive empty, unprepared. But, Gnaeus [Pompeius] was said to be at Luceria and to be visiting the cohorts of the Appian legions, not the most solid ones. But they report that he [Caesar] is rushing ahead and is present any minute now, not that he may engage battle—with whom, for instance?—but that he may cut off escape.

CICERO ATTICO SAL.: *Cicero Attico salutem*

breviloquentem, "short-talking [tweeting]": this participle is a creation of Cicero and appears only once in all of Latinity, while its verb does not. This participle from a presumed verb "*breviloquor, breviloqui, brevilocutus*" was then used by this author to describe "tweeting" in our own day, and from it the whole verb system was created so that this once in a lifetime verb could provide our tweeting terminology, briefly speaking, that is.

→ **696** contemporaneous active participle, deponents, 50, 51.2.1.

tempus, "circumstance": also meaning "the situation."

→ **697** dict., *tempus, oris*, n., I., B., 2., a. "the times, circumstances."

Cave ... putes, "be careful lest you think": *cave*, "beware," is a verb of preventing that can be used with *ne*, "that not," which is normally omitted. For example, we can say *cave cadas*, "beware lest you fall," "watch your step."

→ **698** commands: first, second, 17; verbs of prohibiting, 101, GL n° 632.

putes quidquam esse, "lest you think that there is anything": the main verb *putes*, "lest you think," in T.1s is a verb of M & M producing a statement in OO where *quidquam*, "anything" in the object form functions as the subject of the inf. *esse*, "that there is anything."

→ **699** M & M, 60, 71, GL n° 527, remarks 1–2; OO, 71–73.

minoris, "of lesser value": this is the form of-possession, also called the gen. of value, and here it is in the comparative degree, so we might humorously say the gen. of lesser value. The other degrees are *parvi*, "of little value," and *minimi*, "of the very least value."

→ **700** gen. of indefinite price, 75.2; adj.: comp. and superl., 36.

his consulibus, "than these consuls": an abl. of comparison.

→ **701** abl.: comparison, 90.2, GL n° 398.

quorum ... spe audiendi aliquid, "of whom ... in the hope ... of hearing something": the complement of *spe*, "in the hope," is the gerund *audiendi*, "of hearing," in the gen., and its object is *aliquid*, "[of hearing] something," which goes with *quorum*, "[something] of whom," at the beginning of the clause, because the gen. of part is typically separated and often out front of the word on which it depends.

→ **702** gerund, 77.1; gen. of part, 99; sentence structure, 1.

spe ... cognoscendi nostri apparatus, "in the hope ... of getting to know our preparation": a gerundive combination in the gen. The Romans far preferred the gerundive; nevertheless, we can construct the gerund here as *cognoscendi nostrum apparatum*, with the same meaning, but you can clearly see the object of *cognoscendi* is *nostrum apparatum*. The form *nostri* can function both as a pronoun meaning "of us," but here it is the adjective "our."

→ **703** gerundive, 77.2; gerund, 77.1;
personal pronouns: function of-possession, 24.2;
20% of nouns: *apparatus, us*, m., 35.

maximo imbri, "there being a tremendous rain shower": these two words constitute an A A, where the participle from the verb *esse*, "to be" is not expressed. They could also be an abl. of time at which, "at the time of a tremendous shower."

→ **704** ablative absolute, 54–55; abl.: time at which, 70.1.

Capuam, "to Capua": this form without a preposition indicates the place to where or the end of a journey.

→ **705** function: place to where, *Capuam*, 69.1.2.

veni … ut eram iussus, "I came … as I had been commanded": *veni*, "I came," is T.4b and *eram iussus*, "I had been commanded" in the passive is T.5i, because it occurred before the time of *veni*. Here *ut* followed by an indicative time means "as."

→ **706** times-tenses of the indicative mode and their vernacular meaning, 7; verb T.4, T.5, T.6: 8; dict., *ut*, I., B. meaning "as."

venerant, sed erant venturi, "They … had [not yet] arrived, but they were set to arrive": *venerant*, "they had arrived," in T.5i occurs before the time of *erant venturi*, the futurity formula where the verb, *erant*, is T.2i and the future active participle *venturi* means "set to arrive," "on the point of arriving," "fixing to arrive," thus, "they were set to arrive."

→ **707** futurity participle, 50, 51.1.3; verb: subsequent active infinitive, 72.1; futurity formula, active, 53.3.

Be careful about Latin verb times and their similar appearances!

While *erant venturi* is T.2i, T.5i would be *fuerant venturi*, "they had been set to arrive."

While *eram iussus* is T.5i, T.2i would be *iubebar*, "I was being commanded."

→ **708** times-tenses of the indicative mode and their vernacular meaning, 7; verb formation T.2, 12.2.1; verb formation T.5, 8.2; verb meaning T.2, T.5, 7.

Gnaeus … dicebatur esse, "Gnaeus [Pompeius] was said to be": the Romans prefer the personal construction *Gnaeus dicebatur*, "Gnaeus was said to be," rather than the impersonal verb *dicebatur*, "it was said," accompanied by the object and inf., as in *Gnaeum dicebatur esse*, "it was said that Gnaeus was." In that *dicebatur* is used personally, its subject is the nom. subject of the infinitive *esse*.

→ **709** personal construction, *dici*, 73.3, GL n° 528.1 and remark 2 and note 1; nom. with the inf., 73.3, GL n° 528.1.

Luceriae, "at Luceria": this form indicates place at which, place where, also called the locative. Again there is no preposition.

→ **710** function: place at which, names of cities and small islands, singular, *Luceriae*, 69.3.2.

firmissimarum, "the most solid ones": the superlative degree, whose positive degree is *firmarum*, "the solid ones," and comparative degree *firmiorum* "more solid ones."

→ **711** adj.: comp. and superl., 36.

At, "But": the force of this is extremely strong.

→ **712** dict., *at*, conj. I. "moreover, but."

illum ruere nuntiant, "they report that he [Caesar] is rushing ahead": the main verb *nuntiant*, "they report," in T.1i is a verb of M & M producing a statement in OO where *illum* in the object form functions as the subject of the inf. *ruere*, "that he is rushing ahead."

→ **713** M & M, 60, 71, GL n° 527, remarks 1–2; OO, 71–73.

illum … nuntiant … adesse, non ut manum conserat … sed ut fugam intercludat, "they report that he … is present … , not that he may engage battle … but that he may cut off escape": again the M & M verb *nuntiant*, "they report" in T.1i produces a second statement in OO where *illum* functions also as the subject of the inf. *adesse*, "that he is present." Although *ut … conserat* and *ut … intercludat* both in T.1s depend on OO, the reason for the subjunctive in both is not MA, but a statement of purpose. Caesar's intention in being present is reported in two purpose clauses, the first one negated, *non ut manum conserat*, "not so that he may engage battle [with Pompeius]," where the verb *conserat*, in T.1s, comes from one of two dictionary entries, both *consĕro, conserĕre*, one meaning "to plant," "to sow seed" and the other "to entwine" and thus with *manum*, "the hand," "to engage in close combat," as here. His second intention is *ut fugam intercludat*, "that he may cut off escape [of Pompeius]," where *intercludat*, "he may cut off," is T.1s, that is to say, "he may cut off the escape of Pompeius."

→ **714** M & M, 60, 71, GL n° 527, remarks 1–2; OO, 71–73;
subjunctive use: purpose clause, 58.1;
subjunctive use: modal attraction, 83;
dict., *consero, sevi, situm* or *satum*, 3, "to sew";
dict., *consero, serui, sertum*, 3, "to entwine."

quicum enim, "with whom, for instance?": the *qui* is an old abl. and Cicero and others prefer *quicum* to *quocum*, which we might write today. The plural of *quicum* is *quibuscum*. The *quo* or the old *quī* is the object of the prep. *cum*, "with [whom]." The *qui* as old abl. can also mean "how," "why" as in the sentence of Plautus, "*Qui sciam*?," "How should I know?" See your dict. under *Quī* in the abl.

→ **715** dict., *quī*, adv., interrog., rel. and indef. (old abl. of 1. *qui*).

❧

Ego autem in Italia κἂν ἀποθανεῖν nec te id consulo—sin extra, quid ago?—
Ad manendum hiems, lictores, improvidi et neglegentes duces; ad fugam

hortatur amicitia Gnaei, causa bonorum, turpitudo coniungendi cum tyranno: qui quidem incertum est Phalarimne an Pisistratum sit imitaturus.
Haec velim explices et me iuves consilio, etsi te ipsum istic iam calere puto.
Sed tamen quantum poteris. Ego si quid hic hodie novi cognoro, scies. Iam
enim aderunt consules ad suas Nonas. Tuas cotidie litteras exspectabo. Ad
has autem cum poteris rescribes. Mulieres et Cicerones in Formiano reliqui.   (*Att.* VII, 20, 2)

I, however, in Italy—*bid me to die and I will dare*—nor do I ask you for
that advice—but if abroad, what am I doing? For remaining there, winter
moves me, the public attendants, leaders without foresight and careless; for
flight the friendship of Gnaeus [Pompeius], the cause of the good guys, the
disgrace of joining up with the tyrant [Caesar], who indeed it is uncertain
whether [he] is going to imitate Phalaris or Pisistratus. I would like that
you unravel these things and help me with your advice, although I think
you yourself are already hot with trouble there. But, nevertheless, as much
as you will be able. If I shall have learned about something new here today,
you will know. For, the consuls will already be present at their own Nones.
I shall be awaiting your letter every day. You will write back to this one,
however, when you will be able. I have left the women [his wife Terentia and
daughter Tullia] and the Ciceros [his son Marcus and nephew Quintus] in
my Formian villa.

> *te id consulo*, "I ask you for that advice": a double acc. is extremely rare, as
> mentioned in the dict., and here is one example where the verb *consulo*, "I
> am asking," takes the object of the person, *te*, "you," and the object of the
> thing asked, *id*, "this thing" or here "some advice."
>   → **716** double acc., GL nº 339; dict., *consulo, lui, ltum*, 3., I., B., 1., a.,—with two acc.

> κᾰν ἀποθανεῖν, "*bid me to die and I will dare*": This rendering is suggested in
> Tyrrell and Purser as an explanation to an enigmatic partial quotation of a
> Greek text no longer extant.
>   → **717** Tyrrell and Purser 4:49, fn. 2.

> *sin extra*, "but if abroad": some verb is missing here, and you can just hear
> Cicero skipping through his thoughts and jotting them down as fast as his
> hand can keep up. We have supplied a verb in the English, "do I ask."
>   → **718** sentence structure, 1.

> *ad manendum*, "For remaining there": a gerund combination of the preposi-
> tion *ad*, "for," with its object, *manendum*, "remaining," a gerund.
>   → **719** gerund, 77.1.

> *hortatur*, "… moves me": the main is verb *hortatur*, "… moves me," and it
> has two complements, first, *Ad manendum*, "for remaining," and second
> *ad fugam*, "for flight." Although Cicero places the verb with this second

complement, in our English rendering we moved it up to the beginning of
the first complement for clarity. After each of these complements is a list of
several motives, each a subject of *hortatur*. Thus, winter, the public attendants, and leaders without foresight and careless, each moves Cicero for
remaining where he is. Conversely, the friendship of Gnaeus, the cause of
the good guys and the disgrace of joining up with the tyrant all move Cicero
for flight. Again, Cicero is skipping from one motive to another as fast as his
hand can keep up writing.

→ **720** sentence structure, 1.

coniungendi, "of joining up": a gerund in the gen.

→ **721** gerund, 77.1.

qui ... incertum est Phalarimne an Pisistratum sit imitaturus, "who ... it
is uncertain whether [he] is going to imitate Phalaris or Pisistratus": the
main verbal expression *incertum est*, "it is uncertain," in T.1i is neuter, so its
subject is not *qui*. Rather, *incertum est* is an expression of M & M producing
an IQ whose question word is the suffix *–ne*, "whether," joined to the end
of *Phalarim-*. The entire IQ is the subject of *incertum est*, which produces
the IQ. The subject of the IQ is *qui*, a connective meaning "and he, who,"
and whose verb is *sit imitaturus*, "[who] is going to imitate," "will imitate,"
"has in mind to imitate" in T.1s where the future active participle *imitaturus*
means variously "on the verge of imitating," "on the point of imitating,"
"about to imitate." This futurity formula is the only way to express futurity
explicitly in the subjunctive because there is no future form in the subjunctive. We might render the English thus: "and whether who is going to imitate Phalaris or Pisistratus is uncertain." The *–ne* begins a disjunction whose
other part begins with *an*, "[whether] ... or" and the choice is between
imitating Phalaris or Pisistratus. Thus, in Latin the main verb, *incertum est*,
is set inside its own indirect question, and the main verb produces an IQ as
its own subject.

→ **722** M & M, 60, 71, GL n° 527, remarks 1–2; IQ, 60;
futurity participle, 50, 51.1.3;
consecutio: futurity formula in the subjunctive, 61.3;
dict., 2. *–ne*, I. enclitic particle;
dict., *qui, quae, quod*, pron., II., C. serves as a connective.

velim explices et me iuves, "I would like that you unravel ... and help me":
Cicero and other authors use all the time *velim*, "I would like," in T.1s as the
potential subjunctive of the present followed by the simple subjunctive, here
explices, "that you unravel," and *iuves*, "[and] help," both in T.1s, without
any other particle such as *ut* to emphasize the force of the wish.

→ **723** subjunctive use: purpose clause without *ut*, 58, GL n° 546, remark 2;
commands: other expressions, *velim*, 85.1.7;
subjunctive use: potential of the present or future, *velim* in T.1s,
GL n° 257.2.

etsi te … calere puto, "although I think you … are … hot with trouble": *etsi* is one of three related terms, with *tametsi* and *etiamsi*, which mean "even if," "even though," "although"; each ends with *–si*, and so they follow the exceptional sequence of the conditional sentences with the result that they are usually in the ind. as here with the verb *puto*, "I think," in T.1i and a verb of M & M producing a statement in OO where *te* in the object form functions as the subject of the inf. *calere*, "to be hot."

→ **724** subjunctive use: concessive *etsi* = "although," 64; conditionals: factual, 86.1; M & M, 60, 71, GL nº 527, remarks 1–2; OO, 71–73.

poteris, "you will be able": this form is T.3i, and T.6i is *potueris*, with a difference of only one letter.

→ **725** see the verb "to be" in the indicative, 9.1; conjugation of *possum*, GL nº 119.

Ego si … cognoro, scies, "If I shall have learned … , you will know": the first word is the subject of the last word of this condition, and even precedes the *si*, as if Cicero, first asking Atticus to help him out with his advice, then turns to himself and says, "I, if I shall have learned." The verb *cognoro* is a syncopated form of *cognovero*, "I shall have learned," in T.6i. The consequence is *scies*, "you will know," in T.3i, paired with T.6i *cognoro*, "I shall have learned."

→ **726** sentence structure, 1; conditionals: factual, 86.1; contractions: verbs, 39.2, GL nº 131; T.3i and T.6i paired: 7, Time 6, and GL nº 244, remark 2.

quid … novi, "something new": the *quid* stands for *aliquid*, "something," "some bit," but after the particle *si*, the prefix *ali–* is dropped. The noun *novi*, "of new" is the gen. of part and together they mean "some bit of news," "anything of news."

→ **727** pronouns: indefinite, 42.4; after *si* the *ali*-s fly away, 42.5; gen. of part, 99.

ad suas Nonas, "at their own Nones": this is a reference to the date they decided upon.

→ **728** about the Roman calendar, pp. 605–608; GL appendix: Roman Calendar, pp. 491–92; reflexive pron.: third person, 31.

Tuas, "your": with the first word, Cicero turns his thought away from himself and back to Atticus.

→ **729** sentence structure, 1.

Note all the future indicative times possible in the language in the last three
lines of the letter:

poteris T.3i

cognoro T.6i with *scies* T.3i (verb groups 3 and 4)

aderunt T.3i

exspectabo T.3i (verb groups 1 and 2)

poteris T.3i with *rescribes* T.3i (group 3 and 4)

→ **730** verb formation T.3 in groups I and II, 12.3.1;
 verb formation T.3 in groups III and IV, 12.3.2; verb formation T.6, 8.2;
 see the verb "to be" in the indicative, 9.1; conjugation of *possum*, GL nº 119.

This is a real Latin example and consequently super teaching tool. There
is one pair of T.6i with T.3i, and even a pairing of T.3i with T.3i. Learn the
forms.

→ **731** T.3i and T.6i paired: 7, Time 6, and GL nº 244, remark 2;
 T.3i and T.3i: GL nº 242, remark 1, example.

LETTER 405 T-P
AD FAMILIARES XIV, 7

TULLIUS TERENTIAE SUAE S. P.

Omnis molestias et sollicitudines, quibus et te miserrimam habui, id quod mihi molestissimum est, *et* Tulliolam, quae nobis nostra vita dulcior est, deposui et eieci. Quid causae autem fuerit postridie intellexi quam a vobis discessi. Χολὴν ἄκρατον noctu eieci: statim ita sum levatus ut mihi deus aliquis medicinam fecisse videatur. Cui quidem tu deo, quem ad modum soles, pie et caste satis facies [id est Apollini et Aesculapio].   (*Fam.* XIV, 7, 1)

TULLIUS THE BIGGEST GREETING TO HIS TERENTIA

I put aside and cast out all the troubles and worries, by which I found both you most miserable (something which is most annoying to me), and our little Tullia, who is sweeter to us than our life. On the day after I have departed from you, however, I have understood what kind of a reason there was. During the night I vomited *unmixed bile*; thus, I have been so immediately relieved that some god seems to me to have brought the cure, to which god indeed you will piously and purely render satisfaction [that is to Apollo and Aesculapius] as you are accustomed.

TULLIUS TERENTIAE SUAE S. P.: *Tullius Terentiae suae salutem plurimam*

The box system helps to understand the first sentence:

Omnis molestias et sollicitudines,	main sentence begins
{ quibus et te miserrimam habui,	relative clause 1 begins
[id quod mihi molestissimum est,]	relative clause 2
et Tulliolam,	relative clause 1 continues
[quae nobis nostra vita dulcior est,] }	relative clause 3
deposui et eieci.	main sentence concludes

→ **732** structure of Latin sentences, 103 p. 587, *Ossa* Readings: 1-D, 1-I, 3-D, 3-I, 4-D, 4-I;
relative box, 11.4.

Note that the first and last several words go together. To understand this sentence, you must begin in its thought with the last two verbs, on which the whole thought depends.

Omnis, "all": It may be noted that the Oxford edition prefers this form of the object plural *omnīs* instead of *omnes.* School editions will mercifully write *omnes* to make things a bit easier. It agrees with *molestias et sollicitudines,* "all the troubles and worries."

> → **733** Block II adj.: –*is* = –*es,* 38, GL n° 78.

miserrimam, "most miserable": one of about twenty superlatives in the Latin language made from adjectives that end in –*er.* The adjective, *miser, misera, miserum* would produce here the positive *miseram,* the comparative *miseriorem,* and the superlative has that the double –*rr*– instead of the form *miserissimam.*

> → **734** adj.: comp. and superl., 36.

quod, "which": the antecedent is *id,* which refers to the whole main idea, namely that Cicero found his wife and daughter very miserable; thus *id quod* could be translated nicely as "something which."

> → **735** *quod* referring to previous sentence: GL n° 614, remark 2.

molestissimum, "most annoying": this superlative follows the pattern of Block I adjectives such as *molestus, a, um.* The positive here would be *molestum* and the comparative *molestius,* which is not to be confused with the comparative adverb, also *molestius.*

> → **736** adj.: comp. and superl., 36.

quae nobis nostra vita dulcior est, "who is sweeter to us than our life": the trap here is that *nostra vita* looks like the subject form as in "[who is a] sweeter life [for us]," but here it is the ablative of comparison meaning "[who is sweeter to us] than our life." In prose you cannot see whether *nostra vita* is subject or ablative, but in poetry you can see the difference between them from the length of the two final letters. The short –*ă* in *nostră vită* indicates the subject form, but the long –*ā* in *nostrā vitā* indicates the ablative form. Thus, poetry is more helpful in this case than prose.

> → **737** abl.: comparison, 90.2, GL n° 398;
> Block I nouns, 2; abl.: meaning and forms, 27.

quid causae, "what kind of a reason": *causae* is genitive of part.

> → **738** gen. of part, 99.

quid causae ... fuerit, "what kind of a reason there was": IQ on Track I depending on *intellexi,* "I have understood" in T.4a, producing *fuerit* in T.3s describing antecedent action.

> → **739** M & M, 60, 71, GL n° 527, remarks 1–2; IQ, 60.

postridie ... quam, "On the day after that [I have departed]": the awkward idiom directly means "on the day after than I departed." The *post* in *postridie* goes with the adverb *quam,* to mean "later than." Cicero could have written this out more fully as *die postquam discessi,* "on the day after I have departed."

→ **740** dict., *postridie,* adv., I.... with *quam.*

intellexi ... discessi, "I have departed ... I have understood": both verbs can be T.4a or T.4b. But because *Quod ... fuerit,* "what ... there was" is T.3s, on Track I, the verb on which it depends, *intellexi,* must be T.4a, meaning "I have understood," and establishing Track I. The verb *discessi* refers to his departure on the previous day, but he is writing this letter from the boat still in the area, thus also T.4a, and so is given in English as "I have departed."

→ **741** verb T.4a, T.4b: 8; *consecutio,* 47–48.

Χολὴν ἄκρατον, "*unmixed bile*": the Latin equivalent is *bilis mera,* "pure bile."

→ **742** Bibliography: *Onomasticon Tullianum;* Greek expressions, pp. 623–626.

statim ita sum levatus ut ... videatur, "I have been so immediately relieved that [some god] seems": if *sum levatus* is T.4a, "I have been relieved," then it establishes Track I and produces *videatur* in T.1s. But *sum levatus* may also be T.4b, "I was relieved," establishing Track II but it still may produce *ut ... videatur* as the 3% sequence of tenses giving one concrete result in T.1s.

→ **743** verb T.4a, T.4b: 8; *consecutio,* 47–48;
      subjunctive use: pure result (consecutive), 67.1–2, GL n° 552;
      subjunctive use: 3% sequence of tenses, 94.1.

Cui ... deo, "to which god": in the dative because *satis facere,* is one expression of the 65 that take a complement in the form to-for-from, meaning "to do enough for" and thus "to satisfy someone."

→ **744** 65 verbs with dat., 33.7.2, GL n° 346.

soles ... facies, "you will render ... you are accustomed": both verbs end in –*es,* but *soles* from *soleo, solēre,* "to be accustomed," is T.1i and *facies* from *facio, facĕre,* "to render," is T.3i. This one ending for two different times will cause trouble unless you know your vocabulary and the language. By the way, there is a noun *facies,* "face"; another warning for the wise and competent Latinist.

→ **745** verb T.1i, T.2i, T.3i: 12;
      dict., *soleo, itus,* 2; *facio, feci, factum,* 3; 20% of nouns: *facies, ei,* f., 35.

❧

Navem spero nos valde bonam habere: in eam simul atque conscendi haec scripsi. Deinde conscribam ad nostros familiaris multas epistulas quibus te et Tulliolam nostram diligentissime commendabo. Cohortarer vos quo animo fortiores essetis nisi vos fortiores cognossem quam quemquam virum. Et tamen eius modi spero negotia esse ut et vos istic commodissime sperem esse et me aliquando cum similibus nostri rem publicam defensuros.   (*Fam.* XIV, 7, 2)

I hope that we have a very good ship: as soon as I embarked onto it I have written these things. Afterward I shall write many letters to our close relatives and friends to whom I shall recommend you and our little Tullia most diligently. I would exhort you that you might be braver in spirit if I had not come to know you braver than any man. And nevertheless I hope that matters are of such a nature that I hope both that you are there most comfortably and that I (we) some day will defend the state with people like us.

Navem spero nos ... habere, "I hope that we have a ... ship": the M & M verb *spero* produces OO *nos ... habere*, "that we have." Note that the first word *Navem*, "ship," is the object of the last word *habere* in OO.
> → **746** M & M, 60, 71, GL n° 527, remarks 1–2; OO, 71–73.

valde bonam, "very good": the adv. *valide* has a contracted form, *valde*, used here. It can be used with verbs or with adverbs such as *bonam*, meaning "very good."
> → **747** dict., *validus, a, um*, adj., II., B., (β). with adjectives.

simul atque, "as soon as": this expression will cause trouble because it looks like it means "at the same time also." Other expressions also meaning "as soon as" are: *simul, simul ac, cum primum, ut primum*.
> → **748** dict., *simul*, adv., VIII. with *atque*, "as soon as."

conscendi ... scripsi, "I embarked ... I have written": each verb can be T.4a, "I have embarked ... I have written," or T.4b, "I embarked ... I wrote," or one of one time and one of the other time as in the English rendering above, but the Latin will not help you here. You have to see both possibilities and think, and sometimes even then you do not know what the author intended.
> → **749** verb T.4a, T.4b: 8.

conscribam, "I shall write": the form may be either T.3i, as in the English rendering above, or T.1s.
> → **750** verb formation T.3 in groups III and IV, 12.3.2;
>   forms of the subjunctive, T.1s: 44.1.

ad nostros familiaris, "to our close relatives": the variation *familiarīs* with the long –ī– was heard by the Romans as the same thing as *familiares*. This object plural agrees with *nostros*, "our." We have seen this also when the plural object *omnis* is used for *omnes*, "all."
> → **751** Block II adj.: –*is* = –*es*, 38, GL n° 78.

quibus … commendabo, "to whom I shall recommend": here *quibus* may be either the dative meaning "to whom [I shall recommend you and our little Tullia]," as in the English rendering above, or theoretically the ablative, meaning "with which letters [I shall recommend you and our little Tullia]."

→ **752** natural dat., 33.7.1; abl.: meaning and forms, 27.

diligentissime, "most diligently": the comparative adverb is *diligentius*, and the positive adverb *diligenter*.

→ **753** adv.: irregular comp. and superl., 37.3.

cohortarer … nisi … cognossem, "I would exhort you … if I had not come to know": contrary to fact conditionals where *cohortarer* is T.2s, and *cognossem* is an abbreviated form of *cognovissem*, T.4s. We check this by saying, "I would exhort you, but in fact I am not, if I had not come to know, but in fact I have come to know you braver than any man."

→ **754** conditionals: contrary to fact, 86.3;
          contractions: verbs, 39.2, GL n° 131.

quo animo, "that [you might be braver] in spirit": the *quo* is a trap because people will see *quo animo* together and think it means "with what spirit," but the *quo* does not connect with *animo* at all. Rather *quo* is another way of expressing *ut eo* or *ut tanto*, "in order that all the more" or "so that all the more," where the *ut* goes with *essetis* in T.2s to mean, "so that you might be," and *eo* goes with *fortiores* to mean "all the more brave" or "by so much more brave." Sallustius loves this use of *quo*, meaning in the dictionary "in order that."

→ **755** dict., *quo*, adv. II., B., 2. "in order that, so that";
          subjunctive use: relative clause of purpose, *quo = ut eo*, 58.2;
          GL n° 545.2 *quō = ut eō*;
          adj.: comp., 36.

[eo] … fortiores … quam quemquam, "braver … than any [man]": the comparison is made here with *quam*, "than." The particle *quam*, "than," joins two equal things on both sides. Here the object *quemquam* corresponds to the object *vos* on the other side of the comparison.

→ **756** *quam* with the comp., 43.2.

eius modi, "of such a nature": the dictionary says that *eius* can mean "of him, her, it, this, that" or even "of such," as here.

→ **757** dict., *is, ea, id*, pron. demonstr., II. "such."

negotia esse, "that matters are": OO depending on M & M verb *spero*, "I hope."

→ **758** M & M, 60, 71, GL n° 527, remarks 1–2; OO, 71–73.

esse … esse … [esse], "[that matters] are … [that you] are … [that I/we] will": the contemporaneous infinitive *esse* appears twice and is implied once, with different meanings. The first, *negotia esse*, "that matters are," depends on *spero*, "I hope" in T.1i. The second, *vos ... esse*, "that you are," depends on *sperem*, "I hope" in T.1s. Also depending on *sperem*, the third is implied by the futurity participle and means "that I/we are about to defend," "that I/we are on the point of defending," or simply, "that I/we will defend."

→ **759** sentence structure, 1.

ut ... sperem, "that I ... hope": result clause in T.1s depending on *eius modi spero ... esse*, "[I hope that matters] are [of such a nature]." As a result clause, the Latin subjunctive *sperem* sounds indicative in English, just like the verb that begins the sentence, *spero*, "I hope" in T.1i.

→ **760** subjunctive use: pure result (consecutive), 67.1–2, GL n° 552.

et vos ... esse, "both ... you are": the first of two statements in OO depending on *sperem*, "I hope" in T.1s. The choice of words here is weak; instead of *esse*, "you are," he could have said *habitare*, *vivere*, or *degere*, all rendered here as "you live" or "you are living."

→ **761** M & M, 60, 71, GL n° 527, remarks 1–2; OO, 71–73.

et ... et ..., "both ... and ...": these coordinate *vos esse*, "you are," with *me defensuros esse*, "I (we) ... will defend."

→ **762** conjunction: *et ... , et ...* , 3.2.

et me ... cum similibus ... defensuros, "and that I (we) ... will defend ... with people like [us]": the second of two statements in OO depending on *sperem*, "I hope" in T.1s. The full infinitive is *defensuros esse*, "to be about to defend." Any Latin teacher could consider this an unbelievable or intolerable mistake. The singular subject is the accusative *me* which should produce the singular accusative participle *defensurum*, meaning "that I will defend." But between the subject and the participle Cicero adds the idea of other people acting in cohort with him, *cum similibus nostri*, "with people like us." So, he switches to the plural form of the participle *defensuros*, which should have a plural subject such as *nos*, meaning "that we will defend." This is a purely natural or logical *constructio ad sensum*, grammatical construction according to the concept and meaning. Cicero was, after all, in a boat jotting down off the top of his mind this letter to his wife with their family up on the hill.

→ **763** M & M, 60, 71, GL n° 527, remarks 1–2; OO, 71–73.

cum similibus nostri, "with people like us": here *nostri* is the of-possessive form of *nos*, and means "of us." He uses the of form because of the expression formed by *similis* followed by the of-possession, meaning "similar of us." We have the same of-possession form in the English expression "the likes of us." Cicero does this all the time; confirmed by the dict.

→ **764** personal pronouns: function of-possession, 24.2.

Tu primum valetudinem tuam velim cures: deinde, si tibi videbitur, villis iis
utere quae longissime aberunt a militibus. Fundo Arpinati bene poteris uti
cum familia urbana si annona carior fuerit. Cicero bellissimus tibi salutem
plurimam dicit. Etiam atque etiam vale. D. VII. Id. Iun.   (*Fam.* XIV, 7, 3)

First of all I would like that you take care of your health: then, if it will seem
OK to you, you will use those villas which will be the furthest removed from
soldiers. You will be able to use well the estate at Arpinum with the slave
contingent from Rome if the price of living will have been too high. Very
handsome Cicero extends the greatest greeting to you. Take care again and
again. I was (am) sending on the seventh before the June Ides [7 June].

Tu ... cures, "you take care": Cicero is thinking of his wife and so begins
with the word uppermost on his mind *Tu*, "You." The first word is the subject of the last word, *Tu ... cures*, which is T.1s depending on *velim*, "I would
like." Note the use of the subjunctive following *velim* without *ut*. We might
emphasize the first word in English, saying: "You, I would like that (you)
take care of your health."

→ **765** subjunctive use: purpose clause without *ut*, 58, GL nº 546, remark 2;
commands: other expressions, 85.1.7; sentence structure, 1.

si tibi videbitur, "if it will seem OK to you": some readers may think this
says, "if it appears to you," but the dictionary says that the Romans did not
express but understood here the idea, "good, fine, OK." This fuller meaning
is implied in the Latin and expressed in the English rendering.

→ **766** dict., *video, vidi, visum*, 2., II., B., 6., c. *videtur alicui*, "it seems good to
any one."

villis iis, "those villas": the abl. of instrument going with *utére*, one of the
five deponent verbs that have such a complement, here meaning "you will
get use for yourself by/from those villas."

→ **767** famous five verbs with the ablative, 78.1;
abl.: instrument, 28.5.3–4, 89.2, GL nº 401.

utere, "you will use": this one form can be three different words in the Latin
language: *útere*, "you must use" is the command form of a deponent verb,
its plural being *utimini*. *útere*, a alternative form of *úteris*, "you are using,"
which is T.1i of an deponent verb. *utére*, a variant form of *utéris*, "you will
be using," which is T.3i of a deponent verb. This last possibility is how we
understand *utere* here, because there are other future forms in the sentence:
videbitur, "it will seem OK," and *aberunt*, "will be removed" both in T.3i. It
is tempting at this point to add that one speaking to Mother Nature could
say, *Uteris uteris*, "You are using wombs."

→ **768** verb: deponent, 29;
commands: deponent, 34; variation: –*ris*, 39.3.

Fundo Arpinati, "the estate at Arpinum": as above an abl. of instrument going with *uti*, "to use," one of the five deponent verbs with such abl. complements.

> → **769** famous five verbs with the ablative, 78.1;
>   abl.: instrument, 28.5.3–4, 89.2, GL n° 401.

cum familia, "with the slave contingent": this looks like it means "with the family," but your dictionary will tell you that it does not refer to the wife and children, the family; that would be *tua cum domo tota*, "with your whole household," "with your family," or simply *cum tuis*, "with your people." Because a *famulus* is "a servant," the first meaning of *familia* is the servitude or group of servants in the house.

> → **770** dict., *familia, ae*, f., I. not = "family" (*domus*), except by rare exception
>   v. II., A., 3.

annona, "the price of living": the word refers to the price of food, and so to the cost of living.

> → **771** dict., *annona, ae*, f., annual income from natural products.

Cicero bellissimus, "Very handsome Cicero": Here Cicero the father is speaking about his son Marcus, who is 15 years of age.

> → **772** adj.: superlative, 36.

D. VII. Id. Iun, "I was sending on the seventh before the June Ides [7 June]": the full Latin text is *Dabam septimo Idus Iunias*. Note: *Idus* is a feminine object and *Iunias*, "Junian," is an adjective that agrees with it, according to classical use. The verb *Dabam*, "I was sending" is in the epistolary tense which really means "I am sending," but the time is given from the perspective of the reader.

> → **773** about the Roman calendar, pp. 605–608;
>   GL appendix: Roman Calendar, pp. 491–92;
>   20% of nouns: *idus, uum*, f., 35; letter-writer tense, GL n° 252.

LETTER 117 T-P
AD QUINTUM FRATREM II, 6

MARCUS QUINTO FRATRI SALUTEM.

O litteras mihi tuas iucundissimas exspectatas, ac primo quidem cum desiderio, nunc vero etiam cum timore! Atque has scito litteras me solas accepisse post illas, quas tuus nauta attulit Ulbia datas. Sed cetera, ut scribis, praesenti sermoni reserventur. Hoc tamen non queo differre. Id. Maiis senatus frequens divinus fuit in supplicatione Gabinio deneganda. Adiurat Procilius hoc nemini accidisse. Foris valde plauditur. Mihi cum sua sponte iucundum tum iucundius quod me absente. Etenim εἰλικρινὲς iudicium sine oppugnatione, sine gratia nostra erat.   (Q. Fr. II, 6, 1)

MARCUS A GREETING TO BROTHER QUINTUS

O most pleasant letters of yours having been awaited by me, and indeed first of all with longing, now however even with fear! And you must know that I received only this letter after the one, which your sailor brought, having been sent from Ulpia. But the remaining matters, as you write, should be reserved for a discussion face to face. However I am not able to put off this. On the May Ides [15 May] a crowded senate was terrific in denying to Gabinius a supplication. Procilius swears that this has happened to nobody. Outside it is applauded very much. For me [it was] both acceptable on its own accord and more acceptable because [done]—myself being absent. For it was a *pure* judgment without opposition, without our political influence.

> *O litteras*, "O ... letters": the object form is used to express an exclamation, as in English we say "O miserable me" in the object form of exclamation, not "O miserable I."
> → **774** exclamations, GL n° 343.1.

> *mihi ... iucundissimas exspectatas*, "most pleasant ... having been awaited by me": the *mihi* can go two ways here, either with *iucundissimas* as a natural dat. meaning "most pleasant for me," or with *exspectatas* meaning "hav-

ing been awaited by me" as a dat. of agent, normally used with the participle of passive necessity, but also possible with the simple passive.

→ 775 natural dat., 33.7.1; dat. of agent, 53.5;
      participle of passive necessity, 50, 51.1.4.

has scito litteras me solas accepisse, "And you must know that I received only this letter": in early Latin such as Plautus we do have the command form *sci*, "you must know," but then it seems to have gone out of use and *scito*, "you must know," became the standard usage of the second command form, sometimes called the future imperative; its reversed form is *scitote*. The main verb *scito* is a verb of M & M producing a statement in OO where *me* in the object form functions as the subject of the inf. *accepisse* describing antecedent action, "that I received," and its object is *litteras*, "letter."

→ 776 commands: first, second, 17;
      M & M, 60, 71, GL n° 527, remarks 1–2; OO, 71–73.

quas ... attulit, "which [your sailor] brought": here *attulit*, "he brought," is in T.4b, that is, in the indicative. Cicero does not put this verb into the subjunctive, such as *attulisset* in T.4s by MA because this relative clause is just a remark said in passing and does not pertain closely to the total complex of the sentence in indirect discourse on which it depends. MA is not necessarily used, but may be used when the clause sticks closely to the idea of the sentence in indirect discourse on which it depends.

→ 777 relative clauses, 10–11; subjunctive use: modal attraction, 83.

tuus nauta, "your sailor": these two words agree because *nauta, ae* is a Block I masculine noun. The Romans did not have women sailors, but today we might say *tua nauta* to refer to a woman sailor.

→ 778 Block I nouns: variations, 4.1.

Ulbia datas, "having been sent from Ulpia": the form *Ulbia* is an abl. of separation, "from Ulpia." In Shackleton Bailey (2:296) the name of the city is *Olbia*, which L&S says is a city in Sardinia now called *Terranova*.

→ 779 dict., *Olbia, ae*, f., IV., a city in Sardinia, now Terranova;
      function: place from where, names of cities and small islands, *Ulbia*,
      69.2.2; abl. separation from place, 27.

ut scribis, "as you write": with *scribis*, "you write," in T.1i, *ut* here means "as."

→ 780 dict., *ut*, I., B. meaning "as."

Hoc ... non queo differre, "I am not able to put off this": written as two words, *non queo*, is extremely rare, because it is usually written as one word, *nequeo*, "I am unable." Its object is *differre*, a gerund, "to put off," which in turn has as its object the first word in the sentence, *Hoc*, "this."

→ 781 dict., *nequeo, ivi* and *ii, itum*, 4., I.... Cicero always writes "*non queo* ...";
      verb: complementary infinitive, 77; gerund, 77.1; sentence structure, 1.

Id. Maiis, "On the May Ides": the full Latin form is *Idibus Maiis*, where *Mai-is* is used as an adj. describing *Idibus*, as in "on the May Ides," that is, 15 May.

→ **782** about the Roman calendar, pp. 605–608;
   GL appendix: Roman Calendar, pp. 491–92.

in supplicatione Gabinio deneganda, "in denying to Gabinius a supplica-tion": the Romans prefer the gerundive combination as here, whereas the scholastics prefer the clarity of the gerund with its object, which would be here *in supplicationem … denegando*, where the preposition *in*, "in," takes the abl., *denegando*, "in denying," whose object in turn is *supplicationem*, "a supplication." From this we can form the gerundive combination by putting the object of the gerund in the function of the gerund, that is, by putting *supplicationem* in the abl. *supplicatione*, and then making the gerund agree with it, as in *deneganda*. There is no difference in meaning between the two, only of preference and Latin style. The man's name, *Gabinio*, "to Gabinius," is the natural dat. complement of *deneganda*.

→ **783** gerundive, 77.2; gerund, 77.1; prep. with abl., 28.4;
   natural dat., 33.7.1.

The eternal difficulty remains in that the preposition could go with *supplicatione*, "in a supplication," with which the passive necessity participle agrees, *deneganda*, "[in a supplication] needing to be denied." If this were the case, then *Gabinio* could be the dat. of agent and the whole thing would mean "in a supplication needing to be denied by Gabinius." These are Latin possibilities and subtleties which require calm thinking and logical analysis; in Latin nothing is automatic!

→ **784** prep. with abl., 28.4; participle of passive necessity, 50, 51.1.4;
   dat. of agent, 53.5.

Adiurat Procilius hoc nemini accidisse, "Procilius swears that this has happened to nobody": the main verb *adiurat*, "[Procilius] swears," in T.1i is a verb of M & M producing a statement in OO where *hoc* in the object form functions as the subject of the inf. *accidisse*, antecedent to the main action, "that this has happened." The complement of *accidisse* is a natural dat., *nemini*, "to nobody."

→ **785** M & M, 60, 71, GL n° 527, remarks 1–2; OO, 71–73;
   natural dat., 33.7.1.

Foris, "Outside": in the abl. this functions like the locative stating the place where, or in which, so here referring to the place in front of the senate house, the Curia, in the Roman forum. If we want to indicate motion, as in "to go outside," then *foras* is used.

→ **786** function: place at which, *foris*, 69.3.3;
   function: place to where, *foras*, 69.1.3.

plauditur, "it is applauded": in T.1i passive, the verb is used impersonally here, meaning "applause is given."

> → **787** passive Times 1, 2, 3 indicative, 21;
>   passive verb used impersonally, GL nº 208.

cum … tum … , "both … and …": also meaning "not only … but also.…"

> → **788** correlative comparative sentences, 90.5, GL nº 642.

sua sponte, "on its own accord": this idiom is almost the same as the English word "spontaneous." Here, *sua* agrees with *sponte*, which is found in the abl. only in this expression.

> → **789** dict., *sponte*, abl., I. joined with *mea, tua, sua*, "of one's own accord."

quod, "because [done]": we added a few words in here, "[it was] … [done]," because the letter was jotted off without all the verbs explicit. Here *quod* means "because," but nothing more is given.

> → **790** causal: *quod*, "because, since," 59.2.

me absente, "myself being absent": an AA where *me* in the abl. form functions as the subject of the contemporaneous part. *absente*. The English "myself being absent" is simply a smoother way of saying "me being absent."

> → **791** ablative absolute, 54–55.

εἰλικρινὲς, "*pure*": the Latin equivalent is *sincerum* or *purum*, "unmixed," "genuine."

> → **792** Bibliography: *Onomasticon Tullianum*; Greek expressions, pp. 623–626.

❧

Ante quod Idibus et postridie fuerat dictum de agro Campano actum iri, non est actum. In hac causa mihi aqua haeret. Sed plura quam constitueram: coram enim. Vale, mi optime et optatissime frater, et advola; idem te pueri nostri rogant. Illud scilicet: cenabis, cum veneris.   (*Q. Fr.* II, 6, 2)

That which previously on the Ides and the following day had been said would be done about the Campanian land, was not done. In this case "I am stuck." But [I have written] more things than I had decided: for [we shall talk] face to face. Take care, my most wonderful and most longed for brother, and come flying here; our boys ask the same thing of you. This of course: you will have dinner, when you will have arrived.

Ante quod Idibus, "That which previously on the Ides": the combination *Ante* looks like a preposition that goes with *quod*, meaning "Before which." Here, rather, *Ante* is an adv. meaning "previously," and relates to *Idibus*, an abl. of time at which, "on the Ides," whereas *quod* goes with *fuerat dictum*, "[that] which had been said."

> → **793** dict., *ante*, II. adv., B., 1. of time, "before, previously"; abl.: time at which, 70.1;
>   about the Roman calendar, pp. 605–608;
>   GL appendix: Roman Calendar, pp. 491–92.

quod ... fuerat dictum ... actum iri, non est actum, "That which ... had been said would be done ... , was not done": the main sentence is *non est actum,* "[That] was not done," in T.4b passive. Its subject is an unexpressed *id,* "That," the antecedent of *quod,* "That which." The *id* is then expanded in the relative clause *quod ... fuerat dictum,* "[That] which ... had been said," in T.5i passive.

→ **794** passive Times 4, 5, 6 indicative, 26; relative clauses, 10–11.

If this is read too quickly, a reader might say the word *quod* means "that which," but this quick reading is incorrect, because *quod* means simply "which." This distinction is important in this sentence because the unexpressed antecedent *id* is the main subject of the sentence *non est actum,* "[that] was not done," and the *quod* goes with *fuerat dictum,* meaning "which had been said."

→ **795** rel. pron.: omission of the antecedent, 11.2.

Note that in place of *fuerat dictum* the usual classical form as learned in school is *erat dictum* with the same meaning "[which] had been said," in T.5i passive. This rare usage of Cicero will take over in the Middle Ages, because the classical expression *erat dictum* to some people no longer looked or sounded like T.5i, whereas *fuerat dictum* did. Yet, here it is in Cicero much to the displeasure of conservative grammarians.

→ **796** characteristics of later Latin, 105.

Cicero is inconsistent, and this is living, evolving Latin, when he should have said *erat dictum* in T.5i, but he said *fuerat dictum,* then he comes back and says *est actum* in T.4b and not *fuit actum,* jumping around a bit with his forms. Both usages are in the same natural thought, but *fuerat dictum* will become the way to talk from about 3rd–4th c. C.E. until the Renaissance. Latin is a living, growing body, not a dead laboratory frog to be dissected.

→ **797** characteristics of later Latin, 105;
      passive Times 4, 5, 6 indicative, 26.

The verb *fuerat dictum,* "[which] had been said," is a verb of M & M producing a statement in OO in which the verb combination *actum iri* is the futurity passive inf., "[action] would be done," a clumsy solution in the absence of any other Latin forms, as are available in more developed Greek. As an impersonal verb, its subject is contained within itself. The complement of *iri* is the supine *actum,* "to do"; the supine requires a verb of motion, which here is *iri,* meaning "motion is being made," and the whole expression *actum iri* means "motion is being made to do." This is all that Latin could do or produce. Sorry!

→ **798** verb: futurity passive infinitive, 81.3; supine, 81;
      M & M, 60, 71, GL n° 527, remarks 1–2; OO, 71–73.

Many grammars and textbooks say don't worry about this expression because it doesn't exist, but it does, as here before your eyes. We can play with this expression to test ourselves a bit by giving its plural. The plural of *fuerat dictum* is *fuerant dicta,* and the plural of *est actum* is *sunt acta,* but the plu-

ral of *actum iri* is *actum iri*, because here *actum* is an unchangeable supine,
not an adjectival participle. We can put the verbs of the whole sentence in
the plural by saying:

> *Ante quae Idibus et postridie fuerant dicta de agro Campano actum iri,*
> *non sunt acta.*

"Those things which previously on the Ides and the following day had
been said would be done about the Campanian land, were not done."

→ **799** verb: futurity passive infinitive, 81.3; supine, 81.

mihi aqua haeret: for this metaphor Tyrrell and Purser point to the *The-*
saurus Linguae Latinae, which explains it as taken perhaps from the use of
the water clock becoming clogged and no longer functioning. Therefore an
orator had to discontinue his speech because the time clock no longer func-
tioned: "the water clock is stuck," meaning "I am stuck," "I cannot go ahead
because the clock is stuck."

→ **800** dict., *haereo, haesi, haesum*, 2., I., b., (β). *aqua haeret*, "the water (in the
         waterclock) stops";
   dict., *aqua, ae*, f., II., F. the water in the water-clock used to regulate
         speeches, (g) *aqua haeret*, "the water stops," "I am at a loss."

optime et optatissime frater, "my wonderful and most longed for brother":
the other degrees are *bene* and *melior*; *optate* and *optatior*, if they exist in
literature at all.

→ **801** function: direct address, 38.3;
   adj.: irregular comp. and superl., 36.5.

idem te ... rogant, "[our boys] ask the same thing of you": a double object
with *rogant*, literally, "they ask you the same thing." The boys are Cicero's
nephew, age eleven, and Cicero's son, age nine.

→ **802** double acc., GL n° 339; dict., *rogo, avi, atum*, 1., I., A.... *aliquem aliquid*.

cenabis, cum veneris, "you will have dinner, when you will have arrived": the
pair T.3i with T.6i consists of *cenabis*, "you will have dinner," in T.3i followed
by *cum* with the indicative, thus meaning "when," here *veneris*, "you will
have arrived," in T.6i. Today, on the street you might hear, "You'll eat when
you get here."

→ **803** T.3i and T.6i paired: 7, Time 6, and GL n° 244, remark 2.

LETTER 366 T-P
AD ATTICUM IX, 11A

Note: we shall consider here a letter that Cicero sent to Caesar. Cicero sent a copy of that letter also to Atticus along with a cover letter in which Cicero explains to Atticus what he is doing. In our commentary here we shall first present part of one line of the cover letter in which Cicero tells Atticus about the attached letter to Caesar. Thereafter we shall consider the text of the letter to Caesar.

CICERO ATTICO SAL.

[…] Misi ad te exemplum litterarum mearum ad Caesarem quibus me aliquid profecturum puto.   (*Att.* IX, 11, 5)

CICERO TO ATTICUS A GREETING

[…] I have sent to you a copy of my letter to Caesar by which I think I shall be making some progress.

Note: there follows now immediately below that copy of Cicero's letter to Caesar, which is mentioned in the above citation.

ॐ

CICERO IMP. S. D. CAESARI IMP.

Ut legi tuas litteras quas a Furnio nostro acceperam, quibus mecum agebas ut ad urbem essem, te velle uti 'consilio et dignitate mea' minus sum admiratus: de 'gratia' et de 'ope' quid significares mecum ipse quaerebam, spe tamen deducebar ad eam cogitationem ut te pro tua admirabili ac singulari sapientia de otio, de pace, de concordia civium agi velle arbitrarer, et ad eam rationem existimabam satis aptam esse et naturam et personam meam.   (*Att.* IX, 11A, 1)

Cicero, commander, says a greeting
to Caesar, commander

When I read your letter, which I had received from our Furnius, by which you were discussing with me that I might be present around the city [Rome], I was less surprised that you wanted to use "my advice and status": I myself was asking in my own heart what you were hinting by "influence" and by "resources"; however, I was being drawn by hope to such a consideration that I might think that you, according to your admirable and singular wisdom, wanted a discussion to be had about tranquility, about peace, about the agreement of citizens, and for that program I was thinking that both my character and stature were suitable enough.

Cicero imp. s. d. Caesari imp.: *Cicero imperator salutem dicit Caesari imperatori*

ut legi, "When I read": followed by *legi* in T.4b, here *ut* means "when," as will *ubi* also occasionally mean.

→ **804** dict., *ut*, II., conjunction, B. temporal clause where *ut* = *quo tempore*; dict., *ubi*, adv., II., A. when.

quibus ... agebas ut ... essem, "by which you were discussing ... that I might be present": *agebas*, "you were dealing" or "you were negotiating," is T.2i and establishes a purpose clause on Track II, *ut ... essem* in T.2s.

→ **805** subjunctive use: purpose clause, 58.1; *consecutio*, 47–48.

ad urbem, "around the city [Rome]": *ad urbem* also means "near Rome" or "in the vicinity of Rome," in distinction from *in urbe*, "in the city."

→ **806** prep. with obj., 6; prep. with abl., 28.4.

te velle ... sum admiratus, "I was ... surprised that you wanted": the infinitive *velle* sounds past in English, "you wanted," "you were desiring," because it is contemporaneous with *sum admiratus*, a deponent verb in T.4b, where the passive form has active meaning. This is why we do not call this an antecedent *passive* participle.

→ **807** verb: deponent, 29; participle, deponents, 50, 51.2.2.

uti consilio et dignitate mea, "to use 'my advice and status'": *uti* is one of the five deponent verbs that takes its apparent object in the ablative, here *consilio et dignitate mea*, meaning literally "to procure usefulness by my advice and status." The quotation in the original indicates that Cicero is quoting Caesar's letter, offering to us a brief peek into the great Caesar's Latin.

→ **808** famous five verbs with the ablative, 78.1.

sum admiratus, "I was ... surprised": your dictionary will tell you that the verb *admiror, admirari*, "to be surprised," allows three different usages.

First, GL (nº 533) explains that as a verb of emotion, *admirari* may function as a verb of M & M producing OO, as here: *te velle*, "that you wanted."

Second and third, the dictionary also indicates that this verb may be used with *quod*. This is explained further in GL nº 542: *quod*, "that," is used with verbs of emotion followed by either the indicative or the subjunctive, as in *quod volebas* or *quod velles*, with the same meaning. An indication like this in the classroom will reassure students that this is as far as you can go in Latin, and there are not any more secrets: congratulations!

→ **809** dict., *admiror, atus*, 1., II, B. constructed with acc. with inf. ... *quod*;
verbs of emotion + OO, GL nº 533; verbs of emotion + *quod*, GL nº 542;
M & M, 60, 71, GL nº 527, remarks 1–2; OO, 71–73; verb: deponent, 29.

quid significares ... quaerebam, "I ... was asking ... what you were hinting": the M & M verb *quaerebam* in T.2i establishes Track II and produces an IQ *quid significares* in T.2s.

→ **810** M & M, 60, 71, GL nº 527, remarks 1–2;
IQ, 60; *consecutio*, 47–48.

spe tamen deducebar ... ut ... arbitrarer, "however, I was being drawn by hope ... that I was thinking": hope was drawing his consideration toward an intention, a purpose. *deducebar* in T.2i pass. produces a purpose clause *ut arbitrarer* in T.2s. Note the similar construction here to the above *agebas ut ... essem*. Both are based on verbs in T.2i, giving rise to a clause constructed of *ut* and a verb in T.2s.

→ **811** subjunctive use: purpose clause, 58.1;
subjunctive use: complementary result (consecutive), 68.1.

eam cogitationem, "such a consideration": *eam* may mean "this," "that," or as here "such," to coordinate with the *ut* and purpose clause.

→ **812** demonstrative pron.: *is, ea, id*, 3.1, 40.2;
dict., *is, ea, id*, pron. demonstr., II. "such."

te ... velle, "that you ... wanted": OO depending on the M & M verb *arbitrarer*, "I was thinking."

→ **813** M & M, 60, 71, GL nº 527, remarks 1–2; OO, 71–73.

te ... agi velle, "that you ... wanted a discussion to be had": *agi* is OO where the accusative subject is implied in the action of the impersonal infinitive, as in "it to be discussed" or "it to be negotiated" or "discussion to be had" or "dealings to be done."

→ **814** OO, 71–73; verb: contemporaneous passive infinitive, 72.3;
passive verb used impersonally, GL nº 208.

pro, "according to": a glorious example of the meaning of *pro*: "in keeping with," "acccording to," "in proportion to," but here not "for."

→ **815** prep. with abl., 28.4; dict., *pro*, prep. II., B., 6.

singulari sapientia, "singular wisdom": from a human perspective, this statement masks the true feelings of Cicero, who did not think Caesar had much wisdom.

existimabam esse et naturam et personam, "I was thinking that … character and stature were": OO where the infinitive *esse* is contemporaneous with the M & M verb on which it depends, *existimabam* in T.2i, and so in English *esse* is rendered as "were."

→ **816** M & M, 60, 71, GL nº 527, remarks 1–2; OO, 71–73.

Quod si ita est et si qua de Pompeio nostro tuendo et tibi ac rei publicae reconciliando cura te attingit, magis idoneum quam ego sum ad eam causam profecto reperies neminem; qui et illi semper et senatui, cum primum potui, pacis auctor fui, nec sumptis armis belli ullam partem attigi, iudicavique eo bello te violari contra cuius honorem populi Romani beneficio concessum inimici atque invidi niterentur. Sed ut eo tempore non modo ipse fautor dignitatis tuae fui verum etiam ceteris auctor ad te adiuvandum, sic me nunc Pompei dignitas vehementer movet. Aliquot enim sunt anni cum vos duo delegi quos praecipue colerem et quibus essem, sicut sum, amicissimus.   (*Att.* IX, 11A, 2)

Which thing if it is so and if any concern touches you about protecting and reconciling our Pompeius to you and to the country, you will find no one for sure more suitable for this cause than I am; who was the instigator of peace both for him always and for the senate as soon as I was able, nor did I touch any part of the war—after arms had been taken up—and I judged that by that war you were being mistreated against whose honor, bestowed by the kindness of the Roman people, enemies and envious people were working. But as at that time I was not only the promotor of your dignity but also I was for other people an instigator for helping you, thus at this time the dignity of Pompeius moves me tremendously. For it is a few years now that I chose the two of you, whom I would honor especially and to whom I would be most friendly, as I am.

Quod … reperies, "Which thing … you will find": *Quod* refers to the content of the preceding sentence as a whole, namely, Cicero's effort in avoiding the civil war. Some scholars will take the *Quod* as a simple connective and render it in English as "And, [if it is so]."

→ **817** *quod* referring to previous sentence: GL nº 614, remark 2; dict., *qui, quae, quod*, pron., II., C. a connective instead of *is, ea, id* with a conj.

qua … cura, "any … concern": people may initially take *qua* to be the ablative of the relative pronoun *qui, quae, quod*, where the subject is *quae*. Here, however, *qua* is the subject form of the indefinite adjective *aliqui, aliqua, aliquod.* The prefix *ali–* frequently does not appear after the word *si.* Thus, *si qua* here means "if any." The *qua* agrees with *cura,* the eleventh word beyond; good luck!

→ **818** adj.: indefinite, 42.4; after *si* the *ali*-s fly away, 42.5; sentence structure, 1.

de Pompeio nostro tuendo … et … reconciliando, "about protecting and reconciling our Pompeius": both *tuendo* and *reconciliando* may be taken as gerundives as in the English above. In this case the gerund would be *de Pompeium nostrum tuendo … et … reconciliando* with no change in meaning. Conversely they may be taken as participles of passive necessity meaning "about our Pompeius needing to be protected and reconciled." This ambivalence will never go away.

→ **819** gerundive, 77.2; gerund, 77.1; participle of passive necessity, 50, 51.1.4, 51.2.4; participle of passive receptivity, deponents, 50, 51.1.4, 51.2.4.

magis idoneum quam, "more suitable than": with adjectives like *idoneus, impius,* and *industrius,* the comp. and super. are not *idoneor* or *impiior* or *industrior,* but they use *magis idoneum, magis impium, magis industrium* and *maxime idoneum, maxime impium, maxime industrium.*

→ **820** comparative with *magis,* superlative with *maxime,* GL n° 87.6.

auctor, "instigator": upon first sight a person might take *auctor* to refer to the "author" of a book, but it means much more here "an instigator," "the pusher," "the originator."

→ **821** dict., *auctor, oris,* comm., II., C.

sumptis armis, "after arms had been taken up": AA smoothed out in translation. The literal meaning, "arms having been taken up," is the first step in producing a smoothed-out translation according to our method.

→ **822** ablative absolute, 54–55.

te violari, "that … you were being mistreated": OO depending on verb of M & M *iudicavique* … "and I judged," where the *–que,* "and," is added to the end of the first word of this part of the sentence. The infinitive *violari* is contemporaneous with the action of *iudicavi* in T.4b, and thus sounds in English as "[you] were being mistreated."

→ **823** M & M, 60, 71, GL n° 527, remarks 1–2; OO, 71–73; conjunction: *–que,* 3.2.

contra cuius honorem … niterentur, "against whose honor … [people] were working": the main verb *iudicavi,* "I judged," in T.4b establishes Track II, which carries through the contemporaneous infinitive *violari* and produces *niterentur* in T.2s in this relative clause subjunctive by MA.

→ **824** *consecutio,* 47–48; subjunctive use: modal attraction, 83.

beneficio concessum, "bestowed by the kindness": the full and natural meaning of the participle *concessum* is "[the honor] having been conceded." The passive participle is accompanied by an expression of instrumentality *beneficio*, "by the kindness," and thus without the preposition *a* or *ab*, which would be used elsewhere to express personal agent, as in *a populo Romano*, "by the Roman people."

> → **825** antecedent participle, 50, 51.1.2; abl.: instrument, 28.5.3–4, 89.2, GL n° 401.

eo tempore, "at that time": time at which.

> → **826** abl.: time at which, 70.1.

verum, "but": rightly looks like "true" or "truly," nevertheless here it means "but" or "however," according to the dict. It is always the first word in the sentence, and its force is very strong. The form *vero* is always later in the sentence, never first, which is why it is generally called postpositive.

> → **827** dict., *verus, a, um*, adj., II., adv., B. *vero*, "truly," 2. "but" (always placed after a word).

ad te adiuvandum, "for helping you": the gerund and gerundive and participle of passive necessity all look the same here and the polyvalence remains forever. Our rendering follows the first two, which have the same meaning. The third would mean "for you needing to be helped."

> → **828** gerund, 77.1; gerundive, 77.2;
> participle of passive necessity, 50, 51.1.4.

Aliquot ... sunt anni cum ... delegi, "there are a few years now that I chose": the *cum* means "when," "after," "that" or in the temporal meaning of "since," as in the English. We hate to mention the legitimate temporal meaning of the English word "since" here lest it be confused with the causal meaning of "because, since," so we have remained with the rendering "that." The whole phrase in idiomatic English today might be "it is a few years now that I chose."

> → **829** *cum* + indicative = "when": temporal sentences, 66.3.

sunt ... sicut sum, "are ... as I am": the main verb of the sentence, *sunt*, "there are [a few years now]," establishes the sentence on Track I, continuing the time of the previous sentence, which ended in T.1i with *movet*, "[the dignity of Pompeius] moves [me]." This sentence shifts to Track II with the temporal clause *cum ... delegi*, "that I chose," in T.4b and producing the two purpose clauses in T.2s *colerem*, "I would honor," and *essem*, "I would be." Interrupting this second purpose clause is a parenthetical statement, *sicut sum*, "as I am" in T.1i, which returns to Track I and corresponds to the main verb *sunt*, "there are." The effect of this is to bring the time of the message right up to the present situation as Cicero is writing the letter.

> → **830** *consecutio*, 47–48.

The content of this letter may appear to us, as it did to Renaissance scholars, full of hypocrisy, lies, and duplicity in comparison with Cicero's comments after Caesar's death. But Latinists enjoying the linguistic expression
of Cicero will find here a festival meal and dance celebration.

quos ... colerem ... quibus essem, "whom I would honor ... to whom I would
be": two relative expressions of purpose where *quos*, "whom," stands for
ut vos, "so that you." Likewise *quibus*, "to whom," stands for *ut vobis*, "so
that to you." They depend on the verb *delegi*, "I chose," in T.4b, establishing
Track II and thus producing *colerem* and *essem*, both in T.2s.

   → **831** subjunctive use: relative clause of purpose, 58.2;
        consecutio, 47–48.

                                             ⟳

Quam ob rem a te peto vel potius omnibus te precibus oro et obtestor ut in
tuis maximis curis aliquid impertias temporis huic quoque cogitationi ut
tuo beneficio bonus vir, gratus, pius denique esse in maximi benefici memoria possim. Quae si tantum ad me ipsum pertinerent, sperarem me a te
tamen impetraturum, sed, ut arbitror, et ad tuam fidem et ad rem publicam
pertinet me, et pacis et utriusque vestrum *amicum, ad vestram* et ad civium
concordiam per te quam accommodatissimum conservari. Ego, cum antea
tibi de Lentulo gratias egissem cum ei saluti qui mihi fuerat fuisses, tamen
lectis eius litteris quas ad me gratissimo animo de tua liberalitate beneficioque misit, eandem me salutem a te accepisse *putavi* quam ille: in quem si
me intellegis esse gratum, cura, obsecro, ut etiam in Pompeium esse possim.   (*Att.* IX, 11A, 3)

For which reason I ask of you or rather with all supplications I pray you
and implore that in the midst of your very great concerns you assign some
amount of time also to this thought that I may be able to be a good man
by your kindness, grateful, finally dutiful in the recollection of the greatest
kindness. Which things, if they would belong only to me myself, nevertheless I would hope that I would obtain them from you, but, as I believe, it
belongs both to your trustworthiness and to the state that I with your help
be kept *a friend* of peace and of each of you and as suited as possible *for your*
and the citizens' harmony. After I had previously given thanks to you with
regard to Lentulus, since you had been for a salvation to him who had been
to me, nevertheless after his letters had been read which he sent to me with
a most grateful spirit regarding your generosity and kindness, *I thought* that
I had received from you the same salvation which he did: toward whom, if
you understand that I am grateful, take care, I beg, that I may also be able to
be [grateful] toward Pompeius.

Quam ob rem, "For which reason": also written as one word *Quamobrem*, as in the manuscript in part I.

→ **832** dict., *quamobrem*, or *quam ob rem*, adv.

peto ... oro et obtestor, "I ask ... I pray ... and implore": three synonyms in a row meaning "to ask."

→ **833** dict., *peto, ivi* and *ii, itum*, 3.;
    dict., *oro, avi, atum*, 1.;
    dict., *obtestor, atus*, 1., dep.

vel potius, "or rather": here *potius* is the comparative adverb, "rather," "preferably," and not the neuter comparative adjective *potius*, "better, preferable." The dict. says that the adj. *potis* is rarely declined and that there is no positive degree of the adverb, but the superlative is *potissimum*, "most especially."

→ **834** dict., *potis*, adj.; adv.: comparative, superlative 37; adj.: comp., 36.

ut ... impertias, "that ... you assign": purpose clause in T.1s depending on *obtestor*, "I implore," in T.1i and establishing Track I.

→ **835** subjunctive use: purpose clause, 58.1; *consecutio*, 47–48.

aliquid ... temporis, "something of time": also expressed as "some bit of time" or "some amount of time"; the partitive genitive *temporis* is separated from the word on which it depends.

→ **836** gen. of part, 99.

ut ... possim, "that I may be": expression of purpose in T.1s, depending on *ut ... impertias*, "that ... you assign" in T.1s and sustaining Track I established by *obtestor*, "I implore," in T.1i.

→ **837** subjunctive use: purpose clause, 58.1; *consecutio*, 47–48.

si ... pertinerent, sperarem, "if they ... would ... belong ... I would hope": contrary to fact conditions tested by saying "if they would only belong to me myself, but they do not, nevertheless I would hope, which I am hardly doing."

→ **838** conditionals: contrary to fact, 86.3.

me ... impetraturum, "that I would obtain": the full infinitive is *impetraturum esse*, which is OO depending on *sperarem*, "I would hope," the verb of M & M in T.2s. The participle alone *impetraturum* is an indication of futurity, and about the only English version possible here in OO is "I was about to obtain," or "I would obtain." That expression "would" may appear to represent the subjunctive in English, as in "I would hope ... I would obtain," but in Latin these are two different constructions and English fails here. In this case "would" expresses futurity from a point in the past.

> → **839** M & M, 60, 71, GL n° 527, remarks 1–2; OO, 71–73;
>   futurity participle, 50, 51.1.3;
>   verb: subsequent active infinitive, 72.1.

This is more clearly seen in this hypothetical calendar.

March	September
sperarem	*impetraturum esse*
I would hope	that I would obtain
(contrary to fact condition)	(futurity from a point in the past)

> → **840** calendars, 83 pp. 514–15, 103 p. 586.

utriusque vestrum, "and of each of you": *vestrum* is used, rather than *vestri*, because the idea is numerical, referring to two people, Caesar and Pompeius.

> → **841** *nostri**, *vestri**, 24.6.

quam accommodatissimum, "as suited as possible": *quam* followed by the superlative meaning "as possible."

> → **842** *quam* with the superlative, 43.3.

cum ... egissem, "after I had": the three possible meanings for *cum* followed by the subjunctive are "because, since," "although," and "when" or here "after." Here *egissem* is T.4s because it is dependent on *putavi*, "I thought" in T.4b and establishing Track II.

> → **843** subjunctive use: temporal circumstance *cum* = "when," 66.3.2;
>   *consecutio*, 47–48;
>   subjunctive use: causal *cum* = "because, since," 59.1;
>   subjunctive use: concessive *cum* = "although," 64.

cum ... fuisses, "since you had been": the same three possible meanings for *cum* followed by the subjunctive are possible: "because, since" as here, "although," and "when." Here *fuisses* is T.4s because it is dependent on *putavi*, "I thought" in T.4b and establishing Track II. Note: in this and the previous note *cum* is followed by verbs each in T.4s; the first *cum* means "after" and the second "because, since."

> → **844** subjunctive use: causal *cum* = "because, since," 59.1;
>   subjunctive use: concessive *cum* = "although," 64;
>   subjunctive use: temporal circumstance *cum* = "when," 66.3.2;
>   *consecutio*, 47–48.

ei saluti, "for salvation to him": double dative of person and end result depending on *fuisses*, "you had been."

> → **845** double dat., 91.2.

lectis ... litteris: "after ... letters had been read": AA.

→ **846** ablative absolute, 54–55.

quas ... misit, "which he sent": relative clause depending on the AA *lectis ... litteris*, "after letters were read."

→ **847** relative clauses, 10–11; ablative absolute, 54–55.

me ... accepisse, "that I had received": OO depending on *putavi*, "I thought," a verb of M & M in T.4b, establishing Track II.

→ **848** M & M, 60, 71, GL n° 527, remarks 1–2; OO, 71–73; *consecutio*, 47–48.

The boxes of this sentence may be mapped out in this way:

Ego,	main begins
{ cum antea tibi de Lentulo gratias egissem	temporal
[cum ei saluti	causal begins
(qui mihi fuerat)	relative
fuisses,] }	causal concludes
{ tamen lectis eius litteris	AA
[quas ad me gratissimo animo de tua	relative
liberalitate beneficioque misit,] }	
{ eandam me salutem a te accepisse	OO
putavi	main continues
quam ille } :	comparison

→ **849** structure of Latin sentences, 103 p. 587, *Ossa* Readings: 1-D, 1-I, 3-D, 3-I, 4-D, 4-I;
relative box, 11.4.

si ... intellegis ... cura, "If you understand ... take care": factual conditional where *intellegis* is T.1i and *cura* is a command form.

→ **850** conditionals: factual, 86.1;
commands: other expressions, 85.1.7;
consecutio after command form, GL n° 517.

me ... esse, "that I am": OO depending on *intellegis*, a verb of M & M in T.1i.

→ **851** M & M, 60, 71, GL n° 527, remarks 1–2; OO, 71–73.

ut possim, "that I may ... be able": purpose clause depending on *cura*, "take care."

→ **852** subjunctive use: purpose clause, 58.1.

in Pompeium, "toward Pompeius": here the preposition *in* followed by the object refers to moral movement to or toward, as its synonyms: *ad, erga, adversus*.

→ **853** prep. with obj., 6.

LETTER 107 T-P
AD ATTICUM IV, 4B

CICERO ATTICO SAL.

Perbelle feceris, si ad nos veneris. Offendes designationem Tyrannionis mirificam in librorum meorum bibliotheca, quorum reliquiae multo meliores
sunt quam putaram. Et velim mihi mittas de tuis librariolis duos aliquos
quibus Tyrannio utatur glutinatoribus, ad cetera administris, iisque imperes
ut sumant membranulam ex qua indices fiant, quos vos Graeci, ut opinor,
σιττύβας appellatis.   (*Att.* IV, 4b, 1)

CICERO A GREETING TO ATTICUS

You will have done very nicely, if you will have come to us. You will meet
the marvelous cataloguing of Tyrannio in the library of my books, whose
remnants are much better than I had thought. And I would like that you
send to me from your copyists some two whom Tyrannio may use as gluers,
helpers for all the other things, and that you order them that they take a
small piece of parchment from which the indexes may be made, which you
Greeks, as I believe, call *labels*.

CICERO ATTICO SAL.: *Cicero Attico salutem*

SAL., "A GREETING": the verb *dicit*, "he says," is typically missing from these
initial formulae, as here: "CICERO [SAYS] A GREETING TO ATTICUS."
> → **854** dict., *salus, tis*, f., I., B. "S. D. P. (*salutem dicit plurimam*)." v. the
> superscriptions of Cicero's letters. Freq., also elliptically without *dicit*.

feceris… veneris…, "You will have done … you will have come …": in contrast to the more typical combination of T.6i and T.3i, both verbs here are
T.6i, which expresses a strong certainty of a completed action.
> → **855** T.6i and T.6i paired: GL nº 244, remark 4.

offendes, "You will meet": this word looks like it means "you will offend,"
but it means "you will run in to," "you will meet."
> → **856** dict., *offendo, di, sum*, 3.

multo meliores, "much better": the adjective *multo* is an ablative of degree of difference, meaning "by much," and goes with *meliores*, "better," the comparative of *bonus, a, um*, and the superlative is *optimus, a, um*.

→ **857** abl.: comparison, 90.2, GL n° 398;
   adj.: irregular comp. and superl., 36.5, GL n° 90.

Note: Cicero refers to the remnants of his library because he was exiled for one and a half years, and his enemies burned down three of his houses, one on the Palatine, one in Anzio, and his Tusculan villa, where he had a big library.

quam putaram, "than I had thought": the contraction *putaram* stands for *putaveram*, "I had thought." Cicero loves to use this contraction frequently.

→ **858** contractions: verbs, 39.2, GL n° 131.

velim ... mittas ... iisque imperes, "I would like that you send ... and that you order them": a favorite usage of Cicero where *velim*, "I would like," in T.1s is the potential of the present that produces two purpose clauses both given in the subjunctive here without the particle *ut* to emphasize the wish. Cicero's first intention is *mittas*, "that you send," in T.1s, and second is *imperes*, "that you order," which is one of the 65 verbs whose complement is in the dat., here *iis*, "[that you order] them." These two subjunctive verbs are joined by the *–que* attached to the end of the first word of the second element, *iisque*, "and ... them."

→ **859** subjunctive use: potential of the present or future, *velim* in T.1s, GL n° 257.2;
   subjunctive use: purpose clause without *ut*, 58, GL n° 546, remark 2;
   commands: other expressions, *velim*, 85.1.7;
   65 verbs with dat., 33.7.2, GL n° 346; conjunction: *–que*, 3.2.

quibus Tyrannio utatur glutinatoribus ... administris, "whom Tyrannio may use as gluers, helpers": the verb *utatur*, "[Tyrannio] may use," is one of five verbs that have their complement in the abl. of instrument, here *quibus*, "whom" or "with whom," where something happens reflexively for the good of the subject, as in "... the copyists with whom Tyrannio may procure usefulness for himself." As a relative clause of purpose, *quibus* stands for *ut iis*, "[copyists] so that [Tyrannio may use] them [as gluers]." In apposition to *quibus*, "whom," are both *glutinatoribus*, "as gluers," and *administris*, "helpers."

→ **860** famous five verbs with the ablative, 78.1;
   abl.: instrument, 28.5.3–4, 89.2, GL n° 401;
   subjunctive use: relative clause of purpose, 58.2;
   apposition, GL n° 320–21.

iisque imperes ut sumant, "and order them that they take": Cicero wants Atticus to order the two copyists with the intention given in this purpose clause, *ut sumant*, "that they take up," in T.1s given in English also in the subjunctive.

→ **861** subjunctive use: purpose clause, 58.1.

ex qua indices fiant, "from which the indexes may be made": the intention
for which they take the parchment is given in this relative clause of purpose,
where *ex qua*, "from which," followed by *fiant*, "[indexes] may be made" in
T.1s, stands for *ut ex ea … fiant*, "so that from which [parchment indexes]
may be made."

    → **862** subjunctive use: relative clause of purpose, 58.2.

σιττύβας, "*labels*": the Latin equivalent is *indices*, "indicators."

    → **863** Bibliography: *Onomasticon Tullianum*; Greek expressions, pp. 623–626.

৹৴

Sed haec, si tibi erit commodum. Ipse vero utique fac venias, si potes in his
locis adhaerescere et Piliam adducere. Ita enim et aequum est et cupit Tullia. Medius fidius ne tu emisti λόχον praeclarum: gladiatores audio pugnare
mirifice. Si locare voluisses, duobus his muneribus liber esses. Sed haec posterius. Tu fac venias, et de librariis, si me amas, diligenter.   (*Att.* IV, 4b, 2)

But these things, if it will be convenient for you. But you yourself for sure
see to it that you come, if you are able to stick around in these places and
bring along Pilia [the wife of Atticus]. For thus it is both right, and Tullia
wants it. By god really you have bought an outstanding *troupe*: I hear that
the gladiators fight marvelously. If you had wished to rent them out, you
would be debtless—there being these two gladiatorial spectacles. But these
things later. You, see to it that you come, and carefully [see] about the copyists, if you love me.

fac venias, "see to it that you come": this is a shorted expression of *fac ut
venias* with the same meaning. The command form *fac* is one of four that
has lost its final *–e*, the others are *duc, dic, fer*. As a verb of causing, *fac*
produces a result clause *venias* given in English in the ind., "that you come."

    → **864** commands: famous four, 39.4;
           subjunctive use: complementary result (consecutive), 68.1.

medius fidius, "By god": consult the dict. under *fidius*. This expression is a
title of "Faithful Jupiter," and is an exclamation meaning such as "by the
god of truth," "by the gods," or as we might say, "for heaven's sake."

    → **865** dict., *Fidius, ii*, m. I. a surname of Jupiter.

ne tu emisti, "really you have bought": here *ne*—patience, all learners!—has
nothing to do with the negative and it does not mean "that not." Rather *ne*
means "yes indeed." The *ne* is really a Greek expression sometimes written
wholly in Latin as *nae*, "yes, for sure."

    → **866** dict., 3. *ne*, interjection.

λόχον, "*troupe*": The word in Greek letters refers to a troupe of gladiators.

> → **867** See the index of Greek expressions in this volume.

Si ... voluisses ... liber esses, "If you had wished [to rent them out], you would be debtless": a contrary to fact conditional whose consequence is contrary to fact in the present *esses*, "you would be," in T.2s, and whose condition is contrary to fact in the past, *voluisses*, "you had wished." We can test this condition by saying, "If you had wished to rent them out—but you did not—you would be debtless—but you are not debtless."

> → **868** conditionals: contrary to fact, 86.3.

duobus his muneribus, "there being these two gladiatorial spectacles": in the middle of the contrary to fact conditional, these three substantive words function as an AA whose participle is not given, but is felt to be "being," and its subject is in the abl. form *muneribus*.

> → **869** ablative absolute, 54–55.

LETTER 176 T-P
AD FAMILIARES II, 5

M. CICERO S. D. C. CURIONI.

Haec negotia quo modo se habeant ne epistula quidem narrare audeo. Tibi, etsi, ubicumque es, ut scripsi ad te ante, in eadem es navi, tamen quod abes gratulor, vel quia non vides ea quae nos, vel quod excelso et illustri loco sita est laus tua in plurimorum et sociorum et civium conspectu: quae ad nos nec obscuro nec vario sermone sed et clarissima et una omnium voce perfertur.   (*Fam.* II, 5, 1)

MARCUS CICERO SAYS A GREETING
TO CAIUS CURIO

I dare to narrate not even by a letter how these affairs find themselves. To you, although, wherever you are, as I wrote to you before, you are in the same boat, nevertheless I send congratulations, because you are far away, either because you do not see those things which we do, or because your praise has been located in a high and brilliant place in the sight of very many both allies and citizens: which [praise] is being brought in to us with neither an ambiguous nor inconstant report, but with the both most clear and unanimous voice of all.

M. CICERO S. D. C. CURIONI: *Marcus Cicero salutem dicit Caio Curioni*

Caio Curioni, "Caius Curio": his name is written *Caio* but they preferred *Gaio*, and they could not really hear much of a difference.
  → **870** dict., *Gaius*, less correctly *Caius*.

Haec negotia quo modo se habeant, "how these affairs find themselves": the gerund *narrare* is a verb of M & M and produces the IQ which begins the sentence. The question word *quo modo*, also written like the manuscript in part I as one word *quomodo*, begins an IQ on Track I producing *habeant* in T.1s. Note that the subject of *habeant* is *Haec negotia*, which stands first in

the sentence, geographically outside the expression *quo modo ... habeant*.
For the sake of example, all other possible times for *habeant* here are:
habuerint, "they have found themselves" in T.3s and *sint habitura*, "they will
find themselves" in T.1s with the futurity participle, the only explicit way to
express futurity in the subjunctive. Here, T.1s *habeant* refers to a contemporaneous action, whereas *sint habitura* would refer to a future action.

> → **871** M & M, 60, 71, GL nº 527, remarks 1–2; IQ, 60;
>   *consecutio*, 47–48;
>   *consecutio*: futurity in the subjunctive, 61.1;
>   *consecutio*: futurity formula in the subjunctive, 61.3; sentence structure, 1.

narrare audeo, "I dare to narrate": the main verb *audeo*, "I dare," in T.1i
establishes the sentence on Track I. *narrare* is a complementary infinitive
that functions as a gerund object of *audeo*, as in "I dare narrating" or "I dare
to narrate."

> → **872** *consecutio*, 47–48;
>   verb: complementary infinitive, 77; gerund, 77.1.

Tibi ... gratulor, "To you ... I send congratulations": the dep. verb is one of
the 65 that take a dative complement.

> → **873** 65 verbs with dat., 33.7.2, GL nº 346.

The second sentence is one gorgeous Latin sentence spread over four lines.
Welcome aboard! It begins with a clear box structure:

   Tibi,   main begins
      { etsi,   concessive begins
         [ubicumque es,]   relative
         [ut scripsi ad te ante,] comparative
       in eadem es navi, }   concessive concludes
   tamen   main continues
      (quod abes)   causal
   gratulor,   main continues

> → **874** structure of Latin sentences, 103 p. 587, *Ossa* Readings: 1-D, 1-I, 3-D, 3-I,
>   4-D, 4-I;
>   relative box, 11.4.

etsi ... es: "although ... you are": concessive in the indicative. Other particles
related to *etsi* that mean "although" are *tametsi, etiamsi*.

> → **875** subjunctive use: concessive *etsi* = "although," 64.

ut scripsi, "as I wrote": *ut* meaning "as."

> → **876** dict., *ut*, I., B. meaning "as."

in eadem es navi, "you are in the same boat": English has this turn of phrase too, but the Latin beat it by far.

quod abes gratulor, "I send congratulations, because you are far away": the *quod abes* is taken here as a causal clause with *abes* in T.1i, indicating it is the opinion of the author, Cicero. If reporting the speech of another, the subjunctive would be used. For all that, another meaning is very close here, *quod abes*, "the fact that you are far away, [I send congratulations]," which is an object-noun clause where the whole clause functions as a noun, as in "I congratulate your absence" or "I congratulate the fact that you are far away."

→ **877** causal: *quod*, "because, since," + indicative, one's own reason, 59.2;
causal: *quod*, "because, since," + subjunctive, reported reason, 59.2;
quod = "the fact that" as a new subject, GL nº 525.2.

vel quia … vel quod, "either because … or because": *quia* and *quod* both mean "because" and are examples of Cicero's intentional stylistic variation. Both are used with the indicative because each refers to definite solid historical facts that Cicero relies upon.

→ **878** sentence structure, 1;
causal: *quod*, "because, since," + indicative, one's own reason, 59.2.

quae … perfertur, "which [praise] … being brought": Note the architectural beauty of these almost word-for-word parallel phrases:

quae ad nos	nec	obscuro	nec	vario	sermone	
	sed et	clarissima	et	una omnium	voce	perfertur

The two parts are joined by *sed*, "but."

→ **879** conjunction: *sed*, 3.2.

The last word of each part is a noun in the ablative of instrumentality: *sermone … voce*, "with an … report … with the … voice."

→ **880** abl.: instrument, 28.5.3–4, 89.2, GL nº 401.

Each noun of instrumentality is introduced by two adjectives: *obscuro … vario* agree with *sermone*, "with neither an ambiguous nor inconstant report," and *clarissima … una* agree with *voce*, "with the both most clear and unanimous voice."

→ **881** sentence structure, 1;
abl.: instrument, 28.5.3–4, 89.2, GL nº 401.

The first has two negative connectives, *nec … nec*, "neither … nor"; the second two positive ones, *et … et*, "both … and." This is all perfect, insuperable living Latin!

→ **882** conjunction: *nec … , nec … ,* 3.2.

❧

Unum illud nescio, gratulerne tibi an timeam, quod mirabilis est exspectatio reditus tui, non quo verear ne tua virtus opinioni hominum non respondeat, sed mehercule ne, cum veneris, non habeas iam quod cures: ita
sunt omnia debilitata *et* iam prope exstincta. Sed haec ipsa nescio rectene
sint litteris commissa. Qua re cetera cognosces ex aliis. Tu tamen, sive habes
aliquam spem de re publica sive desperas, ea para, meditare, cogita quae
esse in eo civi ac viro debent qui sit rem publicam adflictam et oppressam
miseris temporibus ac perditis moribus in veterem dignitatem et libertatem
vindicaturus.   (*Fam.* II, 5, 2)

That one thing I do not know, whether I should congratulate you or be in
fear, because the expectation of your return is extraordinary, not because
I am afraid that your virtue may not correspond to the idea of people, but,
by george, that, when you will have come, you may not have anything yet
which you may care about: thus all things have been undermined *and* already now nearly wiped out. But I do not know whether these things themselves have been properly entrusted to a letter. For which reason you will get
to know the remaining things from other people. You, however, whether
you have some hope about the republic or are in desperation, prepare, ponder, think of those things which ought to exist in such a citizen and a man
who is going to claim back the republic, afflicted and oppressed by miserable
circumstances and ruined behavior, into the old-time dignity and freedom.

Mapping out the boxes of the first sentence reveals its magnificent structure
clearly:

Unum illud nescio,	main
{ gratulerne tibi }	IQ 1
{ an timeam,	IQ 2
[quod mirabilis est exspectatio reditus tui,] }	causal
{ non quo verear	reported reason
[ne tua virtus opinioni hominum non respondeat,]	purpose 1
[sed mehercule ne,	purpose 2
(cum veneris,)]	temporal
[non habeas iam	purpose 2 continued
(quod cures:)] }	characteristic result

→ **883** structure of Latin sentences, 103 p. 587, *Ossa* Readings: 1-D, 1-I, 3-D, 3-I,
4-D, 4-I.

gratulerne tibi an timeam, "whether I should congratulate you or be in
fear": two IQs depending on the M & M verb *nescio*, "I do not know," in T.1i
establishing Track I. The two questions are posed by the pair *–ne . . . , an,*

"whether … or," where –*ne* is attached as an ending to *gratuler*, "I should congratulate." *gratuler* and *timeam* are both T.1s. The dep. *gratuler* is one of the 65 verbs that takes a dative complement, here *tibi*.

→ **884** M & M, 60, 71, GL nº 527, remarks 1–2; IQ, 60;
consecutio, 47–48;
65 verbs with dat., 33.7.2, GL nº 346;
disjunctive question, GL nº 458 and note 3.

–*ne … an, ne, ne, –ne,* "whether … or," "that," "whether," "that": several occurrences of *ne* with several different meanings. (1) It begins an IQ, *gratulerne … an,* "*whether* I should congratulate … or." (2) After a verb of fearing *ne* establishes a purpose clause, *verear ne respondeat,* "I am afraid *that* [your virtue] may not correspond," (3) and a second purpose clause, *ne … habeas,* "that [your virtue] may not correspond." (4) Finally, for this part of the letter, *ne* continues an IQ, *rectene sint … commissa,* "whether [these things] have been properly entrusted." (5) In the first part of the letter *ne* appears in an adverbial use in *ne quidem,* "not even"; and (6) in the conjunction *nec … nec,* "neither … nor." Congratulations!

→ **885** ways of asking, 13.1; disjunctive question, GL nº 458 and note 3;
subjunctive use: purpose clause, 58.1; IQ, 60; verbs of fearing with *ne,* 95;
dict., *quidem,* adv., I., C., 1. *ne … quidem,* "not even";
dict., *neque,* or *nec,* II. conj., B., 3. *Neque (nec) …, neque (nec) …,* "neither …, nor.…"

timeam … verear, "I should … be in fear … I am afraid": so as not to repeat the same word, Cicero uses two synonyms.

→ **886** sentence structure, 1.

reditus, "of … return": this is one of the –*us, –us* type words. This one form *reditus* can function as of-possession as here, or as subject singular or plural or as object plural, with different vowel length in the –*us.* Only the singular subject has a short –*ŭs,* the rest are long, which you cannot see in prose, but is evident and infallible in poetry.

→ **887** 20% of nouns: *reditus, us,* m., 35.

non quo verear, "not because I am afraid": *verear* is T.1s to indicate reported reason, as in "not because *allegedly, as you might think, as people might say* I am afraid." *quo* means "for the reason that," "because," as a variant of *quod* and *quia* and *quoniam* (GL nº 541, note 2).

→ **888** dict., *quo,* adv., I., B., 2. For the reason that, because; adv., 37;
causal: *quod, quia, quoniam,* "because, since," + subjunctive, reported reason, 59.2;
causal: rejected reason, *non quo,* GL nº 541, note 2.

ne … non respondeat … ne … non habeas, "that [your virtue] may not correspond … that you may not have": the sentence depends on the verb of fearing *timeam,* "I should … be in fear," itself part of an IQ in T.1s. With verbs of fearing *ne* is used to mean "that," as occurs twice here, and is followed by the subjunctive, here *respondeat* and *habeas*, both in T.1s. In this case, instead of the double negative *ne … non*, typically *ut* is used and means "that not." This is deceiving if you don't know that verbs of fearing produce *ne* meaning "that," and instead of *ne non*, they use *ut* to mean "that not." For all that, it is easier to see *ne … non* meaning "that not," than to read *ut* and think "that not," providing another example of the immediacy of these letters to Cicero's thought and daily talk.

→ **889** verbs of fearing with *ne*, 95; IQ, 60.

cum veneris, "when you will have come": although *veneris* could be T.3s in MA, the English text takes it to be T.6i and thus a temporal clause.

→ **890** *cum* + indicative = "when": temporal sentences, 66.3;
   subjunctive use: modal attraction, 83.

quod cures, "which you may care about": this expression of characteristic result is short for *tale ut id cures*, "such a thing that you care for it." The sequence of tenses follows Track I, beginning with *nescio* in T.1i and continuing with *timeam* in T.1s and *habeas* in T.1s and ending with *cures*, also in T.1s.

→ **891** subjunctive use: characteristic result, 68.2; *consecutio*, 47–48.

sunt omnia debilitata … sint litteris commissa, "things have been undermined … have been … entrusted to a letter": in many schools and grammar books the verbs are presented in charts in this format, *debilitata sunt* and *commissa sint*, but that is not how they appear in Cicero's expression, where the elements are given the other way around so as not to end the sentence with *sunt* or *sint*. Furthermore, in the first example the subject comes between the two elements and in the second the natural dative of destination.

→ **892** sentence structure, 1.

haec ipsa … rectene sint … commissa, "whether these things themselves have been properly entrusted": IQ depending on the M & M verb *nescio*, "I do not know" in T.1i establishing Track I thus producing *sint commissa* in T.3s passive. Note that the subject of *sint commissa* is *haec ipsa*, which appears geographically before *nescio*. The question is posed by the ending *–ne*, "whether."

→ **893** M & M, 60, 71, GL n° 527, remarks 1–2; IQ, 60;
   consecutio, 47–48;
   sentence structure, 1; ways of asking, 13.1;
   disjunctive question, GL n° 458 and note 3.

para, meditare, cogita, "prepare, ponder, think": three practically synonymous words used in a row!

→ **894** sentence structure, 1.

meditare, "ponder": the command form of a deponent verb. Its plural is *meditamini*.

→ **895** commands: deponent, 34.

in eo civi ac viro, "in such a citizen and a man": the pronoun *is, ea, id* means "he, she, it," but as an adjective it means "this, that, such" as here. If you hear the meaning "such," then you see the *qui* coming down the line in a result clause where *qui*, "who," stands for *ut is*, "that he."

→ **896** dict., *is, ea, id*, pron. demonstr., II. "such";
subjunctive use: pure result (consecutive), 67.1–2, GL n° 552.

in eo civi ... qui sit ... vindicaturus, "in such a citizen ... who is going to claim back": a pure result clause where *qui sit* stands for *ut is sit*, "with the result that he is." All alone the futurity participle *vindicaturus* has several meanings: "one going to deliver back, about to claim back, fixing to deliver back, on the point of restoring." This is the only way to express futurity in subjunctive because *vindicet* is T.1s and means "[who] is doing this," but according to the account given in the letter Cicero is not even in Rome yet.

→ **897** subjunctive use: pure result (consecutive), 67.1–2, GL n° 552;
futurity participle, 50, 51.1.3;
consecutio: futurity formula in the subjunctive, 61.3.

sit ... vindicaturus, "is going to claim back": one must simply and happily and confidently see that *sit* connects with *vindicaturus* sixteen words later! People must calmly and joyfully see this and then rejoice over their Latin super-training.

→ **898** sentence structure, 1.

in veterem diginitatem, "into the old-time dignity": the preposition *in* followed by the object to express physical or here moral motion to or toward.

→ **899** *in* with object, 6.3.

30

LETTER 717 T-P
AD ATTICUM XIV, 13b

CICERO ANTONIO COS. S. D.

Quod mecum per litteras agis, unam ob causam mallem coram egisses. Non enim solum ex oratione, sed etiam ex vultu et oculis et fronte, ut aiunt, meum erga te amorem perspicere potuisses. Nam cum te semper amavi, primum tuo studio, post etiam beneficio provocatus, tum his temporibus res publica te mihi ita commendavit ut cariorem habeam neminem.   (*Att.* XIV, 13b, 1)

CICERO SAYS A GREETING TO ANTONIUS CONSUL

The fact that you are dealing with me by correspondence, I would prefer that you had done that face to face for one reason. For you would have been able to grasp my love toward you not only from [my] speech but also from the face and eyes and forehead, as they say. For while I always have loved you, challenged first by your interest, afterward also by your kindness, then in these times the state has commended you to me in such a way that I hold no one more dear.

CICERO ANTONIO COS. S. D.: *Cicero Antonio consuli salutem dicit*

COS., "consul": just as the inscription on the facade of the Pantheon, the abbreviation *cos.* here stands for *consul*. The letter *n* was missing because the pronunciation of *cosul* was already nasalized even without the additional letter.

→ **900** dict., *consul, ulis*, m., abbrev. COS.

Quod ... agis, "The fact that you are dealing": explanatory *quod* introduces a new subject, as if to say, "By the way, ... ," so the sentence with *agis*, "you are dealing," in T.1i, stands on its own in front of the main sentence as an object clause, "That you are dealing."

→ **901** *quod* = "the fact that" as a new subject, GL n° 525.2.

mallem egisses, "I would prefer that you had done": this is one half of a
contrary to fact conditional in the present. We might supply a condition
such as "if you had been able" or "if it would have been convenient." The
consequence is *mallem,* "I would prefer" in T.2s. We can test this by saying,
"I would prefer—but I have no choice now." The verb *mallem,* "I would prefer," produces a purpose clause that expresses the intention in wishing, here
egisses, "that you had done," in T.4s given without any particle such as *ut,*
"that." In turn, *egisses* functions as a contrary to fact condition in the past,
which we can test by saying, "that you had done—but you did not."

→ **902** conditionals: contrary to fact, 86.3; GL n° 261, remark;
subjunctive use: purpose clause without *ut,* 58, GL n° 546, remark 2.

egisses … potuisses, "that you had done … you would have been able": here
potuisses, "you would have been able," in T.4s is the consequential half of
a second contrary to fact conditional, this one set in the past. We can test
it by saying, "you would have been able—but you were not." Both *potuisses*
and *egisses* seen previously are in T.4s, but for different reasons. *egisses* is an
expression of purpose which functions as a contrary to fact condition. *potuisses* continues the train of thought of the contrary to fact set in the past.

→ **903** conditionals: contrary to fact, 86.3.

cum … tum …, "while … then": correlatives both with the ind., *cum …
amavi,* "while I … have loved you," and *tum … commendavit,* "then … [the
republic] has commended," both in T.4a; no subjunctive is necessary.

→ **904** correlative comparative sentences, 90.5, GL n° 642.

ita commendavit ut … habeam, "[the state] has commended … in such a
way that I hold": we take *commendavit,* "[the state] has commended," as
T.4a establishing Track I, and the *ita,* "in such a way," prepares for a result
clause, *ut … habeam,* "that I hold," in T.1s, rendered in English in the ind.

→ **905** *consecutio,* 47–48;
subjunctive use: pure result (consecutive), 67.1–2, GL n° 552.

It is conceivable to take *commendavit,* "[the state] commended," as T.4b
establishing Track II, but this could still produce *habeam,* "that I hold," in
T.1s according to the 3% exception whereby one definite, concrete result is
given in T.1s, as if to say, "[the state] recommended you in such a way that
right now I find no one so dear." This reinforces our conviction and teaching
about the infinite, mysterious uses of the Latin subjunctive, and the frequent
impossibility to determine the exact reason and meaning of every subjunctive.

→ **906** *consecutio,* 47–48; subjunctive use: 3% sequence of tenses, 94.1.

Litterae vero tuae cum amantissime tum honorificentissime scriptae sic me adfecerunt ut non dare tibi beneficium viderer, sed accipere a te ita petente ut inimicum meum, necessarium tuum, me invito servare nolles, cum id nullo negotio facere posses.   (*Att.* XIV, 13b, 2)

But your letter, written both most lovingly and most honorably, moved me in such a way that I did not seem to be giving a favor to you, but receiving [one] from you requesting in such a way that you might not want to save my enemy, your close relative—myself being unwilling—although you were able to do that with no bother.

Litterae ... sic me adfecerunt ut non dare tibi beneficium viderer, "[your] letter ... moved me in such a way that I did not seem to be giving a favor to you": the main verb *adfecerunt,* "[your letter] moved [me]," in T.4b establishes Track II. The *sic,* "in such a way," prepares for the result clause with contemporaneous meaning, *ut non ... viderer,* "that I did not seem," where *viderer,* "I did not seem," in T.2s is a personal construction, whereas in many modern languages the impersonal construction would be used here, as in "it did not seem that I." In that *viderer* is used personally, its subject is the nom. subject of the infinitive *dare,* "I did [not] seem to be giving," and this infinitive has its own object, *beneficium,* "a favor," with the natural dat. *tibi,* "to you."

> → **907** *consecutio,* 47–48;
>> subjunctive use: pure result (consecutive), 67.1–2, GL n° 552;
>> personal construction: *videor,* 73.3, GL n° 528.1 and remark 2 and note 1;
>> nom. with the inf., 73.3, GL n° 528.1;
>> verb: complementary infinitive, 77; gerund, 77.1;
>> natural dat., 33.7.1.

vero, "But": never the first word of the sentence, *vero* can mean "truly," but here is a second meaning and forceful way of saying "but," "however."

> → **908** dict., *verus, a, um,* adj., II., adv., B. *vero,* "truly," 2. "but" (always placed after a word).

cum amantissime tum honorificentissime, "both most lovingly and most honorably": *cum ... tum ... ,* "both ... and ..." are correlatives. The superlative adv. *amantissime,* "most lovingly," is from the positive *amanter,* "loving" and the superlative adv. *honorificentissime,* "most honorably," is from the positive degree *honorifice,* "honorably," from which we would expect "*honorificissime,*" but this and a few other adverbs work in this other way. The comparative adverbs are *amantius,* "too loving," "rather loving," and *honorificentius,* "quite honorably," "somewhat honorably," again instead of *honorificius,* which you might expect.

> → **909** correlative comparative sentences, 90.5, GL n° 642;
>> adv.: positive, comp., superl., 37.

sed accipere, "but receiving": a second complement to *viderer*, "I did [not] seem," *accipere* is also a gerund object, "receiving," "to receive."

→ **910** verb: complementary infinitive, 77; gerund, 77.1.

a te ita petente ut ... servare nolles, "from you requesting in such a way that you might not want to save": the natural meaning of the participle *petente* is "[from] one asking." The participle *petente* would normally produce a purpose clause expressing the intention in the asking, here *ut ... nolles*, "that you might not want," in T.2s. However, it is still possible that the verb of asking produce a pure result clause, which depends on the force of the *ita*, "in such a way." If you take *nolles* with *petente*, then it is a purpose clause, and the *ita* is less felt, but if you take *nolles* with *ita* then it is a result clause, and *petente* is less felt, as in "from you requesting in such a way that you did not want to save." This is a human language, however logical it is not mathematics!

→ **911** contemporaneous active participle, 50, 51.1.1;
    subjunctive use: purpose clause, 58.1;
    subjunctive use: pure result (consecutive), 67.1–2, GL n° 552.

The verb *nolles* has its own complement, the gerund *servare*, meaning "you might not want saving," "you might not want to save."

→ **912** verb: complementary infinitive, 77; gerund, 77.1.

me invito, "—myself being unwilling—": a very famous AA where *me* in the abl. form functions as the subj. of the participle "being" only implied but felt. Scholastic, Medieval Latinists will develop a form for that participle, *ente*, which did not exist for Cicero. This phrase is still used in the Code of Canon Law of 1983. Be careful, because *me invitato*, has the opposite meaning "myself having been invited."

→ **913** ablative absolute, 54–55.

cum id ... facere posses, "although you were able to do that": *cum* followed by *posses* in T.4s can give the temporal circumstance "when" something happened, or it may more probably mean "because," or as we have taken it, "although." The complement of *posses* is the gerund *facere*, "to do," with its own object *id*, "that."

→ **914** subjunctive use: causal *cum* = "because, since," 59.1;
    subjunctive use: concessive *cum* = "although," 64;
    subjunctive use: temporal circumstance *cum* = "when," 66.3.2;
    verb: complementary infinitive, 77; gerund, 77.1.

nullo negotio, "with no bother": this expression is in the dict. under *negotium* and also means "with no difficulty," "with no effort."

→ **915** dict., *negotium, ii, n.,* II., A.... *nullo negotio* ... "with little trouble."

Ego vero tibi istuc, mi Antoni, remitto atque ita ut me a te, cum his verbis scripseris, liberalissime atque honorificentissime tractatum existimem, id- que cum totum, quoquo modo se res haberet, tibi dandum putarem, tum do etiam humanitati et naturae meae. Nihil enim umquam non modo acerbum in me fuit, sed ne paullo quidem tristius aut severius quam necessitas rei publicae postulavit. Accedit ut ne in ipsum quidem Clodium meum insigne odium fuerit umquam, semperque ita statui, non esse insectandos inimi- corum amicos, praesertim humiliores, nec his praesidiis nosmet ipsos esse spoliandos.   (*Att.* XIV, 13b, 3)

My dear Anthony, I however entrust that whole thing to you and in such a way that I do consider that I have been treated by you most generously and most honorably because you wrote in these words, and while I would think that whole matter would have to be attributed to you in whatever way the situation found itself, then I attribute it also to my own courtesy and tem- perament. For there was nothing ever in me not only bitter but not even a little more gloomy or severe than the necessity of republic demanded. It is added [to this] that my hatred was never special not even toward Clodius himself, and thus I always decided that the friends of enemies were not to be persecuted, especially those of lower rank, nor that we ourselves were to be deprived of these protections.

> *vero*, "But": never the first word of the sentence, in contrast to *verum*, which also means variously "but," "however," and "truly" and always appears as the first word of the sentence.
> > → **916** dict., *verus, a, um*, adj., II., adv., B. *vero*, "truly," 2. "but" (always placed after a word).

> *istuc*, "the whole thing": a variation of *istud*, as is common in Plautus.
> > → **917** dict., *iste, a, ud*, pron. demonstr., I.... "with affixed *ce*," and v. *Ossa*, 40.3.

> *mi Antoni*, "My dear Anthony": both words are in direct address, also called the vocative. This expression in direct address is more familiar, more intimate, warmer than may be initially apparent. This is reflected in the dictionary entry for *meus, a, um*, where the vocative *mi* is said to mean "*my dear! my beloved!*"
> > → **918** dict., *meus, a, um*, adj., I. –voc.: *mi*;
> > function: direct address, 38.3.

> *remitto ... ita ut ... existimem*, "I entrust ... in such a way that I do consid- er": the particle *ita*, "in such a way," prepares for the expression of the result of Cicero's entrusting the matter to Marcus Antonius, *ut existimem*, "that I do consider," given in English in the ind. Here *atque* is joining *remitto* to a second implied *remitto ita ut ...*, "I entrust ... and [I entrust] in such a way that."
> > → **919** subjunctive use: pure result (consecutive), 67.1–2, GL n° 552.

remitto … idque cum totum … dandum putarem, tum do, "I entrust … and while I would think that whole matter would have to be attributed … then I attribute it": the *–que*, "and," attached to the end of the first word of the second element, *id*, "that matter," joins *remitto*, "I entrust," to *do*, "I attribute." For the *cum … tum …* , "while … and … ," the *cum*, "while [I would think]" correlates the contrary to fact condition to the main sentence *tum do*, "then I attribute."

→ **920** conjunction: *–que*, 3.2; correlative comparative sentences, 90.5, GL n° 642.

ut me a te … tractatum existimem, "that I do consider that I have been treated by you": the verb *existimem*, "I think," is a verb of M & M producing a statement in OO where *me* in the object form functions as the subject of the inf. whose full implied form is *tractatum esse*, "me to have been treated." The personal agent *a te*, "by you," gives the agent of the passive verbal form *tractatum*, "[I] have been treated by you."

→ **921** M & M, 60, 71, GL n° 527, remarks 1–2; OO, 71–73;
abl.: personal agent, 28.5.3–4, 89.2.

cum … scripseris, "because you wrote": the main verb *remitto*, "I entrust," in T.1i establishes Track I carried through in the result clause, *ut … existimem*, "that I do consider," in T.1s producing the statement in OO *me … tractatum* [*esse*], "that I have been treated," describing the previous action as touching on the present, the equivalent of T.4a thus maintaining Track I, resulting in *scripseris*, "you wrote," in T.3s describing an action antecedent to *tractatum* [*esse*]. Here *cum* followed by *scripseris* in T.3s can mean either "because," as we take it, or "although," or it gives the temporal circumstance of another action.

→ **922** M & M, 60, 71, GL n° 527, remarks 1–2; OO, 71–73;
consecutio, 47–48;
subjunctive use: causal *cum* = "because, since," 59.1;
subjunctive use: concessive *cum* = "although," 64;
subjunctive use: temporal circumstance *cum* = "when," 66.3.2.

idque cum totum … tibi dandum putarem, "and while I would think that whole matter would have to be entrusted to you": the first part of the sentence depends on *remitto*, "I entrust," in T.1i, which establishes Track I. The second part of the sentence is the consequence of a contrary to fact condition set in the present, where the main clause is *putarem*, "I would think," in T.2s. Now, *putarem* is also a verb of M & M producing a statement in OO, where *id … totum*, "that whole matter," in the object form functions as the subject of the inf. whose full implied form is *dandum esse*, "would have to be entrusted." In its turn, *dandum* is a participle of passive necessity, which means "needing to be given," "worthy to be given," "to be given." We can test the contrary to fact condition in the following way: "and while I would think—but I do not—that whole matter would have to be entrusted to you—which it does not," and this is further confirmed by the rest of the sentence in which Cicero attributes the matter not to Mark Anthony but to his own courtesy and temperament.

> → **923** M & M, 60, 71, GL n° 527, remarks 1–2; OO, 71–73;
>   *consecutio*, 47–48;
>   conditionals: contrary to fact, 86.3;
>   participle of passive necessity, 50, 51.1.4;
>   passive necessity formula, 53.4.

idque … tum do etiam humanitati et naturae meae, "and … then I attribute this also to my own courtesy and temperament": the *id* also functions as the object of *do*, "I attribute it." Note the natural use of the dative.

> → **924** sentence structure, 1; natural dat., 33.7.1.

quoquo modo se res haberet, "in whatever way the situation found itself": a relative clause whose verb *haberet*, "[the situation] found," is in T.2s due to MA because the clause is dependent upon *totum … dandum* in OO and the idea is closely connected with the whole concept.

> → **925** subjunctive use: modal attraction, 83.

Some simple boxes below will reveal clearly the structure of the previous sentence.

Ego vero tibi istuc,	main 1
mi Antoni,	direct address
remitto	main 1 T.1i
atque [remitto]	main 1b,
ita ut	result
me a te,	OO
cum his verbis scripseris,	causal MA T.3s
⎛liberalissime atque	OO continued
⎝honorificentissime tractatum	
existimem,	result continued T.1s
id–	OO 2
–que cum	conjunction, correlative
totum,	OO 2 continued
quoquo modo se res haberet,	rel. MA T.2s
tibi dandum	OO 2 continued, pass. necessity
putarem,	contrary to fact cond. T.2s
⎛tum [id] do etiam humanitati et	correlative, main 2 T.1i
⎝naturae meae	

> → **926** structure of Latin sentences, 103 p. 587, *Ossa* Readings: 1-D, 1-I, 3-D, 3-I,
>   4-D, 4-I;

Nihil … acerbum … paullo … tristius aut severius, "nothing … bitter … a little more gloomy or severe": the neuter noun *Nihil*, "nothing," is described by the adj. *acerbum*, "bitter," and by two comparative adjectives, *tristius … servius*, "more gloomy … severe"; these last two are the same form as

the comparative adv. meaning "more sadly … severely." The word *paullo*
is an abl. of measure or degree of difference, meaning "by a little," and
corresponds to the two comparative adjectives, "a little [more gloomy and
severe]."

> → **927** adj.: comp., 36; adv.: positive, comp., superl., 37;
>   abl.: measure, 90.3; GL n° 403.

non modo … sed ne paullo quidem, "not only … but not even a little [more]":
here *non modo*, "not only," contrasts with *sed*, "but," which goes with *ne …
quidem*, which together mean "not even." Separating *ne* and *quidem* is *paullo,* an abl. of degree of measure or degree of difference meaning "by a little,"
as in "not even by a little," "not even a little [more gloomy]."

> → **928** *non modo … , sed … ,* GL n° 482.5;
>   dict., *quidem*, adv., I., C., 1. *ne … quidem*, "not even";
>   abl.: measure, 90.3, GL n° 403.

Accedit ut ne … quidem … meum insigne odium … fuerit umquam, "It is
added … that my hatred was never special not even": the main verb *Accedit*,
"It comes besides," "It is added," is T.1i establishing Track I and producing
a result clause *ut … fuerit*, "that [my hatred] was," where *fuerit* is T.3s and
rendered in English in the ind. The subject of *fuerit* is *meum … odium*, "my
hatred [was]." Some people will think that *ut ne* means "that not," but as
above the *ne* goes with *quidem*, the third word down, and means "not even."

> → **929** subjunctive use: complementary result (consecutive), 68.1;
>   *consecutio*, 47–48;
>   dict., *quidem*, adv., I., C., 1. *ne … quidem*, "not even."

semperque ita statui non esse insectandos … amicos, "and I always decided that the friends … were not to be persecuted": the main verb *statui*,
"I decided," a verb of M & M in T.4b produces an object sentence in OO
where *amicos* in the object form functions as the subj. of the inf. whose full
implied form is *esse insectandos*, itself the passive necessity formula where
the passive necessity participle *insectandos* all alone means people "owing to
be persecuted," "having to be persecuted," "needing to be persecuted." The
only time a deponent verb such as *insector, atus,* 1, can be used with passive
meaning is as a participle of passive necessity.

> → **930** M & M, 60, 71, GL n° 527, remarks 1–2; OO, 71–73;
>   dict., *insector, atus,* 1, v. dep.; dict., *insecto, avi, atum,* 1., v. a.;
>   participle of passive necessity, deponents, 50, 51.1.4, 51.2.4;
>   passive necessity formula, 53.4.

When *statui* produces an object statement in OO, as here, it subtly refers
to a mental process, as in "I decided in my own mind that people were not
supposed to be persecuted," whereas when *statui* produces a statement composed of *ut* and the subjunctive, it refers to a decree that something external
happen, outside one's own mental process, as in "I decreed that the persecu-
tion end." The difference is subtle yet significant.

> → **931** dict., *statuo, ui, utum,* 3, II., D. "to decree, order, prescribe," 1. with *ut*; II.,
>   F. "to judge, declare," 1. with acc. and inf.

statui ... nec his praesidiis nosmet ipsos esse spoliandos, "I ... decided ... nor that we ourselves were to be deprived of these protections": the main verb, *statui*, "I decided," a verb of M & M in T.1i, again produces an object statement in OO whose subject *nosmet ipsos*, also written like the manuscript in part I as one word, *nosmetipsos*, "our very selves," in the object form functions as the subject of the inf. *esse spoliandos*, where the contemporaneous inf. *esse* is presented with the participle of passive necessity *spoliandos*, "worthy to be deprived," "owing to be deprived," "having to be deprived." Again the construction of *statui* producing an object sentence in OO refers to a mental process, as in "I decided in my own mind ... nor that we ourselves were to be deprived." The natural abl. of separation *his praesidiis*, means "from these protections," but the English idiom is "to be deprived of something."

→ **932** M & M, 60, 71, GL n° 527, remarks 1–2; OO, 71–73;
participle of passive necessity, 50, 51.1.4;
passive necessity formula, 53.4;
dict., *statuo, ui, utum*, 3: II., F. "to judge, declare," 1. with acc. and inf.;
abl.: separation, 27.

❧

Nam de puero Clodio tuas partis esse arbitror ut eius animum tenerum, quem ad modum scribis, iis opinionibus imbuas ut ne quas inimicitias residere in familiis nostris arbitretur. Contendi cum P. Clodio, cum ego publicam causam, ille suam defenderet. Nostras concertationes res publica diiudicavit. Si viveret, mihi cum illo nulla contentio iam maneret.   (*Att.* XIV, 13b, 4)

For concerning the young Clodius [the son] I think it is your role that you imbue his tender soul, as you write, with those ideas lest he think that any enmities are left over in our families. I struggled with Publius Clodius [the father] when I was defending the public cause, he his own. The republic judged between our contentions. If he were alive, there would no longer remain for me any dispute with him.

tuas partis, "your role": *partis* is another form for *partes*, agreeing with *tuas*. The noun *partes* refers to the role an actor plays on the stage, here referring to the role of Marcus Antonius in the comedy. The plural Latin is rendered in the singular in English for ease of expression and according to the dictionary.

→ **933** Block II nouns: *–is* = *–es*, 38, GL n° 56;
dict., *pars, partis*, f., II., B. in plural, "a part", II., B., 2. in plural, "a function."

tuas partis esse arbitror, "I think it is your role": the main verb *arbitror*, "I think," in T.1i of a deponent verb, is a verb of M & M producing a statement in OO whose subject is *tuas partis*, in the object form functioning as the subject of the inf. *esse*, "it is your role."

→ **934** M & M, 60, 71, GL n° 527, remarks 1–2; OO, 71–73;
verb: deponent, 29.

tuas partis esse ... ut ... imbuas, "it is your role that you imbue": the explanation of Marcus Antonius' role is given in a purpose clause, *ut imbuas*, "that you imbue."

→ **935** subjunctive use: purpose clause, 58.1.

quem ad modum scribis, "as you write": followed here by *scribis*, "you write," in T.1i. The meaning of *quem ad modum*, is easily seen if we say *ad quem modum*, "according to which manner" or simply "how." The antecedent of *quem* is the *modum*, incorporated into the same phrase. It is often, as in the manuscript in part I, written as one word, *quemadmodum*.

→ **936** dict., *quemadmodum*, adv.

ut ne quas inimicitias residere ... arbitretur, "lest he think that any enmities are left over": the *ne* here is not the same as the other *ne ... quidem*, "not even," two lines above. A negative purpose clause may be indicated by either *ut ne* followed by the subjunctive, as here, or as we might use today simply *ne* with the subjunctive. A negative result clause by contrast is indicated by *ut non* with the subjunctive, "with the result that ... not." The subjunctive verb here, *arbitretur*, "lest he think" or "so that he not think," in T.1s of a deponent verb, is a verb of M & M producing a statement in OO where *inimicitias* in the object form functions as the subject of the inf. *residere* describing contemporaneous action, "that enmities are left over." The word *quas* is an abbreviation of *aliquas* as is typical after the *ut ne*.

→ **937** subjunctive use: purpose clause, 58.1; verb: deponent, 29;
        M & M, 60, 71, GL n° 527, remarks 1–2; OO, 71–73;
        adj.: indefinite, 42.4; after *si* the *ali*-s fly away, 42.5.

cum ego publicam causam, ille suam defenderet, "when I was defending the public cause, he his own": the main verb *Contendi*, "I struggled," in T.4b establishes Track II, and *cum* with *defenderet*, "he was defending," in T.2s, may mean either "because" or "although" or as here it may give the temporal circumstance for another action "when." The verb *defenderet* is given only once here with the second part of the sentence, whose full implied form is *cum ille suam causam defenderet*, "when he was defending his own cause," where the *suam* is reflexive referring to the subject of *defenderet*, namely *ille*, "he." The full implied form of the first part of the sentence is *cum ego publicam causam defenderem*, "when I was defending the public cause."

→ **938** consecutio, 47–48;
        subjunctive use: temporal circumstance *cum* = "when," 66.3.2;
        subjunctive use: causal *cum* = "because, since," 59.1;
        subjunctive use: concessive *cum* = "although," 64;
        reflexive pron.: third person, 31.

Si viveret, ... nulla contentio iam maneret, "If he were alive, there would no longer remain ... any dispute": a contrary to fact conditional in the present in which the verbs of both parts are in T.2s, *viveret*, "he were alive," *maneret*, "there would [no longer] remain." We can test this by saying, "If he were alive (but he is not), there would no longer remain (but there does remain) some dispute."

→ **939** conditionals: contrary to fact, 86.3.

Qua re quoniam hoc a me sic petis ut, quae tua potestas est, ea neges te me invito usurum, puero quoque hoc a me dabis, si tibi videbitur, non quo aut aetas nostra ab illius aetate quidquam debeat periculi suspicari aut dignitas mea ullam contentionem extimescat, sed ut nosmet ipsi inter nos coniunctiores simus quam adhuc fuimus; interpellantibus enim his inimicitiis animus tuus *mihi* magis patuit quam domus. Sed haec hactenus. Illud extremum: ego quae te velle quaeque ad te pertinere arbitrabor semper sine ulla dubitatione summo studio faciam. Hoc velim tibi penitus persuadeas.   (*Att.* XIV, 13b, 5)

For which reason, because you request this of me in such a way that—what your authority is—you deny that you will be using it [your authority]—I being unwilling, you will also pass this on to the young boy, if it will seem proper to you, not because either our age group should suspect anything of danger from his age group or that my dignity should fear any confrontation, but that we ourselves may be more united among ourselves than we have been up to this time; for—as these enmities were causing interruption— your spirit lay open to me more than your home. But so far, these matters. That, the final thing: I shall do always without any hesitation with the greatest zeal those things which I shall judge you want and which pertain to you. I would like that you fully convince yourself of this.

> *Qua re*, "For which reason": here this expression connects the preceding to the following and means "wherefore," "therefore." This is not used as an interrogative here meaning "how," "why." The words are sometimes written as one word, *quare*, as in the dict. and the manuscript in part I.
>
> > → **940** dict., *quare* or *qua re*, adv.: I. interrog., "by what means?"; II., B. "wherefore."

> *quoniam hoc a me … petis*, "because you request this of me": the three particles that mean "because" are *quod, quia,* and here *quoniam*. They are followed by the ind. when the stated reason is the speaker's own, as here where *petis*, "you request," is in T.1i. They are followed by the subjunctive when the reason given belongs to someone else, whether it is accepted or not.
>
> > → **941** causal: *quod, quia, quoniam,* "because, since," + subjunctive, reported reason, 59.2;
> > causal: *quod, quia, quoniam,* "because, since," + indicative, one's own reason, 59.2;
> > causal: rejected reason, *non quo,* GL n° 541, note 2.

sic petis ut ... neges, "you request ... in such a way that ... you deny": the
request is made *sic*, "in such a way," that it produces a specific result, given
as a result clause, *ut ... neges*, "[in such a way] that you in fact deny [it]."

→ **942** subjunctive use: pure result (consecutive), 67.1–2, GL n° 552.

quae tua potestas est, "what your authority is": this relative clause shows an
eloquent style which incorporates the antecedent of the *quae* into the clause
itself. Instead of saying *potestas quae tua est*, "the authority which is yours,"
the *potestas* is drawn into the clause to make the statement, "which authority is yours."

→ **943** relative clauses, 10–11; sentence structure, 1.

quae tua potestas est, ea neges te ... usurum, "—what your authority is—you
deny that you will be using it [your authority]": the verb of the result clause,
negas, "you deny," in T.1s is a verb of M & M producing a statement in OO
where *te* in the object form functions as the subject of the inf. whose full
implied form is *usurum esse*, the futurity formula that includes the futurity
active participle *usurum*. This participle is one of five where an action is
done for the good of the subject reflexively, and whose complement is therefore in the abl. of instrument, here *ea*, referring to the *potestas*, "authority,"
mentioned in the relative clause. As a whole the expression means "you deny
that you will procure usefulness for yourself by means of your authority."

→ **944** M & M, 60, 71, GL n° 527, remarks 1–2; OO, 71–73;
futurity participle, deponents, 50, 51.2.3;
verb: subsequent active infinitive, 72.1;
futurity formula, active, 53.3;
famous five verbs with the ablative, 78.1;
abl.: instrument, 28.5.3–4, 89.2, GL n° 401.

me invito, "I being unwilling": an AA where *me* in the abl. form functions
as the subj. of an implied, "being." The word *invito* looks like a participle
meaning "[I] having been invited," which would be *me invitato*, but here it is
an independent adj. with the opposite meaning "[I] being unwilling."

→ **945** dict., *invitus, a, um*, adj., I.—ablative absolute: *me invito*, "against my will";
dict., *invito, avi, atum*, 1, "to invite";
ablative absolute, 54–55.

si tibi videbitur, "if it will seem proper to you": the condition part of a logical
conditional set almost parenthetically into the larger sentence, whose main
verb *videbitur*, "it will seem proper," includes the idea of "right," "good,"
"fit." Its use here is impersonal, "it will seem proper."

→ **946** conditionals: factual, 86.1;
dict., *video, vidi, visum*, 2., II., B., 7., (δ)., c. "it seems proper."

non quo aut ... debeat ... suspicari aut ... extimescat, "not because either
[our age group] should suspect ... or that [my dignity] should fear": here
non quo does not mean "not by which." Rather, the *quo* means "for which

reason," "because" and is the equivalent of *quod, quia,* or *quoniam,* "because," which takes the subjunctive to indicate quoted reason of another, so
we might say *non quo ... debeat suspicari,* "not because some people say
[our age group] should suspect" and *non quo ... extimescat,* "not because
allegedly [my dignity] should fear." Of itself these expressions do not indicate whether the author or speaker agrees with the quoted reason, but here
Cicero says *non quo,* "not because," and so rejects both quoted reasons.

> → **947** dict., *quo,* adv., I., B., 2. "because"; n. b.: II., B., 2. "so that";
>   causal: *quod, quia, quoniam,* "because, since," + subjunctive,
>   reported reason, 59.2;
>   causal: rejected reason, *non quo,* GL n° 541, note 2.

non quo aut ... aut ... sed, "not because either ... or ... but": one set of
correlatives is *non quo ... sed ... ,* "not because ... but ... ," and another set
located within the first is, *aut ... aut ... ,* "either ... or...."

> → **948** correlative comparative sentences, 90.5, GL n° 642.

quidquam debeat periculi suspicari, "[our age group] should suspect
anything of danger": the object of *debeat,* in T.1s, is the gerund *suspicari*
from a deponent verb, meaning "[our age group] should suspect," "[our age
group] must be suspecting of," and *suspicari* has its own object, *quidquam,*
"something," which is separated from its gen. of part, *periculi,* "something
of danger."

> → **949** verb: complementary infinitive, 77; gerund, 77.1;
>   verb: deponent, 29; gen. of part, 99.

sed ut nosmet ipsi inter nos coniunctiores simus, "but that we ourselves may
be more united among ourselves": after rejecting two quoted reasons, Cicero
then gives his own purpose for which he asks Mark Anthony to pass this
on to the young boy, *sed ut ... simus,* "but that we ... may be," where *simus*
is T.1s. The subject *nosmet ipsi* may also be written as one word, *nosmetipsi,*
"we our very selves." There is no reciprocal pronoun in Latin, so in its place
the prepositional phrase is used, *inter nos,* "among ourselves, mutually."
The comparative degree of *coniuncti,* "united, connected," is *coniunctiores,*
meaning variously "more united," "rather united," "too united," "quite united," "somewhat united."

> → **950** subjunctive use: purpose clause, 58.1;
>   dict., *nos, nostrum,* I. "It often takes the suffix *–met*";
>   prep. with obj., 6; adj.: comp., 36.

quam adhuc fuimus, "than we have been up to this time": the comparison
involves both the comparative *coniunctiores,* "more united," and *quam,*
"than." The verb *fuimus,* "we have been" is in T.4a.

> → **951** *quam* with the comp., 43.2; adj.: comp., 36; the verb *esse,* 9.

interpellantibus enim his inimicitiis, "for these enmities causing interruption": an AA where *inimicitiis* in the abl. form functions as the subjunctive

of the participle *interpellantibus*, which is both active and contemporaneous, also meaning "enmities coming between," "enmities disturbing." The word *enim*, "for," gives a reason in a causal expression which begins with this AA and continues with the following sentence.

→ **952** ablative absolute, 54–55.

animus tuus mihi magis patuit quam domus, "your spirit lay open to me more than your home": this causal clause is coordinated with the rest of the larger sentence by the *enim*, "for," that appears in the AA at the beginning of this causal statement. The comparison is made by the comparative *magis*, "more," and *quam*, "than." Here *domus* agrees with *animus tuus* because they are the two items being compared, "your spirit" and so the *tuus* is implied, "your home."

→ **953** *quam* with the comp., 43.2; ablative absolute, 54–55.

Some simple boxes will reveal clearly the structure of the sentence just discussed.

Qua re	connective relative pronoun
quoniam hoc a me sic petis	causal
ut,	purpose
quae tua potestas est,	almost parenthetical rel.
ea	OO begins
neges	purpose continued T.1s
te	OO continues
me invito	AA
usurum,	OO concludes
puero quoque hoc a me dabis,	main T.3i
si tibi videbitur	condition T.3i
non quo	quoted speech begins
⎧aut aetas nostra ab illius aetate	quoted reason 1 T.1s
⎩quidquam debeat periculi suspicari	
⎧aut dignitas mea ullam	quoted reason 2 T.1s
⎩contentionem extimescat,	
⎧sed ut nosmet ipsi inter nos	purpose T.1s
⎩coniunctiores simus	
quam adhuc fuimus;	comparison T.4b
interpellantibus enim his inimicitiis	AA
animus tuus mihi magis patuit	T.1i
quam domus	comparative

→ **954** structure of Latin sentences, 103 p. 587, *Ossa* Readings: 1-D, 1-I, 3-D, 3-I, 4-D, 4-I;
relative box, 11.4.

Note the space before the last three lines, which are coordinated with the previous sentence by the causal particle *enim* situated within the AA. Thus the AA goes with *animus ... patuit*, and not with *quam ... fuimus,* as indicated by the space.

→ **955** ablative absolute, 54–55.

ego ... faciam, "I shall do": the first word is the subject of the last, *faciam*, "I shall do," in T.3i.

→ **956** sentence structure, 1.

quae te velle quaeque ad te pertinere arbitrabor, "those things which I shall judge you want and which pertain to you": the antecedent of *quae* is as so very often an implied *ea*, the object of *faciam*, "I shall do [the things] which." The main verb of the relative clause is *arbitrabor*, "I shall judge," in T.3i and deponent, which as a verb of M & M produces two statements in OO where *te* in the object form functions as the subject of the first whose inf. is *velle*, "you want," and the object of *velle* is *quae*, "which things I shall judge you want." The second statement in OO is *quaeque ad te pertinere,* "and which pertain to you," where the same implied *ea*, the object of *faciam*, "I shall do the things ... and which," is the antecedent of *quaeque*, in the object form but functioning this time as the subject of the inf. *pertinere*, describing contemporaneous action. Thus the first *quae* is the object of *te velle*, whereas the second *quaeque* is the subject of *pertinere*, all depending on *arbitrabor.*

→ **957** rel. pron.: omission of the antecedent, 11.2; verb: deponent, 29;
   M & M, 60, 71, GL n° 527, remarks 1–2; OO, 71–73.

Hoc velim tibi ... persuadeas, "I would like that you ... convince yourself": the main verb *velim*, "I would like," in T.1s expresses the potential of the present and produces a purpose clause expressing Cicero's intention where *persuadeas*, "that you fully convince," in T.1s is given without the particle *ut*, thus emphasizing the wishing. The verb *persuadeas* is complemented both by a dat. of the person *tibi*, and object of the thing, *Hoc*, "that you persuade yourself this thing."

→ **958** subjunctive use: potential of the present or future, *velim* in T.1s,
   GL n° 257.2;
   subjunctive use: purpose clause without *ut*, 58, GL n° 546, remark 2;
   commands: other expressions, *velim*, 85.1.7;
   double dat., 91.2.

LETTER 306 T-P
AD FAMILIARES XIV, 18

TULLIUS TERENTIAE SUAE ET PATER SUAVISSIMAE FILIAE, CICERO MATRI ET SORORI S. P. D.

Considerandum vobis etiam atque etiam, animae meae, diligenter puto quid faciatis, Romaene sitis an mecum an aliquo tuto loco. Id non solum meum consilium est sed etiam vestrum. Mihi veniunt in mentem haec: Romae vos esse tuto posse per Dolabellam, eamque rem posse nobis adiumento esse, si quae vis aut si quae rapinae fieri coeperint. Sed rursus illud me movet, quod video omnis bonos abesse Roma et eos mulieres suas secum habere. Haec autem regio in qua ego sum nostrorum est cum oppidorum tum etiam praediorum, ut et multum esse mecum et, cum abieritis, commode in nostris esse possitis.   (*Fam.* XIV, 18, 1)

TULLIUS [SENIOR] TO HIS TERENTIA AND FATHER TO HIS MOST SWEET DAUGHTER, CICERO [JUNIOR] TO MOTHER AND SISTER SAY A BIG GREETING

My dear souls, I think it must be pondered carefully by you again and again what you are doing, whether you are in Rome or with me or in some safe place. This is not only my decision but also yours. These elements come to me in mind: that you are able to be in Rome safely with the help of Dolabella and this fact is able to be for a help to us, if any violence or if any plunderings will have begun to take place. But again that thing disturbs me, the fact that I see all good people are away from Rome and that they have their women with them. However, this area in which I am belongs to both our cities as well as our estates so that you are able both to be a lot with me and, when you will have been absent, to be conveniently in our estates.

Tullius Terentiae suae et pater suavissimae filiae, Cicero matri
et sorori s. p. d.: *Tullius Terentiae suae et pater suavissimae filiae, Cicero
matri et sorori salutem plurimam dicunt*

Considerandum vobis, "it must be pondered … by you": the participle of
passive necessity *Considerandum*, "consideration has to be made," is in OO
depending on the main verb *puto*, "I think," a verb of M & M in T.1i. The
full infinitive is *Considerandum esse*. Its accusative subject is an understood
id, "it," which stands for the entire IQ *quid … loco*. Thus, you could say, "I
think that what you do must be considered.…" The dat. of agent *vobis*, "by
you," is most often associated with the passive necessity formula, as here.

> → **959** M & M, 60, 71, GL n° 527, remarks 1–2; OO, 71–73; IQ, 60;
> participle of passive necessity, 50, 51.1.4;
> passive necessity formula, 53.4; dat. of agent, 53.5.

quid faciatis, "what you are doing": IQ depending on *puto*, "I think" in T.1i
and establishing Track I, which continues with *faciatis* in T.1s. In Latin indirect questions are expressed in the subjunctive, but they are expressed in the
indicative in English 90% of the time, as in "[I think] what you are doing,"
but 10% of the time the independent question is itself a natural subjunctive
before it is made indirect. Here the original question could be reconstructed
as *Quid faciatis?*, "What should you do?," and thus the IQ rendered as "[I
think] what you should do."

> → **960** M & M, 60, 71, GL n° 527, remarks 1–2; IQ, 60;
> consecutio, 47–48.

Romae, "in Rome": without a preposition, *Romae* expresses place at which.
It is not the genitive, here, but the so-called locative originally written as *Romai*, the locative ending being *–i*, which therefore is not found in the plural,
because they use the abl., and is not the of-possession form.

> → **961** function: place at which, names of cities and small islands, singular,
> *Romae*, 69.3.2.

–ne sitis … an … an …, "whether you are … or … or …": IQ where *–ne* is
the particle introducing the disjunctive question "whether … or … or …,"
and the verb *sitis* in T.1s. It is not always easy to reconstruct the original
question, whether it was *Estisne Romae?*, "Are you in Rome?," in T.1i which
asks a question in the indicative, or *Sitisne Romae?*, "Should you be in
Rome?," in T.1s a natural subjunctive that asks a question.

> → **962** IQ, 60; disjunctive question, GL n° 458.

mecum, "with me": the preposition follows and is attached to its own object,
as with a few others such as *secum, vobiscum, nobiscum, quicum, quibuscum*.

> → **963** dict., *cum*, prep. with abl., II., D., a.… *mecum, tecum, secum,
> nobiscum*, etc.… *quocum (quīcum)*.

aliquo tuto loco, "in some safe place": typically the preposition *in* is used to indicate place in which, but with certain adjectives such as *aliquo*, "some," the abl. was used with no preposition. Other adjectives include *totus, cunctus, omnis* as in *toto orbe*, "in the whole world"; *tota Asia*, "in all Asia."

→ **964** GL n° 387–88.

Mihi veniunt in mentem, "[these elements] come to me in mind": The mihi here is sometimes called an ethical dative and means, "for me," "what concerns me," or a dative that makes reference "to me," as in "it does not come into mind for me." The dat. of reference or the so-called ethical dative, is implied in the example *Magno mihi est honori vos salutare*, "It is for a great honor to me to greet you all," presented in *Ossa* 91.2.

→ **965** dat.: meaning and forms, 33;
ethical dat., see 91.2, GL n° 351; dat. of reference, 91.2, GL n° 352.

Mihi veniunt in mentem haec: ... vos esse tuto posse, "These elements come to me in mind: that you are able to be safely": the first part, *Mihi veniunt in mentem haec*, "These elements come to me in mind," in T.1i, functions as an expression of M & M, giving rise to an expression in OO where the subject is the acc. *vos*, "you," and the inf. *posse*, "to be able." Here *esse*, "to be," is a complementary infinitive, which is described by *tuto*, here an adverb meaning "safely," whereas in the previous sentence *tuto* was an abl. of place in which, meaning "in [some] safe [place]."

→ **966** M & M, 60, 71, GL n° 527, remarks 1–2; OO, 71–73;
verb: complementary infinitive, 77; dict., *tueor, tuitus*, 2., II., B.—adv. *tuto*.

rem posse ... esse, "that ... [this] fact is able to be": also depending on the expression of M & M *Mihi veniunt in mentem haec*, "These elements come to me in mind," in T.1i, is a second OO where the subject is the acc. *rem*, "fact," and the inf. *posse*, "to be able" is complemented by the inf. *esse*, "to be."

→ **967** M & M, 60, 71, GL n° 527, remarks 1–2; OO, 71–73;
verb: complementary infinitive, 77.

nobis adiumento esse, "to be for a help to us": double dative of person and of result.

→ **968** double dat., 91.2.

si ... fieri coeperint, "if ... will have begun to take place": depending on *veniunt*, "they come," in T.1i and establishing Track I which continues in the OO *rem posse*, "that ... [this] fact is able," *si ... coeperint* is a factual conditional for one of two reasons. Either *coeperint* is T.6i meaning "if ... will have begun," or it is T.3s by MA again with future completed meaning in English.

→ **969** M & M, 60, 71, GL n° 527, remarks 1–2; OO, 71–73;
consecutio, 47–48;
conditionals: factual, 86.1; subjunctive use: modal attraction, 83.

The dictionary has an entry for the verb *coepio, coepi, coeptum* 3, "to begin, commence, undertake" and states that the present times of this verb are rare before the classical period and that the historical times are used very frequently in literature. This is an indication that this verb is practically defective because the forms are not found. This being the case, there are other possible meanings to consider. The expression *si ... fieri coeperint*, in T.6i could also be felt as if it were T.3i, meaning "if ... will have begun to take place." Likewise if *coeperint* is T.3s by MA, then it could be felt as T.1i, meaning "if ... are beginning to take place." Lest our zeal lead us to form an absolute rule, there are other verbs with fewer forms and so more consistently defective than *coepio*. Literature, as always, is our guide.

→ **970** defective verbs, 14.4, GL n° 175.5: *coepi, memini, odi*.

si quae vis ... si quae rapinae, "if any violence ... if any plunderings": in both cases the plural feminine subject *quae* stands for the indefinite adjective *aliquae*, "any violence" or "some plunderings." After the word *si*, "if," and similar particles, *ne, ut, num, nisi* the form *aliquae* is often shortened to *quae*.

→ **971** adj.: indefinite, 42.4; after *si* the *ali*-s fly away, 42.5.

fieri coeperint, "will have begun to take place": the infinitive *fieri*, "to take place," completes the action of *coeperint*; it is the passive of *facere*, "to make, do."

→ **972** verb: complementary infinitive, 77.

❧

Mihi plane non satis constat adhuc utrum sit melius. Vos videte quid aliae faciant isto loco feminae et ne cum velitis exire non liceat. Id velim diligenter etiam atque etiam vobiscum et cum amicis consideretis. Domus ut propugnacula et praesidium habeat Philotimo dicetis. Et velim tabellarios instituatis certos, ut cottidie aliquas a vobis litteras accipiam. Maxime autem date operam ut valeatis, si nos vultis valere. VIIII Kal. Formiis.   (*Fam.* XIV, 18, 2)

Thus far it is not certain enough for me which of the two is better. You people see what the other women are doing in your location there, and [see to it] that departure not be not permitted when you wish. This I would like that you consider again and again carefully with yourselves and with friends. You shall give orders to Philotimus that the house have fortifications and a garrison. And I would like that you organize definite letter carriers so that I may receive every day some letter from you. However, especially make an effort that you be in good health, if you wish us to be in good health. On the ninth day before the [February] Kalends [24 January], Formia.

constat, "it is ... certain": when referring to facts and reports, this verb can mean "it is evident," "it is well known," "it is sure." It is used impersonally here.

→ **973** dict., *consto, stiti, statum*, 1., II., B., 2. of facts, "to be established" ... and impers.

utrum sit melius, "which of the two is better": the controlling verb is *constat*, "it is [not] certain," in T.1i, establishing Track I, which verb is used impersonally. The subject of *constat* is this IQ whose verb is the subjunctive, *sit*, rendered in the indicative in English, "is." The expression *utrum melius* means "which of two things," where *melius* is the comparative adj. in the neuter agreeing with *utrum* as in the English rendering above. The positive adj. is *bonum*, and the superlative adj. *optimum*. Conversely *sit melius* means "it exists better," where *melius* is the comparative adv. going with the verb *sit*. The positive adv. is *bene* and the superlative *optime*.

→ **974** IQ, 60; *consecutio*, 47–48; adj.: comp. and superl., 36; adv.: positive, comp., superl., 37.

utrum, "which of the two": from the third dictionary entry for *uter*, a pronoun posing the indirect question. The two options are given in the first sentence of the letter: *Romaene sitis an mecum an aliquo tuto loco*, "whether you are in Rome or with me or in some safe place."

→ **975** dict., 3. *uter, utra, utrum*, pron.

vos videte quid ... et ne ..., "You people see what ... and that ... not": the verb *videte* is used in two ways here. First as a verb of M & M giving rise to an IQ *quid ...* and indicates almost physical perception as in "look and see." Second as a verb of precaution giving rise to a negative purpose clause *ne ...*, meaning "take care that not" or "see to it that not."

→ **976** M & M, 60, 71, GL n° 527, remarks 1–2; IQ, 60; subjunctive use: purpose clause, 58.1.

quid ... faciant, "what [the other women] are doing": IQ in T.1s depending on the M & M command form *videte*, "you ... check."

→ **977** M & M, 60, 71, GL n° 527, remarks 1–2; IQ, 60; commands: first, second, 17.

ne ... exire non liceat, "that departure not be not permitted": a negative purpose clause where *ne* stands for *ut non*, "that not," or "lest," and negates the whole statement. In this case there is a double negative because *ne* is followed by *non liceat*, "it not be permitted." If the term "lest" is understood, one may say, "lest departing not be permitted." The subject of *liceat* is *exire*, "departing," which functions as a subject gerund.

→ **978** subjunctive use: purpose clause, 58.1; gerund, 77.1.

cum velitis, "when you wish": a temporal clause indicating time when, which is normally in the indicative, but here in T.1s by MA.

> → **979** *cum* + indicative = "when": temporal sentences, 66.3;
>> subjunctive use: modal attraction, 83.

Id ... consideretis, "This [I would like] that you consider": the first word, *Id*, "This," is the object of the last word of the sentence *consideretis*, in T.1s, which is a purpose clause without an expressed *ut* and depending on *velim*, "I would like," in T.1s establishing Track I and expressing a wish. He could have said this more directly as *volo*, "I want," but Cicero is using a more gentle form of command, a form of politesse with his wife and daughter.

> → **980** sentence structure, 1;
>> subjunctive use: purpose clause without *ut*, 58, GL n° 546, remark 2;
>> commands: other expressions, *velim*, 85.1.7;
>> *consecutio*: subjunctive depending on a subjunctive, 62.1.

etiam atque etiam, "again and again": it may look like it means "also and also," but this is a famous idiom in your dictionary.

> → **981** dict., *etiam*, conj., II., F. *etiam atque etiam*, "again and again."

Domus ut ... habeat ... dicetis, "You will give orders ... that the house have": the main word is the last one, *dicetis*, T.3i establishing Track I and producing the purpose clause *ut ... habeat*, "that the house have," in T.1s. The first word of the sentence is the subject of *habeat*, but stands geographically before the purpose clause. The verb *dicetis*, "you shall give orders" is an example of T.3i used as a light command.

> → **982** subjunctive use: purpose clause, 58.1;
>> sentence structure, 1; commands: T.3i, 85.1.6.

velim ... instituatis, "I would like that you organize": again *velim*, "I would like," is T.1s and produces a purpose clause *instituatis*, "that you organize," in T.1s without the particle *ut*.

> → **983** subjunctive use: purpose clause without *ut*, 58, GL n° 546, remark 2;
>> commands: other expressions, *velim*, 85.1.7;
>> *consecutio*: subjunctive depending on a subjunctive, 62.1.

ut ... accipiam, "so that I may receive": purpose clause in T.1s depending on *instituatis*, "that you organize," in T.1s.

> → **984** subjunctive use: purpose clause, 58.1;
>> *consecutio*: subjunctive depending on a subjunctive, 62.1.

date operam, "make an effort": this expression of a command is found in the dictionary under *do, dare*, and it refers to bestowing labor and pains on something."

> → **985** dict., *do, dedi, datum, dare*, I. ... *operam*, "to bestow labor and pains on any thing";
>> commands: first, second, 17.

date operam ut valeatis, "make an effort that you be in good health": a purpose clause in T.1s depending on the command *date operam*, "make an effort" establishing Track I.

→ **986** *consecutio* after command form, GL nᵒ 517;
      subjunctive use: purpose clause, 58.1.

si … vultis valere, "if you wish … to be in good health": a factual conditional sentence in T.1i, and not in the subjunctive, as some modern languages would presume or demand.

→ **987** conditionals: factual, 86.1; gerund, 77.1.

VIIII Kal. Formiis, "on the ninth day before the [February] Kalends [24 January]": the full Latin expression is, *(die) nono (ante) Kalendas Februarias. Formiis.*

→ **988** about the Roman calendar, pp. 605–608;
      GL appendix: Roman Calendar, pp. 491–92;
      abl.: time at which, 70.1.

Formiis, "Formia": this form is either "from Formia," as in "a letter sent from Formia," or "in Formia," as in "a letter written in Formia," in the latter case *Formiis* in the abl. pl. is a substitution for the place where function, otherwise called the locative.

→ **989** function: place at which, names of cities and small islands, plural, *Formiis*, 69.3.2.

LETTER 97 T-P
AD FAMILIARES I, 3

M. CICERO S. D. P. LENTULO PROCOS.

A. Trebonio, qui in tua provincia magna negotia et ampla et expedita habet, multos annos utor valde familiariter. Is cum antea semper et suo splendore et nostra ceterorumque amicorum commendatione gratiosissimus in provincia fuit tum hoc tempore propter tuum in me amorem nostramque necessitudinem vehementer confidit his meis litteris se apud te gratiosum fore.   (*Fam.* I, 3, 1)

CICERO SAYS A GREETING TO PUBLIUS
LENTULUS PROCONSUL

I associate very intimately for many years with Aulus Trebonius, who in your province has big and abundant and unencumbered business affairs. While previously he always was most accepted in the province both by his shining character and by our recommendation as well as that of other friends, then at this time, because of your love for me and our close relationship, he strongly hopes that by this letter of mine he will be acceptable in your sight.

M. CICERO S. D. P. LENTULO PROCOS.: *Marcus Cicero salutem dicit Publio Lentulo proconsuli*

A. Trebonio … utor, "I associate … with Aulus Trebonius": the dictionary gives one of the later meanings of *utor* as "to associate with [a person]" or "to get along with [a person]," but certainly not "to use [a person]." *utor* is one of the five deponent verbs that takes an ablative complement, here *A. Trebonio*; they are separated by thirteen words.

> → **990** dict., *utor, usus*, 3., II., A. "to associate with," a. with abl.;
>   famous five verbs with the ablative, 78.1; verb: deponent, 29;
>   sentence structure, 1.

multos annos, "for many years": accusative of extent of time.
> → **991** acc.: time during which, 70.2.

hoc tempore, "at this time": time at which in the ablative with no preposition.
> → **992** abl.: time at which, 70.1.

necessitudinem, "close relationship": the first meaning refers to "necessity," but one of the latter meanings is "relationship, friendship, intimacy."
> → **993** dict., *necessitudo, onis*, f., II. "a close connection, relationship, friendship."

❧

Quae ne spes eum fallat vehementer rogo te, commendoque tibi eius omnia negotia, libertos, procuratores, familiam, in primisque ut quae T. Ampius de eius re decrevit ea comprobes omnibusque rebus eum ita tractes ut intellegat meam commendationem non vulgarem fuisse.   (*Fam.* I, 3, 2)

Which hope, I beg of you strongly that it not deceive him, and I recommend to you all of his business affairs, his freed men, his administrators, his household servants, and first of all that you may approve those things which Titus Ampius decided about his affair and you may treat him with all things in such a way that he may understand that my recommendation was not a commonplace one.

Quae ne spes eum fallat … rogo te, "Which hope, lest it deceive him, I beg of you": the main verb is *rogo*, "I beg [you]," in T.1i establishing Track I. Out front is a negative purpose clause *ne … fallat*, "that [hope] not deceive," or "lest [hope] deceive." The *Quae* is another example of a connecting relative, which stands for *Et ea*, or *Et illa*, meaning "And it," and so we might say, "And I ask you that that hope not deceive him." Old English versions of the Bible which were very close to the Latin Vulgate would say something like, "Jesus remained in the town. Who when he had left, the lepers followed him." Today we might smooth out the initial relative "Who when he" and say instead, "And when he."
> → **994** dict., *qui, quae, quod*, pron., II., C. a connective instead of *is, ea, id* with a conj.;
> subjunctive use: purpose clause, 58.1; *consecutio*, 47–48.

familiam, "household servants": again the earlier meaning of *familia* is not what we mean by "family" but the household servants.
> → **995** dict., *familia, ae*, f., I. not = "family" (*domus*), except by rare exception v. II., A., 3.

ut ... comprobes ... –que ... tractes: "that ... you may approve and you may treat": a double purpose clause whose verbs *comprobes ... tractes* are in T.1s on Track I depending on *commendo*, "I recommend" in T.1i.

→ **996** subjunctive use: purpose clause, 58.1; *consecutio*, 47–48.

ita tractes ut intellegat, "you may treat him ... in such a way that he may understand": this could be taken as a purpose clause, as in the English rendering, if the intention comes to the fore in *tractes*, "you may treat him." Or it may be taken as a result clause if *ita ... ut*, "in such a way that," come to the fore; in this case the Latin subjunctive *intellegat* is rendered in the indicative in English as in "you may treat him in such a way that he does understand." The subtle difference between the two is explained with microscopic letters in GL n° 543 note 2.

→ **997** subjunctive use: purpose clause, 58.1;
    subjunctive use: pure result (consecutive), 67.1–2, GL n° 552;
    difference between purpose and result is perspective, GL n° 543, note 2.

commendationem ... fuisse, "that my recommendation was": OO. The time of *fuisse* is anything before *intellegat*, "he may understand."

→ **998** M & M, 60, 71, GL n° 527, remarks 1–2; OO, 71–73.

LETTER 151 T-P
AD QUINTUM FRATREM III, 3

MARCUS QUINTO FRATRI SALUTEM.

Occupationum mearum tibi signum sit librari manus. Diem scito esse nullum, quo die non dicam pro reo. Ita, quidquid conficio aut cogito, in ambulationis tempus fere confero. Negotia se nostra sic habent, domestica vero, ut volumus. Valent pueri, studiose discunt, diligenter docentur, et nos et inter se amant. Expolitiones utriusque nostrum sunt in manibus: sed tua ad perfectum iam res rustica Arcani et Lateri. Praeterea de aqua, de via nihil praetermisi quadam epistula quin enucleate ad te perscriberem. Sed me illa cura sollicitat angitque vehementer, quod dierum iam amplius L intervallo nihil a te, nihil a Caesare, nihil ex istis locis non modo litterarum sed ne rumoris quidem adfluxit. Me autem iam et mare istuc et terra sollicitat, neque desino, ut fit in amore, ea quae minime volo cogitare. Qua re non equidem iam te rogo ut ad me de te, de rebus istis scribas—numquam enim, cum potes, praetermittis—sed hoc te scire volo, nihil fere umquam me sic exspectasse ut, cum haec scribebam, tuas litteras.   (*Q. Fr.* III, 3, 1)

MARCUS TO BROTHER QUINTUS A GREETING

May the writing of my secretary be a sign for you of my occupations. You must know there is no day on which day I am not giving a speech for someone accused. Thus, whatever I accomplish or think of, I usually assign to the time of my stroll. Our occupations find themselves in this way, but our domestic affairs as we wish. The children are well; they are learning zealously; they are being taught carefully; they both love us and each other. The finishing touches of the works of each one of us are in hand: but your rural project in Arcanum and Laterium is already at the end. Besides concerning the water service, concerning the road I left out nothing that I did not write to you in detail with some letter. But now this worry disturbs and troubles me very much, the fact that in an interval already now of more than fifty days nothing has drifted in from you, nothing from Caesar, nothing from those your areas not only of a letter but not even of a rumor. Already that sea of yours and the land disturbs me, nor do I cease, as happens in the case of love, to think about those things which I absolutely do not want to think of. For which reason I indeed am not asking you any more that you write to me about yourself, your affairs—for, when you are able, you never skip it—but I want you to know this, that, when I was writing these things, I was awaiting nothing almost ever in such a way as your letter.

librari, "of my secretary": until about the second century C.E. the form *librari* was used for the of-possession form, where we would expect *librarii*. Cicero is pacing up and down, dictating here to his secretary because he is busy.

→ **999** early gen. ending in –*i*, GL nº 33, remark 1;
function: of-possession, 20;

Diem scito esse nullum, "You must know there is no day": OO depending on *scito*, "you must know," "you shalt know," the second command form.

→ **1000** commands: first, second, 17;
M & M, 60, 71, GL nº 527, remarks 1–2; OO, 71–73.

quo die non dicam, "on which day I am not giving a speech": *quo die* is ablative of time at which. Two reasons for *quo ... dicam* in T.1s are: it may be a relative clause in the subjunctive by MA, because the clause depends on and the idea is closely associated with *Diem ... esse nullum*, "there is no day," in OO produced by *scito*, "You must know." Or it may be, as the English rendering understands it, a character result clause where the *quo* stands for *talem ut eo*, "such that on it"; *quo ... dicam* in T.1s sounds indicative in English, "such that on which [day] I am [not] giving a speech."

→ **1001** M & M, 60, 71, GL nº 527, remarks 1–2; OO, 71–73;
abl.: time at which, 70.1;
subjunctive use: modal attraction, 83;
subjunctive use: characteristic result, 68.2.

fere, "usually": toward the end of the dictionary entry you will see the temporal meaning "usually" or "almost all the time." Be careful: *ferre*, "to carry"; *ferae*, "wild animals"; *feriae*, "week days." In Medieval Latin the first letters of diphthongs are easily lost, and these are easily confused.

→ **1002** dict., *fere*, adv.; dict., *ferus, a, um*, adj.;
dict., *feriae, arum*, f.; dict., *fero, tuli, latum, ferre*, v. irreg.

studiose ... diligenter, "zealously ... carefully": Students should notice two different forms of the adv. placed near each other, *studiose* from the Block I adj. *studiosus, a, um*, "zealous," and *diligenter* from the Block II adjective, *diligens, –entis*, "careful."

→ **1003** adj.: Block I, 4; Block II adj. in three ways, 18.

inter se amant, "they both love ... mutually": Latin does not have the reciprocal pronoun as does Greek and most modern languages, so the idiom *inter se,* "among themselves" or "between themselves" is used to mean "one another" or "mutually," "each other."

> → **1004** dict., *inter,* prep. with acc., with pronouns.

nihil praetermisi quadam epistula quin ... perscriberem, "I left out nothing that I did not write [to you in detail] with some letter": *praetermisi,* "I left out," is T.4b, establishing Track II. *quin perscriberem,* often rendered as "without writing," in T.2s is a result clause where *quin* stands for *quī non,* as in "that I did not write," where *quī* is an old abl., otherwise expressed as *ut non,* as in "that I did not write [nothing]," where *nihil* is the object of *per-scriberem.* Note that *quadam epistula,* "with some letter" stands geographically in front of its clause, *quin perscriberem.*

> → **1005** subjunctive use: pure result (consecutive), 67.1–2, GL nº 552.3;
>   *consecutio,* 47–48.

quod ... adfluxit, "the fact that ... [nothing] has drifted in from you": here *quod* means "the fact that," "in the circumstance that," "that" and begins an object sentence that gives the content of the worry and trouble, and so de-pends on the verbs *sollicitat angitque,* "[this worry] disturbs ... and troubles," in T.1i. The numeral L stands for *quinquagenta,* which is invariable for "fifty."

> → **1006** *quod* = "the fact that" as a new subject, GL nº 525.2.

nihil ... litterarum ... rumoris, "nothing ... of a letter ... of a rumor": *nihil* is followed by two gen. of part some distance down the sentence.

> → **1007** gen. of part, 99.

mare istuc, "that sea of yours": here *istuc* is an alternative way of writing *istud,* and so goes with *mare.* The form *istuc* is a favorite of Plautus. Quintus is Lieutenant of Caesar in Gaul, who is planning a second invasion of Caesar in the year 54 BCE.

> → **1008** three cousins: *iste–ille–ipse,* 41.3.

ut fit, "as happens": followed by *fit* in T.1i, here *ut* means "as."

> → **1009** dict., *ut,* I., B. meaning "as."

minime, "absolutely ... not": the superlative also means "minimally," "in no way." In the positive degree, the practically nonexistent *parve,* "slightly," is usually substituted by *paulum,* "a little bit"; the comparative adverb is *minus,* "less."

> → **1010** adv.: irregular comp., 37.3, GL nº 93.

ut ... scribas, "that you write": a purpose clause in T.1s and depending on *rogo,* "I ... beg." The English "that you write" is in either the subjunctive or the indicative. The subjunctive is difficult to see in English unless you say, "that you may write." Note that here *ut* means "that," but in the previous sentence *ut* meant "as."

> → **1011** subjunctive use: purpose clause, 58.1.

te scire volo, "I want you to know": OO in which the infinitive *scire* is contemporaneous with *volo* in T.1i.

> → **1012** M & M, 60, 71, GL n° 527, remarks 1–2; OO, 71–73.

me ... exspectasse, "I have ... waited": an abbreviated form of *expectavisse*,
the infinitive may stand for T.4a, "[I] have waited" or T.4b "[I] waited" or
any other time antecedent to *scire*, "[you] to know," which in turn is contemporaneous with *volo*, "I want" in T.1i.

> → **1013** verb: antecedent active infinitive, 72.1.

scribebam, "I was writing": expostulatory tense meaning "as I am writing," but seen from the perspective of Quintus reading the letter. The text
almost ends up saying, "*I have expected* nothing as much as your letter," or
if the epistolary tense is extended to include the infinitive *exspectasse*, the
sentence ends up as "*I am expecting* nothing as much as your letter, as I am
writing these things."

> → **1014** letter-writer tense, GL n° 252.

☙

Nunc cognosce ea quae sunt in re publica. Comitiorum cotidie singuli dies
tolluntur obnuntiationibus, magna voluntate bonorum omnium: tanta invidia sunt consules propter suspicionem pactorum a candidatis praemiorum. Candidati consulares quattuor omnes rei: causae sunt difficiles, sed
enitemur ut Messalla noster salvus sit, quod est etiam cum reliquorum
salute coniunctum. Gabinium de ambitu reum fecit P. Sulla, subscribente
privigno Memmio, fratre Caecilio, Sulla filio. Contra dixit L. Torquatus omnibusque libentibus non obtinuit.   (*Q. Fr.* III, 3, 2)

Now, get to know the things which are in public life. Every day the individual days of voting are being removed by adverse omen-announcements,
with the great willingness of all good people: the consuls are people of such
great unpopularity because of the suspicion of rewards having been agreed
upon by the candidates. The four consular candidates are all accused: the
cases are difficult, but we shall struggle that our Messalla be safe and sound,
something which has been tied up also with the well-being of the rest. Publius Sulla made Gabinius a man accused of corruption, as Memmius the
stepson was endorsing, and his brother Caecilius and Sulla junior. Lucius
Torquatus spoke in opposition and did not win—all people being content.

cognosce, "get to know": simple and direct command form. Here Cicero did
not use the more polite, gentle, indirect expression *velim cognoscas*, "I would
like that you get to know."

> → **1015** commands: first, second, 17.

magna voluntate, "with the great willingness": rendered here as an abl. expressing instrument or accompaniment. Some would take this as an AA, "great being the willingness," "great being the agreement [of all good people]."

> → **1016** abl.: instrument, 28.5.3–4, 89.2, GL n° 401;
> ablative absolute, 54–55.

tanta invidia sunt, "[the consuls] are people of such great unpopularity": the function of description is given in the abl. The adj. *tantus, a, um* means "so great," and here *tanta*, "with so great."

> → **1017** quality in abl., 96.2;
> abl.: quality, 96.2; Block I adj., 4.2–3.

invidia, "with … unpopularity": the noun *invidia, ae*, f. is from the adj. *invidus, a, um*. The noun can refer either to people who practice envy or to people who suffer envy; as a human vice or as the unpopularity that they are suffering, as in the English rendering above.

> → **1018** dict., *invidia, ae*, f.; *invidus, a, um*, adj.; Block I nouns, 2.

rei, "under accusation": from the masculine noun *reus, i*, like the feminine noun *rea, ae*. The form *rei* can mean, as here, "indicted men," or "of a guilty man," or the same form can mean "of a thing" from the feminine noun *res, i*, "a thing, matter, affair" which has nothing to do with the word here. With this ambivalence we can say, *rei rei huius sumus*, "we are guilty of this thing."

> → **1019** dict., *reus, i*, m.; dict., *rea, ae*, f.; dict., *res, i*, f.;
> 20% of nouns: *res, rei*, f., 35.

enitemur ut … sit, "we shall struggle that [Messalla] be [safe]": purpose clause depending on the deponent verb *enitemur*, "we shall struggle," from *enitor, eniti, enixum*, 3 "to push on," "to press," "to strive," not from *eniteo, enitere, enitui*, 2 "to shine forth." Thus *enítens* is "pushing," "striving" from *enítor*, but *énitens* is "shining" from *enitére*.

> → **1020** dict., *enitor, nisus* or *nixus*, 3; dict., *eniteo, tui*, 2;
> subjunctive use: purpose clause, 58.1; verb: deponent, 29.

Messalla … salvus, "Messala [be] safe": Your dictionary indicates that the Roman surname *Messalla* is masculine, as here.

> → **1021** dict., *Messalla, ae*, m.

quod est … coniunctum, "something which has been tied up": the *quod* is neuter because its antecedent is the whole situation explained in the previous sentence.

> → **1022** *quod* referring to previous sentence: GL n° 614, remark 2.

Gabinium ... reum fecit P. Sulla, "Publius Sulla made Gabinius a man accused": *fecit*, T.4b, has a double object, the acc. *Gabinium*, and the acc. *reum*, meaning "he made Gabinius into an accused man."

→ **1023** dict., *facio, feci, factum*, 3., I., B., 1. with a double object; double acc., GL n° 339; dict., *rogo, avi, atum*, 1., I., A.... *aliquem aliquid*.

de ambitu, "of corruption": the dictionary entry is *ambitus, us*, m. and the by-with-from-in form is easy to recognize, ending in the final *–u*. The noun means "a going around" and thus "canvassing for office," and thus "bribery" and "corruption." This noun is part of the 20% of nouns we present during the last encounter of the First Experience, well after we present the 40% of nouns comprising Bk. I and the other 40% of nouns comprising Bk. II.

→ **1024** 20% of nouns, *ambitus, us*, m., 35.

subscribente ... Memmio, ... Caecilio, Sulla, "as Memmius ... was endorsing and ... Caecilius and ... Sulla": AA with three subjects all in a row without connecting words, an example of asyndeton.

→ **1025** ablative absolute, 54–55; asyndeton, GL n° 481.2.

contra dixit, "[Lucius Torquatus] spoke in opposition": written as two words until about the middle of the first century C.E. It does not mean simply "he contradicted," but that he spoke opposite or on behalf of the opposition.

→ **1026** dict., *contra*, adv., and prep. with acc.

omnibus libentibus, "all people being content": AA with the verb implied.

→ **1027** ablative absolute, 54–55.

☙

Quaeris quid fiat de Gabinio? Sciemus de maiestate triduo: quo quidem in iudicio odio premitur omnium generum, maxime testibus caeditur: accusatoribus frigidissimis utitur: consilium varium, quaesitor gravis et firmus, Alfius, Pompeius vehemens in iudicibus rogandis. Quid futurum sit nescio, locum tamen illi in civitate non video. Animum praebeo ad illius perniciem moderatum, ad rerum eventum lenissimum.   (*Q. Fr.* III, 3, 3)

You ask what is going on about Gabinius. We will know within three days about the treason, in which trial, indeed, he is being squashed by the hatred of all classes; he is especially being cut down by witnesses; he has very cool prosecutors; the council [is] unstable; the investigator, Alfius, heavy and unmoved; Pompeius, vehement in begging the judges. I do not know what is going to be; however I do not see a place for him in the state. I show a tempered attitude toward his destruction, a very mild one toward the outcome of things.

quid fiat, "what is going on": IQ depending on M & M *Quaeris,* "You ask."

→ **1028** M & M, 60, 71, GL n° 527, remarks 1–2; IQ, 60.

maiestate, "the treason": here it does not mean "majesty," but refers to *crimen maiestatis,* "high treason" or "an offence against the sovereignty of the people."

→ **1029** dict., *majestas, atis,* f., I., 2.... *crimen majestas,* "high-treason."

triduo, "within three days": the abl. of time within which.

→ **1030** abl.: time within which, 70.3.

in iudicibus rogandis, "in begging the judges": *rogandis* is not a passive necessity participle meaning "in the case of judges needing to be begged." Rather this expression is a gerundive; the gerund would be *in iudices rogando,* with the same meaning. Almost the last meaning in the dictionary of the preposition *in* followed by the abl., here the abl. gerundive, has the special meaning "in the case of."

→ **1031** dict., *in,* prep. with abl. and acc.; gerundive, 77.2; gerund, 77.1.

Quid futurum sit, "what is going to be": IQ depending on M & M verb *nescio,* "I do not know," in T.1i establishing Track I. The form *futurum* means "about to be," "going to be," but some commentaries will say that *futurum sit* is used to express the idea of "what is going to be done," which cannot be said in Latin because it is passive, so they fall back on this active form.

→ **1032** M & M, 60, 71, GL n° 527, remarks 1–2; IQ, 60;
futurity participle, 50, 51.1.3;
consecutio: futurity formula in the subjunctive, 61.3.

in civitate, "in the state": here this does not mean "in the city." The first meaning in the dictionary for *civitas, tis,* f. is "the citizenry," "citizenship," then it means the state. This is why papal documents, using Latin from the 1700s, refer to the United States of America as *Civitates Foederatae Americae Septentrionalis,* in contrast to other modern languages that say, as in Italian, *gli Stati Uniti.*

→ **1033** dict., *civitas, tis,* f.

∾

Habes fere de omnibus rebus. Unum illud addam: Cicero tuus nosterque summe studiosus est Paeoni sui rhetoris, hominis, opinor, valde exercitati et boni. Sed nostrum instituendi genus esse paullo eruditius et Θετικώτερον non ignoras. Qua re neque ego impediri Ciceronis iter atque illam disciplinam volo, et ipse puer magis illo declamatorio genere duci et delectari videtur—in quo quoniam ipsi quoque fuimus, patiamur illum ire nostris itineribus (eodem enim perventurum esse confidimus), sed tamen, si nobiscum

eum rus aliquo eduxerimus, in hanc nostram rationem consuetudinemque
inducemus. Magna enim nobis a te proposita merces est quam certe nostra
culpa numquam minus adsequemur. Quibus in locis et qua spe hiematurus
sis ad me quam diligentissime scribas velim.   (*Q. Fr.* III, 3, 4)

You just about have [the stuff] concerning all matters. I will add that one
item: your and our [nephew] Cicero is super zealous about Paeonius his
teacher of rhetoric, a man, I think, well trained and good. But you realize
that our type of educating is a little more intellectual and *subtle*. For which
reason neither do I wish that Cicero's pathway and that training program be
impeded, and the boy himself seems to be attracted and pleased more with
that declamatory type—in which, because we ourselves also were found, let
us allow him to advance by our pathways (for we are confident that he will
arrive at the same place), but still, if we shall have taken him with us to some
place into the country, we shall draw him into this our system and custom.
For a great reward has been offered to us by you, which certainly we shall
never attain to a lesser degree by our own fault. In which localities and with
what hope you are going to be spending winter, I would like that you write
to me as carefully as possible.

> *summe studiosus ... Paeoni*, "super zealous about Paeonius": the adj.
> *studiosus* is used with the gen., as we might say in English "fond of
> someone," here *Paeoni sui rhetoris, hominis ... exercitati ... boni*, "of
> Paeonius, his rhetorician, a man ... trained ... good." Other expressions for
> this in English include "interested in," "in love with," "devoted to." Cicero's
> nephew, Quintus Cicero, is about eleven years old, and Paeonius is his
> teacher.
>
> → **1034** dict., *studiosus, a, um*, adj.

> *Paeoni*, "about Paeonius": this is the spelling of the gen. until the second
> century, because they did not hear two distinct letters "*–ii*," as it came to be
> written *Paeonii*, "of Paeonius."
>
> → **1035** early gen. ending in *–i*, GL n° 33, remark 1.

> *opinor*, "I think": parenthetically inserted into the list of words describing
> Paeonius.
>
> → **1036** verb: deponent, 29.

> *nostrum ... genus esse*, "that our type ... is": OO depending on M & M
> *non ignoras*, a double negative, thus with positive meaning "you realize."
> Because of the super principle in the neuter, the object form used here is the
> same as the subject form.
>
> → **1037** dict., *genus, eris*, n.; neuter: super principle 2;
>   M & M, 60, 71, GL n° 527, remarks 1–2; OO, 71–73.

instituendi, "of educating": gen. gerund depending on *nostrum ... genus,* "our type."

→ **1038** gerund, 77.1.

paullo eruditius, "a little more intellectual": here *eruditius,* "more intellectual," is the comparative adj. in the neuter to agree with *genus,* "type," but the same form is also the comparative adv. The positive adj. here would be *eruditum,* "learned," and the superlative, *eruditissimum,* "most accomplished." The adverbial use *paullo,* usually written *paulo,* is formed from the abl. and means "by a little"; it is often used with the comparative to show the measure of difference, as here.

→ **1039** adj.: comp., 36; adv.: comp., 37; abl.: measure, 90.3, GL nº 403.

Θετικώτερον, "*more ... subtle*": the equivalent of *subtilius,* "more subtle."

→ **1040** Bibliography: *Onomasticon Tullianum*;
         Greek expressions, pp. 623–626.

neque ego, "neither do I": *neque* means *et non,* "and not." It correlates this sentence with the previous sentence; it does not correlate with *atque* further along in the sentence.

→ **1041** dict., *neque,* adv. and conj., I.... "and not."

Qua re, "For which reason": as in the manuscript in part I, often written as one word *quare,* "by what means," "why."

→ **1042** dict., *quare* or *qua re,* adv.

impediri ... iter ... disciplinam, "that [Cicero's] pathway ... training ... be impeded": OO depending on verb of M & M, *volo,* "I [do not wish]." Note that both acc. subjects follow the passive infinitive.

→ **1043** M & M, 60, 71, GL nº 527, remarks 1–2; OO, 71–73.

atque, "and": joins *iter ... disciplinam,* "pathway ... training program," and does not correlate with *neque,* "and not," "neither."

→ **1044** conjunction: *atque,* 3.2.

ipse puer ... duci et delectari videtur, "the boy himself seems to be attracted and pleased": personal use of *videtur,* "the boy seems." The Romans preferred this personal use of *videtur,* where its subject *ipse puer* is also the nom. subject of the infinitives *duci* and *delectari,* instead of the impersonal use composed of the acc. and inf., as in *ipsum puerum ... duci et delectari videtur,* "it seems that the boy himself is attracted and pleased." The two passive infinitives are *duci,* "to be attracted," and *delectari,* "to be pleased."

→ **1045** personal construction: *videor,* 73.3, GL nº 528.1 and remark 2 and note 1;
         nom. with the inf., 73.3, GL nº 528.1;
         contemporaneous passive infinitive, 72.3.

magis, "[to be pleased] more": the comparative adv. *magis*, "more so," is an irregular form; the positive is *magnopere* and the superlative is *maxime*.

→ **1046** adv.: irregular comp., 37.3, GL n° 93.

quoniam … fuimus, "because we … were": T.4b is used to indicate the opinion of the speaker. Reported or another's opinion would be expressed here with T.3s *fuerimus*, "we [allegedly] were," on Track I.

→ **1047** causal: *quoniam*, "because, since," + indicative, one's own reason, 59.2;
causal: *quoniam*, "because, since," + subjunctive, reported reason, 59.2.

patiamur, "let us allow": T.1s; one letter makes all the difference: T.3i *patiemur*, "we shall allow," T.1i *patimur* "we do allow."

→ **1048** dict., *patior, passus*, 3.

illum ire, "him to advance": OO depending on M & M *patiamur*, "let us allow."

→ **1049** M & M, 60, 71, GL n° 527, remarks 1–2; OO, 71–73.

Note: the expression *puer … duci et delectari videtur* uses the personal construction where *puer*, the subject of the infinitives *duci* and *delectari*, has been made the subject of the personal verb *videtur*, but the same sentence also includes *patiamur* used as a verb of M & M producing OO with the acc. subject *illum* and inf. *ire*, to say *patiamur illum ire*. Both the nom. with the inf. and the acc. with the inf. appear in this one sentence.

→ **1050** personal construction: *videor*, 73.3, GL n° 528.1 and remark 2 and note 1;
nom. with the inf., 73.3, GL n° 528.1;
M & M, 60, 71, GL n° 527, remarks 1–2; OO, 71–73.

eodem, "at the same place": adv. meaning "to the same place"; this used to be a dative but is now considered an adverb.

→ **1051** dict., *eodem*, adv.

perventurum esse, "that he will arrive": OO depending on M & M *confidimus*, "we are confident." The acc. subject *eum*, "he," is implied in the idea expressed. Futurity in OO is specified by the futurity participle *perventurum*, "about to arrive," "going to arrive," "on the point of arriving" coupled with the infinitive *esse*, "to be." We can add the other infinitives possible and their meaning here: the contemporaneous inf. *pervenire*, "he is getting to the same place"; antecedent inf. *pervenisse*, "he has arrived at the same place."

→ **1052** M & M, 60, 71, GL n° 527, remarks 1–2; OO, 71–73.

rus aliquo, "to some place into the country": *rus* is the acc. of place to which; *aliquo* used to be a dative but is now considered an adv. meaning "to some place." We could change the expression to *ad rus aliquod,* "to some country estate."

→ **1053** dict., *aliquis, aliquid,* indef. subst. pron., *aliquo,* adv., old dat.; function: place to where, *rus,* 69.1.3.

quam … adsequemur, "which … we shall … attain": a relative clause where *quam,* "which," is the object of *adsequemur* and its antecedent is *merces,* "a … reward."

→ **1054** rel. pron.: subject or object, 10.

qua spe hiematurus sis, "with what hope you are going to be spending winter": IQ in T.1s depending on *scribas,* "that you write," in T.1s itself a purpose clause without *ut* depending on *velim,* "I would like" in T.1s establishing Track I. The futurity formula *hiematurus sis* means "you are going to winter over," "you will spend the winter," that is, to remain with Caesar in wintery Gaul. We can play with this expression to produce the other times possible and their meaning here: contemporary or subsequent to the writing is *qua spe hiemes,* "with what hope you are spending the winter"; antecedent to the writing is *qua spe hiemaveris,* "with what hope you wintered over." These are the possibilities on Track I.

→ **1055** M & M, 60, 71, GL n° 527, remarks 1–2; IQ, 60; subjunctive use: purpose clause without *ut,* 58, GL n° 546, remark 2.

quam diligentissime, "as carefully as possible": here *quam* is an adv. followed by the superlative and means "as much as possible." We can play with this statement to make a question, *quam diligenter,* "how diligently?," where *quam* is an interrogative meaning "how?"; we can also say, *diligentius quam,* "more diligently than," where *quam* is part of a comparison between two equal elements.

→ **1056** *quam* with the comp. or superl., 43.

LETTER 189 T-P
AD ATTICUM V, 6

CICERO ATTICO SAL.

Tarentum veni a. d. XV Kal. Iunias. Quod Pomptinum statueram exspectare, commodissimum duxi dies eos, quoad ille veniret, cum Pompeio consumere, eoque magis quod ei gratum esse id videbam, qui etiam a me petierit ut secum et apud se essem cotidie: quod concessi libenter. Multos enim
eius praeclaros de re publica sermones accipiam, instruar etiam consiliis
idoneis ad hoc nostrum negotium.   (*Att.* V, 6, 1)

CICERO A GREETING TO ATTICUS

I came to Taranto on the fifteenth day before the June Kalends [18 May]. Because I had decided to wait for Pomptinus, I thought it most convenient to
spend those days, until he would come, with Pompeius, and all the more so
because I was noticing this is pleasing to him, because he asked of me also
that I be with him and at his house every day: that which I willingly allowed.
For I shall take in his many brilliant discourses about the republic, also I
shall be instructed with suitable ideas for this our business.

CICERO ATTICO SAL.: *Cicero Attico salutem*

Tarentum, "to Taranto": the form of motion toward the end of a journey, in
this case the town in southern Italy Taranto.
> → **1057** function: place to where, 69.1.2.

a. d. XV Kal. Iunias, "on the fifteenth day before the June Kalends": the full
form is *ante diem quintum decimum Kalendas Iunias*.
> → **1058** about the Roman calendar, pp. 605–608;
>   GL appendix: Roman Calendar, pp. 491–92.

commodissimum duxi dies eos … consumere, "I thought it most convenient
to spend those days": the tendency is to understand *duxi* to mean "I led," but
here *duxi*, in T.4b, functions as a verb of M & M producing a statement in
OO where the gerund in the object form *consumere* functions as the subject

of an implied inf. *esse* and then *commodissimum* agrees with the gerund
taken as a neuter singular noun, which means "spending those days [to be]
most convenient." The whole expression can also be rendered as "I thought
that spending those days was most convenient." The object of the gerund
consumere is *dies eos*, "spending those days."

> → **1059** dict., *duco, xi, ctum*, 3., II., B., 4., b., (β), "to consider,"—with acc. + inf.;
> M & M, 60, 71, GL n° 527, remarks 1–2; OO, 71–73; gerund, 77.1.

quoad ille veniret, "until he would come": the reason for the subjunctive, *veniret*, "he would come," in T.2s is either by MA because the phrase depends
upon the statement in OO and is closely involved in the whole sentence,
which would be rendered in English in the ind., as in "until he comes." Or it
is in the subjunctive following *quoad*, "until," because the whole expression
indicates the uncertainty of when and even whether he will come, in which
case the subjunctive is expressed in the English as in "until he might some
day come."

> → **1060** subjunctive use: modal attraction, 83;
> *quoad* with an uncertain outcome, 65.2.2.

eoque magis, "and all the more": here *eo* is an abl. of degree of difference or
of measure and means "by that degree," and *eo magis* means "by that
degree more." The form *magis* is an adv. of degree, meaning "to a greater
degree," "more so," "more." The dict. explains that *magis* is an anomalous
form for the adv. A synonym would be *tantoque magis*, "by so much more."
The *–que*, "and," attached to the end of *eo*, joins both *quod* statements,
Quod ... statueram, "because I had decided" and *quod ... videbam*,
"because I was noticing."

> → **1061** abl.: measure, 90.3, GL n° 403; conjunction: *–que*, 3.2;
> dict., *magnus, a, um*, adj., II., B., 3....—*magis*, adv. comp., *magis*, "more";
> adv.: irregular comp., 37.3, GL n° 93.

ei gratum esse id videbam, "I saw this is pleasing to him": the verb *videbam*,
"I was noticing," in T.2i is a verb of M & M that gives rise to a statement in
OO where *id* in the object form functions as the subject of *esse*, and agrees
with *gratum* in the predicate, "this to be pleasing." The adj. *gratum*, "pleasing," is complemented by the natural dat. *ei*, "to him."

> → **1062** M & M, 60, 71, GL n° 527, remarks 1–2; OO, 71–73;
> natural dat., 33.7.1.

ei gratum esse id videbam, qui ... a me petierit, "I was noticing this is pleasing to him, because he asked of me": the reason for the subjunctive *petierit*,
"he asked," in T.3s is because this is a relative causal sentence where *qui*
stands for *cum is*, "because he [asked]" or "inasmuch as he asked."

> → **1063** subjunctive use: causal *qui, quae, quod* = "because, since," 59.4.

The explanation for the sequence of tenses here is as follows. The main
verb *videbam*, "I was noticing," in T.2i sets the sentence on Track II, and as a

verb of M & M it gives rise to a sentence in OO *ei gratum esse id*, "that this is pleasing to him," where the inf. *esse* is not only contemporaneous with *videbam*, which would logically produce the clause *qui me petivisset*, "because he asked of me." Here, however, Cicero's text unexpectedly uses *petierit*, "he asked of me," in T.3s, and thus on Track I. If we are forced to defend Cicero from conservative grammarians, one justification is that *gratum esse* is not only contemporaneous, but also open ended, ongoing, incomplete and here is equivalent to T.1s, meaning "it is pleasing to him," because Cicero is taking *gratum esse* out of the historical context and saying that right up to the present moment it has been and indeed is pleasing to him, which would produce *petierit*, "because he asked" in T.3s on Track I. There is no note explaining the text in either Tyrrell and Purser nor in the Oxford edition. Shackleton Bailey points to the word *cotidie*, "every day," suggesting continuance into the present moment of writing the letter.

→ **1064** M & M, 60, 71, GL n° 527, remarks 1–2; OO, 71–73;
  consecutio, 47–48.

Another possibility is that *videbam*, "I was noticing," is in the epistolary tense. That is Cicero is writing about what he was at that very moment noticing, from the later perspective of the reader. It is as though Cicero were writing *video*, "I am noticing," which would be in T.1i, establishing the sentence on Track I. The epistolary tense tends to be used with only one or a few verbs at the beginning of a thought, and does not continue throughout a letter, as here where Cicero continues the sentence on Track I with *petierit*, "he asked," in T.3s.

→ **1065** letter-writer tense, GL n° 252.

petierit ut ... essem cotidie, "he asked ... that I be ... every day": the act of requesting is stated as *petierit*, "he asked," in T.3s, and thus to that point the sentence is on Track I. But the asking occurred in the past and so the content or concept of *petierit* produces a purpose clause on Track II expressing the intention of the request, *ut ... essem*, "that I be," where *essem* is in T.2s.

→ **1066** subjunctive use: purpose clause, 58.1;
  consecutio: subjunctive depending on a subjunctive, 62.1.

quod concessi libenter, "that which I willingly allowed": the antecedent of *quod*, "something which," a relative pronoun, is the whole sentence before it. Here *quod* does not stand for *aliquod*, "something," the indefinite pronoun.

→ **1067** rel. pron.: subject or object, 10;
  quod referring to previous sentence: GL n° 614, remark 2.

accipiam, instruar, "I shall take ... I shall be instructed": both verbs in T.3i, the first T.3i active, the second T.3i pass. This gives us opportunity to flip these verbs from active to passive and vice versa to say, *accipiar, instruam*, "I shall be accepted ... I shall instruct."

→ **1068** verb formation T.3 in groups III and IV, 12.3.2;
  passive Times 1, 2, 3 indicative, 21;
  T.3i and T.3i: GL n° 242, remark 1, example.

❧

Sed ad te brevior iam in scribendo incipio fieri, dubitans Romaene sis an iam profectus. Quod tamen quoad ignorabo, scribam aliquid potius quam committam ut tibi, cum possint reddi a me litterae, non reddantur. Nec tamen iam habeo quod aut mandem tibi aut narrem. Mandavi omnia, quae quidem tu, ut polliceris, exhauries: narrabo, cum aliquid habebo novi. Illud tamen non desinam, dum adesse *te* putabo, de Caesaris nomine rogare, ut confectum relinquas. Avide exspecto tuas litteras et maxime ut norim tempus profectionis tuae.   (*Att.* V, 6, 2)

But I am already beginning to become shorter in writing to you, doubting whether you are in Rome or already have set out; which thing, however, as long as I shall not know, I shall write something rather than I should allow that letters not be delivered to you, although they are able to be delivered from me. Right now, however, I do not have something which I may order or narrate to you. I have instructed all the things which indeed you will carry out as you promise: I shall report when I shall have some bit of news. However, as long as I shall think you are nearby, I shall not stop at that one thing, to ask about Caesar's financial affair so that you leave the business finished. Eagerly I am waiting for your letter and especially that I may know the time of your departure.

> *Sed ... brevior iam ... incipio fieri*, "But I am already beginning to become shorter": the main verb here is *incipio*, "I am beginning," whose object is *fieri*, "to be made," or "to become," a gerund. The form *brevior*, "shorter," is a comparative adjective and agrees with *ego*, "I," the subject of *incipio*, "I am beginning."
>
> → **1069** verb: complementary infinitive, 77; gerund, 77.1; adj.: comp., 36.

> *ad te ... in scribendo*, "in writing to you": the gerund *scribendo*, "writing," is in the abl. after the preposition *in*, "in writing," and its complement is *ad te*, "to you," which appears at the beginning of the sentence and is separated by two words.
>
> → **1070** gerund, 77.1; prep. with abl., 28.4; sentence structure, 1.

Note the interweaving of words that go together

| **main sentence** | *Sed* | ... | *brevior iam* | ... | *incipio fieri* |
| **gerund expression** | | *ad te* | ... | *in scribendo* | |

> → **1071** sentence structure, 1.

> *dubitans*, "doubting": this contemporaneous participle agrees with the same subject of the previous verbs, the implied *ego*, "I."
>
> → **1072** contemporaneous active participle, 50, 51.1.1.

Romaene sis an iam profectus, "whether you are in Rome or already have set
out": the participle *dubitans* is a verbal expression of M & M giving rise to
an IQ where the question word is *–ne*, "whether," attached to the first word
of the IQ *Romae*, which functions as the place where or in which, "at Rome."
The verb *sis*, "you are," in T.1s is due to the IQ. The full implied form of the
second verb is *profectus sis*, "you have set out," in T.3s. He is very clever to
use the same form *sis* both as a full verb in T.1s and as part of a verb in T.3s:
two so completely different verbs and verbal times with completely different
meanings.

> → **1073** M & M, 60, 71, GL n° 527, remarks 1–2; IQ, 60;
> forms of the subjunctive, T.1s, 44.1; forms of the subjunctive, T.3s, 44.3;
> passive and deponent forms of T.3s, 46;
> disjunctive question: *–ne*, GL n° 458;
> function: place at which, names of cities and small islands, singular,
> *Romae*, 69.3.2.

Quod ... quoad ignorabo, "which thing ... as long as I shall not know": here
quoad, "as long as," is followed by *ignorabo*, "I shall not know," in T.1i, and
so expresses a definite time as in "as long as I shall not know." The object
of the verb is *Quod*, "[I shall not know] which thing," the first word in the
sentence appearing even before the *quoad*, and so functioning as a relative
connective, meaning almost, "And which thing as long as I shall not know
it."

> → **1074** *quoad* with ind., 65.2.2;
> relative clauses, 10–11;
> dict., *qui, quae, quod*, pron., II., C. a connective instead of *is, ea, id* with a
> conj.

scribam aliquid potius quam committam, "I shall write something rather
than I should allow": here *scribam*, "I shall write," is in T.3i. The comparison begins with the expression *potius quam*, "rather than," which takes the
subjunctive, here *committam*, "I should allow," in T.1s, although this is the
same form as T.3i.

> → **1075** *quam* with the comp., 43.2.

committam ut tibi ... non reddantur, "I should allow that letters not be
delivered to you": at first sight people may misunderstand the verb *committam* to mean "I should commit." Rather here we have rendered *committam*
as "I should allow," in light of the definition in the dictionary "I should
give occasion"; it is in T.1s establishing Track I, and produces a clause that
describes the result of Cicero's allowing, *ut ... reddantur*, "that [letters] not
be delivered," in T.1s passive.

> → **1076** dict., *committo, misi, missum*, 3., I., B., 4., (δ). with *ut*, "to give occasion,
> cause";
> subjunctive use: complementary result (consecutive), 68.1;
> *consecutio*: subjunctive depending on a subjunctive, 62.1.

cum possint reddi a me litterae, "although they are able to be delivered from
me": here *cum* followed by *possint* in T.1s can mean "because" or "although."

Note that the form *reddi*, "to be delivered," is the contemporaneous inf. in the passive, whose active form is *reddere*. Here *a me*, "from me," could also mean "by me" if Cicero were the letter carrier!

> → **1077** subjunctive use: causal *cum* = "because, since," 59.1;
> subjunctive use: concessive *cum* = "although," 64;
> verb: contemporaneous passive infinitive, 72.3;
> verb: contemporaneous active infinitive, 72.1;
> prep. + abl. of separation or agent, 28.5.2.

habeo quod aut mandem tibi aut narrem, "I do [not] have something which I may order or narrate to you": both *mandem*, "I may order," and *narrem*, "I may narrate," are in T.1s because this is a relative sentence of characteristic result where *quod* stands for *tale ut id aut mandem tibi aut narrem*. A Latin sentence of result is rendered in English in the ind., but here there is an underlying potential, which is expressed in English in the subjunctive, "such that I may order or narrate it to you."

> → **1078** subjunctive use: characteristic result, 68.2;
> subjunctive use: underlying potential of the present or future, 94.3,
> GL n° 257.

ut polliceris, exhauries, "you will carry out as you promise": the form *exhauries*, "you will carry out," is T.3i. Here *ut* is followed by *polliceris*, "you promise," which is T.1i of a deponent verb, and so *ut* here means "as." We can reverse both of these as *pollicemini*, "you all promise," and *exhaurietis*, "you all will carry out," and this reveals how we understand the original forms.

> → **1079** verb meaning T.1, T.2, T.3, 7; verb formation T.1, T.2, T.3, 12;
> verb: deponent, 29; dict., *ut*, I., B. meaning "as."

narrabo, cum aliquid habebo novi, "I shall report when I shall have some bit of news": the verb *narrabo*, "I shall report," is T.3i. Here *cum* followed by *habebo*, "I shall have," in T.3i means "when"; both "because" and "although" are excluded because of the ind. verb. The word *novi*, "of news," is a gen. of part separated, as typical, from the word on which it depends, here *aliquid*, meaning "something of news" or "some bit of news."

> → **1080** verb formation T.3 in groups I and II, 12.3.1;
> *cum* + indicative = "when": temporal sentences, 66.3; gen. of part, 99.

Illud ... non desinam ... de Caesaris nomine rogare, "I shall not stop at that one thing, to ask about Caesar's financial affair": the main verb *desinam*, "I shall not stop," in T.3i, has as its object the pronoun *Illud*, "that one thing," whose content is given in the gerund *rogare*, "asking" or "to ask." A *nomen* is a "financial debt," "stock bond," "promissory note," according to the dict. A little outside research can discover the financial affairs that Cicero is talking about here, while we remain focused here on his manner of Latin expression.

> → **1081** verb formation T.3 in groups III and IV, 12.3.2; gerund, 77.1;
> three cousins: *iste–ille–ipse*, 41.3;
> dict., *nomen, inis*, n., I., B., 2. "a bond, debt."

dum adesse te putabo, "as long as I shall think you nearby": the verb *putabo*, "I shall think," in T.3i, is a verb of M & M producing a sentence in OO where *te* in the object form functions as the subject of the inf. *adesse*, "you to be present" or "you to be nearby."

> → **1082** M & M, 60, 71, GL n° 527, remarks 1–2; OO, 71–73.

rogare, ut confectum relinquas, "to ask … that you leave the business finished": the gerund *rogare*, "to ask," produces a purpose clause that gives the intent in asking, *ut … relinquas*, "that you leave." Here *confectum* is a participle meaning "having been settled," "having been completed," and it agrees with *nomen*, "financial affair."

> → **1083** gerund, 77.1; subjunctive use: purpose clause, 58.1;
> antecedent participle, 50, 51.1.2; dict., *conficio, feci, fectum*, 3.

exspecto … ut norim, "I am waiting … that I may know": Cicero's intention in waiting for the letter is given in a purpose clause, *ut norim*, in which the form *norim* is a syncopated form of *noverim*, in T.3s, with present meaning because this verb *novi* in T.4i means "I have gotten to know" or "I have come to know" and thus in the present, "I know," as described in the dict. This is a defective verb with an extremely rare present system, thus the perfect system has to work for the present.

> → **1084** subjunctive use: purpose clause, 58.1;
> contractions: verbs, 39.2, GL n° 131;
> dict., *nosco, novi, notum*, 3, "to come to know."

LETTER 281 T-P
AD ATTICUM VI, 8

CICERO ATTICO SAL.

Cum instituissem ad te scribere calamumque sumpsissem, Batonius e navi recta ad me venit domum Ephesi et epistulam tuam reddidit pridie Kal. Octobris. Laetatus sum felicitate navigationis tuae, opportunitate Piliae, etiam hercule sermone eiusdem de coniugio Tulliae meae.   (*Att.* VI, 8, 1)

CICERO A GREETING TO ATTICUS

When I had begun to write to you and had taken up a pen, Batonius came home to me in Ephesus by a straight road from the ship and he delivered your letter on the day before the Kalends of October [30 September]. I was happy about the success of your sailing, and the opportune meeting of Pilia, even, by george, the talk of the same woman about the marriage of my Tullia.

CICERO ATTICO SAL.: *Cicero Attico salutem*

Cum instituissem ad te scribere calamumque sumpsissem, "When I had begun to write to you and had taken a pen": the main verb is *venit*, "[Batonius] came," in T.4b and establishing Track II. Here *cum* followed by *instituissem*, "I had begun," and *sumpsissem*, "I had taken up," both in T.4s, can mean "because" or "although" or it can give the temporal circumstance for another action "when," as here. The object of *instituissem* is the gerund *scribere*, "[I had begun] writing" or "[I had begun] to write." The *–que*, "and," is attached to the end of the first word of the second element and joins the two verbs *instituissem* and *sumpsissem*.

> → **1085** subjunctive use: temporal circumstance *cum* = "when," 66.3.2;
> subjunctive use: causal *cum* = "because, since," 59.1;
> subjunctive use: concessive *cum* = "although," 64;
> *consecutio*, 47–48; gerund, 77.1; conjunction: *–que*, 3.2.

e navi recta, "by a straight road from the ship": the phrase does not mean "from a straight ship" and the two words *navi recta* do not go together. Rather, *recta* goes with an implied *via*, "by a straight road," "on a straight path," meaning "directly"; see the dict. where you will find *rectā* with a long *ā*, but no noun around and it means all by itself, "by a straight road." The preposition *e*, "out of," "from," goes with *navi*, "from the ship."

> → **1086** dict., *rectā*, v.: *rego, xi, ctum*, 3,—adv., *rectā* (undoubtedly *viā*), "directly"; sentence structure, 1; prep. with abl., 28.4.

domum Ephesi, "home ... in Ephesus": the form *domum* all alone means "to home" and gives the place of destination. The form *Ephesi* is the place where or at which, also called the loc., "in Ephesus."

> → **1087** function: place to where, *domum*, 69.1.3;
> function: place at which, names of cities and small islands, singular, *Ephesi*, 69.3.2.

pridie Kal. Octobris, "on the day before the Kalends of October ": the full form is *pridie Kalendas Octobris*. The classical practice is to say *Kalendas Octobres*, "the October Kalends," where *Octobres* is an adj. that agrees with *Kalendas*. Here *Octobris* is an alternative form for *Octobres*. In passing we should say that in later Latin and church Latin and even today we use *Octobris*, "of October," as a noun in the form of-possession also called the gen.

> → **1088** about the Roman calendar, pp. 605–608;
> GL appendix: Roman Calendar, pp. 491–92;
> function: of-possession, 20.

༄

Batonius autem meros terrores ad me attulit Caesarianos, cum Lepta etiam plura locutus est, spero falsa, sed certe horribilia, exercitum nullo modo dimissurum, cum illo praetores designatos, Cassium tribunum pl., Lentulum consulem facere, Pompeio in animo esse urbem relinquere.   (*Att.* VI, 8, 2)

However, Batonius has brought to me pure Caesarian horrors, and he has discussed with Lepta quite a few things, I hope false, but certainly terrifying: that he [Caesar] is in no way going to disband the army; that the designated praetors, Cassius the tribune of the people [and] Lentulus the Consul, are acting with him [Caesar]; that it is in the mind of Pompeius to abandon the city of Rome.

> *terrores ad me attulit ... cum Lepta etiam plura locutus est*, "[Batonius] has brought to me ... horrors, and he has discussed with Lepta quite a few things": Cicero tells of receiving the news of Caesarian horrors from Batonius when Cicero says: *terrores ad me attulit*, "[Batonius] has brought to me ... horrors," in T.4a. The content of these Caesarian horrors was also the subject of discussion between Batonius and Lepta, as Cicero says: *locutus*

est, "he has discussed," also in T.4a. Then Cicero gives this content in three expressions composed in indirect discourse.

→ **1089** verb meaning T.4a, 7; verb formation T.4a, 8.2; M & M, 60, 71;
GL n° 527, remarks 1–2.

The first of these three statements in OO involves the inf., whose full implied form is *dimissurum esse*, with the subsequent active participle, *dimissurum*, "about to disband," "on the verge of disbanding," "on the point of disbanding," and its subject is an implied *Caesarem*, "Caesar to be about to disband," and its object is *exercitum*, "the army."

→ **1090** OO, 71–73; futurity participle, 50, 51.1.3;
verb: subsequent active infinitive, 72.1.

If the above controlling verbs, *attulit* and *locutus est*, are both understood to be in T.4a, that is, touching on the present, then the contemporaneous infinitive *esse* can mean "is [in no way going to disband the army]," expressing the immediate and present telling of the horrors that have been just now brought and discussed, as in our translation. Otherwise, if the two controlling verbs are T.4b, considered as past events not touching on the present, then the infinitive *esse* is translated as "was [in no way going to disband the army]," and the entire story is set in the past and recounts the past receiving of the news and discussing it with Lepta.

→ **1091** verb: T.4a, T.4b, 8.

cum illo praetores designatos, Cassium tribunum pl., Lentulum consulem facere, "that the designated praetors, Cassius the tribune of the people [and] Lentulus the Consul, are acting with him [Caesar]": the subject of the first of these three statements in OO was an implied Caesar. The change of subject in the second of these statements in OO is indicated initially by *cum illo*, "with him [Caesar]." The *praetores* in the object form function as the subject of the inf. *facere*, which is contemporaneous to the two verbs in T.4a given previously in the sentence, thus here *facere* can express the present telling of the news just received and thus mean "are acting [with him]." The participle *designatos*, "designated," is not part of the verb, rather it has become part of a technical term such as "praetors designate." The abbreviation *pl.* stands for *plebis*, "of the people."

When a statement in OO involves an abundance of object forms it may be difficult if not impossible to identify with clarity which object form functions as the subject of the verb and which functions as its object. This is heightened here with the word *facere*, which can mean "to act [with him]" or "to make" as in "to make Cassius a tribune, to make Lentulus a consul." A thorough knowledge of history is needed to fill out the story mentioned only partially in these letters. But even then there are few assurances. If you give only a cursory reading to this phrase: Good luck!

→ **1092** OO, 71–73;
dict., *designo* or *dissigno, avi, atum*, 1, II., B., 2., b. *designatus*, "elect";
dict., *plebs, bis*, f.

Pompeio in animo esse urbem relinquere, "that it is in the mind of Pompeius to abandon the city of Rome": the third of these statements in OO involves the gerund *relinquere*, "to abandon," "abandoning," whose object is *urbem*, "[abandoning] the city." The expression *urbem relinquere* functions as the subject of the inf. *esse*, "[abandoning the city] is." The form *Pompeio* is a dat. of personal interest, meaning "as far as Pompeius is concerned," which in effect means here "in the mind of Pompeius." An example from the field of sport is to say, "that was a good pitch for you," where "for you" is the dat. of personal interest.

→ **1093** OO, 71–73; dat. of personal interest, GL n° 350.

☙

Sed heus tu, num quid moleste fers de illo, qui se solet anteferre patruo sororis tuae fili? At a quibus victus! Sed ad rem.   (*Att.* VI, 8, 3)

But, hey you, don't you take it badly about him [Caesar], who is accustomed to prefer himself to the uncle of the son of your sister? And beaten by whom!? But to the matter.

num quid, "don't": the expression *num quid*, also written as one word *numquid*, as in the manuscript in part I, is the same as *num*, anticipating a negative answer, as in the expressions, "you don't mean to say that … ," "surely not … ," "of course not …."

→ **1094** dict., *numquid*, adv. interrog.; ways of asking, 13.1.

moleste fers, "you take it badly": the expression, where *fers* means "you take," "you bear," in T.1i, as a whole means "you take badly," "you take amiss." The dict. entry for *molestus, a, um*, gives *moleste fero*, "I take it ill," "it vexes me," "it annoys me."

→ **1095** dict., *molestus, a, um*, adj., II., B., 1.

se … anteferre patruo, "to prefer himself to the uncle": the compound verb *ante–ferre* means "to bear before," "to place before," thus "to prefer." As a compound verb, its complement *patruo*, "the uncle," is in the dat., which can be difficult to hear in English. We can reconstruct the expression to say *ferre ante patruum*, "to bear before the uncle," but when the preposition *ante* is attached as the prefix to *ferre*, then its object, *patruum*, becomes the dat. complement of the compound verb.

→ **1096** dat. with compound verbs, 33.7.3, GL n° 347.

patruo sororis tuae fili, "to the uncle of the son of your sister": namely Cicero. Caesar prefers himself to Cicero.

At a quibus victus!, "And beaten by whom!?": the difference between
an exclamation and a question is fine and often conveyed in the tone of
voice—O to hear such a voice!

→ **1097** exclamations, GL n° 343.1.

☙

Nos etesiae vehementissime tardarunt. Detraxit XX ipsos dies etiam
aphractus Rhodiorum. Kal. Octobr. Epheso conscendentes hanc epistulam
dedimus L. Tarquitio, simul e portu egredienti sed expeditius naviganti.
Nos Rhodiorum aphractis ceterisque longis navibus tranquilitates aucupaturi eramus: ita tamen properabamus ut non posset magis.   (*Att.* VI, 8, 4)

The trade winds slowed us down very significantly. Also the longboat of
the Rhodians took us off course exactly 20 days. On the October Kalends
[1 October], we, boarding the ship out of Ephesus, gave this letter to Lucius
Tarquitius, leaving at the same time from the harbor but sailing more lightly. We are about to watch for calm seas with the longboats of the Rhodians
and other warships, nevertheless we are hastening in such a way that more
is not possible.

tardarunt, "[winds] slowed [us] down": a contraction of *tardaverunt* in T.4b.
→ **1098** contractions: verbs, 39.2, GL n° 131.

XX ipsos dies, "exactly 20 days": *dies* is in the object form to indicate extent
of time. *ipsos* adds the idea of "exactly," "precisely."
→ **1099** acc.: time during which, 70.2.

Kal. Octobr., "On the October Kalends [1 October]": the full form is *Kalendis*
Octobribus, in the abl. of time at which and rendered into English as above.
→ **1100** abl.: time at which, 70.1.

Epheso, "out of Ephesus": the name of the town in the abl. without a preposition, meaning "from Ephesus."
→ **1101** function: place from where, names of cities and small islands, *Epheso*,
       69.2.2;
    abl. separation from place, 27.

expeditius, "more lightly": here the comparative degree of the adv., but the
same form as the comparative degree of the adjective in the neuter.
→ **1102** adv.: positive, comp., superl., 37; adj.: comp., 36.

aucupaturi eramus: ita … properabamus ut non posset magis, "We are about
to watch … we are hastening in such a way that more is not possible": all
three verbs are in the epistulary tense. While writing the letter, he thinks,
"*aucupaturi sumus,*" "we are about to watch," the futurity formula in T.1i,
but then he takes the perspective of Atticus reading the letter a few days

later and he puts the verb typically in T.2i, here *aucupaturi eramus*, literally, "we were about to watch," but its meaning remains "we are about to watch" as in the translation. The deponent verb *aucupor, atus, 1*, produces the future active participle *aucupaturi* with both active form and active meaning all alone, "ones about to watch."

> → **1103** letter-writer tense, GL n° 252;
>   futurity participle, 50, 51.1.3;
>   verb: subsequent active infinitive, 72.1;
>   futurity formula, active, 53.3.

This is the same for *properabamus*, in T.2i, as in "we were hastening," but actually describing the action at the time of writing the letter, thus, "we are hastening." The particle *ita*, "in such a way," prepares for the result clause depending on *properabamus*, namely *ut non posset*, whose verb *posset* is in T.2s, suggesting a translation such as "[we were hastening in such a way] that more was not possible," but once again describing the current action and so, "[we were hastening in such a way] that more is not possible." Typically the epistolary tense is in T.2i, but here we also see *posset* in T.2s. The epistolary tense is difficult to sustain for the whole letter, and so is often used only in the concluding remarks. *magis* is an adv. of degree or measure meaning "to a greater degree," "more so," "more."

> → **1104** letter-writer tense, GL n° 252;
>   subjunctive use: pure result (consecutive), 67.1–2, GL n° 552;
>   abl.: measure, 90.3, GL n° 403; adv.: irregular comp., 37.3, GL n° 93.

⌒

De raudusculo Puteolano gratum. Nunc velim dispicias res Romanas, videas quid nobis de triumpho cogitandum putes, ad quem amici me vocant. Ego, nisi Bibulus qui, dum unus hostis in Syria fuit, pedem porta non plus extulit quam *domi* domo sua, adniteretur de triumpho, aequo animo essem. Nunc vero αἰσχρὸν σιωπᾶν. Sed explora rem totum, ut quo die congressi erimus consilium capere possimus. Sat multa, qui et properarem et ei litteras darem qui aut mecum aut paullo ante venturus esset. Cicero tibi plurimam salutem dicit. Tu dices utriusque nostrum verbis et Piliae tuae et filiae.   (*Att.* VI, 8, 5)

It was pleasing about the brass coin of Puzzuoli. Now I would like you to discern Roman matters, that you see what you consider should be thought by us about a triumph, to which friends are summoning me. I would be of tranquil spirit, if Bibulus, who did not put his foot more outside the town gate than from his own house at home, as long as there was one enemy in Syria, were not working on the triumph. Now, however, *it is shameful to be silent*. But look into the whole matter so that we may be able to make a decision on the day when we will have met. Many things enough, inasmuch as I was both hastening and I was entrusting the letter to him who was about to arrive either with me or a little bit sooner. Cicero [son] says a very big greeting to you. You shall say in the words of each one of us [a greeting] both to your Pilia and your daughter.

> *gratum*, "It was pleasing": the verb is only implied, perhaps *erat*, "it was."
> → **1105** ellipsis—omission of the verb, GL n° 209.

> *velim dispicias*, "I would like you to discern": a favorite expression of Cicero combines *velim*, "I would like," in T.1s with the subjunctive, here *dispicias*, "that you discern," without an intervening *ut*, to give greater emphasis on the wish. The verb *dispicias*, "that you see the difference between things," is sadly confused with the verb *despicere*, with one letter difference, meaning "that you scorn," and so neither is used in elevated formal papal documents.
> → **1106** subjunctive use: purpose clause without *ut*, 58, GL n° 546, remark 2; commands: other expressions, *velim*, 85.1.7; dict., *dispicio, spexi, spectum*, 3; dict., *despicio, exi, ectum*, 3.

> *velim ... videas quid nobis ... cogitandum putes*, "I would like ... that you see what you consider should be thought by us": the verb *velim*, "I would like," in T.1s goes with a second verb *videas*, "that you see," also in T.1s without an intervening *ut*, once again to give greater emphasis on the wish.
> → **1107** subjunctive use: purpose clause without *ut*, 58, GL n° 546, remark 2; commands: other expressions, *velim*, 85.1.7.

Next, *videas*, "that you see" is a verb of M & M which gives rise to an IQ whose interrogatory pronoun *quid* goes with the verb *putes*, "what you consider," in T.1s. In turn, *putes* is a verb of M & M whose complement is an entire statement in OO, whose subject is the same interrogatory word *quid*, "what," and whose verb is given in full as *cogitandum esse*, using the con-temporaneous inf. *esse* with the participle of passive necessity, "needing to be thought" or "should be thought," whose agent is typically in the dat., here *nobis*, "by us." You can see here that *videas* gives rise to an IQ *quid putes*, but that the interrogative pronoun *quid* is itself the subject of *cogitandum*, and so the subject of the subordinate clause in OO depending on *putes*.

> → **1108** M & M, 60, 71, GL n° 527, remarks 1–2; IQ, 60;
> OO, 71–73; dat. of agent, 53.5;
> participle of passive necessity, 50, 51.1.4;
> passive necessity formula, 53.4.

This next sentence offers a good occasion to illustrate the construction of a sentence naturally and without effort by Cicero, which construction shows the importance of subordinated sections and boxes magnificently—while it signifies the apparent challenge and diffuses any terror in first readers and learners.

Ego,	contrary to fact consequence
nisi Bibulus	contrary to fact condition
qui,	relative
dum unus hostis in Syria fuit,	temporal
pedem porta non plus extulit	relative
quam *domi* domo sua,	*plus … quam* comparative
adniteretur de triumpho,	contrary to fact condition
aequo animo essem.	contrary to fact consequence

→ **1109** structure of Latin sentences, 103 p. 587, *Ossa* Readings: 1-D, 1-I, 3-D, 3-I,
4-D, 4-I;
relative box, 11.4.

Ego … essem, "I would be": during the First Encounter of the First Experience of Latin we would not hesitate to point out that the first word of this sentence is the subject of the last word of a three-line sentence. Later in Latin we would point out that *essem*, "I would be," in T.2s is one half of a counter to fact conditional, the consequence, and we can test this by saying, "I would be of tranquil spirit—but I am not."

→ **1110** sentence structure, 1; conditionals: contrary to fact, 86.3.

nisi Bibulus … adniteretur, "if Bibulus were not working": the other half of the contrary to fact condition, the condition is given as a negative clause where *nisi* means "unless" or "if … not," and is followed by *adniteretur*, "were [not] working," in T.2s of the deponent verb *annitor* also written as *adnitor*. Again we can confirm our understanding of this condition by saying, "If Bibulus were not working—but he is, I would be of tranquil spirit—but I am not."

→ **1111** conditionals: contrary to fact, 86.3; verb: deponent, 29.

domi, "at home": this is the form of place where, at which. This works with only a select number of words: *ruri*, "in the country," *humi*, "on the ground."

→ **1112** function: place at which, *domi*, 69.3.3 .

αἰσχρὸν σιωπᾶν, "*it is shameful to be silent*": a fragment from Isocrates, rendered in Latin as *turpe est tacere*, "It is shameful to keep silent."

→ **1113** Bibliography: *Onomasticon Tullianum*;
Greek expressions, pp. 623–626.

explora … ut … possimus, "look into [the whole matter] so that we may be able": a purpose clause where the main verb *explora*, "look," as a direct command establishes Track I producing *possimus*, "we may be able," in T.1s.

→ **1114** subjunctive use: purpose clause, 58.1;
commands: first, second, 17; *consecutio* after command form, GL nº 517.

congressi erimus, "we will have met": T.6i of a deponent verb. The action is logically prior to making a decision, *consilium capere possimus*, "we may be able to make a decision," in T.1s, which is not only contemporaneous with the main verb *explora*, "Look into," but also ongoing, open ended, continuing, unfinished, and future.

> → 1115 *consecutio*: futurity in the subjunctive, 61.1;
> T.3i and T.6i paired: 7, Time 6, and GL n° 244, remark 2;
> verb: deponent, 29.

consilium capere, "to make a decision": the dict. entry for *consilium, ii*, n. gives the expression *consilium capere*, "to form a purpose," "to decide." The form *capere* functions here as a gerund, the object of *possimus*, "we may be able to make a decision."

> → 1116 dict., *consilium, ii*, n., II., A., 1., b., (α). *consilium capere*, "to form a purpose";
> gerund, 77.1; verb: complementary infinitive, 77.

Sat multa, qui et properarem et ... darem, "Many things enough, inasmuch as I was both hastening and I was entrusting": the main verb here is only implied, perhaps *dixi*, "I said," or *scripsi*, "I wrote." The reason for the two verbs in T.2s is for sure because this is a relative causal clause where *qui*, "who," stands for *cum ego*, "because I," "inasmuch as I," as in the translation above.

> → 1117 ellipsis—omission of the verb *dicere*, GL n° 209, note 5;
> subjunctive use: causal *qui, quae, quod* = "because, since," 59.4.

qui ... venturus esset, "who was about to arrive": a causal clause where *qui* stands for *cum is*, "inasmuch as I," "because I," followed here by the futurity formula *venturus esset* in T.2s meaning "because he was about to arrive," "inasmuch as he was going to come."

> → 1118 subjunctive use: causal *qui, quae, quod* = "because, since," 59.4;
> futurity participle, 50, 51.1.3;
> futurity formula, active, 53.3.

plurimam salutem dicit, "[Cicero the son] says a very big greeting to you": here we see spelled out what is often abbreviated at the top of the letters as *s. p. d.*, "*salutem plurimam dicit*." We might make our own sentence from his to say, "Say a greeting to him in my words," *Dic ei meis verbis salutem.*

> → 1119 dict., *salus, tis*, f., I., B.: S. D. P., *salutem dicit plurimam*.

dices, "You shall say": in T.3i this is a light imperative meaning something more than the simple future, "You will say," but "You shall be sure to say" or understood as an imperative in very correct English "You shall say."

> → 1120 commands T.3i, 85.1.6.

utriusque nostrum, "of each one of us": *nostrum* is numerical, thus "of us," and we are several.

> → 1121 *nostri**, *vestri**, 24.6.

LETTER 239 T-P
AD FAMILIARES XV, 10

M. CICERO IMP. S. D. C. MARCELLO C. F. COS.

Quoniam id accidit, quod mihi maxime fuit optatum, ut omnium Marcellorum, Marcellinorum etiam—mirificus enim generis ac nominis vestri
fuit erga me semper animus—quoniam ergo ita accidit ut omnium vestrum
studio tuus consulatus satis facere posset, in quem meae res gestae lausque
et honos earum potissimum incideret, peto a te id, quod facillimum factu
est non aspernante, ut confido, senatu, ut quam honorificentissime senatus
consultum litteris meis recitatis faciundum cures.   (*Fam.* XV, 10, 1)

MARCUS CICERO COMMANDER SAYS A GREETING TO
GAIUS MARCELLUS THE SON OF GAIUS, CONSUL

Because that thing happened, which was most acceptable to me, that of all
the Marcelluses, even the Marcellinuses—for the attitude of your family and
name has always been wonderful toward me—because therefore it so happened that your consulship was able to satisfy the zeal of all of you, with
which my exploits and their praise and honor was most especially coinciding, I ask of you that which is the easiest thing to do—the senate not rejecting, as I trust—that you take care realizing the decision of the senate most
honorably as possible, after my letter has been recited.

M. Cicero imp. s. d. C. Marcello C. f. cos.: *Marcus Cicero imperator
salutem dicit Gaio Marcello Gaii filio consuli*

f., "the son": as in the inscription on the façade of the Pantheon, f. stands
for FILIUS.
→ **1122** dict. entry for the letter F: the abbreviation "F" stands for "*fili ... filius.*"

Cicero's expression is very eloquent and he obviously wants to use lavish
speech in the hope of obtaining a triumph in Rome. Here is the box effect of
the first paragraph in one gorgeous Latin sentence:

Quoniam id accidit,	causal
quod mihi maxime fuit optatum,	relative 1
ut omnium Marcellorum, Marcellinorum etiam	result 1
(—mirific<u>us</u> enim generis ac nominis vestri	parenth. 1
<u>fuit</u> erga me semper animus—	
quoniam ergo ita accidit	resumed causal
(ut omnium vestrum studio tuus consulatus	result 2
satis facere posset,	
(in quem meae res gestae lausque et	relative MA
honos earum potissimum incideret,	
peto a te id,	main sentence
quod facillimum factu est	relative 3
non aspernante,	AA 1
ut confido,	parenthetical 2
senatu,	AA 1 continued
ut quam honorificentissime	purpose
senatus consultum	gerundive
litteris meis recitatis	AA 2
faciundum	gerundive continued
cures.	purpose continued

→ **1123** structure of Latin sentences, 103 p. 587, *Ossa* Readings: 1-D, 1-I, 3-D, 3-I,
    4-D, 4-I;
    relative box, 11.4.

Note: Just about the whole sequence of tenses is represented in this one
sentence. The main verb *peto*, "I ask," in T.1i establishes Track I. Depending
on *peto*, the sentence begins with *accidit*, "it happened," in T.4b, shifting the
first part of the sentence to Track II, thus producing *posset*, "was able," and
in MA *incideret*, "was coinciding." The second half of the sentence continues
from *peto*, "I ask," producing a purpose clause *ut … cures*, "that you take
care," in T.1s, with three parenthetical clauses intervening, the relative *quod
… est*, "that which is"; and an AA, *non aspernante … senatu*, "the senate not
rejecting"; and *ut confido*, "as I hope."

→ **1124** *consecutio*, 47–48;
    consecutio: subjunctive depending on a subjunctive, 62.1;
    subjunctive use: complementary result (consecutive), 68.1;
    subjunctive use: modal attraction, 83; subjunctive use: purpose clause, 58.1;
    relative clauses, 10–11; ablative absolute, 54–55;
    dict., *ut*, I., B. meaning "as."

Quoniam … accidit … quoniam ergo … accidit, "Because [that thing]
happened … because therefore it happened": the causal clause begins and
then is interrupted, and then it begins again reinforced with *ergo*, "therefore," used like *igitur* with similar meaning to resume an interrupted idea.
Cicero repeats this thought a second time as a reminder to the reader. Both
causal clauses depend on the main verb, *peto*, "I ask," in T.1i establishing
Track I, but the track then changes with both occurrences of *accidit* in T.4b

establishing Track II. Note: in both causal statements, the indicative *accidit* is used to express the idea of the author; to have said *acciderit* in T.3s would have indicated reported speech or the idea of another person or a discounted idea.

> → **1125** dict., *igitur*, conj., II., D. resuming interrupted thought;
> consecutio, 47–48;
> causal: *quoniam*, "because, since," + indicative, one's own reason, 59.2;
> causal: *quoniam*, "because, since," + subjunctive, reported reason, 59.2;
> causal: rejected reason, *non quo*, GL n° 541, note 2.

Quoniam id accidit … quoniam ergo ita accidit, "Because that thing happened … because therefore it so happened": Cicero begins his statement, but after mentioning the Marcelluses, he diverts to a long parenthetical sentence. Finally he picks up his main sentence once again by repeating almost verbatim the first words. The *ergo*, "therefore," indicates that he is taking up his main thought once again.

> → **1126** dict., *igitur*, conj., II., D. resuming interrupted thought;
> sentence structure, 1.

quod … fuit, "which was": here *quod* is the subject of *fuit*, and the whole expression develops the idea expressed in *id*, the subject of *accidit*, "that thing happened."

> → **1127** rel. pron.: brevity, 11.3.

ut … ut … posset, "that … that … [your consulship] was able": as Cicero begins his sentence, he quickly turns to a result clause, which he begins but does not finish when he diverts to comment on the Marcelluses. When he begins the sentence again, he picks up the result clause again and carries it through to its completion. The main verb is one of causing or bringing about, *id accidit*, "this happened," in T.4b establishing Track II. The result clause is *ut … posset*, "that [your consulship] was able," in T.2s.

> → **1128** subjunctive use: complementary result (consecutive), 68.1;
> consecutio, 47–48.

mirificus … animus, "the attitude … wonderful": the first and last words of this parenthetical statement going together naturally, although nine words separate them—this is natural Latin.

> → **1129** sentence structure, 1.

consulatus, "consulate": the dictionary gives the noun as *consulatus, us*, so this form could be either the subject singular as here, or elsewhere the subject plural, of-possession singular or object plural.

> → **1130** 20% of nouns, *consulatus, us*, m., 35.

satis facere, "to satisfy": the contemporaneous infinitive *facere* complements *posset*, "was able to satisfy."

> → **1131** verb: complementary infinitive, 77.

in quem ... incideret, "with which ... was ... coinciding": relative clause in MA because it depends on and is closely associated with the idea expressed in *ut posset*, "that ... was able," in T.2s, itself depending on *accidit*, "it happened," in T.4b establishing Track II. The several subjects, *res gestae laus ... honos*, "exploits ... praise ... honor," might seem to demand a plural verb, however, as in many languages the verb *incideret* follows the last one, which is singular.

> → **1132** subjunctive use: modal attraction, 83;
>   *consecutio*: subjunctive depending on a subjunctive, 62.1;
>   relative clauses, 10–11;
>   verb agrees with the nearest subject, GL n° 285, exception 1.

potissimum, "most especially": this is the usual form of the adv., also written as *potissime*. The comparative is *potius*, "rather," "preferably." The positive adv. does not exist.

> → **1133** dict., *potis*, adj., III., B.—hence adv. only in the *comp.* and *sup.*: A. *potius*, B. *potissime*, adv.: positive, comp., superl., 37.

peto, "I ask": the main verb in T.1i, establishing Track I.

> → **1134** *consecutio*, 47–48.

peto ... id ... ut ... cures, "I ask ... that ... that you take care": what Cicero asks, *peto*, "I ask," is stated first as an *id*, "that," which in turn is expanded by a purpose clause giving his intention in asking, the content of his petition, namely *ut ... cures*, "that you take care," in T.1s.

> → **1135** subjunctive use: purpose clause, 58.1.

id, quod ... est, "that which is": *id* is the object of *peto*, "I ask," which is expanded further down the sentence in a purpose clause *ut ... cures*, "that you take care." Before he states the content of the *id*, he first gives a few parenthetical descriptions of the request, beginning with this rel. clause, *quod ... est*, "which is."

> → **1136** relative clauses, 10–11; subjunctive use: purpose clause, 58.1.

facillimum factu, "the easiest thing to do": *factu* is a remnant of a verbal noun originally *factus, us*, "to do," where the abl. in *–u* is used with a number of standard adjectives, *facile, iucundum, pulchrum, mirabile, suave*, and it sounds like the gerund inf. "to do," as in *pulchrum visu*, "beautiful to see," *iucundum gustatu*, "pleasant to taste." There are about ten real tight stock phrases *facile dictu, difficile factu*, "easy to say, hard to do." These are commonly called the abl. of the supine and they are very easy to spot and are unmistakable.

> → **1137** supine, 81.

non aspernante ... senatu, "the senate not rejecting": a second parenthetical description of the request is given in an AA with contemporaneous time frame, which can be smoothed out to say, "as long as the senate is not rejecting."

→ **1138** ablative absolute, 54–55.

ut confido, "as I trust": a third element is interjected within the AA. Here *ut* with T.1i means "as."

→ **1139** dict., *ut*, I., B. meaning "as"; ablative absolute, 54–55.

quam honorificentissime, "most honorably as possible": *quam* followed by the superlative means "as much as possible." The adverb in the positive degree is *honorifice*, "honorably," and in the comparative *honorificentius*, "more honorably."

→ **1140** *quam* with the superlative, 43.3.

senatus, "of the senate": the dictionary gives the class of this noun as *senatus, us*, thus its of-possessive form as here is *senatus consultum*, "the decision of the senate." However, rarely we read *senati consultum*, with the same meaning, as the dict. will tell you.

→ **1141** dict., *senatus, us*, m., I. gen. *senati*;
        20% of nouns: *senatus, us*, m., 35.

senatus consultum … faciendum, "making the decision of the senate": an example of a gerundive depending on a verb of handing over or of undertaking or here of taking care, *cures*, "you take care," whose object is put in the gerundive to mean "*take care* doing something," in this case, "you take care making the decision of the senate."

→ **1142** gerundive with certain verbs, 80.

Si mihi tecum minus esset quam est cum tuis omnibus, adlegarem ad te illos a quibus intellegis me praecipue diligi. Patris tui beneficia in me sunt amplissima neque enim saluti meae neque honori amicior quisquam dici potest; frater tuus quanti me faciat semperque fecerit esse hominem qui ignoret arbitror neminem; domus tua denique tota me semper omnibus summis officiis prosecuta est: neque vero tu in me diligendo cuiquam concessisti tuorum. Qua re a te peto in maiorem modum ut me per te quam ornatissimum velis esse meamque et in supplicatione decernenda et in ceteris rebus existimationem satis tibi esse commendatam putes.   (*Fam.* XV, 10, 2)

If there were less for me [in common] with you than there is with all of your people, I would delegate to you those people by whom you understand that I am especially esteemed. The good acts of your father toward me are most noble, for anyone is able to be called more friendly neither to my well-being nor to honor; I think there is no individual who does not know how much your brother values me and has always valued me; finally your whole household has always accompanied me with all the highest favors: nor, however, have you taken second place to anyone of your own people in appreciating me. For which reason I ask of you to a greater degree that you wish me to be as distinguished as possible with your help and that both in decreeing the supplication and in other things you consider my reputation has been recommended enough to you.

si ... esset ... adlegarem ... , "If there were ... I would delegate": contrary to fact condition where *esset*, "there were," in T.2s, gives the condition, and *adlegarem*, "I would delegate," also in T.2s, gives the consequence. We can test the conditional statement to confirm that it is contrary to fact by adding: "If there were, but there is not ... I would delegate, but I am not."

→ **1143** conditionals: contrary to fact, 86.3.

si ... minus esset quam est, "If there were less ... than there is": *minus ... quam*, "less ... than." Cicero changes the verbal time from *esset*, "there were," in T.2s, to *est*, "there is," in T.1i, to compare the contrary to fact condition, which he is denying, with current factual reality.

→ **1144** *quam* with the comp., 43.2; conditionals: contrary to fact, 86.3.

adlegarem ... illos a quibus intellegis, "I would delegate ... those people by whom you understand": the time changes from *adlegarem*, "I would delegate," in T.2s, giving the consequence of the contrary to fact conditional, to *intellegis*, "you understand," in T.1i because the relative clause has no reason for a subjunctive.

→ **1145** relative clauses, 10–11.

intellegis me ... diligi, "you understand that I am ... esteemed": the M & M verb *intellegis*, "you understand," in T.1i produces a statement in OO where the subject in the object form is *me*, and the contemporaneous inf. *diligi*, is passive, "that I am ... esteemed."

→ **1146** M & M, 60, 71, GL n° 527, remarks 1–2; OO, 71–73; verb: contemporaneous passive infinitive, 72.3.

amplissima, "most noble": superlative adj., whose positive degree is *ampla*, "esteemed," and comparative degree is *ampliora*, "more renowned," "noble after a fashion." This is all in the dict.

→ **1147** dict., *amplus, a, um*, adj., I.—comp.,—sup.; adj.: comp. and superl., 36.

neque ... neque ... , "neither ... nor ...": each negates its respective dative: *neque ... saluti meae*, "neither ... to my well-being," and *neque honori*, "nor honor."

→ **1148** dict., *neque*, adv. and conj., II., B., 3. *neque ... , neque ...* , "neither ... , nor ..."; GL n° 445.

amicior ... dici, "to be called more friendly": the predicate of the pass. inf.
dici, "to be called," is the rather rare form *amicior*, "more friendly," an adj.
in the comparative degree, whose positive degree is *amicus*, "a friend," and
superlative degree *amicissimus*, "best friend," which prompts two natural
datives, *saluti meae ... honori*, "to my well-being ... honor."

→ **1149** verb: contemporaneous passive infinitive, 72.3; adj.: comp. and superl., 36;
       natural dat., 33.7.1.

The magnificent architecture of Latin at its best is seen in five little lines as
this box structure of the following sentence makes clear:

[(frater tuus quanti me faciat semperque fecerit)	IQ depending on *ignoret*
<u>esse hominem</u>	OO depending on *arbitror*
qui ignoret]	characteristic result depending on OO
arbitror	main; T.1i Track I
<u>neminem</u>	OO continued

→ **1150** structure of Latin sentences, 103 p. 587, *Ossa* Readings: 1-D, 1-I, 3-D, 3-I,
       4-D, 4-I;
       relative box, 11.4.

If you begin translating this sentence with the first word *frater*, you will
be misled time and again, because what may initially appear to be the subject of the sentence is the subject of a double IQ, depending on a characteristic result, which in turn depends on OO all produced from the main word
arbitror, whose subject *ego*, "I," is implied. Alleluia!

→ **1151** sentence structure, 1.

frater tuus quanti me faciat semperque fecerit ... qui ignoret: "who does not
know how much your brother values me and has always valued me": the
verb of M & M *ignoret*, "[who] does not know," in T.1s establishes Track I
and gives rise to a double IQ prompted by the question word *quanti*, "how
much," "how dear," followed by two verbs *faciat*, "[your brother] values,"
in T.1s and *fecerit*, "[your brother] has ... valued me." The dictionary tells
you that the verb *facio, facere* means "to value," "to esteem," "to regard"
especially when accompanied by a gen. of price, as in the English phrase
"to make much of," or we might say, "to knock up a price." Here the gen.
of price *quanti*, "how dear," also prompts the question, "how much your
brother values me."

→ **1152** M & M, 60, 71, GL nᵒ 527, remarks 1–2; IQ, 60;
       consecutio, 47–48;
       consecutio: subjunctive depending on a subjunctive, 62.1;
       gen. of indefinite price, 75.2.

esse hominem ... arbitror neminem, "I think there is no individual": the
main verb of this sentence is *arbitror*, "I think," in T.1i, a deponent verb of
M & M producing a statement in OO whose subject in the object form is *ho-*

minem ... neminem, "nobody individual," "no individual," where *neminem* is used as an adj. to describe *hominem,* and whose inf. is contemporaneous, *esse,* "to be," "is"; we might say, "there is nobody, human person."

→ **1153** M & M, 60, 71, GL n° 527, remarks 1–2; OO, 71–73; verb: deponent, 29.

qui ignoret, "who does not know," a characteristic result where *qui* followed by the subjunctive here stands for *talem ut is ignoret,* "such that he does not know."

→ **1154** subjunctive use: characteristic result, 68.2.

in me diligendo, "in appreciating me": in the singular here the gerund and gerundive appear the same, but in the plural the gerund would be *in nos diligendo,* and the gerundive *in nobis diligendis,* both with the meaning "in appreciating us" or "in loving us."

→ **1155** gerund, 77.1; gerundive, 77.2.

cuiquam concessisti, "[nor] have you taken second place to anyone": the natural use of the dat. *cuiquam,* "to anyone," with the verb *concessisti,* "[nor] have you taken second place."

→ **1156** natural dat., 33.7.1.

Qua re, "For which reason": a relative phrase, "by means of which reason," "out of which reason."

→ **1157** dict., *quare* or *qua re,* adv.: I. interrog., "by what means?", and II., B. "wherefore."

a te peto, "I ask of you": that *peto* with the acc. of the person would mean "I head for," "I attack you."

→ **1158** dict., *peto, ivi* and *ii, itum,* 3., II., A. "to attack," B., 2., b. "to beg," with acc. of person.

peto ... ut ... velis ... –que ... [ut] ... putes, "I ask ... that you wish ... and that ... you consider": the main verb *puto,* "I ask," in T.1i establishing Track I gives rise to a double purpose clause in which *velis,* "you wish," and *putes,* "you consider," both in T.1s, are joined together by the *–que* attached to the end of the first word in the second element, *meamque,* which does not mean "and my," but "and ... my."

→ **1159** subjunctive use: purpose clause, 58.1; conjunction: *–que,* 3.2.

in maiorem modum, "to a greater degree": the preposition *in* followed by the acc. indicates motion to or toward, either geographical or moral. Here, one might express that motion by saying, "unto a greater degree." However, the idea of motion to or toward "a greater degree" is as odd in English as in Latin, yet the expression is long-standing. This expression is the comparative degree, whose positive degree is *magnum in modum*, "to a great extent," and superlative, *maximum in modum*, "to the greatest extent."

> → **1160** dict., *modus, i*, m., II., B., 2., *in modum*;
>   prep. with obj., 6; adj.: comp., 36.

ut me ... quam ornatissimum velis esse, "that you wish me to be as distinguished as possible": The intention for asking, *peto*, "I ask," in T.1i and establishing Track I, is given in a purpose clause where *velis*, "you wish," in T.1s is rendered in the subjunctive in English although this cannot be distinguished from the ind. As a verb of M & M, *velis*, "you wish," produces a statement in OO, whose subject is in the object form, *me*, and whose inf., *esse*, is contemporaneous, "me to be." In the predicate is the special use of *quam* with the superlative *ornatissimum*, meaning "as distinguished as possible."

> → **1161** subjunctive use: purpose clause, 58.1; *consecutio*, 47–48;
>   M & M, 60, 71, GL nº 527, remarks 1–2; OO, 71–73;
>   *quam* with the superlative, 43.3.

meam ... existimationem ... esse commendatam putes, "you consider my reputation has been recommended": the verb of the second purpose clause *putes*, "you consider," in T.1s is a verb of M & M producing a statement in OO where the subject in object form is *meam existimationem*, and the infinitive *esse commendatam* is both antecedent and passive and agrees with its subject, "my reputation has been recommended."

> → **1162** M & M, 60, 71, GL nº 527, remarks 1–2; OO, 71–73.

et in supplicatione decernenda et in ceteris rebus, "both in decreeing the supplication and in other things": the double *et ... et ...*, means "both ... and ...." Both introduce prepositional phrases whose object in the first is a gerundive and in the second the simple abl. The gerundive *in supplicatione decernenda* could be turned into a gerund, *in supplicationem decernendo*, with no change in meaning, but the Romans prefer the gerundive style, and medieval and scholastic Latin prefer the gerund style because the object is easier to catch immediately.

> → **1163** conjunction: *et ... , et ...* , 3.2; prep. with abl., 28.4;
>   gerundive, 77.2; characteristics of later Latin, 105.

Note: Cicero is writing this letter in the year 58–57 BCE as proconsul, military governor, in Cilicia, today squeezed between Turkey and Syria, whose capital was Tarsus, where Cicero might have known the father of a certain Paul of Tarsus.

In this letter Cicero is begging the Consul in Rome to organize a triumphal procession—a *supplicatio*, a public day of prayer to celebrate victories or lament defeats—processing through the city to celebrate his administration and one military victory in the province, something which never happened, because the civil war broke out and Cicero's dream was dashed.

LETTER 839 T-P
AD BRUTUM II, 2

CICERO BRUTO SAL.

Planci animum in rem publicam egregium, legiones, auxilia, copias ex litteris eius, quarum exemplum tibi missum arbitror, perspicere potuisti. Lepidi, tui necessarii, qui secundum fratem adfinis habet quos oderit proximos,
levitatem et inconstantiam animumque semper inimicum rei publicae iam
credo tibi ex tuorum litteris esse perspectum.   (*Brut.* II, 2, 1)

CICERO A GREETING TO BRUTUS

You were able to grasp the outstanding attitude of Plancus toward the state,
the legions, the auxiliaries, the troops from his letters, a copy of which I
think has been sent to you. From the letters of your people I think that the
fickleness and the inconstancy of Lepidus your relative, who next to his
brother has very close people whom he hates, as well as his attitude, always
hostile to the state, has been understood by you.

CICERO BRUTO SAL.: *Cicero Bruto salutem*

Planci animum ... perspicere potuisti, "You were able to grasp the [outstand-
ing] attitude of Plancus": the second word, *animum*, "the ... attitude," is the
object of the second to last word, *perspicere*, "to grasp." The sentence begins
with *Planci*, "of Plancus," the of-possession form out front.
  → **1164** sentence structure, 1; function: of-possession, 20.

in rem publicam ... legiones, auxilia, copias, "toward the state, the legions,
the auxiliaries, the troops": the preposition *in* is followed by four objects all
lined up without connecting words, an example of asyndeton.
  → **1165** prep. with obj., 6; asyndeton, GL nº 481.2.

quarum exemplum tibi missum arbitror, "a copy of which I think has been
sent to you": *arbitror*, "I think," in T.1i, is an M & M verb. The content of

the thought is given in OO, where the full infinitive is *missum esse*, both antecedent and passive, in the sentence *exemplum ... missum*, "a copy ... has been sent."

→ **1166** M & M, 60, 71, GL n° 527, remarks 1–2; OO, 71–73.

Lepidi, tui necessarii ... levitatem et inconstantiam animumque ... credo ... esse perspectum, "I think that the fickleness and the inconstancy of Lepidus your relative ... as well as his attitude ... has been understood": the main verb is *credo*, "I think," in T.1i a verb of M & M. The content of his thought is given in OO. The acc. subject are three: *levitatem*, "the fickleness," *inconstantiam*, "the inconstancy," both of which are feminine nouns, and *animum*, "attitude," which is a masculine noun. The infinitive agrees with the nearest one *animum ... esse perspectum*, "[his] attitude ... has been understood," both antecedent and passive. Note that the first words *Lepidi, tui necessarii*, "of Lepidus your relative," begin the sentence but depend on the three nouns in its middle, which are the subjects of the last two words in the sentence.

→ **1167** M & M, 60, 71, GL n° 527, remarks 1–2; OO, 71–73;
        sentence structure, 1;
        verb agrees with the nearest subject, GL n° 285, exception 1.

qui secundum fratrem adfinis habet quos oderit proximos, "who next to his brother has very close people whom he hates": *secundum* does not mean "second" or "according to," but "following" or "after." *adfinis* is another form of *adfines*, "associates," and agrees with *proximos*, "very close people," the object of *habet*, "[his brother] has," in T.1i establishing Track I. The relative clause *quos oderit* with the subjunctive is a result clause that describes the character of *quos*, "[people] whom." Here *quos* stands for *tales ut eos*, "such that [he hates] them." *oderit* is in T.3s because the verb is defective and does not have the T.1s form given in the English rendering above, "whom he hates," which is also given in the indicative according to the expression of a result clause in English. If the time of the defective verb is confusing, then we could supply a different verb in a time that we would expect, for example: *adfinis habet quos odio habeat proximos*, "he has associates very close people whom he has for a hatred," where *habeat*, "he has," is in T.1s as would be expected. In time the defective verbs will pose no problem to understanding.

→ **1168** dict., *secundum,* I. adv., II. prep. with acc., A., 1., a. "following after," and
        A., 2. "next to";
        Block II adj.: *–is = –es*, 38, GL n° 78;
        subjunctive use: characteristic result, 68.2;
        defective verbs, 14.4, GL n° 175.5: *coepi, memini, odi*.

credo tibi ... esse perspectum, "I think ... has been understood by you": *tibi* is understood here as the dat. of agent "by you," which is on the rare side. Others would legitimately take it with ethical reference to mean, "it has been understood with your regard" or "... if you are interested."

→ **1169** dat. of agent, 53.5;
        ethical dat., see 91.2, GL n° 351; dat. of reference, 91.2, GL n° 352.

∾

Nos exspectatio sollicitat, quae est omnis iam in extremum adducta discrimen. Est enim spes omnis in Bruto expediendo, de quo vehementer timebamus.   (*Brut.* II, 2, 2)

Expectation is worrying us, which all has already been brought into the
greatest crisis. For our total hope is in freeing Brutus, about whom we were
sorely afraid.

> Note: We can see a leap-frog style of alternative positions between the nomi-
> nal and verbal elements of this sentence. If we place the nominal elements of
> the sentence on the top line, and the verbal elements on the bottom line, we
> can see this alternation:

nominal	*quae*		*omnis*		*in extremum*		*discrimen*
verbal		*est*		*iam*		*adducta*	

So many things that naturally go together are separated here by other
elements. Beginning with the top line, *omnis* goes with *quae*, but between
them is *est*, and again *in extremum* goes with *discrimen*, but between them
is *adducta*. Looking at the bottom line, *est* goes with *adducta*, but they are
separated by four other words. What was pointed out on the first day of the
whole Corpus of Latinity is precisely what you see here. If students catch on
to this mode of speaking, they will have the trick of the Latin language.

→ **1170** sentence structure, 1.

in Bruto expediendo, "in freeing Brutus": a gerundive which can be re-
phrased as a gerund, *in Brutum expediendo* with the same meaning. If in
the gerund you were to take *in* with *Brutum*, meaning "unto Brutus," then
how would you account for *expediendo*? Rather, the gerund makes clear
that *in* goes with *expediendo*, whose object is *Brutum*. The Romans much
preferred the gerundive as better style; the scholastics preferred the gerund
for the sake of students in order that the object be seen more clearly.

→ **1171** gerundive, 77.2; gerund, 77.1; characteristics of later Latin, 105.

∾

Ego hic cum homine furioso satis habeo negotii, Servilio, quem tuli diutius
quam dignitas mea patiebatur, sed tuli rei publicae causa, ne darem perditis civibus hominem, parum sanum illum quidem sed tamen nobilem, quo
concurrerent, quod faciunt nihilio minus; sed eum alienandum a re publica
non putabam. Finem feci eius ferendi. Coeperat enim esse tanta insolentia
ut neminem liberum duceret. In Planci vero causa exarsit incredibili dolore,
mecumque per biduum ita contendit et a me ita fractus est ut eum in perpetuum modestiorem sperem fore. Atque in hac contentione ipsa, cum maxime res ageretur, a. d. V. Idus Aprilis litterae mihi in senatu redditae sunt a

Lentulo nostro de Cassio, de legionibus de Syria: quas statim cum recitavissem, cecidit Servilius, complures praeterea—sunt enim insignes aliquot qui
improbissime sentiunt—, sed acerbissime tulit Servilius adsensum esse mihi
de Planco. Magnum illud monstrum in re publica est [...]   (*Brut.* II, 2, 3)

Here I have enough trouble with a wild man, Servilius, whom I have tol-
erated longer than my dignity was permitting, but I put up [with him] for
the sake of the state, lest I hand over to ruined citizens a person, him not
sufficiently sane, indeed, but nevertheless noble to whom they might gather,
which they do nonetheless, but I was not thinking that he had to be turned
away from the state. I have made an end of tolerating him. For he had begun
to be a person of such great haughtiness that he was considering nobody
free. But in the cause of Plancus, he broke out with incredible grief, and over
a period of two days he fought with me in such a way and was broken by me
in such a way that I hope he will be more modest forever. And in this confrontation itself, when precisely the matter was being discussed, on the fifth
day before the April Ides [9 April] a letter was delivered to me in the senate
from our Lentulus concerning Cassius, concerning the legions, concerning
Syria: which when I had recited immediately, Servilius collapsed, besides
quite a few others—for there are some noteworthy people who are thinking
most wickedly—but Servilius took it most bitterly that consent was given to
me about Plancus. That is a big monstrosity in the republic ...

> *cum homine furioso ... Servilio*, "with a wild man, Servilius": *Servilio*,
> "Servilius," is abl. to agree with *homine*, "a ... man," itself the object of
> *cum*, "with." Between these elements are the verb and its object, *satis habeo
> negotii*, "I have enough of trouble."
> → **1172** prep. with abl., 28.4; sentence structure, 1.
>
> *satis ... negotii*, "enough trouble": *negotii* is the gen. of part, typically sepa-
> rated from the word it depends upon, here *satis*, as in "enough of trouble."
> → **1173** gen. of part, 99.
>
> *quem ... quam ... quidem ... quo... quod*, "whom ... than ... indeed ... to
> whom ... which": note all the words beginning *qu–*, which the Romans
> heard as *–kw–*, as you are likely to pronounce it as well; the Romans loved
> this sound and the sentences are full of these words.
> → **1174** sound *qu–*, 10.2.
>
> *diutius quam*, "longer than": a comparison. The *quam* balances two equal
> elements, the verbs *tuli*, "I have tolerated," and *patiebatur*, "[dignity] was
> permitting."
> → **1175** *quam* with the comp., 43.2.
>
> *rei publicae causa*, "for the sake of the state": here *causa*, "for the sake," in
> the abl. is preceded by *rei publicae*, "of the republic," in the gen. according to

the expression. This expression is also found with *gratia* and *ergo*, both also meaning "for the sake [of something or someone]," as in *gratitudinis ergo*, "for the sake of gratitude."

→ **1176** abl.: meaning and forms, 27; function: of-possession, 20.

ne darem, "lest I hand over": a negative purpose clause where *darem*, "I hand over," is T.2s on Track II established by *tuli*, "I put up," in T.4b.

→ **1177** subjunctive use: purpose clause, 58.1; *consecutio*, 47–48.

parum sanum illum, "not sufficiently sane": the adv. *parum* means neither "a little bit" nor "slightly," but "too little" and "not enough."

→ **1178** dict., *parum*, subst. indecl. and adv., "too little, not enough."

quo concurrerent, "to whom they might gather": *concurrerent*, "[to whom] they might run together," in T.2s is subjunctive because this is a relative clause of purpose, where *quō* is an adv. meaning "whither," "to whom," and stands for *ut eō* or for *ut ad eum*, "so that to him," "so that to that place."

→ **1179** dict., *quo*, adv., II. "to which place, whither";
   eō, adv., I., A. of place—*in eo loco*, "there";
   subjunctive use: relative clause of purpose, *quo* = *ut eo*, 58.2;
   GL n° 545.2 *quō* = *ut eō*.

nihilo minus, "nonetheless": sometimes written as one word *nihilominus*, *nihilo* is an abl. of measure meaning "[less] by no degree," "in no degree [less]."

→ **1180** dict., *nihil*, n., indecl., II. *nihilum, i*, n., (δ) adv.: *nihilo minus* or *nihilominus*, "none the less";
   abl.: measure, 90.3, GL n° 403.

eum alienandum a re publica non putabam, "I was not thinking that he had to be turned away from the republic": *putabam*, "I was thinking," in T.2i and a verb of M & M. The content of Cicero's thought is given in OO where the full inf. is *alienandum esse*, and its subj. is *eum* in the object form, meaning "that he must be estranged."

→ **1181** M & M, 60, 71, GL n° 527, remarks 1–2; OO, 71–73;
   participle of passive necessity, 50, 51.1.4;
   passive necessity formula, 53.4.

Finem feci eius ferendi, "I have made an end of tolerating him": a mysterious expression for most people. This gerundive is in the of-possession form or gen. because the gerundive depends on *finem*, "an end." The Romans preferred the gerundive, but the scholastics preferred the clarity of the gerund, *Finem feci eum ferendi*, with the same meaning but with such a clear object *eum*, "him."

→ **1182** gerundive, 77.2; gerund, 77.1; characteristics of later Latin, 105.

Coeperat enim esse tanta insolentia, "For he had begun to be a person of such great haughtiness": it may look like the subject of *Coeperat* is *tanta insolentia*, but its subject is rather *is*, "he [had begun]," and *tanta insolentia* is an abl. of description, "of such great haughtiness." Cicero could have used the preferred gen. *tantae insolentiae* with the same meaning, or even *tantus insolentia*, where *insolentia* is an abl. of limitation, meaning "[a person] so great in haughtiness." These are the three options to express quality in Latin, all three given here together. Knowing the limits and extent of what can be expressed in Latin is its own consolation for all learners; Latin is totally learnable, manageable,

→ **1183** quality in gen., 96.1; quality in abl., 96.2;
  quality in adj. + abl. noun, 96.3.

tanta ... ut neminem liberum duceret, "of such great [haughtiness] that he was considering nobody free": the main verb *coeperat*, "he had begun," is T.5i, establishing Track II, and is followed by a result clause whose verb *duceret*, in T.2s, is on Track II. The combination *tanta ... ut ...* "of such great ... that ...," prepares for the pure result. The Latin subjunctive is rendered in the indicative in English according to the nature of a result clause.

→ **1184** subjunctive use: pure result (consecutive), 67.1–2; GL n° 552.

In Planci vero causa exarsit incredibili dolore, "But in the cause of Plancus, he broke out with incredible grief": note the word order. The object of *in* is *causa* in the abl. "in the case," and depending on this is *Planci*, "of Plancus," the gen. placed out front, and inserted in the midst is *vero*, "but," used postpositively. *incredibili dolore* is an abl. of instrumentality.

→ **1185** dict., *verus, a, um*, adj., II., adv., B. *vero*, "truly," 2. "but" (always placed after a word);
  sentence structure, 1; prep. with abl., 28.4;
  abl.: instrument, 28.5.3–4, 89.2, GL n° 401.

per biduum, "over a period of two days": people will say, "for two days," but that would be expressed by *biduum*, the acc. of extent of time, without *per*. In Latin *per* never means "for," and if it appears to do so, then check your dictionary.

→ **1186** acc.: time during which, 70.2; dict., *per*, prep. with acc.

mecumque ... ita contendit et a me ita fractus est ut ... sperem, "and ... he fought with me in such a way and was broken by me in such a way that I hope": the *–que* is attached to the first word of the second element *mecum*, "with me," and joins *exarsit*, "he broke out," with *contendit*, "he fought." The *et*, "and," also joins two equal elements, *contendit*, "he fought," with *fractus est*, "he was broken." All three of these verbs are T.4b, establishing Track II. Accordingly, one might expect the pure result clause to follow on Track II with T.2s, such as *ita fractus est ut sperarem*, "he was broken in such a way that I was hoping" or "... that I hoped." Here, rather, *ut sperem*, "that I hope," in T.1s describes one concrete result, and so brings the time right up to the present, as an example of the 3% exception to the sequence of tenses. As an expression of result, the Latin subjunctive *sperem* is rendered in the indicative in English, "I do hope," "I am hoping."

> → **1187** conjunction: –*que*, 3.2; conjunction: *et*, 3.2;
>   subjunctive use: 3% sequence of tenses, 94.1;
>   subjunctive use: pure result (consecutive), 67.1–2, GL n° 552.

ut eum in perpetuum modestiorem sperem fore, "that I hope he will be more modest forever": *sperem*, "I hope," in T.1s, is a verb of M & M. The content of that hope is given in OO, *eum … fore*, "he will be," where the infinitive *fore* stands for *futurum esse*, and *eum futurum esse* means "him to be about to be," "that he is going to be," "that he will be." Placed in the middle of the expression is the comparative adj. describing *eum*, "him," the predicate *modestiorem*, "more modest."

> → **1188** M & M, 60, 71, GL n° 527, remarks 1–2; OO, 71–73;
>   futurity participle, 50, 51.1.3; *futurum esse* (*fore*), 72.1;
>   futurity formula, active, 53.3; adj.: comp., 36.

a. d. V. Idus Aprilis, "on the fifth day before the April Ides [9 April]": the abbreviation is *ante diem quintum Idus Aprilis*. This expression is a set formula where the word *ante* is really felt before *Idus*, as in *die quinto ante Idus Aprilis*, "on the fifth day before the April Ides." *Aprilis* here is not of-possession form "of April" found in later church expression, but is rather the alternative form of *Apriles*, the object plural agreeing with *Idus*, as we have seen when *omnis* stands for *omnes*.

> → **1189** about the Roman calendar, pp. 605–608;
>   GL appendix: Roman Calendar, pp. 491–92;
>   Block II adj.: –*is* = –*es*, 38, GL n° 78.

cum maxime res ageretur … litterae … redditae sunt, "when precisely the matter was being discussed … a letter was delivered": the main verb is *redditae sunt*, "[a letter] was delivered," in T.4b in the passive, thus establishing Track II. The closely related temporal circumstances are indicated in the clause *cum … ageretur*, "when [the matter] was being discussed," with the verb in T.2s, and the English rendering in the indicative according to the nature of a temporal clause. Had Cicero used the indicative here, as in *cum agebatur*, he would have indicated a mere coincidence of time, as at noon or 5:00 p.m.

> → **1190** subjunctive use: temporal circumstance *cum* = "when," 66.3.2.

quas statim cum recitavissem, cecidit Servilius, "which when I had recited immediately, Servilius collapsed": the main verb *cecidit*, "[Servilius] collapsed" in T.4b establishes Track II. The temporal circumstances are so closely related in the clause *cum recitavissem*, "when I had recited," that its meaning is almost causal, "because I had recited." Here *recitavissem* in T.4s indicates any time prior or up to the time of *cecidit*. *Quas* is the object of *recitavissem,* "which I had received," and *quas statim,* "which immediately," stand geographically in front of the clause on which they depend. The antecedent of *quas* is *litterae,* "a letter," in the previous sentence, but in its own clause *quas* functions as the object of *recitavissem,* dependent on *cecidit.*

> → **1191** *consecutio,* 47–48;
> > subjunctive use: temporal circumstance *cum* = "when," 66.3.2;
> > subjunctive use: causal *cum* = "because, since," 59.1;
> > sentence structure, 1; relative clauses, 10–11.

sed acerbissime tulit Servilius adsensum esse, "but Servilius took it most bitterly that agreement was given": the main verb is *tulit,* "[Servilius] took," which functions as a verb of M & M in T.4b establishing Track II. The content of the idea is given in OO, *adsensum esse,* "that agreement had been given," used impersonally here, and so without a separate subject in the object form. The dictionary gives *assentior, sensus,* 4, a deponent verb, which would normally have passive form and active meaning, but is used here passively, as happens also with other verbs, for example *adipiscor, eptus,* 3, "to attain," when Cicero says *adeptam,* "[when people get old they criticize the age] having been attained," which he really should not do according to some peoples' preconceptions and rules, but nevertheless Cicero does it, as is mentioned in the dictionary. This is the Latin language, not phony grammar.

Note: *assentiri* is one of the 65 verbs whose object is given in the dat. Gildersleeve and Lodge has this one note in tiny print at the bottom of the page that says: "Of course the passives of these verbs are used impersonally (208)" (GL n° 346, remark 1). Good luck!

> → **1192** dict., *assentior, sensus,* 4, I.... pass....—and impers. *Bibulo adsensum est* (Cic. *Fam.* I, 2);
> > M & M, 60, 71, GL n° 527, remarks 1–2; OO, 71–73;
> > *consecutio,* 47–48;
> > 65 verbs with dat., 33.7.2, 89.3.3, GL n° 346, remark 1;
> > passive of intransitive verbs used impersonally, GL n° 208.2;
> > dict., *adipiscor, eptus,* 3, "to arrive at, reach," II., c. pass.

Note: The text at the end of the letter is uncertain, and so is not considered here.

LETTER 70 T-P
AD ATTICUM III, 14

CICERO ATTICO SAL.

Ex tuis litteris plenus sum exspectatione de Pompeio quidnam de nobis velit
aut ostendat. Comitia enim credo esse habita: quibus absolutis scribis illi
placuisse agi de nobis. Si tibi stultus esse videor qui sperem, facio tuo iussu,
et scio te me iis epistulis potius et meas spes solitum esse remorari. Nunc
velim mihi plane perscribas quid videas. Scio nos nostris multis peccatis in
hanc aerumnam incidisse. Ea si qui casus aliqua ex parte correxerit, minus
moleste feremus nos vixisse et adhuc vivere.   (*Att.* III, 14, 1)

CICERO A GREETING TO ATTICUS

From your letters I am full of expectation concerning Pompeius, what in the
world he wants in our regard or is indicating. For I believe that the elections
have been conducted: which having been finished, you write that it was
pleasing to him that negotiations be made about us. If I seem to you to be
foolish because I am hoping, I am doing this at your command, and I know
that you have been accustomed to slow me and my hopes down rather by
those letters. Now I would like that you clearly write out for me what you are
noticing. I know that we have come into this tribulation by our many mistakes. If any happening will have corrected them to some extent, we shall
take less badly that we have lived and are still living.

CICERO ATTICO SAL.: *Cicero Attico salutem*

quidnam ... velit ... ostendat, "what in the world he wants ... is indicating":
IQ depending on the M & M idea expressed in the noun *exspectatione,*
"expectation." Both verbs are T.1s.

   → **1193** M & M, 60, 71, GL n° 527, remarks 1–2; IQ, 60.

nam, "in the world": not used alone, but only attached to question words
to give emphasis, almost indignation, as in *quidnam,* "what in the world";

Ubinam latitat?, "Where in the world is he hiding?"; *Quonam modo hoc explicabis?*, "In what ever way are you going to explain this?"

→ **1194** dict., *nam*, conj.

Comitia … esse habita, "that the elections have been conducted": OO depending on the M & M verb *credo*, "I believe."

→ **1195** M & M, 60, 71, GL n° 527, remarks 1–2; OO, 71–73.

quibus absolutis, "which having been finished": an ablative absolute. To understand this construction, we may reconstruct the two independent sentences. The first sentence is given directly in the text: *Comitia enim credo esse habita*, "For I believe that the elections have been conducted." The second sentence begins with an ablative absolute, so we can reconstruct the independent sentence as follows: *Comitiis absolutis, scribis illi placuisse agi de nobis*, "The elections having been finished, you write that it was pleasing to him that negotiations be made about us." Now, the two sentences are joined by making *Comitiis* into a relative pronoun *quibus*, whose antecedent is *Comitia* in the first sentence, thereby producing the given text. Note: the subject of the AA is not the subject or object of the main sentence grammatically, even though logically they are the same thing or reality. Here, *quibus* is the subj. of the AA, and does not enter the main sentence, although the antecedent to *quibus* is *Comitia*. The *quibus* may also be considered as a connecting relative where *quibus absolutis* stands for *et iis absolutis*, [*scribis illi placuisse*], "and—the elections having been finished—[you write that it was pleasing to him]." Another way to write this is *quae cum absoluta essent* [*scribis illi placuisse*], "which—when they had been finished—[you write it was pleasing to him]."

→ **1196** ablative absolute with relative subject, 55.3;
   subjunctive use: temporal circumstance *cum* = "when," 66.3.2;
   dict., *qui, quae, quod*, pron., II., C. a connective instead of *is, ea, id* with a
   conj.

placuisse agi, "it was pleasing … that negotiations be made": depending on the main verb of this second part of the sentence, *scribis*, "you write," in T.1i, the antecedent infinitive *placuisse*, "to have met the approval of," "to have been decided," is impersonal OO, and its subject is the passive infinitive *agi*, "negotiating to be done," functioning as a subject gerund. This produces the English sentence "That negotiations be made was pleasing [to Pompeius]," or "It was pleasing [to Pompeius] that negotiations be made," where "It" functions as a placeholder for the entire phrase "that negotiations be made."

→ **1197** M & M, 60, 71, GL n° 527, remarks 1–2; OO, 71–73;
   verb: contemporaneous passive infinitive, 72.3;
   verb: antecedent active infinitive, 72.1; gerund, 77.1.

stultus esse videor, "I seem … to be foolish": the Romans preferred the personal construction of *videor*, "I seem," rather than the impersonal use many people would say today, "if it seems that I am stupid." Agreeing with the subject of both *videor* and of the inf. *esse*, is the nom. adj. *stultus*, "foolish."

→ **1198** personal construction: *videor*, 73.3, GL n° 528.1 and remark 2 and note 1; nom. with the inf., 73.3, GL n° 528.1.

qui sperem, "because I am hoping": a causal relative sentence where *qui* stands for *cum ego*, "because I," followed by *sperem*, "I am hoping," in T.1s and depending on the M & M verb *videor*, "I seem," in T.1i establishing Track I. The subjunctive *sperem* in Latin sounds indicative in English, "I am hoping," because of the nature of a causal clause in each language. The relative sentence means "inasmuch as I am hoping," "because I am hoping," "seeing that I am hoping."

→ **1199** subjunctive use: causal *qui, quae, quod* = "because, since," 59.4; M & M, 60, 71, GL n° 527, remarks 1–2; *consecutio*, 47–48.

facio ... , et scio, "I am doing ... , and I know": this *et* joins *facio*, "I am doing," to *scio*, "I know."

→ **1200** conjunction: *et*, 3.2.

scio te me ... solitum esse remorari, "I know that you have been accustomed to slow [me] ... down": the verb of M & M *scio*, "I know," produces OO. Then immediately two acc. are given in a row, *te me* and at the end of the sentence two infinitives in a row, *solitum esse remorari*. The two accusatives *me* and *te* serve one as the acc. subject of *solitum esse*, whose complementary infinitive is *remorari*, whose object is the other acc.; there is eternal ambiguity here; good luck! The Latin will not help you decide, only by knowing the history can you decide which is the subject, which the object. By the way, *solitum esse* is from *soleo, solere, solitus*, one of some five semi-deponent verbs.

→ **1201** M & M, 60, 71, GL n° 527, remarks 1–2; OO, 71–73; verb: complementary infinitive, 77; semi-deponent verbs, GL n° 167.

me ... et meas spes, "me and my hopes": this *et* joins *me*, "me," and *meas spes*, "my hopes."

→ **1202** conjunction: *et*, 3.2.

velim ... perscribas quid videas, "I would like that you ... write out ... what you are noticing": every verb in this sentence is T.1s. The verb *velim*, "I would like," produces a purpose clause *perscribas*, "that you write out," without the particle *ut*. The IQ *quid videas*, "what you are noticing," is given in the indicative in English according to the nature of an IQ. We could play with the IQ here and say "what you have seen" is *quid videris*, and "what you are going to see" is *quid sis visurus*.

→ **1203** subjunctive use: purpose clause without *ut*, 58, GL n° 546, remark 2; commands: other expressions, *velim*, 85.1.7; IQ, 60; *consecutio*: futurity formula in the subjunctive, 61.3.

nos ... incidisse, "that we have come into": OO depending on the M & M verb *Scio*, "I know," in T.1i.

→ **1204** M & M, 60, 71, GL n° 527, remarks 1–2; OO, 71–73.

nostris multis peccatis, "by our many mistakes": the cause is given in the abl., namely *peccatis*, "faults," "mistakes."

→ **1205** abl.: meaning and forms, 27.

Ea, "them": these are the *peccata*. Note that *Ea* stands geographically before its clause *si ... correxerit*, "If [any happening] will have corrected them."

→ **1206** sentence structure, 1.

si qui casus, "If any happening": beginning a conditional sentence, following the word *si*, "if," here *qui* stands for *aliqui*, "any [happening]," not for *aliquis*, which will shock some people who expect *aliquis, aliquid*, the indefinite pronoun, whereas here we have the adj. *aliqui, aliqua, aliquod*.

→ **1207** dict., *aliquis, aliquid*, indef. subst. pron., "some one, any one";
dict., *aliqui, aliqua, aliquod*, indef. adj. "some, any";
pronouns: indefinite, 42.4; after *si* the *ali*-s fly away, 42.5.

si ... correxerit, ... feremus, "if ... will have corrected, we will take [it]": the condition *si ... correxerit*, "if ... will have corrected," is given in T.6i, and the consequence *feremus*, "we will take [it]," in T.3i.

→ **1208** conditionals: factual, 86.1;
T.3i and T.6i paired: 7, Time 6, and GL n° 244, remark 2.

feremus, "we will take [it]": in T.3i, functions as an M & M verb producing an OO. The idea of suffering, bearing, allowing produces OO, just as would here *patiemur*, "we shall allow."

→ **1209** dict., *fero, tuli, latum, ferre*, v. irreg., mentions "object-clause" several times;
dict., *patior, passus*, 3., II., A.,—with acc. and inf. M & M, 60, 71,
GL n° 527, remarks 1–2; OO, 71–73.

nos vixisse et adhuc vivere, "that we have lived and are still living": OO depending on the M & M idea expressed in *feremus*, "we will take [it]," in T.3i. The acc. subject *nos*, "we," has first an antecedent inf. *vixisse*, "to have lived," and then its contemporaneous form *vivere*, "to live." The human story here is that Cicero did contemplate suicide at one time.

→ **1210** M & M, 60, 71, GL n° 527, remarks 1–2; OO, 71–73.

❧

Ego propter viae celebritatem et cotidianam exspectationem rerum novarum non commovi me adhuc Thessalonica. Sed iam extrudimur, non a Plancio—nam is quidem retinet—verum ab ipso loco minime apposito ad tolerandam in tanto luctu calamitatem. In Epirum ideo, ut scripseram, non ii, quod subito mihi universi nuntii venerant et litterae qua re nihil esset

necesse quam proxime Italiam esse. Hinc si aliquid a comitiis audierimus,
nos in Asiam convertemus neque adhuc stabat quo potissimum, sed scies.
Data XII Kal. Sext. Thessalonicae.   (*Att.* III, 14, 2)

Because of the heavy traffic of the road and the daily expectation of new
developments, I have not thus far moved myself from Thessalonica. But already we are being kicked out, not by Plancius—for he indeed is holding us
back—but by the very geographical location in no way adapted to tolerating
a calamity in such mourning. Therefore, I did not go to Epirus, as I had
written, because all of a sudden all the announcements had arrived for me
and letters for which reason it was in no way necessary to be as close as
possible to Italy. If we shall have heard anything from the elections, we shall
turn ourselves from here to Asia Minor, nor up to this point was it certain
to where most especially, but you will know. Given in Thessalonica on the
twelfth day before the August Kalends [21 July].

> *celebritatem,* "the heavy traffic": the dictionary indicates a great number of
> people, thus a crowded street.
>> → **1211** dict., *celebritas, atis,* f., I. "a numerous concourse, a crowd."

> *Thessalonica,* "from Thessalonica": in the abl. indicting separation, "from."
> Note: Cicero was living at the house of Plancius.
>> → **1212** function: place from where, names of cities and small islands,
>>   *Thessalonica,* 69.2.2; abl. separation from place, 27.

> *verum,* "but": it can mean "true" or "truly"; here rather it means "but."
>> → **1213** dict., *verus, a, um,* adj., II., adv., A. *verum,* 2., a. In gen., "but."

> *ad tolerandam ... calamitatem,* "to tolerating a calamity": a gerundive. The
> gerund would be *ad tolerandum ... calamitatem,* with the same meaning.
>> → **1214** gerundive, 77.2; gerund, 77.1.

> *ut scripseram,* "as I had written": here *ut* with T.5i means "as."
>> → **1215** dict., *ut,* I., B. meaning "as."

> *non ii,* "I did not go": many will think *ii* means "they," "the people." Here it
> is T.4b, another form is *ivi,* "I went." Note: the shortest sentence in Latin is
> the command, *I!,* "You must go!"
>> → **1216** dict., *eo, ivi* or *ii, ire, itum,* "to go," GL n° 169.2.

> *quod ... venerant,* "because [the announcements] had arrived": a causal
> clause in T.5i, giving the reason of the writer. A reported reason or the
> reason of another would be in the subjunctive, here *venissent,* "because
> [allegedly, as they say] the announcements had arrived," in T.4s depending
> on *non ii,* "I did not go," in T.4b establishing Track II.
>> → **1217** causal: *quod,* "because, since," + indicative, one's own reason, 59.2;
>>   causal: *quod,* "because, since," + subjunctive, reported reason, 59.2;
>>   *consecutio,* 47–48.

nuntii venerant et litterae qua re nihil esset necesse, "announcements had arrived … and letters for which reason it was in no way necessary": the reason for the subjunctive *esset* here could be twofold. On the one hand *nuntii venerant et litterae*, "announcements had arrived and letters," may function as an expression of M & M producing an IQ where *qua re* means "why": "announcements had arrived … and letters why it was in no way necessary." On the other hand, *qua re … esset* could be a result clause where *qua re* stands for *ut ea re*, "by that fact," "that," "for which reason," as in the translation.

→ **1218** dict., *quare* or *qua re*, adv.: II. "why," and II., B. "for which reason";
M & M, 60, 71, GL n° 527, remarks 1–2; IQ, 60;
subjunctive use: pure result (consecutive), 67.1–2, GL n° 552;
subjunctive use: relative clause of pure result (consecutive), 79.6.

nihil, "in no way": here adverbial.

→ **1219** dict., *nihil*, n., indecl., I., B. adv. "not at all," *et passim*.

quam proxime Italiam, "as close as possible to Italy": *quam* followed by the superlative *proxime* means "as close as possible." Cicero is using *proxime* not as a preposition but as an adv. nevertheless with the object *Italiam*, "to Italy." This phenomenon is based on the use of *prope* as a preposition that takes the object as in *prope Italiam*, "close to Italy." Here, rather, Cicero has used the superlative of *prope* as an adverb *proxime*, but he keeps the same construction with an acc. as if it were an object. It ends up meaning "as close as possible to Italy."

→ **1220** *quam* with the superlative, 43.3;
dict., *prope*, adv. and prep. with acc.;
dict., *propior, ius*, adj. comp., II., B., 4.—adv.: *proxime*, 1.—with acc.;
prep. with obj., 6.

esse, "to be": the subject of *esset* is *esse*, used as a subject gerund meaning "to be as close as possible to Italy was not necessary."

→ **1221** gerund, 77.1.

Hinc, "from here": that is, from Thessalonica.

→ **1222** dict., *hinc*, adv. for *hince*, locative form from *hic*, I. "from this place, hence."

si … audierimus, … convertemus, "If we will have heard … we shall turn": a conditional sentence with *audierimus* in T.6i and *convertemus* in T.3i.

→ **1223** conditionals: factual, 86.1;
T.3i and T.6i paired: 7, Time 6, and GL n° 244, remark 2.

nos … convertemus, "we shall turn ourselves": here *nos* can mean either "ourselves" as the object of *convertemus*, as in the English rendering above, or it can mean "we" as the subject of the same verb, as in "we shall turn [from here to Asia Minor]."

→ **1224** reflexive pron.: first and second person, 30.

neque adhuc stabat, "nor up to this point was it certain": here *adhuc* is an adv. meaning "so far." This text is cited in the Lewis and Short dictionary as an example of a particular meaning for *stabat*, which we render here as "it was certain."

> → **1225** dict., *sto, steti, statum*, 1., II., B. b. (δ);
> dict., *adhuc*, adv. I. "to this place," II. "until now";
> dict., *sto, steti, statum*, 1., II., B., c., (δ), "the determination stands, holds good."

quo, "to where": the IQ begins and just ends without a verb. *quo* means "whither," "to where"; *eo*, "thither," "to there"; *huc*, "hither," "to here."

> → **1226** dict., *quo*, adv., II. "to where";
> dict., *eo*, adv., II. "to that place"; dict., *huc*, adv., I. "to this place"; IQ, 60.

potissimum, "most especially": adv. in superlative. The other superlative form is *potissime*, the comparative is *potius*, and the positive adv. does not exist.

> → **1227** dict., *potis*, adj., III., B.—hence adv. only in the comp. and sup., B. Sup., *potissimum*, "most especially": this is the usual form of the adv., also *potissime*.

scies, "you shall know": T.3i.

> → **1228** verb formation T.3 in groups III and IV, 12.3.2.

Data XII Kal. Sext., "Given on the twelfth day before the August Kalends [21 July]": the full Latin form is: *Data duodecimo Kalendas Sextiles*. The English word for "date," as in 21 July, comes from this Latin word *data*, "having been given," "having been sent."

> → **1229** about the Roman calendar, pp. 605–608;
> GL appendix: Roman Calendar, pp. 491–92.

Thessalonicae, "in Thessalonica": the place at which function, that in this case may look like the gen., but is not. Also called traditionally the locative.

> → **1230** function: place at which, names of cities and small islands, singular, *Thessalonicae*, 69.3.2.

LETTER 104 T-P
AD FAMILIARES I, 6

M. CICERO S. D. P. LENTULO PROCOS.

Quae gerantur accipies ex Pollione, qui omnibus negotiis non interfuit
solum sed praefuit. Me in summo dolore, quem in tuis rebus capio, maxime
scilicet consolatur spes, quod valde suspicor fore ut infringatur hominum
improbitas et consiliis tuorum amicorum et ipsa die, quae debilitat cogitationes et inimicorum et proditorum tuorum.   (*Fam.* I, 6, 1)

MARCUS CICERO SAYS A GREETING TO
PUBLIUS LENTULUS PROCONSUL

What things are being done, you will learn from Pollio, who was not only
present at but presided over all the dealings. In the greatest pain which I am
feeling in your matters, hope certainly consoles me to the greatest degree,
because I seriously suspect that it will be that the wickedness of people is
broken both by the decisions of your friends and by time itself, which weak-
ens the thoughts both of your enemies and of your betrayers.

M. CICERO S. D. P. LENTULO PROCOS.: *Marcus Cicero salutem dicit Publio
Lentulo proconsuli*

Quae gerantur, "What things are being done": an IQ depending on the M &
M verb *accipies,* "you will learn," in T.3i, establishing Track I and producing
gerantur, "[things] are being done," in T.1s. The entire letter begins with
Quae out front.

> → **1231** M & M, 60, 71; GL nº 527, remarks 1–2; IQ, 60;
>   *consecutio,* 47–48;
>   sentence structure, 1.

omnibus negotiis ... interfuit ... sed praefuit, "[who] was [not only] present at
but presided over all the dealings": both *inter-fuit* and *prae-fuit* are compound verbs and so take the dat. We may test this by restoring the prefixes

as prepositions with their natural complements, either plural objects, as in
inter negotia fuit, "he was in the midst of the dealings," or plural ablatives,
as in *prae negotiis fuit*, "he was over the dealings." When these prepositions
are prefixed to their verbs, the objects of the previous prepositional phrases
are put into this dat. usage; thus, *negotia* and *negotiis* now become *negotiis*
in the dat. plural.

→ **1232** dat. with compound verbs, 33.7.3, GL n° 347.

Me … consolatur spes, "the hope … consoles me": the sentence begins with
Me, "me," the object of *consolatur*, "[hope] consoles [me]," whose subject is
spes, "the hope," the last word of the phrase.

→ **1233** sentence structure, 1.

quod … suspicor, "because I … suspect": Cicero gives his reason for "hope,"
spes, in this sentence of cause where *quod* means "because" or even "seeing
that," and is followed by the ind. because Cicero is giving his own opinion.

→ **1234** relative clauses, 10–11;
    causal: *quod*, "because, since," + indicative, one's own reason, 59.2.

suspicor fore ut infringatur … improbitas, "I … suspect that it will happen that wickedness is broken": this construction is an alternative way of
expressing what would otherwise have been an awkward expression of OO.
The M & M verb *suspicor*, "I suspect," produces OO, which we can reconstruct here with the acc. subj. *improbitatem*, but the future passive infinitive
would be expressed with the supine, *infractum iri*, literally, "motion is being
made to break," producing *suspicor infractum iri hominum improbitatem*,
literally, "I suspect that motion is being made to break the wickedness of
people," or more smoothly, "I suspect the wickedness of people will be
broken." This direct way of speaking is quite heavy, and not too pleasing
to many Latin writers. Consequently, Cicero and others often preferred
the present paraphrase in which *suspicor* is followed by *fore*, which is an
alternative way of saying *futurum esse*, literally, "to be about to be," itself an
impersonal infinitive in OO. In that *fore* sets the time in the future, Cicero
provides the passive action in a complementary result clause *ut* with the
passive verb *infringatur*, "that [wickedness] is broken," in T.1s, which complements or completes the verb *fore*.

→ **1235** M & M, 60, 71, GL n° 527, remarks 1–2; OO, 71–73;
    futurity participle, 50, 51.1.3; *futurum esse (fore)*, 72.1;
    futurity formula, active, 53.3; *futurum esse (fore)* + *ut*, 92;
    subjunctive use: complementary result (consecutive), 68.1.

∾

Facile secundo loco me consolatur recordatio meorum temporum, quorum
imaginem video in rebus tuis. Nam etsi minore in re violatur tua dignitas quam mea adflicta est, tamen est tanta similitudo ut sperem te mihi
ignoscere, si ea non timuerim, quae ne tu quidem umquam timenda dux-

isti. Sed praesta te eum qui mihi a teneris, ut Graeci dicunt, unguiculis es cognitus. Illustrabit, mihi crede, tuam amplitudinem hominum iniuria. A me omnia summa in te studia officiaque exspecta: non fallam opinionem tuam. (*Fam.* I, 6, 2)

In the second place the recollection of my times easily consoles me, the image of which I see in your life. For even though your dignity is being mistreated in a lesser matter than mine has been afflicted, nevertheless there is such a likeness that I do hope you are forgiving me if I have not feared the things which not even you ever thought had to be feared. But show yourself the person who have been well known to me from tender baby-nails, as the Greeks say [from infancy]. Believe me, the injustice of people will enhance your grandeur. You must await from me all the highest signs of devotion and kindnesses toward you: I shall not disappoint your expectation.

facile, "easily": this is normally the adv. for *facilis, facile,* adj., but the form *faciliter* is rarely found.

> → **1236** dict., *facilis, e,* adj., II., B.,—Adv: *facile, facul, faculter, faciliter,* 1. *facile* (the class. form).

etsi ... tamen, "even though ... nevertheless": of the seven words for "although," three related conditional particles—*etsi, tametsi, etiamsi,* "even if"—follow the rules of the conditionals, most of which are in the indicative, as here *violatur,* "[your dignity] is being violated," in T.1i. The main sentence is introduced by *tamen,* "nevertheless."

> → **1237** conditionals: factual, 86.1; concessive particles, 64;
> subjunctive use: concessive *etsi* = "although," 64.

minore in re violatur tua dignitas quam mea adflicta est, "your dignity is being mistreated in a lesser matter than mine has been afflicted": the *quam* compares two balanced elements. Compared is *tua dignitas,* "your dignity," with *mea,* "mine," that is, "my dignity." The dignity of Lentulus "is being mistreated," *violatur* in T.1i; whereas Cicero's dignity "has been afflicted," *adflicta est* in T.4a. The *quam* is comparative and goes with *minore,* "lesser," but what is only implied is that Cicero's dignity has been afflicted in a greater matter.

> → **1238** *quam* with the comp., 43.2; adj.: comp., 36.

tanta ... ut sperem, "such ... that I do hope": a pure result clause where *sperem,* "I do hope," "I am hoping," T.1s, is subjunctive in Latin but indicative in English according to the nature of a result clause.

> → **1239** subjunctive use: pure result (consecutive), 67.1–2, GL n° 552.

te ... ignoscere, "that you are forgiving": OO depending on the M & M verb *sperem* in T.1s.

> → **1240** M & M, 60, 71, GL n° 527, remarks 1–2; OO, 71–73.

mihi ignoscere, "[you] forgive me": one of the 65 verbs whose complement is in the dat., here *mihi*. In the English rendering, "you forgive me," you cannot hear the dat. because "me" sounds like the object in the acc.

→ **1241** 65 verbs with dat., 33.7.2, GL n° 346.

si ea non timuerim, "if I have not feared the things": the main verb *est*, "there is," in T.1i establishes Track I and produces *tanta ... ut sperem*, "such ... that I do hope," a result clause in T.1s. In its turn *sperem* is a verb of M & M that produces *te mihi ignoscere*, "that you forgive me," in OO with a contemporaneous infinitive that continues Track I. The factual condition is *si ea non timuerim*, "if I have not feared the things," where *timuerim* in T.3s is subjunctive by MA, because the idea expressed is closely associated with and the clause depends upon the OO, which depends on the result clause, which depends on the main verb. Unlike the word order, the action behind *timuerim* in T.3s occurs previous to that behind *te mihi ignoscere*, "you forgive me," which is one of the 65 verbs whose complement is in the dat.

→ **1242** subjunctive use: pure result (consecutive), 67.1–2, GL n° 552;
M & M, 60, 71, GL n° 527, remarks 1–2; OO, 71–73; *consecutio*, 47–48;
conditionals: factual, 86.1; subjunctive use: modal attraction, 83;
65 verbs with dat., 33.7.2, GL n° 346.

ea ... quae ... timenda duxisti, "the things, which ... you ... thought had to be feared": the M & M verb *duxisti*, "you thought," produces OO in which the full infinitive is *timenda esse*, literally "to be having to be feared," "to be needing to be feared." Its subject is *quae*, "which [things]" in the acc., whose antecedent is *ea*, "the things," in the previous clause.

→ **1243** dict., *duco, xi, ctum*, 3., II., B., 4., (β).—with acc. and inf.;
M & M, 60, 71, GL n° 527, remarks 1–2; OO, 71–73; relative clauses, 10–11;
participle of passive necessity, 50, 51.1.4;
passive necessity formula, 53.4.

quae ne tu quidem umquam ... duxisti, "which not even you ever thought": *duxisti* is in T.4b with this meaning, which may be a surprise to people with foolish one-to-one vocabulary lists. Much further down the dictionary entry of *duco, ducere* is this other meaning "to reckon," "to consider," and so "to think." This relative sentence depends on *si ... non timuerim*, "If I have not feared," in T.3s by MA. Cicero considers it an explanatory sentence, more or less in passing, which does not affect the meaning of the rest of the sentence, and thus expresses it in the indicative.

→ **1244** dict., *duco, xi, ctum*, 3., II., B., 4. "to reckon," (α). "to consider," (β). "account";
relative clauses, 10–11.

ne tu quidem, "not even you": the thing negated, *tu*, "you," is put in the middle of the expression *ne ... quidem*, "not even." Here *ne* does not mean what is often blindly attributed to this particle, "lest," "that not."

→ **1245** dict., *quidem*, adv., I., C., 1. *ne ... quidem*, "not even."

praesta te eum, "show yourself the person": the command *praesta*, "show," takes a double object here, both the reflexive *te*, "yourself," and *eum*, "such a man," "this person," "that one." This very occurrence is mentioned in the dictionary.

> → **1246** dict., *praesto, sti, atum* or *itum*, 1., II., C., 2., b.... *praesta te eum*, "show thyself such";
> commands: first, second, 17;
> reflexive pron.: first and second person, 30;
> demonstrative pron.: *is, ea, id*, 3.1, 40.2.

es cognitus, "[who] have been known": T.4a which brings the moment in the past right up to the present moment. Latin manuals give this passive form in reversed order, *cognitus es*, but not Cicero here.

> → **1247** passive Times 4, 5, 6 indicative, 26; sentence structure, 1.

ut ... dicunt, "as [the Greeks] say": followed by T.1i, here *ut* means "as." This phrase is inserted parenthetically into the sentence, which can stand without this statement. The phrase *ut ... dicunt* is a sign that Cicero is quoting a proverb or a saying.

> → **1248** *ut* I., B. meaning "as."

Illustrabit ... non fallam, "[the injustice] will enhance ... I shall not disappoint": a good example for Latin learners that both systems of the future coexist without difficulty. We can make these two verbs plural for practice and say, *illustrabunt*, "they will enhance," and *fallemus*, "we shall not disappoint."

> → **1249** verb formation T.3 in groups I and II, 12.3.1;
> verb formation T.3 in groups III and IV, 12.3.2.

mihi crede, "Believe me": this command is set parenthetically into the sentence, which could stand on its own without this interjection. *crede* is one of the 65 verbs whose complement is in the dat., here *mihi*. The difficulty with these verbs is that the dat. complement is not heard in English: "Believe me," which sounds acc. Note: the Romans did not say *crede mihi* in that word order, because it sounds like the beginning of an hexameter Latin verse. They always preferred the less metric word order *mihi crede*.

> → **1250** commands: first, second, 17;
> 65 verbs with dat., 33.7.2, GL n° 346.

studia officiaque, "signs of devotion and kindness": the plural is difficult to express directly in English as if "zeals, zealous expressions," so we have eased our English rendering as "signs of devotion."

LETTER 320 T-P
AD ATTICUM VII, 22

CICERO ATTICO SAL.

Pedem in Italia video nullum esse qui non in istius potestate sit. De Pompeio scio nihil, eumque, nisi in navim se contulerit, exceptum iri puto. O celeritatem incredibilem! huius autem nostri—sed non possum sine dolore accusare eum de quo angor et crucior. Tu caedem non sine causa times, non quo minus quidquam Caesari expediat ad diuturnitatem victoriae et dominationis, sed video quorum arbitrio sit acturus. Recte sit; *sed* censeo cedendum.   (*Att.* VII, 22, 1)

CICERO A GREETING TO ATTICUS

I see there is no foot [twelve inches] in Italy which is not in the control of that guy [Caesar]. I know nothing about Pompeius, and I think that, unless he will have gotten himself onto a ship, he will be cut off. O unbelievable swiftness [of Caesar]! but of this our man [Pompeius]—but I am not able without grief to accuse him [Pompeius] about whom I am worried and tormented. Not without a reason do you fear a slaughter, not because anything is supposedly less advantageous to Caesar for the durability of victory and of domination, but I see by whose judgment he is going to be acting. Let it be all right; *but* I believe a concession has to be made.

CICERO ATTICO SAL.: *Cicero Attico salutem*

video nullum esse, "I see there is no [foot]": *video*, "I see," in T.1i and a verb of M & M produces *nullum esse*, "none to be," in OO.
  → **1251** M & M, 60, 71, GL nº 527, remarks 1–2; OO, 71–73.

qui ... sit, "which is": result clause describing the character of the place. Here *qui* stands for *talem ut is sit*, "such that it is" or "such which is."
  → **1252** subjunctive use: characteristic result, 68.2.

istius, "of that guy [Caesar]": the first normal, natural meaning in the dictionary of *iste, a, ud* is "that by you" or more specifically "that of yours." The dictionary also gives a second, derogatory use meaning "that lousy guy," "that bad thing of yours." Because of this pejorative sense which seems persistently among Latinists to be its principal meaning, the normal use of this pronoun may be have to be avoided in formal discourse such as Vatican documents. For example, the Pope does not send a greeting by saying, *Salutem nuntiamus isti dioecesi*, which is good Latin and so should not but unfortunately does sound like it means "We are sending a greeting to that lousy diocese of yours." Rather than say in correct Latin, *Benedictionem impertimur dioecesi isti*, "We impart a blessing to the diocese of yours," the Pope would have to say, *Benedictionem impertimur illi tuae dioecesi*, "We impart a blessing to that your diocese," which is bad Latin because *illi* refers to the diocese in another place, not "yours."

→ **1253** dict., *iste, a, ud*, pron. demonstr., I.... "with affixed *ce*," and v. *Ossa*, 40.3.

scio ... eumque ... exceptum iri puto, "I know ... and I think that ... he will be cut off": *puto*, "I think," is a M & M verb in T.1i. Depending on *puto* is an idea whose action is future passive, expressed here in OO, where *iri* is the passive infinitive of a verb of motion and means "motion is being made." Connected with *iri* is the object supine of purpose *exceptum*, "to intercept" or "to cut off," which looks like a participle, but as a supine is unchangeable. The object of *exceptum* is *eum*, "him" or here "he." Thus, the phrase *eum exceptum iri* may be understood to say, "[I think] that motion is being made to cut him off." Its plural is *eosque exceptum iri putamus*, "we think they will be intercepted." This construction is used in a letter to Atticus where his thought, as we shall see, skips along almost faster than he can write it. Rather than a more difficult expression, this is the ready and natural way of expressing his thought.

→ **1254** M & M, 60, 71, GL n° 527, remarks 1–2; OO, 71–73; verb: futurity passive infinitive, 81.3.

scio ... que ... puto, "I know ... and ... I think": *-que*, "and," joins *scio*, "I know" and *puto*, "I think"; true to style, the *-que* is attached to the first word of the second element, which in this case is *eum*, the object of *exceptum*, depending on *iri*, itself depending on *puto*.

→ **1255** conjunction: *-que*, 3.2.

nisi ... se contulerit, "unless he will have gotten himself": *nisi*, "if not," "unless," begins a factual conditional, where *contulerit*, "he will have taken [himself]," is taken as T.6i here because of the magnetic force of *exceptum iri*, providing the combination of T.3i with T.6i. But *contulerit* could also be T.3s by MA with the same future completed meaning; in this case, *puto*, a verb of M & M, establishes the action in T.1i on Track I, and produces a future action *exceptum iri* given in OO; but before that future occurs, another action may occur before; that action is put in the future completed time, *contulerit*, which is either T.6i, or by MA on Track I is T.3s, both meaning the same in English, "he will have taken [himself]."

> → **1256** conditionals: factual, 86.1; conditionals in OO, 103;
> M & M, 60, 71, GL nº 527, remarks 1–2; OO, 71–73;
> verb: futurity passive infinitive, 81.3; *consecutio*, 47–48;
> T.3i and T.6i paired: 7, Time 6, and GL nº 244, remark 2;
> subjunctive use: modal attraction, 83.

in navim, "onto a ship": rather than the form *navem*, the alternative *navim* is the object form of a group of nouns in –*is*, –*is*; another example is *turrim* from *turris, is* f. "a tower," as is *securim* from *securis, is*, f. "an axe." This use of *navim* is mentioned in the dictionary.

> → **1257** dict., *navis, is*, f. (I. acc. sing. usually *navem*, but *navim*).

O celeritatem incredibilem, "O unbelievable swiftness [of Caesar]": the object form is used in exclamations, just as we say in English: "O miserable me," where "me" is in the object form, not "O miserable I," where "I" is in the subject form.

> → **1258** exclamations, GL nº 343.1.

huius autem nostri, "but of this our man [Pompeius]": an incomplete sentence that contrasts with the previous idea. Thus, in contrast to Caesar's swiftness perhaps he implies "but what of the slowness of this our man [Pompeius]," but Cicero does not finish his thought, as though his thoughts skip along ahead of his need to write every word.

non quo … expediat, "not because [anything] is [less] advantageous": people may initially take *quo minus*, also written as one word *quominus* to mean "that not," but there is no verb of hindering or preventing here to produce that expression. Rather, here *non quo* is like *non quod, non quia, non quoniam*, "not because," and *expediat*, "[anything] is [less] advantageous," is in T.1s to indicate an outside quoted reason. Because of its nature, this subjunctive in Latin is expressed in the indicative in English, but Cicero's intent in using the subjunctive we might express in English as "allegedly," "as they say," "as is said," as in "not because anything is allegedly less advantageous." The reported speech may be discounted or reported neutrally. Cicero could have claimed this comment as his own by saying, *non quo … expediat*, "not because, as I believe, [anything] is [less] advantageous," where *expediat* is T.1s. Cicero is quoting himself, as if a third person.

> → **1259** causal: *quod*, "because, since," + subjunctive, reported reason, 59.2;
> causal: rejected reason, *non quo*, GL nº 541, note 2.

Caesari expediat, "[anything] is [less] advantageous to Caesar": *expediat* is one of the 65 verbs whose natural complement is in the dat., here *Caesari*. In the English rendering above the dat. is heard, "to Caesar," but other ways of rendering it into English mask the dat., as in "it promotes Caesar," "it furthers Caesar."

> → **1260** 65 verbs with dat., 33.7.2, GL nº 346.

video quorum arbitrio sit acturus, "[but] I see by whose judgment he is going to be acting": *video*, "I see," in T.1i is a verb of M & M establishing Track I. The expression of futurity in the subjunctive, *sit acturus*, means "he is about to act," "he is going to act," "he is on the point of acting," "he will act." *quorum ... sit acturus*, is an IQ; its direct question would be *Quorum arbitrio est acturus?*, "By whose judgment is he going to act?," or *Quorum arbitrio aget?*, "By whose judgment will he be acting?" Tyrrell and Purser indicate that there is a textual problem with the reading *sit* or *sed*, so we shall not comment further here.

> → **1261** M & M, 60, 71, GL n° 527, remarks 1–2; IQ, 60;
>   futurity participle, 50, 51.1.3;
>   *consecutio*: futurity formula in the subjunctive, 61.3.

censeo cedendum, "I believe a concession has to be made": *censeo* in T.1i is a verb of M & M and gives rise to OO where the full infinitive is *cedendum esse*, which includes the participle of passive necessity *cedendum*. No subject is given, because the infinitive is used here impersonally, and so means "a concession has to be granted." *cedo, cessi, cessum*, 3, is one of the 65 verbs whose object is given in the dat. Gildersleeve and Lodge has this one note in tiny print at the bottom of the page that says: "Of course the passives of these verbs are used impersonally (208)" (GL n° 346, remark 1). Good luck!

> → **1262** M & M, 60, 71, GL n° 527, remarks 1–2; OO, 71–73;
>   65 verbs with dat., 33.7.2, 89.3.3, GL n° 346, remark 1;
>   passive of intransitive verbs used impersonally, GL n° 208.2;
>   participle of passive necessity, 50, 51.1.4.

☙

De Oppiis egeo consili. Quod optimum factu videbitur facies. Cum Philotimo loquere, atque adeo Terentiam habebis Idibus. Ego quid agam? qua aut terra aut mari persequar eum qui ubi sit nescio? Etsi terra quidem qui possum? mari quo? Tradam igitur isti me? Fac posse tuto—multi enim hortantur—num etiam honeste? Nullo modo quidem. A te petam consilium, ut soleo? Explicari res non potest. Sed tamen si quid in mentem venit velim scribas et ipse quid sis acturus.   (*Att.* VII, 22, 2)

As to the Oppii [people], I need advice. You will do what will appear the best thing to do. You shall speak with Philotimus, and so you shall have Terentia there on the Ides. What shall I do? by what either land or sea shall I follow him who I do not know where [he] is? Even if by land, indeed, how can I do it? by sea, to what place? Therefore shall I hand myself over to that guy [Caesar]? Imagine that I can do this safely—for many are encouraging—you don't mean even honorably? In no way, indeed. Shall I ask advice of you, as I am accustomed? The matter is not able to be resolved. But nevertheless if anything comes to mind, I would like that you write also what you yourself are going to do.

egeo consili, "I need advice": the verb *egeo,* "I want," "I lack," has the comple-ment *consili,* an early way of writing *consilii,* in the gen. and so literally, "of advice." The difficulty in English is that you cannot hear the gen. in "I need advice" unless you say, "I am in need of advice." This same verb also takes the abl. as in *egeo consilio,* "I need advice."

→ **1263** dict., *egeo, ui,* 2., I., b., (a). in the abl., (b). in the gen.;
early gen. ending in *–i,* GL n° 33, remark 1.

Quod … videbitur facies, "You will do what will appear": *facies,* "you will do," is T.3i, and *Quod … videbitur,* also in T.3i, is perhaps more properly expressed in English as "that which will appear," but more colloquially as "what will appear." The latter rendering is problematic in English because it appears to be an IQ, but there is no verb of M & M to give rise to an IQ, and the Latin indicative indicates that it is a simple relative sentence.

→ **1264** verb formation T.3 in groups I and II, 12.3.1;
verb formation T.3 in groups III and IV, 12.3.2; relative clauses, 10–11;
IQ, 60.

optimum factu, "the best thing to do": *factu,* "to do," is the abl. supine that is used with a number of adjectives in almost set phrases.

→ **1265** supine, 81.

Cum Philotimo loquere, "You shall speak with Philotimus": the form *loquere* can mean one of three things in Latin. First, *lóquere,* "you must speak," is the command form of a deponent verb. Second, *lóquere* is a variation of *lóqueris,* "you are speaking," in T.1i. Third, *loquére* is a variation form of *loquéris,* "you shall speak," in T.3i and also serving as a light command. We took this as T.3i because there are other verbs in T.3i in the sentence.

→ **1266** commands: deponent, 34;
commands: T.3i, 85.1.6; variation: *–ris,* 39.3.

Idibus, "on the Ides": function of time at which, abl. Implied here is *Febru-ariis,* "February Ides" [13 February], where *Februariis* is an adj. going with *Idibus* according to classical usage. Church usage is *Idibus Februarii,* "on the Ides of February."

→ **1267** abl.: time at which, 70.1;
about the Roman calendar, pp. 605–608;
GL appendix: Roman Calendar, pp. 491–92.

Ego quid agam?, "What shall I do?": *agam* is either T.3i as in the English rendering above, or it is T.1s and means "What should I do?"

→ **1268** verb formation T.3 in groups III and IV, 12.3.2;
forms of the subjunctive, T.1s, 44.1.

aut terra aut mari, "by … either land or sea": no prepositions for this famous idiom-phrase.

→ **1269** dict., *terra, ae,* f., I. numerous variations on this idiom are given.

persequar, "shall I follow": again this is either T.3i as in the English rendering above, or it is T.1s and means "should I follow [him—Pompeius]?"

→ **1270** verb formation T.3 in groups III and IV, 12.3.2;
forms of the subjunctive, T.1s, 44.1.

qui ubi sit nescio, "who I do not know where [he] is": *qui* is the subject of *sit* in the IQ *ubi sit*, "where [who] is," depending on *nescio*, "I do not know," in T.1i, a verb of M & M.

→ **1271** M & M, 60, 71, GL n° 527, remarks 1–2; IQ, 60.

qui possum?, "how can I do it?": *qui possum* is one of the most difficult elements in the letter so far. You must look in your dictionaries where you will find this entered separately as *quī*. This is an old abl. interrogative, "by what means," "in what way," "how," and its plural is *quibus*. This is not the relative *qui, quae, quod*. This *quī* has its own entry in the dictionary.

→ **1272** dict., *quī*, adv. interrog. "in what manner? How?"

mari quo?, "by sea, to what place?": this expression does not mean "by what sea." Rather it picks up the previous phrase and begins *mari*, "by sea," and then asks *quo*, "to where." Here *quo*, "to what place," "whither," is an adv., as in *Quo vadis*, "Whither goest thou." Related are *eo*, "to that place," "thither," and *huc*, "to this place," "hither."

→ **1273** dict., *quo*, adv., II. "to where";
eo, adv., II. "to that place"; dict., *huc*, adv., I. "to this place."

Tradam … isti me?, "shall I hand myself over to that guy?": The object *me*, "myself," is reflexive because it refers to *ego*, "I," the subject of *Tradam*, "I shall hand over." The natural dat. *isti* means both "to that man" and in a derogatory sense "to that bum [Caesar]." If we reverse *Tradam isti me* by making all of the words plural, we get, *Trademus istis nos?*, "Shall we hand ourselves over to those lousy people," also in T.3i. *Tradam me* could also mean "should I hand myself over," in T.1s, in which the subjunctive is used to engage another person in a deliberative question. When we make this sentence plural the result is *Tradamus istis nos?*, "Should we give ourselves over to those lousy people?" We can never know whether *Tradam me* here means "I shall hand myself over" in T.3i, or "Should I hand over" in T.1s.

→ **1274** reflexive pron.: first and second person, 30;
verb formation T.3 in groups III and IV, 12.3.2;
forms of the subjunctive, T.1s, 44.1;
independent subjunctive, 45.6, deliberative question, GL n° 265;
natural dat., 33.7.1.

Fac posse tuto, "Imagine that I can do this safely": about the tenth meaning of *facio, feci, factum*, 3 in the dictionary is "suppose," "assume," "imagine." As in one of the examples given in the dictionary, here *Fac* is used with OO where the infinitive is *posse*, and its subject *me* is implied from the whole idea. The other form of the adv. *tuto* is *tute*, "safely." The hypothetical idea,

Fac [me] posse tuto, goes back to *Tradam*, as in "Imagine that I can safely hand myself over to Caesar."

→ **1275** commands: famous four, 39.4;
    M & M, 60, 71, GL n° 527, remarks 1–2; OO, 71–73;
    dict., *tueor, tuitus*, 2., II., B.—adv. *tuto*.

num etiam honeste?, "you don't mean even honorably?": the *num* asks a question that presumes a negative answer. You really have to work the English around to express this: "surely not even honorably?," or "you can't mean even honorably?" The idea that he is rejecting goes back to *Tradam*, namely, that he could honorably turn himself over to Caesar—surely not!

→ **1276** ways of asking, 13.1.

Nullo modo, "In no way": the answer to his command *Fac [me] posse tuto ... num etiam honeste?*, meaning "Imagine that [I] can safely [hand myself over to Caesar] ... surely you don't mean [I can do so] even honorably?," is "In no way!" This is a natural meaning of the abl.

→ **1277** abl.: meaning and forms, 27.

ut soleo, "as I am accustomed": followed by the indicative *soleo*, "I am wont," in T.1i; here *ut* means "as."

→ **1278** *ut*, I., B. meaning "as."

A te petam consilium ... ?, "Shall I ask advice of you ... ?," the question is formed here with the use of *petam*, "Shall I ask [of you] ... ?," in T.3i, which could also be taken as T.1s, also asking a question, "Should I ask of you ... ?"

→ **1279** verb formation T.3 in groups III and IV, 12.3.2;
    forms of the subjunctive, T.1s, 44.1.

explicari res non potest, "The matter is not able to be resolved": the passive inf. *explicari* complements the action of the main verb *potest*, "[the matter] is able," and means "to be unraveled," thus, "to be solved."

→ **1280** verb: complementary infinitive, 77.

si quid in mentem venit, "if anything comes to mind": here *si quid* stands for *si aliquid*, "if anything," and begins a factual conditional sentence whose verb *venit*, "[anything] comes," is T.1i. Note the preposition *in* with the object *mentem* to indicate geographical or moral motion to or toward, as in "into the mind."

→ **1281** conditionals: factual, 86.1;
    pronouns: indefinite, 42.4; after *si* the *ali*-s fly away, 42.5;
    prep. with obj., 6.

si quid ... quid sis acturus, "if anything ... what you ... are going to do": the word *quid* appears twice in this sentence with two different meanings. First, *si quid*, as an indefinite pronoun, stands for *si aliquid*, "if anything," and the

interrogative *quid* in the IQ *quid sis acturus*, "what you are going to do," is
an IQ where *quid* asks the question "what."

> → **1282** pronouns: indefinite, 42.4; after *si* the *ali*-s fly away, 42.5; IQ, 60;
> dict., 1. *quis, quid,* pron. interrog.;
> dict., 2. *quis, quid,* pron. indef.;
> dict., *aliquis, aliquid,* indef. subst. pron.

velim scribas, "I would like that you write": *velim,* "I would like," is T.1s and
is complemented by *scribas,* "that you write," in T.1s without *ut.* This is a
polite form of command that expresses a polite request.

> → **1283** commands: other expressions, *velim,* 85.1.7;
> subjunctive use: purpose clause without *ut,* 58, GL n° 546, remark 2.

et ipse quid sis acturus, "also what you yourself are going to do": Cicero
would like not only that Atticus write, but also that in his writing Atticus
tell Cicero what he himself intends to do. The complement of *velim,* "I would
like," is *scribas,* "that you write," which in turn has two objects. The first is
the *aliquid,* in the condition *si quid in mentem venit,* "if anything comes
to mind." The second, a verb of M & M, *scribas,* produces the IQ *quid sis
acturus,* "what you are going to do," which gives the content of the writing.
These two objects of *scribas,* "that you write," are joined by an *et,* meaning
either "and" or "also." We may play with this expression of futurity in the
subjunctive by changing *quid sis acturus* "what you are going to do," to say,
quid agas, "what you are doing" in T.1s, and *quid egeris,* "what you have
done" in T.3s.

> → **1284** subjunctive use: purpose clause without *ut,* 58, GL n° 546, remark 2;
> commands: other expressions, *velim,* 85.1.7;
> pronouns: indefinite, 42.4; after *si* the *ali*-s fly away, 42.5;
> conditionals: factual, 86.1;
> M & M, 60, 71, GL n° 527, remarks 1–2; IQ, 60;
> futurity participle, 50, 51.1.3;
> *consecutio:* futurity formula in the subjunctive, 61.3;
> conjunction: *et,* 3.2.

LETTER 72 T-P
AD QUINTUM FRATREM I, 4

MARCUS QUINTO FRATRI SALUTEM.

Amabo te, mi frater, ne, si uno meo facto et tu et omnes mei corruistis, improbitati et sceleri meo potius quam imprudentiae miseriaeque adsignes. Nullum est meum peccatum nisi quod iis credidi a quibus nefas putaram esse me decipi, aut etiam quibus ne id expedire quidem arbitrabar. Intimus, proximus, familiarissimus quisque aut sibi pertimuit aut mihi invidit: ita mihi nihil misero praeter fidem amicorum, cautum meum consilium *de*fuit.   (*Q. Fr.* I, 4, 1)

MARCUS A GREETING TO BROTHER QUINTUS

Please, my dear brother, if by one deed of mine both you and all my people have crashed, do not attribute [that] to my wickedness and crime rather than to lack of foresight and to misery. There is no mistake of mine except that I trusted those people by whom I had thought that it was a crime that I be deceived, or also to whom I was thinking that it was not even advantageous. Every most intimate, nearest, and most familiar person either feared for himself or envied me: thus nothing was lacking to miserable me besides the trustworthiness of my friends, [and] my own cautious program.

> *Amabo te*, "Please": literally "I shall love you," this idiom more or less means "please." It stands parenthetical to this sentence. It is most frequent in comic writers and colloquial speech.
>
> → **1285** dict., *amo, avi, atum*, 1., II., D., c.—*amo*, or *amabo te* (never *amabo vos*, etc.), "I shall like you."

> *mi frater*, "my dear brother": direct address, Cicero is talking directly to his brother Quintus. The expression "dear" is supplied to express the tenderness of the petition, *Amabo te*, "Please." This is reflected in the dictionary entry for *meus, a, um*, where the vocative *mi* is said to mean "*my dear! my beloved!*"
>
> → **1286** dict., *meus, a, um*, adj., –voc.; function: direct address, 38.3.

ne … adsignes, "do not attribute [that]": a negative command composed of *ne* followed by *adsignes* in T.1s. Note the word order and the opening of boxes at the beginning of this letter, *Amabo te, mi frater, ne, si … ,* "Please, my brother, don't, if …." The object of *adsignes* is not explicit, but felt "[that]."

→ **1287** negative command T.1s: 85.2.3.

ne … improbitati et sceleri meo potius quam imprudentiae miseriaeque adsignes, "do not attribute [that] to my wickedness and crime rather than to lack of foresight and misery": note the natural use of the dat. placed in front with the verb coming last. The comparative *potius quam*, "rather than" or "sooner than," stands between the two equal elements. *et* joins the first pair, *improbitati et sceleri*, "to my wickedness and crime," whereas *–que* is attached to the second member of the second pair just for variety: *imprudentiae miseriaeque*, "to lack of foresight and misery." Tyrrell and Purser says that *imprudentiae miseriaeque* is a hendiadys, where two words are used to express the one idea, "my pitiable shortsightedness."

→ **1288** natural dat., 33.7.1; *quam* with the comp., 43.2;
conjunction: *et,* 3.2; conjunction: *–que,* 3.2; hendiadys, GL n° 698.

ne … adsignes … ne … quidem, "do not attribute … not even": two uses of *ne* with different meanings. At the beginning of the sentence it goes with *adsignes* to form the negative command, "do not attribute." At the end of the sentence *ne* goes with *quidem* and the two words surround the idea they negate, *id expedire*, "that it was advantageous not even [to them]."

→ **1289** negative commands: other expressions, 85.4;
dict., *quidem,* adv., I., C., 1. *ne … quidem,* "not even."

et tu et omnes mei corruistis, "both you and all of my people have crashed": *et … et … ,* "both … and … ," join *tu*, "you," with *omnes mei*, "all my people." This last noun *omnes* is plural, and the verb agrees with it *corruistis*, "you-all have crashed." Here *mei*, "my people," is subject plural of *meus, a, um*.

→ **1290** conjunction: *et … , et … ,* 3.2;
verb agrees with the nearest subject, GL n° 285, exception 1.

nisi quod iis credidi, "except that I trusted those people": *nisi quod*, "except for the fact that" or "save only that," refers to the whole previous statement and develops its content, *Nullum est meum peccatum*, "There is no mistake of mine." In T.4b *credidi* is one of the 65 verbs that takes a complement in the dat.; the difficulty is that the dat. cannot be heard in the English rendering, "I trusted those people."

→ **1291** 65 verbs with dat., 33.7.2, GL n° 346;
quod = "the fact that" as a new subject, GL n° 525.2.

a quibus nefas putaram esse me decipi, "by whom I had thought that it was a crime that I be deceived": the main verb is *putaram*, a contracted form of *putaveram*, "I had thought," in T.5i and a verb of M & M. The content of the thought is given in OO where the infinitive is *esse*, "to be," meaning here "[it] was" because the infinitive is contemporaneous to *putaram*, "I had thought." The subject of *esse* is the whole statement given in OO, *me decipi*, "that I be deceived," where *me* is the acc. subj. of the inf. *decipi*. Equal to *me decipi* is the predicate *nefas*, "a crime." The statement begins with the relative *a quibus*, "by whom," which depends on the passive infinitive *decipi*, "[I had thought that it was a crime that I] be deceived [by whom]"; the relative expresses the personal agent doing the deceiving.

> → **1292** contractions: verbs, 39.2, GL n° 131;
> M & M, 60, 71, GL n° 527, remarks 1–2; OO, 71–73;
> verb: contemporaneous passive infinitive, 72.3;
> verb: contemporaneous active infinitive, 72.1;
> relative clauses, 10–11; abl.: personal agent, 28.5.3–4, 89.2.

aut etiam quibus ne id expedire quidem arbitrabar, "or even to whom I was thinking that was not even advantageous": the *aut*, "or," adds this second possibility to the first, both describing Cicero's belief in *iis*, "those people," first *a quibus*, "by whom," or now *quibus*, "to whom." The main verb is *arbitrabar*, "I was thinking," in T.2i and a verb of M & M. The content of his thought is given in OO, *id expedire*, "[I was thinking] that it was [not even] advantageous." *expedire* is one of the 65 verbs whose complement is given in the dat., here *quibus*, "[I was thinking that it was advantageous] to whom."

> → **1293** M & M, 60, 71, GL n° 527, remarks 1–2; OO, 71–73;
> verb: deponent, 29;
> 65 verbs with dat., 33.7.2, GL n° 346; relative clauses, 10–11.

Intimus, proximus, familiarissimus quisque, "Every most intimate, nearest, and most familiar person": *quisque* is placed after the superlatives, here *intimus*, "most intimate," *proximus*, "nearest," and *familiarissimus*, "most familiar," not to convey the expected meaning "each [most intimate … person]," but to convey universality, as in "all the most intimate, nearest, and most familiar." We do this in English when we say, "all the best people" rather than "each best person."

> → **1294** dict., *quisque, quaeque, quodque*, pron. indef. I.—with sup. to express
> universality (placed after sup.);
> adj.: superlative, 36.

aut sibi pertimuit aut mihi invidit, "either feared for himself or envied me": *aut … aut …*, "either … or" coordinate the two verbs. The first verb, *pertimuit*, "[Every … person] feared," in T.4b takes the natural dat., *sibi*, "for himself," which is reflexive because it refers back to the subject of *pertimuit*, namely, *quisque*, "Every." We can play with this and say "he feared for the other guy," *ei pertimuit*, and "he feared for them over there," *illis pertimuit*. The second verb, *invidit*, "[Every … person] envied," is T.4b and is one of the 65 verbs that take a complement in the dat., here *mihi*, "[envied] me."

Students have difficulty with the English expression "Every person envied me," because they cannot hear the Latin dat. in the English "me."

→ **1295** disjunctive sentence: *aut . . . , aut . . .* , GL n° 493.3;
natural dat., 33.7.1; reflexive pron.: third person, 31;
65 verbs with dat., 33.7.2, GL n° 346.

mihi nihil misero . . . defuit, "nothing was lacking to miserable me": the combination *mihi nihil misero* does not mean here "to me miserable in no way," because *nihil* is logically the subject of *defuit*, "nothing was lacking," and *defuit* takes the dat. here, *mihi . . . misero*, "[nothing] was lacking to miserable me." Thus, the two words *mihi . . . misero* are separated by the subject *nihil* of their verb *defuit*.

→ **1296** dict., *desum, fui, esse*, v. irreg., I., (β). with dat. (so most freq.).

praeter fidem amicorum, cautum meum consilium, "besides the trustworthiness of my friends, [and] my own cautious program": the objects of *praeter* are juxtaposed without a connecting word such as "and," giving an example of asyndeton. First *fidem*, "the trustworthiness," is given, then *consilium*, "program."

→ **1297** prep. with obj., 6; asyndeton, GL n° 481.2.

❧

Quod si te satis innocentia tua et misericordia hominum vindicat hoc tempore a molestia, perspicis profecto ecquaenam nobis spes salutis relinquatur. Nam me Pomponius et Sestius et Piso noster adhuc Thessalonicae retinuerunt, cum longius discedere propter nescio quos motus vetarent. Verum ego magis exitum illorum litteris quam spe certa exspectabam. Nam quid sperem potentissimo inimico, dominatione obtrectatorum, infidelibus amicis, plurimis invidis?   (*Q. Fr.* I, 4, 2)

But if your innocence and the compassion of people frees you enough at this time from trouble, by all means you do understand whether any-in-the-world hope of salvation is left over for us. For Pomponius and Sestius and our Piso so far kept me back in Thessalonica, when they were forbidding [me] to depart further away because of some-I-don't-know-which rumblings. However I was awaiting the outcome more by their letters than with a sure hope. For what should I hope—my enemy being very powerful—there being the control of my detractors—my friends being unfaithful—very many people being envious.

Quod si te . . . vindicat . . . , perspicis, "But if [innocence . . .] frees you . . . you do understand": a factual conditional where the verbs of both clauses are T.1i in the indicative. *Quod si*, "But if," is sometimes written as one word *Quodsi* because the expression is so standardized. Note the word order: *te*, "you," is the object of *vindicat*, "it frees," and they stand separated by the five words that express the subject.

→ **1298** conditionals: factual, 86.1; sentence structure, 1.

perspicis … ecquaenam nobis spes salutis relinquatur, "you do understand whether any-in-the-world hope of salvation is left over for us": the main verb is *perspicis*, "you do understand," a verb of M & M in T.1i establishing Track I. The content of the understanding is given in an IQ introduced by the question word *quae* in *ecquaenam*, "whether any-in-the-world [hope]," accompanied by the verb *reliquatur*, "is left over," in T.1s, which is complemented by the natural dat., *nobis*, "for us."

→ **1299** M & M, 60, 71, GL nº 527, remarks 1–2; IQ, 60;
consecutio, 47–48;
natural dat., 33.7.1.

ecquaenam … spes, "any-in-the-world hope": this expression is composed of three elements: *ec quae nam*. The dictionary explains that *ec* is combined with any form of *qui, quae, quod* to ask "is there any," as here where *ec* is followed by *quae* that agrees with *spes* to ask "is there any hope." The addition of *nam* increases the desperation as in the English expression "in the world."

→ **1300** dict., *ecqui, ecquae* or *ecqua, ecquod*, pron. interrog. adj., I.—with suffixed *nam*.

Nam me Pomponius … adhuc Thessalonicae retinuerunt, "For Pomponius … so far kept me back in Thessalonica": note the word order: *retinuerunt* is separated from its object *me* by the eight words of the rest of the sentence. *Thessalonicae* is not the gen., but the form of place at which, the proper locative, which was originally written as *Thessalonicai* but sounded like the present spelling.

→ **1301** sentence structure, 1;
function: place at which, names of cities and small islands, singular, *Thessalonicae*, 69.3.2.

cum longius discedere propter nescio quos motus vetarent, "when they were forbidding me to depart further away because of some-I-don't-know-which rumblings": depending on the main verb *retinuerunt*, "[Pomponius …] kept me back," in T.4b establishing Track II. Here *cum … vetarent*, in T.2s is either a temporal clause giving the circumstance, "when they were forbidding," or a causal clause giving the reason why, "because they were forbidding"; the other possibility, a clause making a concession, does not make sense here: "although they were forbidding." Had the indicative been used, for example *vetabant*, "they were forbidding," it would have indicated the mere coincidence of time, rather than temporal circumstance.

→ **1302** subjunctive use: temporal circumstance *cum* = "when," 66.3.2;
subjunctive use: causal *cum* = "because, since," 59.1;
subjunctive use: concessive *cum* = "although," 64;
cum + historical times of indicative = "when": temporal coincidence, 66.3.1.

The M & M verb *vetarent*, "they were forbidding," produces OO, where the infinitive *discedere* has the implied subject *me*, "[me] to depart." The expression *nescio quos*, "some-I-don't-know-which," may also be written as one word *nescioquos* and is taken as the object of *propter*, "because of." Here *nescio* does not function as an independent verb but as part of the pronoun *nescioqui*, as found in the dictionary, and *quos* agrees with *motus*, "rumblings," the object plural of the *–us*, *–us* noun *motus*. *longius* is a comparative adv. meaning "further off."

> → **1303** M & M, 60, 71, GL n° 527, remarks 1–2; OO, 71–73;
> *consecutio*, 47–48;
> dict., *nescio, ivi* or *ii, itum*, 4., I., (γ). *nescio quis, quid*;
> dict., *motus, us*, m.; 20% of nouns: *motus, us*, m., 35;
> adv.: positive, comp., superl., 37.

Nam quid sperem, "For what should I hope": the verb *sperem* is T.1s, a natural subjunctive that asks the question "what may I hope," "what should I hope."

> → **1304** independent subjunctive, 45.6, deliberative question, GL n° 265;
> dict., *nam*, conj., III. in interrogations.

potentissimo inimico, dominatione obtrectatorum, infidelibus amicis, plurimis invidis, "my enemy being very powerful—there being the control of my detractors—my friends being unfaithful—very many people being envious": each pair of words is an AA without the verb expressed, a sign that the implied verb is "being."

> → **1305** ablative absolute, 54–55.

❧

De novis autem tribunis plebis est ille quidem in me officiosissimus Sestius et, spero, Curius, Milo, Fadius, Fabricius, sed valde adversante Clodio, qui etiam privatus eadem manu poterit contiones concitare, deinde etiam intercessor parabitur.   (*Q. Fr.* I, 4, 3)

However, out of the new tribunes of the people there is that Sestius indeed most obliging toward me, and, I hope, Curius, Milo, Fadius, Fabricius, but Clodius strongly opposing, who even as a private citizen with the same band of men will be able to stir up the popular assemblies, and even after that he will be prepared as an obstructionist.

sed valde adversante Clodio, "but Clodius strongly opposing": an AA that is strongly adversative. It could be smoothed out more by saying, "but while Clodius is in opposition."

> → **1306** ablative absolute, 54–55.

qui ... poterit contiones concitare, "who ... will be able to stir up the popular assemblies": this relative clause depends on the AA and continues its

thought. The verb *poterit*, "[who] will be able," is T.3i and is completed with
an infinitive *concitare*, "to stir up," which has its own object, *contiones*, "the
popular assemblies." The idea continues with *parabitur*, "he will be prepared," also in T.3i.

> → **1307** ablative absolute, 54–55; relative clauses, 10–11;
>   the verb "to be" in the indicative, 9.1; conjugation of *possum*, GL n° 119;
>   verb: complementary infinitive, 77; passive T.1i, T.2i, T.3i, 21;
>   verb formation T.3 in groups I and II, 12.3.1.

∽

Haec mihi proficiscenti non proponebantur, sed saepe triduo summa cum
gloria dicebar esse rediturus. Quid tu igitur? inquies. Quid? multa convenerunt quae mentem exturbarent meam: subita defectio Pompei, alienatio
consulum, etiam praetorum, timor publicanorum, arma. Lacrimae meorum me ad mortem ire prohibuerunt, quod certe et ad honestatem et ad
effugiendos intolerabilis dolores fuit aptissimum. Sed de hoc scripsi ad te
in ea epistula quam Phaëthonti dedi. Nunc tu, quoniam in tantum luctum
laboremque detrusus es quantum nemo umquam, si levare potest communem casum misericordia hominum, scilicet incredibile quiddam adsequeris:
sin plane occidimus—me miserum!—ego omnibus meis exitio fuero quibus
ante dedecori non eram.   (*Q. Fr.* I, 4, 4)

These things were not being put before me setting out [into exile], but often
I was being said to be about to return with the greatest glory within three
days. You will say, "You, therefore, what?" What? many things came together which were totally disturbing my mind: the sudden defection of Pompeius, the estrangement of the consuls, even of the praetors, the fear of the tax
collectors, the weapons. The tears of my people stopped me going to death,
something which for sure was most suitable both for respectability and for
escaping intolerable pains. But I wrote to you about this in that letter which
I gave to Phaëthon. Now, because you have been cast down into so great an
affliction and hardship as much as no one ever, if the sympathy of people
is able to relieve our common disaster, of course you will attain some sort
of incredible thing: but if we have totally fallen—O miserable me!—I shall
have been for a destruction to all my people for whom previously I was not
for a dishonor.

> *dicebar esse rediturus*, "I was being said to be about to return": the personal
> use of the rather rare form *dicebar*, "I was being said," and the content of
> the M & M verb is given in OO, where the infinitive *esse rediturus* is in
> the subject form and its subject is the implied *ego* contained both in the
> infinitive and in the main verb *dicebar*, "I was being said." This personal
> construction was preferred by the Romans to the impersonal construction,
> *me dicebatur esse rediturum*, "it was said that I would return," where the

infinitive and its subject are both in the acc. or object form. The expression here is called in certain books the nominative with the infinitive.

> → **1308** personal construction: *videor*, 73.3, GL n° 528.1 and remark 2 and note 1;
> nom. with the inf., 73.3, GL n° 528.1;
> M & M, 60, 71, GL n° 527, remarks 1–2; OO, 71–73.

multa convenerunt quae mentem exturbarent meam, "many things came together which were totally disturbing my mind": the main verb is *convenerunt*, "[many things] came together," in T.4b establishing Track II. The relative statement *quae … exturbarent*, in T.2s, is a result clause that expresses the character of the *multa*, "many things." What is implied in that *quae* is *talia ut ea*, "[many things came together] such that they [were disturbing my mind]." The subjunctive in Latin, *exturbarent*, is given in the indicative in English, "they were disturbing," according to the nature of a result clause. A list of the "many things" then follows, in the nom. subject form, as is *multa*.

> → **1309** *consecutio*, 47–48; subjunctive use: characteristic result, 68.2.

Lacrimae meorum me ad mortem ire prohibuerunt, "The tears of my people stopped me going to death": as for verbs of hindering or prohibiting, *prohibuerunt*, "[tears] stopped me," in T.4b produces a statement in OO, *me … ire*, "me going" or "me to go." As a verb of prohibiting, it could also be rendered in English as "[tears] kept me from going [to death]." Other ways to express this include: *ne*, "that," or *quominus*, "how much less" or "that not," followed by the subjunctive, as in *lacrimae meorum ne (quominus) irem ad mortem prohibuerunt*, "the tears of my people prohibited that I go to death," or "kept me from going to death"; in Latin the idea of "from" is not expressed but contained in the verb of prohibiting itself and in the *ne*.

> → **1310** verbs of prohibiting, 101, GL n° 632; OO, 71–73.

quod … fuit aptissimum, "something which … was most suitable": the *quod* here is not causal and does not mean "because." Rather it is relative, "something which," which is neuter and refers to the whole idea of going to death expressed previously. Likewise *aptissimum* is neuter because it agrees with *quod*, "something which … most suitable."

> → **1311** relative clauses, 10–11;
> *quod* referring to previous sentence: GL n° 614, remark 2.

et ad honestatem et ad effugiendos intolerabilis dolores, "both for respectability and for escaping intolerable pains": the repetition of *et … et … ,* "both … and … ," joins the two phrases beginning with *ad*. The first has a simple object, *ad honestatem*, "for respectability." The second as an object gerundive, *ad effugiendos intolerabilis dolores*, "for escaping intolerable pains." Here *intolerabilis* is an alternative form of *intolerabiles* agreeing with *dolores*, "intolerable pains." We can restore the gerund as *ad effugiendum intolerabiles dolores*, with the same meaning.

> → **1312** conjunction: *et … , et … ,* 3.2; prep. with obj., 6;
> gerundive, 77.2; gerund, 77.1;
> Block II adj.: *–is* = *–es*, 38, GL n° 78.

quoniam in tantum luctum laboremque detrusus es quantum nemo um-
quam, "because you have been cast down into so great an affliction and
hardship as much as no one ever": the sentence begins with an explanation
of the cause or reason for what follows, *quoniam ... detrusus es,* "because
you have been cast down," in T.4a. The pair *tantum ... quantum ... ,* "so
great ... as much ... ,"* are correlatives. What is implied is *in quantum luc-*
tum laboremque nemo umquam detrusus est, "into as much affliction and
hardship no one ever has been cast down," but there was no need to repeat
the whole statement. The statement, however, could benefit from the repetition of *in* before *quantum,* as *in quantum nemo umquam,* "into so much as
no one ever."

→ **1313** causal: *quoniam,* "because, since," + indicative, one's own reason, 59.2;
correlative comparative sentences, 90.5, GL n° 642.

si levare potest communem casum misericordia hominum, "if the sympathy of people is able to relieve our common disaster": before continuing to
the independent statement, a factual condition is given, *si levare potest,* "if
[sympathy] is able to relieve," where *potest,* "[sympathy] is able," is T.1i and
is complemented by the infinitive *levare,* "to relieve."

→ **1314** conditionals: factual, 86.1; verb: complementary infinitive, 77.

scilicet incredibile quiddam adsequeris, "of course you will attain some sort
of incredible thing": Cicero finally arrives at the independent statement,
which is also the second half of the factual conditional. The form *adsequeris*
may be *adséqueris,* "you do attain," in T.1i, but here it is *adsequéris,* "you
will attain," in T.3i. This future time corresponds in what follows to *fuero,*
"I shall have been," T.6i. The adverb *scilicet,* "of course," goes with the verb,
adsequéris, "of course you will attain."

→ **1315** conditionals: factual, 86.1; verb formation T.3 in groups III and IV, 12.3.2;
the verb "to be" in the indicative, 9.1; passive Times 1, 2, 3 indicative, 21;
T.3i and T.6i paired: 7, Time 6, and GL n° 244, remark 2;
verb: deponent, 29.

sin plane occidimus, "but if we have been totally ruined": this states the contrary condition. The positive condition was previously given, *si levare potest,*
"if [sympathy] is able to relieve," and is followed here by *sin,* the equivalent
of *si non,* "if not" or "if on the contrary." This is followed by *occidimus,*
"we have fallen," "we have collapsed," "we have sunk," "we have set," in
T.4a from *óccĭdo, cĭdi, casum,* 3, which in turn is from *cado, cádĕre,* "I fall,"
distinguished in your dict. from *occído, cīdi, cīsum,* 3, "to cut down," which
in its turn is from *caedo, cĕcīdi, caesum,* 3, "to slash," "to cut." Thus, we can
say: *sol occídit multos et óccidit,* "the sun has killed many people and has set
in the west."

→ **1316** conditionals: factual, 86.1;
dict., *óccĭdo, cĭdi, cāsum,* 3, "to fall down";
dict., *occído, cīdi, cīsum,* 3, "to cut down," "to kill."

me miserum!, "O miserable me!": an exclamation expressed in object form, as we say in English, "O miserable me!," not "O miserable I!"; or "Woe is me!," not "Woe is I!"

→ **1317** exclamations, GL n° 343.1.

ego omnibus meis exitio fuero, "I shall have been for a destruction to all my people": the verb *fuero*, "I shall have been," in T.6i, produces a double dative where the dat. of the person involved is *omnibus meis*, "to all my people," and the dat. expressing the outcome or result is *exitio*, "for a ruination." Cicero did not use here T.3i, which would express a future idea; T.6i indicates that Cicero considered this a certain, completed act.

→ **1318** double dat., 91.2; verb T.6i: GL n° 244.

quibus ante dedecori non eram, "for whom previously I was not for a dishonor": the verb *eram*, "I was," in T.2i, gives rise to another double dative. The dat. of the person involved is *quibus*, "to whom," and the dat. of the outcome or result is *dedecori*, "for a disgrace."

→ **1319** double dat., 91.2.

❧

Sed tu, ut ante ad te scripsi, perspice rem et pertempta et ad me, ut tempora nostra non ut amor tuus fert, vere perscribe. Ego vitam, quoad putabo tua interesse aut ad spem servandam esse, retinebo. Tu nobis amicissimum Sestium cognosces: credo tua causa velle Lentulum, qui erit consul. Quamquam sunt facta verbis difficiliora. Tu et quid opus sit et quid sit videbis. Omnino, si tuam solitudinem communemque calamitatem nemo dispexerit, aut per te aliquid confici aut nullo modo poterit: sin te quoque inimici vexare coeperint, ne cessaris: non enim gladiis tecum sed litibus agetur. Verum haec absint velim. Te oro ut ad me de omnibus *rebus* rescribas et in me animi aut potius consili minus putes esse quam antea, amoris vero et offici non minus.   (*Q. Fr.* I, 4, 5)

But you, as I wrote to you before, must ascertain the whole matter and try everything and write everything to me truly, as our circumstances not as your love allows. I shall hold on to life, as long as I shall consider that it is a concern to you or it is to be maintained according to our hope. You will get to know Sestius most friendly toward us: I believe that Lentulus, who will be consul, is disposed on your behalf. But still, deeds are more difficult than words. You will see both what is necessary and what the situation is. In general, if nobody will have discerned your isolation and our common calamity, either something will be able to be concluded with your help or in no way, but if also [our] enemies will have begun to bother you: don't stop, for it will be decided with you not by swords but by court cases. However, I would like these things to be far away. I beg you that you write back to me about all things and that you think that in me there is a smaller amount of

courage or rather of prudent-judgment than before, however not less of love
and dutifulness.

ut ... scripsi ... ut tempora nostra non ut amor tuus fert, "as I wrote ... as
our circumstances not as your love allows": *ut* appears three times meaning
"as," twice with a verb in the indicative, *scripsi*, "as I wrote," and *fert*, "as
... allows," and once without an expressed verb, *ut tempora nostra*, "as our
circumstances."

→ **1320** dict., *ut*, I., B meaning "as."

perspice ... et pertempta et ... perscribe, "must ascertain the whole ... and
try everything and write everything": Cicero liked the prefix *per–* used in all
three main verbs of this sentence and with it created innumerable Latin adjectives and verbs. This text is cited in L&S under verb *pertento, avi, atum*, 1.

→ **1321** dict., *pertento, avi, atum*, 1., I., B., *rem*, "to consider well," "to weigh well."

Ego vitam ... retinebo, "I shall hold on to life": the main sentence compris-
es the first two and last word, with the subject, *Ego*, "I," and object, *vitam*,
"life," out front.

→ **1322** sentence structure, 1.

quoad putabo, "as long as I shall consider": *quoad* is an adv. originally from
quod ad, "how long." Like *dum* and *donec* so too *quoad* means "as long as,"
"while," and is usually with the indicative, as here *putabo*, "I shall consider,"
in T.3i and a verb of M & M.

→ **1323** *quoad* with ind., 65.2.2; verb formation T.3 in groups I and II, 12.3.1;
M & M, 60, 71, GL n° 527, remarks 1–2.

quoad putabo tua interesse, "as long as I shall consider that it is a concern
to you": *putabo*, "I shall consider," in T.3i and a verb of M & M. The content
of the consideration is given in two expressions of OO. First, *tua interesse*,
"that it is a concern to you," is an impersonal infinitive that takes *tua*, due
to a transference from the verb *refert*, which also takes *tua* to agree with its
prefix *rē*. Thus, what is understood here is *tua re interesse*, "that it has bearing out of your matter." This is all explained in *Ossa* and found in L&S.

→ **1324** M & M, 60, 71, GL n° 527, remarks 1–2; OO, 71–73;
dict., *intersum, fui, esse*, v. irreg.;
dict., *rē-fert, rē-tuli, rē-latum, rē-ferre*, v. irreg.;
interest and *refert*, 102; GL n° 381.

quoad putabo ... aut ad spem servandam esse, retinebo, "I shall hold on [to
life], as long as I shall consider that ... or to be maintained according to our
hope": *putabo*, "I shall consider," in T.3i and a verb of M & M producing a
second expression of OO, *esse*, an impersonal infinitive.

→ **1325** verb formation T.3 in groups I and II, 12.3.1;
M & M, 60, 71, GL n° 527, remarks 1–2; OO, 71–73;
dict., *sum, fui, esse*, v. irreg., I., B., 5., b., (ζ). *in eo esse ut* (impers. or with
res etc. as subj.).

Note the typing or printing error in Lewis and Short, replicated in digital versions of the same, in which the entry for *sum, fui, esse*, says at I., B., 5., b., (ζ). *in eo ease ut*, where we believe it should read *in eo esse ut* (v. p. 1797, half way down column 1, following the Greek letter zeta).

The participle *servandam* can be understood in the English rendering above to be part of the infinitive *servandam esse*, literally, "to be needing to be maintained," whose subject is logically *vitam*, "life," in the main sentence producing *servandam*. Otherwise, it works as part of *ad spem servandam*, as a participle of passive necessity, "for hope needing to be maintained" or as a gerundive, "for maintaining hope," in which cases *esse* stands on its own.

→ **1326** participle of passive necessity, 50, 51.1.4;
    passive necessity formula, 53.4;
    gerundive, 77.2.

credo tua causa velle Lentulum, "I believe that Lentulus … is disposed on your behalf": *credo* in T.1i is a verb of M & M, and the content of Cicero's belief is given in OO, *velle Lentulum*, "that Lentulus … is disposed" or "that Lentulus … wishes." You might expect here *tui causā* where *causa* is in the abl. and *tui* in the gen., meaning "for the sake of you," but the Latin authors make *tuus, a, um* and the other possessive pronouns agree with *causa*, as here *tua causa*, as we nicely do in English, "for your sake."

→ **1327** M & M, 60, 71, GL nº 527, remarks 1–2; OO, 71–73;
    dict., *tuus, a, um*, pron. poss., II. for the obj. gen. *tui*.

credo … velle Lentulum, qui erit consul, "I believe that Lentulus, who will be consul, is disposed": in *qui erit consul*, "who will be consul," the verb *erit*, "[who] will be," in T.3i, could have been in the subjunctive by MA, because the relative clause depends on *velle Lentulum*, "Lentulus is disposed," in OO, which depends on *credo*, "I believe," a verb of M & M. Cicero does not do this, however, because he himself sees it as an historical fact in passing, and not closely integrated into the thought on which it depends.

→ **1328** M & M, 60, 71, GL nº 527, remarks 1–2; OO, 71–73;
    subjunctive use: modal attraction, 83; the verb "to be" in the
    indicative, 9.1.

Quamquam sunt facta verbis difficiliora, "But still, deeds are more difficult than words": here *Quamquam* does not mean "although," because there is no subordinate verb. Rather, it goes with the main verb and provides a transition to an objection, "But still," according to its secondary meaning in the dictionary. *verbis* is an abl. of comparison equivalent to *quam verba*, "than words." *factum, i, n.*, "a deed" is a noun, so here *sunt facta* is not T.4i passive; rather, *sunt* is T.1i active, and its subject is *facta*, "deeds are."

→ **1329** dict., *quamquam*, conj., I., "although" and II. as a rhetor. particle of
    transition, "yet";
    abl.: comparison, 90.2, GL nº 398.

Tu et quid opus sit et quid sit videbis, "You will see both what is necessary and what the situation is": the first word on his mind is *Tu*, "You," the sub-

ject of the last word of the sentence, *videbis*, "You will see," a verb of M & M
in T.3i establishing Track I and producing two IQs. The first is *quid opus sit*,
which does not mean "what the work is," but "what the need is" or "what is
necessary." The second is *quid sit*, "what the situation is."

> → **1330** sentence structure, 1; verb formation T.3 in groups I and II, 12.3.1;
>   M & M, 60, 71, GL n° 527, remarks 1–2; IQ, 60; *consecutio*, 47–48.

si ... nemo dispexerit, "if nobody will have discerned": a factual condition
where *dispexerit* is T.6i. Be careful about vocabulary; *dispicio* means "to
see the difference" or "to discern," *despicio* means "to look down on," "to
scorn," the difference of only one letter.

> → **1331** conditionals: factual, 86.1;
>   dict., *dispicio, spexi, spectum*, 3; *despicio, exi, ectum*, 3.

aut per te aliquid confici aut nullo modo poterit, "either something will be
able to be concluded with your help or in no way": the consequence of the
factual conditional where *póterit* is T.3i, as in the English rendering above,
"[something] will be able." Note the one letter difference in spelling with
potúerit which is T.6i. Here *aut ... aut ...*, "either ... or ...," correlate *per
te*, "through you" and *nullo modo*, "in no way." *confici* is a passive infinitive
completing the idea of *poterit*, "[something] will be able to be concluded."

> → **1332** conditionals: factual, 86.1; conjugation of *possum*, GL n° 119;
>   disjunctive sentence: *aut ... , aut ...* , GL n° 493.3.

sin te quoque inimici vexare coeperint, "but if also [our] enemies will have
begun to bother you": a second factual conditional that begins with *sin*, "but
if" or "if however," followed by *coeperint*, a defective verb that still follows
the nondefective system and here is T.6i both in form and meaning "[ene-
mies] will have begun." *vexare* is an infinitive complementary to *coeperint*,
"[enemies] will have begun to bother." We have added the word "our" in
square brackets to the translation for smooth reading and clarification,
although it is not given in the Latin text.

> → **1333** conditionals: factual, 86.1;
>   defective verbs, 14.4, GL n° 175.5: *coepi, memini, odi*;
>   verb: complementary infinitive, 77.

ne cessaris, "don't stop": *cessaris* is the contracted form of *cessaveris*, in T.3s.
This is a negative command form composed of *ne* with T.3s, whereas this
same epistle began with a similar command, equivalent in meaning but
composed of *ne* and *adsignes*, "don't attribute," in T.1s. This command is
the second part of the factual condition. Thus, in the conditional phrase,
coeperint, "[enemies] will have begun," is T.6i and not T.3s. This is reinforced
in the following clause where *agetur*, "it will be decided," is T.3i.

> → **1334** contractions: verbs, 39.2, GL n° 131;
>   negative command T.3s: 85.2.5; negative command T.1s: 85.2.3;
>   conditionals: factual, 86.1.

Verum … amoris vero, "But … but … of love": both mean "but," where *Verum* is always used as the first word of the sentence, whereas *vero* is any but the first, and is, as they say, postpositive.

> → **1335** dict., *verus, a, um*, adj., II., adv., A. *verum*, 2., a. In gen., "but" and II., adv., B. *vero*, "truly," 2. "but" (always placed after a word).

haec absint velim, "I would like these things to be far away": the main verb *velim*, "I would like," in T.1s produces a purpose clause in the subjunctive, *absint*, "[things] to be far away," but without *ut*.

> → **1336** subjunctive use: purpose clause without *ut*, 58, GL n° 546, remark 2; commands: other expressions, *velim*, 85.1.7.

Te oro ut … rescribas, "I beg you that you write back …": the main verb *oro*, "I beg," in T.1i produces a purpose clause giving the intention of the request, *ut … rescribas*, "that you write back," in T.1s and given in the subjunctive both in Latin and English according to the nature of a purpose clause.

> → **1337** subjunctive use: purpose clause, 58.1; *consecutio*, 47–48.

Te oro ut … et … animi … minus putes esse quam antea, "I beg you … and that you think that … there is a smaller amount of courage … than before": *oro*, "I beg," produces a second purpose clause *ut … et … putes*, "and that you think," in T.1s. The content of the thinking is given in OO, *minus … esse*, "that … there is a smaller amount [of courage]," where *minus*, "less," "a smaller amount," "a smaller bit," is the neuter subject of *esse*.

> → **1338** subjunctive use: purpose clause, 58.1; *consecutio*, 47–48;
> M & M, 60, 71, GL n° 527, remarks 1–2; OO, 71–73;
> adj.: irregular comp. and superl., 36.5, GL n° 90; gen. of part, 99.

et in me animi aut potius consili minus putes esse quam antea, amoris vero et offici non minus, "and that you think that in me there is a less amount of courage or rather of prudent-judgment than before, however not less of love and dutifulness": *animi* and *consili* are partitive genitives going with *minus*, literally, "a less amount of courage … of prudent-judgment." A comparison is made by *minus … quam*, "less … than." *potius* is also a comparative neuter, used here as an adv. with *aut*, to strengthen the comparison, "or rather." In the final clause he repeats the subject *non minus*, "not less," without the verb *esse*. Again, *amoris* and *offici* are two partitive genitives going with *non minus*, literally, "not less of love and of dutifulness."

> → **1339** adj.: irregular comp. and superl., 36.5, GL n° 90; gen. of part, 99;
> *quam* with the comp., 43.2; adv.: positive, comp., superl., 37.

LETTER 42 T-P
AD ATTICUM II, 15

CICERO ATTICO SAL.

Ut scribis, ita video non minus incerta in re publica quam in epistula tua, sed tamen ista ipsa me varietas sermonum opinionumque delectat. Romae enim videor esse cum tuas litteras lego et, ut fit in tantis rebus, modo hoc, modo illud audire. Illud tamen explicare non possum, quidnam inveniri possit nullo recusante ad facultatem agrariam.   (*Att.* II, 15, 1)

CICERO A GREETING TO ATTICUS

As you write, so I see things not less uncertain in the state than in your letter, but however, that variation of conversations and opinions itself delights me. For I seem to be in Rome when I read your letters and, as happens in such important things, to hear now this, now that. However, I am not able to resolve that fact: what-in-the-world is able to be found for the agrarian facilitation—no one being opposed.

CICERO ATTICO SAL.: *Cicero Attico salutem*

Ut scribis, ita video, "As you write, so I see": here *ut* is followed by *scribis,* "you write," in T.1i, and so means "as." The main verb is *video,* "I see," in T.1i.

> → **1340** dict., *ut*, I., B. meaning "as."

video ... sed tamen ... delectat, "I see ... but however ... [change] delights [me]": the two independent verbs are coordinated by *sed tamen,* "but however."

non minus incerta ... quam ... , "things not less uncertain ... than ...": an expression of comparison. The object of *video,* "I see," is *incerta,* "uncertain things."

> → **1341** *quam* with the comp., 43.2.

Romae ... videor esse, "I seem to be in Rome": the Romans prefer the personal construction here, where many modern languages prefer the impersonal, such as "it seems that I." The complement of *videor* is the inf. *esse*, "to be," and both the infinitive and the verb *videor* share the same subject, *ego*, as in "I seem to be." The form *Romae* indicates the place where or at which, "in Rome." The original loc. was *Romai*, which the Romans heard as *Romae*, which here is the loc. not the gen.

→ **1342** personal construction: *videor*, 73.3, GL n° 528.1 and remark 2 and note 1;
    nom. with the inf., 73.3, GL n° 528.1; verb: complementary infinitive, 77;
    function: place at which, names of cities and small islands, singular,
    Romae, 69.3.2.

videor esse ... et ... audire, "I seem to be ... and ... to hear": the main verb *videor*, "I seem," has two complementary infinitives, first *esse*, "to be," and the last word in the sentence *audire*, "to hear." Again, the subject of *audire* is the same as the subject of *videor*, as in "I seem to hear." The *et* joins the two infinitives.

→ **1343** personal construction: *videor*, 73.3, GL n° 528.1 and remark 2 and note 1;
    nom. with the inf., 73.3, GL n° 528.1;
    verb: complementary infinitive, 77; conjunction: *et*, 3.2.

cum ... lego, "when I read": here *cum* followed by *lego*, "I read," in T.1i, means "when," and excluded are "because" and "although," which take the subjunctive.

→ **1344** *cum* + indicative = "when": temporal sentences, 66.3.

ut fit, "as happens": here *ut* is followed by *fit*, "it is done," "it happens," in T.1i, a verb used as the passive form of *facio, facere, feci, factum*, 3, "to make," and so *ut* means "as."

→ **1345** dict., *ut*, I., B. meaning "as."

tantis, "such important": agreeing with *rebus*, "things," "matters," this adj. means "such great," "such important," "such big."

→ **1346** dict., *tantus, a, um*, adj., I. "of such size" *et passim*.

modo ... modo ..., "now ... now ...": here *modo* is not the abl. of *modus*, but an adv. meaning "just now [this] ... just now [that] ..." or "just now ... only."

→ **1347** dict., *mŏdŏ*, adv., II., B., 1. *modo ... , modo ...*, "now ... , now...."

quidnam inveniri possit, "what-in-the-world is able to be found": the main verb *possum*, "I am [not] able," in T.1i, establishes Track I and has as its object *explicare*, "to resolve," a gerund and verb of M & M whose object is *Illud*, "that," which in turn is expanded in the IQ presented here, whose question word is *quid*– "what ...," which functions as the subject of the verb *possit*, "[what] is able," in T.1s and complemented by the inf. *inveniri*, "to be found," which is contemporaneous and passive.

> → **1348** verb: complementary infinitive, 77; gerund, 77.1;
> M & M, 60, 71, GL nº 527, remarks 1–2; IQ, 60; *consecutio*, 47–48;
> verb: contemporaneous passive infinitive, 72.3;
> verb: contemporaneous active infinitive, 72.1.

Added to the end of *quid*, "what," is the expression –*nam* "in-the-world," which is not used alone, but only attached to question words to give emphasis, as in *Ubinam latitat?*, "Where in the world is he hiding?"; *Quonam modo hoc explicabis?*, "In whatever-in-the-world way are you going to explain this?"

> → **1349** dict., *quisnam, quaenam, quidnam*, pron. interrog., "who, which, what pray."

nullo recusante, "no one being opposed": the pronoun *nemo* is not found in certain forms; for example, instead of *neminis*, "of no one," they use *nullius*. Here in place of *nemine*, "no one" in the abl., we find *nullo*, in the abl. form, which functions in this AA as the subject of the participle, also in the abl. form *recusante* and describing contemporaneous action. Cicero naturally reflects the oddities of the Latin language.

> → **1350** ablative absolute, 54–55; contemporaneous active participle, 50, 51.1.1.

⁓

Bibuli autem ista magnitudo animi in comitiorum dilatione quid habet nisi ipsius iudicium sine ulla correctione rei publicae? Nimirum in Publio spes est. Fiat, fiat tribunus pl., si nihil aliud, ut eo citius tu ex Epiro revertare. Nam ut illo tu careas non video posse fieri, praesertim si mecum aliquid volet disputare. Sed id quidem non dubium est quin, si quid erit eius modi, sis advolaturus. Verum ut hoc non sit, tamen sive ruet sive eriget rem publicam, praeclarum spectaculum mihi propono, modo te consessore spectare liceat.   (*Att.* II, 15, 2)

But what does that magnanimity of Bibulus in the postponement of the elections contain if not the judgment of him himself without any correction of the people. Of course there is hope in Publius. Let him be made, let him be made tribune of the people, if nothing else, so that you may return all the more quickly from Epirus. For I do not see it can happen that you live without him, especially if he will want to discuss something with me. But that fact indeed is not doubtful: that if there will be anything of this nature, you will be flying in. Although this is not the case, nevertheless, whether he will tear down or lift up the state, I put before myself a wonderful show, provided that viewing be allowed—you sitting next to me.

quid habet, "what does [magnanimity] … contain": the question is asked by these two words in the middle of this long sentence, which words in English we can separate and place at both ends of this expression. Two lines previously *quidnam* followed by the subjunctive, *possit*, "what-in-the-world is able," was an IQ, but here a direct question is asked this time with the simple *quid* followed by *habet*, in T.1i.

→ **1351** other similar questions 13.2, 42.3.

Fiat, fiat, "Let him be made, let him be made": here *fiat, fiat* are two independent jussive subjunctives, rendered in English as either "Let him be made" or "he should be made." The optative subjunctive would be rendered "may he be"; the potential subjunctive, "perhaps he might be" or "perhaps he could be"; a deliberative subjunctive asks a question, "should he not be?" Another example is the concessive subjunctive *fuerit fur*, "so what if he was a criminal" or "suppose that he was a criminal," and *sit fur*, "granted that he be a thief." See more in GL n° 257–65.

→ **1352** independent subjunctive, 45.6, concessive, GL n° 264.

tribunus pl., "tribune of the people": now we say *tribunus plebis*, "tribune of the people," but in older Latin the form of-possession was *plebei* with the same meaning.

→ **1353** dict., *plebs, bis,* and *ei,* f.; GL n° 68.8.

eo citius, "all the more quickly": with the comparative adv. *citius*, "more quickly," *eo* in the abl. means "by so much [more quickly]," "so much [more quickly]." A synonym would be *tanto citius*, "by so much more quickly."

→ **1354** adv.: positive, comp., superl., 37;
 abl.: comparison, 90.2, GL n° 398;
 dict., *eo*, adv., I., C. with words of comparison, "so much," "by so much."

revertare, "you may return": Cicero loves this alternative form for *revertaris* in T.1s, a passive form of a verb that has both deponent and active forms with similar meanings. In T.4 we can say, *reversus est* or *revertit* with the same meaning, "he came back."

→ **1355** variation: –*ris*, 39.3.

ut illo tu careas, "that you live without him": the verb of causing, *fieri*, produces a clause that describes the result where the verb *careas*, in T.1s, is one of three related words that have their complement in the abl.: *careo, ui, itum,* 2, "to be without," "to lack," here *illo*, "to be without him," "to lack him." The other two verbs are *egeo, ui,* 2, "to be in need of," "to need" and *indigeo, ui, ēre,* 2, "to be in need of," "to need."

→ **1356** subjunctive use: complementary result (consecutive), 68.1;
 verbs with the abl., 78.3.

non video posse fieri, "I do not see it can happen [that you live without him]": the object of *video* is *posse*, and the subject of *posse* is *fieri*, thus *posse fieri* go together and mean "happening is possible," thus, "I see that happening is [not] possible."

→ **1357** gerund, 77.1.

si ... aliquid volet disputare, "if he will want to discuss something": this is
the conditional half of a factual or logical conditional in which the verb
volet, "he will want," is in T.3i. The object of *volet* is the gerund *disputare*,
"he will want discussing," "he will want to discuss," and its object in turn is
aliquid, "something," which is not abbreviated to *quid*, "something," after
the particle *si*, "if," as is common. The consequential half of this logical or
factual condition is the main sentence, *non video*, "I do not see."

> → **1358** conditionals: factual, 86.1; irregular verbs: *volo*, 82;
>   verb: complementary infinitive, 77; gerund, 77.1;
>   pronouns: indefinite, 42.4; after *si* the *ali*-s fly away, 42.5.

id ... non dubium est quin ... sis advolaturus, "that fact ... is not doubtful: that ... you will be flying in": this expression of negative doubt *id non
dubium est*, "that fact is not doubtful" is followed by a result clause whose
particle is *quin*, with positive meaning "that," and the subjunctive, here *sis
advolaturus*, the futurity formula consisting of *sis* in T.1s and the future
active participle, "about to fly in," "going to fly in." The futurity formula is
an explicit way to indicate futurity in the subjunctive.

> → **1359** negative *dubitare* + *quin* + subjunctive, 93.4, 101.2, GL n° 555.2;
>   subjunctive use: complementary result (consecutive), 68.1;
>   futurity participle, 50, 51.1.3;
>   *consecutio*: futurity formula in the subjunctive, 61.3.

quin, si quid erit ... , sis advolaturus, "that, if there will be anything ... , you
will be flying in": the result clause *quin ... sis advolaturus*, "that you will be
flying in" is the consequence part of a factual conditional whose other half,
the condition, is *si quid erit*, "if there will be anything," where *erit*, "there
will be," is T.3i. Contrary to the use of *quid* above in *quidnam*, "what-in-the-
world," and *quid [habet]*, "what [does it contain]," here *quid* means "anything," as an alternative way of writing *aliquid*, "something."

> → **1360** conditionals: factual, 86.1; the verb "to be" in the indicative, 9.1;
>   pronouns: indefinite, 42.4; after *si* the *ali*-s fly away, 42.5.

verum ut hoc non sit, tamen, "Although this is not the case, nevertheless":
The sentence begins with *verum*, which can mean "however," "but," or even
"truly," but here it functions as an adjective going with *hoc*, literally, *verum
... hoc non sit*, "this is not true." This sentence is in the Latin dictionary
by Lewis and Short as an example of *ut* meaning "even if," "although," as
a concessive expression. The subjunctive *sit* in T.1s is due to the concessive
nature of the *ut*, "even if [this] is [not]." In this case the *ut* correlates with
the *tamen*, "although ... , nevertheless." The most famous example of this is
in Ovid, *ut desint vires tamen est laudanda voluntas*, "although powers be
lacking, goodwill must be praised."

> → **1361** dict., *verus, a, um*, adj., I. "true," II., adv., A. *verum*, 2., a. In gen., "but";
>   dict., *ut*, II., conj., A., 2., a., (β). concessive, = *etsi ... , tamen ... ,*
>   "although ... , yet ...."

modo ... spectare liceat, "provided that viewing be allowed": here *modo* is
not the abl. of *modus*. Rather it is an adv. meaning "provided that [this is
done]." The synonyms for *modo* here are *dum* followed by the subjunctive
or *dummodo* followed by the subjunctive, both meaning "just so that [this is
done]," "provided that." The subject of *liceat* is the gerund *spectare*, "viewing
be allowed." The context for this sentence is that Cicero, sitting with Atticus
by his side, is going to watch other politicians either tearing down or build-
ing up the republic.

> → **1362** dict., *mŏdŏ*, adv., I., B., d. a conj. with subjunctive for *dummodo*,
>   "provided that";
>   *dummodo*, "provided that," GL n° 573.

te consessore, "you sitting next to me": this text is also mentioned in the Latin dictionary by Lewis and Short. This is an AA where both *te* and *consessore* in the abl. form function as the subject and predicate of a participle
that is felt but not expressed, "being." Medieval Latinists will supply the
participle as *ente*, but that form does not exist for Cicero.

> → **1363** ablative absolute, 54–55.

☙

Cum haec maxime scriberem, ecce tibi Sebosus! Nondum plane ingemueram, 'Salve,' inquit Arrius. Hoc est Roma decedere! Quos ego homines effugi, cum in hos incidi? Ego vero

> in montis patrios et ad incunabula nostra

pergam. Denique, si solus non potuero, cum rusticis potius quam cum his
perurbanis, ita tamen ut, quoniam tu certi nihil scribis, in Formiano tibi
praestoler usque ad *a. d.* III. Nonas Maias.   (*Att.* II, 15, 3)

Precisely when I was writing these things, there is Sebosus for you! I had not
yet completely groaned; Arrius says "Hi there." This is to depart from Rome!
What kind of people did I escape when I fell upon these guys? I, however,

> to the ancestral mountains and our birth cradle

shall move on. Finally, if I shall not have been able all alone, with country
people rather than with these city slickers, in such a way however that, because you write nothing certain, I await you in my Formian villa all the way
up to the third day before the May Nones [5 May].

Cum haec maxime scriberem, "Precisely when I was writing these things":
here *cum* followed by *scriberem*, "I was writing," in T.2s, can mean "because" or "since" or it can give the temporal circumstance for another

action and mean "when." The adv. *maxime* in this expression of time means "precisely when."

> → **1364** subjunctive use: temporal circumstance *cum* = "when," 66.3.2;
>   subjunctive use: causal *cum* = "because, since," 59.1;
>   subjunctive use: concessive *cum* = "although," 64;
>   dict., *magnus, a, um*, adj., II....—sup. *maxime*, B., 1....—with *nunc*,
>   "precisely."

tibi, "for you": this is a natural meaning of the dat., sometimes called the ethical dat. or dat. of interest or of reference (see GL nº 350–53), meaning "if it concerns you," "if you are interested," "for you." In the field of sport, a person may say, "There's a good play for you," where "for you" is a dative of reference.

> → **1365** natural dat., 33.7.1; dat. of personal interest, GL nº 350;
>   ethical dat., GL nº 351; dat. of reference, GL nº 352.

Nondum plane ingemueram, "I had not yet completely groaned": Cicero had not yet finished moaning about the presence of his one neighbor Sebosus, and then in walks his other neighbor on the other side of his villa, Arrius. The verb *ingemueram*, in T.5i, means "to begin to groan." This verb also appears in the Roman funeral rite, in the *Dies ire*, in the phrase *ingemisco tamquam reus*, "I am groaning like a guilty person."

> → **1366** dict., *ingemo, ui*, 3., "to groan, lament."

Hoc est Roma decedere!, "This is to depart from Rome!": the main verb is *est*, "this is," and its subject is *decedere*, "departing," "to depart," a gerund, accompanied by *Roma*, "from Rome," an abl. of separation. We again can hear Cicero joking and reacting in living Latin—if getting out of Rome means going to Formia and finding things worse there.

> → **1367** gerund, 77.1; function: place from where, names of cities and small
>   islands, *Roma*, 69.2.2;
>   abl. separation from place, 27.

Quos, "What kind of": the dict. gives the meaning of *qui, quae, quod* not only as "who?," but also "what kind of," "what sort of."

> → **1368** dict., *qui, quae, quod*, pron., I. interrog., "what kind of," "what sort of."

cum in hos incidi?, "when I fell upon these guys?": above we saw *cum* meaning "when" and giving the temporal circumstance for another action, *Cum haec maxime scriberem*, "Precisely when I was writing these things." Here *cum* is followed by *incidi*, in T.4b, also meaning "when" but not giving temporal circumstance. In this case, *cum*, "when," indicates the pure temporal coincidence, suggesting that Cicero is startled by the coincidence of events.

> → **1369** *cum* + historical times of indicative = "when": temporal coincidence, 66.3.1.

in montis patrios, "to the ancestral mountains": here *montis* is another form for *montes*, in the object form and so agrees with *patrios*, "the ancestral mountains." Cicero was born in Arpinum, which lies at the foot of these mountains. The preposition *in* is followed by object forms to indicate motion to or toward, here geographical but elsewhere even moral movement.

→ **1370** Block II nouns: *–is = –es*, 38, GL n° 56;
   prep. with obj., 6.

si solus non potuero, "if I shall not have been able all alone": the conditional half of a factual or logical conditional with the verb *potuero*, "I shall have been able," in T.6i.

→ **1371** conditionals: factual, 86.1.

cum rusticis potius quam cum his perurbanis, "with country people rather than with those city slickers": the consequential half of the factual conditional is given without a verb, which we might supply as *potero*, "I shall be able," in T.3i to coordinate with *potuero*, "I shall have been able," in T.6i in the condition. At this point, Tyrrell and Purser comment, "the verb is sometimes strangely missing" (1:306, note 3, *si solus non potuero*). The comparison is made with *potius quam*, "rather than," balancing two equal elements.

→ **1372** conditionals: factual, 86.1; *quam* with the comp., 43.2;
   T.3i and T.6i paired: 7, Time 6, and GL n° 244, remark 2.

ita … ut … tibi praestoler, "in such a way … that … I await you": the *ita* prepares for the result clause *ut … praestoler*, whose dep. verb is T.1s and is one of the 65 verbs whose complement is in the dat., here *tibi*. While it is proper to render this as "I am awaiting you," the dat. form of *tibi* cannot be heard, so if you say "I am waiting for you," then you can see and hear the dat. in English as well.

→ **1373** subjunctive use: pure result (consecutive), 67.1–2, GL n° 552;
   65 verbs with dat., 33.7.2, GL n° 346.

quoniam tu certi nihil scribis, "because you write nothing certain": *quoniam* is one of the three related words that begin a causal sentence; the other two are *quod, quia*. Here it is followed by *scribis*, "you write," in T.1i, indicating that the opinion is that of the author or speaker, Cicero. The expression *nihil certi* means "nothing of certainty," where *certi* is a gen. of part, meaning "of what is certain."

→ **1374** causal: *quod, quia, quoniam*, "because, since," + indicative, one's own
   reason, 59.2;
   gen. of part, 99.

usque ad a. d. III. Nonas Maias, "all the way up to the third day before the May Nones": the full form is *usque ad ante diem tertium Nonas Maias*. That is 5 May. It is clear that the date is given as a set formula that is not touched, because otherwise you could not have the expression *usque ad ante*. Rather *usque ad* has as its complement the whole formula and *ante* is the beginning of the formula.

→ **1375** about the Roman calendar, pp. 605–608;
   GL appendix: Roman Calendar, pp. 491–92.

෧

Terentiae pergrata est adsiduitas tua et diligentia in controversia Mulviana. Nescit omnino te communem causam defendere eorum qui agros publicos possideant. Sed tamen tu aliquid publicanis pendis: haec etiam id recusat. Ea tibi igitur et Κικέρων ἀριστοκρατικώτατος παῖς, salutem dicunt.   (*Att.* II, 15, 4)

Your constant presence and diligence in the Mulvian controversy is very pleasing to Terentia. She does not know at all that you are defending the common cause of these people who possess public lands. But you, however, pay something to tax collectors; this woman even refuses that. She therefore and *Cicero, a most aristocratic boy*, express a greeting to you.

> *Terentiae pergrata est*, "is very pleasing to Terentia": the expression is composed of the verb *est*, "[it] is," in T.1i with the adj. *pergrata*, "most pleasing," which is complemented by *Terentiae*, "to Terentia," in the dat.
>   → **1376** Block I adj., 4.2–3; dat.: meaning and forms, 33.

> *Nescit ... te ... defendere ... qui ... possideant*, "She does [not] know ... that you are defending [people] who possess": the main verb is *nescit*, "she does not know," in T.1i, a verb of M & M producing a statement in OO where *te* in the object form functions as the subject of the inf. *defendere* describing contemporaneous action. Depending on this statement in OO, and closely related to the whole thought is the relative statement, *qui ... possideant*, "who possess," where *possideant* is T.1s due to MA. It is also possible that *qui ... possideant* is an expression of characteristic result where *qui* stands for *tales ut ii*, "such that they [possess]."
>   → **1377** M & M, 60, 71, GL n° 527, remarks 1–2; OO, 71–73;
>   subjunctive use: modal attraction, 83;
>   subjunctive use: characteristic result, 68.2.

> *aliquid publicanis pendis*, "you ... pay something to tax collectors": namely a bribe.

> Κικέρων ἀριστοκρατικώτατος παῖς, "*Cicero, a most aristocratic boy*": the Greek phrase has the following Latin equivalent: *Cicero optimatium studiosissimus puer*, "Cicero, a boy most devoted to the first citizens" or perhaps "Cicero, a boy most devoted to to the elite."
>   → **1378** Bibliography: *Onomasticon Tullianum*;
>   Greek expressions, pp. 623–626.

43

LETTER 214 T-P
AD FAMILIARES XV, 7

M. CICERO PROCOS. S. D. C. MARCELLO COS. DESIG.

Maxima sum laetitia adfectus cum audivi consulem te factum esse, eumque
honorem tibi deos fortunare volo atque a te pro tua parentisque tui dignitate
administrari. Nam cum te semper amavi dilexique tum mei amantissimum
cognovi in omni varietate rerum mearum, tum patris tui pluribus beneficiis
vel defensus tristibus temporibus vel ornatus secundis et sum totus vester et
esse debeo, cum praesertim matris tuae, gravissimae atque optimae feminae, maiora erga salutem dignitatemque meam studia quam erant a muliere
postulanda perspexerim. Quapropter a te peto in maiorem modum ut me
absentem diligas atque defendas.   (*Fam.* XV, 7)

MARCUS CICERO PROCONSUL SAYS A GREETING TO
GAIUS MARCELLUS ELECTED CONSUL

I was moved with the greatest joy when I heard that you had been created
consul, and I want the gods to prosper that honor for you and that it be administered by you in keeping with your and your father's dignity. For while
I have always loved and esteemed you, then I have known you most fond of
me in all the change of my life, then both I am and ought to be all yours,
having been either defended in sad times by the many kindnesses of your
father or honored in prosperous times, since I fully grasped especially the
greater interests of your mother, a most serious and outstanding woman,
toward my well-being and dignity than had to be demanded of a woman.
For which reason I ask of you to a greater degree that you love and defend
me being absent.

M. Cicero procos. s. d. C. Marcello cos. desig.: *Marcus Cicero proconsul salutem dicit Gaio Marcello consuli designato*

Maxima sum laetitia adfectus, "I was moved with the greatest joy": this has the feel of a form letter and fills it nicely. *Maxima* goes with *laetitia*, and *sum* goes with *adfectus*. Thus, the four words alternate *a, b, a, b.*

→ **1379** sentence structure, 1.

cum audivi, "when I heard": here *cum* is followed by *audivi*, "I heard," in T.4b, expresses simple coincidence of "clock" time, meaning "when," for example at 10:00 A.M., and does not imply circumstance.

→ **1380** *cum* + historical times of indicative = "when": temporal coincidence, 66.3.1.

audivi consulem te factum esse, "I heard that you had been created consul": the verb *audivi*, "I heard," in T.4b, is a verb of M & M producing a statement in OO where *te* in the object form functions as the subject of the passive inf. *factum esse*, expressing antecedent action, and in turn its predicate is *consulem.*

→ **1381** M & M, 60, 71, GL n° 527, remarks 1–2; OO, 71–73;
  verb: antecedent passive infinitive, 72.3.

eumque honorem tibi deos fortunare volo, "I want the gods to prosper that honor for you": the *-que* is joined to the end of the first word of the second part, *eum.* The *-que* connects the two main verbs, *sum … adfectus*, "I was moved," and *volo*, "I want," in T.1i, itself a verb of M & M producing a statement in OO where *deos* in the object form functions as the subject of the inf. *fortunare*, expressing contemporaneous action, whose object is *eumque honorem.*

→ **1382** dict., *fortuno, avi, atum*, 1.; conjunction: *-que*, 3.2;
  M & M, 60, 71, GL n° 527, remarks 1–2; OO, 71–73.

eumque honorem … volo atque … administrari, "I want … and that it be administered": the M & M verb *volo*, "I want," in T.1i produces a second statement in OO where *honorem* in the object form functions as the object of *fortunare* in the first statement in OO, but here functions as the subject of the inf. *administrari*, which is passive both in form and in meaning and describes contemporaneous action, meaning "I want … and that that honor be administered." The *atque*, "and," joins the two statements in OO.

→ **1383** M & M, 60, 71, GL n° 527, remarks 1–2; OO, 71–73;
  As a verb, *fortunare* also means "to second a motion";
  conjunction: *-que*, 3.2;
  conjunction: *atque*, 3.2.

pro tua parentisque tui dignitate, "in keeping with your and your father's dignity": the preposition *pro* is one of the richest words in the Latin language and thus most difficult. Here it means "in keeping with," "in proportion to," and its complement is *tua … dignitate*, "your dignity." Agreeing with *dignitate* in the abl., the possessive adj. *tua*, "your," is an expression of possession, just as *patrisque tui*, "and of your father," where *tui* agrees with *patris*. The *–que* at the end of *patris*, "of [your] father," joins the two expressions of possession, *tua* and *patris*.

> → **1384** prep. with abl., 28.4; adj.: possessive, 24.3, 100.2;
> conjunction: *–que*, 3.2.

cum ... tum ... tum ... cum ... , "while ... then ... then ... since": the first three of these go together and can also mean "not only ... but also ... but also ..." or "now ... now ... now ...."

> → **1385** correlative comparative sentences, 90.5, GL n° 642.

cum te semper amavi dilexique, "while I have always loved and esteemed you": the first *cum* is followed by *amavi dilexique*, "I have ... loved and esteemed," both verbs in T.4a.

> → **1386** *cum* + historical times of indicative = "when": temporal coincidence,
> 66.3.1.

tum mei amantissimum cognovi, "then I have known you most fond of me": the first *tum* goes with *cognovi*, "I have known," in T.4a also meaning "I have come to know," and thus with present meaning "I now know." The object of *cognovi* is *te*, "you," given in the first clause as the object of *amavi*. Here *mei*, "of me," goes with *amantissimum*, which agrees with *te* from the first clause, meaning "you most fond of me." We can test our understanding of *mei*, "of me," by stating its plural *nostri*, "of us," not *meorum*, "of my people."

> → **1387** personal pronoun: object form, 3;
> personal pronouns: function of-possession, 24.1; adj.: possessive, 24.1,
> 100.2.

tum ... vel ... vel ... et sum ... et esse debeo, "then both I am and I ought ... either ... or ...": the second *tum* goes with the two verbs *et sum ... et esse debeo*, "both I am and ought to be." This phrase also includes connecting pairs, *vel ... vel ...* , "either ... or ... ," and *et ... et ...* , "both ... and ...." Only strict logic will help you see the whole sentence clearly.

> → **1388** conjunction: *et ... , et ...* , 3.2;
> dict., *vel*, conj., I., B., 1. *vel ... , vel ...* , "either ... , or...."

Some simple boxes will make the logical clarity of this sentence readily evident. The brackets on this one are different than the others because there are three main sentences coordinated by *cum ... tum ... tum....* Each of these is placed in its own set of brackets { ... }; the third of these continues to the end of the sentence.

{ Nam cum te semper amavi dilexique }	*cum* coordinate 1
{ tum mei amantissimum cognovi in omni	*tum* coordinate 2
varietate rerum mearum, }	
{ tum patris tui pluribus beneficiis	*tum* coordinate 3
vel defensus tristibus temporibus	*vel* coordinate 1
vel ornatus secundis	*vel* coordinate 2
et sum totus vester	*et* coordinate 1
et esse debeo,	*et* coordinate 2
[cum praesertim matris tuae,	*cum* causal begins
(gravissimae atque optimae feminae,)	apposition
maiora	causal continues
(erga salutem dignitatemque meam)	*erga* preposition
studia	causal continues
(quam erant a muliere postulanda)	*quam* comparison
perspexerim.] }	causal concludes

→ **1389** structure of Latin sentences, 103 p. 587, *Ossa* Readings: 1-D, 1-I, 3-D, 3-I, 4-D, 4-I;

vel defensus tristibus temporibus vel ornatus secundis, "having been either defended in sad times … or honored in prosperous times": the two participles *defensus*, "having been defended" and *ornatus*, "having been honored," describe *ego*, "I," the subject of the two verbs *sum … esse debeo*, "I am … I ought to be." The expression *tristibus temporibus*, "in sad times," is the abl. of time when or in which, as is also *secundis*, "in prosperous times." The adj. *secundis* comes from the verb *sequor, sequi*, "to follow," and refers to the favorable currents of water or of wind that follow and so push a ship along its course. In this sense, in parliamentary procedure to second a motion is to favor it, to come from behind and push it forward. Here *secundis* does not mean "second."

→ **1390** antecedent participle, 50, 51.1.2;
Block I adj., 4.2–3; abl.: time at which, 70.1;
dict., *secundus, a, um*, adj., I., B. (v. *sequor*, II), nautical, currents of water, "favorable."

cum … perspexerim, "since I fully grasped": the second *cum* is followed by *perspexerim*, "I fully grasped," in T.3s and so can mean "because," "since" as here, or "although."

→ **1391** subjunctive use: causal *cum* = "because, since," 59.1.

matris tuae … maiora erga salutem dignitatemque meam studia, "the greater interests of your mother … toward my well-being and dignity": the object of *perspexerim*, "I fully grasped," in T.3s, is *maiora … studia*, both in the neuter plural and rendered in English expression by a clumsy plural, "greater interests." Depending on *maiora studia* is *matris tuae … feminae*, "of your mother … woman," and this string of genitives is put out in front of the words on which it depends. The preposition *erga* takes the object form, *salutem signitatemque meam*, "toward my well-being and dignity," and this phrase is placed between *maiora* and *studia*.

→ **1392** adj.: irregular comp. and superl., 36.5;
function: of-possession, 20; prep. with obj., 6; sentence structure, 1.

maiora ... studia quam erant a muliere postulanda, "the greater interests ... than had to be demanded of a woman": the comparative *maiora*, "greater," corresponds with the comparison *quam*, "than," whose verb is the passive necessity formula where *erant* in T.2i is followed by the participle of passive necessity *postulanda*, "having to be demanded," "owing to be demanded," "needing to be demanded." With the participle of passive necessity the agent is usually given in the dat. form, which confirms that *a muliere* means "from a woman" and does not mean "by a woman," which would be *mulieri* in the dat. without a preposition.

→ **1393** adj.: comp., 36; *quam* with the comp., 43.2;
participle of passive necessity, 50, 51.1.4;
dat. of agent, 53.5; prep. + abl. of separation or agent, 28.5.2;
dat.: meaning and forms, 33.

Note, this man, Gaius Marcellus, is the brother of Marcus Marcellus, for whom Cicero gave an immortal, laudatory oration, which was totally ineffective, because Marcus Marcellus was killed in Athens by republicans on his way to Rome to accept Caesar's pardon against the protest of conservatives.

LETTER 11 T-P
Ad Atticum I, 2

CICERO ATTICO SAL.

L. Iulio Caesare C. Marcio Figulo consulibus filiolo me auctum scito salva Terentia. Abs te tam diu nihil litterarum? Ego de meis ad te rationibus
scripsi antea diligenter. Hoc tempore Catilinam, competitorem nostrum,
defendere cogitamus. Iudices habemus quos voluimus, summa accusatoris
voluntate. Spero, si absolutus erit, coniunctiorem illum nobis fore in ratione
petitionis: sin aliter acciderit, humaniter feremus.   (*Att.* I, 2, 1)

CICERO A GREETING TO ATTICUS

Lucius Iulius Caesar, Gaius Marcius Figulus being consuls—you must know
that I have been blessed with a little son—Terentia being safe and sound.
From you so long not a bit of a letter? Previously I wrote to you carefully
about my plans. At this time we are planning to defend Catilina, our com-
petitor. We have the judges whom we have wanted—the favorable disposition of the prosecutor being the greatest. If he will have been acquitted, I
hope he will be closer united to us in the program of canvassing for office;
but if it will have happened otherwise, we shall bear it in a humane way.

CICERO ATTICO SAL.: *Cicero Attico salutem*

L. Iulio Caesare C. Marcio Figulo consulibus, "Lucius Iulius Caesar, Gaius
Marcius Figulus being consuls": an AA where the proper names are in the
abl. form and function as the subjects of an implied participle "being."
The predicate is *consulibus,* "consuls." The whole first sentence is a solemn
announcement of the birth of his son. Normally one would not quote
the consuls at the birth of your little boy, but this expression blows the
announcement up suitable for a billboard, or an engraved almost mock
announcement of birth on the part of a proud father.

We might say today, even as we are writing this sentence—*Elisabetha regina, Barack presidente, tractatum persoluimus*, "Elizabeth being Queen, Barack being President—we completed the commentary."

→ **1394** ablative absolute, 54–55.

filiolo me auctum scito, "thou shalt know that I have been blessed with a little son": the second command, called by some others the future imperative, gives the impression of a decree, *scito*, "thou shalt know," "you must know." This is a verb of M & M producing a statement in OO where *me* in the object form functions as the subject of the inf. whose full implied form is *auctum esse*, describing antecedent action, "me to have been increased," "me to have been blessed." The form *filiolo* is an abl. of means or instrument meaning "with a baby son," because the father was blessed by means of the son. The form *filiolo* here is almost an instrument "with a son"; it is not an abl. of agent meaning "by a son," which would imply that his son Marcus leaving the womb raised his hand to bless and amplify his father.

→ **1395** commands: first, second, 17;
M & M, 60, 71, GL nº 527, remarks 1–2; OO, 71–73;
abl.: instrument, 28.5.3–4, 89.2, GL nº 401.

salva Terentia, "Terentia being safe and sound": an AA where *Terentia* is in the abl. form functioning as the subj. of a participle that is not there, but is felt, whose predicate is *salva*. This whole first statement could be adapted and printed on a card announcing the arrival of a child with the imprint of the baby's little foot or hand and the current year, say 2017 when this text was first written or 2019 when the editing process was brought to its conclusion, shall we say *magna non sine difficultate*, "not without great difficulty," quoting the immortal words chiseled in stone in the cathedral of Milwaukee that greet all who enter.

→ **1396** ablative absolute, 54–55.

Abs te, "From you": the *abs* is a rather rare form of the preposition instead of *ab* or *a*. Perhaps ten years later Cicero appears to have practically abandoned this form *abs*.

→ **1397** dict., *ab, a, abs*, prep. with abl.;
prep. + abl. of separation or agent, 28.5.2.

nihil litterarum, "not a bit of a letter": here *litterarum* is a gen. of part, "of a letter."

→ **1398** gen. of part, 99.

Catilinam … defendere cogitamus, "we are planning to defend Catilina": the main verb *cogitamus*, "we are planning," in T.1i has as its object *defendere*, a gerund, whose object is *Catilinam*, "we were thinking of defending Catilina," "we were planning on defending Catilina."

→ **1399** verb: complementary infinitive, 77; gerund, 77.1.

summa ... voluntate, "the favorable disposition ... being the greatest": an
AA where *voluntate* in the abl. form functions as the subject of a participle
which is not there but felt, "being," whose predicate is *summa*. The noun
voluntate refers also to the "good disposition."

> → **1400** dict., *voluntas, atis*, f., I., B., 1. "disposition good or bad";
>   ablative absolute, 54–55.

Spero ... illum nobis fore, "I hope he will be": the main verb *Spero*, "I hope,"
is a verb of M & M producing a statement in OO where *illum* in the object
form functions as the subject of the inf. *fore*, which stands for *futurum esse*,
"to be about to be," an expression of futurity in the inf.

> → **1401** M & M, 60, 71, GL n° 527, remarks 1–2; OO, 71–73;
>   futurity participle, 50, 51.1.3;
>   *futurum esse* (*fore*), 72.1; futurity formula, active, 53.3.

si absolutus erit, "If he will have been acquitted": because this clause depends on the statement in OO *illum ... fore*, "he will be," and it is closely
involved in the thought of the whole expression, Cicero could have used MA
here to say *absolutus sit* with the same meaning in completed futurity, but
he did not, preferring concrete, direct talk.

> → **1402** OO, 71–73; subjunctive use: modal attraction, 83;
>   conditionals: factual, 86.1.

coniunctiorem, "closer united": a comparative also meaning "more intimate," "more closely joined."

> → **1403** adj.: comp., 36.

acciderit ... feremus, "it will have happened ... we shall bear": we see the
combination of T.6i and T.3i respectively.

> → **1404** T.3i and T.6i paired: 7, Time 6, and GL n° 244, remark 2.

humaniter, "in a humane way": from the adj. *humanus, a, um* we get the adv.
humane, "in a humane way," but the alternative form of the adv. is *humaniter*. A few words work this way; they switch from one group of adverbs
ending in –*e* to another group of adverbs ending in –*iter*, such as *luculente*
and its alternative form *luculenter*.

> → **1405** dict., *humanus, a, um*, adj., II., B.,—adv. (α) *humane*, (β) *humaniter*;
>   adv., 37.

❧

Tuo adventu nobis opus est maturo: nam prorsus summa hominum est
opinio tuos familiaris, nobilis homines, adversarios honori nostro fore. Ad
eorum voluntatem mihi conciliandam maximo te mihi usui fore video. Qua
re Ianuario mense, ut constituisti, cura ut Romae sis.   (*Att.* I, 2, 2)

There is need for us of your speedy arrival; for absolutely it is the most prev-
alent opinion of people that your friends, noble people, are going to be op-

posed to our honor. I see that you will be for the greatest help to me for winning over to me their goodwill. For which reason, take care that you be in Rome in the month of January, as you have decided.

Tuo adventu ... opus est maturo, "There is need ... of your speedy arrival": the expression *opus est* means "There is need," not, "it is work," where *opus* is the subject of *est*. Here it is used with the abl. *Tuo adventu ... maturo* "of your speedy arrival," but he could also have used the gen. and said *Tui adventus ... maturi*, with the same meaning, or he could have placed the expression in the predicate, *Tuus adventus opus est maturus*, "Your speedy arrival is necessary." The adj. *maturo* agrees with *tuo adventu* and it means "seasonable," "timely," "soon."

> → **1406** dict., *opus, eris*, n. III., A. *opus est*, "there is need," (β). with abl., (γ). with
>   gen.,(δ). with acc.;
>   *opus est*, 75.3.

est opinio tuos familiaris, nobilis homines ... fore, "it is the ... opinion ... that your friends, noble people, are going to be": the subject of *est*, "it is," in T.1i, is *opinio*, "the opinion," which even as a noun is an expression of M & M producing a statement in OO where *tuos familiaris* in the object form functions as the subject of the inf. *fore*, an alternative form of the futurity inf. *futurum esse*, "to be about to be," "to be going to be." The form *familiaris* is an alternative form of *familiares*, in the object form agreeing with *tuos*, "your friends." Likewise *nobilis* is the alternative form of *nobiles*, in the object form agreeing with *homines*, "noble people."

> → **1407** M & M, 60, 71, GL n° 527, remarks 1–2; OO, 71–73;
>   futurity participle, 50, 51.1.3; *futurum esse (fore)*, 72.1;
>   futurity formula, active, 53.3;
>   Block II adj.: *–is = –es*, 38, GL n° 78.

Ad ... voluntatem ... conciliandam, "for winning over ... [their] goodwill": we can make this gerundive expression a gerund to see its object more clearly, *Ad voluntatem conciliandum*, where the complement of the preposition *Ad*, "for," is *conciliandum*, "winning over," and its object is *voluntatem*, "[their] goodwill," with the same meaning but used much less by the Romans. Of course, the other possibility is always present which would take the complement of *Ad* to be *voluntatem* which is complemented by the passive necessity participle *conciliandam*, meaning "for [their] goodwill needing to be won over." As a gerundive expression, this is one of the ways to express purpose, but not if taken to be a participle of passive necessity.

> → **1408** prep. with obj., 6; gerundive, 77.2; gerund, 77.1;
>   participle of passive necessity, 50, 51.1.4;
>   14 ways to express purpose, 84.

maximo ... mihi usui, "for the greatest help to me": the double dat. where *mihi*, "to me," is the dat. of the person affected and *maximo usui*, "for the greatest help," is the dat. of the goal.

> → **1409** double dat., 91.2.

te … fore video, "I see that you will be": the main verb is *video*, "I see," in T.1i, which is a verb of M & M producing a statement in OO where *te* in the object form functions as the subject of the inf. *fore*, an alternative form of *futurum esse*, "to be about to be."

> → **1410** M & M, 60, 71, GL n° 527, remarks 1–2; OO, 71–73;
> futurity participle, 50, 51.1.3; *futurum esse (fore)*, 72.1;
> futurity formula, active, 53.3.

Ianuario mense, "in the January month": the abl. of time when.

> → **1411** abl.: time at which, 70.1.

ut constituisti, "as you have decided": followed by *constituisti*, "you have decided," in T.4a, here *ut* means "as."

> → **1412** dict., *ut*, I., B. meaning "as."

cura ut sis, "take care that you be": the command form *cura*, "take care," produces a purpose clause *ut sis*, where the verb *sis* is T.1s, "that you be."

> → **1413** commands: other expressions, 85.1.7;
> subjunctive use: purpose clause, 58.1;
> *consecutio* after command form, GL n° 517.

Romae, "in Rome": the form of place where, the so-called locative.

> → **1414** function: place at which, names of cities and small islands, singular,
> *Romae*, 69.3.2.

LETTER 134 T-P
AD FAMILIARES VII, 5

CICERO CAESARI IMP. S. D.

Vide quam mihi persuaserim te me esse alterum non modo in iis rebus quae ad me ipsum sed etiam in iis quae ad meos pertinent. C. Trebatium cogitaram quocumque exirem mecum ducere, ut eum meis omnibus studiis, beneficiis quam ornatissimum domum reducerem. Sed postea quam et Pompei commoratio diuturnior erat quam putaram et mea quaedam tibi non ignota dubitatio aut impedire profectionem meam videbatur aut certe tardare, vide quid mihi sumpserim. Coepi velle ea Trebatium exspectare a te quae sperasset a me, neque mehercule minus ei prolixe de tua voluntate promisi quam eram solitus de mea polliceri.   (*Fam.* VII, 5, 1)

CICERO SAYS A GREETING TO
CAESAR, COMMANDER

Look how much I have convinced myself that you are another I [*alter ego*] not only in those matters which pertain to me myself, but also in those which pertain to my people. I had planned to take with me Gaius Trebatius to whatever place I would go so that I might bring him back home as decorated as possible with all my attentions, kindnesses. But after both the sojourn of Pompeius was longer than I had thought and a certain hesitation of mine not unknown to you either seemed to impede my departure or certainly slow down, look what I have dared for myself. I began to wish that Trebatius was expecting from you the things which he had hoped from me, nor by george did I promise him less extensively out of your goodwill than I had been accustomed to promise out of my own.

CICERO CAESARI IMP. S. D.: *Cicero Caesari imperatori salutem dicit*

Vide quam mihi persuaserim, "Look how much I have convinced myself": *Vide*, "Look," is a command form and a verb of M & M that establishes Track I producing an IQ. *quam ... persuaserim*, "how much I have convinced," in T.3s, rendered in the indicative in English. *persuaserim* is one of the 65 verbs whose complement in the dat. is not often heard because English uses the acc., here "myself."

> → **1415** commands: first, second, 17;
>   M & M, 60, 71, GL nº 527, remarks 1–2; IQ, 60;
>   65 verbs with dat., 33.7.2, GL nº 346.

te me esse alterum, "that you are another I": *persuaserim*, "I have convinced [myself]," in T.3s is a verb of M & M, whose content is given in OO, *te esse*, "that you are." *me ... alterum*, "another I," is in the predicate to go with *te*, "you." The English may parallel the Latin use of the acc. with the inf. if we say, "you to be another me," where both "you" and "me" are in the acc., but this construction is difficult to maintain given the full sentence.

> → **1416** M & M, 60, 71, GL nº 527, remarks 1–2; OO, 71–73.

non modo ... sed etiam, "not only ... but also": adversative copulative sentences.

> → **1417** *non modo ... , sed ... ,* GL nº 482.5.

quae ad me ipsum ... quae ad meos pertinent, "which pertain to me myself ... which pertain to my people": Cicero uses *pertinent*, "[which] pertain," in T.1i, rather than *pertineant*, in T.1s by MA, to indicate that he does not see these comments as a complicated part of a whole mental idea, but as an explanation in passing.

> → **1418** subjunctive use: modal attraction, 83.

C. Trebatium cogitaram ... mecum ducere, "I had planned to take with me Gaius Trebatius": *cogitaram* is a contracted form of *cogitaveram*, "I had planned," in T.5i, and it combines with a complementary infinitive to mean "I had something in mind," "I planned to do something," here *ducere*, "[I planned] to take." The object of *ducere* is *Gaium Trebatium*, "to take Gaius Trebatius," placed first in the sentence.

> → **1419** contractions: verbs, 39.2, GL nº 131;
>   verb: complementary infinitive, 77; gerund, 77.1; sentence structure, 1.

quocumque exirem, "to whatever place I would go": *quocumque*, "to whatever place" or "whithersoever," begins a clause whose verb *exirem*, "I would go," is in T.2s. In standard Latin you would expect the indicative here, but all authors make exceptions. The subjunctive here is justified by a long explanation, but more simply imitating the Greek use of the subjunctive with what they call the iterative pronouns, such as "whensoever," "whithersoever," "-soever." Use of the subjunctive in such expressions becomes more common in later Latin and in modern languages including English; see the remarks on *quicumque* in GL nº 254 and nº 625.

> → **1420** *quicumque*, GL nº 254, 625.

ut eum ... domum reducerem, "so that I might bring him back home": The intention contained in *cogitaram*, "I had planned," in T.5i establishing Track II, is expressed in a purpose clause *ut ... reducerem*, "so that I might bring ... back," in T.2s. *domum* implies the idea of motion "to home." The two words *ornatissimum domum* look like they go together, meaning "to a most decorated house," but they do not. Here *domum* goes with the verb *reducerem*, "to bring him home" and *ornatissimum* goes with *eum ... quam ornatissimum*, "him ... as decorated as possible."

> → **1421** subjunctive use: purpose clause, 58.1; *consecutio*, 47–48;
> function: place to where, *domum*, 69.1.3;
> *quam* with the superlative, 43.3.

Note the many uses and meanings of *quam*: *Vide quam*, "[Look] how much"; *quam ornatissimum*, "as [decorated] as possible"; *postea quam*, sometime written as *postquam*, "later than" or "after," *diuturnior quam putaram*, "[longer] than [I had thought]"; these are the subtleties in Latin.

> → **1422** dict., *quam*, adv., I. "how much"; *postquam*, 65.1;
> *quam* with the comp., 43.2; *quam* with the superlative, 43.3.

postea quam et ... commoratio ... erat ... et ... dubitatio aut impedire ... videbatur aut ... tardare, vide ..., "after both the sojourn ... was ... and a ... hesitation of mine ... either seemed to impede ... or ... slow down, look ...": the main verb is the command *vide*, "look." The temporal clause has two parts coordinated by *et ... et ...*, "both ... and ...," which join *commoratio ... erat*, "the sojourn ... was," to *dubitatio ... videbatur*, "hesitation ... seemed." *videbatur* is used personally here with the subject *dubitatio*, according to the preference of the Romans, whereas other languages use the impersonal followed by OO, as in *dubitationem impedire videbatur*, "it seemed that hesitation was impeding." *videbatur* is complemented by two infinitives correlated by "aut ... aut ...," "either ... or ...," namely *aut impedire ... aut ... tardare*, whose subject in the nom. is also *dubitatio*, the subject of *videbatur*, as in "either a hesitation seemed to impede or to slow down."

> → **1423** *postquam*, 65.1; commands: first, second, 17;
> personal construction: *videor*, 73.3, GL n° 528.1 and remark 2 and note 1;
> nom. with the inf., 73.3, GL n° 528.1;
> conjunction: *et ... , et ... ,* 3.2;
> disjunctive sentence: *aut ... , aut ... ,* GL n° 493.3;
> verb: complementary infinitive, 77.

vide quid mihi sumpserim, "look what I have dared for myself": the command *vide*, "look," is a verb of M & M that established Track I and produces an IQ, *quid ... sumpserim*, "what I have dared," in T.3s.

> → **1424** commands: first, second, 17;
> M & M, 60, 71, GL n° 527, remarks 1–2; IQ, 60; *consecutio*, 47–48.

Coepi velle ... Trebatium exspectare, "I began to wish that Trebatius was expecting": the independent verb *Coepi*, "I began," in T.4b is complemented by an infinitive, *velle*, "to wish," which is a sort of M & M verb. The content of the wish is expressed in OO, *Trebatium exspectare*, "that Trebatius was expecting."

> → **1425** verb: complementary infinitive, 77; gerund, 77.1;
> irregular verbs: *volo*, 82;
> M & M, 60, 71, GL n° 527, remarks 1–2; OO, 71–73.

Coepi … neque … promisi, "I began … nor … did I promise": the *neque*, "nor," "and not" joins these two verbs, both in T.4b.

> → **1426** *neque … , neque …* , GL n° 445.

quae sperasset a me, "[the things] which he had hoped from me": a simple relative clause *ea … quae speraverat a me*, "the things which [Trebatius] had hoped from me," is given in the subjunctive by MA where *sperasset* is the contracted form of *speravisset*, "[Trebatius] had hoped" in T.4s because *Coepi*, "I began," in T.4b sets the sentence on Track II, which carries through both contemporaneous infinitives *velle … exspectare*. Here *sperasset* may look like an unreal condition meaning "which he would have hoped," but the subjunctive is due to MA.

> → **1427** *consecutio*, 47–48; verb: complementary infinitive, 77; gerund, 77.1;
> subjunctive use: modal attraction, 83;
> contractions: verbs, 39.2, GL n° 131;
> conditionals: contrary to fact, 86.3.

minus ei prolixe de tua voluntate promisi quam eram solitus de mea polliceri, "did I promise him less extensively out of your goodwill than I had been accustomed to promise out of my own": *minus … quam …* , "less … than …," compare two verbs: *minus … promisi*, "did I promise … less," and *quam eram solitus … polliceri*, "than I had been accustomed to promise." The verb *eram solitus*, "I had been accustomed," is from a semi-deponent verb, *soleo, itus*, 2, also meaning "to use," "to be wont," and here its form and meaning are both T.5i. It is complemented by the infinitive *polliceri*, "to promise," which as a deponent verb is passive in form but active in meaning. *de tua voluntate*, "out of your goodwill," goes with *de mea [voluntate]*, "out of my [goodwill]."

> → **1428** *quam* with the comp., 43.2;
> dict., *soleo, itus*, 2., "to use, be wont, be accustomed";
> semi-deponent verbs, GL n° 167;
> verb: complementary infinitive, 77; gerund, 77.1; verb: deponent, 29.

❧

Casus vero mirificus quidam intervenit quasi vel testis opinionis meae vel sponsor humanitatis tuae. Nam cum de hoc ipso Trebatio cum Balbo nostro loquerer accuratius domi meae, litterae mihi dantur a te quibus in extremis scriptum erat "M. † itfiuium quem mihi commendas vel regem Galliae faciam, vel hunc Leptae delega, si vis. Tu ad me alium mitte quem ornem."

Sustulimus manus et ego et Balbus: tanta fuit opportunitas ut illud nescio quid non fortuitum sed divinum videretur. Mitto igitur ad te Trebatium atque ita mitto ut initio mea sponte, post autem invitatu tuo mittendum duxerim.   (*Fam.* VII, 5, 2)

However, a certain marvelous event intervened as either a witness of my own idea or a surety of your graciousness. For when I was speaking more specifically at my house with our Balbo about this very Trebatius, letters are handed to me from you at the end of which had been written, "Marcus ... whom you recommend to me, either I will make the king of Gaul, or you delegate this man to Lepta if you wish. You must send to me some other person whom I may decorate." We threw up our hands both I and Balbus: for it was such a favorable circumstance that it seemed a certain I-know-not-what not chance but divine thing. Therefore I am sending to you Trebatius, and I am sending in such a way that in the beginning I thought he had to be sent on my own accord, but afterward at your invitation.

> *cum ... cum Balbo ... loquerer accuratius domi meae*, "when I was speaking more specifically at my house with ... Balbo": the first *cum* goes with *loquerer*, "when I was speaking," in T.2s and so on Track II. The second *cum* is a preposition, "with [Balbo]." *accuratius*, "more carefully," "more specifically," is a comparative adverb. *domi meae*, "at my house," is the function of place at which, or locative with the word *domus*, f. "house."
>
>> → **1429** subjunctive use: temporal circumstance *cum* = "when," 66.3.2;
>>   *consecutio*, 47–48;
>>   prep. with abl., 28.4; adv.: positive, comp., superl., 37;
>>   function: place at which, *domi*, 69.3.3.

> *cum ... loquerer ... litterae mihi dantur*, "when I was speaking ... letters are handed to me": *dantur*, "[letters] are handed [to me]," in T.1i passive, is an historical present, whereby T.1i is used in the place of an historical time such as *sunt datae*, "[letters] were handed," in T.4b passive, to make the content more vivid, graphic, actual; see GL n° 229. Otherwise the sequence of tenses would not produce *cum loquerer*, "when I was speaking," in T.2s.
>
>> → **1430** historical present, GL n° 229;
>>   passive Times 1, 2, 3 indicative, 21;
>>   subjunctive use: temporal circumstance *cum* = "when," 66.3.2;
>>   *consecutio*, 47–48.

> *M. † itfiuium:* The † indicates the text is corrupt, marking a *locus desperatus*, "despaired-of text," that is, a text which is hopeless to restore.

> *vel ... faciam, vel ... delega, si vis*, "either I will make ... or you delegate ... if you wish": the correlatives *vel ... vel ...*, "either ... or ...," correlate the two

verbs, *faciam,* "I will make," in T.3i and *delega,* "you delegate," the command
form, softened by the polite form *si vis,* "if you wish," "please."

> → **1431** disjunctive sentence: *vel . . . , vel . . . ,* GL n° 494.2;
>> commands: first, second, 17;
>> dict., *volo, velle, volui,* v. irreg., 2., II., E. *si vis* parenthetically, I. "if you
>> please";
>> conditionals: factual, 86.1.

quem ornem, "whom I may decorate": a purpose clause where *quem* stands
for *ut eum,* "so that [I may decorate] him."

> → **1432** subjunctive use: relative clause of purpose, 58.2.

sustulimus manus, "We threw up our hands": a delightful expression that
even children show at play. The dictionary entry for *sustulimus* in T.4b is
tollo, sustuli, sublatum, 3, "to lift up."

> → **1433** dict., *tollo, sustuli, sublatum,* 3, "to lift up."

tanta fuit opportunitas ut illud . . . non fortuitum sed divinum videretur, "for
it was such a favorable circumstance that it seemed a certain . . . not chance
but divine thing": the main verb *fuit,* "it was," in T.4b establishes Track II.
The result of this circumstance is given as *tanta . . . ut . . . videretur,* "such
. . . that it seemed," in T.2s. Because the Romans preferred to take *videretur*
personally, its subject here is presumed to be *illud,* "something," "a certain
. . . thing."

> → **1434** subjunctive use: pure result (consecutive), 67.1–2, GL n° 552;
>> *consecutio,* 47–48;
>> personal construction: *videor,* 73.3, GL n° 528.1 and remark 2 and note 1.

illud nescio quid, "a certain I-know-not-what . . . thing": it is less misleading when *nescio quid* is written as one word *nescioquid.* Here *nescio* is not
functioning as a verb and does not mean "I do not know what." Rather
nescioquid functions as an indefinite pronoun meaning "I-know-not-what"
or here "something I-do-not-know-what." The expression indicates uncertainty with regard to something specific in the clause but does not have
an effect on the rest of the sentence, as a verb would produce an IQ in the
subjunctive.

> → **1435** dict., *nescio, ivi* or *ii, itum,* 4., I., (γ); GL n° 467, remark 1 and note; IQ, 60.

ita mitto ut . . . mittendum duxerim, "I am sending in such a way that . . . I
thought he had to be sent": *mitto,* "I am sending," in T.1i establishes Track
I. The result of the sending is given in the expression *ita . . . ut . . . duxerim,*
"in such a way that . . . I thought," in T.3s. The mental operation of the M &
M verb *duxerim* is given in OO, where the full infinitive is *mittendum esse,*
"to be needing to be sent," and its felt subject is *eum* referring to *Trebatium.*
Note the frequent but not recognized meaning of *duco, ducere,* not "to lead,"

but "to think," or "to judge"; see this variation in this very lengthy text, where Cicero jumps from "leading" to "judging."

> → **1436** subjunctive use: pure result (consecutive), 67.1–2, GL n° 552;
> M & M, 60, 71, GL n° 527, remarks 1–2; OO, 71–73;
> participle of passive necessity, 50, 51.1.4;
> passive necessity formula, 53.4;
> dict., *duco, xi, ctum*, 3., II., B., 4., b. (α) "to consider, calculate," (β) "to reckon, consider."

initio mea sponte, post autem invitatu tuo, "in the beginning . . . on my own accord, but afterward at your invitation": the two words *initio* in the abl. and the adverb *post*, "in the beginning . . . afterward . . . ," correlate the two elements. People may initially see *post . . . invitatu tuo*, and think "after your invitation," but *post* is used as an adverb here, meaning "afterward," "later," and *invitatu tuo*, "by your invitation," is not the object of *post*, but a natural abl.

> → **1437** abl.: meaning and forms, 27; abl.: time at which, 70.1;
> dict., *post*, I. adv., B. "after," II. prep. with acc. "behind," B. "after."

☙

Hunc, mi Caesar, sic velim omni tua comitate complectare ut omnia quae per me possis adduci ut in meos conferre velis in unum hunc conferas. De quo tibi homine haec spondeo non illo vetere verbo meo quod, cum ad te de Milone scripsissem, iure lusisti, sed more Romano quo modo homines non inepti loquuntur, probiorem hominem, meliorem virum, pudentiorem esse neminem. Accedit etiam, quod familiam ducit in iure civili, singulari memoria, summa scientia. Huic ego neque tribunatum neque praefecturam neque ullius benefici certum nomen peto, benevolentiam tuam et liberalitatem peto, neque impedio quo minus, si tibi ita placuerit, etiam hisce eum ornes gloriolae insignibus: totum denique hominem tibi ita trado, de manu, ut aiunt, in manum tuam istam et victoria et fide praestantem. Simus enim putidiusculi quamquam per te vix licet, verum, ut video, licebit. Cura ut valeas et me, ut amas, ama. (*Fam.* VII, 5, 3)

My dear Caesar, I would like that you may embrace this man with all your affability in such a way that all the things which through me you are able to be persuaded that you may want to bestow on my people, you may bestow on this man alone. About which person I promise you these things not with that old-time phrase of mine, which, when I had written to you about Milo, you deservedly mocked, but in the Roman fashion just as not-foolish people speak: that no one is a more honest person, a better man, more modest. It is added also besides, that he leads the pack in civil law, a person of exceptional memory, of the greatest knowledge. I ask for this man neither the tribunate, neither the prefecture, nor a certain title of any favor; I am seeking your benevolence and generosity, nor am I keeping you from decorating him even with these sort of medals of little glory, if it will have pleased you in this way. Finally, I hand over to you the whole person, outstanding both by victory and trustworthiness, in this way from one hand as they say into that hand of yours. For let us be a little tedious, although through you it is hardly permitted, still, as I see, it will be permitted. Take care that you be well and love me as you do love.

Note: Five subjunctive verbs and two infinitives alone in the first sentence devoid of indicative verbs gives an opportunity to understand the infinite uses of only one subjunctive time here. The box effect of the first sentence is indicated below:

Hunc,	purpose 1
mi Caesar, sic velim	main sentence; potential
omni tua comitate complectare	purpose 1 continued
[ut omnia	purpose 2
(quae per me possis adduci	relative in MA
< ut in meos conferre velis >)	purpose 3
in unum hunc conferas.]	purpose 2 continued

→ **1438** structure of Latin sentences, 103 p. 587, *Ossa* Readings: 1-D, 1-I, 3-D, 3-I, 4-D, 4-I;
relative box, 11.4.

Hunc … velim omni tua comitate complectare, "I would like that you may embrace [this man] with all your affability": the main verb *velim*, "I would like," produces a purpose statement that gives Cicero's intention. It is constructed without *ut*, but with the subjunctive alone, *complectare*, an alternative form for *complectaris*, "that you may embrace." Its object Cicero says first in the sentence, *Hunc*, "this man."

→ **1439** subjunctive use: purpose clause without *ut*, 58, GL n° 546, remark 2;
commands: other expressions, *velim*, 85.1.7;
variation: –*ris*, 39.3; demonstrative pron.: *hic, haec, hoc*, 40.3.

mi Caesar, … velim, "My dear Caesar, I would like": Cicero addresses Caesar directly as *mi Caesar*, "My dear Caesar." This is reflected in the dictionary entry for *meus, a, um*, where the vocative *mi* is said to mean "*my dear! my beloved!*" The main verb *velim*, "I would like," in T.1s, expresses a possible wish.

→ **1440** function: direct address, 38.3; dict., *meus, a, um*, adj., –voc.;
commands: other expressions, *velim*, 85.1.7.

sic … complectare ut omnia … in unum hunc conferas, "that you may embrace this man … in such a way that all the things … you may bestow on this man alone": Cicero suggests Caesar's intention in embracing Trebatius, with the purpose clause *ut … conferas*, "so that … you may bestow," in T.1s; its verb's object, *omnia*, "all things," is separated by thirteen words and two subordinate clauses describing the *omnia*.

→ **1441** sentence structure, 1.

omnia quae per me possis adduci ut in meos conferre velis, "all the things which through me you are able to be persuaded that you want to bestow on my people": the relative clause *quae … possis adduci* is in T.1s by MA because Cicero considered this idea closely integrated with the series of purpose clauses it depends on. *adduci*, "to be persuaded," is a passive infinitive and a verb of M & M producing a purpose clause *ut … velis*, "that you may want," "that you may wish," and the idea of this verb is completed by *conferre*, "to bestow," a complementary infinitive.

> → **1442** relative clauses, 10–11;
>   subjunctive use: modal attraction, 83;
>   verb: contemporaneous passive infinitive, 72.3;
>   verb: contemporaneous active infinitive, 72.1;
>   M & M, 60, 71, GL n° 527, remarks 1–2;
>   subjunctive use: purpose clause, 58.1;
>   verb: complementary infinitive, 77; gerund, 77.1.

Notice how the type of subjunctive in Latin influences its expression in the English vernacular. The following chart indicates the corresponding boxes of the English sentence. The Latin subjunctive verbs are inserted in parentheses next to their English equivalents, whether subjunctive or indicative.

My dear Caesar, *I would like* (*velim* T.1s; potential)
> { that *you may embrace* (*complectare* T.1s; purpose 1) this man with all
>   your affability
>   [so that all the things
>   (which through me *you are able* (*possis* T.1s; MA) to be persuaded
>   < that *you may want* (*velis* T.1s; purpose 3) to bestow on my
>   people, >)
>   *you may bestow* (*conferas* T.1s; purpose 2) on this man alone.] }

A comparative explanation for each pair of verbs in English and Latin follows:

I would like (*velim* T.1s; potential): the natural subjunctive expression of a wish comes through in both languages.

> → **1443** commands: other expressions, *velim*, 85.1.7.

you may embrace (*complectare* T.1s; purpose 1): the purpose clause is subjunctive in both languages. The use of "may" is not necessary in the English because "you embrace" is already subjunctive, but because this is often not recognized by the reader, we have not hesitated to make the subjunctive even more clear with the addition of "may."

> → **1444** principles of the subjunctive, 45;
>   subjunctive use: purpose clause without *ut*, 58, GL n° 546 remark 2.

you are able (*possis* T.1s; MA): the verb subjunctive by MA, but rendered in the indicative in English as a normal relative clause.

> → **1445** subjunctive use: modal attraction, 83.

you may want (*velis* T.1s; purpose): the verb is subjunctive in both Latin and English according to the nature of a purpose clause. Of course, there is always the possibility that this is a result clause and the difference is sometimes only a matter of perspective.

→ **1446** principles of the subjunctive, 45;
subjunctive use: purpose clause, 58.1;
difference between purpose and result is perspective, GL n° 543 note 2.

you may bestow (*conferas* T.1s; purpose 2): the purpose clause is subjunctive in both languages. Again, the use of "may" is not necessary in the English because "you bestow" is already subjunctive, but we have not hesitated to emphasize the subjunctive with the addition of "may."

→ **1447** principles of the subjunctive, 45;
subjunctive use: purpose clause, 58.1.

quod, cum ad te de Milone scripsissem, iure lusisti, "which, when I had written to you about Milo, you deservedly mocked": the dictionary gives a special meaning for the combination of *ludere aliquem* or *aliquid*, meaning "to mock," "to imitate," as here, where *quod ... lusisti* means "which ... you mocked," in T.4b establishing Track II. The temporal circumstances of Caesar mocking Cicero's old-time phrase are given in the clause *cum ... scripsissem*, "when I had written," in T.4s. Tyrrell and Purser say that we do not know what old saying Cicero is referring to here.

→ **1448** dict., *ludo, si, sum*, 3., II., C. *ludere aliquem, aliquid*, "to play, mock a person";
subjunctive use: temporal circumstance *cum* = "when," 66.3.2;
consecutio, 47–48.

sed more Romano, "in the Roman fashion": a reference to straight speaking or honest talk, as we might refer to speaking in "plain English."

→ **1449** abl.: meaning and forms, 27.

De quo tibi homine haec spondeo ... probiorem hominem, meliorem virum, pudentiorem esse neminem, "About which person I promise you these things ... that no one is a more honest person, a better man, more modest": the main verb of the sentence is *spondeo*, "I promise," in T.1i and a verb of M & M followed by an object *haec*, "these things." Cicero then explains what he means by "these things," and he details the content of the promise in OO, *esse neminem*, "no one is." This is said of three comparative descriptions, *probiorem hominem, meliorem virum, pudentiorem*, "a more honest person, a better man, more modest." These comparisons refer back to the beginning of the sentence *De quo ... homine*, "About which person."

→ **1450** M & M, 60, 71, GL n° 527, remarks 1–2; OO, 71–73;
adj.: comp., 36; prep. with abl., 28.4; relative clauses, 10–11.

Accedit ... quod ... ducit, "It is added also ... that he leads": the expression *Accedit ... quod* has the special meaning "there is added, the fact that" or "there comes besides, the fact that," when followed by the indicative, as here, *ducit*, "he leads." The subject of *Accedit* is the whole expression *quod...ducit*, as in "the fact that he is leading the crowd is in addition."

→ **1451** dict., *accedo, cessi, cessum*, 3., II., B., 2.... *accedit quod*, "add to this, that"; GL n° 525.

ducit ... singulari memoria, summa scientia, "he leads ... a person of exceptional memory, the greatest knowledge": the subject of *ducit*, "he leads," is *is*, "he," referring to Trebatius. His characteristics are described by these words given in the abl., so we do not hesitate to make that subject more explicit by adding a few words here, "a man of," "a person of" to convey what these ablatives are doing.

→ **1452** quality in abl., 96.2.

neque ... neque ... neque ... neque ..., "neither ... neither ... nor ... nor ...": this conjunction is repeated four times here.

→ **1453** *neque ... , neque ...*, GL n° 445.

neque impedio quo minus ... eum ornes, "nor am I keeping you from distinguishing him": *quo minus* is usually written as one word, *quominus*, "that not," as in the manuscript in part I, and it stands for *ut eo minus*, "so that by that much less," followed by the subjunctive *ornes*, "you decorate." Thus here he says *neque impedio ut eo minus eum ornes*, "nor do I impede that by that much less you decorate him." Sometimes the *quominus* is substituted by *ne*, "that not," or *quin*, also meaning "that not," as in "nor do I impede that you not decorate him," which means in clearer English, "I am not keeping you from decorating him."

→ **1454** dict., *parvus, a, um*, adj., III., B., 3., b. *quo minus, quominus*, "that not," "from";
subjunctive use: relative clause of purpose, *quo = ut eo*, 58.2;
GL n° 545.2 *quō = ut eō*;
ne, quominus, quin, 101.1, GL n° 547.

si tibi ita placuerit, "if it will have pleased you in this way": the factual condition with *placuerit*, "it will have pleased" in T.6 has as its consequence *quo minus ... ornes*, "[nor am I keeping] you from decorating [him]."

→ **1455** conditionals: factual, 86.1.

ut aiunt, "as they say": also "as people say," used when quoting a proverb or a saying, this expression can also be rendered, "as the saying goes."

→ **1456** dict., *ut*, I., B. meaning "as."

putidiusculi, "a little tedious": this text is cited in the dictionary to mean "somewhat of a bore."

→ **1457** dict., *putidiusculus, a, um*, adj., "rather more tedious."

quamquam, "although": usually with the indicative, this is one of several words meaning "although": *quamvis, quantumvis, cum, licet,* and *ut* usually take the subjunctive; and the three *etsi, etiamsi,* and *tametsi* follow the rules of the conditionals.

> → **1458** concessive particles, 64;
>   subjunctive use: concessive *quamquam* = "although," 64.

per te, "through you": almost meaning "with your permission."

> → **1459** prep. with obj., 6.

verum, "still": it looks like it means "truly" but it means "nevertheless," "but," and it is always placed as the first word in the sentence.

> → **1460** dict., *verus, a, um,* adj., II., adv., A. *verum,* 2., a. In gen., "but."

ut video . . . ut valeas . . . ut amas, "as I see [it] . . . that you be well . . . as you do love": the word *ut* meaning "as" is used here twice, with the indicatives *video* and *amas,* "as I see . . . as you do love"; and used once here meaning "so that" or "in order that," with the subjunctive *valeas,* "that you be well."

> → **1461** dict., *ut,* I., B. meaning "as"; subjunctive use: purpose clause, 58.1.

LETTER 348 T-P
AD ATTICUM VIII, 13

CICERO ATTICO SAL.

Lippitudinis meae signum tibi sit librari manus et eadem causa brevitatis, etsi nunc quidem quod scriberem nihil erat. Omnis exspectatio nostra erat in nuntiis Brundisinis. Si nactus hic esset Gnaeum nostrum, spes dubia pacis; sin ille ante tramisisset, exitiosi belli metus. Sed videsne in quem hominem inciderit res publica? quam acutum, quam vigilantem, quam paratum? Si mehercule neminem occiderit nec cuiquam quidquam ademerit, ab iis qui eum maxime timuerant maxime diligetur.   (*Att.* VIII, 13, 1)

CICERO A GREETING TO ATTICUS

May the writing of my secretary be a sign for you of my eye inflammation, and the same, the motive of the brevity, although now indeed there was nothing which I should write. All of our expectation was in the Brindisi news: if this man [Caesar] would have found our Gnaeus [Pompeius], a dubious hope of peace; but if the latter [Pompeius] would have crossed over ahead of time, the fear of a disastrous war. But do you see upon what kind of a man the state has fallen? how sharp, how vigilant, how ready? If, by george, he will have killed no one, nor taken away anything from anyone, he will be esteemed mostly by those who had feared him mostly.

CICERO ATTICO SAL.: *Cicero Attico salutem*

Lippitudinis meae signum tibi sit librari manus et eadem causa brevitatis, "May the writing of my secretary be a sign for you of my eye inflammation, and the same, the motive of the brevity": the stylish chiasm begins and ends with *Lippitudinis ... brevitatis,* "of ... eye inflammation ... of the brevity," and in the middle is *manus,* "the writing," the subject of *sit,* "May the writing ... be" in T.1s to express a wish. The *et* joins the sentence that precedes it with the sentence that follows it; much of the latter is implied. The subject of the second sentence is éadem, "the same," referring either to the closest feminine noun, *manus,* or possibly to *Lippitudinis,* the eye condition. The verb *sit* is felt but not repeated. The predicate *causa,* "the motive," agrees with *eadem.* A fuller version of the second sentence would be: *et lippitudo tibi causa sit brevitatis,* "and may the eye inflammation be for you the motive of brevity." Until about the second century c.e. *librarii* the gen. was spelled *librari* because that is how it was heard.

→ **1462** sentence structure, 1; early gen. ending in *–i,* GL n° 33, remark 1.

signum tibi sit librari manus ... etsi nunc ... quod scriberem nihil erat, "May the writing of my secretary be a sign for you ... although now ... there was nothing which I should write": the main verb is the independent subjunctive expressing a wish, *sit,* "May [the writing] be," in T.1s, indicating Track I. The concessive clause *etsi ... erat,* "although ... there was," in T.2i, establishes Track II and indicates a switch to the epistolary tense. Were Cicero simply commenting about the task of writing at the moment, he could have simply said, *etsi nunc ... quod scribam nihil est,* "although now ... there is nothing which I may write." Rather he recounts his present moment from the perspective of the reader looking back at the time when Cicero was writing this letter and had not yet received any news from Brindisi.

→ **1463** subjunctive use: concessive *etsi* = "although," 64; *consecutio,* 47–48; letter-writer tense, GL n° 252.

quod scriberem nihil erat, "there was nothing which I might write": *erat,* "there was," in T.2i establishes Track II, producing *ut scriberem,* "which I might write," in T.2s, a result clause that describes the characteristic of *nihil,* "nothing." Here *quod* stands for *tale ut id,* "[nothing] such that [I might write] it." The English rendering is in the subjunctive because of the felt presence of a natural subjunctive underlying the idea expressed.

→ **1464** subjunctive use: characteristic result, 68.2; *consecutio,* 47–48; subjunctive use: underlying potential of the past, 94.3, GL n° 258.

exspectatio nostra erat in nuntiis Brundisinis, "our expectation was in the Brindisi news": *erat,* "[the news] was," in T.2i continues the epistolary tense. As he writes he is expecting news from Brindisi. Perhaps the news will be known by the time the letter is read, thus suggesting the use of the epistolary tense to distance the present writing from its future reading. *in nuntiis Brundisinis,* "in the Brundisian news," here the name of the town functions as an adjective describing *nuntiis.*

→ **1465** letter-writer tense, GL n° 252; prep. with abl., 28.4; Block I adj., 4.2–3; dict., *Brundisium, ii,* n., II. *Brundisinus, a, um,* adj.

Si nactus hic esset Gnaeum nostrum, spes dubia pacis; sin ille ante tramisisset, exitiosi belli metus, "if this man [Caesar] would have found our Gnaeus [Pompeius], a dubious hope of peace; but if the latter [Pompeius] would have crossed over ahead of time, the fear of a disastrous war": the verbs *nactus*

... *esset* and *transisset* are both T.4s, which we insist on not calling the pluperfect subjunctive because it is also the natural way of expressing future completed action in the subjunctive on Track II, as we shall see here.

→ **1466** principles of the subjunctive, 45; *consecutio*, 47–48; *consecutio*: completed futurity in the subjunctive, 61.1.

The verbs establish two factual conditions. If the first condition occurs, and Caesar finds Gnaeus, the consequence is *spes dubia pacis*, "a dubious hope of peace," given without an expressed verb. If the second condition occurs, and Pompeius crosses over to Greece, then the consequence is *exitiosi belli metus*, "the fear of a disastrous war," also given without an expressed verb.

Factual conditions are normally given in the indicative, but here in the subjunctive by MA. This may be explained in one of two ways.

→ **1467** conditionals: factual, 86.1; subjunctive use: modal attraction, 83.

First, the English rendering above does not follow the real possibility that these conditional sentences depend on *erat* in the previous sentence, meaning "[expectation] was [in the news]," in T.2i, thereby establishing Track II. Since *erat* is the time when Cicero wrote the letter, he used T.4s to indicate an action that he believed had already occurred, namely that either Caesar had already found Gnaeus or Pompeius had already crossed over to Greece. Relative to *erat* in T.2i, these subjunctive verbs have the equivalent of T.5i. This possibility suggests the English rendering: "if this man [Caesar] had found our Gnaeus [Pompeius] ... ; but if the latter [Pompeius] had crossed over ahead of time ...."

→ **1468** letter-writer tense, GL nº 252.

Second, the option followed in the English rendering above is based in the previous sentence less on the verb *erat* than on the idea contained in the subject, *exspectatio*, "[our] expectation [was]." This indicates that Cicero did not know what was happening. He accounts for his expectation that either the hope of a future peace will be dubious or there will be a fear of a disastrous war. Given his expectation of one or the other future possibility, he then states the respective conditions that will have to have already occurred to bring about each expectation. Thus, both factual conditions, if rewritten as independent sentences, would be written in T.6i and T.3i, as in the following reconstruction: *Si nactus hic erit Gnaeum nostrum, spes erit dubia pacis; sin ille ante tramiserit, exitiosi erit belli metus*, "if this man [Caesar] *will have found* our Gnaeus [Pompeius], there *will be* a dubious hope of peace; but if the latter [Pompeius] *will have crossed over* ahead of time, there *will be* the fear of a disastrous war." When these conditions are made to depend on the epistolary time *erat*, they are put into the subjunctive by MA, and then both conditions are given in T.4s because this is the natural way to express future completed action in the subjunctive on Track II. The result is *nactus esset ... tramisisset*, with several possibilities in English: first the simple future completed time, "[Caesar] will have found ... [Pompeius] will have crossed over," second future completed action from a point in the past where "would have" is not a sign of the subjunctive but of completed futurity, "[Caesar] would have found … [Pompeius] would have crossed over," third, a natural subjunctive may still come through, as in "[Caesar] should have found … [Pompeius] should have crossed over."

→ **1469** conditionals: factual, 86.1;
 letter-writer tense, GL n° 252; subjunctive use: modal attraction, 83;
 principles of the subjunctive, 45; *consecutio*, 47–48;
 consecutio: completed futurity in the subjunctive, 61.1.

Sed videsne in quem hominem inciderit res publica?, "But do you see upon what kind of a man the state has fallen?": the rather extended use of the epistolary time ends, and Cicero brings the reader to the present time of the writer with the verb *vides*, "do you see," an M & M verb in T.1i establishing Track I. *inciderit* is from *íncĭdo, cĭdi, cāsum*, 3 from *in-cado*, "to fall into," "to fall upon," but, in the name of honesty, it has the same form as another verb in the dictionary, *incído, cídi, císum*, 3 from *in-caedo*, "to cut into," "inscribe." Here *inciderit*, "[the state] has fallen upon" is T.3s because it is part of an IQ that begins with the question word *in quem hominem*, which does not mean only "unto which man," but even "upon what kind of man," where *quem* is an interrogative in the dictionary and means "what kind of," "what sort of."

→ **1470** M & M, 60, 71, GL n° 527, remarks 1–2; IQ, 60;
 consecutio, 47–48;
 dict., *incido, cidi, casum*, 3 from *in-cado*, "to fall into," "to fall upon";
 dict., *incído, cídi, císum*, 3 from *in-caedo*, "to cut into," "inscribe";
 dict., *qui, quae, quod*, pron., I. interrog., "what kind of," "what sort of."

quam acutum, quam vigilantem, quam paratum?, "how sharp, how vigilant, how ready?": *quam* may appear to agree with *res publica*, "the state," that immediately precedes, but here *quam* is an adv. that means "how." Each adjective further describes *eum*, referring to Caesar, contained in the *quem*, in the expression *in quem hominem*, "upon what kind of man."

→ **1471** dict., *quam*, adv., "in what manner," "how";
 Block I adj., 4.2–3; Block II adj. in three ways, 18.

Si … occiderit nec … ademerit … diligetur, "If … he will have killed … nor taken away … he will be esteemed": the first two verbs are conditions *Si … occiderit*, "If … he will have killed," in T.6i, and *nec … ademerit*, meaning "and [if he will have] not taken away," also in T.6i. The consequence is given in T.3i, *diligetur*, "he will be esteemed." N.B.: Cicero has a premonition of the possible greatness of Caesar, who did not kill anyone in reprisal and was esteemed in fact.

→ **1472** conditionals: factual, 86.1.

nec cuiquam quidquam ademerit, "nor taken away anything from anyone": two pronouns back to back *cuiquam quidquam*, "anything from anyone."

ademerit, "[he will have ... nor] taken away," is one of the 65 whose complement is in the dat., here *cuiquam*, "from anyone." This expression is counterintuitive because the ad, "for," in *ademerit* looks like it refers to taking toward not from someone. Rather, it refers to taking *ad* "for [one's self]" and thus away from another. It is also counterintuitive because here *cuiquam* does not mean "for anyone," but instead "from anyone," according to the natural meaning of the dat. This is why in our system from the beginning we call this the to-for-from function. The meaning "from" is typical with words of privation that are among the 65 that take the dat. complement.

→ **1473** dict., *quisquam, quaequam, quicquam* or *quidquam*, pron. indef.,
  "any one, any thing";
  natural dat., 33.7.1; 65 verbs with dat., 33.7.2, GL n° 346.

maxime ... maxime, "mostly ... mostly": the adv. is repeated here.

→ **1474** adv.: positive, comp., superl., 37.

❧

Multum mecum municipales homines loquuntur, multum rusticani. Nihil prorsus aliud curant nisi agros, nisi villulas, nisi nummulos suos. Et vide quam conversa res sit; illum quo antea confidebant metuunt, hunc amant quem timebant. Id quantis nostris peccatis vitiisque evenerit non possum sine molestia cogitare. Quae autem impendere putarem scripseram ad te et iam tuas litteras exspectabam.   (*Att*. VIII, 13, 2)

The townsfolk speak much with me, the country people much. They care for absolutely nothing else except their fields, their little villas, their little coins. And look how much the situation has been turned around. They fear that man [Pompeius] whom before they were trusting, they love this man [Caesar] whom they were fearing. I am not able to think without grief by what great mistakes and faults of ours that has come about. I had written to you, however, what things I was thinking were imminent, and already I was awaiting your letter.

Multum ... multum, "much ... much": the adverb of *multus, a, um*.
→ **1475** dict., *multus, a, um*, adj., I., B., 3. adv., A. *multum*, B. *multō*: A. *multum*,
  "much, very much," B. *multo*, "by much";
  adv.: irregular comp. and superl., 37.3, GL n° 93.

prorsus, "absolutely": an adv. also meaning "straight away."
→ **1476** dict., *prorsus*, adv., I. "forwards," II. "straight on," B. "absolutely"
  [as people say today];
  adv.: positive, comp., superl., 37.

nisi agros, nisi villulas, nisi nummulos suos, "except their fields, their little villas, their little coins": Cicero uses the diminutives *villulas*, "little villas," and *nummulos*, "little coins" to show scorn or contempt, as in "their stupid little villas and stupid little coins of money."

> → **1477** dict., *villula, ae,* f. dim. of *villa, ae,* f.;
> dict., *nummulus, i,* m. dim. *nummus, i,* m.;
> diminutive adj., GL n° 181.12, 182.12.

vide quam conversa res sit, "look how much the situation has been turned around": here *quam* means "how much," and begins an IQ whose verb is *conversa … sit*, "[the situation] has been turned around," "was being changed," "had been changed," or any other expression of time antecedent to the M & M verb it depends on, the command form *vide*, "look," "see." Note that the subject *res*, "the situation," is placed in the middle of the compound verb.

> → **1478** commands: first, second, 17; M & M, 60, 71, GL n° 527, remarks 1–2;
> dict., *quam*, adv., I. "how much"; IQ, 60; sentence structure, 1.

illum … hunc, "that man … this man": one way of taking these is to say that *illum* means "the former" or "the previous" or "the further," and hunc "the latter," "the more recent," or "the nearer"; here *illum* refers to Pompeius and *hunc* to Caesar. But sometimes this is reversed and depends on the perspective of the speaker-writer or the reader-hearer or on a logical not geographical distinction. If you consult Lewis & Short, this is explained that sometimes the traditional order, "this one … that one … ," is reversed where "this one" is far away and "that one" is further away.

> → **1479** dict., *hic, haec, hoc,* pron. demonstr., I., D. "this, the latter" or "that, the former";
> dict., *ille, a, ud,* pron. demonstr., something more remote or regarded as more remote;
> three cousins: *iste–ille–ipse*, 41.3.

Id quantis nostris peccatis vitiisque evenerit, "by what great mistakes and faults of ours that has come about": the main verb, *possum*, "I am [not] able," in T.1i establishes Track I and is complemented by the infinitive *cogitare*, "[I am not able] to think," a verb of M & M that produces this IQ. The question word is *quantis*, "by what great," and the verb is *evenerit*, "it has come about," in T.3s.

> → **1480** verb: complementary infinitive, 77; gerund, 77.1;
> M & M, 60, 71, GL n° 527, remarks 1–2;
> dict, *quantus, a, um,* adj., I. "how great"; IQ, 60; consecutio, 47–48.

Quae … impendere putarem, "what things I was thinking were imminent": the verb of M & M *scripseram*, "I had written," in T.5i, continuing Track II produces an IQ where the question word is *Quae*, "what things," and the verb *putarem*, "I was thinking," in T.2s. If *Quae* were a relative pronoun, "[things] which," and not an interrogative pronoun, then there would be

no reason for the subjunctive here, but it would produce *ea quae impende-*
re putabam scripseram, meaning "I had written those things which I was
thinking were threatening." *putarem*, "I was thinking," is a verb of M & M
and provides OO where the interrogative *quae* in the object form functions
as the subj. of the infinitive *impendere*, which is contemporary to *putarem*
and thus set in the past, "things … were imminent."

> → **1481** M & M, 60, 71, GL n° 527, remarks 1–2; IQ, 60;
>   *consecutio*, 47–48;
>   dict., *qui, quae, quod*, pron., I. interrog., "who? which? what?".

scripseram ad te, "I had written to you": the action of *scripseram*, "I had
written," in T.5i is prior to the epistolary time in *exspectabam*, "I was awaiting," in T.2i.

> → **1482** letter-writer tense, GL n° 252.

iam tuas litteras exspectabam, "already I was awaiting your letter": epistolary tense. At the time Cicero is writing he would say *exspecto*, "I am expecting," but he writes from the perspective of the one reading the letter and so
uses *exspectabam*, "I was awaiting," in T.2b establishing Track II, to refer to
his present action of writing.

> → **1483** letter-writer tense, GL n° 252.

LETTER 381 T-P
AD ATTICUM X, 3A

CICERO ATTICO SAL.

A. d. VII Id. alteram tibi eodem die hanc epistulam dictavi, et pridie dederam mea manu longiorem. Visum te aiunt in regia nec reprehendo, quippe cum ipse istam reprehensionem non fugerim. Sed exspecto tuas litteras, neque iam sane video quid exspectem, sed tamen, etiam si nihil erit, id ipsum ad me velim scribas.   (*Att.* X, 3a, 1)

CICERO A GREETING TO ATTICUS

On the seventh day before the Ides [7 April] I have dictated to you this second letter on the same day, and on the day before I had sent you a longer one in my own hand. People say you were seen in the palace, and I do not criticize inasmuch as I myself have not escaped that criticism. But I am waiting for your letter, nor do I already of course see what I am awaiting, but nevertheless, even if there will be nothing, I would like that you write that very thing to me.

CICERO ATTICO SAL.: *Cicero Attico salutem*

A. d. VII Id., "On the seventh day before the Ides [7 April]": the full formula is *Ante diem septimum Idus Apriles.* This is a set formula, but the word *ante* is felt before the word *Idus,* as in *die septimo ante Idus Apriles,* "on the seventh day before the April Ides." Eventually this system was relinquished and medieval and church calendar Latin says *die septimo mensis Aprilis,* "on the seventh day of the month of April."
> → **1484** about the Roman calendar, pp. 605–608;
>   GL appendix: Roman Calendar, pp. 491–92.

hanc epistulam dictavi, et pridie dederam, "I have dictated … this … letter, and on the day before I had sent": *dictavi,* "I have dictated," is T.4a and expresses a present action of writing this letter. *dederam*, "I had sent," is T.5i, but describes writing a longer letter on the previous day.

> → **1485** times-tenses of the indicative mode and their vernacular meaning, 7.

longiorem, "a longer one": comparative adjective whose positive degree is *longam* and superlative *longissimam*.

> → **1486** adj.: comp. and superl., 36.

Visum te aiunt, "People say you were seen": *aiunt*, "People say" is a verb of M & M in T.1i. The content of their speech is given in OO *Visum te*, where the full infinitive is *visum esse*, "you to have been seen," "you were seen."

> → **1487** M & M, 60, 71, GL n° 527, remarks 1–2; OO, 71–73.

nec reprehendo, quippe cum ... non fugerim, "and I do not criticize inasmuch as I ... have not escaped": *reprehendo*, "I do [not] criticize," is T.1i establishing Track I. The causal clause *cum ... fugerim*, "because I have [not] escaped," in T.3s represents anterior action. The *quippe*, "as someone who," strengthens the *cum* and together they are rendered here as "inasmuch as I." The combination *quippe cum* could also be written as *utpote qui* or *ut qui*, "as someone who" followed by the subjunctive.

> → **1488** subjunctive use: causal *cum* = "because, since," 59.1;
>   *consecutio*, 47–48;
>   subjunctive use: causal *quippe qui*, 59.5; GL n° 633.

neque ... video quid exspectem, "nor do I ... see what I am awaiting": the main verb here is *video*, "I do [not] see," a verb of M & M in T.1i establishing Track I. It produces an IQ *quid exspectem*, "what I am awaiting," in T.1s. Discerning whether the original independent question is indicative or subjunctive is not always evident from the IQ, as here. We expect the original question to be indicative 90% of the time, as in *Quid exspecto?*, "What am I expecting?," then the IQ in English is in the indicative, as in "what I am awaiting." We are aware that 10% of the time the original question is in the subjunctive, as in *Quid exspectem?*, "What should I expect?," then the subjunctive comes through the IQ in English as "[nor do I see] what I should await."

> → **1489** M & M, 60, 71, GL n° 527, remarks 1–2; IQ, 60;
>   *consecutio*, 47–48;
>   independent subjunctive, 45.6, deliberative question, GL n° 265.

sane, "of course": from the adjective *sanus, a, um*, this popular adv. has many different meanings in the dictionary, but here it does not mean "in a healthy way." It can also mean "naturally."

> → **1490** dict., *sanus, a, um*, adj., II., B. ... —adv.: A. *saniter*, B. *sane*, "healthily," 2., b. "of course."

velim scribas, "I would like that you write": following *velim*, "I would like,"
in T.1s, is a purpose clause given without the *ut*, but the subjunctive alone,
scribas, "that you write."

→ **1491** subjunctive use: purpose clause without *ut*, 58, GL n° 546, remark 2;
commands: other expressions, *velim*, 85.1.7.

☙

Caesar mihi ignoscit per litteras quod non venerim seseque in optimam
partem id accipere dicit. Facile patior, quod scribit, secum Tullum et Servium questos esse quia non idem sibi quod mihi remisisset. Homines ridiculos! qui cum filios misissent ad Cn. Pompeium circumsedendum, ipsi in
senatum venire dubitarint. Sed tamen exemplum misi ad te Caesaris litterarum.   (*Att.* X, 3a, 2)

Caesar forgives me by letter that I did not come, and he says that he is taking that in the best way. I easily allow, that which he writes, that Tullus and
Servius complained with him [Caesar] that he did not respond the same
thing to them which he had to me. O laughable people! who although they
had sent their sons to blockade Gaius Pompeius, they themselves hesitated
to come into the senate. But nevertheless I have sent you a copy of Caesar's
letter.

Caesar mihi ignoscit, "Caesar forgives me": *ignosco* is one of the 65 verbs
whose complement is in the dat., here *mihi*. The problem in English is that
you cannot hear that dat. *mihi* in the rendering "me" because in English it
sounds like the acc. object.

→ **1492** 65 verbs with dat., 33.7.2, GL n° 346.

Caesar mihi ignoscit … quod non venerim, "Caesar forgives me … that I did
not come": *ignoscit*, "[Caesar] forgives," in T.1i producing Track I. Caesar's
reason for forgiving is given in the clause *quod non venerim*, "that I did not
come," where *venerim* is T.3s. The reason for that subjunctive is because
Cicero is quoting Caesar's reason for forgiving, a quoted reason which may
be expressed as "Caesar forgives me … that, as he says, I did not come." Had
Cicero used the indicative here, *quod non veni*, then Cicero would be own-
ing the statement explaining why Caesar forgave him, as in "Caesar forgives
me … that, as I say, I did not come."

→ **1493** causal: *quod*, "because, since," + subjunctive, reported reason, 59.2;
causal: *quod*, "because, since," + indicative, one's own reason, 59.2.

quod non venerim … quia non … remisisset, "that I did not come … that
he did not respond": the reason for the subjunctive in the first example is
because Cicero is quoting the written comment of Caesar, and in the second
Cicero is stating the complaint which Tullus and Servius made to Caesar, as

in "that as Caesar said I did not come … that as Tullus and Servius complained to [Caesar] that he [Caesar] had not responded."

> → **1494** causal: *quod, quia, quoniam,* "because, since," + subjunctive,
> reported reason, 59.2.

seseque in optimam partem id accipere dicit, "and he says that he is taking that in the best way": the main verb *dicit,* "he says," is a verb of M & M in T.1i. The content of his speech is given in OO, *sese … accipere,* "that he is taking," where *sese,* "he," refers to *is,* "he," the subject of *dicit,* and so functions as a direct reflexive. The expression *in optimam partem accipere* means "to receive into the best part" or "in the best way"; the positive degree is *in bonam partem accipere,* "to receive it well," and the comparative, *in meliorem partem accipere,* "to take it better."

> → **1495** M & M, 60, 71, GL n° 527, remarks 1–2; OO, 71–73;
> reflexive pron.: third person, 31;
> adj.: irregular comp. and superl., 36.5.

sese … secum … sibi, "that he … with him [Caesar] … to them": we have already seen that *sese* refers to the subject of the verb *dicit,* Caesar, and so functions as a direct reflexive.

In the cases of *secum* and *sibi,* the reflexive pronoun refers not to the subject of their clauses, but to the person or persons whose speech Cicero is quoting. In the first example, *secum* does not refer to the subject of *questos esse,* that is, to Tullus and Servius; rather *secum* refers indirectly to the subject of *scribit,* Caesar, whose speech Cicero is reporting. Here *sibi* does not refer to the subject of *remisisset,* but indirectly to the subject of *questos esse,* Tullus and Servius, whose speech Cicero is reporting. Thus, here *sese* means "that he," *secum* means "with him," but *sibi* means "to them."

The third option is not presented here, where the reflexive pronoun refers logically to the subject of the whole story, which is very common in later Latin, early Christian writers, and medieval Latin. As always with reflexive pronouns the magical word is "the subject," but you have to figure out which subject: the grammatical subject, the indirect subject, or the logical subject.

> → **1496** reflexive pron.: third person, 31.

patior … secum Tullum et Servium questos esse, "I … allow … that Tullus and Servius complained with him [Caesar]": the main verb, *patior,* "I allow," is T.1i of a deponent verb, thus with passive form and active meaning. As a verb of M & M, the content of the mental operation is expressed in OO where two objects *Tullum* and *Servium* are the subjects of the infinitive *questos esse,* "[they] complained," from the deponent verb *queror, questus,* 3, "to complain, lament," not from the active verb *quaero, sivi, situm,* 3, "to seek."

> → **1497** verb: deponent, 29;
> M & M, 60, 71, GL n° 527, remarks 1–2; OO, 71–73;
> dict., *queror, questus,* 3., "to complain, lament";
> dict., *quaero, sivi, situm,* 3., "to seek."

Here *secum,* "with him," refers to Caesar. This is called an indirect reflexive because it does not refer to the subject of its own verb, *questos esse,* that
is, to *Tullum* and *Servium;* rather, it refers outside of its immediate clause to
the subject of *scribit,* "he [Caesar] writes."

→ **1498** reflexive pron.: third person, 31;
　　　dict., *cum,* prep. with abl., II., D., a.... *mecum, tecum, secum, ... quocum*
　　　(*quīcum*).

quod scribit, "what he writes": also rendered as "that which he writes" or
"something which he writes." That *quod* refers to the whole story that Caesar mentions in his letter.

→ **1499** *quod* referring to previous sentence: GL n° 614, remark 2.

quia non idem sibi quod mihi remisisset, "that he did not respond the same
thing to them which he had to me": the main verb, *patior,* "I allow," in T.1i
establishes Track I and produces the OO whose infinitive verb describes an
antecedent action, *questos esse,* "[they] complained," which, as the equivalent
of T.4b, changes the rest of the sentence to Track II. *questos esse* is a verb of
M & M and the content of the complaint made by Tullus and Servius is given
in the statement *quia ... remisisset,* "that he [Caesar] had not responded."
The reason for the T.4 subjunctive *remisisset* is because Cicero is quoting the
speech of Tullus and Servius. Furthermore, *sibi* refers not to Caesar, the subject of *remisisset,* and so does not function as a direct reflexive; rather it is an
indirect reflexive referring to the subject of the quoted speech, to Tullus and
Servius, as in "which—as Tullus and Servius said—Caesar had responded to
me." The verb in quoted speech, *remisisset,* is not repeated for the first part of
the expression, for which we hesitate to supply the verb Cicero left out: *quia
non idem sibi remisit,* "which as I say he sent to them," where the indicative
indicates Cicero's own statement. The whole statement would be, then: *quia
non idem sibi remisit quod mihi remisisset,* "that he did not respond the same
thing to them which [they said] he had responded to me."

→ **1500** verb: deponent, 29;
　　　M & M, 60, 71, GL n° 527, remarks 1–2; OO, 71–73;
　　　consecutio, 47–48; reflexive pron.: third person, 31;
　　　causal: *quia,* "because, since," + subjunctive, reported reason, 59.2;
　　　causal: *quia,* "because, since," + indicative, one's own reason, 59.2.

The box structure of the third sentence is made clear with a simple chart:

Homines ridiculos!	main; T.1i Track I
{ qui	causal
[cum filios misissent	concessive; T.4s Track II
(ad Cn. Pompeium	
circumsedendum,)]	gerund or gerundive
ipsi in senatum venire	
dubitarint. }	causal cont.; T.3s Track I producing Track II

→ **1501** structure of Latin sentences, 103 p. 587, *Ossa* Readings: 1-D, 1-I, 3-D, 3-I,
　　　4-D, 4-I; relative box, 11.4.

Homines ridiculos!, "O laughable people!": an exclamation in the acc. just as when we say in English, "O miserable me!" not "O miserable I!"

→ **1502** exclamations, GL nº 343.1.

qui ... ipsi in senatum venire dubitarint, "who ... they themselves hesitated to come into the senate": the main verb is only felt in this sentence, such as *Homines ridiculos*! [i.e., *Sunt* ...], "O laughable people! [They are ...]" in T.1i establishing Track I. Cicero then explains the reason why they are so laughable in a causal clause where *qui* stands for *cum ii*, "because they," followed by *dubitarint*, the contracted form of *dubitaverint*, in T.3s, rendered in English in the indicative according to the nature of a causal clause, "who ... hesitated." The reason for the use of *qui* here rather than *cum ii* is to avoid the expression *cum ii cum filios misissent*, ... , "because they, although they had sent sons, ..."

→ **1503** subjunctive use: causal *qui, quae, quod* = "because, since," 59.4; *consecutio*, 47–48.

cum filios misissent, "although they had sent their sons": Here *cum* does not mean "when" or "because" but "although." A note about the sequence of tenses: the felt main verb *sunt*, "they are," is T.1i, establishing Track I. Depending on it is the causal clause whose antecedent action *dubitarint*, "they ... hesitated," is given in T.3s, which, although on Track I, is the equivalent of T.4b, which sets the rest of the sentence on Track II thereby producing this causal clause whose antecedent action *misissent* is given in T.4s, here the equivalent of T.5i.

→ **1504** subjunctive use: concessive *cum* = "although," 64; *consecutio*, 47–48;
   cum + historical times of indicative = "when": temporal coincidence, 66.3.1;
   subjunctive use: causal *cum* = "because, since," 59.1.

ad Cn. Pompeium circumsedendum, "to blockade Gaius Pompeius": the gerund looks the same as the gerundive here because its object is masculine singular. *Cn.* stands for *Gnaeum*.

→ **1505** gerund, 77.1; gerundive, 77.2.

A simple calendar can clarify the timeline of this sentence.

February	March	May
		Homines ridiculos!
		[i.e., *Sunt* ...]
	qui dubitarint	
cum misissent		

→ **1506** calendars, 83 pp. 514–15, 103 p. 586.

Note, *cum misissent* is geographically placed in the sentence before the verb it depends on, *dubitarint*, because Cicero has the whole sentence in mind and the change from Track I to Track II before he starts writing the first word.

→ **1507** sentence structure, 1.

LETTER 15 T-P
AD FAMILIARES V, 7

M. TULLIUS M. F. CICERO S. D. CN.
POMPEIO CN. F. MAGNO IMPERATORI.

S. T. E. Q. V. B. E. Ex litteris tuis quas publice misisti cepi una cum omnibus incredibilem voluptatem: tantam enim spem oti ostendisti quantam ego
semper omnibus te uno fretus pollicebar. Sed hoc scito, tuos veteres hostis,
novos amicos, vehementer litteris his perculsos atque ex magna spe deturbatos iacere.   (*Fam.* V, 7, 1)

MARCUS TULLIUS CICERO, THE SON OF MARCUS, SAYS
A GREETING TO GNAEUS POMPEIUS MAGNUS, THE SON
OF GNAEUS, COMMANDER IN CHIEF

If you and the army are well, it is well. From your letter, which you sent
officially, I together with all people got an unbelievable pleasure: for you
showed so great a hope of peace, how great I, relying on you alone, was
always promising to all people. But you must know this, that your old enemies, new friends, having been profoundly shaken by this letter and having
been cast off from a great hope, are flat on their backs.

M. TULLIUS M. F. CICERO S. D. CN. POMPEIO CN. F. MAGNO IMPERATORI:
*Marcus Tullius Marci filius Cicero salutem dicit Gnaeo Pompeio Gnaei filio,
Magno imperatori*

S. T. E. Q. V. B. E., "If you and the army are well, it is well": *Si tu exercitusque
valetis, bene est.*

una cum omnibus, "together with all people": Here *una* means "at the same
time," "in company," "together"; with the long vowel *unā* here it is the feminine abl. and stands for *unā* agreeing perhaps with *opera* as in "with one
effort." The same thing appears in the church phrase *unā cum Patre et Filio,*

where, instead of saying "together with the Father and Son" (which would be *simul cum Patre et Filio*), the Latin says "with one effort with the Father and the Son."

→ **1508** dict., *unus, a, um*, num. adj., II., C....—adv., *unā*, "in company, together."

tantam ... quantam ... , "so great ... how great ...": correlatives.

→ **1509** correlative comparative sentences, 90.5, GL n° 642.

scito, tuos veteres hostis, novos amicos ... iacere, "you must know ... that your old enemies, new friends ... are flat on their backs": the command *scito*, "you must know," is the second imperative form, sometimes called the future imperative. As a verb of M & M the content of the knowledge is given in OO, *hostis ... iacere*, where *hostis* is an alternative form of *hostes*, agreeing with *tuos veteres ... novos amicos*, and serves as the acc. subject of the infinitive *iacére*. Reading the sentence out loud will help clarify whether the reader understands *iacere* to be as here *iacére* meaning "to lie flat," or if the reader is confused with *iácere*, "to throw," "to cast," which would be ridiculous here.

→ **1510** commands: first, second, 17;
       M & M, 60, 71, GL n° 527, remarks 1–2; OO, 71–73;
       dict., *jaceo, cui, citum*, 2., "to be thrown," thus, "to lie";
       dict., *jacio, jeci, jactum*, 3., I. "to throw, cast, fling, hurl."

◆

Ad me autem litteras quas misisti, quamquam exiguam significationem tuae erga me voluntatis habebant, tamen mihi scito iucundas fuisse: nulla enim re tam laetari soleo quam meorum officiorum conscientia, quibus si quando non mutue respondetur, apud me plus offici residere facillime patior. Illud non dubito quin, si te mea summa erga te studia parum mihi adiunxerint, res publica nos inter nos conciliatura coniuncturaque sit.   (*Fam.* V, 7, 2)

However, know that the letter which you sent to me, although it continued to have a thin hinting of your disposition toward me, nevertheless was pleasing to me: for I am accustomed to rejoice in no thing so much as in the awareness of my own services, to which, if at times an answer is not given mutually, I very easily allow that a greater amount of dutifulness rests with me. That thing I do not doubt: that, if my very great signs of enthusiasm toward you will have joined you to me not enough, public concern is going to unite and bind us mutually.

Ad me autem litteras quas misisti ... iucundas fuisse, "However ... the letter, which you sent to me ... was pleasing to me": note the word order. *Ad me*, "to me," precedes the relative clause it depends on, *quas misisti*, "which you sent [to me]." Geographically between the two is *litteras*, "the letter," which serves as the antecedent of *quas*, "which [letter]," and goes with, the fourteenth word further along, *iucundas*, and in the object form serves as the subject of the infinitive verb *fuisse*, "was." Should someone think that this word order is "mixed up," as we see time and again, this is the natural expression of Latin, depending on the endings.

> → **1511** sentence structure, 1.

litteras ... mihi scito iucundas fuisse, "know that the letter ... was pleasing to me": *scito*, "know," is a second command form and a verb of M & M. The content of the knowledge is given in OO, *litteras ... iucundas fuisse*, "the letter ... was pleasing," "... had been pleasing," "... has been pleasing," where the infinitive describes antecedent action.

> → **1512** commands: first, second, 17;
> M & M, 60, 71, GL nᵒ 527, remarks 1–2; OO, 71–73.

quamquam ... habebant, "although it continued to have": *quamquam*, usually with the indicative, is one of several words meaning "although": *quamvis, quantumvis, cum, licet, ut* usually take the subjunctive; and *etsi, etiamsi, tametsi* follow the rules of conditionals.

> → **1513** subjunctive use: concessive *quamquam* = "although," 64.

nulla ... re tam ... quam ... conscientia, "in no thing so much as in the awareness": the correlatives *tam ... quam ...*, "so much ... as ... ," balance two equal elements in the abl. *nulla ... re*, "by no thing" and *conscientia*, "by the awareness."

> → **1514** correlative comparative sentences, 90.5, GL nᵒ 642.

quibus si ... respondetur, "to which, if ... an answer is not given": *quibus* is in front of the *si*, "if," but goes with *respondetur*. The antecedent of *quibus* is of-*ficiorum*, "services," and *quibus* stands for *et iis*, "and to them," as a connection with the previous sentence. The dat. *quibus* is natural with *respondetur*, as in "and if an answer is not given to them."

> → **1515** dict., *qui, quae, quod*, pron., II., C. a connective instead of *is, ea, id* with a
> conj., "and this";
> relative clauses, 10–11; natural dat., 33.7.1;
> conditionals: factual, 86.1.

si quando, "if at times": how many people will take *quando* to mean "when," but here after *si* it stands for *aliquando* and means "if ever."

> → **1516** adv.: indefinite, 42.4; after *si* the *ali*-s fly away, 42.5.

mutue, "mutually": the normal adv. is *mutuo*.

> → **1517** dict., *mutuus, a, um*, adj., II, adv., A. *mutuō*, B. *mutue*, "mutually,"
> C. *mutuiter*.

non dubito quin ... res publica ... conciliatura coniuncturaque sit, "I do not doubt: that ... public service is going to unite and bind": *res publica* means variously, "public life," "public concern," "the republic," "the commonweal." Following an expression of negative doubting, *non dubito*, there follows *quin* and the subjunctive, where *quin* is rendered "that," and the subjunctive, here, *conciliatura coniuncturaque sit*, sounds indicative in English as "[service] is going to unite and bind," according to the nature of a result clause. We can play with this expression of futurity in the subjunctive to express a present time, as in *conciliet coniungatque*, "is reconciling and binding," or antecedent action, as in *conciliaverit coniunxeritque*, "has reconciled and bound," or any other antecedent possibility.

> → **1518** negative *dubitare* + *quin* + subjunctive, 93.4, 101.2, GL n⁰ 555.2;
>   futurity participle, 50, 51.1.3;
>   *consecutio*: futurity formula in the subjunctive, 61.3.

si ... studia ... adiunxerint, "[I do not doubt: that,] if ... signs of enthusiasm ... will have joined ... [public concern is going to unite and bind]": the main verbal construction *non dubito*, "I do not doubt," is T.1i and establishes Track I. As a verb of M & M it gives rise to a result clause *quin ... res publica ... conciliatura coniuncturaque sit*, "that ... public concern is going to unite and bind," where *quin* means "that," following a verb of prohibition. The subjunctive *sit* in T.1s, maintains Track I, and is part of the futurity formula with two future active participles. The factual condition *si ... adiunxerint*, "if ... [signs of enthusiasm] ... will have joined," expresses future completed action either as a simple T.6i or as T.3s by MA according to the natural future-completed time frame of T.3s.

> → **1519** M & M, 60, 71, GL n⁰ 527, remarks 1–2;
>   *consecutio*, 47–48; futurity participle, 50, 51.1.3;
>   *consecutio*: futurity formula in the subjunctive, 61.3;
>   *consecutio*: completed futurity in the subjunctive, 61.1;
>   conditionals: factual, 86.1; subjunctive use: modal attraction, 83.

inter nos, "mutually": there is no reciprocal pronoun in Latin, so in its place the prepositional phrase is used, *inter nos*, "among ourselves," "mutually." Here *inter nos* could also be rendered as "between ourselves" or "us, one to the other."

> → **1520** dict., *inter*, prep. with acc., II., B., 2. (α)., with *pronouns*, to express all reciprocal relations.

❧

Ac ne ignores quid ego in tuis litteris desiderarim, scribam aperte, sicut et mea natura et nostra amicitia postulat. Res eas gessi quarum aliquam in tuis litteris et nostrae necessitudinis et rei publicae causa gratulationem exspectavi: quam ego abs te praetermissam esse arbitror quod vererere ne cuius animum offenderes. Sed scito ea quae nos pro salute patriae gessimus orbis terrae iudicio ac testimonio comprobari. Quae, cum veneris, tanto consilio tantaque animi magnitudine a me gesta esse cognosces ut tibi multo maiori quam Africanus fuit iam me non multo minorem quam Laelium facile et in re publica et in amicitia adiunctum esse patiare.   (*Fam.* V, 7, 3)

And lest you be unaware what I missed in your letter, I shall write openly, as both my character and our friendship demands. I have accomplished those things of which I expected some congratulations in your letter both on account of our closeness and of public concern: which I believe was omitted by you because you were fearing that you were hurting somebody's feelings. But you must know that those things which we carried out for the well-being of the fatherland are being approved by the judgment and the testimony of the whole world. Which things, when you will have come, you will understand have been done by me with such great prudence and such great courage that you allow me both in public life and in friendship already to have been joined easily to you much greater than Africanus was, [me] not much lesser than Laelius.

Ac ne ignores quid ego in tuis litteris desiderarim, scribam aperte, "And lest you be unaware what I missed in your letter, I shall write openly": the main verb is *scribam*, "I shall write," in T.3i establishing Track I. Depending on this is *ne ignores*, "lest you be unaware," a negative purpose clause in T.1s expressing incomplete action. The content of the M & M verb *ignores*, "[lest] you be unaware," is given in an IQ *quid … desiderarim*, "what I missed," in T.3s and so expressing antecedent action, all on Track I.

> → **1521** subjunctive use: purpose clause, 58.1;
> M & M, 60, 71, GL n° 527, remarks 1–2; IQ, 60; *consecutio*, 47–48.

aliquam … gratulationem, "some congratulations": eleven words later *gratulationem* goes with *aliquam*.

> → **1522** sentence structure, 1.

quam ego abs te praetermissam esse arbitror, "which I believe was omitted by you": the main verb is *arbitror*, "I believe," a deponent in T.1 and a verb of M & M whose content is given in OO where the acc. subject is *quam*, "which," and infinitive verb *praetermissam esse*, describing antecedent and passive action, here "which … was omitted." The variant *abs* is used here where he could have used *a te*, "by you."

> → **1523** M & M, 60, 71, GL n° 527, remarks 1–2; OO, 71–73;
> verb: deponent, 29; rel. pron.: subject or object, 10;
> dict., *ab, a, abs*, prep. with abl.; abl.: personal agent, 28.5.3–4, 89.2.

quod vererere, "because you were fearing": *vererére* is an alternative form for *verereris*, "you were fearing," which is T.2s from *vereor, itus*, 2, a deponent verb meaning "to revere," "to fear." The causal clause depends on the statement in OO, *quam … abs te praetermissam esse*, "which … was omitted by you," which puts this clause on Track II. The reason for the subjunctive is either by MA or by quoted reason because Cicero is quoting Pompeius, as in "which I believe was omitted by you because, as you, Pompeius, say, you were fearing."

> → **1524** variation: *–ris*, 39.3; verb: deponent, 29;
> subjunctive use: modal attraction, 83;
> causal: *quod*, "because, since," + subjunctive, reported reason, 59.2.

quod vererere ne cuius animum offenderes, "because you were fearing that you were hurting somebody's feelings": the verb of fearing *vererere*, "[because] you were fearing" produces a purpose clause that looks negative, *ne offenderes*, but has affirmative meaning, "that you were hurting somebody." After *ne* the form *cuius* stands for *alicuius*, "somebody's."

→ **1525** subjunctive use: purpose clause, 58.1; verbs of fearing with *ne*, 95.

scito ea ... comprobari, "you must know that those things ... are being approved": the main verb *scito*, "you must know," is a second command form and the content of the knowing is given in OO, *ea ... comprobari*, "those things ... are being approved," where *comprobari* is a contemporaneous infinitive in the passive. We can change this to an antecedent time frame by saying *ea comprobata esse*, "those things were being approved," or set it in futurity by saying *ea comprobatum iri*, "motion is being made to approve those things," or more smoothly, "those things will be approved," where *iri*, "motion is being made," is the passive infinitive of the verb *eo, ire*, "to go," and *comprobatum* the invariable supine after verbs of motion and its object is *ea*. This may make no sense, but it is all the Romans had at the cliff-edges of their expression, at the exhaustion of their language's forms.

→ **1526** commands: first, second, 17;
M & M, 60, 71, GL nº 527, remarks 1–2; OO, 71–73;
verb: futurity passive infinitive, 81.3; supine, 81.

orbis terrae, "of the whole world": more directly this means "of the circle of the earth," which has stuck for the idiom referring to the whole planet, the whole earth.

→ **1527** dict., *orbis, is*, m., I.... "the circle of the world, the world, the universe."

Some simple boxes will reveal clearly the glorious structure of the last sentence.

Quae,	relative OO
[cum veneris,]	temporal T.6i
tanto consilio	relative OO continued
tantaque animi magnitudine a me gesta esse	
cognosces	main; T.3i; Track I
[ut	result
< tibi	OO 2
(multo maiori quam Africanus fuit)	apposition 1
iam me	OO 2 continued
(non multo minorem quam Laelium)	apposition 2
facile et in re publica et in amicitia adiunctum esse >	OO 2 concluded
patiare]	result concluded

→ **1528** structure of Latin sentences, 103 p. 587, *Ossa* Readings: 1-D, 1-I, 3-D, 3-I, 4-D, 4-I;
relative box, 11.4.

cognosces, "you will understand": the main verb, one of M & M in T.3i, establishes Track I.

→ **1529** M & M, 60, 71, GL n° 527, remarks 1–2.

Quae ... gesta esse, "Which things have been done": the content of that understanding (*cognosces*) is given in OO, where the subject is *Quae,* "Which things," and the infinitive *gesta esse.* The antecedent of that *Quae* is the *ea,* "the things," in the previous sentence, and the relative *Quae* serves as a connective, meaning *Et ea,* "And those things."

→ **1530** OO, 71–73;
  dict., *qui, quae, quod,* pron., II., C. a connective instead of *is, ea, id* with a conj.

cum veneris, "when you will have come": this clause is placed geographically at the head of the OO, immediately following the connective relative *Quae,* but logically it is a temporal clause in T.6i connected with *cognosces,* "you will understand," in T.3i, and so stands parallel to *cognosces.*

→ **1531** dict., *qui, quae, quod,* pron., II., C. a connective instead of *is, ea, id* with a conj.;
  cum + indicative = "when": temporal sentences, 66.3;
  T.3i and T.6i paired: 7, Time 6, and GL n° 244, remark 2.

ut ... patiare, "that you ... allow": separated by 23 words, this result clause depends on the OO, *Quae ... gesta esse,* and coordinates with the expressions *tanto ... tantaque ... ,* "with such great ... and such great ...." As a result clause, it sounds indicative in English, even though the verb *patiare* is an alternative form of *patiaris,* "you allow," in T.1s on Track I.

→ **1532** sentence structure, 1; OO, 71–73; *consecutio,* 47–48;
  subjunctive use: pure result (consecutive), 67.1–2, GL n° 552;
  correlative comparative sentences, 90.5, GL n° 642;
  verb: deponent, 29; variation: *–ris,* 39.3.

tibi ... iam me ... facile et in re publica et in amicitia adiunctum esse, "me both in public life and in friendship ... already to have been joined easily to you": OO depending on *ut ... patiare,* "that you ... allow." The object form *me,* "me," is the subject of the infinitive *adiunctum esse,* "to have been joined." The idea *iam,* "already," can just as easily describe *ut patiare,* "that already you allow."

→ **1533** M & M, 60, 71, GL n° 527, remarks 1–2; OO, 71–73.

multo maiori quam Africanus fuit, "much greater than Africanus was": following *tibi,* "to you," is not a normal box but a parenthetical expression in apposition. *multo maiori* do not go together; *multo* is an abl. describing the degree of difference as "by much" and *maiori,* "greater," agrees with *tibi,* meaning "to you, greater by much." This comparison is continued with *quam Africanus fuit,* "than Africanus was." Thus, Cicero compares Pompeius more favorably to Africanus.

→ **1534** apposition, GL nº 320–21;
  abl.: measure, 90.3, GL nº 403; adj.: irregular comp. and superl., 36.5;
  quam with the comp., 43.2.

non multo minorem quam Laelium, "not much lesser than Laelius": following *me,* "me," the acc. subject of the OO, is not a normal box but a second parenthetical expression in apposition. Again, *non multo* is an abl. describing the degree of difference as "not by much" and *minorem,* "lesser," agrees with *me,* meaning "me, lesser not by much." This comparison is continued with *quam Laelium,* "than Laelius." Thus, Cicero compares his relationship to Pompeius more favorably than that of the two close, very famous associates Africanus and Laelius.

→ **1535** apposition, GL nº 320–21;
  abl.: measure, 90.3, GL nº 403; adj.: irregular comp. and superl., 36.5;
  quam with the comp., 43.2.

LETTER 913 T-P
AD BRUTUM I, 14

CICERO BRUTO SAL.

Breves litterae tuae, breves dico? immo nullae: tribusne versiculis his temporibus Brutus ad me? nihil scripsissem potius. Et requiris meas! Quis
umquam ad te tuorum sine meis venit? Quae autem epistula non pondus
habuit? quae si ad te perlatae non sunt, ne domesticas quidem tuas perlatas
arbitror. Ciceroni scribis te longiorem daturum epistulam: recte id quidem,
sed haec quoque debuit esse plenior. Ego autem, cum ad me de Ciceronis abs
te discessu scripsisses, statim extrusi tabellarios litterasque ad Ciceronem,
ut, etiamsi in Italiam venisset, ad te rediret; nihil enim mihi iucundius, nihil illi honestius. Quamquam aliquoties ei scripseram sacerdotum comitia
mea summa contentione in alterum annum esse reiecta—quod ego cum Ciceronis causa elaboravi, tum Domiti, Catonis, Lentuli, Bibulorum; quod ad
te etiam scripseram—: sed videlicet, cum illam pusillam epistulam tuam ad
me dabas, nondum erat tibi id notum.   (*Brut.* I, 14, 1)

CICERO A GREETING TO BRUTUS

Your short letter, do I say short? indeed nonexistent: Brutus [writes] to me
with three little verses in these circumstances? I would have preferably
written nothing. And you are looking for mine! Who of your people ever
came to you without a letter from me? However what epistle has not had
weightiness? which if they have not been delivered to you, I believe not even
your household letters were delivered. You write that you will be sending a
longer letter to Cicero [junior]: that, rightly indeed; but this one was also
supposed to be fuller. But when you had written to me about Cicero's departure from you, I immediately pushed out the letter carriers and letters to
Cicero so that, even if he should have come to Italy, he would return to you;
for there is nothing more pleasant to me, nothing more honorable for him.
And yet I had written a few times to him that the elections of the priests had
been postponed for the next year by my extreme confrontation—something

which I worked out both for the sake of Cicero, then of Domitius, Cato, Lentulus, the Bibuli; something which I had also written to you—; but of course when you were sending to me that tiny letter of yours, this was not yet known to you.

Cᴵᴄᴇʀᴏ Bʀᴜᴛᴏ sᴀʟ.: *Cicero Bruto salutem*

Breves litterae tuae, "Your short letter": there is no expressed verb in these initial statements as Cicero runs through his thoughts.

→ **1536** sentence structure, 1.

nullae ... meas ... sine meis, "nonexistent ... mine ... without a letter from me": all agreeing with some form of *litterae,* "a letter," as in *litterae nullae,* "not any letter"; *meas litteras,* "my letter" or "a letter from me"; or *sine litteris meis,* "without my letter" or "without a letter from me." The same word *litterae* is used in the plural to refer to several letters of the alphabet, or to a collection of letters and thus to an epistle, or to more than one epistle; see your dictionary. Cicero freely alternates between the two here.

→ **1537** sentence structure, 1.

tribusne versiculis his temporibus Brutus ad me? "Brutus [writes] to me with three little verses in these circumstances?": again we might supply a verb here. He is not referring to poetic verses, but to simple lines of text.

→ **1538** sentence structure, 1.

nihil scripsissem potius, "I would have preferably written nothing": *scripsissem,* "I would have written," in T.4s, is the consequential half of a contrary to fact conditional set in the past. We can test that it is contrary to fact by adding, "if I had been in this position, I would have preferably written nothing."

→ **1539** conditionals: contrary to fact, 86.3.

quae si ad te perlatae non sunt, "which if they have not been delivered to you": *si,* "if," begins a factual condition where *perlatae non sunt,* "they have not been delivered," is in T.4a in the passive. The *quae* here is connective, meaning *et eae,* "and ... they," referring now to the felt word *litterae,* now, "letters."

→ **1540** conditionals: factual, 86.1;
    dict., *qui, quae, quod,* pron., II., C. a connective instead of *is, ea, id* with a conj.

ne domesticas quidem tuas perlatas arbitror, "I believe not even your household letters were delivered": the main verb *arbitror,* "I believe," is the consequence of a factual condition and a verb of M & M in T.1i. The content of his judgment is given in OO where the subject is in the object form *domesticas* and the full form of the infinitive is *perlatas esse. ne ... quidem* negate the

word between them, here *domesticas*, "not even [your] household letters."
The idea involves multiple letters, *domesticas*, "household letters."

> → **1541** conditionals: factual, 86.1;
> M & M, 60, 71, GL n° 527, remarks 1–2; OO, 71–73;
> dict., *quidem*, adv., I., C., 1. *ne ... quidem*, "not even."

Ciceroni scribis te longiorem daturum epistulam, "You write that you will be
sending a longer letter to Cicero [junior]": the main verb *scribis*, "You write,"
is a verb of M & M in T.1i, and the content of his writing is given in OO
where the acc. *te* functions as the subject of the full infinitive in the futurity
formula *daturum esse* and together they mean "you to be about to send" or
"that you are going to send" or "you will be sending."

> → **1542** M & M, 60, 71, GL n° 527, remarks 1–2; OO, 71–73;
> futurity participle, 50, 51.1.3;
> verb: subsequent active infinitive, 72.1;
> futurity formula, active, 53.3.

sed haec quoque debuit esse plenior, "but this one was also supposed to be
fuller": *haec*, "this one," referring to the short epistle Cicero received from
Brutus, is the subject of *debuit*, "this one was supposed," and *esse*, "to be," is
a complementary infinitive with *plenior*, "fuller," in the subject form. Now
haec ... debuit in the singular refers to *epistula*, as in "but this epistle was."

> → **1543** dict., *debeo, ui, itum*, 2., II., A., (β) with inf. "to be bound, must, should";
> verb: complementary infinitive, 77; adj.: comp., 36.

The box structure of the next half-sentence is more easily understood in this
way:

Ego autem,	main
{ cum ad me de Ciceronis abs te	circumstantial; when T.4s
discessu scripsisses, }	
statim extrusi tabellarios	
litterasque ad Ciceronem,	main continued; T.4b
{ ut,	purpose—factual consequence
[etiamsi in Italiam venisset,]	factual condition; T.4s by MA
ad te rediret; }	purpose continued—factual
	consequence; T.2s

> → **1544** structure of Latin sentences, 103 p. 587, *Ossa* Readings: 1-D, 1-I, 3-D, 3-I,
> 4-D, 4-I;

extrusi, "I pushed out": the main verb is T.4b establishing Track II, and also
means "I threw out."

> → **1545** *consecutio*, 47–48.

cum ... scripsisses, "when ... you had written": describing the temporal
circumstance of the main verb, here *scripsisses* is T.4s to indicate antecedent
action on Track II.

> → **1546** subjunctive use: temporal circumstance *cum* = "when," 66.3.2.

ut ... ad te rediret, "so that he would return to you": Cicero's intention in kicking out the letter carriers with letters is given in this purpose clause, where *rediret*, "he would return," is in T.2s, indicating here subsequent action on Track II.

> → **1547** subjunctive use: purpose clause, 58.1; *consecutio*, 47–48;
>   *consecutio*: futurity in the subjunctive, 61.1.

etiamsi in Italiam venisset, "even if he should have come to Italy": this may mistakenly look like a contrary to fact condition set in the past, meaning "even if he had come to Italy, but he did not." To understand this, we begin with the main verb *extrusi*, "I shoved out," in T.4b establishing Track II. With regard to that moment in the past, the purpose clause of its very nature expresses futurity, here *ut ... rediret*, "so that he would return." The clause *etiamsi ... venisset*, here in the subjunctive by MA, expresses an action that happens in the meanwhile, that is, between the time of *extrusi*, when Cicero shoved out letters to his son, but before the future time when his son would return. Of the four times of the subjunctive, the only one to express this future completed action from a point in the past is T.4s, here *venisset*, "he would have come." This is why in our system we insist on not calling *venisset* the pluperfect subjunctive because here it is the only possible way to express future perfect action on Track II. Its natural meaning here is "even if he might have come," "even if he would have come," "even if he should have come," but it is not a contrary to fact conditional set in the past.

> → **1548** subjunctive use: purpose clause, 58.1; *consecutio*, 47–48;
>   *consecutio*: futurity in the subjunctive, 61.1;
>   *consecutio*: completed futurity in the subjunctive, 61.1;
>   subjunctive use: modal attraction, 83; conditionals: contrary to fact, 86.3.

Like *tametsi* and *etsi*, so *etiamsi*, "even if," like the other concessive sentences means "although," but because these three are formed with the particle *–si* they follow the rules of conditional sentences, most of which are factual and thus in the indicative. Accordingly, this phrase straddles the fence between the concessive sentences meaning "although," giving greater force to the "even" in "even if," and the conditional sentences giving greater emphasis to the "if"; nevertheless, it is in the subjunctive by MA.

> → **1549** concessive particles, 64; conditionals, 86;
>   subjunctive use: modal attraction, 83.

Quamquam ... scripseram, "And yet I had written": here *Quamquam* does not mean "although." Rather it has the secondary meaning of "and still," "however," as a particle of transition.

> → **1550** dict., *quamquam*, conj., I., "although"; and II. as a rhetor. particle of
>   transition, "yet."

scripseram ... comitia ... esse reiecta, "I had written ... that the elections ... had been postponed": *scripseram*, "I had written," is a verb of M & M in T.5i, and the content of what he wrote is given in OO where the object *comitia*, "the elections," functions as the subject of the infinitive *esse reiecta*, "had been postponed," which expresses antecedent and passive action.

→ **1551** M & M, 60, 71, GL n° 527, remarks 1–2; OO, 71–73.

comitia mea summa contentione, "by my extreme confrontation": the superlative *summa* or *suprema*, "extreme," has the comparative *superiore* and the positive *supera*.

→ **1552** adj.: comp. and superl., 36.

cum Ciceronis causa elaboravi, tum Domiti, Catonis, Lentuli, Bibulorum, "I worked out both for the sake of Cicero, then of Domitius, Cato, Lentulus, the Bibuli": *cum … tum …*, "both … and …," are coordinating conjunctions here. *causa* is preceded by the of-possession form to mean "for the sake of Cicero," and then *causa* is followed by four more genitives in succession without further connective words, thus in asyndeton. This expression can also be constructed as *Ciceronis gratia* or *Ciceronis ergo* with the same meaning.

→ **1553** correlative comparative sentences, 90.5, GL n° 642;
      dict., *causa, ae*, f., I., b. *causā* in abl. with gen or possess. adj., "for the sake of";
      function: of-possession, 20; asyndeton, GL n° 474.

cum … dabas, "when you were sending": *cum* with the indicative *dabas* in T.2b is a good example of the simple coincidence of time, namely for example at 10:30 A.M. when Brutus had his tiny letter in hand ready to be sent, but the news had not yet arrived with the postman.

→ **1554** *cum* + historical times of indicative = "when": temporal coincidence, 66.3.1.

❧

Quare omni studio a te, mi Brute, contendo ut Ciceronem meum ne dimittas tecumque deducas, quod ipsum, si rem publicam, cui susceptus es, respicis, tibi iam iamque faciendum est. Renatum enim bellum est, idque non parvum scelere Lepidi; exercitus autem Caesaris, qui erat optimus, non modo nihil prodest, sed etiam cogit exercitum tuum flagitari; qui si Italiam attigerit, erit civis nemo, quem quidem civem appellari fas sit, qui se non in tua castra conferat. Etsi Brutum praeclare cum Planco coniunctum habemus, sed non ignoras quam sint incerti et animi hominum infecti partibus et exitus proeliorum. Quin etiam si, ut spero, vicerimus, tamen magnam gubernationem tui consilii tuaeque auctoritatis res desiderabit: subveni igitur, per deos, idque quam primum, tibique persuade non te Idibus Martiis, quibus servitutem a tuis civibus depulisti, plus profuisse patriae quam, si mature veneris, profuturum. II. Idus Quintilis.   (*Brut.* I, 14, 2)

For this reason with all energy I beg of you, my dear Brutus, that you not dismiss my Cicero, and take him along with you, something itself which, if you consider the republic for whom you were raised, must be done by you precisely now. For the war has been reborn, and that not a small one by the criminal action of Lepidus; however [Octavian] Caesar's army, which was very good, not only profits you nothing but even forces your army to be put on demand, if which [army] will have touched Italy, there will be no citizen, whom indeed it may be legitimate to be called a citizen, who does not bring himself into your camp. And yet we find Brutus wonderfully associated with Plancus, but you are not ignorant of how uncertain are both the sentiments of people tainted by factions and the outcomes of battles. Indeed, even if as I hope we shall have won, nevertheless the situation will be requiring the great guidance of your counsel and your authority. Therefore, for heaven's sake come to help, and that as soon as possible, and convince yourself that you, on the March Ides on which you cast off slavery from your citizens, were not more useful to the fatherland than, if you will have come soon, you will be useful. On the second day before the July Ides [14 July].

The box system of part of the first sentence is presented below in its different parts:

contendo	main
ut Ciceronem meum ne dimittas	purpose part 1; T.1s
tecumque deducas,	purpose part 2; T.1s
quod ipsum,	relative, factual consequence; necessity
si rem publicam,	factual conditional
cui susceptus es,	relative
respicis,	factual conditional continued
tibi iam iamque faciendum est	relative, factual consequence; necessity continued

→ **1555** structure of Latin sentences, 103 p. 587, *Ossa* Readings: 1-D, 1-I, 3-D, 3-I, 4-D, 4-I;
relative box, 11.4.

mi Brute, "my dear Brutus": the friendship between Cicero and Brutus is reflected in this warm address as mentioned in the dictionary under *meus, a, um*, where the vocative *mi* is said to mean *"my dear! my beloved!"*

→ **1556** dict., *meus, a, um*, adj., –voc.;
function: direct address, 38.3.

contendo, "I beg": the main verb in T.1i produces a purpose clause that presents Cicero's intention.

→ **1557** subjunctive use: purpose clause, 58.1.

ut Ciceronem meum ne dimittas tecumque deducas, "that you not dismiss my Cicero, and take him along with you": the *ut*, "that," begins a double purpose clause. First, *ut ... ne dimittas* in T.1s gives a negative intention "that you not dismiss," and second *ut ... deducas*, "that you take [him]," in T.1s gives a positive intention. We can confirm this in Gildersleeve and

Lodge n° 545, remark 1, which says that the "*ut ne* is found for *ne* with apparently no difference in signification."

→ **1558** subjunctive use: purpose clause, 58.1, GL n° 545, remark 1.

quod ipsum ... tibi iam iamque faciendum est, "something itself which ... must be done by you precisely now": *quod ipsum* refers to the whole previous discussion about Brutus and his bringing Cicero's son. The necessity formula *faciendum est*, "[which] has to be done," in T.1i, is neuter to agree with its subject, *quod*, "something which." 90% of the time this passive necessity formula uses the dat. of agent, as here *tibi*, "by you." This clause gives the factual consequence of the conditional *si ... respicis*, "if you consider."

→ **1559** *quod* referring to previous sentence: GL n° 614, remark 2;
        participle of passive necessity, 50, 51.1.4;
        passive necessity formula, 53.4;
        dat. of agent, 53.5; conditionals: factual, 86.1.

si rem publicam, cui susceptus es, respicis, "if you consider the republic for whom you were raised": *si ... respicis*, "if you consider," gives the factual condition in T.1i, the indicative as most conditionals appear in Latin. *cui* is a natural dative, "for whom."

→ **1560** conditionals: factual, 86.1.

susceptus es, "you were raised": *suscipere* is what a father does when a newborn child is put at his feet. If the father takes the child up, then he supports and rears him; if not, the child is abandoned.

→ **1561** dict., *suscipio, cepi, ceptum*, 3., II., B., 1. "to take up" a new-born child
        from the ground.

exercitus autem Caesaris,	main 1
qui erat optimus,	relative; T.2i
non modo nihil prodest,	main 1 continued; T.1i
sed etiam cogit	main 2; T.1i
exercitum tuum flagitari;	OO
qui si Italiam attigerit,	relative factual condition; T.6i
erit civis nemo,	factual consequence; T.3i
quem quidem civem appellari	OO relative subject
fas sit,	relative restrictive continued; T.1s
qui se non in tua castra conferat.	characteristic result; T.1s

→ **1562** structure of Latin sentences, 103 p. 587, *Ossa* Readings: 1-D, 1-I, 3-D, 3-I,
        4-D, 4-I;
        relative box, 11.4.

cogit exercitum tuum flagitari, "forces your army to be put on demand": the independent verb *cogit*, "[Caesar's army] forces," functions here as a verb of M & M in T.1i, and the object of this compelling is given in OO, *exercitum tuum* with the passive infinitive *flagitari*, "your army to be put on demand."

→ **1563** M & M, 60, 71, GL n° 527, remarks 1–2; OO, 71–73;
        verb: contemporaneous passive infinitive, 72.3.

qui si Italiam attigerit, erit, "if which [army] it will have touched Italy, there will be": *attigerit,* "it will have touched," is T.6i and correlates with the T.3i right next to it, *erit,* "there will be." The factual condition is *qui si ... attigerit,* "if which will have touched" or "which if it will have touched," where the subject of *attigerit* is *qui* placed before the *si.* The antecedent of *qui,* "which," is *exercitus tuus* "your army [Brutus]." The factual consequence is *erit,* "there will be."

→ **1564** T.3i and T.6i paired: 7, Time 6, and GL n° 244, remark 2;
conditionals: factual, 86.1; relative clauses, 10–11; sentence structure, 1.

erit civis nemo, quem quidem civem appellari fas sit, "there will be no citizen, whom indeed it may be legitimate to be called a citizen": the sentence *erit civis nemo,* "there will be no citizen," produces two descriptions of that citizen, each given in relative clauses. The first begins with the relative pronoun *quem,* which functions as the subject of the verb *appellari* and this statement *quem ... appellari* depends on the rather rare, almost parenthetical expression *fas sit,* which is given in the subjunctive perhaps to express potentiality. The *fas sit* almost means "[who indeed] *I hope* it may be legitimate [to be called a citizen]," but it is difficult to get any closer to this Latin expression in English.

→ **1565** rel. pron.: subject or object, 10;
subjunctive use: potential of the present or future, *fas sit* in T.1s,
GL n° 257.2;
dict., *fas,* indecl. n., II., B. usually translated as an adjective, "right, fit,
permitted";
fas: a defective substantive with only this form, a neuter subject or object,
GL n° 70.B.

erit civis nemo, ... qui se non in tua castra conferat, "there will be no citizen ... who does not bring himself into your camp": the second description of the character of that citizen is also a relative clause, where *qui* stands for *talis ut is,* "such that he [does not bring himself]." The reflexive *se* is direct here, referring to the subject of *conferat,* "[who] does ... bring himself," that is, to the *is,* "he," contained in the *qui,* "who."

→ **1566** subjunctive use: characteristic result, 68.2;
reflexive pron.: third person, 31.

quem quidem civem appellari fas sit, "whom indeed it may be legitimate to be called a citizen": the subject or predicate of *sit* is the entire expression of the relative sentence in indirect discourse. The relative *quem* given in the object form functions as the subject of the passive infinitive *appellari.*

→ **1567** OO, 71–73.

Etsi Brutum praeclare cum Planco coniunctum habemus, "And yet we find Brutus wonderfully associated with Plancus": here the clause *Etsi ... habemus,* "And yet we find ..." refers to what is the main tenor of the preceding. The expression is left hanging just a bit, just as we have seen above with *Quamquam,* "And yet," functioning as an article of transition, as confirmed in your dictionary. The object of *habemus*, "we find," is *Brutum* described by *coniunctum*, "Brutus ... associated."

→ **1568** dict., *etsi*, conj., II. like *quamquam*, "and yet, but."

non ignoras quam sint incerti, "you are not ignorant of how uncertain are": the main verb *ignoras*, "you are [not] ignorant of," is a verb of M & M in T.1i establishing Track I. The content of the knowledge is given as an IQ, *quam sint incerti*, "how uncertain are." The two subjects of the IQ are *et animi ... et exitus*, "both the sentiments ... and the outcomes."

→ **1569** M & M, 60, 71, GL n° 527, remarks 1–2; IQ, 60.

Quin, "Indeed": *Quin* connects with what has already been said and adds a stronger assertion meaning "Indeed, rather," "yea indeed," "nay, rather." The dictionary says that *Quin* is used with *etiam* when adding a stronger assertion, but here we take the *etiam* with the next word *si*.

→ **1570** dict., *quin*, conj., II., C., 1. "but, indeed."

etiam si, ut spero, vicerimus, tamen ... res desiderabit, "rather, if as I hope we shall have won, nevertheless the situation will be requiring": the factual condition, *si ... vicerimus*, "If we shall have won," is given in T.6i and its factual consequence *res desiderabit*, "the situation will be requiring." Set into the factual condition is the expression *ut spero*, where *ut* means "as" followed by the indicative *spero*, "I hope."

→ **1571** conditionals: factual, 86.1; dict., *ut*, I., B. meaning "as."

subveni, "come to help": the accent distinguishes the command form *súbveni*, from the statement *subvéni* "I have come to help," in T.4a, or "I came to help" in T.4b, and their reversed forms are *subveníte* and *subvénimus*.

→ **1572** dict., *subvenio, vēni, ventum*, 4; verb T.4a, T.4b: 8;
commands: first, second, 17.

tibique persuade, "and convince yourself": *persuade*, "convince," is the command form of one of the 65 verbs whose natural object is in the dat., here *tibi*, "yourself."

→ **1573** 65 verbs with dat., 33.7.2, GL n° 346;
commands: first, second, 17.

non te ... plus profuisse patriae quam, si mature veneris, profuturum, "that you ... were not more useful to the fatherland than, if you will have come soon, you will be useful": the main verb, *persuade*, "convince," is a verb of M & M whose content is given in OO where the object form *te* functions as the subject of two verbs: *profuisse*, "that you were [not] ... useful," and *profuturum* [*esse*], "you will be useful." The two verbs express two ideas that are correlated by the comparison *plus ... quam ...*, "more ... than ...." The first of these expresses antecedent action, *te ... profuisse*, "you were [not] ... useful," where *profuisse* is one of the 65 verbs whose complement is in the dat., here *patriae*, "to the fatherland," which sounds like a natural dat. The second of these, *te ... profuturum*, expresses future action, as the equivalent of T.3i, and functions as the consequence of a factual condition, *si ... veneris*, "If you will have come," which is either T.6i or T.3s by MA, both with the same future completed meaning natural to these two times. This is an example of how synthetic Latin can be.

> → **1574** M & M, 60, 71, GL n° 527, remarks 1–2; OO, 71–73;
>   futurity participle, 50, 51.1.3;
>   verb: subsequent active infinitive, 72.1;
>   futurity formula, active, 53.3; *quam* with the comp., 43.2;
>   65 verbs with dat., 33.7.2, GL n° 346; conditionals: factual, 86.1;
>   subjunctive use: modal attraction, 83;
>   *consecutio*: completed futurity in the subjunctive, 61.1.

Idibus Martiis, quibus servitutem a tuis civibus depulisti, "on the March Ides on which you cast off slavery from your citizens": the reference to casting off slavery refers to the assassination of Julius Caesar. *Idibus Martiis, quibus*, are all three the abl. of time at which, "on the March Ides on which."

> → **1575** abl.: time at which, 70.1.

II. Idus Quintilis, "On the second day before the July Ides [14 July]": the expression *II Idus* does not really exist in Latin. Perhaps Cicero was distracted or confused, weeping or despairing. The expression for the day before the Ides is *pridie Idus*. Here *Quintilis* is the alternative form of *Quintiles*, which the Romans heard as the same.

> → **1576** about the Roman calendar, pp. 605–608;
>   GL appendix: Roman Calendar, pp. 491–92.

LETTER 166 T-P
AD FAMILIARES II, 1

M. CICERO S. D. C. CURIONI.

Quamquam me neglegentiae nomine suspectum tibi esse doleo, tamen non tam mihi molestum fuit accusari abs te officium meum quam iucundum requiri, praesertim quom in quo accusabar culpa vacarem, in quo autem desiderare te significabas meas litteras prae te ferres perspectum mihi quidem, sed tamen dulcem et optatum amorem tuum. Equidem neminem praetermisi, quem quidem ad te perventurum putarem, cui litteras non dederim. Etenim quis est tam in scribendo impiger quam ego? A te vero bis terve summum et eas perbrevis accepi. Qua re si iniquus es in me iudex, condemnabo eodem ego te crimine: sin me id facere noles, te mihi aequum praebere debebis. Sed de litteris hactenus: non enim vereor ne non scribendo te expleam, praesertim si in eo genere studium meum non aspernabere.   (*Fam.* II, 1, 1)

CICERO SAYS GREETING TO ATTICUS

Although I am sorry that I am suspect to you under the title of negligence, nevertheless it was not so annoying to me that my duty was being accused by you as it was pleasant that [it] was being sought out, especially since I was free from fault in which thing I was being accused; however you, in which thing you were indicating that you were missing my letters, were demonstrating your love fully understood by me indeed, but yet sweet and desired. I indeed left out no one, who indeed I was thinking was going to get to you, to whom I did not entrust a letter. For who is so energetic in writing as I? But from you twice or thrice at the most I have gotten [letters] and those very short. For which reason, if you are an unjust judge toward me, I shall condemn you with the same accusation; but if you will not want me to do that, you will have to show yourself to me as just. But about letters so far enough; for I am not afraid that I may not satisfy you by writing, especially if you will not scorn my fervor in that area.

M. Cicero s. d. C. Curioni: *Marcus Cicero salutem dicit Gaio Curioni*

me ... suspectum tibi esse doleo, "I am sorry that I am suspect to you": *doleo*, "I am sorry," in T.1i, is a verb of emotion like *gaudeo*, "I rejoice," and it is used here as a similar expression; Cicero explains his sentiment in OO where the object form *me* functions as the subject of the infinitive *esse*, "that I am." GL says that verbs of emotion "may be considered as" M & M verbs. *suspectum* is an adj. here that has a natural dat. complement, *tibi*, "suspect to you."

> → **1577** verbs of emotion + OO, GL n° 533;
> M & M, 60, 71, GL n° 527, remarks 1–2; OO, 71–73;
> natural dat., 33.7.1.

non tam mihi molestum fuit accusari abs te officium meum quam iucundum requiri, "it was not so annoying to me that my duty was being accused by you as it was pleasant that [it] was being sought out": the main verb *fuit*, "it was," in T.4b, together with *molestum*, "[it was not] a bother," is used as an expression of M & M whose mental content is given in OO where *officium* is the object form functioning as the subject of the passive infinitive *accusari*, "that ... duty was being accused." The last two words replace their counterparts in the previous sentence to produce the statement *mihi iucundum fuit requiri abs te officium meum*, "it was pleasant to me that my duty was being sought out by you." The *tam ... quam ...* , "so ... as ...," correlate the two parts of the sentence, and this sentence is correlated with the previous by *Quamquam ... , tamen ...* , "Although ... , nevertheless ...."

> → **1578** dict., *molestus, a, um*, adj. "troublesome, annoying";
> M & M, 60, 71, GL n° 527, remarks 1–2; OO, 71–73;
> verb: contemporaneous passive infinitive, 72.3;
> correlative comparative sentences, 90.5, GL n° 642;
> dict., *quamquam*, conj., I., "although."

quom ... vacarem ... autem ... prae te ferres, "since I was free ... however you ... were demonstrating": *quom* can also be written *quum* or most frequently as *cum*, and they mean "although" or "when" or as here "because" followed by the subjunctive *vacarem*, rendered in the indicative according to the nature of a causal clause, "I was being accused." The *quom* has a second verb joined to *vacarem*, "I was free," by *autem*, "however," in the expression *prae te ferres*, "you were demonstrating." The dictionary gives *prae se ferre* as an idiom sometimes written as one word, as in the image of the manuscript at part I of this volume, meaning "to hold out in front of yourself," "to show off," "to demonstrate," "to manifest."

> → **1579** dict., *cum*, sometimes *quom* or *quum*;
> subjunctive use: causal *cum* = "because, since," 59.1;
> subjunctive use: concessive *cum* = "although," 64;
> subjunctive use: temporal circumstance *cum* = "when," 66.3.2;
> dict., *fero, tuli, latum, ferre*, v. irreg., II., B., 6., b. *prae se ferre*, "to show, manifest."

quom ... culpa vacarem, "since I was free from fault in which thing I was being accused": the antecedent of *quo* is *eo*, as in *in eo in quo accusabar culpa vacarem*, "I did not have any fault in that thing in which I was being accused." The verb *vaco, avi, atum,* 1, "to be empty" may go with the to-for-from function as in "to be free for [something]" or with the by-with-from-in function, as here meaning "to be free from [something]." The form *culpā* is in the abl. here. We can playfully say, *scholis vacabo sed ludis vacabo*, "I will be free from school but free for games" or the opposite.

> → **1580** dict., *cum*, sometimes *quom* or *quum*;
> rel. pron.: omission of the antecedent, 11.2; rel. pron.: brevity, 11.3;
> dict., *vaco, avi, atum,* 1., I., B., 1. with abl., II., A., 2., a. *vacare alicui rei.*

in quo autem desiderare te significabas meas litteras, "in which thing however you were indicating that you were missing my letters": the main verb *significabas*, "you were indicating," is an M & M verb in T.2i. Curio's thinking is developed in OO where the object form *te* functions as the subject of the infinitive *desiderare*, which is contemporaneous with *significabas* in T.2i and so sounds in English like, "that you felt a lack of." The object of *desiderare* is *meas litteras*, "[that you] felt a lack of my letters"; the other meaning of *desiderare te* is not helpful here, "that you were desiring."

> → **1581** M & M, 60, 71, GL nº 527, remarks 1–2; OO, 71–73;
> dict., *desidero, avi, atum,* 1., I. "to long for," II. "to miss [anything]."

The antecedent of *quo* is *eo*, as in *prae te ferres autem in eo in quo desiderare te significabas meas litteras*, "however, you were demonstrating your love in that thing in which you were indicating that you felt a lack of my letters."

> → **1582** rel. pron.: omission of the antecedent, 11.2; rel. pron.: brevity, 11.3.

perspectum mihi quidem ... amorem tuum, "your love fully understood by me indeed": here *mihi* is either a dat. of agent meaning "by me," as in the translation, which also takes *perspectum* as a participle, "having been understood," or *mihi* is a natural dat., and gives moral reference meaning "your love clear to me," or "obvious to me," where *perspectum* is an adjective, "clear," "obvious."

> → **1583** dat. of agent, 53.5; natural dat., 33.7.1;
> dict., *perspicio, spexi, spectum,* 3., II., ...—*perspectus, a, um,* P. a., "clearly perceived."

neminem praetermisi, quem quidem ad te perventurum putarem, "I ... left out no one, who indeed I was thinking was going to get to you": the main verb, *praetermisi*, "I ... left out," is T.4b establishing Track II, and its object is *neminem*, "no one," which is then amplified by two result clauses that describe the character of such a person. First, *quem*, standing for *talem ut eum*, is in the object form because it functions as the acc. subject of the infinitive whose full form is *perventurum esse*, "such that he ... was going to get," and this whole statement in OO gives the content of Cicero's thinking stated as *putarem*, "I was thinking," in T.2s on Track II. The use of the second subjunctive to express ongoing action on Track II gives the impression that Cicero may have waited for several days for someone to pass by.

> → **1584** subjunctive use: characteristic result, 68.2;
> M & M, 60, 71, GL n° 527, remarks 1–2; OO, 71–73;
> *consecutio*, 47–48.

neminem praetermisi, quem quidem ad te perventurum putarem, cui litteras non dederim, "I left out no one, who indeed I was thinking was going to get to you, to whom I did not entrust a letter" or "to whom I did not entrust a letter, who I was thinking would indeed arrive at your house." The main verb *praetermisi*, "I … left out," in T.4b establishing Track II, is followed by a second description of the character of *neminem*, "no one," given in the relative expression *cui … dederim*, "to whom I did [not] entrust," where *cui* stands for *talem ut ei*, "such that to him," which functions as the natural dat. going with *dederim* in T.3s.

Because this sentence is on Track II, the use of *dederim*, "I did [not] entrust," can be explained as an example of the 3% use of the sequence of tenses where one concrete result is given in T.3s.

> → **1585** subjunctive use: characteristic result, 68.2;
> *consecutio*, 47–48; subjunctive use in 3% sequence of tenses, 94.1.

quis est tam in scribendo impiger quam ego?, "For who is so energetic in writing as I?": the correlatives *tam … quam …*, "so … as …," balance two equal elements, *quis … ego*, "who … [as] I [am]." *in scribendo*, "in writing," is a gerund.

> → **1586** correlative comparative sentences, 90.5, GL n° 642; gerund, 77.1.

bis terve summum et eas perbrevis accepi, "twice or thrice at the most I have gotten [letters] and those very short": *summum* is an adv. meaning "at the most." *perbrevis* is an alternate form for *perbreves* agreeing with *eas*, referring to "those very short letters."

> → **1587** dict., *superus, a, um*, adj., III., C., 2.…—adv. *summum*, "at the utmost";
> Block II adj.: *-is = -es*, 38, GL n° 78.

si iniquus es in me iudex, condemnabo eodem ego te crimine, "if you are an unjust judge toward me, I shall condemn you with the same accusation": the factual condition *si … es*, "if you are," in T.1i, leads to the factual consequence *condemnabo*, "I shall condemn," in T.3i. *in me* indicates here moral motion "toward me." Note the word order of the second part where *eodem* is separated from *crimine* by the verb's subject and object in contrast to one another.

> → **1588** conditionals: factual, 86.1; prep. with obj., 6; sentence structure, 1.

sin me id facere noles, te mihi aequum praebere debebis, "but if you will not want me to do that, you will have to show yourself to me as just": another factual condition *sin … noles*, "if you will not want," in T.3i, leads to the

factual consequence *debebis*, "you will have to," also in T.3i. *te* goes with
aequum, and *te mihi* contrast with one another as the object and dat., "yourself to me."

> → **1589** conditionals: factual, 86.1; personal pronoun: object form, 3;
>   natural dat., 33.7.1.

non enim vereor ne non scribendo te expleam, praesertim si in eo genere
studium meum non aspernabere, "for I am not afraid that I may not satisfy
you by writing, especially if you will not scorn my fervor in that area":
non ... vereor, "I am not afraid," gives rise to a statement of the fear. More
commonly if the object of fear is positive, it begins with *ne*, meaning "that,"
and if it is negative, it begins with *ut*, meaning "that not." The simplicity of
these expressions was encumbered by their apparent reversal of meaning,
so here instead of *ut*, meaning "that not," Cicero uses *ne non*, "that not." The
apparent clarity, however, produces the confusion of having three negatives
in a row *non vereor ne non*, "I am not afraid that not." *ne ... expleam*, "that
I may not satisfy," is in T.1s. Cicero had to work with the same difficulties in
the language as do we. *scribendo*, "by writing," is a gerund with the natural
meaning of the form by-with-from-in.

> → **1590** verbs of fearing with *ne*, 95; gerund, 77.1.

si ... non aspernabere, "if you will not scorn": a factual condition where *as-*
pernábere is an alternative for *aspernáberis*, in T.3i of a deponent verb whose
plural is *aspernabimini*.

> → **1591** conditionals: factual, 86.1; variation: *–ris*, 39.3;
>   verb: deponent, 29.

❧

Ego te afuisse tam diu a nobis et dolui quod carui fructu iucundissimae
consuetudinis, et laetor quod absens omnia cum maxima dignitate es consecutus quodque in omnibus tuis rebus meis optatis fortuna respondit.
Breve est quod me tibi praecipere meus incredibilis in te amor cogit. Tanta
est exspectatio vel animi vel ingeni tui ut ego te obsecrare obtestarique non
dubitem, sic ad nos conformatus revertare ut, quam exspectationem tui concitasti, hanc sustinere ac tueri possis. Et quoniam meam tuorum erga me
meritorum memoriam nulla umquam delebit oblivio, te rogo ut memineris,
quantaecumque tibi accessiones fient et fortunae et dignitatis, eas te non
potuisse consequi, nisi meis puer olim fidelissimis atque amantissimis consiliis paruisses. Qua re hoc animo in nos esse debebis ut aetas nostra iam
ingravescens in amore atque in adulescentia tua conquiescat.   (*Fam.* II, 1, 2)

I both have been sad that you have been away from us so long, because I
have gone without the enjoyment of a most pleasant relationship, and I am
happy that being absent you have attained all things with the greatest dignity, and that in all your concerns good luck has corresponded to my wishes.

There is a short thing which my unbelievable love toward you forces me to command you. There is such a great awaiting of your either spirit or intelligence that I do not hesitate to beg and implore you, that you may return to us well formed in such a way that you are able to maintain and safeguard this expectation which you have awakened of your very self. And because no forgetfulness will ever wipe out my recollection of your merits toward me, I ask you that you remember, no matter how great additions will happen to you both of success and dignity, that you were not able to attain them, if as a child once upon a time you had not obeyed my most trustworthy and loving counsels. For which reason you will have to be of this attitude toward us that our age of life already increasing in weight may totally rest in your love and your youth.

Ego ... et dolui ... et laetor, "I both have been sad ... and I am happy": in this main sentence *et ... et ...*, "both ... and ...," join *dolui,* "I have been sad," in T.4a, and *laetor,* "I am happy," a deponent verb in T.1i. Both are verbs of emotion that function as expressions of M & M producing the next statement.
> → **1592** conjunction: *et ... , et ... ,* 3.2; verb: deponent, 29;
> verbs of emotion + OO, GL nº 533;
> M & M, 60, 71, GL nº 527, remarks 1–2; OO, 71–73.

Ego te afuisse tam diu a nobis et dolui ... et laetor, "I both have been sad that you been away from us so long ... and I am happy": Cicero gives the reason both for his sadness (*dolui;* T.4a) and joy (*laetor;* T.1i) in OO set at the beginning of the sentence. The object form *te* functions as the subject of the infinitive *afuisse,* which describes any antecedent time, given in the English rendering as the equivalent of T.4a, "that you have been away."
> → **1593** M & M, 60, 71, GL nº 527, remarks 1–2; OO, 71–73.

Ego ... et dolui quod carui ... et laetor quod ... es consecutus quodque ... fortuna respondit, "I both have been sad ... because I have gone without the enjoyment ... and I am happy that ... you have attained ... and that ... good luck has corresponded": here Cicero does not use the subjunctive by MA with these three verbs, but uses instead the indicative, all Time 4a, so his speech is much clearer and direct that these are his own personal reasons for being sad and rejoicing: *carui,* "I have gone without"; *es consecutus,* "you have attained"; *respondit,* "[lady fortune] has corresponded."
> → **1594** causal: *quod,* "because, since," + indicative, one's own reason, 59.2;
> subjunctive use: modal attraction, 83.

in omnibus tuis rebus meis optatis ... respondit, "in all your concerns ... [good luck] has corresponded to my wishes": the phrase *omnibus tuis rebus* is in the abl. as the object of *in,* "in all your concerns," but *meis optatis* is in the dat. as the natural complement of the verb *respondit,* "[lady fortune] has corresponded to my wishes." This distinction can be heard when the text is read out loud if the reader is looking to the end of the sentence and sees what is happening.

→ **1595** prep. with abl., 28.4; natural dat., 33.7.1; sentence structure, 1.

me tibi praecipere … amor cogit, "love … forces me to command you": the verb *cogit*, "[love] forces," is used as an M & M verb in T.1i and its complement is an object sentence where the object form *me* functions as the subject of the infinitive *praecipere*, which is one of the 65 verbs whose complement is in the dat., here *tibi*, "me to order you" or "that I order you."

→ **1596** M & M, 60, 71, GL n° 527, remarks 1–2; OO, 71–73;
      65 verbs with dat., 33.7.2, GL n° 346.

Tanta est exspectatio … ut ego te obsecrare obtestarique non dubitem, "There is such a great awaiting … that I do not hesitate to beg and implore you": the main verb, *est*, "There is," in T.1i is followed by a result clause *Tanta … ut … dubitem*, in T.1i but rendered in the indicative according to the nature of a result clause, "[There is] such … that I do not hesitate." *dubitem* is complemented by two infinitives *obsecrare obtestarique*, "to beg and implore," joined by the final *-que*, "and"; their object is *te*, "you."

→ **1597** subjunctive use: pure result (consecutive), 67.1–2, GL n° 552;
      verb: complementary infinitive, 77; gerund, 77.1; conjunction: *-que*, 3.2.

ut ego te obsecrare obtestarique non dubitem … ad nos conformatus revertare, "that I do not hesitate to beg and implore you, that you may return to us well formed": Cicero's intention in begging and imploring (*obsecrare obtestarique*) is given in a purpose clause whose verb is *revertare*, a favorite alternate form of Cicero here for *revertaris*, "that you may return," in T.1s. Depending on *te obsecrare obtestarique*, "[I do not hesitate] to beg and implore you [that]," the *ut* that goes with *revertare*, "[that] you may return," is not expressed, as in other instances where the verb of asking is strongly felt. The participle *conformatus* agrees with the *tu*, "you," the subject of *revertare*, "you … [having been] well formed."

→ **1598** subjunctive use: purpose clause without *ut*, 58, GL n° 546, remark 2;
      commands: other expressions, 85.1.7;
      variation: *-ris*, 39.3; antecedent participle, 50, 51.1.2.

sic … revertare ut … hanc sustinere ac tueri possis, "that you may return … in such a way that you are able to maintain and safeguard this expectation": after his experience abroad, the result when he returns home is *sic … ut … possis*, in T.1s, but given in the indicative as the expression of a result clause in English, "in such a way that you are able."

→ **1599** subjunctive use: pure result (consecutive), 67.1–2, GL n° 552.

ut, quam exspectationem tui concitasti, hanc sustinere ac tueri possis, "that you are able to maintain and safeguard this expectation which you have awakened of your very self": The object of *sustinere ac tueri*, "to maintain and safeguard," is *hanc* [*exspectationem*], which has been incorporated into the relative sentence, *quam exspectationem*, "which expectation."

→ **1600** relative clause: incorporation of the antecedent, GL n° 616; verb: deponent, 29.

Et quoniam meam tuorum erga me meritorum memoriam nulla umquam delebit oblivio, "And because no forgetfulness will ever wipe out my recollection of your merits toward me": note the word order, where *meam* goes with *memoriam*, "my recollection," and between them are *tuorum … meritorum*, "of your merits," and between them *erga me*, "toward me." Also *nulla* goes with *oblivio*, "no forgetfulness." This is forever typical, normal Latin, which thrives on "hyperbaton," the separation of sentence elements naturally going together!

→ **1601** sentence structure, 1; GL n° 696.

te rogo ut memineris, "I ask you that you remember": the main verb *rogo*, "I ask," in T.1i establishing Track I, is followed by a purpose clause that gives the content or intention in asking, *ut memineris*, where the defective verb has no T.1s, so Cicero must use T.3s with the same meaning as T.1s, "that you remember" or to make the subjunctive more evident in English, "that you may remember." Often the subjunctive cannot be heard when present in English.

→ **1602** subjunctive use: purpose clause, 58.1; *consecutio*, 47–48; defective verbs, 14.4, GL n° 175.5: *coepi, memini, odi*.

ut memineris … eas te non potuisse consequi, "that you remember … that you were not able to attain them": *memineris*, "[that] you remember," is a verb of M & M, and the content of the recollection is given in OO where the object form *te* functions as the subject of the infinitive *potuisse*, whose action is completed by the deponent infinitive *consequi*. The English rendering is given in the following.

→ **1603** M & M, 60, 71, GL n° 527, remarks 1–2; OO, 71–73.

eas te non potuisse consequi, nisi … paruisses, "that you were not able to attain them, if … you had not obeyed": these two statements comprise a conditional sentence, but the condition is contrary to fact, whereas the consequent is logical or factual. The condition *nisi … paruisses*, "if you had not obeyed," is in T.4s, and so is contrary to fact in the past, which we can test by saying, "if you had not obeyed—but you did."

The consequence half of the conditional statement, *te non potuisse*, "you were not able," is a factual statement, and therefore not contrary to fact. At this point Latin runs out of forms to distinguish between the contrary to fact and the factual action in an antecedent infinitive. When the ability is real, the verb *possum, posse*, "to be able," resists being made into a contrary to fact statement. We can test this here by rendering *te non potuisse* as a contrary to fact consequence, "that you would not have been able," but in fact

he was not able, so it is not contrary to fact, but a factual statement. Here
the ability was not possible, so stating that reality is factual. The question is
whether the ability is contrary to fact, then the statement is contrary to fact,
but a factual statement about the ability is a factual statement.

→ **1604** conditionals: contrary to fact, 86.3; conditionals: factual, 86.1.

nisi meis puer olim fidelissimis atque amantissimis consiliis paruisses, "if as a
child once upon a time you had not obeyed my most trustworthy and loving
councils": *paruisses* is one of the 65 verbs whose complement is given in the
dat., here *meis ... fidelissimis ... amantissimis consiliis*, "my most trustworthy ... loving counsels."

→ **1605** 65 verbs with dat., 33.7.2, GL n° 346.

hoc animo in nos esse debebis, "you will have to be of this attitude toward
us": *hoc animo* is the abl. of description, meaning exactly "with this attitude," but rendered into English idiom as "of this attitude," which can also
be said exactly in Latin as *huius animi*, the gen. of description.

→ **1606** quality in abl., 96.2; quality in gen., 96.1.

esse debebis ut aetas nostra ... in amore ... tua conquiescat, "you will have
to be ... that our age of life ... may totally rest in your love": the main verb
debebis, "you will have," in T.3i, is complemented by the infinitive *esse*, "to
be." These are followed by *ut ... conquiescat*, in T.1s, which exemplifies the
ambiguity between a result and a purpose clause. If taken as a result clause
it is rendered in the indicative in English, "that [our age] is totally resting
in your love," but if taken as an expression of purpose, the English is also
in the subjunctive, as in "that [our age] may rest totally in your love." The
difference may simply be one of perspective. Latin allows this ambiguity, but
English often requires deciding one way or the other.

→ **1607** verb: complementary infinitive, 77;
           difference between purpose and result is perspective, GL n° 543, note 2.

It might interest some readers to know that the historical document of
Pope Paul VI issued at his own initiative on 21 November 1970, by which the
cardinals at the age of 80 are relieved of their responsibilities and the right
of electing the Pope, begins with the words of Cicero here, *ingravescentem
aetatem*, which the new papal Latinist happily remembered and thought
to employ for this his own first Latin papal document from this letter of
Cicero.

LETTER 770 T-P
AD ATTICUM XVI, 5

CICERO ATTICO SAL.

Tuas iam litteras Brutus exspectabat: cui quidem ego [non] novum attuleram de "Tereo" Acci. Ille "Brutum" putabat. Sed tamen rumoris nescio
quid adflaverat commissione Graecorum frequentiam non fuisse, quod
quidem me minime fefellit. Scis enim quid ego de Graecis ludis existimem.   (*Att.* XVI, 5, 1)

CICERO A GREETING TO ATTICUS

Brutus was already awaiting your letters, to whom indeed I had brought
something new from the "Tereus" of Accius. He was thinking of "Brutus."
But still something I-know-not-what of a rumor had blown in, that at the
presentation of the Greeks there had not been a crowd, something which
disappointed me to the least degree indeed. For you know what I think
about Greek plays.

CICERO ATTICO SAL.: *Cicero Attico salutem*

cui ... ego [*non*] *novum attuleram*, "to whom ... I had brought something
new": the word [non] is to be ignored according to Tyrrell and Purser,
something which we have done in the English rendering. *cui* shows the
natural to-for-from function. The discussion is about plays named *Tereus*
and *Brutus*, and a production of the Greeks.

→ **1608** natural dat., 33.7.1.

rumoris nescio quid, "something I-know-not-what of a rumor": it is less
misleading when *nescio quid* is written as one word *nescioquid*, as in many
dictionaries and some editions. Here *nescio* is not functioning as a verb and
does not mean "I do not know." Rather *nescioquid* functions as an indefinite
pronoun meaning "I-know-not-what" or here "something I-do-not-know-
what." The expression indicates uncertainty with regard to something
specific in the clause but does not have an effect on the rest of the sentence,

whereas a genuine verb would otherwise produce an IQ in the subjunctive. Here *rumoris*, "of a rumor," is a gen. of part and depends on the *quid*,
"something," to which *nescio* is attached but just hanging there.

> → **1609** dict., *nescio, ivi* or *ii, itum,* 4., I., (γ); GL n° 467, remark 1 and note;
> gen. of part, 99.

rumoris nescio quid … frequentiam non fuisse, "something I-know-not-what
of a rumor … there had not been a crowd": the content of the rumor is given
in OO depending not on a verb but on the M & M idea in the word *rumoris*, "of a rumor." The object form *frequentiam*, "a crowd," functions as the
subject of the infinitive *fuisse*, "there had not been a crowd."

> → **1610** M & M, 60, 71, GL n° 527, remarks 1–2; OO, 71–73.

quod … fefellit, "something which disappointed me": *quod* refers to the
whole preceding idea as in "which thing" or "something which."

> → **1611** *quod* referring to previous sentence: GL n° 614, remark 2.

Scis enim quid ego de Graecis ludis existimem, "For you know what I think
about Greek plays": the independent verb *Scis*, "you know," is a verb of M
& M in T.1i establishing Track I. The content of the knowledge appears in
an IQ, *quid … existimem*, "what I think," in T.1s. We may play with this
and say, *scis quid existimaverim*, "you know what I have thought"; *quid sim
existimaturus*, "you know what I will be thinking"; on Track II we can say,
sciebas quid existimarem, "you knew what I was thinking"; *sciebas quid
existimavissem*, "you knew what I had thought"; *sciebas quid existimaturus
essem*, "you knew what I was going to think" or "you knew what I would
think."

> → **1612** M & M, 60, 71, GL n° 527, remarks 1–2; IQ, 60;
> *consecutio*, 47–48.

෨

Nunc audi quod pluris est quam omnia. Quintus fuit mecum dies compluris, et si ego cuperem, ille vel pluris fuisset, sed, quantum fuit, incredibile
est quam me in omni genere delectarit, in eoque maxime in quo minime satis faciebat. Sic enim commutatus est totus et scriptis meis quibusdam quae
in manibus habebam et adsiduitate orationis et praeceptis, ut tali animo
in rem publicam quali nos volumus futurus sit. Hoc cum mihi non modo
confirmasset sed etiam persuasisset, egit mecum accurate multis verbis tibi
ut sponderem se dignum et te et nobis futurum, neque se postulare ut statim crederes, sed, cum ipse perspexisses, tum ut se amares. Quod nisi fidem mihi fecisset iudicassemque hoc quod dico firmum fore, non fecissem
id quod dicturus sum. Duxi enim mecum adulescentem ad Brutum. Sic ei
probatum est quod ad te scribo ut ipsi crediderit, me sponsorem accipere
noluerit eumque laudans amicissime mentionem tui fecerit, complexus osculatusque dimiserit. Quam ob rem etsi magis est quod gratuler tibi quam

quod te rogem, tamen etiam rogo ut, si quae minus antea propter infirmitatem aetatis constanter ab eo fieri videbantur, ea iudices illum abiecisse
mihique credas multum adlaturam vel plurimum potius ad illius iudicium
confirmandum auctoritatem tuam.   (*Att.* XVI, 5, 2)

Now hear that which is of greater value than all things. Quintus [junior-
nephew to Cicero] was with me quite a few days, and if I were willing he
would have been even more days, but how much he was [present], it is incredible how much he delighted me in every respect, and in that respect
mostly in which he used to satisfy me to the least degree. For the whole of
him has been so changed both by certain of my writings which I was handling in my hands and by a constant application of talk and by precepts, that
he is going to be of such an attitude toward the republic of which we want
him [to be]. After he had not only assured me but also had convinced me of
this, he negotiated with me carefully in many words that I would promise
you that he would be worthy both of you and of us and that he was not asking that you might believe this immediately, but that you should love him
then, when you yourself would have totally understood this. But if he had
not given me a word of honor and if I had not judged this which I am saying
would be solid in the future, I would not have done that which I am about to
explain. For I took the young man with me to Brutus. That which I am writing to you [Atticus] was made acceptable to him [Brutus] in such a way that
he [Brutus] believed him himself [Quintus], that he [Brutus] did not want to
accept me as a sponsor and that praising him [Quintus] he [Brutus] made a
mention of you in a most friendly way, and that [Brutus] having embraced
and given a kiss dismissed him [Quintus]. For which reason, although it is
supposedly more important that I congratulate you [Atticus] than that I implore you, nevertheless I am even asking that, if some things were appearing
previously to have been done by him [Quintus] less solidly because of the
weakness of his age, you may judge that he has cast those things off and
that you may believe me that your authority is going to contribute much or
rather the most for strengthening that estimation of him.

Nunc audi quod pluris est quam omnia, "Now hear that which is of greater
value than all things": *audi quod* does not mean "hear what," as if opening
an IQ, which would require that the verb be in the subjunctive *audi quid
… sit,* "hear what is," in T.1s. But the verb *est* is in the indicative, *quod …
est,* T.1i, and this is a relative statement where the antecedent of *quod* is not
expressed, *id,* which is the object of *audi,* as in "hear that which."

→ **1613** rel. pron.: omission of the antecedent, 11.2.

pluris … pluris, "of greater value … more": the same word *pluris* occurs
twice in two lines for two completely different reasons. In the first sentence
pluris is in the of-possession form and means "of greater value," as a gen. of
evaluation. In the second, *pluris* is the alternative form for *plures,* the object

plural that agrees with *dies* previously in the sentence, meaning "a few [days]." This is Latin and will drive people crazy because first they will not understand the function of *pluris* and second they will not understand the form *pluris*. This is about as much as you can demand of people on earth.

→ **1614** gen. of indefinite price, 75.2; variation: *–ris*, 39.3.

Quintus fuit mecum dies compluris, et si ego cuperem, ille vel pluris fuisset, "Quintus [junior] was with me quite a few days, and if I were willing he would have been even more days": an alternative meaning of *vel* is "even," as an intensive particle in your dictionary. The main verb *fuit*, "[Quintus] was," in T.4b.

→ **1615** dict., *vel*, conj. and adv. II., A. "even," *et passim.*

Cicero is writing to Atticus and says, *nunc audi,* "Now hear," T.1i and so establishes the present perspective.

→ **1616** commands: first, second, 17.

Next, Cicero reflects back in time and describes a contrary to fact statement set just after the departure of Quintus, during his absence, *ille vel pluris fuisset,* "[Quintus] would have been even more days," where the verb *fuisset* is in T.4s. We can test this unreal consequence by saying, "Quintus would have been present with me even more days, but he was not able."

Unreal conditionals stand independent from the rest of the sentence, as here it stands independent from *fuit*, "[Quintus] was," in T.4b. Typically unreal conditionals set in the past have both verbs, the condition and its consequence, in T.4s … T.4s…. Here only the consequence *fuisset*, "he would have been," is T.4s.

→ **1617** conditionals: contrary to fact, 86.3.

The time of *cuperem* is determined by its relation to the verb on which it depends. Here *si cuperem* in T.2s could be mistaken as a contrary to fact condition set in the present, when Cicero is writing the letter, meaning "if I were willing at this time, but I am not." However, *cuperem* does not depend on the present moment, represented by *Nunc audi*, "Now hear."

In this case a somewhat special sequence of tenses is established by *fuisset* in T.4s, in regard to which the condition is contemporaneous and ongoing and thus in T.2s, producing *cuperem*, "if I were willing at that time." This can be tested by saying, "if I were willing at that time, but I was not willing, Quintus would have been present with me even more days, but he was not."

→ **1618** conditionals: contrary to fact, 86.3; *consecutio*, 47–48.

A simple calendar can clarify the times of these verbs. Cicero is writing this letter on 9 July 44. Say that Quintus visited until the last day of April. *Animi causa, interpretationem nostram praeter consuetudinem addidimus vernaculam,* "just for kicks we have added the vernacular interpretation beyond our own custom."

April	May	9 July
		[*Nunc audi*]
fuit		
	cuperem	
	fuisset	
		[Now listen]
Quintus was with me		
	if I were willing	
	he would have been	

→ **1619** calendars, 83 pp. 514–15, 103 p. 586.

quantum fuit, "but how much he was [present], it is incredible": this is half of a correlative where *quantum* means "how much," and the other half is not given.

→ **1620** correlative comparative sentences, 90.5, GL nº 642.

incredibile est quam me in omni genere delectarit, "it is incredible how much he delighted me in every respect": *incredibile est*, "it is incredible," in T.1i implies a mental operation of M & M whose content is given in an IQ where the question word is *quam*, "how much," followed by the antecedent action *delectarit*, a syncopated form of *delectaverit*, "he delighted me," in T.3i.

→ **1621** M & M, 60, 71, GL nº 527, remarks 1–2; IQ, 60;
contractions: verbs, 39.2, GL nº 131.

in eoque maxime in quo minime satis faciebat, "and in that respect mostly in which he used to satisfy me to the least degree": the one verb *faciebat*, "he used to," goes with both clauses *in eo ... in quo ...*, "in that respect ... in which ...." The main verb *incredibile est*, "it is incredible," in T.1i functions as an expression of M & M and produces an IQ *quam delectarit*, "how much he delighted me," in T.3s describing antecedent action. The verb *faciebat* in T.2i describes the state of things as they were at some time in the past, and according to the idea of the story *faciebat* is previous to *delectarit*. Cicero makes the contrast with two adverbs *maxime ... minime*, "mostly ... to the least degree."

→ **1622** dict., *eo*, adv., II. "to that place";
dict., *huc*, adv., I. "to this place";
dict., *quo*, adv., II. "to where";
M & M, 60, 71, GL nº 527, remarks 1–2; IQ, 60;
adv.: positive, comp., superl., 37.

Sic ... commutatus est ... ut tali animo ... futurus sit, "[the whole of him] has been so changed ... that he is going to be of such an attitude": the main verb *commutatus est*, "[the whole of him] has been ... changed," is T.4a in the passive, establishing Track I. Cicero describes the result of this change in a result clause *sic ... ut ... futurus sit*, "that he is going to be," "that he will be." We can play with the sentence, where *futurus sit* is in the subjunctive in a result clause, and construct an independent sentence in the indicative by changing only three words: *ut* becomes *et*, "and," and *futurus sit* become *erit*, "he will be," in T.3i, as in *Sic ... commutatus est ... et tali animo ... erit*, "He has been changed in such a way, and he will be of such a spirit."

> → **1623** passive Times 4, 5, 6 indicative, 26; *consecutio*, 47–48;
> subjunctive use: pure result (consecutive), 67.1–2, GL n° 552;
> futurity participle, 50, 51.1.3;
> *consecutio*: futurity formula in the subjunctive, 61.3.

et scriptis ... et adsiduitate ... et praeceptis, "both by ... writings ... and by a constant application ... and by precepts": a sequence of *et ... et ... et ...*, "both ... and ... and," each followed by the by-with-from-in form describing three means by which Quintus was changed, *commutatus est*.

> → **1624** conjunction: *et ..., et ...*, 3.2;
> quality in abl., 96.2.

quae in manibus habebam, "which I had in my hands": Cicero uses *habebam*, "I was handling," in T.2i, to describe the manuscripts and writings he was handling and working on for a long period of time. This is a good example of how T.2i is used to record as it were a moving film or video of action over a period of time.

> → **1625** times-tenses of the indicative mode and their vernacular meaning, 7.

commutatus est totus et scriptis meis quibusdam, "the whole of him has been so changed both by certain of my writings": the main verb, *commutatus est*, "[the whole of him] has been so changed," is T.4a in the passive establishing Track I.

tali animo in rem publicam quali nos volumus, "of such an attitude toward the republic of which we want him [to be]": the correlatives *tali ... quali ...* both agree with *animo*, in the abl. of quality or description, which you can hear in the English expression "with such an attitude ... with which [attitude]." The alternative is the gen. of description *talis animi ... qualis ...*, "[he will be] of such an attitude ... of which...."

> → **1626** correlative comparative sentences, 90.5, GL n° 642;
> quality in abl., 96.2; quality in gen., 96.1.

The next sentence is in good order as the boxes in this chart indicate:

{ Hoc cum mihi non modo confirmasset	temporal circumstance; T.4s
sed etiam persuasisset,	
egit mecum accurate multis verbis	main; T.4b
{ tibi ut sponderem	purpose 1; T.2s
[se dignum et te et nobis futurum,]	OO; futurity
[neque se postulare	OO; contemporaneous
(ut statim crederes,	purpose 2; T.2s
(sed,	purpose 3
< cum ipse perspexisses, >	temporal circumstance; T.4s = future completed
tum ut se amares.)] }	purpose 3 continued; T.2s

→ **1627** structure of Latin sentences, 103 p. 587, *Ossa* Readings: 1-D, 1-I, 3-D,
3-I, 4-D, 4-I.

Hoc cum mihi non modo confirmasset sed etiam persuasisset, egit, "After he
had not only assured me but also had convinced me of this, he negotiated":
the main verb *egit,* "he negotiated," in T.4b establishes the sentence on Track
II. The circumstance for the negotiations is given in the temporal clause
cum, followed by two verbs *confirmasset,* "he had … assured" and *persuasisset,* "he … had convinced" in T.4s describing antecedent action; thus *cum* is
rendered as "After." The two verbs are correlated by *non modo … sed etiam
…,* "not only … but also.…" The object of both verbs is *Hoc,* "this," which
is placed out in front, and *mihi,* "to me," is the natural dative for both verbs,
which can be more easily heard if we were to say, for example, *Hoc cum mihi
confirmasset,* "After he confirmed this for me."

→ **1628** subjunctive use: temporal circumstance *cum* = "when," 66.3.2;
consecutio, 47–48;
non modo … , sed … , GL n° 482.5; sentence structure, 1;
natural dat., 33.7.1.

egit mecum accurate multis verbis tibi ut sponderem, "he negotiated with me
carefully in many words that I would promise you": the main verb *egit,* "he
negotiated," is T.4b establishing Track II. His intention in negotiating was
tibi ut sponderem, "that I would promise you," "that I might promise you,"
in T.2s and so describing ongoing or future action. Note that *tibi* as a natural dative means "to you," but this is not heard in the English idiom, and it
is placed at the front of its clause.

→ **1629** subjunctive use: purpose clause, 58.1; *consecutio,* 47–48;
consecutio: futurity in the subjunctive, 61.1; natural dat., 33.7.1.

tibi ut sponderem se dignum et te et nobis futurum, neque se postulare, "that
I would promise you that he would be worthy both of you and of us and that
he was not asking": *sponderem,* "[that] I would promise" is a verb of M & M
and the content of the promise is given in two statements in OO. The subject
of the first is given in the object form *se,* an indirect reflexive referring to

Quintus, who is the subject of the main verb *egit*, as in "Quintus negotiated that I would promise that Quintus would be." The full infinitive is *futurum esse*, "[that he] would be," expressing futurity from a point in the past established by *sponderem*, depending on *egit*. The dictionary indicates that *dignum*, here in the predicate agreeing with *se*, is complemented by the gen. or the abl. as here, *et te et nobis*, meaning exactly, "worthy both by you and by us," but the English idiom is "worthy both of you and of us."

→ **1630** M & M, 60, 71, GL nº 527, remarks 1–2; OO, 71–73;
    reflexive pron.: third person, 31;
    futurity participle, 50, 51.1.3; *futurum esse (fore)*, 72.1;
    futurity formula, active, 53.3;
    dict., *dignus, a, um*, adj., I., (α) with abl., (ζ) with gen.

The subject of the second is given in the object form *se* with the infinitive *postulare*, rendered in the past as "that he was [not] asking" because it is contemporaneous with *sponderem*, "I would promise," depending on *egit*, "he negotiated," to which the subject *se* again refers indirectly, "that he [Quintus] was not asking."

→ **1631** M & M, 60, 71, GL nº 527, remarks 1–2; OO, 71–73;
    reflexive pron.: third person, 31.

neque se postulare ut statim crederes, "and that he was not asking that you might believe this immediately": the statement in OO *se postulare*, "that he was [not] asking," produces a purpose clause that gives the content or intention for which Quintus was not asking, *ut ... crederes*, in T.2s. *crederes* may also be taken as an imaginary "you" meaning "that one might believe"; see GL nº 258.

→ **1632** OO, 71–73; subjunctive use: purpose clause, 58.1;
    imaginary "you," GL nº 258.

neque se postulare ... sed, cum ipse perspexisses, tum ut se amares, "and that he was not asking ... but that you should love him then, when you yourself would have totally understood this": the statement in OO *se postulare*, "that he was [not] asking," produces a purpose clause that gives the content or intention for which Quintus was asking, *ut ... amares*, "that you should love," referring to Atticus. The *se* does not refer to the subject of *amares*, which is *tu*, "you [Atticus]," but it is an indirect reflexive referring all the way back to the subject of the sentence *is*, "he [Quintus]," implied in *egit*, "he negotiated." *cum ... tum ...* correlate the two phrases given in reverse order in English, "... then, when ...." Because the nature of the purpose clause *ut ... amares*, "that you should love," has futurity in it, *cum ... perspexisses*, "when you ... would have totally understood," in T.4s by MA expresses completed futurity, which here is in no sense what others incorrectly call "pluperfect" and therefore projected back to some remote past. Rather, this clause is projected out into future completed action, as in "when in the meanwhile you yourself would have understood this, then you might love him."

> → **1633** OO, 71–73; subjunctive use: purpose clause, 58.1;
> reflexive pron.: third person, 31; correlative comparative sentences, 90.5,
> GL n° 642;
> subjunctive use: modal attraction, 83;
> *consecutio*: completed futurity in the subjunctive, 61.1.

If some of the essential aspects of this sentence will not have been complete-ly comprehended and calculated, no one will understand this Latin sen-tence, but a sort of calendar may be helpful. This is very demanding Latin, but completely logical and humanly possible.

February	May	June	July	September	October	December
confirmasset						
persuasisset						
	egit →					
		ut sponderem →				
			se dignum futurum			
		se postulare →				
				ut crederes		
						ut amares
					cum perspexisses	

> → **1634** calendars, 83 pp. 514–15, 103 p. 586.

Thus, we might say: "After he had assured and convinced (*confirmasset, per-suasisset*) in February, he dealt with me (*egit*) in May that I would promise you (*ut sponderem*) in June that he would be worthy (*se dignum futurum*) in July and that also in June he was asking (*se postulare*) that in September you might not believe this (*ut crederes*) immediately but that you would love him (*ut amares*) in December, when in the meanwhile in October you might have understood (*cum perspexisses*) his conversion."

Calendar notes:

The arrow after *egit* indicates the action is going over into the purpose clause *ut sponderem*.

The arrow after *ut sponderem* is pointing to the effect of the promising *se futurum*.

The arrow after *se postulare* is going over into the contents of his asking, *ut crederes* and *ut amares*.

Quod nisi, "But if … not": the negative of *Quodsi*, "but if," and the introduction to a contrary to fact statement "explained below."

Quod nisi fidem mihi fecisset iudicassemque hoc quod dico firmum fore, "But if he had not given me a word of honor and if I had not judged this which I am saying would be solid in the future": *nisi fecisset* and *iudicassem*, both in T.4s, are the conditions of a contrary to fact statement set in the past, which we may test: "if he had not given, but he gave, … and if I had not judged, but I did judge." The second of these, *iudicassem*, is a verb of M & M. The content of his judging is given in OO where the subject *hoc* is in the object form and the infinitive *fore* is more fully given as *futurum esse*, "to be about to be," the futurity infinitive. *quod dico*, "which I am saying," is a relative clause whose antecedent is *hoc*, "this thing," the subject of *fore*.

→ **1635** conditionals: contrary to fact, 86.3;
M & M, 60, 71, GL nᵒ 527, remarks 1–2; OO, 71–73;
futurity participle, 50, 51.1.3; *futurum esse (fore)*, 72.1;
futurity formula, active, 53.3;
relative clauses, 10–11.

non fecissem id quod dicturus sum, "I would not have done that which I am about to explain": going with *nisi fecisset iudicassemque*, "if he had not given … and if I had not judged," is the consequence *non fecissem*, "I would not have done"; all three in T.4s indicating a contrary to fact conditional set in the past. The time of the sentence changes to the present moment as Cicero is writing in the relative clause, *quod dicturus sum*, "which I am about to explain," the futurity formula in the indicative.

→ **1636** conditionals: contrary to fact, 86.3; *consecutio*, 47–48;
futurity participle, 50, 51.1.3;
futurity formula, active, 53.3.

Sic ei probatum est … ut … crediderit, … noluerit … fecerit, … dimiserit, "[it] was made acceptable to him [Brutus] in such a way that he [Brutus] … believed, he [Brutus] did not want … he [Brutus] made a mention … that [Brutus] … dismissed": the structure of this sentence is clear when you see that the main verb, *probatum est*, "[it] was made acceptable," in T.4b establishes Track II, and that all four of the subjunctive verbs are in T.3s, which appears to jump tracks to Track I. This is, rather, another example of the 3% peculiarity of the sequence of tenses in which a pure result clause (*sic … ut …*) is used to express one concrete result, or in this case the four single concrete results, as if presenting four photographs of these results. The subject of all four of these verbs in the Latin is Brutus.

→ **1637** *consecutio*, 47–48; subjunctive use: 3% sequence of tenses, 94.1;
subjunctive use: pure result (consecutive), 67.1–2, GL nᵒ 552.

Sic … ut ipsi crediderit, "in such a way that he [Brutus] believed him himself [Quintus]": *crediderit* is one of the 65 verbs whose complement is in the dat., here *ipsi*, but in English this dat. is not heard, as in "he believed him."

→ **1638** 65 verbs with dat., 33.7.2, GL nᵒ 346;
three cousins: *iste–ille–ipse*, 41.3.

Sic … ut … me sponsorem accipere noluerit, "in such a way … that he [Bru-tus] did not want to accept me as a sponsor": although *noluerit* is a verb of M & M that produces a statement in OO, here *accipere* is a complementary infinitive, and *me* is the object of *accipere*, "to accept me." *sponsorem* agrees with *me*, in apposition.

→ **1639** M & M, 60, 71, GL n° 527, remarks 1–2;
verb: complementary infinitive, 77; gerund, 77.1;
apposition, GL n° 320–21.

ei probatum est quod ad te scribo, "That which I am writing to you [Atti-cus] was made acceptable to him [Brutus]": the main verb is *probatum est*, "… was made acceptable," in T.4b, a passive verb in the neuter. Its subject grammatically is an implied *id*, the antecedent of *quod*, "that which," which begins the relative clause *quod … scribo*, "that which I am writing to you," in T.1i and the rest of the sentence, all of which is philosophically the subject of *probatum est*, "[it all] was made acceptable." Expressing this passive *pro-batum est* is difficult in clear English as the dictionary points out the clumsy meaning of *probo, probare*, "to make something approved by someone," which in the passive is heavy, "to be made approved." Alas, each language has its own different limits.

→ **1640** dict., *probo, avi, atum, are*, 1., III. "to make acceptable";
rel. pron.: omission of the antecedent, 11.2.

magis est quod gratuler tibi quam quod te rogem, "it is supposedly more important that I congratulate you [Atticus] than that I implore you": the main verb, *est*, "it is," in T.1i is followed by two clauses coordinated by the comparison *magis … quam …*, "more … than …." Both clauses *quod gratuler* and *quod … rogem*, are in the subjunctive, perhaps because they are reporting the speech of others, or of some imagined opinion. This use of the subjunctive is expressed in our English rendering above by the addition of the word "supposedly," or we could have said, "allegedly." The dep. *gratuler*, "that I congratulate you," in T.1s is one of 65 verbs whose complement is in the dat., here *tibi*, and the entire clause *quod gratuler tibi*, "that I congratu-late you," is structurally the subject of *est*, "it is." Likewise the entire clause *quod te rogem*, "that I implore you," is also the subject of *est*.

→ **1641** *quam* with the comp., 43.2;
adv.: irregular comp., 37.3, GL n° 93;
object sentence: *quod* = "that," GL n° 524;
65 verbs with dat., 33.7.2, GL n° 346,
causal: *quod*, "because, since," + subjunctive, reported reason, 59.2.

tamen etiam rogo ut … iudices, "nevertheless I am even asking that … you may judge": *rogo*, "I am asking," in T.1i establishes Track I. Cicero's intention in asking is given in a purpose clause with two verbs. First, *ut … iudices*, "that you may judge," where the verb *iudices* in T.1s looks like it means "judges," the plural subject or object from *iudex, icis*, f., "a judge."

→ **1642** subjunctive use: purpose clause, 58.1; *consecutio*, 47–48;
dict., *judex, icis*, comm., "a judge";
dict., *judicio, avi, atum*, 1., "to examine judicially."

rogo ut ... ea iudices illum abiecisse, "I am ... asking that you may judge that he has cast those things off": *iudices*, "that you judge," is a verb of M & M in T.1s. Cicero requests a judgment of Atticus given in OO. The object form *illum* is the subject of the infinitive *abiecisse* describing antecedent action, "that he has cast ... off."

→ **1643** M & M, 60, 71, GL nº 527, remarks 1–2; OO, 71–73.

rogo ut ... mihique credas, "I am ... asking ... and that you may believe me": the *-que*, "and," attached to *mihi* joins *iudices* to *credas*, which gives the second intention for Cicero's request. *credas*, "that you believe," in T.1s is one of the 65 whose complement is in the dat., here *mihi*, where the dat. function is not evident in the English expression "that you believe me."

→ **1644** 65 verbs with dat., 33.7.2, GL nº 346.

si quae ... ab eo fieri videbantur, "if some things were appearing ... to have been done by him": *videbantur* in T.2i is used personally here, where *quae*, "some things," is its subject and the complement of *videbantur* is the infinitive *fieri* the passive form of the verb *facio*. The subject of *fieri* is given in the nom., the same *quae*, the subject of *videbantur*. Because the infinitive *fieri* is contemporaneous with *videbantur*, "[some things] were happening," the infinitive *fieri* too is set in the past, but its passive voice is difficult to express fully in English, such as "if some things were appearing to be being done by him." This factual condition in T.2i corresponds with its consequence expressed in the purpose clause, *ut ... iudices*, "that ... you may judge."

→ **1645** personal construction: *videor*, 73.3, GL nº 528.1 and remark 2 and note 1;
nom. with the inf., 73.3, GL nº 528.1;
pronouns: indefinite, 42.4; after si the *ali*-s fly away, 42.5;
conditionals: factual, 86.1.

credas multum adlaturam vel plurimum potius ... auctoritatem tuam, "you may believe me that your authority is going to contribute much or rather the most": *credas* is also a verb of M & M, and the content of this mental operation is given in OO, where the object form *auctoritatem*, "authority," functions as the subject of the infinitive, whose full form is *adlaturam esse*, "that [your] authority is going to contribute," expressing futurity action.

→ **1646** M & M, 60, 71, GL nº 527, remarks 1–2; OO, 71–73.

ad illius iudicium confirmandum, "for strengthening that estimation of him": *iudicium* is the object of the gerund or gerundive *confirmandum*, "strengthening [that] estimation." The gen. *illius*, "of him," is out front in this expression.

→ **1647** gerund, 77.1; gerundive, 77.2;
three cousins: *iste–ille–ipse*, 41.3.

◦~

Bruto cum saepe iniecissem de ὁμοπλοίᾳ, non perinde atque ego putaram adripere visus est. Existimabam μετεωρότερον esse, et hercule erat et maxime de ludis. At mihi, cum ad villam redissem, Cn. Lucceius, qui multum utitur Bruto, narravit illum valde morari, non tergiversantem sed exspectantem si qui forte casus. Itaque dubito an Venusiam tendam et ibi exspectem de legionibus: si aberunt, ut quidam arbitrantur, Hydruntem: si neutrum erit ἀσφαλές, eodem revertar. * * Iocari me putas? Moriar si quisquam me tenet praeter te. Etenim † circumspice, sed ante quam erubesco †   (*Att.* XVI, 5, 3)

Although I had hinted often to Brutus about *the companionship of sailing*, he seemed to catch it not exactly as I had thought. I was thinking that he was *of a more dubious spirit*, and by george he was and especially concerning the games. But when I had come back to the villa, Gnaeus Lucceius, who hangs around much with Brutus, narrated to me that he [Brutus] was delaying very much, not vacillating but awaiting, if perhaps some event.... Thus, I am hesitant whether I should head for Venusia and there await [news] about the legions. If they will not be there, as some people think, [I'll head out] to Otranto: if neither will be *safe*, I shall return to the same place. * * Do you think I am kidding? May I perish if anyone is holding me back besides you. For † look around, but before I blush †

> *Bruto cum saepe iniecissem*, "Although I had hinted often to Brutus":
> followed by *iniecissem*, "I had hinted," in T.4s, *cum* can mean "because,"
> "although," or circumstantial "when."
>
> → **1648** subjunctive use: concessive *cum* = "although," 64;
>   subjunctive use: causal *cum* = "because, since," 59.1;
>   subjunctive use: temporal circumstance *cum* = "when," 66.3.2.

> *de* ὁμοπλοίᾳ, "about *the companionship of sailing*": the Latin equivalent is *de societate navigandi*.
>
> → **1649** Bibliography: *Onomasticon Tullianum*; Greek expressions, pp. 623–626.

> *non perinde atque ego putaram adripere visus est*, "he seemed to catch it not
> exactly as I had thought": used personally, the subject of *visus est* is contained in the verb, namely *is*, "he," referring to Brutus, as the story indicates.
> Here *atque* does not mean "and," but "as," which the dictionary indicates.
> The dictionary entry for *perinde* indicates that *non perinde atque* means
> here "not exactly as." *putaram* is the syncopated form of *putaveram*, "I had
> thought." *adripere*, "to catch [it]," is a complementary infinitive whose subject is the same as that of *visus est*, namely the nom. *is* referring to Brutus,
> producing "he seemed to catch."
>
> → **1650** personal construction: *videor*, 73.3, GL n° 528.1 and remark 2 and note 1;
>   nom. with the inf., 73.3, GL n° 528.1; dict., *atque*, conj., II. in comparisons,
>   A. "as";
>   dict., *perinde*, adv., II., (α) with *atque*, "just as."

Existimabam μετεωρότερον *esse*, "I was thinking that he was *of a more dubious spirit*": *Existimabam*, "I was thinking," is an M & M verb in T.2i, and the content of Cicero's thought is given in OO where the subject of the verb *esse*, "to be," is an implied *eum*, "him," because the Greek term is masculine. The Latin equivalent of the Greek term μετεωρότερον is *suspensiore animo*, an abl. of description meaning exactly *with a more dubious spirit*, or in English idiom "of a more dubious spirit."

> → **1651** M & M, 60, 71, GL n° 527, remarks 1–2; OO, 71–73;
>   Bibliography: *Onomasticon Tullianum*;
>   Greek expressions, pp. 623–626; quality in abl., 96.2.

cum ad villam redissem, "when I had come back to the villa": with the subjunctive *redissem*, "I had come back" in T.4s, according to the story *cum* can mean either "because," "although," or as here circumstantial "when."

> → **1652** subjunctive use: temporal circumstance *cum* = "when," 66.3.2;
>   subjunctive use: causal *cum* = "because, since," 59.1;
>   subjunctive use: concessive *cum* = "although," 64.

Cn. Lucceius ... narravit illum valde morari, "Gnaeus Lucceius ... narrated to me that he [Brutus] was delaying very much": *narravit*, "[Lucceius] narrated," is an M & M verb in T.4b, and the content of the account of Lucceius is given in OO where the object form *illum* functions as the subject of *morari*, a deponent verb and so passive in form but active in meaning, as in "that he was delaying." *illum* refers to "that one over there," "the former," "that illustrious one."

> → **1653** M & M, 60, 71, GL n° 527, remarks 1–2; OO, 71–73;
>   three cousins: *iste–ille–ipse*, 41.3; verb: deponent, 29.

qui multum utitur Bruto, "who hangs around much with Brutus": here *utitur Bruto* does not mean "[who] uses Brutus," according to the special meaning, given in the dictionary way down the entry, of "to get along with" or "to be familiar with."

> → **1654** dict., *utor, usus*, 3., II., A. "to be familiar with";
>   famous five verbs with the ablative, 78.1.

si qui forte casus, "if perhaps some event ...": a condition begins but is not finished, as there is no verb. The sentence just floats off.

> → **1655** conditionals, 86.

dubito an Venusiam tendam et ibi exspectem, "I am hesitant whether I should head for Venusia and there await": the verb of doubting *dubito*, "I am hesitant," is followed by *an*, "whether," which introduces an IQ and so is followed by the subjunctive in Latin, here *tendam*, "I should head," in T.1s, which only 10% of the time is rendered in the subjunctive in English due to an underlying independent subjunctive. The dictionary states that *dubito* followed by *an* indicates that the writer favors this outcome, as in "I am inclined to think." The same can be said of *dubito an … ibi expectem*, meaning "I am hesitant whether I should await there."

> → **1656** negative *dubitare* + *quin* + subjunctive, 93.4, 101.2, GL n° 555.2; IQ, 60; dict., *an*, disjunctive conj., II. "or," E. *dubito an*, "I am inclined to think"; disjunctive question: *an*, GL n° 458.

si aberunt, ut quidam arbitrantur, Hydruntem, "If they will not be there, as some people think, [I'll head out] to Otranto": the conditional *si aberunt*, "If they will not be there," in T.3i, is followed by the consequence, which depends on the previous statement, *Hydruntem tendam*, taken as T.3i in the English rendering, "I shall head out to Otranto." *áberunt* is T.3i. *ut* means "as," here followed by the indicative *arbitrantur*, "[as people] think."

> → **1657** conditionals: factual, 86.1; dict., *ut*, I., B. meaning "as."

ἀσφαλές, "*safe*": the Latin equivalent is *tutum*, "safe." Cicero wanted to avoid the legions and the civil war.

> → **1658** Bibliography: *Onomasticon Tullianum*; Greek expressions, pp. 623–626.

eodem revertar, "I shall return to the same place": *eodem*, "to the same place," is an adv.

> → **1659** dict., *eodem*, adv., II., A. "to the same place."

Iocari me putas?, "Do you think I am kidding?": *putas*, "Do you think," is an M & M verb and the content of the thought is in OO, where the object form *me* functions as the subject of the deponent infinitive *Iocari*, so the passive form has active meaning.

> → **1660** M & M, 60, 71, GL n° 527, remarks 1–2; OO, 71–73; verb: deponent, 29.

moriar, "May I perish": either an optative subjunctive expressing a wish or T.3i; in either case *moriar* is almost an oath or curse word.

> → **1661** dict., *morior, mortuus*, 3., I.… *moriar, si*, "may I die, if"; independent subjunctive, 45.6, optative subjunctive with asseverations, GL n° 262.

The indications * * and † a *locus desperatus*, "despaired of text," are in the cited text from T-P, where a discussion about textual difficulties can be found.

ᘒ

O dies in auspiciis Lepidi *lepide* descriptos et apte ad consilium reditus nostri! Magna ῥοπὴ ad proficiscendum *in* tuis litteris. Atque utinam te illic! Sed ut conducere putabis.   (*Att. XVI, 5, 4*)

O the days having been *charmingly* noted down in the auguries of Lepidus, and suitably for the decision of our return! There is a great *inclination* for setting out *in* your letter. And would that [I see] you there! But as you will think to be advantageous.

O dies … descriptos, "O the days having been … noted down": an exclamation in the object case just as in the English expression, "Woe is me!" not "Woe is I!"

→ **1662** exclamations, GL n° 343.1.

reditus nostri, "of our return": the dictionary entry is *reditus, us*, n., "a returning," so the form here agrees.

→ **1663** 20% of nouns: *reditus, us*, m., 35.

ῥοπὴ, "an … *inclination*": the Latin equivalent is *momentum* or *inclinatio*, which describes the hand on a balance scale that tips toward the heavier weight. Cicero leaves out the verb, perhaps *est*, "there is." On the scale, the weight is moving toward setting out.

→ **1664** Bibliography: *Onomasticon Tullianum*; Greek expressions, pp. 623–626.

ad proficiscendum, "for setting out": a gerund.

→ **1665** gerund, 77.

Atque utinam te illic!, "And would that [I see] you there!": the sentence does not have a verb, so we can say that Cicero quickly skips along in his thoughts and moves beyond the verb as well. *utinam* follows the rules of potential subjunctives where T.1s expresses a possible wish or the possible fulfilment of a wish, and T.2s is an impossible wish as seen from the perspective of the present moment, as in "I wish it were snowing now, but it is not," and T.4s to express impossibility set in the past. Cicero leaves out the verb, so we suggest *videam*, whose subjunctive in English is more clearly expressed as "[would that] I may see [you there]."

We can add here that *utinam viderem* means "would that I would see, but I am not seeing"; and *utinam vidissem*, "would that I had seen, but I did not."

→ **1666** subjunctive use: *utinam*, 88.

Sed ut conducere putabis, "But as you will think is advantageous": the main verb *putabis*, "you will think," is a verb of M & M in T.3i. The content of the thought is given in OO, where *conducere* is used impersonally, meaning "to be advantageous" or "it is advantageous." Cicero gives here only the second half of a correlative sentence. The *ut* is missing its correlative *ita*, which should produce *ita … , ut …*. In both the previous and this sentence Cicero is talking so excitedly to Atticus that he skips along in his thought, which we might complete as "But [I'll do exactly] as you will think to be advantageous."

→ **1667** M & M, 60, 71, GL n° 527, remarks 1–2; OO, 71–73; passive verb used impersonally, GL n° 208.

Nepotis epistulam exspecto. Cupidus ille meorum? Qui ea quibus maxime γαυριῶ legenda non putet? Et ais μετ' ἀμύμωνα. Tu vero ἀμύμων : ille quidem ἄμβροτος. Mearum epistularum nulla est συναγωγή, sed habet Tiro instar septuaginta. Et quidem sunt a te quaedam sumendae: eas ego oportet perspiciam, corrigam; tum denique edentur.   (*Att.* XVI, 5, 5)

I am waiting for the letter of Nepos. Is he interested in my stuff? Who [although Nepos] does not think that those things must be read in which *I boast* most of all? And you say *after the greatest one*. But you are *the greatest*, he however *immortal*. Of my letters there is no *collection*, but Tiro has the amount of seventy. And indeed certain ones have to be taken from you: it is necessary that I look through, correct them; then finally they will be published.

> *Qui ea quibus maxime* γαυριῶ *legenda non putet?*, "Who [although Nepos] does not think that those things must be read in which *I boast* most of all?": *Qui* does not function as an interrogative meaning "Who?," because *Qui ... non putet*, reliant on an M & M verb in T.1s, is concessive, where *Qui* stands for *cum is*, "although he [Nepos ... does not think]." The editor indicates this is a question with the final punctuation, not because there is an interrogative word, but because the whole sentence asks a question. The content of the thinking is given in OO, where the object form *ea* functions as the subject of the infinitive whose full form is *legenda esse*, "that those things must be read." The Latin equivalent of γαυριῶ is *glorior*, "I boast."
>
> → **1668** subjunctive use: concessive *qui, quae, quod* = "although," 64;
>   M & M, 60, 71, GL n° 527, remarks 1–2; OO, 71–73;
>   participle of passive necessity, 50, 51.1.4;
>   passive necessity formula, 53.4;
>   Bibliography: *Onomasticon Tullianum*;
>   Greek expressions, pp. 623–626.

> μετ' ἀμύμωνα, "*after the greatest one*": the Latin equivalent is *post egregium*. We could also say, "following the greatest one," or "next to the greatest one."
>
> → **1669** Bibliography: *Onomasticon Tullianum*; Greek expressions, pp. 623–626.

> ἀμύμων, "*the greatest*": the Latin equivalent is *egregius, praeclarus*.
>
> → **1670** Bibliography: *Onomasticon Tullianum*; Greek expressions, pp. 623–626.

> ἄμβροτος, "*immortal*": the Latin equivalent is *immortalis, divinus*.
>
> → **1671** Bibliography: *Onomasticon Tullianum*; Greek expressions, pp. 623–626.

> συναγωγή, "*collection*": the Latin equivalent is *collectio*. This is the same word as the English word for a Jewish "synagogue," a word that came to refer also to a liturgical assembly.
>
> → **1672** Bibliography: *Onomasticon Tullianum*; Greek expressions, pp. 623–626.

instar, "the amount": other meanings include "as many as," "as big as," "the equivalent of," "the size [of 70]."

→ **1673** dict., *instar*, n. indecl.

sunt a te quaedam sumendae, "certain ones have to be taken from you": the passive necessity formula *sunt sumendae*, "[ones] have to be taken," is T.1i and agrees with *quaedam*, "certain ones." *a te* means "from you," because the letters are in his archives; to say the letters must be taken "by you" would be *tibi*, the dat. of agent with the necessity formula *sunt sumendae*.

→ **1674** participle of passive necessity, 50, 51.1.4;
   passive necessity formula, 53.4;
   prep. + abl. of separation or agent, 28.5.2; dat. of agent, 53.5.

eas ego oportet perspiciam, corrigam, "it is necessary that I look through, correct them": *oportet*, "it is necessary," is an impersonal verb in T.1i and also means "it is behooving." Both *perspiciam*, "that I look through" and *corrigam*, "that I . . . correct," are given in T.1s without *ut*, as mentioned in the dictionary, and they are placed next to each other without a connecting word by asyndeton. The subject of these two verbs is expressed, *ego*, "I," and their object is *eas*, "them," referring to certain letters to be taken from Atticus.

→ **1675** dict., *oportet, tit*, 2., I. v. impers.,—constr. class. with subjunctive,
   GL n° 535, remark 2;
   asyndeton, GL n° 473, remark.

tum denique edentur, "then finally they will be published": we end this presentation of 51 letters of Cicero with his insistence that "they shall be published," *edentur*. The same spelling can be one of two forms. If the initial letter is a short *ĕ*, then the form *ĕdentur* is from *ĕdo, ĕdere, edi, esum*, 3, "to eat," and is T.3i giving either a light imperative, "They shall be eaten" or the simple future meaning "they will be eaten." If the initial letter is a long *ē*, then it is from *ēdo, ēdere, edidi, editum*, 3, "to give out," "put forth," and is T.3i used as a light imperative meaning "they shall be published" or again as a simple future meaning "they will be published." The accents of these two forms are identical, but the Romans heard the difference in that initial letter *e*.

→ **1676** dict., *ĕdo, ĕdere, edi, esum*, 3, "to eat";
   dict., *ēdo, ēdere, edidi, editum*, 3, "to give out," "put forth."

Thus, we might say the following, with which we conclude this discourse staying ever close to the words of Cicero.

EDENTUR A NOBIS AT A POSTERIS EDENTUR

THEY WILL BE PUBLISHED BY US
BUT BY POSTERITY THEY WILL BE EATEN UP.

AMEN, AMEN!

QVINGENTA INSTAR EXEMPLORVM INCISA SEV BREVILOQVIA CICERONIS EPISTVLARIS

~

part III: five hundred clauses or tweets of Cicero in his letters in the manner of examples

As a second thought and a second attempt to provide help to self-learners and teachers of Latin there now follows Part III, a collection made many years ago of Ciceronian examples. The idea here is to present five hundred complete, untouched sentences of Cicero drawn from his letters almost in succession by anyone paging through the letters. They are complete sentences with complete thoughts, and each one exhibits a special beautiful use of the Latin language. The word order has not been changed, nothing has been omitted, nothing has been added, and each sentence consists of at the most six words; many are shorter yet, short enough that numbered entries pack in more than one adjacent tiny sentence, but completely intelligible and imitable. You will see there are two hundred statements or declaratory sentences numbered 1–200, followed by one hundred questions numbered 201–300, and then one hundred commands numbered 301–400, and finally one hundred exclamations numbered 401–500. Elsewhere in this volume we refer to these sentences by their "B" number for *Breviloquia* 1–500. The intent here is to give the learner and the teacher immediate access to the language and material for personal review and play and expansion of the whole language from real words of Cicero. These things can be appreciated in themselves and on one's own or in the classroom. They may be expanded to include every use and form, or the verbs, nouns, and adjectives replaced with counterparts drawn from the whole language. So nothing will be added because the sentences are obvious and self-explanatory. The thought is that we take what Cicero said on his phone or his twitter message as an inspiration and a guide to fill out our own complete sentences and consequently our knowledge and use of the language. Experience has shown that these five hundred sentences are extremely useful and highly appreciated by people who just want to hear Cicero talking and who want to imitate Cicero and to master the Latin language from Cicero's letters, as one source of the Latin experience. Some sentences are brilliant and magnificent, others are banal and empty, but they are all real expressions of Cicero as he wrote formal letters or intimate letters or empty letters to anyone. All of Latin literature for the past 2,200 years can be subjected to this same treatment at the hands of competent teachers or experts.

AFFIRMATIONES BREVES FACILESQVE EX
Ciceronis perscriptae epistvlis

*short and easy declarative sentences written
out from the letters of Cicero*

(A) AD ATTICUM

1. MULTUM TE AMAMUS.
    (I, 1, 5)

2. QUINTUM FRATREM COTIDIE EXSPECTAMUS.
    (I, 5, 8)

3. APUD TE EST UT VOLUMUS.
    (I, 8, 1)

4. ACTA RES EST.
    (I, 14, 5)

5. NOSTER AUTEM STATUS EST HIC.
    (I, 16, 11)

6. NON SUNT HAEC RIDICULA, MIHI CREDE.
    (I, 17, 11)

7. VIDES ENIM CETERA.
    (II, 3, 2)

8. TERENTIA TIBI SALUTEM DICIT.
    (II, 7, 5)

9. NIHIL ME EST INERTIUS.
    (II, 8, 1)

10. POMPEIUS AMAT NOS CAROSQUE HABET.
    (II, 20, 1)

11. A VIBIO LIBROS ACCEPI.
    (II, 20, 6)

12. ID EST MIHI GRATISSIMUM.
    (III, 5)

13. MEOS TIBI COMMENDO.
    (III, 6)

14. VIDERE TE CUPIO.
    (III, 7, 3)

15. TERENTIA TIBI SAEPE AGIT GRATIAS.
    (III, 9, 3)

16. AMAMUR A FRATRE ET A FILLA.
    (IV, 2, 7)

17. PERBELLE FECERIS, SI AD NOS VENERIS.
    (IV, 4A, 1)

18. NOS HIC CUM POMPEIO FUIMUS.
    (IV, 9, 1)

19. DOMUS TE NOSTRA TOTA SALUTAT.
    (IV, 12)

20. SUSPENSO ANIMO EXSPECTO QUID AGAT.
    (IV, 15, 10)

21. DE ANNIO SATURNINO CURASTI PROBE.
    (V, 1, 2)

22. DIONYSIUS NOBIS CORDI EST.
    (V, 3, 3)

23. NARRABO CUM ALIQUID HABEBO NOVI.
    (V, 6, 2)

24. SUMMA ERIT HAEC.
    (V, 8, 3)

25. ABSTULI, APERUI, LEGI.
    (V, 11, 7)

26. LEPTA NOSTER MIRIFICUS EST.
    (V, 17, 2)

27. PERSCRIBAM AD TE PAUCIS DIEBUS OMNIA.
    (V, 17, 2)

28. RELIQUA SUNT DOMESTICA.
    (V, 21, 14)

29. OMNIA SUM DILIGENTISSIME PERSECUTUS.
    (VI, 1, 3)

30. SUMUS ENIM AMBO BELLE CURIOSI.
    (VI, 1, 25)

31. EQUIDEM VALDE IPSAS ATHENAS AMO.
    (VI, 1, 26)

32. ID SCIRE TE ARBITROR.
    (VI, 2, 2)

33. HOC EST IGITUR EIUS MODI.
    (VI, 3, 3)

34. ABIIT IRATUS.
    (VI, 3, 7)

35. NUNC QUIDEM PROFECTO ROMAE ES.
    (VI, 5, 1)

36. CONFIDO REM UT VOLUMUS ESSE.
    (VI, 7, 1)

37. RIDEBIS HOC LOCO FORTASSE.
    (VII, 1, 5)

38. VERUM DICEBAT.
    (VII, 1, 8)

39. NIHIL VIDI MELIUS.
    (VII, 2, 3)

40. FUIMUS UNA HORAS DUAS FORTASSE.
(VII, 4, 2)

41. PACE OPUS EST.
(VII, 5, 4)

42. EQUIDEM DIES NOCTESQUE TORQUEOR.
(VII, 9, 4)

43. IN EO AESTUAVI DIU.
(VII, 13A, 1)

44. DEFICIT ENIM NON VOLUNTAS SED SPES.
(VII, 21, 1)

45. VICTI, OPPRESSI, CAPTI PLANE SUMUS.
(VII, 23, 1)

46. EGO NAVEM PARAVI.
(VIII, 4, 3)

47. EGO NON PUTO.
(VIII, 7, 1)

48. EGO TECUM TAMQUAM MECUM LOQUOR.
(VIII, 14, 2)

49. PLURA SCRIBEREM, SI IPSE POSSEM.
(VIII, 15, 3)

50. MIHI NIHIL POTEST ESSE GRATIUS.
(IX, 9, 1)

51. PLANE SIC FACIENDUM.
(IX, 9, 2)

52. DO, DO POENAS TEMERITATIS MEAE.
(IX, 10, 2)

53. SPEM AUTEM PACIS HABEO NULLAM.
(IX, 13, 8)

54. QUICQUID EGERO CONTINUO SCIES.
(IX, 15, 4)

55. NULLUM VIDEO FINEM MALI.
(IX, 18, 2)

56. RES SUNT INEXPLICABILES.
(X, 2, 2)

57. SINE SPE CONAMUR ULLA.
(X, 2, 2)

58. SED HAEC VIDEBIMUS.
(X, 4, 11)

59. CRAS IGITUR AD ME FORTASSE VENIET.
(X, 10, 3)

60. VIDES ENIM PROFECTO ANGUSTIAS.
(X, 11, 2)

61. SED SATIS LACRIMIS.
(X, 12, 2)

62. SCIES QUICQUID ERIT.
(X, 12, 4)

63. VETTIENUM DILIGO.
(X, 13, 2)

64. NOS TAMEN ALIQUID EXCOGITABIMUS.
  (X, 13, 2)

65. SED VIX ERIT TAM CITO.
  (X, 15, 3)

66. EST ENIM RUMOR.
  (X, 16, 3)

67. HABES CAUSAM OPINIONIS MEAE.
  (X, 17, 4)

68. NON POSSUM PLURA SCRIBERE.
  (XI, 2, 3)

69. PECUNIA APUD EGNATIUM EST.
  (XI, 3, 3)

70. HAEC ME EXCRUCIANT.
  (XI, 7, 3)

71. DE EA RE SCRIPSI AD TERENTIAM.
  (XI, 11, 2)

72. VIDEO DIFFICILE ESSE CONSILIUM.
  (XI, 15, 1)

73. IPSUM AGUSIUM AUDIES.
  (XI, 23, 2)

74. HOC IGITUR HABEBIS, NIHIL NOVI.
  (XII, 1, 2)

75. TU INTEREA DORMIS.
  (XII, 2, 2)

76. TE EXSPECTABO POSTRIDIE.
  (XII, 5C)

77. EGO ISTA NON NOVI.
  (XII, 6, 1)

78. DE CICERONE MULTIS RES PLACET.
  (XII, 8)

79. SED ADSUM. CORAM IGITUR.
  (XII, 11)

80. ATTICAE HILARITATEM LIBENTER AUDIO.
  (XII, 11)

81. EAS LITTERAS CRAS HABEBIS.
  (XII, 15)

82. HERI ENIM VESPERI VENERAT.
  (XII, 16)

83. ILLIS EGI GRATIAS.
  (XII, 19, 2)

84. RATIONES MEAS NOSTI.
  (XII, 21, 2)

85. ET EI SALUTEM DICES ET PILIAE.
  (XII, 24, 3)

86. SEQUOR CELEBRITATEM.
  (XII, 27, 1)

87. CAPUT ILLUD EST QUOD SCIS.
  (XII, 29, 2)

88. SED FACIES UT VIDEBITUR.
   (XII, 37, 3)

89. NULLO PACTO PROBO.
   (XII, 38A, 2)

90. TRIGINTA DIES IN HORTIS FUI.
   (XII, 40, 2)

91. SED CERTUM NON HABEO.
   (XII, 40, 5)

92. NIHIL ERAT QUOD SCRIBEREM.
   (XII, 41, 1)

93. DOMI TE LIBENTER ESSE FACILE CREDO.
   (XII, 48)

94. TU IGITUR ID CURABIS.
   (XII, 51, 2)

95. MISI TIBI TORQUATUM.
   (XIII, 5, 1)

96. TE IDIBUS VIDEBO CUM TUIS.
   (XIII, 8)

97. MIHI ARPINUM EUNDUM EST.
   (XIII, 9, 2)

98. PLANE QUID SIT NON INTELLEGO.
   (XIII, 10, 3)

99. DIES ADEST.
   (XIII, 12, 4)

100. ID EGO PLANE NOLO.
   (XIII, 13, 4 [OLIM 14, 1])

101. ID SCIRE SANE VELIM.
   (XIII, 20, 1)

102. SED NIMIUM MULTA DE NUGIS.
   (XIII, 20, 4)

103. DE DOLABELLA TIBI ADSENTIOR.
   (XIII, 21A, 3)

104. QUOD EGERIS ID PROBABO.
   (XIII, 24, 1)

105. SIC AGES IGITUR.
   (XIII, 26, 1)

106. SED CRAS SCIES.
   (XIII, 26, 2)

107. HOC PUTAVI TE SCIRE OPORTERE.
   (XIII, 28, 4)

108. DE HORTIS SATIS.
   (XIII, 29, 2)

109. PUDET ME PATRIS.
   (XIII, 31, 4)

110. RESCRIBES SI QUID VOLES.
   (XIII, 31, 4)

111. SED COMPLERE PAGINAM VOLUI.
   (XIII, 34)

112. UTAR EO QUOD DECREVERIS.
 (XIII, 38, 2)

113. MAGNA ENIM RES ET MULTAE CAUTIONIS.
 (XIII, 41, 2)

114. FACIAM QUOD VOLUNT.
 (XIII, 42, 1)

115. VIDEBIMUS TE IGITUR.
 (XIII, 43, 3)

116. LEGI EPISTULAM.
 (XIII, 46, 2)

117. DE DOMO ARPINI NIL SCIO.
 (XIII, 46, 4)

118. PUTO EQUIDEM NIHIL ESSE.
 (XIII, 47A, 2)

119. FUIT ENIM PERIUCUNDE.
 (XIII, 52, 1)

120. SEMEL SATIS EST.
 (XIII, 52, 2)

121. SED AD PROPOSITUM.
 (XIV, 1, 2)

122. DUAS A TE ACCEPI EPISTULAS HERI.
 (XIV, 2, 1)

123. TRANQUILLAE TUAE QUIDEM LITTERAE.
 (XIV, 3, 1)

124. TUMENT NEGOTIA.
 (XIV, 4, 1)

125. EXSULTANT LAETITIA IN MUNICIPIIS.
 (XIV, 6, 2)

126. POSTRIDIE IDUS PAULUM CAIETAE VIDI.
 (XIV, 7, 1)

127. ET BALBUS HIC EST MULTUMQUE MECUM.
 (XIV, 9, 3)

128. HAEC ET TALIA FERRE NON POSSUM.
 (XIV, 10, 1)

129. VEHEMENTER DELECTOR TUIS LITTERIS.
 (XIV, 10, 4)

130. REDEO NUNC AD EPISTULAM TUAM.
 (XIV, 13, 5)

131. EXPLANABIS IGITUR HOC DILIGENTIUS.
 (XIV, 14, 1)

132. INCIPIT RES MELIUS IRE QUAM PUTARAM.
 (XIV, 15, 2)

133. MULTUM PROFECTO PROFICIAM.
 (XIV, 17, 2)

134. NOS PILIAM DILIGENTER TUEBIMUR.
 (XIV, 19, 6)

135. MEUM MIHI PLACEBAT, ILLI SUUM.
 (XIV, 20, 3)

136. CUM PANSA VIXI IN POMPEIANO.
     (XIV, 20, 4)

137. STOMACHOR OMNIA.
     (XIV, 21, 3)

138. NAM APERTE LAETATI SUMUS.
     (XIV, 22, 2)

139. DOLABELLAM SPERO DOMI ESSE.
     (XV, 1, 2)

140. DE REGINA RUMOR EXSTINGUITUR.
     (XV, 1, 5)

141. ITAQUE ALIA COGITAT.
     (XV, 2, 3)

142. COGNOVI DE ALEXIONE QUAE DESIDERABAM.
     (XV, 3, 2)

143. EXCISA ENIM EST ARBOR, NON EVULSA.
     (XV, 4, 2)

144. EPISTULAM TIBI MISI.
     (XV, 5, 1)

145. NUNC EXSPECTO A TE LITTERAS.
     (XV, 6, 4)

146. NEC AUDENT NEC IAM POSSUNT.
     (XV, 10)

147. ID MIHI HERI VESPERI NUNTIATUM EST.
     (XV, 11, 4)

148. INTEREA IN ISDEM LOCIS ERANT FUTURI.
     (XV, 12, 1)

149. SCRIBES IGITUR QUICQUID AUDIERIS.
     (XV, 13, 2)

150. REGINAM ODI.
     (XV, 15, 2)

151. SEMEL EUM OMNINO DOMI MEAE VIDI.
     (XV, 15, 2)

152. NON PLACET.
     (XV, 17, 1)

153. PRORSUS NON MIHI VIDEOR ESSE TUTUS.
     (XV, 18, 2)

154. FACIES OMNIA MIHI NOTA.
     (XV, 19, 2)

155. SED HUMANA FERENDA.
     (XV, 20, 3)

156. SED VIDEBIMUS.
     (XV, 21, 3)

157. MAGNA RES EST.
     (XV, 25)

158. BRUTI AD TE EPISTULAM MISI.
     (XV, 29, 1)

159. QUAESIVIT EX ME PATER QUALIS ESSET FAMA.
     (XV, 29, 2)

160. MEAM PROFECTIONEM LAUDARI GAUDEO.
    (XVI, 1, 3)

161. BRUTO TUAE LITTERAE GRATAE ERANT.
    (XVI, 2, 3)

162. NOSTI RELIQUA.
    (XVI, 2, 4)

163. ATTICAM NOSTRAM CUPIO ABSENTEM SUAVIARI.
    (XVI, 3, 6)

164. MIRIFICE EST CONTURBATUS.
    (XVI, 4, 1)

165. SED HAEC HACTENUS; RELIQUA CORAM.
    (XVI, 7, 6)

166. MAGNA MOLITUR.
    (XVI, 8, 1)

167. IAM IAMQUE VIDEO BELLUM.
    (XVI, 9)

168. GRAVEDO TUA MIHI MOLESTA EST.
    (XVI, 11, 3)

169. NIHIL LEGI HUMANIUS.
    (XVI, 13, 1)

170. REM TIBI TIRO NARRABIT.
    (XVI, 13A, 1)

171. VIDEBIS IGITUR ET SCRIBES.
    (XVI, 14, 4)

172. IUCUNDISSIMAS TUAS LEGI LITTERAS.
    (XVI, 16, 1)

(B) AD QUINTUM FRATREM

173. SAEPE AD TE SCRIPSI.
    (I, 2, 3 §8)

174. IBATUR IN EAM SENTENTIAM.
    (II, 1, 3)

175. SED EGO ADHUC EMI NIHIL.
    (II, 2, 1)

176. TUI NOSTRIQUE VALENT.
    (II, 2, 4)

177. IS ERAT AEGER.
    (II, 3, 5)

178. RES AUTEM ROMANAE SESE SIC HABENT.
    (II, 5, 2)

179. POSTEA SUNT HAEC ACTA.
    (II, 6, 1)

180. CONSOLABOR TE ET OMNEM ABSTERGEBO DOLOREM.
    (II, 9, 4)

181. HOC ENIM UTITUR VERBO.
    (II, 16, 5)

182. SED AD TUAS VENIO LITTERAS.
     (III, 1, 5 §17)

183. HABES FORENSIA.
     (III, 2, 3)

184. NIHIL DICAM GRAVIUS.
     (III, 4, 2)

185. SINE ULLA ME HERCULE IRONIA LOQUOR.
     (III, 4, 4)

186. SED HAEC NON CURARE DECREVI.
     (III, 5, 9)

(C) **AD TERENTIAM UXOREM** [AD FAMILIARES]

187. SED VIDEO IN TE ESSE OMNIA.
     (XIV, 2, 3)

188. SED HAEC MINORA SUNT.
     (XIV, 4, 4)

189. NAVEM SPERO NOS VALDE BONAM HABERE.
     (XIV, 7, 2)

190. SI VALES, BENE EST, EGO VALEO.
     (XIV, 8)

191. SI VOS VALETIS, NOS VALEMUS.
     (XIV, 14, 1)

192. TULLIAM ADHUC MECUM TENEO.
     (XIV, 15)

(D) **AD TIRONEM** [AD FAMILIARES]

193. HAEC PRO TUO INGENIO CONSIDERA.
     (XVI, 1, 3)

194. NOS AGEMUS OMNIA MODICE.
     (XVI, 9, 3)

195. EQUUM ET MULUM BRUNDISI TIBI RELIQUI.
     (XVI, 9, 3)

196. NOS ADSUMUS.
     (XVI, 10, 2)

197. HAEC TE SCIRE VOLUI.
     (XVI, 11, 3)

198. SED HAEC CORAM.
     (XVI, 17, 1)

199. ANTERUM TIBI COMMENDO.
     (XVI, 21, 8)

200. MECUM ES, SI TE CURAS.
     (XVI, 22, 1)

INTERROGATIONES BREVES FACILESQVE
EX CICERONIS COLLECTAE EPISTVLIS

*short and easy questions gathered
from the letters of Cicero*

(A) AD ATTICUM

201. NOVI TIBI QUIDNAM SCRIBAM?
(I, 13, 6)

202. QUIDNAM ID EST?
(II, 7, 4)

203. QUO ME VERTAM?
(II, 14, 2)

204. QUID ENIM SUM?
(III, 15, 2)

205. QUID IGITUR CAUSAE FUIT?
(IV, 2, 5)

206. QUID QUAERIS ALIUD?
(IV, 17, 5)

207. HUNC TU NON AMES?
(IV, 19, 2)

208. SED QUID PLURA?
(IV, 19, 2)

209. QUID EST PRAETEREA?
(V, 10, 5)

210. QUID EGO FACIAM?
(V, 20, 1)

211. QUID EST IGITUR QUOD LABOREM?
(VI, 3, 5)

212. PLACET HOC TIBI?
(VI, 6, 2)

213. QUAESO, QUID NOBIS FUTURUM EST?
(VI, 9, 5)

214. QUID DICAM?
(VII, 1, 4)

215. QUID SUPEREST?
(VII, 3, 12)

216. QUID MULTA?
    (VII, 4, 3)

217. QUID NUNC PUTAS?
    (VII, 9, 3)

218. QUAESO, QUID EST HOC?
    (VII, 11, 1)

219. VIDESNE ME ETIAM IOCARI?
    (VII, 17, 1)

220. EGO QUID AGAM?
    (VII, 22, 2)

221. SED QUID FACIAMUS?
    (VII, 23, 1)

222. QUO IGITUR HAEC SPECTAT ORATIO?
    (VIII, 2, 4)

223. QUID ENIM FIERI POTEST?
    (VIII, 3, 6)

224. ACCIPIAM? QUID FOEDIUS?
    (IX, 2A, 1)

225. QUID FECI NON CONSIDERATISSIME?
    (IX, 10, 2)

226. ECQUID ACERBIUS, ECQUID CRUDELIUS?
    (IX, 14, 2)

227. SED QUID REFERT?
    (IX, 19, 2)

228. QUID TURPIUS?
    (X, 8, 4)

229. DE PUERIS QUID AGAM?
    (X, 11, 4)

230. QUO ME NUNC VERTAM?
    (X, 12, 1)

231. QUID PROVIDEAM?
    (X, 12A, 1)

232. QUID SCRIBAM AUT QUID VELIM?
    (XI, 7, 6)

233. QUID MIHI IGITUR PUTAS AGENDUM?
    (XI, 15, 1)

234. SED QUID ME ID LEVAT?
    (XI, 15, 2)

235. QUID ERGO OPUS EST EPISTULĀ?
    (XII, 1, 2)

236. AIN TU? VERUM HOC FUIT?
    (XII, 6, 2)

237. SED QUID DIFFERO?
    (XII, 7, 1)

238. QUAMQUAM QUID AD ME?
    (XII, 17)

239. SED TAMEN ECQUID IMPURIUS?
    (XII, 38, 2)

240. SED QUID SIMILE?
   (XII, 40, 2)

241. QUID ENIM HABEBAS QUOD SCRIBERES?
   (XII, 42, 1)

242. SED QUID EST, QUAESO?
   (XII, 44, 3)

243. QUID ENIM INDIGNIUS?
   (XIII, 2)

244. ATTICA MEA, OBSECRO TE, QUID AGIT?
   (XIII, 13, 3)

245. DE CAESARE QUID AUDITUR?
   (XIII, 16, 2)

246. QUID TIBI DE VARRONE RESCRIBAM?
   (XIII, 24, 1)

247. SED QUID ARGUMENTOR?
   (XIII, 29, 2)

248. SED TU QUID AIS?
   (XIII, 33A, 1)

249. SED QUID FACIAT?
   (XIII, 40, 1)

250. ADVOLONE AN MANEO?
   (XIII, 40, 2)

251. TU QUID DICIS?
   (XIII, 45, 3)

252. SED QUID HAEC AD NOS?
   (XIV, 3, 2)

253. UBI TANDEM EST FUTURUS?
   (XIV, 7, 1)

254. QUID FIERI TUM POTUIT?
   (XIV, 10, 1)

255. NAUSEA IAMNE PLANE ABIIT?
   (XIV, 10, 2)

256. AN CENSEBAS ALITER?
   (XIV, 11, 1)

257. QUID AUTEM ABSURDIUS?
   (XIV, 21, 3)

258. SANUM PUTAS?
   (XV, 5, 1)

259. QUID FACIAM? PLORANDO FESSUS SUM.
   (XV, 9, 1)

260. QUID FOEDIUS?
   (XV, 10)

261. QUID ERGO AGIS?
   (XV, 11, 1)

262. QUID NOCET?
   (XV, 12, 1)

263. QUID ENIM DICAM ALIUD?
   (XV, 13, 3)

264. QUOUSQUE LUDEMUR?
(XV, 22)

265. QUID AD HAEC PANSA?
(XV, 22)

266. QUID ENIM MIHI MEIS IUCUNDIUS?
(XV, 29, 1)

267. OBSECRO TE, QUID EST HOC?
(XV, 29, 3)

268. VIDESNE QUAM BLANDE?
(XVI, 2, 2)

269. IOCARI ME PUTAS?
(XVI, 5, 3)

270. CUR EGO TECUM NON SUM?
(XVI, 6, 2)

271. TERENTIAE VERO QUID EGO DICAM?
(XVI, 6, 3)

272. ITANE, MI ATTICE?
(XVI, 7, 3)

273. NUM REDIIT IPSE POSTRIDIE?
(XVI, 7, 7)

274. O BRUTE, UBI ES?
(XVI, 8, 2)

275. QUIS VENIET?
(XVI, 11, 6)

276. DE RELIQUO QUID TIBI EGO DICAM?
(XVI, 13B, 2)

(B) AD QUINTUM FRATREM

277. EGO TIBI IRASCERER?
(I, 3, 1)

278. TIBI EGO POSSEM IRASCI?
(I, 3, 1)

279. EGO TE VIDERE NOLUERIM?
(I, 3, 1)

280. QUID QUOD EODEM TEMPORE DESIDERO FILIAM?
(I, 3, 3)

281. TU METUIS NE ME INTERPELLES?
(II, 9, 1)

282. SED QUID AGO?
(II, 14, 2)

283. QUID PRAETEREA? QUID?
(III, 1, 6 §24)

284. QUID PLURA DE IUDICIBUS?
(III, 4, 1)

(C) **AD APPIUM** [AD FAMILIARES]

285. FACTA NECNE FACTA LARGITIO, IGNORARI POTEST?
(III, 11, 2)

(D) **AD VOLUMINUM** [AD FAMILIARES]

286. QUID? TU ID PATERIS?
(VII, 32, 1)

287. NON ME DEFENDIS? NONNE RESISTIS?
(VII, 32, 1)

(E) **AD PLANCUM** [AD FAMILIARES]

288. QUID ERGO POTISSIMUM SCRIBAM?
(IX, 3)

(F) **AD PAPIRIUS PAETUS** [AD FAMILIARES]

289. SED QUID HAEC LOQUIMUR?
(IX, 16, 9)

(G) **AD TERENTIAM UXOREM** [AD FAMILIARES]

290. NAM QUID EGO DE CICERONE DICAM?
(XIV, 1, 1)

291. QUID FUTURUM EST?
(XIV, 1, 5)

292. NON ROGEM?
(XIV, 4, 3)

293. SINE TE IGITUR SIM?
(XIV, 4, 3)

294. SED QUID TULLIOLĀ MEĀ FIET?
(XIV, 4, 3)

295. QUID? CICERO MEUS QUID AGET?
(XIV, 4, 3)

296. NUNC MISER QUANDO TUAS LITTERAS ACCIPIAM?
(XIV, 4, 5)

297. QUIS AD ME PERFERET?
(XIV, 4, 5)

(H) **AD TIRONEM** [AD FAMILIARES]

298. NON SIC OPORTET?
    (XVI, 18, 1)

299. ISTE NOS TANTA IMPENSA DERIDEAT?
    (XVI, 18, 2)

300. AN PANGIS ALIQUID SOPHOCLEUM?
    (XVI, 18, 3)

IVSSA BREVIA FACILIAQVE EX
CICERONIS DELIBATA EPISTVLIS

short and easy commands gleaned
from the letters of Cicero

(A) AD ATTICUM

301. NUNC COGNOSCE REM.
    (I, 1, 3)

302. CURA UT ROMAE SIS.
    (I, 2, 2)

303. TOTUM INVESTIGA, COGNOSCE, PERSPICE.
    (I, 12, 2)

304. TU ISTA CONFICE.
    (I, 13, 6)

305. TU MANDATA EFFICE QUAE RECEPISTI.
    (I, 14, 7)

306. VIDE QUAE SINT POSTEA CONSECUTA.
    (I, 18, 3)

307. CURA, AMABO TE, CICERONEM NOSTRUM.
    (II, 2, 1)

308. VIDE LEVITATEM MEAM.
    (II, 5, 2)

309. NUNC AUDI QUOD QUAERIS.
    (II, 9, 4)

310. AC VIDE MOLLITIEM ANIMI.
    (II, 21, 3)

311. TU ISTA OMNIA VIDE ET GUBERNA.
    (III, 8, 4)

312. QUINTUM FRATREM MEUM FAC DILIGAS.
    (III, 13, 2)

313. TU, QUAESO, FESTINA AD NOS VENIRE.
    (III, 26)

314. TU MODO AD NOS VENI.
    (IV, 2, 5)

315. QUA RE ADPROPERA.
    (IV, 3, 6)

316. DIC, ORO TE, CLARIUS.
    (IV, 8A)

317. PERGE RELIQUA.
    (IV, 11, 1)

318. DIONYSIUM IUBE SALVERE.
    (IV, 14, 2)

319. NUNC ROMANAS RES ACCIPE.
    (IV, 15, 4)

320. SEQUERE NUNC ME IN CAMPUM.
    (IV, 15, 7)

321. NUNC TE OBIURGARI PATERE, SI IURE.
    (IV, 16, 7)

322. COGNOSCE CETERA.
    (IV, 17, 6)

323. SED ACCIPE ALIA.
    (IV, 18, 3)

324. LOQUERE CUM DURONIO.
    (V, 8, 3)

325. QUA RE BONO ANIMO ES.
    (V, 18, 3)

326. PERFER, SI ME AMAS.
    (V, 21, 7)

327. SED EXTREMUM AUDI.
    (VI, 1, 25)

328. COGNOSCE NUNC CETERA.
    (VI, 2, 10)

329. ADDE ILLUD.
    (VI, 6, 4)

330. NUNC AUDI RELIQUA.
    (VII, 1, 2)

331. AGE, A CAELIO MUTUABIMUR.
    (VII, 3, 11)

332. DATE IGITUR OPERAM UT VALEATIS.
    (VII, 5, 2)

333. CURA IGITUR UT VALEAS.
    (VII, 5, 5)

334. AD SUMMAM, DIC, M. TULLI.
    (VII, 7, 7)

335. HABE MEAM RATIONEM.
    (VII, 9, 4)

336. HAEC TU MIHI EXPLICA QUALIA SINT.
    (VII, 11, 4)

337. ET VIDE QUAM CONVERSA RES SIT.
    (VIII, 13, 2)

338. TU, QUAESO, COGITA QUID DEINDE.
    (IX, 17, 2)

339. TU ANTONI LEONES PERTIMESCAS CAVE.
    (X, 13, 1)

340. ORO, OBSECRO, IGNOSCE.
     (XI, 2, 3)

341. TUIS SALUTEM DIC.
     (XI, 3, 3)

342. IGNOSCE, OBSECRO TE.
     (XI, 7, 6)

343. QUOQUO MODO CONFICE.
     (XII, 12, 1)

344. PILIAM ANGI VETA.
     (XII, 14, 4)

345. COCCEIUS VIDE NE FRUSTRETUR.
     (XII, 18, 2)

346. MODERARE IGITUR, QUAESO, UT POTES.
     (XII, 22, 1)

347. TU TAMEN, SI QUID POTES, ODORARE.
     (XII, 22, 3)

348. DE OVIA CONFICE, UT SCRIBIS.
     (XII, 24, 1)

349. DE HORTIS, QUAESO, EXPLICA.
     (XII, 29, 2)

350. VIDE, QUAESO, QUID AGENDUM SIT.
     (XII, 32, 1)

351. QUA RE ETIAM OTHONEM VIDE.
     (XII, 37A, 4)

352. PERFICE IGITUR ALIQUID.
     (XII, 44, 2)

353. HIRTI LIBRUM, UT FACIS, DIVULGA.
     (XII, 48, 3)

354. DE LINGUA LATINA SECURI ES ANIMI.
     (XII, 52, 3)

355. MEA MANDATA, UT SCRIBIS, EXPLICA.
     (XIII, 23, 3)

356. CONFICE, MI ATTICE, ISTAM REM.
     (XIII, 31, 4)

357. IUVA ME, QUAESO, CONSILIO.
     (XIII, 38, 2)

358. SUBACCUSA, QUAESO, VESTORIUM.
     (XIII, 46, 3)

359. RECORDARE TUA.
     (XIV, 14, 3)

360. SEQUERE NUNC ME IN CAMPUM.
     (XIV, 15, 7)

361. AUDI IGITUR AD OMNES.
     (XIV, 20, 2)

362. NUNC AUDI AD ALTERAM.
     (XV, 17, 2)

363. VIDE, QUAESO, NE QUID TEMERE FIAT.
     (XV, 19, 1)

364. NOMINA MEA, PER DEOS, EXPEDI, EXSOLVE.
(XVI, 6, 3)

365. NUNC NEGLEGENTIAM MEAM COGNOSCE.
(XVI, 6, 4)

366. AD HAEC RESCRIBE.
(XVI, 9)

367. QUAESO, ADHIBE QUAM SOLES DILIGENTIAM.
(XVI, 11, 3)

368. GRAVEDINI, QUAESO, OMNI RATIONE SUBVENI.
(XVI, 14, 4)

369. DA OPERAM UT VALEAS.
(XVI, 16A, 7)

370. OMITTE ATTICUM.
(XVI, 16C, 10)

(B) AD QUINTUM FRATREM

371. MI FRATER, VALE.
(II, 5, 5)

372. VALE, MI SUAVISSIME ET OPTIME FRATER.
(III, 5, 9)

373. CURA, MI CARISSIME FRATER, UT VALEAS.
(III, 6, 6)

374. MI SUAVISSIME ET OPTIME FRATER, VALE.
(III, 7, 9)

(C) AD CURIUM [AD FAMILIARES]

375. ITA CANINIO CONSULE SCITO NEMINEM PRANDISSE.
(VII, 30, 1)

(D) AD SILIUM [AD FAMILIARES]

376. FAC, QUOD FACIS UT ME AMES.
(XIII, 47)

(E) AD TERENTIAM UXOREM [AD FAMILIARES]

377. TULLIOLAE ET CICERONI SALUTEM DIC.
(XIV, 1, 6)

378. VALETE, MEA DESIDERIA, VALETE.
(XIV, 2, 4)

379. CURA UT VALEAS. VALE.
(XIV, 8)

380. VALETUDINEM TUAM CURA DILIGENTER.
(XIV, 11)

381. QUA RE QUANTUM POTES ADIUVA.
   (XIV, 12)

382. VALETUDINEM TUAM FAC UT CURES.
   (XIV, 24)

(F) AD TIRONEM [AD FAMILIARES]

383. CURA ERGO POTISSIMUM UT VALEAS.
   (XVI, 1, 3)

384. MI TIRO, CONSULITO NAVIGATIONI.
   (XVI, 4, 3)

385. VALE, MI TIRO, VALE, VALE ET SALVE.
   (XVI, 4, 3)

386. VIDE QUANTA SIT IN TE SUAVITAS.
   (XVI, 5, 1)

387. EI TE TOTUM TRADE.
   (XVI, 5, 2)

388. ETIAM ATQUE ETIAM, TIRO NOSTER, VALE.
   (XVI, 7)

389. AMA NOS ET VALE.
   (XVI, 8, 2)

390. VALE, SALVE.
   (XVI, 9, 4)

391. FAC PLANE UT VALEAS.
   (XVI, 10, 2)

392. CONSERVA TE MIHI.
   (XVI, 14, 2)

393. CURA TE ETIAM ATQUE ETIAM DILIGENTER.
   (XVI, 15, 2)

394. FAC OPUS APPAREAT.
   (XVI, 18, 3)

395. TE QUANDO EXSPECTEMUS FAC UT SCIAM.
   (XVI, 18, 3)

396. CURA TE DILIGENTER.
   (XVI, 18, 3)

397. SED CONFICE.
   (XVI, 19)

398. CURA TE, SI ME AMAS, DILIGENTER.
   (XVI, 20)

399. DE TRICLINIO CURA, UT FACIS.
   (XVI, 22, 1)

400. ME AMA. VALE. (QUINTUS CICERO.)
   (XVI, 27, 2)

EXCLAMATIONES BREVES FACILESQVE EX

CICERONIS EXCERPTAE EPISTVLIS

short and easy exclamations taken out
of the letters of Cicero

(A) **AD ATTICUM**

401. ABS TE TAM DIU NIHIL LITTERARUM!
    (I, 2, 1)

402. HOC EST ROMĀ DECEDERE!
    (II, 15, 3)

403. ITERUM DICO "UTINAM ADESSES!"
    (II, 19, 5)

404. UTINAM MODO AGATUR ALIQUID!
    (III, 15, 6)

405. UTINAM MODO CONATA EFFICERE POSSIM!
    (IV, 16, 2)

406. O REM MINIME APTAM MEIS MORIBUS!
    (V, 10, 3)

407. QUOD SUPEREST, DI IUVENT!
    (V, 11, 4)

408. SED HEUS TU!
    (VI, 1, 13)

409. O REM TOTAM ODIOSAM!
    (VI, 4, 1)

410. ID QUIDEM, INQUIS, DI ADPROBENT!
    (VI, 6, 1)

411. PER FORTUNAS!
    (VII, 1, 2)

412. SIBI HABEAT SUAM FORTUNAM!
    (VII, 11, 1)

413. REDEAMUS AD NOSTRUM. PER FORTUNAS!
    (VII, 11, 3)

414. O PERDITUM LATRONEM!
    (VII, 18, 2)

415. O REM MISERAM ET INCREDIBILEM!
(VII, 21, 1)

416. O CELERITATEM INCREDIBILEM!
(VII, 22, 1)

417. O ME MISERUM!
(VII, 23, 1)

418. DE QUA UTINAM ALIQUANDO TECUM LOQUAR!
(VIII, 2, 4)

419. SED EN MEAM MANSUETUDINEM!
(VIII, 5, 1)

420. O REM TURPEM ET EĀ RE MISERAM!
(VIII, 8, 1)

421. O REM LUGUBREM!
(VIII, 8, 2)

422. UTINAM ALIQUID PROFECTUM ESSET!
(VIII, 9, 2)

423. O REM DIFFICILEM PLANEQUE PERDITAM!
(IX, 2A, 1)

424. QUANTO NUNC HOC IDEM ACCIPIET ASPERIUS!
(IX, 2A, 1)

425. MISEROS NOS!
(IX, 12, 1)

426. O TEMPUS MISERUM!
(IX, 17, 1)

427. RELIQUA, O DI!
(IX, 18, 2)

428. O REM PERDITAM!
(IX, 18, 2)

429. O COPIAS DESPERATAS!
(IX, 18, 2)

430. HOMINES RIDICULOS!
(X, 3A, 2)

431. O REM FOEDAM!
(X, 4, 8)

432. O VIM INCREDIBILEM MOLESTIARUM!
(X, 10, 6)

433. O REM UNDIQUE MISERAM!
(X, 11, 4)

434. SIT MODO RECTE IN HISPANIIS!
(X, 12, 2)

435. UTINAM PROFICERE POSSIM!
(X, 12, 3)

436. SED DI ISTOS!
(X, 15, 4)

437. O, SI ID FUERIT, TURPEM CATONEM!
(X, 16, 3)

438. O MULTAS ET GRAVES OFFENSIONES!
(XI, 7, 3)

439. QUOD UTINAM ITA ESSET!
     (XI, 12, 3)

440. QUAE CENAE, QUAE DELICIAE!
     (XII, 2, 2)

441. O GRATAS TUAS MIHI IUCUNDASQUE LITTERAS!
     (XII, 4, 1)

442. O HOMINEM CAVENDUM!
     (XII, 38, 2)

443. O TEMPORA!
     (XII, 49, 2)

444. ID HERCLE RESTABAT!
     (XIII, 13, 1)

445. HUI, QUAM DIU DE NUGIS!
     (XIII, 21A, 2)

446. O REM ACERBAM!
     (XIII, 22, 3)

447. O GULAM INSULSAM!
     (XIII, 31, 4)

448. O NEGLEGENTIAM MIRAM!
     (XIII, 33, 1)

449. O REM INDIGNAM!
     (XIII, 35, 1)

450. O INCREDIBILEM VANITATEM!
     (XIII, 39, 1)

451. O SUAVES TUAS LITTERAS!
     (XIII, 44, 1)

452. TU TAMEN AUSUS ES VARRONI DARE!
     (XIII, 44, 2)

453. O MAGISTRUM MOLESTUM!
     (XIII, 47)

454. QUOD UTINAM! ITERUM UTINAM!
     (XIII, 48, 1)

455. O PRUDENTEM OPPIUM!
     (XIV, 1, 1)

456. QUOD UTINAM DIUTIUS!
     (XIV, 3, 1)

457. O MEAM STULTAM VERECUNDIAM!
     (XIV, 5, 2)

458. O SOCRATE ET SOCRATICI VIRI!
     (XIV, 9, 1)

459. O DI BONI!
     (XIV, 9, 2)

460. VIVIT TYRANNIS, TYRANNUS OCCIDIT!
     (XIV, 9, 2)

461. QUAE MIHI ISTIM ADFERUNTUR!
     (XIV, 12, 1)

462. QUAE HIC VIDEO!
     (XIV, 12, 1)

463. O MIRIFICUM DOLABELLAM MEUM!
(XIV, 15, 1)

464. O HOMINEM IMPRUDENTEM!
(XIV, 18, 1)

465. ATQUE UTINAM LICEAT ISTI CONTIONARI!
(XIV, 20, 3)

466. O FACTUM MALE DE ALEXIONE!
(XV, 1, 1)

467. O REM ODIOSAM ET INEXPLICABILEM!
(XV, 4, 5)

468. DI IMMORTALES!
(XV, 9, 2)

469. O BRUTI AMANTER SCRIPTAS LITTERAS!
(XV, 10)

470. ET HEUS TU!
(XV, 11, 4)

471. O NEGOTIA NON FERENDA!
(XV, 12, 2)

472. CAUTUM MARCELLUM!
(XV, 13, 3)

473. HUI, QUAM TIMEO QUID EXISTIMES!
(XV, 13, 7)

474. O TURPEM SORORIS TUAE FILIUM!
(XV, 27, 3)

475. QUOD PROMITTIS DI FAXINT!
(XV, 29, 1)

476. MACTE!
(XV, 29, 3)

477. DI HERCULE ISTIS!
(XVI, 1, 1)

478. QUAM ILLE DOLUIT DE NONIS IULIIS!
(XVI, 4, 1)

479. ATQUE UTINAM TE ILLIC!
(XVI, 5, 4)

480. DI ISTIS!
(XVI, 11, 5)

481. MORIAR NISI FACETE!
(XVI, 11, 1)

482. O QUALES TU SEMPER ISTOS!
(XVI, 11, 5)

483. O CASUM MIRIFICUM!
(XVI, 13, 1)

484. O SESTI TABELLARIUM HOMINEM NEQUAM!
(XVI, 14, 2)

485. AT QUAE CONTIO!
(XVI, 15, 3)

(B) **AD QUINTUM FRATREM**

486. QUEM HOMINEM, QUĀ IRĀ, QUO SPIRITU!
(I, 2, 2 §6)

487. SED HAEC UTINAM NE EXPERIARE!
(I, 3, 9)

488. QUID QUAERIS? NIHIL FESTIVIUS!
(II, 6, 2)

489. O ME SOLLICITUM!
(III, 1, 5 §17)

490. O DI!
(III, 2, 2)

(C) **AD APPIUS** [AD FAMILIARES]

491. ME MISERUM, QUI NON ADFUERIM!
(III, 11, 3)

492. QUOS EGO RISUS EXCITASSEM!
(III, 11, 3)

(D) **AD BRUTUM** [AD FAMILIARES]

493. QUAM MULTA QUAM PAUCIS!
(XI, 24,1)

494. QUI UTINAM IAM ADESSET!
(XI, 25)

(E) **AD TERENTIAM UXOREM** [AD FAMILIARES]

495. UTINAM EA RES EI VOLUPTATI SIT!
(XIV, 1, 4)

496. QUOD UTINAM MINUS VITAE CUPIDI FUISSEMUS!
(XIV, 4, 1)

497. O ME PERDITUM! O ADFLICTUM!
(XIV, 4, 3)

498. HUIC UTINAM ALIQUANDO GRATIAM REFERRE POSSIMUS!
(XVI, 4, 2)

(F) **AD TIRONEM** [AD FAMILIARES]

499. SI VERO ETIAM TUSCULANUM, DEI BONI!
(XVI, 18, 1)

500. QUANTO MIHI ILLUD ERIT AMABILIUS!
(XVI, 18, 1)

ADDITAMENTVM
ROMANORVM DE KALENDARIO

an addition
about the Roman calendar

Cicero dates many of his letters, so we offer here in one place a few comments on the Roman calendar in four little principles.

One caution must be noted inasmuch as the calendar was radically changing almost from year to year until the year 46 BCE, when Julius Caesar with the help of Egyptian astronomers established the Julian calendar, which was corrected in 1582 by Pope Gregory XIII. Consequently for the sake of coherence the chronology of the letters is the same as that presented in Tyrrell and Purser as well as Shackleton Bailey, which was calculated according to the Julian calendar. The date of any letter written before 46 BCE may be off by as many as two months from the date we give according to the Julian calendar, and again the calendar varied every year until 46 BCE. Historians will find invaluable the compete table provided by William Korb in the *Onomasticon Tullianum*.

A. The first little principle on the Roman calendar is that dates are basically given in the by-with-from-in function, that is, the abl. of time at which.

B. The incredible phenomenon of this Roman calendar is that they calculate days by counting the days backward from three pivotal days of the month. These three pivotal days of the whole month are:

The *Kalendae, Kalendarum*, f., pl., "the Kalends" are the 1st day of the month.

The *Nonae, Nonarum*, f., pl., "the Nones" are usually the 5th day of the month, but they are the 7th day of the months of March, May, July, and October.

The *Idus, Iduum*, f., pl., "the Ides" are usually the 13th day of the month, but the 15th day of the months of March, May, July, and October. How they ever lived with this!

Putting the first and second principle together, if the Romans want to say "on the Kalends" or "on the Nones" or "on the Ides," they use these three words in the abl. of time, namely *Kalendis, Nonis, Idibus*. We can also add that in classical not ecclesiastical Latin the names of the months are adjectives, namely, *Kalendis Ianuariis*, "on the January Kalends" or "on 1 January"; *Nonis Martiis*, "on the March Nones" or "on 7 March"; *Idibus Septembribus*, "on the September Ides" or "on 13 September."

C. All the other days of the month are calculated by counting backwards from these three pivotal days, with the reminder that the Romans include in their calculation both days, the pivotal one and the one they wish to designate. For example, given that the March Nones are on the 7th, the Romans calculate the date 2 March by starting with the Nones and counting backward: 7th, 6th, 5th, 4th, 3rd, 2nd, for a total of six days, so they call 2 March, "the sixth day before the March Nones." We'll get to the Latin formulae in a minute. The March Ides are on the 15th, so they calculate 10 March by starting with the Ides and counting backward: 15th, 14th, 13th, 12th, 11th, 10th, for a total of six days, so they call 10 March, "the sixth day before the March Ides." The days after the Ides are calculated by counting backward from the following Kalends, the Kalends of the next month. March has 31 days, so they calculate 23 March by beginning with 1 April and counting backward thus: 1st April, 31st March, 30th, 29th, 28th, 27th, 26th, 25th, 24th, 23rd March, for a total of ten days, so they call 23 March, "the tenth day before the April Kalends."

To calculate the same dates in September, we begin with the September Nones on the 5th, and then we count backward: 5th, 4th, 3rd, 2nd, for a total of four days, so we can call 2 September, "the fourth day before the September Nones." The September Ides are on the 13th, so we can calculate 10 September by starting with the Ides and counting backward, 13th, 12th, 11th, 10th, for a total of four days, so we can call 10 September, "the fourth day before the September Ides." September has 30 days, so we can calculate 23 September by beginning with 1 October and counting backward thus: 1st October, 30th September, 29th, 28th, 27th, 26th, 25th, 24th, 23rd September, for a total of nine days. So we can call 23 September, "the ninth day before the October Kalends."

There is arithmetic for calculating the same dates. The March Nones are on the 7th, so we can calculate 2 March by subtracting 2 from 7, which equals 5, but then we must add 1 so that we include the day on each end. Thus, $7 - 2 = 5$ and then $5 + 1 = 6$, which tells us that 2 March is the sixth day before the March Nones. The March Ides are on the 15th, so we can calculate 10 March following the arithmetic $15 - 10 = 5$ and $5 + 1 = 6$, which tells us that 10 March is the sixth day before the March Ides. The dates after the Ides are calculated differently, beginning with the last day of the month. Thus, March has 31 days, so we can calculate 23 March by subtracting 23 from 31, and then adding 2, because we began our calculation not with the Kalends but with the last day of March. Thus, 31 − 23 = 8 and 8 + 2 = 10, which tells us that 23 March is the tenth day before the Kalends of April.

The January Nones are on the 5th, so we can calculate 2 January by subtracting 2 from 5, which equals 3, but then we must add 1. Thus, 5 − 2 = 3 and then 3 + 1 = 4, which tells us that 2 January is the fourth day before the January Nones. The January Ides are on the 13th, so we can calculate 10 January following the arithmetic 13 − 10 = 3 and 3 + 1 = 4, which tells us that 10 January is the fourth day before the January Ides. January has 31 days, so we can calculate 23 January by subtracting 23 from 31, and then adding 2. Thus, 31 − 23 = 8 and 8 + 2 = 10, which tells us that 23 January is the tenth day before the Kalends of February.

D. The final principle gives the Latin forms to express these dates. We have said that the dates which fall on the pivotal days are expressed in the abl. of time without a preposition.

Dates which do not fall on the pivotal dates are expressed in two ways. One is to combine the ordinal number, such as "on the fourth day," given in the abl. of time and combined with the object form of the pivotal day and the month, so 2 March is (*die*) *sexto Nonas Martias*, where *die*, "on the day," may be omitted; *sexto*, "on the sixth," is the ordinal number in the abl. of time; and *Nonas Martias* is the object form of the pivotal day with which the month agrees as an adjective. For example, 10 March is (*die*) *sexto Idus Martias*, and 23 March is (*die*) *decimo Kalendas Apriles*.

The reason the pivotal day and its adjective month are in the object form is because the phenomenon above is a simplification of the fuller formula where the preposition *ante*, "before," produces the object form, *die decimo ante Kalendas Apriles* or *die sexto ante Idus Martias* or *die sexto ante Nonas Martias*.

The second phenomenon found in Cicero's letters and everywhere really has no justification. The word *ante* is placed in front of the date, and the entire date was put in the object form and this entire expression became a stock formula. For example, the Romans say *ante diem quartum Nonas Septembres*, "before the fourth day, the Nones of September," where you almost feel that the word *ante* should be before *Nonas*, but they put it out in front and made the whole expression a set formula. For example, 10 September is *ante diem quartum Idus Septembres*, "before the fourth day, the September Ides," and 23 September is *ante diem nonum Kalendas Octobres*.

Both of these formulae the *die septimo . . .*, and *ante diem septimum . . .* are found in Cicero's letters. That is why we have spent so much time, energy, and space expounding this as simply as possible.

The Romans did not assign a number to the day before the Kalends, Nones or Ides. Rather, the adverb *pridie*, "the day before," accompanies the pivotal day, so the date *pridie Kalendas Ianuarias* is 31 December, and *pridie Nonas Ianuarias* is 4 January and *pridie Idus Ianuarias* is 12 January. For the month of September *pridie Kalendas Septembres* is 31 August. *Pridie Idus Septembres* is 12 September.

No wonder later Latin, including church Latin from the fourth century, took refuge in a simpler formula that some non-classicists are using all around the world today. We say, "on the fourth day of August," *die quarto (mensis) Augusti*, where the abl. of time is used for the number and the name of the month is given as a noun in the of-possession form, sometimes with the word *mensis* as in "of the month of August."

Lest anyone think this insanity has run its course, they may be encouraged to see that the correspondence of the old Roman calendar to the current ecclesiastical designations is still given in the most recent Latin editions of the liturgical books of the Church of Rome. This old system is still used with great beauty and solemnity at the beginning of Mass on Christmas Eve, when the sung martyrology begins: *Octavo Kalendas Ianuarii*, "on the eighth day before the Kalends of January," that is to say on 25 December. The phrase mixes *octavo Kalendas*, of the Roman system, with *Ianuarii*, "of January," according to the later Italian, ecclesiastical system.

APPENDICES

BIBLIOGRAPHIA

bibliography

The letters of Cicero were taken from the following volumes.

The Correspondence of M. Tullius Cicero: Arranged According to Its Chronological Order; with a Revision of the Text, a Commentary, and Introductory Essays. Edited by Robert Yelverton Tyrrell and Louis Claude Purser. Hodges, Figgis & Co.–Longmans, Green & Co.: Dublin–London, 1904 (vol. 1, 3rd ed.), 1906 (vol. 2, 2nd ed.), 1914 (vol. 3, 2nd ed.), 1918 (vol. 4, 2nd ed.), 1915 (vol. 5, 2nd ed.), 1933 (vol. 6, 2nd ed.), 1901 (vol. 7, 1st ed.); repr. Georg Olms, Hildesheim, 1969.

OTHER PRIMARY REFERENCES

HORATIUS FLACCUS, QUINTUS. *Opera.* Edited by E. C. Wickham and H. W. Garrod. Scriptorum classicorum bibliotheca oxoniensis. Oxford: Clarendon Press, 1901.

CICERO, MARCUS TULLIUS. *Oratio Philippica.* In *M. Tulli Ciceronis Orationes.* Edited by A. C. Clark. Scriptorum classicorum bibliotheca oxoniensis. 2nd ed. Oxford: Clarendon Press, 1918, repr. 1956.

INSTRUMENTA

W. A. OLDFATHER, H. V. CANTER, and K. M. ABBOT. *Index Verborum Ciceronis Epistularum.* Hildesheim: Georg Olms, 1965; repr. Urbana, Ill.: University of Illinois Press, 1938.

H. MERGUET. *Handlexikon zu Cicero.* Hildesheim: Georg Olms, 1962; repr. Leipzig, 1905–1906.

Onomasticon Tullianum continens M. Tullii Ciceronis vitam historiam litterariam, indicem geographicum et historicum indicem legum et formularum indicem graeco-latinum, fastos consulares. 3 vols. Edited by I. C. Orellius and I. G. Baiterus. Hildesheim: Georg Olms, 1965.

The five hundred sentences of Cicero were first presented by R. Foster at the International Congress for the Promotion of Latin Letters and Language held in Malta 30 August–4 September 1973, published in *Acta omnium gentium ac nationum conventus latinis litteris linguae fovendis: A die XXX mensis Augusti ad diem IV mensis Septembris A. D. MDCCCCLXXIII* (Malta: University of Malta, 1973), pp. 338–69.

The sentences are taken from the following editions:

M. Tulli Ciceronis Epistulae. Vol. 1, *Epistulae ad familiares.* Edited by L. C. Purser. Scriptorum classicorum bibliotheca oxoniensis. Oxford: Clarendon Press, 1901; repr. with corrections, 1957.

M. Tulli Ciceronis Epistulae. Vol. 2, *Epistulae ad Atticum,* published in 2 parts. Edited by L. C. Purser. Scriptorum classicorum bibliotheca oxoniensis. Oxford: Clarendon Press, 1903; repr. 1956 (pt. II) and 1958 (pt. I).

M. Tulli Ciceronis Epistulae. Vol. 3, *Epistulae ad Quintum fratrem; Epistulae ad M. Brutum; Fragmenta epistularum; Accedunt commentariolum petitionis et pseudo-Ciceronis epistula ad Octavianum.* Edited by W. S. Watt. Scriptorum classicorum bibliotheca oxoniensis. Oxford: Clarendon Press, 1901; repr. with corrections, 1958.

Another version

M. Tulli Ciceronis, *Epistulae.* Vol. 2, *Epistulae ad Atticum.* 2 vols. Edited by W. S. Watt. Scriptorum classicorum bibliotheca oxoniensis. Oxford: Clarendon Press, 1963; repr., 2007.

OTHER PUBLICATIONS BY THE AUTHORS:

Foster, R. T., and D. P. McCarthy. "Collectarum latinitas." In *Appreciating the Collect: An Irenic Methodology.* Edited by J. G. Leachman and D. P. McCarthy, 27–56. Documenta rerum ecclesiasticarum instaurata. Liturgiam aestimare: Appreciating the Liturgy 1. Farnborough, England: St. Michael's Abbey Press, 2008.

Leachman, J. G., and D. P. McCarthy, eds. *Appreciating the Collect: An Irenic Methodology.* Documenta rerum ecclesiasticarum instaurata. Liturgiam aestimare: Appreciating the Liturgy 1. Farnborough, England: St. Michael's Abbey Press, 2008. http://www.liturgyinstitute.org/appreciating-the-collect

McCarthy, D. P. "Seeing a Reflection, Considering Appearances: The History, Theology, and Literary Composition of the *Missale Romanum* at a Time of Vernacular Reflection." *Questions Liturgiques / Studies in Liturgy* 94 (2013): 109–43.

———. *Verbum ac Spiritus: Duplici de munere praesidendi coetui orationemque dirigendi = Word and Spirit: On the Double Role of Presiding in the Assembly and Directing the Prayer.* Documenta rerum ecclesiasticarum instaurata, Liturgiam artibus provehens architectura: Architecture with Arts for Liturgy 2. Farnborough, England: St. Michael's Abbey Press, forthcoming. http://www.liturgyinstitute.org/verbum

McCarthy, D. P., and J. G. Leachman. *Listen to the Word: Commentaries on Selected Opening Prayers of Sundays and Feasts with Sample Homilies; Revised from Articles That Appeared in* The Tablet, *18 March 2006–15 September 2007 Augmented with Five Homilies.* Documenta rerum ecclesiasticarum instaurata, varia. London: The Tablet Trust, 2009. http://www.liturgyinstitute.org/listen-to-the-word

———. "Listen to the Word." [Series of commentaries on the Latin texts of the proper prayers of select Sundays and feasts.] *The Tablet.* 18 March 2006–27 November 2011. http://www.danielmccarthyosb.com/prayer-commentaries

———, eds. *Transition in the Easter Vigil: Becoming Christians = Paschali in vigilia Christiani nominis fieri.* Documenta rerum ecclesiasticarum instaurata, Liturgiam aestimare: Appreciating the Liturgy 2. Farnborough, England: St. Michael's Abbey Press, 2014. http://www.liturgyinstitute.org/transition-in-the-easter-vigil

———. *Come into the Light: Church Interiors for the Celebration of Liturgy.* Documenta rerum ecclesiasticarum instaurata, Liturgiam artibus provehens architectura: Architecture with Arts for Liturgy 1. Canterbury, London: Canterbury Press in association with The Tablet, 2014. http://www.liturgyinstitute.org/come-into-the-light/

McCarthy, D. P., J. G. Leachman, and R. T. Foster. *Companion to the Missal: Reprints from The Tablet of London, Originally Published from 18 March 2006 to 26 November 2011.* Documenta rerum ecclesiasticarum instaurata, Liturgiam aestimare: Appreciating Liturgy, Varia 2. Rome: published privately at Pontificium Athenaeum Sancti Anselmi de Urbe, 2019. https://www.liturgyinstitute.org/companion/

Websites

www.thelatinlanguage.org
www.indiegogo.com/at/OSSA
www.liturgyinstitute.org
www.liturgyhome.org
www.benedictine-institute.org
www.londonspring.org
www.ealingmonks.org.uk
www.stbedelibrary.org
www.kansasmonks.org
www.jamesleachman.com
www.danielmccarthyosb.com

INDICES

INDICES VNAS AD EPISTVLAS

indices for the letters alone

❧

INDEX EPISTOLARVM HODIERNO MODO MEMORATARVM

index of letters by modern-day reference

Ossium letter n°	*Reference*	Heading	T-P n°	page
44.	*Att.* I, 2	Cicero Attico sal.	11	139
11.	*Att.* I, 3	Cicero Attico sal.	8	31
2.	*Att.* I, 5	Cicero Attico sal.	1	5
4.	*Att.* I, 6	Cicero Attico sal.	2	13
6.	*Att.* I, 7	Cicero Attico sal.	3	17
13.	*Att.* I, 11	Cicero Attico sal.	7	35
42.	*Att.* II, 15	Cicero Attico sal.	42	133
38.	*Att.* III, 14	Cicero Attico sal.	70	119
28.	*Att.* IV, 4b	Cicero Attico sal.	107	83
20.	*Att.* IV, 10	Cicero Attico sal.	121	55
34.	*Att.* V, 6	Cicero Attico sal.	189	107
35.	*Att.* VI, 8	Cicero Attico sal.	281	109
23.	*Att.* VII, 15	Cicero Attico sal.	311	65
24.	*Att.* VII, 20	Cicero Attico sal.	318	69
40.	*Att.* VII, 22	Cicero Attico sal.	320	123
46.	*Att.* VIII, 13	Cicero Attico sal.	348	149
27.	*Att.* IX, 11A	Cicero imp. s. d. Caesari imp.	366	79
47.	*Att.* X, 3a	Cicero Attico sal.	381	151
15.	*Att.* XI, 3	Cicero Attico sal.	411	41
17.	*Att.* XI, 4	Cicero Attico sal.	413*b*	47

Ossium letter nº	*Reference*	HEADING	T-P nº	page
30.	*Att.* XIV, 13b	CICERO ANTONIO COS. S. D.	717	87
51.	*Att.* XVI, 5	CICERO ATTICO SAL.	770	167
49.	*Brut.* I, 14	CICERO BRUTO SAL.	913	157
37.	*Brut.* II, 2	CICERO BRUTO SAL.	839	117
32.	*Fam.* I, 3	M. CICERO S. D. P. LENTULO PROCOS	97	97
39.	*Fam.* I, 6	M. CICERO S. D. P. LENTULO PROCOS.	104	121
8.	*Fam.* I, 10	M. CICERO S. D. L VALERIO IURIS CONSULTO	162	23
50.	*Fam.* II, 1	M. CICERO S. D. C. CURIONI	166	161
19.	*Fam.* II, 3	M. CICERO S. D. C. CURIONI	169	51
29.	*Fam.* II, 5	M. CICERO S. D. C. CURIONI	176	85
48.	*Fam.* V, 7	M. TULLIUS M. F. CICERO S. D. CN. POMPEIO CN. F MAGNO IMPERATORI	15	153
45.	*Fam.* VII, 5	CICERO CAESARI IMP. S. D.	134	141
7.	*Fam.* VII, 10	CICERO S. D. TREBATIO	161	19
10.	*Fam.* VII, 11	CICERO TREBATIO	167	27
22.	*Fam.* IX, 5	CICERO VARRONI	463	63
9.	*Fam.* XIII, 49	CICERO CURIO PROCOS.	163	25
12.	*Fam.* XIII, 60	M. CICERO C. MUNATIO C. F. S.	164	33
18.	*Fam.* XIV, 6	SUIS S. D.	414	49
25.	*Fam.* XIV, 7	TULLIUS TERENTIAE SUAE S. P.	405	73
14.	*Fam.* XIV, 8	TULLIUS TERENTIAE SUAE S.	410	39
5.	*Fam.* XIV, 12	TULLIUS TERENTIAE SUAE S. D.	415	15
16.	*Fam.* XIV, 16	TULLIUS TERENTIAE SUAE S. D.	424	45
31.	*Fam.* XIV, 18	TULLIUS TERENTIAE SUAE ET PATER SUAVISSIMAE FILIAE, CICERO MATRI ET SORORI S. P. D.	306	93
43.	*Fam.* XV, 7	M. CICERO PROCOS. S. D. C. MARCELLO COS. DESIG.	214	137
36.	*Fam.* XV, 10	M. CICERO IMP. S. D. C. MARCELLO C. F. COS	239	113
3.	*Fam.* XVI, 4	TULLIUS TIRONI SUO S. P. D. ET CICERO ET Q. FRATER ET Q. F.	288	9
41.	*Q. Fr.* I, 4	MARCUS QUINTO FRATRI SALUTEM	72	125
26.	*Q. Fr.* II, 6	MARCUS QUINTO FRATRI SALUTEM	117	77
21.	*Q. Fr.* II, 7 [9]	MARCUS QUINTO FRATRI SALUTEM	120	57
1.	*Q. Fr.* II, 9 [11]	MARCUS QUINTO FRATRI SALUTEM	132	3
33.	*Q. Fr.* III, 3	MARCUS QUINTO FRATRI SALUTEM	151	99

∾

INDEX EARVMDEM EX TEMPORIS RATIONE
AB TYRRELL ET PVRSER VSVRPATA

index of the same according to the chronology employed by Tyrrell and Purser

Ossium letter nº	*Reference*	HEADING	T-P nº	page
2.	*Att.* I, 5	CICERO ATTICO SAL.	1	5
4.	*Att.* I, 6	CICERO ATTICO SAL.	2	13
6.	*Att.* I, 7	CICERO ATTICO SAL.	3	17
13.	*Att.* I, 11	CICERO ATTICO SAL.	7	35
11.	*Att.* I, 3	CICERO ATTICO SAL.	8	31
44.	*Att.* I, 2	CICERO ATTICO SAL.	11	139
48.	*Fam.* V, 7	M. TULLIUS M. F. CICERO S. D. CN. POMPEIO CN. F MAGNO IMPERATORI	15	153
42.	*Att.* II, 15	CICERO ATTICO SAL.	42	133
38.	*Att.* III, 14	CICERO ATTICO SAL.	70	119
41.	*Q. Fr.* I, 4	MARCUS QUINTO FRATRI SALUTEM	72	125
32.	*Fam.* I, 3	M. CICERO S. D. P. LENTULO PROCOS.	97	97
39.	*Fam.* I, 6	M. CICERO S. D. P. LENTULO PROCOS.	104	121
28.	*Att.* IV, 4b	CICERO ATTICO SAL.	107	83
26.	*Q. Fr.* II, 6	MARCUS QUINTO FRATRI SALUTEM	117	77
21.	*Q. Fr.* II, 7 [9]	MARCUS QUINTO FRATRI SALUTEM	120	57
20.	*Att.* IV, 10	CICERO ATTICO SAL.	121	55
1.	*Q. Fr.* II, 9 [11]	MARCUS QUINTO FRATRI SALUTEM	132	3
45.	*Fam.* VII, 5	CICERO CAESARI IMP. S. D.	134	141
33.	*Q. Fr.* III, 3	MARCUS QUINTO FRATRI SALUTEM	151	99
7.	*Fam.* VII, 10	M. CICERO S. D. TREBATIO	161	19
8.	*Fam.* I, 10	M. CICERO S. D. L VALERIO IURIS CONSULTO	162	23
9.	*Fam.* XIII, 49	CICERO CURIO PROCOS.	163	25
12.	*Fam.* XIII, 60	M. CICERO C. MUNATIO C. F. S.	164	33
50.	*Fam.* II, 1	M. CICERO S. D. C. CURIONI	166	161
10.	*Fam.* VII, 11	CICERO TREBATIO	167	27
19.	*Fam.* II, 3	M. CICERO S. D. C. CURIONI	169	51
29.	*Fam.* II, 5	M. CICERO S. D. C. CURIONI	176	85
34.	*Att.* V, 6	CICERO ATTICO SAL.	189	107
43.	*Fam.* XV, 7	M. CICERO PROCOS. S. D. C. MARCELLO COS. DESIG.	214	137

Ossium letter n°	*Reference*	Heading	T-P n°	page
36.	*Fam.* XV, 10	M. Cicero imp. s. d. C. Marcello C. f. cos.	**239**	113
35.	*Att.* VI, 8	Cicero Attico sal.	**281**	109
3.	*Fam.* XVI, 4	Tullius Tironi suo s. p. d. et Cicero et Q. frater et Q. f.	**288**	9
31.	*Fam.* XIV, 18	Tullius Terentiae suae et pater suavissimae filiae, Cicero matri et sorori s. p. d.	**306**	93
23.	*Att.* VII, 15	Cicero Attico sal.	**311**	65
24.	*Att.* VII, 20	Cicero Attico sal.	**318**	69
40.	*Att.* VII, 22	Cicero Attico sal.	**320**	123
46.	*Att.* VIII, 13	Cicero Attico sal.	**348**	149
27.	*Att.* IX, 11A	Cicero imp. s. d. Caesari imp.	**366**	79
47.	*Att.* X, 3a	Cicero Attico sal.	**381**	151
25.	*Fam.* XIV, 7	Tullius Terentiae suae s. p.	**405**	73
14.	*Fam.* XIV, 8	Tullius Terentiae suae s.	**410**	39
15.	*Att.* XI, 3	Cicero Attico sal.	**411**	41
17.	*Att.* XI, 4	Cicero Attico sal.	**413***b*	47
18.	*Fam.* XIV, 6	suis s. d.	**414**	49
5.	*Fam.* XIV, 12	Tullius Terentiae suae s. d.	**415**	15
16.	*Fam.* XIV, 16	Tullius Terentiae suae s. d.	**424**	45
22.	*Fam.* IX, 5	Cicero Varroni	**463**	63
30.	*Att.* XIV, 13b	Cicero Antonio cos. s. d.	**717**	87
51.	*Att.* XVI, 5	Cicero Attico sal.	**770**	167
37.	*Brut.* II, 2	Cicero Bruto sal.	**839**	117
49.	*Brut.* I, 14	Cicero Bruto sal.	**913**	157

≈

INDEX IPSAS SECVNDVM EXCIPIENTES

index according to the ones receiving them

Ossium letter n°	Reference	HEADING	T-P n°	page
		Antonio		
30.	*Att.* XIV, 13b	CICERO ANTONIO COS. S. D.	717	87
		Attico		
44.	*Att.* I, 2	CICERO ATTICO SAL.	11	139
11.	*Att.* I, 3	CICERO ATTICO SAL.	8	31
2.	*Att.* I, 5	CICERO ATTICO SAL.	1	5
4.	*Att.* I, 6	CICERO ATTICO SAL.	2	13
6.	*Att.* I, 7	CICERO ATTICO SAL.	3	17
13.	*Att.* I, 11	CICERO ATTICO SAL.	7	35
42.	*Att.* II, 15	CICERO ATTICO SAL.	42	133
38.	*Att.* III, 14	CICERO ATTICO SAL.	70	119
28.	*Att.* IV, 4b	CICERO ATTICO SAL.	107	83
20.	*Att.* IV, 10	CICERO ATTICO SAL.	121	55
34.	*Att.* V, 6	CICERO ATTICO SAL.	189	107
35.	*Att.* VI, 8	CICERO ATTICO SAL.	281	109
23.	*Att.* VII, 15	CICERO ATTICO SAL.	311	65
24.	*Att.* VII, 20	CICERO ATTICO SAL.	318	69
40.	*Att.* VII, 22	CICERO ATTICO SAL.	320	123
46.	*Att.* VIII, 13	CICERO ATTICO SAL.	348	149
47.	*Att.* X, 3a	CICERO ATTICO SAL.	381	151
15.	*Att.* XI, 3	CICERO ATTICO SAL.	411	41
17.	*Att.* XI, 4	CICERO ATTICO SAL.	413*b*	47
51.	*Att.* XVI, 5	CICERO ATTICO SAL.	770	167
		Bruto		
49.	*Brut.* I, 14	CICERO BRUTO SAL.	913	157
37.	*Brut.* II, 2	CICERO BRUTO SAL.	839	117
		Caesari		
45.	*Fam.* VII, 5	CICERO CAESARI IMP. S. D.	134	141
27.	*Att.* IX, 11A	CICERO IMP. S. D. CAESARI IMP.	366	79

Ossium letter n°	Reference	HEADING	T-P n°	page
		Curio		
9.	*Fam.* XIII, 49	CICERO CURIO PROCOS.	163	25
		Curiono		
50.	*Fam.* II, 1	M. CICERO S. D. C. CURIONI	166	161
19.	*Fam.* II, 3	M. CICERO S. D. C. CURIONI	169	51
29.	*Fam.* II, 5	M. CICERO S. D. C. CURIONI	176	85
		Lentulo		
32.	*Fam.* I, 3	M. CICERO S. D. P. LENTULO PROCOS	97	97
39.	*Fam.* I, 6	M. CICERO S. D. P. LENTULO PROCOS.	104	121
		Marcello		
36.	*Fam.* XV, 10	M. CICERO IMP. S. D. C. MARCELLO C. F. COS	239	113
43.	*Fam.* XV, 7	M. CICERO PROCOS. S. D. C. MARCELLO COS. DESIG.	214	137
		Munatio		
12.	*Fam.* XIII, 60	M. CICERO C. MUNATIO C. F. S.	164	33
		Pompeio		
48.	*Fam.* V, 7	M. TULLIUS M. F. CICERO S. D. CN. POMPEIO CN. F MAGNO IMPERATORI	15	153
		Quinto Fratri		
41.	*Q. Fr.* I, 4	MARCUS QUINTO FRATRI SALUTEM	72	125
26.	*Q. Fr.* II, 6	MARCUS QUINTO FRATRI SALUTEM	117	77
21.	*Q. Fr.* II, 7 [9]	MARCUS QUINTO FRATRI SALUTEM	120	57
1.	*Q. Fr.* II, 9 [11]	MARCUS QUINTO FRATRI SALUTEM	132	3
33.	*Q. Fr.* III, 3	MARCUS QUINTO FRATRI SALUTEM	151	99
		Suis		
18.	*Fam.* XIV, 6	SUIS S. D.	414	49

Ossium letter n°	Reference	HEADING	T-P n°	page
		Terentiae		
25.	*Fam.* XIV, 7	TULLIUS TERENTIAE SUAE S. P.	405	73
14.	*Fam.* XIV, 8	TULLIUS TERENTIAE SUAE S.	410	39
5.	*Fam.* XIV, 12	TULLIUS TERENTIAE SUAE S. D.	415	15
16.	*Fam.* XIV, 16	TULLIUS TERENTIAE SUAE S. D.	424	45
31.	*Fam.* XIV, 18	TULLIUS TERENTIAE SUAE S. ET PATER SUAVISSIMAE FILIAE, CICERO MATRI ET SORORI S. P. D.	306	93
		Tiro		
3.	*Fam.* XVI, 4	TULLIUS TIRONI SUO S. P. D. ET CICERO ET Q. FRATER ET Q. F.	288	9
		Trebatio		
7.	*Fam.* VII, 10	CICERO S. D. TREBATIO	161	19
10.	*Fam.* VII, 11	CICERO TREBATIO	167	27
		Valerio		
8.	*Fam.* I, 10	M. CICERO S. D. L VALERIO IURIS CONSULTO	162	23
		Varroni		
22.	*Fam.* IX, 5	CICERO VARRONI	463	63

∾

INDEX VOCVM GRAECARVM

index of Greek expressions

The Greek term is given to the left as it appears in the letter by Cicero. To its immediate right is our rendering of the term in the letter of Cicero. Beneath the Greek expression is the Latin equivalent to the term as it appears in the *Onomasticon Tullianum*. To the right of the Latin equivalent is our rendering of the Latin equivalent. Finally, following the arrow is the cross-reference to the source of our understanding of the Greek term. This cross-reference includes the citation of the letter.

αἰσχρὸν σιωπᾶν   it is shameful to be silent

turpe est tacere   it is shameful to keep silent

Letter 35.5, pp. 111, 431 → **1113**

   → *Onomasticon Tullianum*;
    Att. VI, 8, 5

ἄμβροτος	immortal
immortalis	immortal
divinus	divine

Letter 51.5, pp. 175, 571 → **1671**
    → *Onomasticon Tullianum*;
    Att. XVI, 5, 5

ἀμύμων	the greatest
egregius, praeclarus	outstanding, extraordinary

Letter 51.5, pp. 175, 571 → **1670**
    → *Onomasticon Tullianum*;
    Att. XVI, 5, 5

ἀσφαλές	safe
tutum	safe
securitas	security

Letter 51.3, pp. 173, 567 → **1658**
    → *Onomasticon Tullianum*;
    Att. XVI, 5, 3

γαυριῶ	*I boast*
glorior	I boast

Letter 51.5, pp. 175, 571 → **1668**
    → *Onomasticon Tullianum*;
    Att. XVI, 5, 5

γυμνασιώδη	suitable for a gymnasium (lecture hall)
apta gymnasio	suitable for a gymnasium (academic hall)

Letter 4.2, pp. 13, 212 → **161**
    → *Onomasticon Tullianum*;
    Att. I, 6, 2

Θετικώτερον	more subtle
subtilius	more subtle

Letter 33.4, pp. 103, 412 → **1040**
    → *Onomasticon Tullianum*;
    Q. Fr. III, 3, 4

εἰλικρινὲς	pure
sincerum	genuine
purum	unmixed

Letter 26.1, pp. 77, 354 → **792**
    → *Onomasticon Tullianum*;
    Q. Fr. II, 6, 1

κακοστόμαχος	someone having a weak stomach
imbecilium stomachum habens	having a weak stomach
imbecilium ventriculum habens	having a weak belly

Letter 3.1, pp. 9, 195 → **103**

    → *Onomasticon Tullianum*;
      Fam. XVI, 4, 1

κἂν ἀποθανεῖν	bid me to die and I will dare

This rendering is suggested in Tyrrell and Purser as an explanation to an enigmatic partial quotation of a Greek text no longer extant

Letter 24.2, pp. 71, 341 → **717**

    → Purser-Tyrrell 4, p. 49, fn. 2;
      Att. VII, 20, 2

Κικέρων ἀριστοκρατικώτατος παῖς	Cicero, a most aristocratic boy
Cicero optimatium studiosissimus puer	Cicero, a boy most devoted to the first citizens
	Cicero, a boy most devoted to the elite

Letter 42.4, pp. 135, 492 → **1378**

    → *Onomasticon Tullianum*;
      Att. II, 15, 4

λόχον	troupe, assembly, gathering, family [here, of gladiators]
	a troupe of gladiators

Letter 28.2, pp. 83, 372 → **867**

    → *Tyrrell-Purser*, 2:56, on letter 107;
      Att. IV, 4b, 2

μετ' ἀμύμωνα	*after the greatest one*
post egregium	following the greatest one
	next to the greatest one

Letter 51.5, pp. 175, 571 → **1669**

    → *Onomasticon Tullianum*;
      Att. XVI, 5, 5

μετεωρότερον	*of a more dubious spirit*
suspensiore animo	with a more dubious spirit
	with a more dubious spirit

Letter 51.3, pp. 171, 567 → **1651**

    → *Onomasticon Tullianum*;
      Att. XVI, 5, 3

ὁμοπλοίᾳ — the companionship of sailing

[de] societate navigandi — about the sailing society

Letter 51.3, pp. 171, 567 → **1649**

→ *Onomasticon Tullianum;*
Att. XVI, 5, 3

ῥοπὴ — a tilting

momentum — a "movement" of the arrow on the balance scale

movimentum — the "movement" on the balance scale

inclinatio — "inclination" describing the hand on a balance scale that tips toward the heavier weight

Letter 51.4, pp. 175, 569 → **1664**

→ *Onomasticon Tullianum;*
Att. XVI, 5, 4

σιττύβας — labels

indices — indicators

Letter 28.1, pp. 83, 370 → **863**

→ *Onomasticon Tullianum;*
Att. IV, 4b, 1

συναγωγή — collection

collectio — gathering, cf. synagogue

Letter 51.5, pp. 175, 571 → **1672**

→ *Onomasticon Tullianum;*
Att. XVI, 5, 5

Χολὴν ἄκρατον — unmixed bile

bilis mera — pure bile

Letter 25.1, pp. 73, 346 → **742**

→ *Onomasticon Tullianum;*
Fam. XIV, 7, 1

INDICES NOSTRAM AD EARVM TRACTATIONEM SPECTANTES

indices referring to our treatment of them

࿇

KALENDARIA AD NOSTRAM COMPOSITA VTILITATEM

calendars composed for our own use

The following sentences are presented as calendars in the commentaries of part 2.

Ac ne illud mirere cur, cum ego antea significarim tibi per litteras me sperare illum in nostra potestate fore, nunc idem videar diffidere, incredibile est quanto mihi videatur illius voluntas obstinatior et in hac iracundia obfirmatior: sed haec aut sanabuntur cum veneris aut ei molesta erunt in utro culpa erit.

Letter 13.1 (*Att.* I, 11, 1), pp. 35, 258 → **393**

... sed nec mihi placuit nec cuiquam tuorum quidquam te absente fieri quod tibi, cum venisses, non esset integrum.

Letter 19.1 (*Fam.* II, 3, 1), pp. 51, 296 → **528**

... aut certe testatum apud animum tuum relinquam quid senserim, ut, si quando—quod nolim—displicere tibi tuum consilium coeperit, possis meum recordari.

Letter 19.1 (*Fam.* II, 3, 1), pp. 51, 296 → **538**

Plerique negant Caesarem in condicione mansurum postulataque haec ab eo interposita esse quo minus quod opus esset ad bellum a nobis pararetur.

Letter 23.3 (*Att.* VII, 15, 3), pp. 65, 334 → **684**

... sperarem me a te tamen impetraturum ....

Letter 27.3 (*Att.* IX, 11A, 3), pp. 81, 366 → **840**

627

Homines ridiculos! qui cum filios misissent ad Cn. Pompeium circumsedendum, ipsi in senatum venire dubitarint.

Letter 47.2 (*Att.* X, 3a, 2), pp. 151, 524 → **1506**

Nunc audi quod pluris est quam omnia. Quintus fuit mecum dies compluris, et si ego cuperem, ille vel pluris fuisset ....

Letter 51.2 (*Att.* XVI, 5, 2), pp. 169, 556 → **1619**

Hoc cum mihi non modo confirmasset sed etiam persuasisset, egit mecum accurate multis verbis tibi ut sponderem se dignum et te et nobis futurum, neque se postulare ut statim crederes, sed, cum ipse perspexisses, tum ut se amares.

Letter 51.2 (*Att.* XVI, 5, 2), pp. 169, 556 → **1634**

$$\sim$$

INDEX STRVCTVRARVM

index of the structures

The following sentences are mapped out in the commentaries of part 2.

Qua re non dubito quin tibi quoque id molestum sit, cum et meo dolore moveare et ipse omni virtute officioque ornatissimum tuique et sua sponte et meo sermone amantem, adfinem, amicumque amiseris.

Letter 2.1 (*Att.* I, 5, 1), pp. 5, 186 → **47**

Omnem spem delectationis nostrae, quam cum in otium venerimus habere volumus, in tua humanitate positam habemus.

Letter 6 (*Att.* I, 7), pp. 17, 219 → **197**

Tametsi iactat ille quidem illud suum arbitrium et ea quae iam tum cum aderas offendere eius animum intellegebam, tamen habet quiddam profecto quod magis in animo eius insederit, quod neque epistulae tuae neque nostra *ad*legatio tam potest facile delere quam tu praesens non modo oratione sed tuo vultu illo familiari tolles, si modo tanti putaris, id quod, si me audies et si humanitati tuae constare voles, certe putabis.

Letter 13.1 (*Att.* I, 11, 1), pp. 35, 258 → **377**

Ac ne illud mirere cur, cum ego antea significarim tibi per litteras me sperare illum in nostra potestate fore, nunc idem videar diffidere, incredibile est quanto mihi videatur illius voluntas obstinatior et in hac iracundia obfirmatior: sed haec aut sanabuntur cum veneris aut ei molesta erunt in utro culpa erit.

Letter 13.1 (*Att.* I, 11, 1), pp. 35, 258 → **392**

Suscepit rem dixitque esse quod Clodius hoc tempore cuperet per se et per Pompeium consequi: putare se, si ego eum non impedirem, posse me adipisci sine contentione quod vellem. Totum ei negotium permisi meque in eius potestate dixi fore.

Letter 21.2 (*Q. Fr.* II, 7 [9], 2), pp. 59, 313 → **604**

Consili nostri, ne si eos quidem qui id secuti non sunt non paeniteret, nobis paenitendum putarem.

Letter 22.2 (*Fam.* IX, 5, 2), pp. 63, 322 → **636**

Ut ab urbe discessi, nullum adhuc intermisi diem quin aliquid ad te litterarum darem, non quo haberem magno opere quod scriberem sed ut loquerer tecum absens, quo mihi, cum coram id non licet, nihil est iucundius.

Letter 23.1 (*Att.* VII, 15, 1), pp. 65, 326 → **647**

Omnis molestias et sollicitudines, quibus et te miserrimam habui, id quod mihi molestissimum est, *et* Tulliolam, quae nobis nostra vita dulcior est, deposui et eieci.

Letter 25.1 (*Fam.* XIV, 7, 1), pp. 73, 346 → **732**

Ego, cum antea tibi de Lentulo gratias egissem cum ei saluti qui mihi fuerat fuisses, tamen lectis eius litteris quas ad me gratissimo animo de tua liberalitate beneficioque misit, eandem me salutem a te accepisse *putavi* quam ille . . . .

Letter 27.3 (*Att.* IX, 11A, 3), pp. 81, 366 → **849**

Tibi, etsi, ubicumque es, ut scripsi ad te ante, in eadem es navi, tamen quod abes gratulor . . . .

Letter 29.1 (*Fam.* II, 5, 1), pp. 85, 374 → **874**

Unum illud nescio, gratulerne tibi an timeam, quod mirabilis est exspectatio reditus tui, non quo verear ne tua virtus opinioni hominum non respondeat, sed mehercule ne, cum veneris, non habeas iam quod cures . . . .

Letter 29.2 (*Fam.* II, 5, 2), pp. 85, 377 → **883**

Ego vero tibi istuc, mi Antoni, remitto atque ita ut me a te, cum his verbis scripseris, liberalissime atque honorificentissime tractatum existimem, idque cum totum, quoquo modo se res haberet, tibi dandum putarem, tum do etiam humanitati et naturae meae.

Letter 30.3 (*Att.* XIV, 13b, 3), pp. 87, 385 → **926**

Qua re quoniam hoc a me sic petis ut, quae tua potestas est, ea neges te me invito usurum, puero quoque hoc a me dabis, si tibi videbitur, non quo aut aetas nostra ab illius aetate quidquam debeat periculi suspicari aut dignitas mea ullam contentionem extimescat, sed ut nosmet ipsi inter nos coniunctiores simus quam adhuc fuimus; interpellantibus enim his inimicitiis animus tuus *mihi* magis patuit quam domus.

Letter 30.5 (*Att.* XIV, 13b, 5), pp. 89, 391 → **954**

Ego, nisi Bibulus qui, dum unus hostis in Syria fuit, pedem porta non plus extulit quam *domi* domo sua, adniteretur de triumpho, aequo animo essem.

Letter 35.5 (*Att.* VI, 8, 5), pp. 111, 429 → **1109**

Quoniam id accidit, quod mihi maxime fuit optatum, ut omnium Marcellorum, Marcellinorum etiam—mirificus enim generis ac nominis vestri fuit erga me semper animus— quoniam ergo ita accidit ut omnium vestrum studio tuus consulatus satis facere posset, in quem meae res gestae lausque et honos earum potissimum incideret, peto a te id, quod facillimum factu est non aspernante, ut confido, senatu, ut quam honorificentissime senatus consultum litteris meis recitatis faciundum cures.

Letter 36.1 (*Fam.* XV, 10, 1), pp. 113, 433 → **1123**

… frater tuus quanti me faciat semperque fecerit esse hominem qui ignoret arbitror neminem ....

Letter 36.2 (*Fam.* XV, 10, 2), pp. 113, 437 → **1150**

Nam cum te semper amavi dilexique tum mei amantissimum cognovi in omni varietate rerum mearum, tum patris tui pluribus beneficiis vel defensus tristibus temporibus vel ornatus secundis et sum totus vester et esse debeo, cum praesertim matris tuae, gravissimae atque optimae feminae, maiora erga salutem dignitatemque meam studia quam erant a muliere postulanda perspexerim.

Letter 43.7 (*Fam.* XV, 7), pp. 137, 493 → **1389**

Hunc, mi Caesar, sic velim omni tua comitate complectare ut omnia quae per me possis adduci ut in meos conferre velis in unum hunc conferas.

Letter 45.3 (*Fam.* VII, 5, 3), pp. 145, 509 → **1438**

Homines ridiculos! qui cum filios misissent ad Cn. Pompeium circumsedendum, ipsi in senatum venire dubitarint.

Letter 47.2 (*Att.* X, 3a, 2), pp. 151, 524 → **1501**

Quae, cum veneris, tanto consilio tantaque animi magnitudine a me gesta esse cognosces ut tibi multo maiori quam Africanus fuit iam me non multo minorem quam Laelium facile et in re publica et in amicitia adiunctum esse patiare.

Letter 48.3 (*Fam.* V, 7, 3), pp. 155, 531 → **1528**

Ego autem, cum ad me de Ciceronis abs te discessu scripsisses, statim extrusi tabellarios litterasque ad Ciceronem, ut, etiamsi in Italiam venisset, ad te rediret ....

Letter 49.1 (*Brut.* I, 14, 1), pp. 157, 536 → **1544**

… contendo ut Ciceronem meum ne dimittas tecumque deducas, quod ipsum, si rem publicam, cui susceptus es, respicis, tibi iam iamque faciendum est.

Letter 49.2 (*Brut.* I, 14, 2), pp. 159, 540 → **1555**

… exercitus autem Caesaris, qui erat optimus, non modo nihil prodest, sed etiam cogit exercitum tuum flagitari; qui si Italiam attigerit, erit civis nemo, quem quidem civem appellari fas sit, qui se non in tua castra conferat.

Letter 49.2 (*Brut.* I, 14, 2), pp. 159, 540 → **1562**

Hoc cum mihi non modo confirmasset sed etiam persuasisset, egit mecum accurate multis verbis tibi ut sponderem se dignum et te et nobis futurum, neque se postulare ut statim crederes, sed, cum ipse perspexisses, tum ut se amares.

Letter 51.2 (*Att.* XVI, 5, 2), pp. 169, 556 → **1627**

∽

INDEX EXEMPLORVM E LEXICO LEWIS ET SHORT
HVC ADLATORVM

index of examples quoted here from the Lewis and Short dictionary

a, ab, abs, prep. with abl.: → 461, 1397, 1523
accedit quod: → 1450
accedo, cessi, cessum, 3: → 370, 1451
adhuc, adv.: → 1225
adipiscor, eptus, 3: → 1192
admiror, atus, 1: → 809
aequus, a, um, adj.: → 278
aliquando, adv.: → 549
aliqui, aliqua, aliquod, indef. adj.: → 1207
aliquis, aliquid, indef. subst. pron.: → 157, 205, 1053, 1207, 1282
aliquo, adv., old dat.: → 1053
alius, alia, aliud, adj. and subst.: → 40
alīus, rare, see: *alius, alia, aliud,* adj. and subst.: → 40
alterius, common, see: *alius, alia, aliud,* adj. and subst.: → 40
amabo te, "I shall like you," see: *amo, avi, atum,* 1: → 1285
amo, avi, atum, 1: → 1285
amo te, "I like you", see: *amo, avi, atum,* 1: → 1285
amplus, a, um, adj.: → 1147
an, disjunctive conj.: → 1656
anni tempora, "the seasons," see: *tempus, oris,* n.: → 630
annona, ae, f.: → 771
ante, II., adv.: → 646, 793
aqua, ae, f.: → 800

aqua haeret, "the water stops," see: *haereo, haesi, haesum*, 2: → 800

assentior, sensus, 4: → 1192

at, conj.: → 712

atque, conj.: → 1650

auctor, oris, comm.: → 821

bene maturum, "just at the right time," see: *maturus, a, um*, adj.: → 627

benevolus, a, um, adj.: → 347

brevi, adv., see: *brevis, e*, adj.: → 552

brevis, e, adj.: → 552

Brundisium, ii, n.: → 1465

causa, ae, f.: → 1553

celebritas, atis, f.: → 1211

certiorem facere aliquem, "to inform, appraise one of a thing," see: *certus, a, um*, adj.: → 171

certus, a, um, adj.: → 171, 429

civitas, tis, f.: → 1033

committo, misi, missum, 3: → 1076

conficio, feci, fectum, 3: → 1083

consero, serui, sertum, 3: → 714

consero, sevi, situm or satum, 3: → 714

consilium, ii, n.: → 1116

consilium capere, "to form a purpose," see: *consilium, ii*, n.: → 1116

constituo, ui, utum, 3: → 188

consto, stiti, statum, 1: → 973

consul, ulis, m.: → 900

consulo, lui, ltum, 3: → 298, 716

contendo, di, tum, 3: → 73

continuus, a, um, adj.: → 695

contra, adv. and prep. with acc.: → 1026

coram, adv. and prep. with abl.: → 657

crimen majestas, "high treason," see: *majestas, atis*, f.: → 1029

cum, prep. with abl.: → 307, 467, 576, 963, 1498

cum, sometimes *quom* or *quum*: → 1579, 1580

cum primum, "as soon as," see: *primus, a, um*, adj.: → 70

Cumae, arum, f.: → 645

Cumanus, a, um, adj., see: *Cumae, arum*, f.: → 645

debeo, ui, itum, 2: → 1543

desidero, avi, atum, 1: → 1581

designatus, "elect," see: *designo or dissigno, avi, atum*, 1: → 1092

designo or dissigno, avi, atum, 1: → 1092

despicio, exi, ectum, 3: → 1106, 1331

desum, fui, esse, v. irreg.: → 9, 529, 1296

dignus, a, um, adj.: → 1630

dispicio, spexi, spectum, 3: → 1106, 1331

do, dedi, datum, dare: → 180, 985

domus, "family," see: *familia, ae*, f.: → 995

dubito an, "I am inclined to think," see: *an*, disjunctive conj.: → 1656

duco, xi, ctum, 3: → 1059, 1243, 1244, 1436

dum, conj.: → 141

dummodo, "provided that," see: *modo*, adv.: → 1362

ecqui, ecquae or *ecqua, ecquod*, pron. interrog. adj.: → 1300

ĕdo, ĕdere, edi, esum, 3: → 1676

ēdo, ēdere, edidi, editum, 3: → 1676

egeo, ui, 2: → 465, 1263

eniteo, tui, 2: → 1020

enitor, nisus or *nixus*, 3: → 1020

eo, adv.: → 1226, 1273, 1354, 1622

eo, adverbially with the comp., see: *is, ea, id*, pron. demonstr.: → 369

eo, ivi or *ii, ire, itum*, v. irreg.: → 369, 1216

eodem, adv.: → 1051, 1659

etiam, conj.: → 981

etiam atque etiam, "again and again," see: *etiam*, conj.: → 981

etsi, conj.: → 1568

ex, prep. with abl.: → 321

existimo, avi, atum, 1: → 101

exlex, egis, adj.: → 321

F, entry for the letter: → 270, 1122

facies, ei, f.: → 745

facilis, e, adj.: → 1236

facio, feci, factum, 3: → 147, 293, 1023

familia, ae, f.: → 770, 995

fas, indecl. n.: → 1565

fere, adv.: → 1002

feriae, arum, f.: → 1002

fero, tuli, latum, ferre, v. irreg.: → 1209, 1579

ferus, a, um, adj.: → 1002

Fidius, ii, m.: → 865

fio, factus, fieri, pass., see: *facio, feci, factum,*
     3 init.: → 147, 293, 516

fors, adv., see: *fors, fortis*, f.: → 571

fors, fortis, f.: → 571

forsan, adv.: → 571

forsitan, adv.: → 571

fortasse (also *fortassis*), adv.: → 571

forte, adv., see: *fors, fortis*, f.: → 571

fortuno, avi, atum, 1: → 1382

fruiturus, see: *fruor, fructus*, 3: → 499

fruor, fructus, 3: → 499

Gaius, Gai, m., less correctly *Caius*: → 870

gaudeo, gavisus, 2: → 590

genus, eris, n.: → 1037

gratus, a, um, adj.: → 431

habeo, ui, itum, 2: → 134

haereo, haesi, haesum, 2: → 800

hic, haec, hoc, pron. demonstr.: → 1479

hinc, adv. for *hince,* locative form from *hic:* → 1222

hince, locative form from *hic:* → 1222

huc, adv.: → 1226, 1273, 1622

humane, adv.: → 1405

humaniter, adv.: → 1405

humanus, a, um, adj.: → 1405

igitur, conj.: → 1125, 1126

ille, a, ud, pron. demonstr.: → 168, 1479

illō, adv., see *ille, a, ud,* pron. demonstr.: → 168

immutatus, a, um, adj.: → 376

immuto, avi, atum, 1, see: *immutatus, a, um,* adj: → 376

imparatus, a, um, adj.: → 689

in, prep. with abl. and acc.: → 341, 1031

in eo esse ut (impers. or with res etc. as subj.), see: *sum, fui, esse,* v. irreg.: → 1325

in modum, see: *modus, i,* m.: → 1160

incido, cidi, casum, 3, from *in–cado:* → 1470

incído, cídi, císum, 3, from *in–caedo:* → 1470

ingemo, ui, 3: → 1366

insector, atus, 1, v. dep.: → 930

instar, n. indecl.: → 1673

integer, tegra, tegrum, adj.: → 535

inter, prep. with acc., with pronouns: → 1004, 1520

interdum, adv.: → 10

intersum, fui, esse, v. irreg.: → 138, 1324

invidia, ae, f.: → 1018

invidus, a, um, adj., see: *invidia, ae,* f.: → 1018

invito, avi, atum, 1: → 945

invitus, a, um, adj.: → 945

ipse, a, um, pron. demonstr.: → 350

is, ea, id, pron. demonstr.: → 369, 389, 480, 757, 812, 896

iste, a, ud, pron. demonstr.: → 917, 1253

jaceo, cui, citum, 2: → 1510

jacio, jeci, jactum, 3: → 1510

judex, icis, comm.: → 1642

judicio, avi, atum, 1: → 1642

laboro, avi, atum, 1: → 132, 617

licet, licuit and *citum est,* 2: → 210, 657

littera, ae, f.: → 486, 495

ludere aliquem, aliquid, "to play, mock a person": → 1448

ludo, si, sum, 3: → 1448

magis, adv. comp.: → 1061

Magnesia, ae, f.: → 17

magnopere, I. adv.: → 368, 641, 654

magnus, a, um, adj.: → 1061, 1364

magnus-opus, "with great labor; greatly," see: *magnopere*, I. adv.: → 368, 641, 654

majestas, atis, f.: → 1029

maturus, a, um, adj.: → 627

maxime, sup. from *superus, a, um*, adj.: → 820, 1364

me invito, "against my will": → 945

mereo, ui, itum, 2: → 357, 522

mereor, itus, 2 dep.: → 357, 522

meritum, i, n.: → 522

Messalla, ae, m.: → 1021

meus, a, um, adj.: → 117, 130, 918, 1286, 1440, 1556

mi, voc.: → 918

minor, us, "less, lesser," comp. of *parvus, a, um*, adj.: → 217

minus, comp. adv. of *parvus, a, um*, adj.: → 618

mirum in modum, see: *modum, i*, m., and *mirus, a, um*, adj.: → 333

mirum quam, or *quantum*, see: *mirus, a, um*, adj.: → 415

mirus, a, um, adj.: → 333, 415

mŏdŏ and *modus, i*, m.: → 373

mŏdŏ, adv., orig. abl. of *modus, i*, m.: → 691, 1347, 1362

modum, i, m.: → 333

modus, i, m.: → 691, 1160

molestus, a, um, adj.: → 1095, 1578

morior, mortuus, 3: → 1661

motus, us, m.: → 1303

multō, adv.: → 1475

multum, adv.: → 1474

multus, a, um, adj.: → 625, 1475

munus, eris, n.: → 530

mutue, adv.: → 1517

mutuiter, adv.: → 1517

mutuō, adv.: → 1517

mutuus, a, um, adj.: → 1517

nam, conj.: → 1194, 1304

navem, from *navis, is*, f.: → 1257

navim, from *navis, is*, f.: → 1257

navis, is, f.: → 1257

–ne (2), enclitic particle: → 722

ne (3), interjection.: → 866

ne ... quidem: → 375, 885, 928, 929, 1245, 1289, 1541

necessitudo, onis, f.: → 993

negotium, ii, n.: → 915

neque, adv. and conj.: → 63, 225, 1041, 1148

neque, or *nec*: → 885

nequeo, ivi and *ii, itum*, 4: → 781

nescio, ivi or *ii, itum*, 4: → 485, 1303, 1435, 1609

nescio quis, quid: → 485

nihil, adv., "in no respect, not at all," see: *nihil*, n., indecl.: → 73, 1219

nihil, n. indecl.: → 73, 180, 1180, 1219

nihil est: → 180

nihilo minus, "none the less," see: *nihil*, n., indecl.: → 1180

nihilominus, "none the less," see: *nihil*, n., indecl.: → 1180

nihilum, i, n., see: *nihil*, n., indecl.: → 1180

nomen, inis, n.: → 1081

nominatim, adv.: → 674

non queo, see: *nequeo, ivi* and *ii, itum*, 4: → 781

nondum, adv.: → 63

nos, nostrum, pers. pron.: → 950

nosco, novi, notum, 3: → 1084

nullo negotio, see: *negotium, ii*, n.: → 915

nummulus, i, m. dim. of *nummus, i*, m.: → 1477

numquam, adv.: → 141

numquid, adv. interrog.: → 1094

obtestor, atus, 1., dep.: → 833

óccĭdo, cĭdi, cāsum, 3: → 1316

occído, cīdi, cīsum, 3: → 1316

offendo, di, sum, 3: → 544, 856

Olbia, ae, f.: → 779

olim, adv.: → 507

oportet, tit, 2., impers.: → 1675

opus, eris, n.: → 73, 432, 672, 1406

opus est, "it is needful", see: *opus, eris*, n.: → 73, 432, 672, 1406

orbis, is, m.: → 1527

oro, avi, atum, 1: → 833

ostendo, di, sum, and *tum*, 3: → 561

paeniteo, ui, 2: → 633

pars, partis, f.: → 933

parum, subst. indecl. and adv.: → 1178

parvus, a, um, adj.: → 217, 618, 681, 1454

patior, passus, 3: → 1048, 1209

paulus, a, um, adj.: → 96

per, prep. with acc.: → 1186

pereo, ĭi (īvi), ĭtum, īre: → 516

perinde, adv.: → 1650

perspectus, a, um, P. a. from *perspicio, spexi, spectum*, 3: → 1582

perspicio, spexi, spectum, 3: → 1583

pertento, avi, atum, 1: → 1321

pertineo, ui, 2: → 441

peto, ivi and *ii, itum*, 3: → 833, 1158

placeo, cui and *citus, citum*, 2: → 56, 332

placo, avi, atum, 1: → 56, 332

plebs, bis, and *ei*, f.: → 1353

plebs, bis, f.: → 1092

plenus, a, um, adj.: → 616

possum, potui, posse, v. irreg.: → 582

post, I. adv., II. prep. with acc.: → 366, 1437

postridie, adv.: → 740

potis, adj.: → 508, 834, 1133, 1227

potissime, sup. adv., see: *potis*, adj.: → 1133, 1227

potissimum, sup. adv., see: *potis*, adj.: → 1227

potius, adv. comp., see: *potis*, adj.: → 508, 1133

prae se ferre, "to show, manifest," see: *fero, tuli, latum, ferre*, v. irreg.: → 1579

praesta te eum, "show thyself such," see: *praesto, sti, atum* or *itum*: → 1246

praesto, sti, atum or *itum*, 1: → 1246

pridie, adv.: → 660

primum, adv., see: *primus, a, um*, adj.: → 70, 248

primus, a, um, adj.: → 70, 248

pro, prep.: → 815

probo, avi, atum, are, 1: → 1640

prope, adv. and prep. with acc.: → 1220

propior, ius, adj. comp.: → 1220

prorsus, adv.: → 1476

proxime, comp. adv. of *proprior, ius*, adj. comp.: → 1220

putidiusculus, a, um, adj.: → 1457

puto, avi, atum, 1: → 35

quaero, sivi, situm, 3: → 1497

quam, adv.: → 1422, 1471, 1478

quamobrem, or *quam ob rem*, adv.: → 832

quamquam, conj.: → 222, 261, 490, 1329, 1550, 1568, 1578

quantum potest, see: *possum, potui, posse*, v. irreg.: → 582

quantus, a, um, adj.

quare or *qua re*, adv.: → 98, 178, 940, 1042, 1157, 1218

quemadmodum, adv.: → 6, 196, 419, 936

queror, questus, 3: → 1497

quī, adv.: → 466, 715, 1272

qui, quae, quod, pron.: → 467, 722, 817, 994, 1074, 1196, 1368, 1470, 1481, 1515, 1530, 1531, 1540

quid multa, see: *multus, a, um*, adj.: → 625

quidem, adv.: → 375, 885, 928, 929, 1245, 1289, 1541

quin, conj.: → 1570

quis, quid (1), pron. interrog. : → 1282

quis, quid (2), pron. indef.: → 207, 1282

quisnam, quaenam, quidnam, pron. interrog.: → 1349

quisquam, quaequam, quicquam or *quidquam*, pron. indef.: → 1473

quisque, quaeque, quodque, pron. indef.: → 1294

quo, adv.: → 652, 755, 888, 947, 1179, 1226, 1273, 1622

quo minus, quominus, "that not," "from," see: *parvus, a, um*, adj.: → 681, 1454

quod ad aliquem (aliquid) pertinet: → 441

quom, see: *cum* sometimes *quom* or *quum*: → 1578, 1579

quum, see: *cum* sometimes *quom* or *quum*: → 1578, 1579

rea, ae, f.: → 1019

recordor, atus, 1, dep.: → 551

rectā (undoubtedly *viā*), adv. from *rego, xi, ctum*, 3: → 1086

rē-fert, rē-tuli, rē-latum, rē-ferre, v. irreg.: → 138, 1324

rego, xi, ctum, 3: → 1086

res, i, f.: → 1019

resisto, resistere, stiti, 3: → 20

resto, restare, stiti, 1: → 20

reus, i, m.: → 1019

rogo, avi, atum, 1: → 115, 116, 802, 1023

S, entry for the letter: → 270

salus, tis, f.: → 854, 1119

sane, adv. from *sanus, a, um*, adj.: → 1490

saniter, adv. from *sanus, a, um*, adj.: → 1490

sanus, a, um, adj.: → 1490

S. D. P. (*salutem dicit plurimam*), see: *salus, tis*, f.: → 854

secundum, I. adv., II. prep. with acc.: → 1168

secundus, a, um, adj.: → 1390

senatus, us, m.: → 1141

sestertius, a, um, num. adj. contr. from *semis-tertius*: → 185

sextus (abbrev. *Sex.*), *i*, m.: → 270

si vis, "if you please," see: *volo, velle, volui*, v. irreg.: → 1431

signum, i, n.: → 296

simul, adv.: → 748

soleo, itus, 2: → 745, 1428

spatium, ii, n.: → 644

sponte, abl.: → 789

statuo, ui, utum, 3: → 931, 932

sto, steti, statum, 1: → 1225, 1225

studiosus, a, um, adj.: → 614, 1034

subinvideo, no perf., *subinvisum*, 2: → 211

subirascor, atus, 3: → 211

subiratus, a, um, P. a. of *subirascor, atus*, 3: → 211

submolestus, a, um, adj.: → 211

subodiosus, a, um, adj.: → 87

subvenio, vēni, ventum, 4: → 1572

sum, fui, esse, v. irreg.: → 1325

    with the gen.: → 163

summum, adv. from *superus, a, um*, adj.: → 1586

summus, a, um, sup. from *superus, a, um*, adj.: → 364

superus, a, um, adj.: → 364, 1587

suscipio, cepi, ceptum, 3: → 1561

tantus, a, um, adj.: → 1346

tempus, oris, n.: → 630, 697

terra, ae, f.: → 1269

testatus, a, um, P. a. with pass. force from *testo, are*, 1, active form of *testor, atus*, 1:
    → 546

testo, are, 1., active form of *testor, atus*, 1: → 546

testor, atus, 1: → 546

tollo, sustuli, sublatum, 3: → 1433

tot, num. adj. indecl.: → 284

tu, pers. pron.: → 229

tueor, tuitus, 2: → 229, 966, 1275

tum, adv. demonstr.: → 129, 137, 166

tute, emphatic form of *tu*, pers. pron., and adv. from *tueor, tuitus*, 2: → 229

tuto, adv. from *tueor, tuitus*, 2: → 229, 966, 1275

tuus, a, um, pron. poss.: → 1327

ubi, adv.: → 258, 259, 804

ultra, adv. and prep. with acc.: → 213

ultro, adv.: → 213

unā, adv. from *unus, a, um*, num. adj.: → 1508

unde, adv.: → 285

unus, a, um, num. adj.: → 1508

ut: → 31, 58, 125, 127, 460, 471, 476, 706, 780, 804, 876, 1009, 1079, 1124, 1139, 1215, 1320, 1340, 1345, 1361, 1412, 1456, 1461, 1571, 1657

    ut = quo tempore, see: *ut*, II: → 804

    ut = ex quo tempore, see: *ut*, II: → 649

    ut potest, "as much or as far as possible," see: *possum, potui, posse*, v. irreg.: → 582

uter, utra, utrum (3), pron.: → 403, 975

utor, usus, 3: → 990, 1654

vacare alicui rei, see: *vaco, avi, atum*, 1: → 1580

vaco, avi, atum, 1: → 1580

validus, a, um, adj.: → 96, 747

vapulo, avi, 1: → 516

vel, conj.: → 446, 1388, 1615

vēnĕo, vĕnīre, īvi or *ii, ītum*, 4, "to be on sale" (not *vĕnĭo, veni, ventum*, 4, "to come"): → 496, 516

vĕnĭo, vĕnīre, vēni, ventum, 4, "to come" (not *vēnĕo, īvi* or *ii, ītum*, 4, "to be on sale"): → 167, 496, 516, 519

vero, adv. from *verus, a, um*, adj.: → 105, 411, 416, 595, 827, 908, 916, 1185, 1334

verum, adv. from *verus, a, um*, adj.: → 374, 411, 1213, 1335, 1361, 1460

verus, a, um, adj.: → 105, 374, 411, 411, 416, 595, 827, 908, 916, 1185, 1213, 1335, 1361, 1460

video, vidi, visum, 2: → 766, 946

videtur alicui, "it seems good to any one," see: *video, vidi, visum*, 2: → 766

villa, ae, f.: → 1477

villula, ae, f. dim. of *villa, ae*, f.: → 1477

volo, velle, volui, v. irreg.: → 1431

voluntas, atis, f.: → 1400

INDEX DOCTRINARVM GRAMMATICO E LIBRO
GILDERSLEEVE ET LODGE DEPROMPTARVM

index of the teachings taken from the grammar book
of Gildersleeve and Lodge

n° 33

    remark 1

        consili: → 76, 631, 1263

        ingeni: → 32

        librari: → 999, 1462

        offici: → 106

        Paeoni: → 1035

n° 56: → 81, 933, 1370

n° 61

    note 2: → 116

n° 68.8: → 1353

n° 70.B: → 1565

n° 78

    adfinis: → 1168

    Aprilis: → 1189

    familiaris: → 751, 1407

    intolerabilis: → 1312

    omnis: → 626, 733

    perbrevis: → 1587

n° 87

    remark 6: → 820

n° 87.4: → 347

n° 90

    facillime: → 354, 458

    meliora: → 296

    meliores: → 857

    minora: → 459

    minus: → 1338, 1339

    miserrimum: → 478

    summa: → 352

n° 93

    bene: → 101

    magis: → 596, 1046, 1061, 1104, 1641

    magno opere: → 368, 654

    maxime: → 464

    minime: → 1010

    minus ... magis: → 641

    Multum ... multum: → 1475

n° 119: → 725, 730, 1307, 1332

n° 131

　　　cessaris: → 1334
　　　cogitaram: → 1419
　　　cognoro: → 726
　　　cognossem: → 754
　　　delectarit: → 1621
　　　efflagitarunt: → 1
　　　mandaras: → 69
　　　navigarit: → 359
　　　norim: → 1084
　　　parasse: → 192
　　　putaram: → 1292, 858
　　　putaris: → 387
　　　putassem: → 86
　　　repudiarunt: → 624
　　　significarim: → 398
　　　sperasset: → 1427
　　　tardarunt: → 1098
n° 167: → 1201, 1428
　　　note 2: → 546
n° 169
　　　remark 1: → 294, 496, 500, 516
n° 169.2: → 1216
n° 175.5
　　　coeperint: → 970, 1333
　　　meminerim: → 594
　　　memineris: → 1602
　　　memini: → 595
　　　oderit: → 1168
n° 181.12, n° 182.12: → 1477
n° 208
　　　agatur: → 668
　　　agi: → 814
　　　conducere: → 1667
　　　existimari: → 101
　　　plauditur: → 787
　　　sciri: → 407
n° 208.2: → 577, 1192, 1262
n° 209: → 112, 1105
n° 209.5: → 1117
n° 211
　　　remark 1: → 149
n° 214
　　　remark 1: → 294, 496, 516
n° 229: → 1430
n° 242
　　　remark 1: → 731, 1068
n° 244
　　　fuero: → 1318

remark 2

> *acciderit ... feremus:* → 1404
>
> *adsequéris ... fuero:* → 1315
>
> *cenabis, cum veneris:* → 803
>
> *contuleris ... iudicabo:* → 146
>
> *cum veneris ... cognosces:* → 1531
>
> *cum veneris cognosces:* → 335
>
> *feceris ... intellexerit:* → 358
>
> *nisi in navim se contulerit, exceptum iri puto:* → 1256
>
> *potuero, [potero]:* → 1372
>
> *qui si Italiam attigerit, erit:* → 1564
>
> *rettuleris ... erit:* → 303
>
> *sanabuntur cum veneris:* → 402
>
> *si ... audierimus ... convertemus:* → 1223
>
> *si ... cognoro, scies:* → 726, 731
>
> *si ... correxerit, ... feremus:* → 1208
>
> *si ... fuerit ... videbo:* → 642
>
> *si veneris ... cognosces:* → 268
>
> *tolles, si ... putaris:* → 387
>
> *ut quo die congressi erimus ... possimus:* → 1115
>
> *Vicerit ... factus erit ... vicerit:* → 686

remark 4

> *feceris ... intellexerit:* → 358
>
> *feceris ... veneris:* → 855
>
> *Omnia viceris, si ... videro:* → 124
>
> *Vicerit ... factus erit ... vicerit:* → 686
>
> *videro ... videro ... :* → 100

n° 245: → 578

n° 252

> *cogitabam:* → 694
>
> *Dabam:* → 773
>
> *erat:* → 1465
>
> *[erat] Si nactus hic esset ... ; sin ille ante tramisisset, ... :* → 1468, 1469
>
> *exspectabam:* → 1483
>
> *properabamus:* → 1103
>
> *properabamus ut non posset magis:* → 1104
>
> *quod scriberem nihil erat:* → 1463
>
> *scribebam:* → 1014
>
> *scripseram ... exspectabam:* → 1482
>
> *vadebam:* → 588
>
> *videbam:* → 1065

n° 254: → 1420

n° 257

> *cui ... demus:* → 513
>
> *non dubito quin ... committas:* → 98
>
> *quae ... curemus ... doleamus:* → 491
>
> *quam ... velimus:* → 514
>
> *qui ferat:* → 488

quo modo satis fiat: → 518
quod ... exspectem ... scribam: → 484
quod ... mandem ... narrem: → 1078

nº 257.2
dederim: → 287, 288
fas sit: → 1565
velim: → 569, 723, 859, 958

nº 258: → 655, 1464, 1632
nº 261: → 902
nº 262: → 1661
nº 264: → 1352
nº 265: → 1274, 1304, 1489
nº 285
exception 1: → 1132, 1167, 1290
nº 320, nº 321: → 106, 521, 860, 1534, 1535, 1639
nº 339: → 115, 116, 716, 802, 1023
nº 343.1: → 774, 1097, 1258, 1317, 1502, 1662
nº 346
ademerit: → 1473
assentior: → 621
Consuli: → 298
consulueris: → 128
credas: → 1644
crede: → 1250
crediderit: → 1638
credidi: → 1291
deesse: → 142
defuisse: → 345
diffidere: → 233
expediat: → 1260
expedire: → 1293
gratificer: → 252
gratuler: → 884, 1641
gratulor: → 873
ignoscere: → 1241, 1242
ignoscit: → 1492
imperes: → 859
invidit: → 1295
parcas: → 116
paruisses: → 1605
persuade: → 1573
persuadeas: → 238
persuaserim: → 1415
placebat: → 220, 665
Placiturum: → 589
praecipere: → 1596
praecipio: → 309
praestoler: → 1373

profuisse: → 1574

respondit: → 600

restitisse: → 21

satis facere: → 744

suasit: → 602

sub-invideo: → 212

remark 1: → 1192, 1262

n° 347: → 345, 452, 613, 674, 1096, 1232

n° 350: → 1093, 1365

n° 351, n° 352: → 179, 965, 1169, 1365

n° 364

    note 2: → 420

n° 377

    note 2: → 420

n° 381: → 1324

n° 387, n° 388: → 964

n° 398

    duobus nobis ... stultius ... me: → 244, 245

    eo citius: → 1354

    minoris his consulibus: → 701

    multo meliores: → 857

    nostra vita dulcior: → 737

    peritior te: → 209

    quo ... iucundius: → 656

    te ... cariorem: → 566

    verbis difficiliora: → 1329

n° 401

    aut consolando aut consilio aut re: → 249

    beneficio: → 825

    clarissima ... una ... voce: → 880, 881

    ea: → 944

    filiolo: → 1395

    Fundo Arpinati: → 769

    gratia: → 616

    his rebus: → 572

    iis bonis: → 555

    iis litteris: → 234

    incredibili dolore: → 1185

    magna voluntate: → 1016

    muneribus: → 558

    obscuro ... vario sermone: → 880, 881

    omnibus iniquitatibus: → 410

    priore pagina ... altera: → 97

    quibus: → 860

    securi Tenedia: → 12

    villis iis: → 767

n° 403

    eoque magis: → 1061

    minore scelere ... quam quo: → 687

    multo maiori: → 1534

    multo minorem: → 1535

    ne paullo quidem: → 928

    nihilo minus nihilominus: → 1180

    paullo eruditius: → 1039

    paullo ... tristius aut severius: → 927

    quanto deteriores: → 423

    quanto ... obstinatior et ... obfirmatior: → 401

    ut non posset magis: → 1104

n° 445: → 30, 63, 225, 1148, 1426, 1453

n° 458: → 962, 1073, 1656

    note 3: → 884, 885, 893

n° 467

    remark 1: → 485, 485, 1435, 1609

n° 473: → 342, 343, 361, 1675

n° 474

    note: → 1553

n° 481.2: → 1025, 1165, 1297

n° 482.5: → 928, 1417, 1628

n° 493.3: → 1295, 1332, 1423

n° 494.2: → 1431

n° 517: → 850, 986, 1114, 1413

n° 524: → 202, 1641

n° 525: → 1451

n° 525.2

    est quod gaudeas: → 202

    nisi quod iis credidi: → 1291

    quod abes: → 877

    quod ... adfluxit: → 1006

    Quod ... agis: → 901

    Quod ... agit: → 520

    Quod ... gaudes: → 174

    Quod me admones ... suadesque: → 593

    quod negas: → 451

    Quod ... scribis: → 49

    Quod ... scripsisti: → 331

n° 527

    remark 1, remark 2

        accipies: → 1231

        adduci: → 1442

        adiurat: → 785

        adsensum esse: → 1192

        ait: → 667

        aiunt: → 1487

        arbitrabar: → 1293

        arbitrabor: → 957

        arbitrarer: → 813

arbitrari: → 405

arbitretur: → 937

arbitror: → 84, 319, 934, 1153, 1166, 1523, 1541

audiebamus: → 68

audio: → 101, 223

audivi: → 336, 1381

censeo: → 219, 1262

cogit: → 1563, 1596

cogitare: → 1480

cogites: → 196

cognovi: → 496, 515

confidimus: → 1052

confido: → 57

constitui: → 187, 188

credas: → 1646

credo: → 1167, 1195, 1327, 1328

cupiebant: → 661

dicebar: → 1308

dicit: → 1495

dixi: → 612

dixit: → 601, 606, 607

doleo: → 1577

dolui: → 1592, 1593

dubitans: → 1073

dubito: → 1519

duxerim: → 1436

duxi: → 85, 1059

est quod: → 203

est rumor: → 568

Existimabam, existimabam: → 1651, 816

existimare: → 36, 37

existimem: → 921, 922

existimes: → 474

expertus est: → 342, 343, 344

explicare: → 1348

exspectatione: → 1193

Fac: → 1275

fac nos certiores: → 169

facias me … certiorem: → 235

feremus: → 1209, 1210

fuerat dictum: → 798

gaudeo: → 590, 1577

gaudere: → 266

gaudes: → 173

habeto: → 135

ignoras: → 1037, 1569, 1521

ignoret: → 1152

incertum est: → 722

incredibile est: → 421, 1621, 1622
intellegat: → 275, 280, 998
intellegebam: → 382
intellegis: → 851, 1146
intellexerit: → 360
intellexi: → 201, 739
iudicabis: → 114
iudicabo: → 147
iudicassem: → 1635
iudicavi: → 823
iudices: → 1643
laetor: → 1592, 1593
mallem: → 77, 78
memineris: → 1603
mihi in mentem non venit: → 179
Mihi veniunt in mentem haec: → 966, 967, 969
mirere: → 396
miror: → 521
molestum fuit: → 1578
narrare: → 871
narravit: → 1653
negas: → 944
negat: → 675, 679, 680, 682
nescio: → 251, 884, 893, 1032, 1271
nescit: → 1377
noluerit: → 1639
nuntiant: → 713, 714
nuntii venerant et litterae: → 1218
opinantes: → 468
opinio: → 1407
pati: → 241
patiamur: → 1049, 1050
patiare: → 1533
patior: → 1497
perspicis: → 1299
persuade: → 1574
persuadeas: → 238, 239
persuaserim: → 1416
placebat: → 665
placuit: → 531
putabam: → 1181
putabas: → 572
putabis: → 1667
putabo: → 35, 1082, 1324, 1325
putare se: → 609
putarem: → 635, 923, 1584, 1585
putas: → 1660
putaveram: → 1292

putavi: → 234, 848

putes: → 237, 699, 1108, 1162, 1338

putet: → 1668

puto: → 121, 126, 685, 724, 959, 960, 1254, 1256

quaerebam: → 810

Quaeris: → 1028

questos esse: → 1500

rescribi: → 440, 443

rumoris: → 1610

sciam: → 243

scio, Scio: → 1201, 1204

scire: → 236, 437, 463

scire cupio: → 297

scis, Scis: → 229, 478, 1612

scitis: → 519

scito: → 88, 90, 313, 406, 407, 563, 565, 776, 1000, 1001, 1395, 1510, 1512, 1526

scribas: → 1055, 1284

scribis: → 101, 191, 1197, 1542

scripseram: → 1481, 1551

scriptum erat: → 404

sic habeto: → 553, 554

significabas: → 1581

solacium: → 240

sperare: → 400

sperarem: → 839

sperem: → 761, 763, 1188, 1240, 1242

spero, Spero: → 746, 758, 1401

spondeo: → 1450

sponderem: → 1630, 1631

statuerim: → 75

statui: → 930, 932

subinvideo: → 214

sum admiratus: → 809

suspicabar: → 589

suspicor: → 1235

testatum: → 547

testis erit: → 50

tulit: → 1192

velis: → 1161

velle: → 1425

venerant et litterae: → 1218

vetarent: → 1303

Vide: → 1415, 1424

videas: → 1108

videatis: → 518

videbam: → 1062, 1064

videbis: → 1330

video: → 181, 295, 577, 1251, 1261, 1410, 1489

videor: → 1199

vides: → 457, 1470, 1478

videte: → 976, 977

videtur: → 397

vis: → 142

volo: → 131, 1012, 1043, 1382, 1383

volui: → 155

n° 528.1

 and remark 2 and note 1

  dici: → 709

  videor: → 231, 233, 290, 397, 907, 1045, 1050, 1198, 1308, 1342, 1343, 1423, 1645, 1650

n° 528.2: → 101, 407

n° 533: → 173, 266, 590, 809, 1577, 1592

n° 535

 remark 2: → 1675

n° 541

 note 2: → 652, 888, 941, 947, 1125, 1259

n° 542: → 266, 809

n° 543

 note 2: → 65, 279, 997, 1446, 1607

n° 542: → 266, 809

n° 545

 remark 1: → 1558

n° 545.2: → 122, 681, 755, 1179, 1454

n° 546

 remark 2

  facias me velim certiorem: → 235

  gaudeas velim: → 175

  mallem egisses: → 902

  obsecrare obtestarique ... revertare: → 1598

  persuadeas velim: → 238

  Scripsi ... daret: → 119

  velim cogites: → 195

  velim ... complectare: → 1439, 1444

  velim ... conficias: → 470

  velim ... consideretis: → 980

  velim cures: → 425

  velim ... cures: → 765

  velim desinas ... revisas ... malis: → 257

  velim dispicias: → 1106

  velim explices ... iuves: → 723

  velim ... instituatis: → 983

  velim ... invisas: → 581

  velim ... mittas: → 412

  velim ... mittas ... imperes: → 859

  velim ... perscribas: → 1203

velim ... persuadeas: → 958

velim scribas: → 1283, 1284

velim scribas: → 1336

velim scribas: → 1491

velim ... urgeas: → 583

velim ... videas: → 1107

videatis velim: → 517

n° 547: → 1454

n° 552

[not a result clause]: → 356

a te ita petente ut ... servare nolles: → 911

eius modi ... ut habeam: → 481

in eo civi ... qui sit ... vindicaturus: → 896, 897

ita commendavit ut ... habeam: → 905

ita mitto ut ... mittendum duxerim: → 1436

ita ... properabamus ut non posset magis: → 1104

ita tractes ut intellegat: → 997

ita ... ut ... placeamus: → 165

ita ... ut ... tibi praestoler: → 1373

mecumque ... ita contendit et a me ita fractus est ut ... sperem: → 1187

nuntii venerant et litterae qua re nihil esset necesse: → 1218

remitto ... ita ut ... existimem: → 919

sic ... commutatus est ... ut ... possis: → 1623

Sic ei probatum est ... ut ... crediderit, ... noluerit ... fecerit, ... dimiserit: →
1637

sic me adfecerunt ut non ... viderer: → 907

sic petis ut ... neges: → 942

sic ... revertare ut ... possis: → 1599

sum levatus ut ... videatur: → 743

Tanta est exspectatio ... ut ... non dubitem: → 1597

tanta fuit opportunitas ut ... divinum videretur: → 1434

tanta ... ut neminem liberum duceret: → 1184

tanta ... ut sperem: → 1239, 1242

ut scire iam possim: → 462

ut ... sperem: → 760

ut ... patiare: → 1532

n° 552.3

nihil praetermisi ... quin perscriberem: → 1005

nullum adhuc intermisi diem quin ... darem: → 650

n° 555.2: → 42, 98, 1359, 1518, 1656

n° 573: → 1362

n° 588: → 129, 137, 166

n° 604.3: → 379

n° 614

remark 2

id quod mihi molestissimum est: → 735

quod concessi libenter: → 1067

quod erat subodiosum: → 87

quod est ... coniunctum: → 1022

quod ... fefellit: → 1611

quod ... fuit aptissimum: → 1311

quod ipsum ... faciendum est: → 1559

Quod ... reperies: → 817

quod scribit: → 1499

n° 616: → 118, 1600

n° 625: → 1420

n° 631.2: → 180

n° 632: → 136, 559, 698, 1310

n° 633: → 504, 562, 1488

n° 642

    aut ... aut ... : → 948

    cum ... tum ... : → 129, 137, 690, 788, 904, 920, 1553, 1633

    cum ... tum ... tum ... : → 1385

    ita ... ut ... : → 356

    non quo aut ... aut ... sed ... : → 948

    Quamquam ... , tamen ... : → 1578

    quantum ... : → 1620

    quantam diligentiam ... tanti ... : → 145

    quem ad modum ... sic ... : → 6

    tali ... quali ... : → 1626

    tam ... quam ... : → 386, 408, 591, 1514, 1586

    tanto ... tantaque ... : → 1532

    tantam ... quantam ... : → 1509

    tantum ... quantum ... : → 1313

    ut ... sic ... : → 573

n° 696: → 1601

n° 698: → 1288

Appendix

    Roman Calendar pp. 491–92

        Pridie Id.: → 29

        VII. Idus, Novembr.: → 151

        D. prid. Non. Nov.: → 182

        ad mensem Ianuarium: → 320

        D. IIII. Nonas Iun.: → 435

        Kal. Quinct.,: → 442

        Idibus Quinctilibus: → 527

        A. d. III. Id. Febr.: → 619

        a. d. VI Kal.: → 659

        ad suas Nonas: → 728

        D. VII. Id. Iun: → 773

        Id. Maiis: → 782

        Ante quod Idibus: → 793

        VIIII Kal. Formiis: → 988

        a. d. XV Kal. Iunias: → 1058

        pridie Kal. Octobris: → 1088

        a. d. v. Idus Aprilis: → 1189

Data XII Kal. Sext.: → 1229
Idibus: → 1267
usque ad a. d. III. Nonas Maias: → 1375
A. d. VII Id.: → 1484
II. Idus Quintilis: → 1576
Roman Money p. 493: → 186

INDICES INTER SE AD VOLVMINA
"OSSA" ET "OSSIVM" RELATI

*indices mutually referred back to the volumes
"Ossa" and "Ossium"*

⤳

ARGVMENTA: INDICIA PRIORIS HVIVSQVE VOLVMINIS RERVM

subject matters: indicators of the material of the previous and this volume

Compiled by Daniel Vowles

Below are elements of the Latin language, with *OSSA* (volume I) encounter numbers 1–105 and some references to Gildersleeve and Lodge. Those numbers and references can be used, in turn, to consult INDEX DOCTRINARVM GRAMMATICO E LIBRO GILDERSLEEVE ET LODGE DEPROMPTARVM (*index of the teachings taken from the grammar book of Gildersleeve and Lodge*) and TRANSVERSA RERVM CONSOCIATIO INTER VOLVMINA "OSSA" ET "OSSIVM" (*cross-index of items between the volumes "Ossa" and "Ossium"*) where arrow numbers will lead you to our specific commentary on the expression of Cicero in question.

14 ways to express purpose, 84
65 verbs with the dative, 89.1, GL346
ablative case (*see* function: by-with-from-in)
accusative case (*see* function: object)
ACI—Accusativus Cum Infinitivo—accusative with infinitive (*see oratio obliqua*)
adjectives
    3 ways in dictionary, 18
    Block I in *–us, –a, –um,* 4
        brevity and ambiguity, 5
        used as nouns according to gender, 5
    Block II in *–is,* 18
    comparative and superlative adjectives, 36
        irregularities, 36.5, GL90
    famous 9: *unus–solus . . . ,* 42.6
    joining Blocks I and II, 18

possessive adjectives *meus–tuus–noster–vester*, 24, 100.2

possessive adjectives, reflexive, 41.2

    the reflexive pronoun and adjective in the subjunctive:, 63

pronouns: *iste–ille–ipse*, 41.3

"verbal adjective" (*see* gerundive)

adverbs

    to express futurity, 61.2

    irregular comparison of adverbs, 37.3, GL93

    difficulties in the forms of the neuter, 37

    positive, comparative, and superlative degrees, 37

causal clauses

    with *cum*; *quod, quia, quoniam*; *qui, quae, quod*; *quippe qui, utpote qui*, 59

    reason and reported reason: *quod, quia, quoniam* + indicative or subjuctive, 59.2

characteristic result clauses, 68.2

command forms: where is the first mention of the second imperative?

    command forms of irregular verbs—*fer* and its compounds, 85.2.7

    dic, duc, fac, fer: the famous four command forms, 39.4

    first and second command-imperative forms, including the verb "to be," 17

    other expressions of obligation or of necessity of action, 85.3

    passive and deponent command forms, 34

    summary for affirming and negating, 85

        affirming expressions, 85.1

        negating expressions, 85.2

comparison

    ablative of comparison (without *quam*) and of measure, 90

    of adjectives, 36

    of adverbs, 37

    comparative or superlative after *quam*, 43

complementary infinitive (*see* infinitives: complementary infinitive)

complementary result clauses, *qui*, 68

concessive clauses, 64

conditional clauses

    examples, 87

    in indirect discourse, 103

    with the particle *utinam*, 88

    in three ways, 86

        contrary-to-fact, 86.3

        foggy future, 86.2

        real, factual, logical, 86.1

conjunctions, 3

consecutio temporum

    3% in the sequence of tenses in result sentences, conditionals, and original subjunctives, 94

    97% normally, 47

    in detail, in Latin and English, 48

    in many examples, 49

    sequence in the subjunctive mode after other verb times:, 62 sequence of tenses of a subjunctive depending on a subjunctive, 62.1

sequence of tenses of a subjunctive depending on a participle, 62.2

sequence of tenses in general, 47

consecutive clauses (*see* subjunctive: uses of the subjunctive: pure result clauses), 67

contractions (of verbal forms), 39, GL122–126

um

cum + ablative, *cum* as a preposition, 28

cum + subjunctive, causal. *cum* = since, because, 59

cum + subjunctive, concessive. *cum* = although, 64

summaries

cum temporal, 66

cum + indicative, 66

cum + subjunctive, 66

dative case (*see* function: to-for-from)

demonstrative pronouns, 40

deponent

deponent command forms, 34

deponent participles: forms and meanings, 51.2

deponent verbs, 29

dubitare + infinitive + *num* + *quin*, 93

eis = iis, 40.3

Famous 9: *unus–solus* ..., 42.6

fearing: verbs of fearing and the phrase *periculum ... est*, 95

fero (*see* irregular verbs), 82

final clauses and expressions

ad—finality preposition, 77.1

final clauses: (*ut, ne, ut ... non*; *qui, quae, quod*—relative clauses of purpose), 58

final expressions: 14 ways to express purpose, 84

foggy future (*see* conditional clauses)

fore (*futurum esse*) + *ut* (substitute for the future infinitive), 92

forgetting: verbs of remembering/forgetting with the genitive and even the accusative, 74

function

function: about, 6

their indication and meanings, 6

function: by-with-from-in (= ablative case)

"ablative absolute" (AA), 54

in authors and sheets, 56

expressed in multiple ways, 55

vernacular renderings, 55

without the participle "being", 57

meaning and forms in nouns and adjectives, 27

prepositions with the ablative, 28

in pronouns and relatives, 28

review, 98

special uses

    5 verbs with the ablative and their vernacular difficulties, 78

    ablative of comparison and of measure, 90

    ablative of definite price, 75

    ablative of the instrument, 28.5.3

    ablative of the personal agent, 28.5.3, 89

    other verbs with the ablative, 78

    the passive of intransitive verbs with the ablative, 89.3.4

    place: names of cities and small islands, 69.2.2

    quality statements by the genitive, ablative, and with specification of an adjective, 96

    time at which, 70.1

    time within which, 70.3

function: direct address (vocative case), 38.3

function: place (locative case), 69

function: object (accusative case)

  accusative as object function, 2

  accusative gerund (*see* gerund), 77

  accusative + infinitive (also called *ACI—Accusativus Cum Infinitivo*; *see oratio obliqua*), 71, 72

  accusative supine (*see* supine), 81

  indication and meaning, 6

  prepositions with the object form—4 with motion, 6

  special uses

    accusative after verbs of remembering/forgetting, 74

    time during which, 70.2

function: of-possession (genitive case)

  of-possession in nouns and adjectives, 20

  of-possession in relatives: in Latin and English, 23

  of-possession in the personal pronouns, 24

  special uses

    genitive after verbs of remembering/forgetting, 74

    genitive of indefinite price, 75

    genitive of part, 99

    genitive of possession in the predicate (also known as predicative genitive) with nouns—*iudicis*, 100

      with adjectives of possession—*meum–tuum–eius*, 100.2

    quality statements by the genitive, ablative, and with specification of an adjective, 96

  two usages, 20

function: subject (nominative case)

  meaning and forms in nouns and adjectives, 6

  special uses

    nominative with the infinitive, 73.3

function: to-for-from (dative case)

  to-for-from: meaning and forms in nouns, adjectives, pronouns, relatives, 33

  special uses

    dative of the agent, used with passive necessity participle, 53.4

dative of possession and of purpose, 91

dative with 65 verbs, 89.1, GL346

dative with compound verbs, 89.2, GL347

double dative, 91.2

futurity

futurity in the subjunctive, 44.5, 61

futurity participle, 51

substitute for the future infinitive: *fore* (*futurum esse*) + *ut*, 92

genitive case (*see* function: of-possession)

gerund

forms and meanings of the gerund, 77

to express purpose (*see* 14 ways to express purpose), 84

gerundive

with certain verbs of taking care, handing over, undertaking, 80, GL430,n.1

forms and meanings of the gerundive, 77.2

to express purpose (*see* 14 ways to express purpose), 84

hic–haec–hoc, 40

imperatives (*see* command forms)

impersonal verbs—*paenitet, miseret, pudet, taedet, piget*, 75.4

example: *oportere*, 73.2

forming the impersonal passive of intransitive verbs, 89.3

indefinite pronouns (*see* pronouns: indefinite)

indicative

times—tenses of the indicative mode and their vernacular meanings, 7

indirect discourse

indirect question, not relative, 60

indirect, reported speech (*see oratio obliqua*)

infinitives

ACI—Accusativus Cum Infinitivo—accusative with infinitive, 72, 73

complementary infinitive

after certain verbs, 77.1

dubitare + complementary infinitive, 93.1

verbs of fearing + complementary infinitive, 95.1

final, to express purpose (poor Latin prose), 84

forms, active, 72.1

forms, passive, 72.3

nominative with infinitive, 73.3, GL528

principal parts of verbs, 8

substitute for the future infinitive: *fore* (*futurum esse*) + *ut*, 92

interest and *refert* from the dictionary, 102

interrogative pronouns, 42

review in the dictionary and with *si, nisi, ut, cum, num, ne*, 79

irregularity

irregular comparison of adjectives, 36.5, GL90

irregular comparison of adverbs, 37.3, GL93

irregular verbs *fero, eo, volo* (I carry, I go, I wish), 82

command forms of irregular verbs—*fer* and its compounds, 85.2.7

–is = –es, 38.1, 38.2, GL56, GL78

is–ea–id, 40

iste–ille–ipse, 41

iussive / jussive subjunctive, 85.1

later Latin: characteristics of later Latin literature, 105

locative case (*see* function: place), 69

M & M verbs: verbs of mind and mouth, 60

modal attraction: principles and examples, 83, GL662

necessity

      participle of passive necessity, 51.1.4

      passive necessity formula, 53.4

negating expressions (*see* command forms: negating expressions), 85.2

neuters: super double principle, 2

nominative case (*see* function: subject)

nouns

    Block I, 2

        as they appear in the dictionary = 40%, 2

        variations in Block I nouns, 4

    Block II, 15

        dictionary appearance and examples, 15

        review, 16, 17

        Block II nouns review, 38

        Block II, *–is* = *–es*, 38

        in *–is* = 40%: masculine, feminine, neuter, 15

    remaining 20%: no adjectives, 35

        dictionary is essential: *manus, us*; *species, iei*, 35

    subject and object functions, 2

    verbal noun (*see* gerund)

opus est—with the genitive, dative, or ablative, 75.3

oratio obliqua: (OO)

    ACI—*Accusativus Cum Infinitivo*—accusative with infinitive, 72, 73

        after M & M verbs, 71

        very many examples, 73

    indirect, reported speech, 71

    nominative with infinitive, 73.3, GL528

    review and phenomenon in a later age, 76

    verbs—infinitives, active and passive; *ACI*, 72

participles

    active futurity formula (active periphrastic), 53.3

        with the subjunctive, 61.3

    difficulties and principles, 50

    examples of brevity, 52

    forms, 51

    four in number, 50

    as nouns, 52

    passive necessity formula, 53.4

    use alone or with the verb "to be," 53

    used in direct address form, 38.3

partitive genitive (*see* function: of-possession: special uses: genitive of part), 99

passive voice
    with oblique functions, genitive, dative, ablative, 89
    passive voice in Times 4, 5, 6, 26
    passive and deponent command forms, 34
    phonetic exceptions, 21
    placing of the verbal parts, 26
    review, 22
    in verb Times 1, 2, 3: 21
    in verb Times 4, 5, 6: 26
periculum est, 95.2
personal endings: signs of persons, 1
place, expressions of
    and the locative function, 69
    to where–from where–where, 69
poetic meter briefly: dactylic hexameter, elegiac pentameter, 104
predicative genitive (*see* function: of-possession: special uses: genitive of
    possession in the predicate), 100
prepositions
    with the ablative—4 with place, 28
    with the object form—4 with motion, 6
    personal agency, 28.4, 28.5.3
principal parts of verbs, 8
prohibiting: verbs of prohibiting; *ne–quominus–quin*, 101, GL 632
pronouns
    personal pronouns, 3, 28, 40
        function: by-with-from-in for personal pronouns, 28
        function of-possession for personal pronouns, 24
        function: to-for-from for personal pronouns, 33
    reflexive pronouns
        and adjective in the subjunctive: uncertainties, 63
        difficulties, 31
        meus–mei–me–mihi; *tuus–tui–te–tibi*: my, of me, to me, myself; yours,
            of you, to you, yourself …, 30
        review, 41.1
        suus, a, um—his, her, its, their, one's own; himself, herself, them-
            selves, 31
    relative pronouns
        brevity, 11
        four principles, 10
        function: by-with-from-in for relative pronouns, 28
        function: of-possession in relatives: in Latin and English, 23
        omission of the antecedent, 11
        position, 11
        review, 42
        as subject and object, 10
        various usages, 79
    demonstrative pronouns
        is–ea–id; *hic–haec–hoc*, 40
        iste–ille–ipse, 41

indefinite pronouns, 42, 79, GL107

interrogative pronouns, 42, 79

relative, interrogative, indefinite pronouns after *si, nisi, ut, cum, num, ne,*
    79.5

pure result clauses; *ut–ut non,* 67

purpose

    14 ways to express purpose, 84

    purpose clauses (*see* final clauses), 58

quality: statements of quality by the genitive, ablative, and with specification of an
    adjective, 96

quam with various usages and subtleties; with comparative adjectives or adverbs,
    43

questions

    question particles, 13

    ways of asking, 13

qui, quae, quod; *quippe qui, utpote qui* in causal clauses, 59

quin: verbs of prohibiting; *ne–quominus–quin*; the uses of *quin*, 101, GL 632

quod

    quod, quia, quoniam + indicative—causal: reason, 59.2

    quod, quia, quoniam + subjunctive—causal: reported reason, 59.2

refert: interest and *refert* from the dictionary, 102

reflexive pronoun (*see* pronouns: reflexive)

relative clauses

    relative clauses in the indicative mode, 10, 11

    used in expressions of characteristic result: *qui, quae, quod* + subjunctive,
        68.2

    used in expressions of purpose: *qui, quae, quod* + subjunctive, 58

    used in expressions of reason/cause: *qui, quae, quod* + subjunctive, 59.4

    summary, ten different uses of *qui, quae, quod*; *quis, quid,* 79

remembering: verbs of remembering/forgetting with the genitive and even the
    accusative, 74

reported reason—partially oblique speech (*see quod, quia, quoniam* +
    subjunctive), 59.2

reported speech (*see oratio obliqua*)

sequence of tenses (*see consecutio temporum*)

si, nisi, ut, cum, num, ne—with relative, interrogative, indefinite pronouns, 42.1.5,
    79.5

structure of Latin sentences = terminations and vocabulary, 1

subjunctive

    forms of Time 1s, Time 2s, Time 3s, Time 4s, both actively and passively,
        44.1–44.4

    forms of the subjunctive of the verb to be, *esse,* in all four subjunctive times,
        46

    futurity in the subjunctive—no special forms, 44.5, 61

        active futurity formula with the subjunctive, 61.3

    principles of use of the subjunctive mode, 45

    sequence in the subjunctive mode after other verb times, 62

sequence of tenses of a subjunctive depending on a subjunctive, 62.1

sequence of tenses of a subjunctive depending on a participle, 62.2

sequence of tenses in the subjunctive mode (*consecutio temporum*), 47, 48

uses of the subjunctive

characteristic result clauses, 68.2

commands—affirming expressions; iussive or jussive subjunctive, 85.1

commands—negating expressions, 85.2

complementary result clauses, 68.1

concessive clauses, 64

conditional clauses, 86, 87

conditionals—contrary-to-fact, 86.3

conditionals—foggy future, 86.2

examples, 87

in indirect discourse; examples, 103

particle *utinam*, 88

cum + subjunctive. Summary of the uses of *cum*, 66

final clauses: *ut, ne, ut ... non*; *qui, quae, quod*, 58

indirect question, not relative, 60

modal attraction: attraction of the subjunctive, 83, GL662

pure result clauses (consecutive clauses), 67

summary: *qui, quae, quod*; *quis, quid* + subjunctive, 79

temporal clauses, 65

ten different uses, 79

superlative (*see* comparison)

supine, two forms and uses, 81

suus, a, um—his, her, its, their, one's own; himself, herself, themselves; difficulties, 31

temporal clauses: *postquam, ut, donec, priusquam, antequam*, 65

temporal sentences and *cum*, 66

time: time at which, through which, within which, 70

utinam, 88

verbs

4 types (Groups) of verbs; in the dictionary, 12

commands

command forms—two types, 17

passive and deponent command forms, 34

contractions of verbal forms, 39, GL122–126

deponent verbs, 29

deponent command forms, 34

deponent participles: forms and meanings, 51.2

difficulties of Time 3: 12

impersonal verbs—*paenitet, miseret, pudet, taedet, piget*, 75.4

irregular verbs *eo–fero–volo, nolo, malo*, 82

command forms of irregular verbs—*fer* and its compounds, 85.2.8

M & M verbs—verbs of mind and mouth, 60

personal endings of verbs: signs of persons, 1

principal parts of verbs, 8

special forms of the verbs: *contendo, –ere, –io, –ere*, 14

Times 1, 2, and 3 according to verb type, 12

Times 4, 5, and 6 of all verbs: easy construction, 8

"to be"; *esse* in the whole indicative; no object with the verb "to be", 9

verbs of fearing and the phrase *periculum ... est*, 95

verbs of prohibiting; *ne–quominus–quin*; the uses of *quin*, 101, GL 632

vocative case (*see* function: direct address), 38

❧

TRANSVERSA RERVM CONSOCIATIO INTER VOLVMINA "OSSA" ET "OSSIVM"

cross-index of items between the volumes "Ossa" and "Ossium"

compiled together with Daniel Vowles

PRIMA EXPERIENTIA

first experience

Encounter 1

sentence structure

A. Trebonio ... utor: → 990

ad fugam: → 720

ad te ... in scribendo: → 1070

aliquam ... gratulationem: → 1522

arbitrium et ea: → 381

benevolentiam ... perspicere potui: → 355

Breves litterae tuae: → 1536

C. Trebatium ... ducere: → 1419

consili nostri ... paenitendum: → 632

cuius sermonis genus: → 82

cum filios misissent ... dubitarint: → 1507

cum homine furioso ... satis habeo negotii Servilio: → 1172

de te ad Caesarem quam diligenter scripserim: → 228

Domus ut ... habeat ... dicetis: → 982

e navi recta: → 1086

Ea si ... correxerit: → 1206

Ego ... essem: → 1110

Ego ... exspecto: → 693

ego ... faciam: → 956

Ego si ... cognoro: → 726

Ego vitam ... retinebo: → 1322

Eius rei ... arbitror: → 318

eodem ego te crimine: → 1588

es cognitus: → 1247

es profectus: → 2

frater tuus quanti me faciat semperque fecerit esse hominem qui ignoret
    arbitror neminem: → 1151

fui esse non possum: → 349

haec ipsa ... rectene sint ... commissa: → 893

Haec negotia quo modo se habeant: → 871

Hoc ... non queo differre: → 781

Hoc cum mihi non modo confirmasset sed etiam persuasisset: → 1628

hoc: → 250

Id ... consideretis: → 980

in omnibus tuis rebus meis optatis ... respondit: → 1595

In Planci vero causa: → 1185

ipse ... amiseris: → 45

Is ... debet: → 271

Lepidi, tui necessarii ... levitatem et inconstantiam animumque ... credo ...
    esse perspectum: → 1167

librum ... placuisse ... gaudeo: → 590

Lippitudinis ... manus et ... brevitatis: → 1462

matris tuae ... maiora erga salutem dignitatemque meam studia: → 1392

Maxima sum laetitia adfectus: → 1379

Me ... consolatur spes: → 1233

me ... retinuerunt: → 1301

meam tuorum erga me meritorum memoriam nulla ... oblivio: → 1601

mihi ... accidebant: → 39

mihi ... dabat: → 5

minus ... quam ... magis ... quam: → 641

mirificus ... animus: → 1129

ne causam quidem elicere: → 375

nec obscuro nec vario sermone sed et clarissima et una omnium voce: → 881

nobis constitutis rebus ... honori fore: → 469

Nobis eos ... conserva: → 418

Nos ea: → 324

nullae ... meas ... sine meis: → 1537

omnem spem ... positam habemus: → 198

para, meditare, cogita: → 894

permisi meque ... dixi fore: → 612

Planci animum ... perspicere: → 1164

Pollicem ... extrudas: → 526

propter ... propter ... tempus: → 629

quae est omnis iam in extremum adducta discrimen: → 1170

Quae gerantur accipies: → 1231

quae tua potestas est: → 924

quae tua potestas est: → 943

quas misisti ... iucundas fuisse: → 1511

quas statim cum recitavissem, cecidit: → 1191

quas tu: → 422

qui ... veniunt ... dicunt: → 262

qui si Italiam attigerit, erit: → 1564

Quoniam id accidit ... quoniam ergo ita accidit: → 1126

quorum ... spe audiendi aliquid: → 702

Sallustium restituere ... non potui: → 336

se ... fecisse: → 360

Sed ad te brevior iam in scribendo incipio fieri: → 1071

si qua ... cura: → 818

Signa ... ea: → 322

sin extra: → 718

sit ... vindicaturus: → 898

spatium ... veniendi: → 643

spero negotia esse ut et vos ... sperem esse ... defensuros [esse]: → 759

summa ... officia: → 351

sunt ... exposita. ... curata sunt: → 323

sunt omnia debilitata ... sint litteris commissa: → 892

te ... vindicat: → 1298

timeam ... verear: → 886

tribusne versiculis his temporibus Brutus ad me?: → 1538

Tu ... praetermittas: → 158

Tu ... velim cures: → 765

Tu ... videbis: → 1330

Tu velim ... des operam: → 190

Tuas: → 729

Uni Favonio ... non placebat: → 665

ut ... patiare: → 1532

ut omnia ... conferas: → 1441

valde ... valde: → 592

vel quia ... vel quod: → 878

vide quam conversa res sit: → 1478

OSSIUM GLUTEN, the bones' glue

Section 1 → 232, 500, 502, 509, 510

Section 3

    function: object: → 380, 676

Section 7 → 82

Section 8 → 537

Encounter 2

Section 1 (Block I nouns): → 305, 439

Section 2

    function: object: → 380, 676

Section 4

    function: object: → 380, 676

Section 6

    function: object: → 380, 676

Encounter 3

Section 1

    demonstrative pron.: *is, ea, id:* → 55, 812, 1246

Section 2

　　conjunction: *–que:* → 46, 232, 448, 575, 576, 599, 600, 602, 605, 612, 823, 859, 920, 1061, 1085, 1159, 1187, 1255, 1288, 1382, 1383, 1384, 1597

　　conjunction: *atque:* → 1044, 1383

　　conjunction: *et:* → 46, 380, 381, 573, 1187, 1200, 1202, 1288, 1343

　　conjunction: *et . . . , et . . . :* → 15, 46, 257, 365, 455, 762, 882, 1163, 1290, 1312, 1388, 1423, 1592, 1624

　　conjunction: *nec . . . , nec . . . :* → 882

　　conjunction: *neque . . . , neque . . . :* → 30

　　conjunction: *neque . . . , nequedum . . . :* → 63

　　conjunction: *sed:* → 879

Encounter 4

Section 1

　　Block I nouns: variations: → 778

Section 2

　　acutum: → 1471

　　brundisinus, a, um, adj.: → 1465

　　immutatus, a, um, adj.: → 376

　　imparatus, a, um, adj.: → 689

　　novus, a, um, adj.: → 439

　　opportunus, a, um, adj.: → 501

　　paratum: → 1471

　　pergrata: → 1376

　　secundus, a, um, adj.: → 1390

　　tantus, a, um, adj.: → 1017

Encounter 5

Section 2

　　adj.: used as nouns: → 439

Encounter 6

Section 3

　　in with object: → 123, 899

Encounter 7

times-tenses of the indicative mode and their vernacular meaning: → 304

verb meaning Time 1, Time 2, Time 3: → 292

verb meaning Time 4, Time 5, Time 6: → 292

verb meaning Time 2, Time 5: → 708

verb meaning Time 4a: → 1089

verb meaning Time 6: → 359

Time 6

　　Time 3 and Time 6 paired

　　　　not a pairing: → 686

　　　　　　facies . . . intellexerit: → 358

　　acciderit . . . feremus: → 1404

　　adsequeris . . . fuero: → 1315

attigerit, erit: → 1564

audierimus ... convertemus: → 1223

cenabis, cum veneris: → 803

cognoro, scies: → 726, 731

congressi erimus ... : → 1115

contuleris ... iudicabo: → 146

contulerit ... : → 1256

correxerit, ... feremus: → 1208

fuerit ... videbo: → 642

potuero: → 1372

rettuleris ... erit: → 303

sanabuntur cum veneris: → 402

tolles ... putaris: → 387

veneris ... : → 1531

veneris cognosces: → 335

veneris ... cognosces: → 268

Encounter 8

Section 2

verb formation Time 4, Time 5, Time 6: → 292, 1089

verb formation Time 4a: → 1089

verb formation Time 6: → 359

Encounter 9

Section 1 (the verb "to be" in the indicative): → 725, 730, 1307, 1315, 1328, 1360

Encounter 10

rel. pron.: subject or object

a quibus intellegis ... : → 1145

ad quos ... : → 474

quae accidunt: → 505

quae aguntur: → 505

quae ... intellegebam: → 382

quae me ita conficiunt: → 493

quae ... parasti: → 413

quae ... vides: → 454

quam ... adsequemur: → 1054

quam ... habere volumus: → 199

quam habes: → 575

quam ... offensurus sis: → 421

quam ... praetermissam esse arbitror: → 1523

quem ... appellari fas sit: → 1565

quem ... ignoras: → 164

qui curet: → 579

qui ... detruserunt: → 494

quod concessi: → 1067

quod ... cuperet: → 606, 608

quod erat: → 87

quod mihi mandaras: → 69

quod opus esset: → 682, 683

quod ... potest: → 385

Quod ... scriptum erat: → 404

relative clauses

a quibus intellegis: → 1145

a quibus nefas putaram: → 1292

cuius ... arbitror: → 83

de quo ... decrevit: → 674

De quo ... homine ... spondeo: → 1450

in quem ... incideret: → 1132

quae ... duxisti: → 1244

quae ... est: → 943

quae ... possis adduci: → 1442

quae ... scribis: → 191

quae ... timenda duxisti: → 1243

quam semper fui: → 349

quas ... attulit: → 777

quas ... cum recitavissem: → 1191

quas ... misit: → 847

qui me amet: → 136

qui ... poterit: → 1307

qui si ... attigerit: → 1564

quibus ne id expedire quidem arbitrabar: → 1293

quibus si ... respondetur: → 1515

quin idem te amet: → 136

quod ... cuperet: → 608

quod dico firmum fore: → 1635

quod ... est: → 1124, 1136

quod ... fuerat dictum: → 794

quod ... fuit: → 1311

Quod ... ignorabo: → 1074

quod ... suspicor: → 1234

quod vellem: → 611

Quod ... videbitur: → 1264

Section 2

sound qu–: → 1174

Encounter 11

relative clauses: *see* Encounter 10

Section 2

in quo ... desiderare te significabas meas litteras: → 1582

in quo accusabar: → 1580

quae accidunt: → 505

quae aguntur: → 505

quae ... parasti: → 413

quae te velle ... arbitrabor: → 957

quaeque ... pertinere arbitrabor: → 957

quam qui: → 639

qui ... veniunt: → 262

quod ad te scribo: → 1640

quod ... fuerat dictum ... actum iri: → 795

quod ... mandaras: → 69

quod pluris est: → 1613

Quod ... scriptum erat: → 404

rel. pron.: omission of the antecedent

Section 3 (rel. pron.: brevity): → 1127, 1580, 1582

Section 4 (relative box)

See: INDEX STRVCTVRARVM | *index of the structures*

benevelentior ... esse non possum: → 349

quam semper fui: → 349

Encounter 12

verb formation Time 1, Time 2, Time 3: → 292, 745, 1079

Section 2

Subsection 1 (verb formation Time 2): → 5, 708

Section 3

verb formation Time 3

videbis: → 1330

verb formation Time 3 in groups I and II

exspectabo: → 730

Illustrabit: → 1249

parabitur: → 1307

putabis: → 391

putabo: → 1323, 1325

retinebo: → 1325

videbitur: → 1264

verb formation Time 3 in groups III and IV

accipiam: → 1068

aderunt: → 730

adsequeris: → 1315

agam: → 1268

audies: → 391

conscribam: → 750

desinam: → 1081

facies: → 1264

fallam: → 1249

instruam: → 1068

narrabo ... habebo: → 1080

persequar: → 1270

petam: → 1279

rescribes: → 730

scies: → 1228

scies: → 730

scribam ... offendam ... dicam: → 540, 545

tolles: → 391

Tradam: → 1274

voles: → 391

Encounter 13

Section 1 (ways of asking): → 885, 893, 1094, 1276
Section 2 (other similar questions): → 1351

Encounter 14

Section 4 (defective verbs): → 594, 595, 970, 1168, 1333, 1602

Encounter 15

Block II nouns: → 12
function: object: → 676

Encounter 17

commands: first, second
    age: → 512
    audi: → 1616
    Cave: → 698
    cognosce: → 1015
    consulito: → 129
    crede: → 1250
    date: → 985
    delega: → 1431
    explora: → 1114
    fuge: → 511
    habeto: → 134
    persuade: → 1573
    praesta: → 1246
    scito: → 89, 90, 314, 315, 406, 564, 776, 1000, 1395, 1510, 1512, 1526
    servi, servite: → 144
    subveni: → 1572
    Vide, vide: → 1415, 1423, 1424, 1478
    videte: → 977
    videto: → 153

Encounter 18

Block II adj. in three ways: → 444, 552, 1003, 1471

Encounter 20

function: of-possession
    Ciceronis ... Domiti, Catonis, Lentuli, Bibulorum: → 1553
    L. Sesti Pansae: → 22
    librari: → 999
    matris tuae: → 1392
    Octobris: → 1088
    Planci: → 1164
    rei publicae: → 1176

Encounter 21

passive Times 1, 2, 3 indicative
    dantur: → 1430

deseror ... sustentor et recreor: → 573

impedior: → 502

instruar: → 1068

parabitur: → 1307

pascor: → 570

plauditur: → 787

Encounter 24

Section 1

adj.: possessive

mei: → 1387

objective genitive: → 420

personal pronouns: function of-possession

mei: → 232, 1387

Section 2

adj.: possessive

nostrum: → 311

personal pronouns: function of-possession

nostri: → 311, 614, 703, 764

Section 3

adj.: possessive

tua: → 1384

tui: → 48

tuorum: → 269

tuum: → 301

personal pronouns: function of-possession

tui: → 48, 301

Section 5

personal pronouns: function of-possession

eius: → 337

Section 6

the forms *nostri*, vestri**

vestrum: → 841, 1121

Encounter 26

passive Times 4, 5, 6 indicative: → 556, 794, 797, 1247, 1315, 1623

verb Time 4b passive: → 13, 16, 323

Encounter 27

abl.: meaning and forms

gravi tempore: → 444

causa: → 1176

inopia: → 503

invitatu tuo: → 1437

more Romano: → 1449

nostra vita: → 737

nostris multis peccatis: → 1205

Nullo modo: → 1277

pluribus: → 541

quibus: → 752

abl.: separation: → 38, 227, 932

abl. separation from place: → 150, 183, 779, 1101, 1212, 1367

function: place from where, names of cities and small islands, *Brundisio:* → 183

Encounter 28

Section 1

abl. in pronouns and relatives: → 466

Section 4

prep. with abl.

a militibus ... a pecunia: → 690

a singulis ... abs te: → 289

a te: → 565

ab eo: → 215

abs te ... a Pomponia: → 59

cum Balbo: → 1429

cum homine furioso ... Servilio: → 1172

De quo ... homine: → 1450

de vestra vetere gratia reconcilianda: → 372

e navi: → 1086

ex ... rumore an ex litteris: → 321

illo tempore: → 630

In ... causa: → 1185

in ceteris rebus: → 1163

in nuntiis Brundisinis: → 1465

in omnibus tuis rebus: → 1595

in scribendo: → 1070

in supplicatione ... deneganda: → 783, 784

in supplicatione decernenda: → 1163

in urbe: → 806

pro salute mea: → 362

pro tua admirabili ac singulari sapientia: → 815

pro tua ... benevolentia: → 362

pro tua ... dignitate: → 1384

Section 5

Subsection 2

prep. + abl. of separation or agent: → 574, 1077, 1393, 1397, 1674

Subsection 3

abl.: instrument

beneficio: → 825

bibliotheca: → 570

clarissima ... una: → 881

consolando ... consilio ... re iuvero: → 249

duabus epistulis tuis ... scriptis: → 367

ea: → 944

filiolo: → 1395

Fundo: → 769

gratia plena: → 616

his rebus Puteolanis et Lucrinensibus: → 572

iis bonis: → 555

iis litteris: → 234

incredibili dolore: → 1185

magna voluntate: → 1016

muneribus: → 558

natura, studio, fortuna: → 556

obscuro ... vario: → 881

omnibus iniquitatibus: → 410

priore pagina ... altera: → 97

quibus ... glutinatoribus ... administris: → 860

securi Tenedia: → 12

sermone ... voce: → 880

villis iis: → 767

abl.: personal agent

actually instrumental abl.: → 556

a me: → 474

a quibus: → 1292

a te: → 148

a te: → 921

abs te: → 1523

Encounter 29

verb: deponent

adniteretur: → 1111

adsequeris: → 1315

alucinari: → 11

arbitrabar: → 1293

arbitrabor: → 957

arbitrari: → 404

arbitretur: → 937

arbitror: → 1153, 1523, 319, 934

aspernabere: → 1591

congressi erimus: → 1115

consequere: → 312

enitemur: → 1020

es profectus: → 2

essent adsensi: → 621

expertus est: → 341

gratificer: → 251

ingrediar: → 562

Iocari: → 1660

laetor: → 1592

loquerer: → 653

miror ... mereri: → 521

morari: → 1653

mortuam esse: → 313

opinor: → 1036

pati: → 240

patiare: → 1532

patior ... questos esse: → 1497, 1500

polliceri: → 1428

polliceris: → 1079

profectus esses: → 283

sum admiratus: → 807, 809

suspicabar: → 589

suspicari: → 949

testatum: → 546

tueor: → 509

tueri: → 1600

utere: → 768

utor: → 990

vererere: → 1524

verita sit: → 316

Encounter 30

reflexive pron.: first and second person

me: → 147, 695, 1274

nos: → 1224

te: → 143, 1246

tibi: → 238

Encounter 31

reflexive pron.: third person

ad suas: → 728

de se: → 357

in se ... sibi: → 341

se: → 601, 607, 667, 675, 1566

se ... se: → 1630, 1631, 1633

se ipsum: → 350

secum: → 1498

sese ... secum ... sibi: → 1496

seseque: → 1495

sibi: → 282, 341, 344, 1295, 1500

suam: → 676, 938

Encounter 33

dat.: meaning and forms: → 444, 965, 1376, 1393

Section 3 (pronoun forms to-for-from): → 142, 449

Section 7

Subsection 1 (natural dat.)

corpori: → 144

cui: → 1608

cuiquam: → 1156, 1473

ei: → 1062

Gabinio: → 783

homini: → 41

humanitati et naturae meae: → 924

illi: → 692

isti: → 1274

medico ipsi: → 121

meis optatis: → 1595

mihi: → 5, 127, 775, 1583, 1589, 1628

nemini: → 785

nobis: → 9, 191, 1299

quibus: → 752, 1515

saluti meae … honori: → 1149

sceleri meo … imprudentiae miseriae: → 1288

sibi: → 1295

tibi: → 102, 907, 1365, 1577, 1629

tibi … Pomponio: → 30

Subsection 2 (65 verbs with dat.)

adsensum esse mihi: → 1192

Afranio … adsensi: → 621

Caesari expediat: → 1260

cedendum: → 1262

Cui … deo … satis facies: → 744

cuiquam … ademerit: → 1473

gratuler tibi: → 1641

gratulerne tibi: → 884

iis credidi: → 1291

iisque imperes: → 859

ipsi crediderit: → 1638

meis … fidelissimis … amantissimis consiliis paruisses: → 1605

mihi crede: → 1250

mihi … deesse: → 142

mihi ignoscere: → 1241, 1242

mihi ignoscit: → 1492

mihi invidit: → 1295

mihi persuaserim: → 1415

mihi … respondit: → 600

mihique credas: → 1644

mihique … suasit: → 602

Mucio et Manilio placebat: → 220

Placiturum tibi esse: → 589

postulationi … restitisse: → 21

profuisse patriae: → 1574

quibus … expedire: → 1293

subinvideo tibi: → 212

sumptu ne parcas: → 116

tibi consuli: → 298

tibi defuisse: → 345

tibi … gratificer: → 252

Tibi … gratulor: → 873

tibi persuadeas: → 238

tibi praecipere: → 1596
tibi ... praecipio: → 309
tibi praestoler: → 1373
tibique persuade: → 1573
Uni Favonio ... non placebat: → 665
valetudini tuae ... consulueris: → 128
voluntati erga me diffidere: → 233
Subsection 3 (dat. with compound verbs): → 345, 452, 613, 674, 1096, 1232

Encounter 34

commands: deponent: → 312, 768, 895, 1266

Encounter 35

20% of nouns, *ambitus, us,* m.: → 1024
20% of nouns, *consulatus, us,* m.: → 1130
20% of nouns: *apparatus, us,* m.: → 703
20% of nouns: *facies, ei,* f.: → 745
20% of nouns: *idus, uum,* f.: → 773
20% of nouns: *motus, us,* m.: → 1303
20% of nouns: *reditus, us,* m.: → 887, 1663
20% of nouns: *res, rei,* f.: → 501, 1019
20% of nouns: *senatus, us,* m.: → 1141

primae experientiae lectionum paginulae | *reading sheets - First Experience*

Readings 1-D, 1-I: → 47, 197, 377, 392, 604, 636, 647, 732, 849, 874, 883, 926, 954, 1109, 1123, 1150, 1389, 1438, 1501, 1528, 1544, 1555, 1562, 1627

TERTIA EXPERIENTIA

third experience

Encounter 36

adj.: comp.
benevolentior: → 348
brevior: → 1069
cariorem ... iucundiorem: → 566
cautior: → 224
certius: → 569
coniunctiorem: → 1403
coniunctiores: → 950, 951
deteriores: → 423, 424
eruditius: → 1039
expeditius: → 1102
fortiores: → 755
maiora: → 1393
maiorem: → 276, 1160

   minore: → 1238

   modestiorem: → 1188

   obstinatior ... obfirmatior: → 401

   officiosior: → 489

   officiosiorem: → 346

   plenior: → 1543

   pluribus: → 541

   potius: → 834

   probiorem ... meliorem ... pudentiorem: → 1450

   studiosior: → 122

   stultius: → 244

   tristius aut severius: → 927

   verecundiores ... saniores: → 637

adj.: comp. and superl.

   amicior: → 1149

   amplissima: → 1147

   diutius: → 438

   firmissimarum: → 711

   gravissima: → 456

   liberalissimi ... amantissimi: → 232

   longiorem: → 1486

   melius: → 974

   minore: → 687

   minoris: → 700

   miserrimam: → 734

   molestissimum: → 736

   neglegentior: → 110

   summa: → 1552

   summa: → 352

adj.: superlative

   bellissimus: → 772

   familiarissimus: → 1294

   studiosissimus: → 226

Section 5 (adj.: irregular comp. and superl.)

   facillime: → 354, 458

   maiora: → 1392

   meliora: → 296

   minora: → 459

   minus: → 1338

   minus ... minus: → 1339

   miserrimum: → 478

   multo maiori: → 1534

   multo meliores: → 857

   multo minorem: → 1535

   optatissime: → 801

   optimam: → 1495

   summa: → 352

Encounter 37

adv: → 96, 552, 652, 888, 1405

adv.: comp.: → 244, 569, 1039

adv.: comparative, superlative: → 834

adv.: positive, comp., superl.

      accurate: →104

      accuratius: → 1429

      amantissime tum honorificentissime: → 909

      citius: → 1354

      diligenter: → 229

      diligentissime: → 172, 426

      fere: → 1102

      longius: → 1303

      maxime: → 447

      maxime ... maxime: → 1474

      maxime ... minime: → 1622

      melius: → 974

      potissimum: → 1133

      potius: → 1339

      prorsus: → 1476

      tristius aut severius: → 927

Section 3

      adv.: irregular comp.

      adv.: irregular comp. and superl.: → 101, 368, 430, 464, 753, 1475

      eoque magis: → 1061

      magis: → 596, 1046, 1104, 1641

      magno opere: → 654

      minime: → 1010

      minus ... magis: → 641

Encounter 38

Block II adj.: *–is = –es*

      adfinis: → 1168

      Aprilis: → 1189

      familiaris: → 751, 1407

      intolerabilis: → 1312

      omnis: → 278, 626, 733

      perbrevis: → 1587

Block II nouns: *–is = –es:* → 81, 933, 1370

Section 3 (function: direct address)

      mi Antoni: → 918

      mi Brute: → 1556

      mi Caesar: → 1440

      mi frater: → 1286

      mi Tiro: → 117, 130

      optime et optatissime frater: → 801

Encounter 39

Section 2 (contractions: verbs)

  cessaris: → 1334

  cogitaram: → 1419

  cognoro: → 726

  cognossem: → 754

  delectarit: → 1621

  efflagitarunt: → 1

  mandaras: → 69

  navigarit: → 359

  norim: → 1084

  parasse: → 192

  putaram: → 858, 1292

  putaris: → 387

  putassem: → 86

  repudiarunt: → 624

  significarim: → 398

  sperasset: → 1427

  tardarunt: → 1098

Section 3 (variation: –*ris*)

  aspernabere: → 1591

  complectare: → 1439

  consequere: → 312

  loquere: → 1266

  meditere: → 543

  mirere: → 395

  moveare: → 43

  obsecrare: → 1598

  patiare: → 1532

  pluris: → 1614

  revertare: → 1355

  utere: → 768

  vererere: → 1524

  videare: → 260

  viderere: → 206

Section 4 (commands: famous four)

  dic: → 475

  fac: → 171, 248, 264, 524, 864, 1275

Encounter 40

Section 2 (demonstrative pron.: *is, ea, id*): → 55, 812, 1246

Section 3 (demonstrative pron.: *hic, haec, hoc*): → 1439

Encounter 41

Section 3 (three cousins: *iste–ille–ipse*)

  illius: → 449, 1647

  Illud: → 1081

  illum: → 1479, 1653

  ipse: → 45
  ipsi: → 1638
  istam ... ista: → 300
  istuc: → 1008
  istum: → 237

Encounter 42

Section 2 (rel. pron. + ind.: review): → 385
Section 3 (other similar questions): → 1351
Section 4
  adj.: indefinite: → 818, 937, 971
  adv.: indefinite, see: → 549, 1516
  pronouns: indefinite
    qua: → 160
    quae: → 1645
    qui: → 472, 579, 1207
    quid: → 24, 433, 477, 569, 727, 1281, 1282, 1284, 1358, 1360
Section 5 (after si the ali-s fly away)
  qua: → 160, 818
  quae: → 971, 1645
  quando: → 549, 1516
  quas: → 937
  qui: → 472, 579, 1207
  quid: → 24, 433, 477, 569, 727, 1281, 1282, 1284, 1358, 1360
Section 6 (famous nine): → 40

Encounter 43

quam: → 78, 575, 597, 639
quam with the comp. or superl.: → 1056
Section 2 (*quam* with the comp.)
  benevolentior quam: → 348
  coniunctiores ... quam: → 951
  deteriores ... quam: → 424
  diutius quam: → 1175
  diuturnior quam: → 1422
  facilius ... quam: → 557
  fortiores ... quam: → 756
  magis ... quam: → 596, 953, 1641
  maiora ... quam: → 1393
  minore ... quam: → 1238
  minus ... quam: → 1144, 1339, 1341, 1428
  multo maiori quam: → 1534
  multo minorem quam: → 1535
  pluris erit quam: → 247
  plus ... quam: → 1574
  potius quam: → 508, 1075, 1288, 1372
  pridie quam: → 660
  verecundiores ... quam ... saniores quam: → 637

Section 3 (quam with the superlative)

    quam accommodatissimum: → 842

    quam diligentissime: → 172

    quam honorificentissime: → 1140

    quam ornatissimum: → 1161, 1421, 1422

    quam primum: → 194, 248, 414, 525

    quam proxime: → 1220

Encounter 44

Section 1 (forms of the subjunctive, Time 1s)

    adducam … relinquam: → 545

    agam: → 1268

    conscribam: → 750

    persequar: → 1270

    petam: → 1279

    properet: → 584

    sis: → 1073

    Tradam: → 1274

Section 2 (forms of the subjunctive, Time 2s): → 398, 584

Section 3 (forms of the subjunctive, Time 3s): → 316, 359, 398, 1073

Encounter 45

principles of the subjunctive: → 648, 1444, 1446, 1447, 1466, 1469

    6. independent subjunctive: → 1274, 1304, 1352, 1489, 1661

Encounter 46

forms of the subjunctive, *esse:* → 297

Encounter 47

consecutio

    accedebat … ut agerem: → 371

    Accedit ut … fuerit: → 929

    accidit ut … esset et ut ego, qui … statuerim esse, mallem Peducaeum …
        quam me dare : → 72, 74, 75, 77, 78

    ait … se adesse velle … si Caesar adductus sit ut praesidia deducat: → 669,
        670, 671

    Aviam … scito … mortuam esse … quod verita sit ne … manerent …
        adducerent: → 315

    certior sum factus: → 60

    Coepi velle … exspectare … quae sperasset: → 1427

    cogitaram … ducere, ut … reducerem: → 1421

    cognovi praedia non venisse: → 496

    commendoque … ut … comprobes … -que … tractes: → 996

    commutatus est … ut … futurus sit: → 1623

    constat … utrum sit: → 974

    Contendi cum … defenderet: → 938

    convenerunt quae … exturbarent: → 1309

    cum … confirmasset … persuasisset, egit … ut sponderem: → 1628, 1629 *cum ... dedissem, cuius ... arbitror, ... duxi scribere ... cum ... audire, quod erat ... , ... putassem:* → 79, 83, 86

cum ... egissem cum ... fuisses, ... putavi: → 843, 844

cum ... loquerer ... dantur: → 1429, 1430

cupiebant Caesarem ... stare ... quas tulisset: → 661, 663

dandum ... fuit, quom ... esses: → 103

de quo ... decrevit ut ... iret ... succederet, negat se ... iturum: → 674, 675

dederim ut ... postulent: → 288

dubito quin ... sit, cum et ... moveare et ... amiseris: → 44

duxi dies ... consumere, eoque magis quod ei gratum esse id videbam, qui ... petierit: → 1064, 1085

erit ... quantae fuerit, ut ... esset is qui esse deberet: → 54

es ... qui neque ... natare volueris ... neque spectare : → 225

est ... facta cum te ... dicerent ... restitisse: → 18

est factum ... quam ego dixeram cum tu adesses: → 620

est tanta ... ut sperem te ... ignoscere, si ... timuerim: → 1242

eumque, nisi ... contulerit, exceptum iri puto: → 1256

explicare ... possum, quidnam inveniri possit : → 1348

exspectatio .... Si nactus ... esset ... ; sin ... tramisisset: → 1466, 1469

extrusi ... ut, etiamsi in Italiam venisset, ... rediret : → 1545, 1547, 1548

fuit ... si ... cuperem, ... fuisset: → 1618

habet quiddam ... quod ... insederit: → 384

intermiseram, ne viderer ... diffidere: → 231

intermisi ... quin ... darem, non quo haberem ... sed ut loquerer ... quo: → 650, 652, 653

ita commendavit ut ... habeam: → 905, 906

iudicavique ... te violari ... cuius ... niterentur: → 824

legi ... quibus ... agebas ut ... essem: → 805

me ... accepisse putavi: → 848

metuo ne ... ceperimus quod ... explicare possimus: → 176, 177

mihique ut idem facerem suasit: → 602

misit ad me ... qui salutem nuntiaret: → 587

ne ignores quid ... desiderarim, scribam: → 1521

ne ... mirere cur, cum ... significarim ... me sperare illum ... fore, ... videar diffidere, incredibile est: → 394, 396

negant ... postulataque ... interposita esse quo minus quod opus esset ... pararetur : → 682, 683

... neque ... fuit de qua ... rescribi voluisti quod ... pertinet quid vellem: → 443

nescio ... gratulerne tibi an timeam ... non quo verear ... ne, cum veneris, non habeas ... quod cures: → 884, 891

nescio rectene sint ... commissa: → 893

nisi fecisset iudicassemque ... fecissem: → 1636

non dubito quin, si ... adiunxerint, ... conciliatura coniuncturaque sit : → 1519

non ii, quod ... venerant: → 1217

oro ut ... rescribas ... putes esse: → 1337, 1338

patior secum Tullum et Servium questos esse quia … remisisset : → 1500

peto … oro … obtestor ut … impertias … ut … esse … possim: → 835, 837

peto … ut me … velis esse: → 1161

placuit … quidquam … fieri quod … esset: → 533

praecisa est, cum … defenderet: → 14

praetermisi … quin perscriberem: → 1005

praetermisi, quem … perventurum putarem, cui … dederim: → 1584, 1585

probatum est … ut … crediderit, … noluerit … fecerit, … dimiserit: → 1637

puto facturum ut … deducat: → 685

puto quid faciatis: → 960

Quae … gesta esse cognosces ut … patiare: → 1532

Quae … impendere putarem scripseram: → 1481

Quae gerantur accipies: → 1231

Quae ne spes eum fallat … rogo te: → 994

quanti me faciat semper fecerit … qui ignoret arbitror neminem: → 1152

quantis … evenerit non possum … cogitare: → 1480

quanto … sim privatus … existimare potes: → 37

quantum … acceperim … existimare potes: → 36

quas statim cum recitavissem, cecidit Servilius: → 1191

qui … accusas … scito … redditas esse, cum … habueris: → 88, 90, 91

… qui cum filios misissent … venire dubitarint: → 1503, 1504

Quid … fuerit … intellexi quam … discessi: → 741

Quid agas … et quid acturus sis fac nos … certiores: → 169

quid opus sit et quid sit videbis: → 1330

quid significares … quaerebam: → 810

quid sit scire cupio: → 297

quo modo se habeant … narrare audeo: → 871, 872

Quod si te … vindicat … , perspicis ecquaenam … relinquatur: → 1299

… quoi … dedimus … opinantes nobis … eam rem etiam honori fore: → 468

Quoniam id accidit … ut … quoniam … accidit ut … posset, in quem …
    incideret, peto: → 1124, 1125, 1128, 1134

remitto … ita ut me … , cum … scripseris, … tractatum existimem, idque
    cum totum … dandum putarem: → 922, 923

reprehendo, quippe cum … non fugerim: → 1488

retinuerunt, cum … discedere … vetarent : → 1303

rogo ut … iudices: → 1642

rogo ut memineris: → 1602

Scis … quid … existimem: → 1612

scribam … offendam … dicam, ut … adducam … relinquam … ut, si …
    coeperit … possis: → 540, 545, 548

Scripsi … quod dixisses daret: → 120

scripsi: … ut, si … videretur, … traferret: → 107

sed acerbissime tulit Servilius adsensum esse: → 1192

Si … stultus esse videor qui sperem, facio: → 1199

sic me adfecerunt ut … viderer: → 907

sit … etsi nunc … quod scriberem nihil erat: → 1463, 1464

spondeo … quod, cum … scripsissem, … lusisti: → 1448

sum levatus ut deus aliquis … fecisse videatur: → 743

sunt ... cum ... delegi quos ... colerem et quibus essem, sicut sum: → 830, 831

sunt persecuti ... qui, ... cum essent adsensi, addiderunt ut ... ita crearentur
ut ... essent: → 621, 622

Suscepit rem dixitque esse quod: → 605, 606

tanta fuit ... ut illud ... videretur: → 1434

tuli ... ne darem: → 1177

velim ... ibi malis esse ubi ... sis quam istic ubi ... spaere videare: → 258, 259

veniunt ... eamque rem posse ... esse, si ... fieri coeperint: → 969

vereor ne ... sit; ... quod, cum ... accepisset, ... remisit: → 113

vide quid mihi sumpserim: → 1424

video quid exspectem: → 1489

video quid prodesse possis si veneris: → 181

videsne in quem ... inciderit: → 1470

Encounter 48

consecution: *see* Encounter 47

Encounter 50

antecedent participle: *see* Encounter 51.1.2

antecedent participle, deponents: *see* Encounter 51.2.2

contemporaneous active participle: → 532, 911, 1072, 1350; *see also* Encounter 51.1.1

contemporaneous active participle, deponents: → 696; *see also* Encounter 51.2.1

futurity participle: *see* Encounter 51.1.3

futurity participle, deponents: → 944; *see also* Encounter 51.2.3:

participle of passive necessity: *see* Encounter 51.1.4

participle of passive necessity, deponents: *see* Encounter 51.2.4

Encounter 51

Section 1

    Subsection 1 (contemporaneous active participle)

        absente: → 532

        dubitans: → 1072

        petente: → 911

        recusante: → 1350

    Subsection2 (antecedent participle)

        abductis: → 662

        concessum: → 825

        confectum: → 1083

        conformatus: → 1598

        defensus ... ornatus: → 1390

        immutatae: → 376

    Subsection 3 (futurity participle)

        acturus: → 1261, 1284

        advolaturus: → 1359

        aucupaturi: → 1103

        conciliatura coniuncturaque: → 1518, 1519

        curaturum: → 187

        daturum: → 1542

        decursurum: → 126

dicturus: → 1636

dimissurum: → 1090

facturum: → 685

fore: → 394, 400, 468, 612, 628, 1188, 1235, 1401, 1407, 1410, 1635

futurum: → 237, 1032, 1630

futurus: → 1623

imitaturus: → 722

impetraturum: → 839

iturum: → 675

mansurum: → 679

Placiturum: → 589

profuturum: → 1574

venturi: → 707

venturus: → 1118

vindicaturus: → 897

Subsection 4 (participle of passive necessity)

accipienda: → 688

adiuvandum: → 828

alienandum: → 1181

ambulandum: → 577

cedendum: → 1262

cogitandum: → 1108

commonendum: → 234

conciliandam: → 1408

Considerandum: → 959

dandum: → 102, 103, 121, 923

deneganda: → 784

faciendum: → 114, 1559

legenda: → 1668

mittendum: → 1436

paenitendum: → 635

placando: → 332

postulanda: → 1393

reconcilianda: → 372

reconciliando: → 819

scribendum: → 474

servandama: → 1326

spoliandos: → 932

sumendae: → 1674

timenda: → 1243

Section 2 (deponents)

Subsection 1 (contemporaneous active participle): → 696

Subsection 2 (antecedent participle)

sum admiratus: → 807

testatum: → 546

Subsection 3 (futurity participle)

usurum: → 944

Subsection 4 (participle of passive necessity)

  insectandos: → 930

  tuendo: → 819

  utendum: → 219

Encounter 53

Section 3 (futurity formula, active)

  aucupaturi eramus: → 1103

  daturum [*esse*]: → 1542

  dicturus sum: → 1636

  erant venturi: → 707

  fore [*futurum esse*]: → 394, 400, 468, 612, 628, 1188, 1235, 1401, 1407,
   1410, 1635

  futurum [*esse*]: → 237, 1630

  Placiturum . . . esse: → 589

  profuturum [*esse*]: → 1574

  usurum [*esse*]: → 944

Section 4 (passive necessity formula)

  accipienda . . . est: → 688

  alienandum [*esse*]: → 1181

  cogitandum [*esse*]: → 1108

  commonendum [*esse*]: → 234

  Considerandum [*esse*]: → 959

  dandum . . . fuit: → 102, 103

  dandum [*esse*]: → 923

  dandum esse: → 121

  esse ambulandum: → 577

  esse spoliandos: → 932

  faciendum est: → 1559

  faciendum sit: → 114

  legenda [*esse*]: → 1668

  mittendum [*esse*]: → 1436

  paenitendum [*esse*]: → 635

  scribendum [*esse*]: → 474

  servandam esse: → 1326

  sunt . . . sumendae: → 1674

  timenda [*esse*]: → 1243

  utendum [*esse*]: → 219

Section 5 (dat. of agent)

  Gabinio: → 784

  medico ipsi: → 121

  mihi: → 127, 1583

  mulieri: → 1393

  nobis: → 635, 775, 1108

  tibi: → 102, 1169, 1559, 1674

  vobis: → 959

Encounter 54

ablative absolute

> *abductis praesidiis:* → 662
>
> *amissis opibus:* → 640
>
> *animo abalienato:* → 334
>
> *constitutis rebus:* → 469
>
> *duabus epistulis tuis ... scriptis:* → 367
>
> *dubio rerum exitu:* → 445
>
> *duobus his muneribus:* → 869
>
> *Elisabetha regina, Barrack presidente:* → 1394
>
> *interpellantibus enim his inimicitiis:* → 952, 953, 955
>
> *lectis ... litteris:* → 846, 847
>
> *magna voluntate:* → 1016
>
> *maximo imbri:* → 704
>
> *me absente:* → 791
>
> *me invito:* → 913, 945
>
> *non aspernante ... senatu:* → 1124, 1138, 1139
>
> *nullo recusante:* → 1350
>
> *omnibus libentibus:* → 1027
>
> *potentissimo inimico, dominatione obtrectatorum, infidelibus amicis,*
>   *plurimis invidis:* → 1305
>
> *Remoto ioco:* → 308
>
> *salva Terentia:* → 1396
>
> *sed valde adversante Clodio:* → 1306, 1307
>
> *subscribente privigno Memmio, fratre Caecilio, Sulla filio:* → 1025
>
> *summa accusatoris voluntate:* → 1400
>
> *sumptis armis:* → 822
>
> *te absente:* → 532
>
> *te consessore:* → 1363
>
> *te provinciam obtinente:* → 273

Encounter 55

ablative absolute: *see* Encounter 54
Section 3
> ablative absolute with relative subject: → 1196

Encounter 58

subjunctive use: purpose clause without *ut*

> *absint velim:* → 1336
>
> *facias me velim:* → 235
>
> *gaudeas velim:* → 175
>
> *mallem egisses:* → 902
>
> *persuadeas velim:* → 238
>
> *scribas velim:* → 1055
>
> *Scripsi ... daret:* → 119
>
> *te obsecrare obtestarique ... revertare:* → 1598
>
> *velim cogites:* → 195
>
> *velim ... complectare:* → 1439, 1444

velim ... conficias: → 470

velim ... consideretis: → 980

velim cures: → 425, 765

velim desinas ... et ... revisas et ... malis: → 257

velim dispicias: → 1106

velim explices ... iuves: → 723

velim ... instituatis: → 983

velim ... invisas: → 581

velim ... mittas: → 412

velim ... mittas ... imperes: → 859

velim ... perscribas: → 1203

velim ... persuadeas: → 958

velim scribas: → 1283, 1284, 1491

velim ... urgeas: → 583

videatis velim: → 517

velim ... videas: → 1107

Section 1

    subjunctive use: purpose clause

        ne darem: → 1177

        ne ... desit: → 477

        ne ... fallat: → 994

        ne ... habeas: → 885

        ne ignores: → 1521

        ne ... liceat: → 976, 978

        ne ... meditere: → 542

        ne ... offenderes: → 1525

        ne parcas: → 116

        ne respondeat: → 885

        ne viderer: → 231

        ut ... accipiam: → 984

        ut ... adducam ... relinquam: → 545, 547

        ut agerem: → 371

        ut ... amares: → 1633

        ut ... comprobes ... tractes: → 996

        ut ... conferas: → 1447

        ut ... conserat: → 714

        ut ... crearentur: → 622

        ut ... crederes: → 1632

        ut curem: → 188

        ut ... cures: → 1124, 1135, 1136

        ut ... deducat: → 671

        ut ... essem: → 805, 811, 1066

        ut ... esset: → 52

        ut ... facerem: → 602

        ut ... habeamus: → 193

        ut ... habeat: → 982

        ut ... imbuas: → 935

        ut ... impertias: → 835, 837

ut intellegat: → 997

ut ... intellegat: → 279

ut ... intercludat: → 714

ut ... iret ... succederet: → 674

ut ... iudices: → 1642

ut loquerer: → 653

ut meminerim: → 594

ut memineris: → 1602

ut ne ... arbitretur: → 937

ut ... ne dimittas ... deducas: → 1557, 1558

ut ... nolles: → 911

ut norim: → 1084

ut ... perferas ... augeas ... recipias: → 310

ut ... possim: → 462

ut ... possimus: → 1114

ut possim: → 585, 852

ut possimus: → 265

ut ... possis: → 548

ut ... postulent: → 288

ut properet: → 584

ut ... putes: → 1338

ut ... recipias: → 277

ut ... rediret: → 1547, 1548

ut ... reducerem: → 1421

ut ... relinquas: → 1083

ut ... rescribas: → 1337

ut salvus sis: → 133

ut ... scribas: → 1011

ut ... simus: → 950

ut sis: → 1413

ut ... sit: → 1020

ut sponderem: → 1629

ut sumant: → 861

ut sustentetur: → 498

ut ... traferret: → 107

ut valeas: → 476, 1461

ut valeatis: → 986

ut ... velis: → 1161, 1442, 1446

ut ... velis ... putes: → 1159

velim ... ne praetermittas: → 159

videto ... ut ... sis: → 154

subjunctive use: relative clause of purpose, *ubi:* → 258, 259

Section 2

subjunctive use: relative clause of purpose

ex qua ... fiant: → 862

quem ornem: → 1432

qui ... nuntiaret: → 587

qui ... solveret: → 327

> *quibus ... placarem ... monerem ... obiurgarem:* → 56
> *quibus ... utatur:* → 860
> *quo = ut eo:* → 122, 681, 755, 1179, 1454
> *quod ... esset:* → 534
> *quos ... colerem ... quibus essem:* → 831

Encounter 59

Section 1 (subjunctive use: causal *cum* = "because, since,")

> *cum ... accepisset:* → 113
> *cum ... agatur:* → 668
> *cum ... consuerit:* → 272
> *cum ... consulueris:* → 128
> *cum ... debeas:* → 278
> *cum ... defenderet:* → 14, 938
> *cum ... egissem:* → 843
> *cum essent adsensi:* → 621
> *cum et ... moveare et ... amiseris:* → 44
> *cum ... fugerim:* → 1488
> *cum ... fuisses:* → 844
> *cum ... iniecissem:* → 1648
> *Cum instituissem ... sumpsissem:* → 1085
> *cum ... liceat:* → 254
> *cum ... misissent:* → 1504
> *cum ... perspexerim:* → 1391
> *cum ... posses:* → 914
> *cum possint:* → 1077
> *cum ... putassem:* → 86, 92
> *cum recitavissem:* → 1191
> *cum ... redissem:* → 1652
> *Cum ... scriberem:* → 1364
> *cum ... scripseris:* → 922
> *cum ... significarim:* → 398
> *cum tu adesses:* → 620
> *cum venissem:* → 658
> *cum ... vetarent:* → 1302
> *cumque ego egissem:* → 599
> *quom ... esses:* → 103
> *quom ... vacarem ... ferres:* → 1579

Section 2

> causal: *quia,* "because, since," + indicative, one's own reason: → 1500
> causal: *quia,* "because, since," + subjunctive, reported reason: → 1500
> causal: *quod, quia, quoniam,* "because, since," + indicative, one's own
>   reason: → 941, 1374
> causal: *quod, quia, quoniam,* "because, since," + subjunctive, reported
>   reason: → 652, 888, 941, 947, 1494
> causal: *quod, quia, quoniam,* "because, since": → 111
> causal: *quod,* "because, since," + indicative, one's own reason
>   *quod abes:* → 877

quod ... adierit, ... navigarit: → 361

quod carui: → 1594

quod ... curata sunt: → 328

quod ... es consecutus: → 1594

quod non veni: → 1493

quod ... remisit: → 113

quod ... suspicor: → 1234

quod ... venerant: → 1217

quodque ... respondit: → 1594

vel quia ... vel quod ... : → 878

causal: *quod,* "because, since," + subjunctive, reported reason: → 877, 1217, 1259, 1493, 1524

causal: *quod,* "because, since," + subjunctive, reported reason: → 263, 316, 328, 361, 1641

causal: *quod,* "because, since": → 202, 790

causal: *quoniam,* "because, since," + indicative, one's own reason: → 1047, 1125, 1313

causal: *quoniam,* "because, since," + subjunctive, reported reason: → 1047, 1125

Section 4 (subjunctive use: causal *qui, quae, quod* = "because, since,")

quae ... sint: → 580

qui ... advoles: → 246

qui ... attraham: → 245

qui ... dubitarint: → 1503

qui et properarem et ... darem: → 1117

qui ingrediar: → 562

qui ... non abundares: → 221

qui ... petierit: → 1063

qui sperem: → 1199

qui ... venturus esset: → 1118

qui ... volueris: → 225

quod ... solebat: → 338

Section 5 (subjunctive use: causal *quippe qui*): → 504, 1488

Encounter 60

IQ

not an IQ

nescio quid ... : → 1435

Quod ... videbitur: → 1264

ubi ... sis: → 258

ubi ... videare: → 259

an ... tendam: → 1656

cur ... gratificer: → 251

cur ... videar: → 396, 399

ecquaenam ... relinquatur: → 1299

gratulerne tibi an timeam: → 884, 885, 889

in quem hominem inciderit : → 1470

–ne sint ... commissa: → 893

–ne … sit: → 722
–ne sitis … an … an … : → 962
qua re nihil esset: → 1218
qua re … possim: → 240
qua spe hiematurus sis: → 1055
Quae gerantur: → 1231
Quae … putarem: → 1481
quam conversa res sit: → 1478
quam … delectarit: → 1621, 1622
quam … offensurus sis: → 421, 424
quam mihi persuaserim: → 1415
quam … putes: → 237
quam … scripserim: → 229
quam sint : → 1569
quando futura sint comitia: → 407
quantae … fuerit: → 50
quanti me faciat semper fecerit: → 1152
quantis … evenerit: → 1480
quanto … offensurus sis: → 421
quanto … sim privatus: → 37
quantum … acceperim: → 36
quem ad modum … possis: → 196
quid acturus sis: → 169
quid agas: → 169, 236
quid … agatur: → 437
quid … desiderarim: → 1521
quid … existimem: → 1612
quid exspectem: → 1489
quid exspectes: → 236
quid … faciant: → 976, 977
quid faciatis: → 960
quid faciatis … loco: → 959
quid faciendum sit: → 114
quid fiat: → 1028
quid … fuerit: → 739
Quid futurum sit: → 1032
quid mihi sumpserim: → 1424
quid … opus sit: → 463
quid opus sit et quid sit: → 1330
Quid possis: → 179
quid … possis: → 181
quid … putes: → 1108
Quid profecerim: → 235
quid senserim: → 547
quid significares: → 810
quid sis acturus: → 1282, 1284
quid sit: → 297
quid vellem: → 440, 443

quid videas: → 1203

quidnam ... possit: → 1348

quidnam ... velit ... ostendat: → 1193

quo ... : → 1226

quo modo fecerit: → 485

quo modo satis fiat: → 518

quo modo se habeant: → 871

quod gaudeas: → 202

quorum ... sit acturus: → 1261

Romaene sis an iam profectus: → 1073

ubi sit: → 1271

utrum sit: → 974

M & M: *see* Encounter 71

Encounter 61

Section 1

consecutio: completed futurity in the subjunctive

cum ... perspexisses: → 1633

cum venisses: → 536

etiamsi ... venisset: → 1548

si ... adiunxerint: → 1519

si ... coeperit: → 538, 550

si ... veneris: → 1574

Si nactus hic esset: → 1466, 1469

sin ille ante tramisisset: → 1466, 1469

consecutio: futurity in the subjunctive

etiamsi ... venisset: → 1548

quin ... committas: → 98

quod ... esset: → 533

Scripsi ... daret: → 120

si tibi videretur: → 108

sint habitura: → 871

ut ... possimus: → 1115

ut ... possis: → 548

ut ... rediret: → 1547

ut agerem: → 371

ut sponderem: → 1629

Section 3

consecutio: futurity formula in the subjunctive

not used

ut agerem: → 371

acturus sis: → 170

conciliatura coniuncturaque sit: → 1518, 1519

futura sint: → 407

futurum sit: → 1032

futurus sit: → 1623

offensurus sis: → 421

quid futurum sit: → 297

> *sint habitura:* → 871
> *sis acturus:* → 1284
> *sis advolaturus:* → 1359
> *sis visurus:* → 1203
> *sit acturus:* → 1261
> *sit imitaturus:* → 722
> *sit ... vindicaturus:* → 897

Encounter 62

Section 1

consecutio: subjunctive depending on a subjunctive

> *committam ut ... reddantur:* → 1076
> *des operam ut ... habeamus:* → 193
> *ne ... mirere ... cur cum ... significarim... videar:* → 394, 399
> *quanti me faciat ... fecerit ... qui ignoret:* → 1152
> *qui ... petierit ut ... essem:* → 1066
> *Quid profecerim facias me velim certiorem:* → 235
> *ut ... adducam ... relinquam ... ut ... possis:* → 548
> *ut ... crearentur ut ... essent:* → 622
> *ut ... posset, in quem ... incideret:* → 1124, 1132
> *ut possim:* → 585
> *ut ... respicias ut ... intellegat:* → 279
> *velim cogites ... quem ad modum ... possis:* → 196
> *velim ... consideretis:* → 980
> *velim ... instituatis ... ut ... accipiam:* → 983, 984
> *velim ... ne praetermittas:* → 159
> *velim ... urgeas ... ut properet:* → 584
> *verita sit ... manerent ... adducerent:* → 315

Encounter 64

concessive particles: → 1237, 1458, 1549
subjunctive use: concessive *cum* = "although,"

> *cum ... accepisset:* → 113
> *cum ... agatur:* → 668
> *cum ... consuerit:* → 272
> *cum ... debeas:* → 278
> *cum ... defenderet:* → 938
> *cum ... egissem:* → 843
> *cum essent adsensi:* → 621
> *cum ... fuisses:* → 844
> *cum ... habueris:* → 91, 92
> *cum ... iniecissem:* → 1648
> *cum ... misissent:* → 1504
> *Cum instituissem ... sumpsissem:* → 1085
> *cum ... posses:* → 914
> *cum possint:* → 1077
> *cum ... putassem:* → 86
> *cum ... redissem:* → 1652

Cum ... scriberem: → 1364

cum ... scripseris: → 922

cum ... significarim: → 398, 620

cum venissem: → 658

cum ... vetarent: → 1302

quom ... esses: → 103

quom ... vacarem ... prae te ferres: → 1579

subjunctive use: concessive *etsi* = "although,": → 724, 875, 1237, 1463

subjunctive use: concessive *quamquam* = "although,": → 1458, 1513

subjunctive use: concessive *quamvis* = "although,": → 306

subjunctive use: concessive *qui, quae, quod* = "although,": → 1668

Encounter 65

Section 1 (*postquam*): → 1422, 1423

Section 2

Subsection 2

quoad with an uncertain outcome: → 99, 1060

quoad with ind.: → 1074, 1323

Encounter 66

Section 3

cum + indicative = "when": temporal sentences

cum ... agatur: → 668

cum ... consulueris: → 128

cum ... delegi: → 829

cum ... habebo: → 1080

cum habeo: → 487

cum ... lego: → 1344

cum ... licet: → 657

cum sumus: → 7

cum velitis: → 979

cum ... venerimus: → 200

cum veneris: → 33, 890, 1531

cum ... venimus: → 167

Subsection 1 (*cum* + historical times of indicative = "when": temporal coincidence)

cum aderas: → 383

cum ... amavi dilexique: → 1386

cum audivi : → 1380

cum ... dabas: → 1554

cum ... dicerent: → 18

cum in hos incidi?: → 1369

cum ... misissent: → 1504

cum ... putassem: → 86, 92

cum ... venimus: → 167

cum venisses: → 536

cum ... vetarent: → 1302

Subsection 2 (subjunctive use: temporal circumstance *cum* = "when")

   cum absoluta essent: → 1196
   cum ... accepisset: → 113
   cum ad te de Milone scripsissem: → 1448
   cum ... confirmasset ... persuasisset: → 1628
   cum ... dedissem: → 79
   cum ... defenderet: → 14, 938
   cum ... dicerent: → 18
   cum essent adsensi: → 621
   cum ... fuisses: → 844
   Cum instituissem ... sumpsissem: → 1085
   cum ... loquerer: → 1429, 1430
   cum maxime res ageretur: → 1190
   cum ... posses: → 914
   cum ... putassem: → 86, 92
   cum recitavissem: → 1191
   cum ... redissem: → 1652
   cum saepe iniecissem: → 1648
   Cum ... scriberem: → 1364
   cum ... scripseris: → 922
   cum ... scripsisses: → 1546
   cum tu adesses: → 620
   cum venissem: → 658, 843
   cum ... vetarent: → 1302
   cumque ego egissem: → 599
   quom ... esses: → 103
   quom ... vacarem ... prae te ferres: → 1579

Encounter 67

Section 1 (subjunctive use: pure result [consecutive])

   eius modi ... ut habeam: → 481
   in eo civi ... qui sit ... vindicaturus: → 896, 897
   ita commendavit ut ... habeam: → 905
   ita commendo ut ... debent: → 356
   ita contendit ... ita fractus est ut ... sperem: → 1187
   ita mitto ut ... duxerim: → 1436
   ita petente ut ... nolles: → 911
   ita ... properabamus ut non posset: → 1104
   ita tractes ut intellegat: → 997
   ita ... ut ... placeamus: → 165
   ita ... ut ... tibi praestoler: → 1373
   qua re nihil esset: → 1218
   quin ... darem: → 650
   quin perscriberem: → 1005
   remitto ... ita ut ... existimem: → 919
   Sic ... commutatus est ... ut ... futurus sit: → 1623
   Sic ei probatum est ... ut ... crediderit, ... noluerit ... fecerit, ... dimiserit: →
      1637

sic me adfecerunt ut ... viderer: → 907

sic petis ut ... neges: → 942

sic ... revertare ut ... possis: → 1599

Tanta est ... ut ... dubitem: → 1597

tanta fuit ... ut ... videretur: → 1434

tanta ... ut ... duceret: → 1184

tanta ... ut sperem: → 1239, 1242

ut ... patiare: → 1532

ut ... sperem: → 760

ut ... videatur: → 743

ut scire iam possim: → 462

Encounter 68

Section 1 (subjunctive use: complementary result [consecutive])

accidit ut ... esset et ut ... mallem: → 72

Accedit ut ... fuerit: → 929

accidit ut ... posset: → 1124, 1128

asequi debet, sut ... intellegat: → 274

committam ... ut ... possis: → 152

committam ut ... reddantur: → 1076

deducebar ... ut ... arbitrarer: → 811

fac extrudas: → 524

fac ut ... sciam: → 248

fac ut ... venias ... accedas: → 264

fac venias: → 864

facies ut sciam: → 434

facturum ut ... deducat: → 685

mereri ut ... possit: → 523

non dubium est quin ... sis advolaturus: → 1359

suspicor fore ut infringatur: → 1235

ut ... careas non video posse fieri: → 1356

Section 2 (subjunctive use: characteristic result)

alia sunt quae ... curemus ... doleamus: → 491, 492

cui ... dare ... possem: → 62

cui litteras demus: → 513

Diem ... esse nullum, quo die non dicam: → 1001

habeo quod ... mandem ... narrem: → 1078

is qui esse deberet: → 54

multa convenerunt quae ... exturbarent: → 1309

nec rem habemus ullam quam ... velimus: → 514

neminem praetermisi, quem ... putarem, cui ... dederim: → 1584, 1585

nemo ... qui ... conferat: → 1566

nihil habeam quod ... exspectem ... scribam: → 484

nullum esse qui ... sit: → 1252

quae ... sint: → 162

qui ferat: → 488

qui ignoret: → 1154

qui ... possideant: → 1377

qui ... proficisceretur: → 64
quiddam ... quod ... insederit: → 384
quin ... amet: → 136
quod cures: → 891
quod ... esset: → 533
quod ... possimus: → 177
quod scriberem: → 655
quod scriberem nihil erat: → 1464
quos oderit: → 1168
si qui erunt ad quos ... existimes: → 473
si qui est qui curet: → 579
si quid erit quod ... opus sit: → 25
ubi ... sis: → 258
ubi ... videare: → 259

Encounter 69
Section 1 (function: place to where)
 Subsection 2: → 1057
  Byzantium: → 615
  Capuam: → 658, 705
  Formias: → 695
  Romam: → 71
  ad Brogitarum: → 615
 Subsection 3
  domum: → 603, 615, 638, 1087, 1421
  foras: → 786
  rus: → 1053
Section 2 (function: place from where)
 Subsection 2 (names of cities and small islands)
  Brundisio: → 183
  Epheso: → 1101
  Leucadia: → 150
  Roma: → 326, 1367
  Thessalonica: → 1212
  Ulbia: → 779
 Subsection 3
  domo: → 638
Section 3 (function: place at which)
 Subsection 2 (names of cities and small islands)
  plural
   Athenis: → 67, 567
   Formiis: → 989
   Parisiis: → 67
   Puteolis: → 567
   Syracusis: → 567
  singular
   Ephesi: → 1087
   Luceriae: → 710

Romae: → 409, 961, 1073, 1342, 1414
Thessalonicae: → 1230, 1301

Subsection 3
domi: → 638, 1112, 1429
foris: → 786

Encounter 70

Section 1 (abl.: time at which)
Eo die: → 623
eo tempore: → 826
gravi: → 436
hieme summa: → 363
his temporibus: → 255
hoc tempore: → 992
Ianuario mense: → 1411
Idibus: → 793, 1267
Idibus Februariis: → 189
Idibus Iuniis: → 479
Idibus Martiis: → 1575
Idibus Quinctilibus: → 527
iis nostris temporibus quibus: → 353
illo tempore: → 630
initio: → 1437
interregnis: → 284
Kal. Octobr.: → 1100
maximo imbri: → 704
multa nocte: → 598
Parilibus: → 586
quo: → 2
quo die: → 1001
Reliquis diebus: → 23
tristibus temporibus: → 1390
VIIII Kal.: → 988
Section 2 (acc.: time during which): → 80, 991, 1099, 1186
Section 3 (abl.: time within which): → 424, 1030

tertiae experientiae lectionum paginulae | *reading sheets—Third Experience*
Readings 3-D, 3-I: → 47, 197, 377, 392, 604, 636, 647, 732, 849, 874, 883, 926, 954,
1109, 1123, 1150, 1389, 1438, 1501, 1528, 1544, 1555, 1562, 1627

QVARTA EXPERIENTIA

fourth experience

Encounter 71
M & M
accipies: → 1231
adduci: → 1442

adiurat: → 785

adsensum esse: → 1192

ait: → 667

aiunt: → 1487

arbitrabar: → 1293

arbitrabor: → 957

arbitrarer: → 813

arbitrari: → 405

arbitretur: → 937

arbitror: → 84, 319, 934, 1153, 1166, 1523, 1541

audiebamus: → 68

audio: → 101, 223

audivi: → 336, 1381

censeo: → 219, 1262

cogit: → 1563, 1596

cogitare: → 1480

cogites: → 196

cognosces: → 1529

cognovi: → 496, 515

confidimus: → 1052

confido: → 57

constitui: → 187, 188

credas: → 1646

credo: → 1167, 1195, 1327, 1328

cupiebant: → 661

dicebar: → 1308

dicit: → 1495

dixi: → 612

dixit: → 601, 606, 607

doleo: → 1577

dolui: → 1592, 1593

dubitans: → 1073

dubito: → 1519

duxerim: → 1436

duxi: → 85, 1059

duxisti: → 1243

est quod: → 203

est rumor: → 568

Existimabam, existimabam: → 1651, 816

existimare: → 36, 37

existimem: → 921, 922

existimes: → 474

expertus est: → 342, 343, 344

explicare: → 1348

exspectatione: → 1193

Fac: → 1275

fac nos certiores: → 169

facias me ... certiorem: → 235

feremus: → 1209, 1210

fuerat dictum: → 798
gaudeo: → 590, 1577
gaudere: → 266
gaudes: → 173
habeto: → 135
ignoras: → 1037, 1569, 1521
ignoret: → 1152
incertum est: → 722
incredibile est: → 421, 1621, 1622
intellegat: → 275, 280, 998
intellegebam: → 382
intellegis: → 851, 1146
intellexerit: → 360
intellexi: → 201, 739
iudicabis: → 114
iudicabo: → 147
iudicassem: → 1635
iudicavi: → 823
iudices: → 1643
laetor: → 1592, 1593
locutus est: → 1089
mallem: → 77, 78
memineris: → 1603
mihi in mentem non venit: → 179
Mihi veniunt in mentem haec: → 966, 967, 969
mirere: → 396
miror: → 521
molestum fuit: → 1578
narrare: → 871
narravit: → 1653
negas: → 944
negat: → 675, 679, 680, 682
nescio: → 251, 884, 893, 1032, 1271
nescit: → 1377
noluerit: → 1639
nuntiant: → 713, 714
nuntii venerant et litterae: → 1218
opinantes: → 468
opinio: → 1407
pati: → 241
patiamur: → 1049, 1050
patiare: → 1533
patior: → 1497
perspicis: → 1299
persuade: → 1574
persuadeas: → 238, 239
persuaserim: → 1416
placebat: → 665

placuit: → 531

putabam: → 1181

putabas: → 572

putabis: → 1667

putabo: → 35, 1082, 1323, 1324, 1325

putare se: → 609

putarem: → 635, 923, 1584

putas: → 1660

putaveram: → 1292

putavi: → 234, 848

putes: → 237, 699, 1108, 1162, 1338

putet: → 1668

puto: → 121, 126, 685, 724, 959, 960, 1254, 1256

quaerebam: → 810

Quaeris: → 1028

questos esse: → 1500

rescribi: → 440, 443

rumoris: → 1610

sciam: → 243

scio, Scio: → 1201, 1204

scire: → 236, 437, 463

scire cupio: → 297

scis, Scis: → 229, 478, 1612

scitis: → 519

scito: → 88, 90, 313, 406, 407, 563, 565, 776, 1000, 1001, 1395, 1510, 1512, 1526

scribas: → 1055, 1284

scribis: → 101, 191, 1197, 1542

scripseram: → 1481, 1551

scriptum erat: → 404

sic habeto: → 553, 554

significabas: → 1581

solacium: → 240

sperare: → 400

sperarem: → 839

sperem: → 761, 763, 1188, 1240, 1242

spero, Spero: → 746, 758, 1401

spondeo: → 1450

sponderem: → 1630, 1631

statuerim: → 75

statui: → 930, 932

subinvideo: → 214

sum admiratus: → 809

suspicabar: → 589

suspicor: → 1235

testatum: → 547

testis erit: → 50

tulit: → 1192

velis: → 1161

velle: → 1425

venerant et litterae: → 1218

vetarent: → 1303

Vide: → 1415, 1424

videas: → 1108

videatis: → 518

videbam: → 1062, 1064

videbis: → 1330

video: → 181, 295, 577, 1251, 1261, 1410, 1489

videor: → 1199

vides: → 457, 1470, 1478

videte: → 976, 977

videtur: → 397

vis: → 142

volo: → 131, 1012, 1043, 1382, 1383

volui: → 155

OO

[id] esse: → 606, 608

[infractum iri]: → 1235

accusari abs te officium: → 1578

actum iri: → 798

adesse te: → 1082

adlaturam… auctoritatem: → 1646

adsensum esse: → 1192

aliquid dandum esse: → 121

aliquid scribendum: → 474

Aviam … mortuam esse: → 313

bene maturum … fore: → 628

Caesarem … mansurum: → 679

Caesarem … stare: → 661, 663, 664

cedendum: → 1262

cogitandum: → 1146

Comitia … esse: → 1195

comitia … esse reiecta: → 1551

commendationem … fuisse: → 998

conducere: → 1667

Considerandum: → 959

Consuli … te: → 298

consumere [esse]: → 1059

deos fortunare: → 1382

desiderare te: → 1581

designatum esse: → 405

Diem … esse nullum: → 1000, 1001

dimissurum: → 1090

discedere: → 1303

domesticas … perlatas: → 1541

ea … comprobari: → 1526

ea … legenda: → 1668

eam rem ... fore: → 460, 468

emisse te et parasse: → 191

esse: → 61, 1325, 1651

esse ambulandum: → 577

esse et naturam et personam: → 816

esse hominem commonendum: → 234

esse hominem ... neminem: → 1153

esse id: → 243

esse insectandos ... amicos: → 930

esse omnia: → 57, 58

esse rediturus: → 1308

esse urbem relinquere: → 1093

eum alienandum: → 1181

eum ... facturum: → 685

eum ... fore: → 1188

exceptum iri: → 1254, 1256

exemplum ... missum: → 1166

exercitum tuum flagitari: → 1563

existimari: → 101

frequentiam non fuisse: → 1610

gratum esse id: → 1062, 1064

hoc ... fore: → 1635

honorem ... administrari: → 1383

hostis ... iacere: → 1510

id expedire: → 1293

idque ... totum ... tibi dandum: → 923

illum abiecisse: → 1643

illum ... adesse: → 714

illum esse: → 342

illum ... fore: → 1401, 1402

illum ire: → 1049, 1050

illum ruere: → 713

illum valde morari: → 1653

impediri ... iter ... disciplinam: → 1043

inimicitias residere: → 937

Iocari me: → 1660

istum tuum discessum ... futurum: → 237

L. Saufeium missurum esse: → 319

leges ... imponi: → 665

levitatem et inconstantiam animumque ... esse perspectum: → 1167

librum ... placuisse: → 590

litteras ... iucundas fuisse: → 1512

litteras redditas esse: → 88, 90

me ... accepisse: → 776, 848

me ... adiunctum esse: → 1533

me ... arbitrari: → 404

me auctum: → 1395

me curaturum: → 187, 188

me dare: → 78

me decipi: → 1292

me ... defensuros: → 763

me ... esse: → 851, 1161, 1577

me fieri: → 147

me ... impetraturum: → 839

me ... ire: → 1310

me miserrimum esse: → 478

me pasci: → 572

me satis fieri velle: → 519

me sperare: → 394

me sperare illum ... fore: → 400

me tibi praecipere: → 1596

me ... tractatum: → 921, 922

me ... vitare potuisse: → 457

meam ... existimationem ... esse commendatam: → 1162

meque ... fore: → 612

meum studium nec ... defuisse: → 343, 344

minus ... esse: → 1338

mittendum: → 1436

negotia esse: → 758

neminem esse: → 135, 136

nihil ... exercitum esse: → 406

nos ... habere: → 746

nos ... incidisse: → 1204

nos ... venisse: → 173

nos vixisse et adhuc vivere: → 1209, 1210

nosmet ipsos esse spoliandos: → 932

nostrum ... genus esse: → 1037

notum esse: → 84

nullam rem ... esse potuisse: → 280

nullum esse: → 1251

paenitendum: → 635

Peducaeum ... dare: → 77

perventurum esse: → 1052

Placiturum tibi esse librum meum: → 589

placuisse agi: → 1197

posse: → 1275

postulataque ... interposita esse: → 680, 682, 683

praedia non venisse: → 496, 497

praedium nullum venire potuisse: → 515

praetores ... facere: → 1092

probiorem hominem, meliorem virum, pudentiorem esse neminem: → 1450

Ptolomaeum esse: → 568

putare se: → 607

putare se ... posse me adipisci: → 609, 611

Quae ... gesta esse: → 1530, 1532

quae ... offendere: → 382

quae ... timenda: → 1243

quam ... praetermissam esse: → 1523

quem ... appellari: → 1567

quem ... perventurum: → 1584

quid ... cogitandum: → 1108

quidquam ... fieri: → 531, 536

quidquam esse: → 699

reditum incidere: → 553, 554

rem posse ... esse: → 967, 969

Sallustium ... restituere: → 336

salvum venisse: → 266

satis ... esse: → 75

sciri: → 407

scribere [esse]: → 85

se adesse velle: → 667, 669

se dixit loqui velle: → 601

se ... fecisse: → 360

se ... fuisse: → 275

se ... futurum, ... se postulare: → 1630, 1631, 1632, 1633

se ... iturum: → 675

sese ... accipere: → 1495

te afuisse: → 1592, 1593

te ... agi velle: → 814

te ... arcessitum: → 214

te ... calere: → 724

te ... daturum: → 1542

te ... decursurum: → 126

te ... defendere: → 1377

te esse: → 241

te ... esse: → 68, 563

te ... esse ... contumeliosum: → 263

te exspectari: → 565

te factum esse: → 1381

te festinare: → 131

te ... fore: → 1410

te ... ignoscere: → 1240

te ... incidisse: → 428

te ... iocari: → 295

te me esse: → 1416

te me ... solitum esse remorari: → 1201

te mereri: → 521

te mihi ignoscere: → 1242

te non potuisse: → 1603

te ... profuisse: → 1574

te scire: → 26, 155, 156, 1012

te superbum esse: → 263

te ... usurum: → 944

te valere: → 139

te velle: → 809, 957

te ... velle: → 813

te ... venisse: → 203, 204

te ... videri: → 201

te violari: → 823

Trebatium exspectare: → 1425

tua interesse: → 1324

tuas partis esse: → 934

Tullum et Servium questos esse: → 1497, 1500

tuos familiaris ... fore: → 1407

unum ... restitisse: → 19

unum mihi esse solacium: → 239

utendum [esse]: → 219

velle Lentulum: → 1327, 1328

videar diffidere: → 397

Virum te putabo ... hominem non putabo: → 35

Visum te: → 1487

vos ... calere: → 223

vos ... esse: → 761

vos esse tuto posse: → 966

Encounter 72

OO: *see* Encounter 71

Section 1

futurum esse (fore)

    fore: → 394, 400, 468, 612, 628, 1188, 1235, 1401, 1407, 1410, 1635

    futurum: → 237, 1630

verb: active infinitive: → 667

verb: antecedent active infinitive: → 291, 455, 1013, 1197

verb: contemporaneous active infinitive

    adesse velle: → 667

    conferre: → 1442

    esse: → 455, 478, 1292

    explicare: → 1348

    putare: → 607

    putare ... posse: → 609

    reddere: → 1077

verb: subsequent active infinitive

    aucupaturi: → 1103

    curaturum: → 187

    daturum: → 1542

    dimissurum: → 1090

    facturum: → 685

    impetraturum: → 839

    iturum: → 675

    mansurum: → 679

    missurum esse: → 319

    Placiturum ... esse: → 589

> *profuturum:* → 1574
> *usurum:* → 944
> *venturi:* → 707

Section 3
>   contemporaneous passive infinitive: → 512, 1045
>   verb: antecedent deponent infinitive: → 313
>   verb: antecedent passive infinitive: → 405, 680, 1381
>   verb: contemporaneous active infinitive: → 1146
>   verb: contemporaneous deponent infinitive: → 404, 405, 521, 609
>   verb: contemporaneous passive infinitive
>
>>   *accusari … requiri:* → 1578
>>   *adduci:* → 1442
>>   *agi:* → 814, 1197
>>   *Consuli … consuli:* → 298
>>   *decipi:* → 1292
>>   *dici:* → 1149
>>   *fieri:* → 531
>>   *flagitari:* → 1563
>>   *inveniri:* → 1348
>>   *reddi:* → 1077
>>   *rescribi:* → 440
>>   *videri* : → 201

Encounter 73

OO: *see* Encounter 71

Section 1
>   verb: contemporaneous active infinitive: → 1292

Section 3 (nom. with the inf.)
>   *adripere visus est:* → 1650
>   *dare … viderer:* → 907
>   *dicebar esse rediturus:* → 1308
>   *dicebatur esse:* → 709
>   *dubitatio aut impedire … videbatur aut … tardare:* → 1423
>   *ipse puer … duci et delectari videtur:* → 1045, 1050
>   personal construction, *dici:* → 709
>   personal construction: *videor*
>
>>   *videar:* → 397
>>   *videbantur:* → 1645
>>   *videbatur:* → 1423
>>   *videor:* → 290, 1198, 1342, 1343
>>   *viderer:* → 231, 233, 907
>>   *videretur:* → 1434
>>   *videtur:* → 1045, 1050
>
>   *visus est:* → 1650
>   *quae … fieri videbantur:* → 1645
>   *stultus esse videor:* → 1198
>   *videar diffidere:* → 397
>   *videor … didicisse:* → 290

> *videor esse:* → 1342
> *videor esse ... et ... audire:* → 1343
> *viderer ... diffidere:* → 231, 233

Encounter 74

verbs of remembering and forgetting: → 551, 594

Encounter 75

abl.: definite price: → 329
Section 2 (gen. of indefinite price)
> *magni:* → 677
> *minoris:* → 700
> *pluris:* → 247, 302, 1614
> *quanti:* → 1152
> *tanti:* → 145, 388
Section 3 (*opus est*)
> *opus erit:* → 432
> *opus esset:* → 73, 683
> *opus est:* → 672, 1406
> *opus sit:* → 25, 118

Encounter 77

verb: complementary infinitive
> *accipere:* → 910, 1639
> *accusare:* → 339
> *adduci ... conferre:* → 1442
> *adipisci:* → 609
> *alucinari:* → 11
> *capere:* → 1116
> *cogitare:* → 1480
> *concitare:* → 1307
> *consequi:* → 608
> *dare:* → 907
> *deesse:* → 8
> *defendere:* → 1399
> *differre:* → 781
> *disputare:* → 1358
> *ducere:* → 1419
> *esse:* → 966, 967, 1342, 1543, 1607
> *esse ... audire:* → 1343
> *explicare:* → 177
> *explicari:* → 1280
> *facere:* → 914, 1131
> *fieri:* → 972, 1069
> *gaudere:* → 267
> *impedire ... tardare:* → 1423
> *inveniri:* → 1348
> *levare:* → 1314
> *loqui:* → 601

narrare: → 872

natare ... spectare: → 225

obsecrare obtestarique: → 1597

pati: → 240

perspicere: → 355

polliceri: → 1428

remorari: → 1201

restituere: → 336

Scire: → 236, 237

scribere: → 230

servare: → 912

suspicari: → 949

velle: → 1425, 1427

venisse: → 266

vexare: → 1333

vitare: → 457

Section 1 (gerund)

accipere: → 910, 1639

ad ... circumsedendum: → 1505

Ad ... conciliandum: → 1408

ad ... confirmandum: → 1647

ad effugiendum: → 1312

ad manendum: → 719

ad proficiscendum: → 1665

ad scribendum: → 3, 94

ad te adiuvandum: → 828

ad tolerandum: → 1214

adduci ... conferre: → 1442

adesse: → 667

adipisci: → 609

agi: → 1197

audiendi: → 702

capere: → 1116

cogitare: → 1480

cognoscendi: → 703

confirmare: → 143

coniungendi: → 721

consequi: → 608

consolando: → 249

consumere: → 1059

dandi: → 95

dare: → 907

decedere: → 1367

declarandi: → 529

deesse: → 142

defendere: → 1399

denegando: → 783

differre: → 781

diligendo: → 1155

disputare: → 1358

ducere: → 1419

esse: → 1221

exeundi: → 325, 326

exire: → 978

expediendo: → 1171

facere: → 914

ferendi: → 1182

fieri: → 1069, 1357

instituendi: → 1038

inveniri: → 1348

loqui: → 601

narrare: → 872

natandi: → 226

natare . . . spectare: → 225

obsecrare obtestarique: → 1597

pati: → 240

polliceri: → 1428

recipere: → 695

reconciliando: → 372

rogando: → 1031

rogare: → 1081, 1083

Scire, scire: → 236, 237, 569

scribendo: → 1070, 1586, 1590

scribere: → 85, 230, 1085

sedere: → 575

servare: → 912

suspicari: → 949

tuendo . . . reconciliando: → 819

uti: → 253

valere: → 987

velle: → 1425, 1427

veniendi: → 643

verb: infinitive as gerund: → 85

Section 2 (gerundive)

ad Cn. Pompeium circumsedendum: → 1505

ad effugiendos intolerabilis dolores: → 1312

ad . . . iudicium confirmandum: → 1647

ad spem servandam: → 1326

ad te adiuvandum: → 828

ad tolerandam . . . calamitatem: → 1214

Ad . . . voluntatem . . . conciliandam: → 1408

cognoscendi nostri apparatus: → 703

de nostro amico placando: → 332

de Pompeio nostro tuendo . . . ac . . . reconciliando: → 819

de vestra vetere gratia reconcilianda: → 372

declarandorum munerum: → 529

    eius ferendi: → 1182

    in Bruto expediendo: → 1171

    in iudicibus rogandis: → 1031

    in me diligendo: → 1155

    in supplicatione decernenda: → 1163

    in supplicatione ... deneganda: → 783

Encounter 78

Section 1 (famous five verbs with the ablative)

    A. Trebonio ... utor: → 990

    audacia ... uti: → 256

    camino luculento utendum: → 219

    ea ... usurum: → 944

    egeo rebus omnibus: → 465

    Fundo ... uti: → 769

    utatur glutinatoribus ... administris: → 860

    uti consilio et dignitate mea: → 808

    utitur Bruto: → 1654

    villis iis utere: → 767

Section 3 (verbs with the abl.): → 1356

Encounter 79

1. *qui, quae, quod* and *quis, quid:* indefinite: → 474

2. rel. pron. + ind.: review: → 385

5. *qui, quae, quod* and *quis, quid:* relative clause of purpose: → 534

6. subjunctive use: relative clause of pure result (consecutive): → 650, 1218

10. *qui, quae, quod* and *quis, quid:* modal attraction: → 534

Encounter 80

gerundive with certain verbs: → 1142

Encounter 81

supine: → 798, 799, 1137, 1265, 1526

Section 3 (verb: futurity passive infinitive): → 798, 799, 1254, 1256, 1526

Encounter 82

irregular verbs: *malo:* → 299, 575, 666

irregular verbs: *volo:* → 142, 519, 1358, 1425

Encounter 83

calendars

See the index: KALENDARIA AD NOSTRAM COMPOSITA VTILITATEM | *calendars composed for our own use*

subjunctive use: modal attraction

    not modal attraction

        credo ... velle Lentulum, qui erit consul: → 1328

        illum ... nuntiant ... adesse, non ut manum conserat ... sed ut fugam intercludat: → 714

        scito ... accepisse ... quas ... attulit: → 777

Spero si absolutus erit ... illum ... fore: → 1402

te afuisse ... dolui quod carui ... et laetor quod ... es consecutus quod-
que ... respondit: → 1594

Vide quam ... persuaserim te ... esse quae ... pertinent: → 1418

ait ... se adesse velle ... si Caesar adductus sit: → 669, 670

ait ... se adesse velle, cum ... agatur: → 668

Aviam ... scito mortuam esse ... quod verita sit: → 316

Coepi velle ... exspectare ... quae sperasset: → 1427

confido ita esse omnia ut ... oporteat et velimus: → 58

cupiebant Caesarem ... stare ... quas tulisset: → 663, 664

dicam, ut ... adducam ... relinquam ... ut, si ... coeperit ... possis: → 550

Diem scito esse nullum quo die non dicam: → 1001

dixitque ... putare se, si ... impedirem, posse: → 610

dixitque ... putare se, si ... impedirem, posse me adipisci ... quod vellem: →
611

dixitque esse quod ... cuperet: → 608

duxi ... , quoad ... venire, ... consumere: → 1060

egit ... ut sponderem ... se postulare ... , cum ... perspexisses, tum ut se
amares: → 1633,

est ... ut sperem te ... ignoscere, si ... timuerim: → 1242

eumque, nisi ... contulerit, exceptum iri puto: → 1256

exspectatio .... Si nactus ... esset ... ; sin ... tramisisset: → 1467, 1469

extrusi ... ut, etiamsi in Italiam venisset, ... rediret : → 1548, 1549

fuerit, ut ... esset is qui esse deberet: → 54

habeto ... neminem esse qui me amet: → 136

idque cum totum, quoquo modo ... haberet, ... dandum putarem, tum do: →
925

intellexerit se ... quod ... adierit ... navigarit ... fecisse: → 361

iudicavique ... te violari ... cuius ... niterentur: → 824

negant ... postulataque ... interposita esse quo minus quod opus esset...
pararetur : → 683

nescio ... an timeam ... non quo verear ... ne, cum veneris, non habeas : →
890

Nescit ... te ... defendere ... qui ... possideant: → 1377

non dubito quin, si ... adiunxerint, ... conciliatura coniuncturaque sit : →
1519

persuade ... te ... , si mature veneris, profuturum: → 1574

persuadeas velim ... esse solacium qua re ... possim pati te esse ... si ... sciam:
→ 242

placuit ... quidquam ... fieri quod ... cum venisses, non esset: → 536

placuit ... quidquam ... fieri quod ... non esset: → 534

puto te ... si ... erit, ... decursurum: → 126

quam ... praetermissam esse arbitror quod vererere : → 1524

Quoniam ... accidit ut ... posset, in quem ... incideret, peto: → 1124, 1132

rogo ... ne parcas ... quod ... opus sit: → 118

Scripsi ... quod dixisses daret: → 120

scripsi: ... ut, si ... videretur, ... traferret: → 108

te ... esse dicunt quod ... respondeas ... quod ... respondeas: → 263 *te scire volui, si … pertineret:* → 156

velim … complectare ut … quae … possis adduci: → 1442, 1445

velim … ibi malis esse ubi … sis: → 258

velim … malis esse … ubi … videare: → 259

veniunt … eamque rem posse … esse, si … fieri coeperint: → 969

video quid prodesse possis si veneris: → 181

videte quid … ne scum velitis exire non liceat: → 979

Encounter 84

ways to express purpose: → 1408

Encounter 85

commands: summary: → 578

Section 1

Subsection 6 (commands Time 3i): → 434, 982, 1120, 1266

Subsection 7 (commands: other expressions): → 765, 850, 1413, 1598

      similar example *Scripsi … daret:* → 119

      velim

            absint velim: → 1336

            facias me velim: → 235

            gaudeas velim: → 175

            persuadeas velim: → 238

            velim cogites: → 195

            velim … complectare: → 1439, 1440, 1443

            velim … conficias: → 470

            velim … consideretis: → 980

            velim cures: → 425

            velim desinas … et … revisas et … malis: → 257

            velim dispicias: → 1106

            velim explices … iuves: → 723

            velim … instituatis: → 983

            velim … invisas: → 581

            velim … mittas: → 412

            velim … mittas … imperes: → 859

            velim … perscribas: → 1203

            velim … persuadeas: → 958

            velim scribas: → 1283, 1284, 1491

            velim … urgeas: → 583

            velim … videas: → 1107

            videatis velim: → 517

Section 2 (negative commands)

    Subsection 3 (Time 1s): → 1287, 1334

    Subsection 5 (Time 3s): → 1334

    Subsection 7 (other expressions): → 417

Section 4

    negative commands: other expressions: → 1289

Encounter 86

conditionals: → 1549, 1655

Section 1 (conditionals: factual)

    dabis, si tibi videbitur: → 946

    date operam ut valeatis, si ... vultis valere: → 987

    delega, si vis: → 1431

    etsi ... violatur ..., tamen est: → 1237

    etsi egeo rebus omnibus: → 465

    exspectatio .... Si nactus ... erit ... erit dubia ...; sin ... tramiserit: → 1469

    exspectatio .... Si nactus ... esset ...; sin ... tramisisset ... : → 1467

    impedio quo minus, si ... placuerit, ... ornes: → 1455

    me adesse volo, ... si ... adductus est: → 670

    nisi ... contulerit, exceptum iri puto: → 1256

    non video posse fieri, ... si ... volet disputare: → 1358

    non video quid prodesse possis si veneris: → 181

    puto te ..., si recte erit, ... decursurum: → 126

    quin, si quid erit ..., sis advolaturus: → 1360

    quod ipsum, si ... respicis, ... faciendum est: → 1559, 1560

    Quod si te ... vindicat ..., perspicis: → 1298

    rem posse ... esse, si quae ... fieri coeperint: → 969

    se adesse velle, ... si ... adductus sit : → 669

    si ad te perlatae non sunt, ... arbitror: → 1540, 1541

    si ... audierimus, ... convertemus: → 1223

    si ... audies et si ... voles, ... putabis: → 390

    si ... coeperit, possis: → 550

    si ... cognoro, scies: → 726

    si ... correxerit, ... feremus: → 1208

    si ... es ..., condemnabo: → 1588

    si ... est profectus, ... fac extrudas: → 524

    si ... impedirem, posse me: → 610

    si ... intellegis ... cura: → 850

    si Italiam attigerit, erit: → 1564

    si levare potest ... adsequeris: → 1314, 1315

    si ... nemo dispexerit, ... poterit: → 1331, 1332

    Si ... occiderit nec ... ademerit ... diligetur: → 1472

    si quae ... fieri videbantur, ... iudices: → 1645

    si quando ... respondetur, ... residere ... patior: → 1515

    si qui est qui curet deus: → 579

    si quid ... venit velim scribas: → 1281, 1284

    si quid erit ... si nihil erit, tamen scribam: → 24, 27, 28

    Si quid habes ..., velim scire: → 569

    si solus non potuero, ... : → 1371, 1372

    si ... studia ... adiunxerint, ... conciliatura coniuncturaque sit: → 1519

    si ... veneris, profuturum: → 1574

    si ... vicerimus, tamen ... desiderabit: → 1571

    sin ... noles, ... praebere debebis: → 1589

    sin ... vexare coeperint, ne cessaris: → 1333, 1334

    sin plane occidimus ... fuero: → 1316

    Spero, si absolutus erit, ... illum ... fore: → 1402

    Tametsi iactat ... tamen habet: → 378

te ... ignoscere, si ... timuerim: → 1242

te non potuisse consequi, nisi ... paruisses: → 1604

tendam ... si aberunt ... , Hydruntem: → 1657

tolles, si ... putaris: → 387

velim explices ... iuves ... , etsi ... puto: → 724

vereor ... , praesertim ... aspernabere: → 1591

viceris, si ... videro: → 124

Virum te putabo, si ... legeris, hominem non putabo: → 34

Section 2 (conditionals: foggy future): → 124, 126, 242, 610

Section 3 (conditionals: contrary to fact): → 108

    not an example

        etiamsi ... venisset: → 1548

        quae sperasset: → 1427

        si tibi videretur: → 208

    perhaps not an example: si ... impedirem: → 610

    cohortarer ... nisi ... cognossem: → 754

    consuluissem ... , si ... deliberavissem: → 450

    egisses ... potuisses: → 903

    essem: → 1110

    fecissem: → 1636

    fuisset: → 1617, 1618

    mallem: → 299

    mallem egisses: → 902

    nisi ... adniteretur: → 1111

    nisi ... fecisset iudicassemque: → 1635

    nisi ... paruisses: → 1604

    paeniteret ... putarem: → 634

    profectus esses ... relinqueres: → 283

    putarem: → 923

    scripsissem: → 1539

    si ... esset ... adlegarem: → 1143

    si ... minus esset: → 1144

    si ... pertinerent, sperarem: → 838

    Si viveret, ... maneret: → 939

    Si ... voluisses ... esses: → 868

Encounter 88

subjunctive use: utinam: → 506, 1666

Encounter 89

Section 2

    abl.: instrument: *see* Encounter 28.5.3–4

    abl.: personal agent: → 148, 474, 556, 921, 1292, 1523; *see also* Encounter

                38.5.3–4

Section 3

    Subsection 3

        65 verbs with dat.: → 1192, 1262

Encounter 90

Section 2 (abl.: comparison)

> *duobus nobis … stultius:* → 244
> *duobus nobis … stultius: … te:* → 246
> *duobus nobis … stultius: me:* → 245
> *eo citius:* → 1354
> *minoris his consulibus:* → 701
> *multo meliores:* → 857
> *nostra vita dulcior:* → 737
> *peritior te:* → 209
> *quo … iucundius:* → 656
> *te … cariorem … iucundiorem:* → 566
> *verbis difficiliora:* → 1329

Section 3 (abl.: measure)

> *eoque magis:* → 1061
> *magis:* → 1104
> *minore scelere:* → 687
> *multo:* → 1534
> *multo minorem:* → 1535
> *nihilo minus:* → 1180
> *paullo:* → 928
> *paullo eruditius:* → 1039
> *paullo … tristius aut severius:* → 927
> *quanto deteriores:* → 423
> *quanto … obstinatior … obfirmatior:* → 401

Section 5 (comparative correlative sentences): → 6

> *cum … tum …:* → 129, 137, 690, 788, 904, 909, 920, 1553, 1633
> *cum … tum … tum … cum …:* → 1385
> *ita … ut …:* → 356
> *non quo aut … aut … sed …:* → 948
> *Quamquam …, tamen …:* → 1578
> *quantum …:* → 1620
> *quantam … tanti:* → 145
> *tali … quali …:* → 1626
> *tam … quam …:* → 386, 408, 591, 1514, 1586
> *tantam … quantam …:* → 1509
> *tanto … tantaque …:* → 1532
> *tantum … quantum …:* → 1313
> *ut … sic …:* → 573

Encounter 91

Section 2

> dat. of reference: → 179, 965, 1169
> double dat.
>
> > *ei saluti … fuisses:* → 845
> > *Hoc … tibi … persuadeas:* → 958
> > *maximo … mihi usui fore:* → 1409
> > *mihi non minori curae:* → 217

> *multis est curae:* → 140
> *nobis adiumento esse:* → 968
> *nobis curae est:* → 184
> *nobis ... honori fore:* → 468, 469
> *omnibus meis exitio fuero:* → 1318
> *quantae mihi curae fuerit:* → 51
> *quibus ... dedecori ... eram:* → 1319
> *sibi maiori usui aut ornamento:* → 281
> *tibi esse ... emolumento:* → 243

ethical dat.: → 179, 965, 1169

Encounter 92

futurum esse (fore) + ut: → 1235

Section 4 (negative *dubitare + quin* + subjunctive): → 42, 98, 1359, 1518, 1656

Encounter 94

Section 1
  subjunctive use in 3% sequence of tenses: → 283, 743, 906, 1187, 1585, 1637
Section 3
  subjunctive use: underlying potential of the past: → 655, 1464
  subjunctive use: underlying potential of the present or future
> *alia sunt quae ... curemus ... doleamus:* → 491
> *habeo quod aut mandem tibi aut narrem* → 1078
> *nec rem habemus ullam quam scribere velimus:* → 514
> *Nec saepe est cui litteras demus:* → 513
> *nihil habeam quod ... exspectem ... scribam:* → 484
> *non dubito quin ... committas:* → 98
> *scribo ... cum habeo qui ferat:* → 488
> *videatis velim quo modo satis fiat:* → 518

Encounter 95

verbs of fearing with *ne*
> *metuo ne ... ceperimus:* → 176, 177
> *metuo ne frigeas:* → 218
> *non ... vereor ne ... expleam:* → 1590
> *quod metuo ne obsit:* → 673
> *quod vererere ne ... offenderes:* → 1525
> *verear ne ... respondeat ... ne ... non habeas:* → 885, 889
> *vereor ne ... sit:* → 109
> *verita sit ne ... non manerent:* → 317

Encounter 96

Section 1
  quality in gen.: → 32, 106, 1183, 1606, 1626
Section 2
  abl.: quality: → 1017
  Bibliography: Onomasticon Tullianum; quality in abl.: → 1651
quality in abl.

μετεωρότερον, *suspensiore animo:* → 1651
animo abalienato: → 334
hoc animo: → 1606
multis luminibus: → 32
scriptis ... adsiduitate ... praeceptis: → 1624
singulari memoria, summa scientia: → 1452
tali animo ... quali: → 1626
tanta invidia: → 1017, 1183

Section 3
quality in adj. + abl. noun: → 1183

Encounter 99

gen. of part
animi: → 1338
animi ... consili: → 1339
argumenti: → 4
causae: → 738
certi: → 1374
consili: → 76, 176, 286
consolationis: → 453
litterarum: → 483, 651, 1398
litterarum ... rumoris: → 1007
negotii: → 1173
novi: → 433, 439, 727, 1080
oti: → 93
periculi: → 949
quorum: → 702
rumoris: → 1609
temporis: → 836

Encounter 100

Section 1
gen. of possession: → 311
Section 2
adj.: possessive: → 48, 269, 301, 1384, 1387
possessive adj.: used as nouns: → 269

Encounter 101

verbs of prohibiting: → 698, 1310
Section 1 (*ne, quominus, quin*): → 1454
Section 2
negative characteristic result: *quin* (= talis ut is non) + subjunctive: → 136, 559
negative *dubitare* + *quin* + subjunctive: → 42, 98, 1359, 1518, 1656

Encounter 102

interest and *refert:* → 138, 1324

Encounter 103

calendars: *see* KALENDARIA AD NOSTRAM COMPOSITA VTILITATEM, *calendars composed for our own use*

conditionals in OO: → 610, 669, 670, 1256

structure of Latin sentences: *see* INDEX STRVCTVRARVM, *index of the structures*

Encounter 105

characteristics of later Latin: → 796, 797, 1163, 1171, 1182

quartae experientiae lectionum paginulae | *reading sheets - Fourth Experience*

Readings 4-D, 4-I: → 47, 197, 377, 392, 604, 636, 647, 732, 849, 874, 883, 926, 954, 1109, 1123, 1150, 1389, 1438, 1501, 1528, 1544, 1555, 1562, 1627

OTHER REFERENCES

asyndeton: examples in *Ossa*, p. 754, 755, 757, 766: → 607

Tyrrell and Purser 4:49, fn. 2: → 482

Tyrrell and Purser, Adnotatio Critica, Ep. 424, 4:596: → 482

INDICES MATERIAM TANGENTES QUINGENTORVM INCISORVM SEV BREVILOQVIORVM CICERONIS EPISTVLARIS

indices touching on the content of five hundred clauses or tweets of Cicero in his letters

꩜

INDEX SVMMATIM SVMPTVS QVINGENTORVM INCISORVM SEV BREVILOQVIORVM CICERONIS EPISTVLARIS ORDINE ALPHABETICO

index of the five hundred clauses or tweets of Cicero in his letters taken together in alphabetic order

In the list below, B marks the Breviloquium or tweet number in part III of this volume.

A VIBIO LIBROS ACCEPI.   B11

ABIIT IRATUS.   B34

ABS TE TAM DIU NIHIL LITTERARUM!   B401

ABSTULI, APERUI, LEGI.   B25

AC VIDE MOLLITIEM ANIMI.   B310

ACCIPIAM? QUID FOEDIUS?   B224

ACTA RES EST.   B4

AD HAEC RESCRIBE.   B366

AD SUMMAM, DIC, M. TULLI.   B334

ADDE ILLUD.   B329

ADVOLONE AN MANEO?   B250

AGE, A CAELIO MUTUABIMUR.   B331

AIN TU? VERUM HOC FUIT?   B236

AMA NOS ET VALE.   B389

AMAMUR A FRATRE ET A FILLA.   B16

AN CENSEBAS ALITER?   B256

AN PANGIS ALIQUID SOPHOCLEUM?   B300

ANTERUM TIBI COMMENDO.   B199

720

APUD TE EST UT VOLUMUS. B3
AT QUAE CONTIO! B485
ATQUE UTINAM LICEAT ISTI CONTIONARI! B465
ATQUE UTINAM TE ILLIC! B479
ATTICA MEA, OBSECRO TE, QUID AGIT? B244
ATTICAE HILARITATEM LIBENTER AUDIO. B80
ATTICAM NOSTRAM CUPIO ABSENTEM SUAVIARI. B163
AUDI IGITUR AD OMNES. B361

BRUTI AD TE EPISTULAM MISI. B158
BRUTO TUAE LITTERAE GRATAE ERANT. B161

CAPUT ILLUD EST QUOD SCIS. B87
CAUTUM MARCELLUM! B472
COCCEIUS VIDE NE FRUSTRETUR. B345
COGNOSCE CETERA. B322
COGNOSCE NUNC CETERA. B328
COGNOVI DE ALEXIONE QUAE DESIDERABAM. B142
CONFICE, MI ATTICE, ISTAM REM. B356
CONFIDO REM UT VOLUMUS ESSE. B36
CONSERVA TE MIHI. B392
CONSOLABOR TE ET OMNEM ABSTERGEBO DOLOREM. B180
CRAS IGITUR AD ME FORTASSE VENIET. B59
CUM PANSA VIXI IN POMPEIANO. B136
CUR EGO TECUM NON SUM? B270
CURA ERGO POTISSIMUM UT VALEAS. B383
CURA IGITUR UT VALEAS. B333
CURA TE DILIGENTER. B396
CURA TE ETIAM ATQUE ETIAM DILIGENTER. B393
CURA TE, SI ME AMAS, DILIGENTER. B398
CURA UT ROMAE SIS. B302
CURA UT VALEAS. VALE. B379
CURA, AMABO TE, CICERONEM NOSTRUM. B307
CURA, MI CARISSIME FRATER, UT VALEAS. B373

DA OPERAM UT VALEAS. B369
DATE IGITUR OPERAM UT VALEATIS. B332
DE ANNIO SATURNINO CURASTI PROBE. B21
DE CAESARE QUID AUDITUR? B245
DE CICERONE MULTIS RES PLACET. B78
DE DOLABELLA TIBI ADSENTIOR. B103
DE DOMO ARPINI NIL SCIO. B117
DE EA RE SCRIPSI AD TERENTIAM. B71
DE HORTIS SATIS. B108
DE HORTIS, QUAESO, EXPLICA. B349
DE LINGUA LATINA SECURI ES ANIMI. B354
DE OVIA CONFICE, UT SCRIBIS. B348
DE PUERIS QUID AGAM? B229

DE QUA UTINAM ALIQUANDO TECUM LOQUAR! B418

DE REGINA RUMOR EXSTINGUITUR. B140

DE RELIQUO QUID TIBI EGO DICAM? B276

DE TRICLINIO CURA, UT FACIS. B399

DEFICIT ENIM NON VOLUNTAS SED SPES. B44

DI HERCULE ISTIS! B477

DI IMMORTALES! B468

DI ISTIS! B480

DIC, ORO TE, CLARIUS. B316

DIES ADEST. B99

DIONYSIUM IUBE SALVERE. B318

DIONYSIUS NOBIS CORDI EST. B22

DO, DO POENAS TEMERITATIS MEAE. B52

DOLABELLAM SPERO DOMI ESSE. B139

DOMI TE LIBENTER ESSE FACILE CREDO. B93

DOMUS TE NOSTRA TOTA SALUTAT. B19

DUAS A TE ACCEPI EPISTULAS HERI. B122

EAS LITTERAS CRAS HABEBIS. B81

ECQUID ACERBIUS, ECQUID CRUDELIUS? B226

EGO ISTA NON NOVI. B77

EGO NAVEM PARAVI. B46

EGO NON PUTO. B47

EGO QUID AGAM? B220

EGO TE VIDERE NOLUERIM? B279

EGO TECUM TAMQUAM MECUM LOQUOR. B48

EGO TIBI IRASCERER? B277

EI TE TOTUM TRADE. B387

EPISTULAM TIBI MISI. B144

EQUIDEM DIES NOCTESQUE TORQUEOR. B42

EQUIDEM VALDE IPSAS ATHENAS AMO. B31

EQUUM ET MULUM BRUNDISI TIBI RELIQUI. B195

EST ENIM RUMOR. B66

ET BALBUS HIC EST MULTUMQUE MECUM. B127

ET EI SALUTEM DICES ET PILIAE. B85

ET HEUS TU! B470

ET VIDE QUAM CONVERSA RES SIT. B337

ETIAM ATQUE ETIAM, TIRO NOSTER, VALE. B388

EXCISA ENIM EST ARBOR, NON EVULSA. B143

EXPLANABIS IGITUR HOC DILIGENTIUS. B131

EXSULTANT LAETITIA IN MUNICIPIIS. B125

FAC OPUS APPAREAT. B394

FAC PLANE UT VALEAS. B391

FAC, QUOD FACIS UT ME AMES. B376

FACIAM QUOD VOLUNT. B114

FACIES OMNIA MIHI NOTA. B154

FACTA NECNE FACTA LARGITIO, IGNORARI POTEST? B285

FUIMUS UNA HORAS DUAS FORTASSE.   B40

FUIT ENIM PERIUCUNDE.   B119

GRAVEDINI, QUAESO, OMNI RATIONE SUBVENI.   B368

GRAVEDO TUA MIHI MOLESTA EST.   B168

HABE MEAM RATIONEM.   B335

HABES CAUSAM OPINIONIS MEAE.   B67

HABES FORENSIA.   B183

HAEC ET TALIA FERRE NON POSSUM.   B128

HAEC ME EXCRUCIANT.   B70

HAEC PRO TUO INGENIO CONSIDERA.   B193

HAEC TE SCIRE VOLUI.   B197

HAEC TU MIHI EXPLICA QUALIA SINT.   B336

HERI ENIM VESPERI VENERAT.   B82

HIRTI LIBRUM, UT FACIS, DIVULGA.   B353

HOC ENIM UTITUR VERBO.   B181

HOC EST IGITUR EIUS MODI.   B33

HOC EST ROMĀ DECEDERE!   B402

HOC IGITUR HABEBIS, NIHIL NOVI.   B74

HOC PUTAVI TE SCIRE OPORTERE.   B107

HOMINES RIDICULOS!   B430

HUI, QUAM DIU DE NUGIS!   B445

HUI, QUAM TIMEO QUID EXISTIMES!   B473

HUIC UTINAM ALIQUANDO GRATIAM REFERRE POSSIMUS!   B498

HUNC TU NON AMES?   B207

IAM IAMQUE VIDEO BELLUM.   B167

IBATUR IN EAM SENTENTIAM.   B174

ID EGO PLANE NOLO.   B100

ID EST MIHI GRATISSIMUM.   B12

ID HERCLE RESTABAT!   B444

ID MIHI HERI VESPERI NUNTIATUM EST.   B147

ID QUIDEM, INQUIS, DI ADPROBENT!   B410

ID SCIRE SANE VELIM.   B101

ID SCIRE TE ARBITROR.   B32

IGNOSCE, OBSECRO TE.   B342

ILLIS EGI GRATIAS.   B83

IN EO AESTUAVI DIU.   B43

INCIPIT RES MELIUS IRE QUAM PUTARAM.   B132

INTEREA IN ISDEM LOCIS ERANT FUTURI.   B148

IOCARI ME PUTAS?   B269

IPSUM AGUSIUM AUDIES.   B73

IS ERAT AEGER.   B177

ISTE NOS TANTA IMPENSA DERIDEAT?   B299

ITA CANINIO CONSULE SCITO NEMINEM PRANDISSE.   B375

ITANE, MI ATTICE?   B272

ITAQUE ALIA COGITAT.   B141

ITERUM DICO "UTINAM ADESSES!"   B403

IUCUNDISSIMAS TUAS LEGI LITTERAS.   B172
IUVA ME, QUAESO, CONSILIO.   B357

LEGI EPISTULAM.   B116
LEPTA NOSTER MIRIFICUS EST.   B26
LOQUERE CUM DURONIO.   B324

MACTE!   B476
MAGNA ENIM RES ET MULTAE CAUTIONIS.   B113
MAGNA MOLITUR.   B166
MAGNA RES EST.   B157
ME AMA. VALE. (QUINTUS CICERO.)   B400
ME MISERUM, QUI NON ADFUERIM!   B491
MEA MANDATA, UT SCRIBIS, EXPLICA.   B355
MEAM PROFECTIONEM LAUDARI GAUDEO.   B160
MECUM ES, SI TE CURAS.   B200
MEOS TIBI COMMENDO.   B13
MEUM MIHI PLACEBAT, ILLI SUUM.   B135
MI FRATER, VALE.   B371
MI SUAVISSIME ET OPTIME FRATER, VALE.   B374
MI TIRO, CONSULITO NAVIGATIONI.   B384
MIHI ARPINUM EUNDUM EST.   B97
MIHI NIHIL POTEST ESSE GRATIUS.   B50
MIRIFICE EST CONTURBATUS.   B164
MISEROS NOS!   B425
MISI TIBI TORQUATUM.   B95
MODERARE IGITUR, QUAESO, UT POTES.   B346
MORIAR NISI FACETE!   B481
MULTUM PROFECTO PROFICIAM.   B133
MULTUM TE AMAMUS.   B1

NAM APERTE LAETATI SUMUS.   B138
NAM QUID EGO DE CICERONE DICAM?   B290
NARRABO CUM ALIQUID HABEBO NOVI.   B23
NAUSEA IAMNE PLANE ABIIT?   B255
NAVEM SPERO NOS VALDE BONAM HABERE.   B189
NEC AUDENT NEC IAM POSSUNT.   B146
NIHIL DICAM GRAVIUS.   B184
NIHIL ERAT QUOD SCRIBEREM.   B92
NIHIL LEGI HUMANIUS.   B169
NIHIL ME EST INERTIUS.   B9
NIHIL VIDI MELIUS.   B39
NOMINA MEA, PER DEOS, EXPEDI, EXSOLVE.   B364
NON PLACET.   B152
NON POSSUM PLURA SCRIBERE.   B68
NON ROGEM?   B292
NON SIC OPORTET?   B298
NON SUNT HAEC RIDICULA, MIHI CREDE.   B6

NON ME DEFENDIS? NONNE? RESISTIS? B287

NOS ADSUMUS. B196

NOS AGEMUS OMNIA MODICE. B194

NOS HIC CUM POMPEIO FUIMUS. B18

NOS PILIAM DILIGENTER TUEBIMUR. B134

NOS TAMEN ALIQUID EXCOGITABIMUS. B64

NOSTER AUTEM STATUS EST HIC. B5

NOSTI RELIQUA. B162

NOVI TIBI QUIDNAM SCRIBAM? B201

NULLO PACTO PROBO. B89

NULLUM VIDEO FINEM MALI. B55

NUM REDIIT IPSE POSTRIDIE? B272

NUNC AUDI AD ALTERAM. B362

NUNC AUDI QUOD QUAERIS. B309

NUNC AUDI RELIQUA. B330

NUNC COGNOSCE REM. B301

NUNC EXSPECTO A TE LITTERAS. B145

NUNC MISER QUANDO TUAS LITTERAS ACCIPIAM? B296

NUNC NEGLEGENTIAM MEAM COGNOSCE. B365

NUNC QUIDEM PROFECTO ROMAE ES. B35

NUNC ROMANAS RES ACCIPE. B319

NUNC TE OBIURGARI PATERE, SI IURE. B321

O BRUTE, UBI ES? B274

O BRUTI AMANTER SCRIPTAS LITTERAS! B469

O CASUM MIRIFICUM! B483

O CELERITATEM INCREDIBILEM! B416

O COPIAS DESPERATAS! B429

O DI BONI! B459

O DI! B490

O FACTUM MALE DE ALEXIONE! B466

O GRATAS TUAS MIHI IUCUNDASQUE LITTERAS! B441

O GULAM INSULSAM! B447

O HOMINEM CAVENDUM! B442

O HOMINEM IMPRUDENTEM! B464

O INCREDIBILEM VANITATEM! B450

O MAGISTRUM MOLESTUM! B453

O ME MISERUM! B417

O ME PERDITUM! O ADFLICTUM! B497

O ME SOLLICITUM! B489

O MEAM STULTAM VERECUNDIAM! B457

O MIRIFICUM DOLABELLAM MEUM! B463

O MULTAS ET GRAVES OFFENSIONES! B438

O NEGLEGENTIAM MIRAM! B448

O NEGOTIA NON FERENDA! B471

O PERDITUM LATRONEM! B414

O PRUDENTEM OPPIUM! B455

O QUALES TU SEMPER ISTOS! B482

O REM ACERBAM!   B446

O REM DIFFICILEM PLANEQUE PERDITAM!   B423

O REM FOEDAM!   B431

O REM INDIGNAM!   B449

O REM LUGUBREM!   B421

O REM MINIME APTAM MEIS MORIBUS!   B406

O REM MISERAM ET INCREDIBILEM!   B415

O REM ODIOSAM ET INEXPLICABILEM!   B467

O REM PERDITAM!   B428

O REM TOTAM ODIOSAM!   B409

O REM TURPEM ET EÃ RE MISERAM!   B420

O REM UNDIQUE MISERAM!   B433

O SESTI TABELLARIUM HOMINEM NEQUAM!   B484

O SOCRATE ET SOCRATICI VIRI!   B458

O SUAVES TUAS LITTERAS!   B451

O TEMPORA!   B443

O TEMPUS MISERUM!   B426

O TURPEM SORORIS TUAE FILIUM!   B474

O VIM INCREDIBILEM MOLESTIARUM!   B432

O, SI ID FUERIT, TURPEM CATONEM!   B437

OBSECRO TE, QUID EST HOC?   B267

OMITTE ATTICUM.   B370

OMNIA SUM DILIGENTISSIME PERSECUTUS.   B29

ORO, OBSECRO, IGNOSCE.   B340

PACE OPUS EST.   B41

PECUNIA APUD EGNATIUM EST.   B69

PER FORTUNAS!   B411

PERBELLE FECERIS, SI AD NOS VENERIS.   B17

PERFER, SI ME AMAS.   B326

PERFICE IGITUR ALIQUID.   B352

PERGE RELIQUA.   B317

PERSCRIBAM AD TE PAUCIS DIEBUS OMNIA.   B27

PILIAM ANGI VETA.   B344

PLACET HOC TIBI?   B212

PLANE QUID SIT NON INTELLEGO.   B98

PLANE SIC FACIENDUM.   B51

PLURA SCRIBEREM, SI IPSE POSSEM.   B49

POMPEIUS AMAT NOS CAROSQUE HABET.   B10

POSTEA SUNT HAEC ACTA.   B179

POSTRIDIE IDUS PAULUM CAIETAE VIDI.   B126

PRORSUS NON MIHI VIDEOR ESSE TUTUS.   B153

PUDET ME PATRIS.   B109

PUTO EQUIDEM NIHIL ESSE.   B118

QUA RE ADPROPERA.   B315

QUA RE BONO ANIMO ES.   B325

QUA RE ETIAM OTHONEM VIDE.   B351

QUA RE QUANTUM POTES ADIUVA. B381

QUAE CENAE, QUAE DELICIAE! B440

QUAE HIC VIDEO! B462

QUAE MIHI ISTIM ADFERUNTUR! B461

QUAESIVIT EX ME PATER QUALIS ESSET FAMA. B159

QUAESO, ADHIBE QUAM SOLES DILIGENTIAM. B367

QUAESO, QUID EST HOC? B218

QUAESO, QUID NOBIS FUTURUM EST? B213

QUAM ILLE DOLUIT DE NONIS IULIIS! B478

QUAM MULTA QUAM PACIS! B493

QUAMQUAM QUID AD ME? B238

QUANTO MIHI ILLUD ERIT AMABILIUS! B500

QUANTO NUNC HOC IDEM ACCIPIET ASPERIUS! B424

QUEM HOMINEM, QUĀ IRĀ, QUO SPIRITU! B486

QUI UTINAM IAM ADESSET! B494

QUICQUID EGERO CONTINUO SCIES. B54

QUID AD HAEC PANSA? B265

QUID AUTEM ABSURDIUS? B257

QUID DICAM? B214

QUID EGO FACIAM? B210

QUID ENIM DICAM ALIUD? B263

QUID ENIM FIERI POTEST? B223

QUID ENIM HABEBAS QUOD SCRIBERES? B241

QUID ENIM INDIGNIUS? B243

QUID ENIM MIHI MEIS IUCUNDIUS? B266

QUID ENIM SUM? B204

QUID ERGO AGIS? B261

QUID ERGO OPUS EST EPISTULĀ? B235

QUID ERGO POTISSIMUM SCRIBAM? B288

QUID EST IGITUR QUOD LABOREM? B211

QUID EST PRAETEREA? B209

QUID FACIAM? PLORANDO FESSUS SUM. B259

QUID FECI NON CONSIDERATISSIME? B225

QUID FIERI TUM POTUIT? B254

QUID FOEDIUS? B260

QUID FUTURUM EST? B291

QUID IGITUR CAUSAE FUIT? B205

QUID MIHI IGITUR PUTAS AGENDUM? B233

QUID MULTA? B216

QUID NOCET? B262

QUID NUNC PUTAS? B217

QUID PLURA DE IUDICIBUS? B284

QUID PRAETEREA? QUID? B283

QUID PROVIDEAM? B231

QUID QUAERIS ALIUD? B206

QUID QUAERIS? NIHIL FESTIVIUS! B488

QUID QUOD EODEM TEMPORE DESIDERO FILIAM? B280

QUID SCRIBAM AUT QUID VELIM? B232

QUID SUPEREST?   B215

QUID TIBI DE VARRONE RESCRIBAM?   B246

QUID TURPIUS?   B228

QUID? CICERO MEUS QUID AGET?   B295

QUID? TU ID PATERIS?   B286

QUIDNAM ID EST?   B202

QUINTUM FRATREM COTIDIE EXSPECTAMUS.   B2

QUINTUM FRATREM MEUM FAC DILIGAS.   B312

QUIS AD ME PERFERET?   B297

QUIS VENIET?   B275

QUO IGITUR HAEC SPECTAT ORATIO?   B222

QUO ME NUNC VERTAM?   B230

QUO ME VERTAM?   B203

QUOD EGERIS ID PROBABO.   B104

QUOD PROMITTIS DI FAXINT!   B475

QUOD SUPEREST, DI IUVENT!   B407

QUOD UTINAM DIUTIUS!   B456

QUOD UTINAM ITA ESSET!   B439

QUOD UTINAM MINUS VITAE CUPIDI FUISSEMUS!   B496

QUOD UTINAM! ITERUM UTINAM!   B454

QUOQUO MODO CONFICE.   B343

QUOS EGO RISUS EXCITASSEM!   B492

QUOUSQUE LUDEMUR?   B264

RATIONES MEAS NOSTI.   B84

RECORDARE TUA.   B359

REDEAMUS AD NOSTRUM. PER FORTUNAS!   B413

REDEO NUNC AD EPISTULAM TUAM.   B130

REGINAM ODI.   B150

RELIQUA SUNT DOMESTICA.   B28

RELIQUA, O DI!   B427

REM TIBI TIRO NARRABIT.   B170

RES AUTEM ROMANAE SESE SIC HABENT.   B178

RES SUNT INEXPLICABILES.   B56

RESCRIBES SI QUID VOLES.   B110

RIDEBIS HOC LOCO FORTASSE.   B37

SAEPE AD TE SCRIPSI.   B173

SANUM PUTAS?   B258

SCIES QUICQUID ERIT.   B62

SCRIBES IGITUR QUICQUID AUDIERIS.   B149

SED ACCIPE ALIA.   B323

SED AD PROPOSITUM.   B121

SED AD TUAS VENIO LITTERAS.   B182

SED ADSUM. CORAM IGITUR.   B79

SED CERTUM NON HABEO.   B91

SED COMPLERE PAGINAM VOLUI.   B111

SED CONFICE.   B397

SED CRAS SCIES. B106

SED DI ISTOS! B436

SED EGO ADHUC EMI NIHIL. B175

SED EN MEAM MANSUETUDINEM! B419

SED EXTREMUM AUDI. B327

SED FACIES UT VIDEBITUR. B88

SED HAEC CORAM. B198

SED HAEC HACTENUS; RELIQUA CORAM. B165

SED HAEC MINORA SUNT. B188

SED HAEC NON CURARE DECREVI. B186

SED HAEC UTINAM NE EXPERIARE! B487

SED HAEC VIDEBIMUS. B58

SED HEUS TU! B408

SED HUMANA FERENDA. B155

SED NIMIUM MULTA DE NUGIS. B102

SED QUID AGO? B282

SED QUID ARGUMENTOR? B247

SED QUID DIFFERO? B237

SED QUID EST, QUAESO? B242

SED QUID FACIAMUS? B221

SED QUID FACIAT? B249

SED QUID HAEC AD NOS? B252

SED QUID HAEC LOQUIMUR? B289

SED QUID ME ID LEVAT? B234

SED QUID PLURA? B208

SED QUID REFERT? B227

SED QUID SIMILE? B240

SED QUID TULLIOLĀ MEĀ FIET? B294

SED SATIS LACRIMIS. B61

SED TAMEN ECQUID IMPURIUS? B239

SED TU QUID AIS? B248

SED VIDEBIMUS. B156

SED VIDEO IN TE ESSE OMNIA. B187

SED VIX ERIT TAM CITO. B65

SEMEL EUM OMNINO DOMI MEAE VIDI. B151

SEMEL SATIS EST. B120

SEQUERE NUNC ME IN CAMPUM. B320

SEQUERE NUNC ME IN CAMPUM. B360

SEQUOR CELEBRITATEM. B86

SI VALES, BENE EST, EGO VALEO. B190

SI VERO ETIAM TUSCULANUM, DEI BONI! B499

SI VOS VALETIS, NOS VALEMUS. B191

SIBI HABEAT SUAM FORTUNAM! B412

SIC AGES IGITUR. B105

SINE SPE CONAMUR ULLA. B57

SINE TE IGITUR SIM? B293

SINE ULLA ME HERCULE IRONIA LOQUOR. B185

SIT MODO RECTE IN HISPANIIS! B434

SPEM AUTEM PACIS HABEO NULLAM.　B53

STOMACHOR OMNIA.　B137

SUBACCUSA, QUAESO, VESTORIUM.　B358

SUMMA ERIT HAEC.　B24

SUMUS ENIM AMBO BELLE CURIOSI.　B30

SUSPENSO ANIMO EXSPECTO QUID AGAT.　B20

TE EXSPECTABO POSTRIDIE.　B76

TE IDIBUS VIDEBO CUM TUIS.　B96

TE QUANDO EXSPECTEMUS FAC UT SCIAM.　B395

TERENTIA TIBI SAEPE AGIT GRATIAS.　B15

TERENTIA TIBI SALUTEM DICIT.　B8

TERENTIAE VERO QUID EGO DICAM?　B271

TIBI EGO POSSEM IRASCI?　B278

TOTUM INVESTIGA, COGNOSCE, PERSPICE.　B303

TRANQUILLAE TUAE QUIDEM LITTERAE.　B123

TRIGINTA DIES IN HORTIS FUI.　B90

TU ANTONI LEONES PERTIMESCAS CAVE.　B339

TU IGITUR ID CURABIS.　B94

TU INTEREA DORMIS.　B75

TU ISTA CONFICE.　B304

TU ISTA OMNIA VIDE ET GUBERNA.　B311

TU MANDATA EFFICE QUAE RECEPISTI.　B305

TU METUIS NE ME INTERPELLES?　B281

TU MODO AD NOS VENI.　B314

TU QUID DICIS?　B251

TU TAMEN AUSUS ES VARRONI DARE!　B452

TU TAMEN, SI QUID POTES, ODORARE.　B347

TU, QUAESO, COGITA QUID DEINDE.　B338

TU, QUAESO, FESTINA AD NOS VENIRE.　B313

TUI NOSTRIQUE VALENT.　B176

TUIS SALUTEM DIC.　B341

TULLIAM ADHUC MECUM TENEO.　B192

TULLIOLAE ET CICERONI SALUTEM DIC.　B377

TUMENT NEGOTIA.　B124

UBI TANDEM EST FUTURUS?　B253

UTAR EO QUOD DECREVERIS.　B112

UTINAM ALIQUID PROFECTUM ESSET!　B422

UTINAM EA RES EI VOLUPTATI SIT!　B495

UTINAM MODO AGATUR ALIQUID!　B404

UTINAM MODO CONATA EFFICERE POSSIM!　B405

UTINAM PROFICERE POSSIM!　B435

VALE, MI SUAVISSIME ET OPTIME FRATER.　B372

VALE, MI TIRO, VALE, VALE ET SALVE.　B385

VALE, SALVE.　B390

VALETE, MEA DESIDERIA, VALETE.　B378

VALETUDINEM TUAM CURA DILIGENTER. B380
VALETUDINEM TUAM FAC UT CURES. B382
VEHEMENTER DELECTOR TUIS LITTERIS. B129
VERUM DICEBAT. B38
VETTIENUM DILIGO. B63
VICTI, OPPRESSI, CAPTI PLANE SUMUS. B45
VIDE LEVITATEM MEAM. B308
VIDE QUAE SINT POSTEA CONSECUTA. B306
VIDE QUANTA SIT IN TE SUAVITAS. B386
VIDE, QUAESO, NE QUID TEMERE FIAT. B363
VIDE, QUAESO, QUID AGENDUM SIT. B350
VIDEBIMUS TE IGITUR. B115
VIDEBIS IGITUR ET SCRIBES. B171
VIDEO DIFFICILE ESSE CONSILIUM. B72
VIDERE TE CUPIO. B14
VIDES ENIM CETERA. B7
VIDES ENIM PROFECTO ANGUSTIAS. B60
VIDESNE ME ETIAM IOCARI? B219
VIDESNE QUAM BLANDE? B268
VIVIT TYRANNIS, TYRANNUS OCCIDIT! B460

❧

INDEX FONTIVM QVINGENTORVM BREVILOQVIORVM ATQUE IIS RESPONDENTIVM CICERONIS EPISTVLARVM A NOBIS INVESTIGATARVM

index of the sources of the five hundred tweets of Cicero and corresponding to them of Cicero's letters studied by us

AD ATTICUM

i	1	*Att.* i, 1, 3: B301
		Att. i, 1, 5: B1
(letter 44 =) 2		*Att.* i, 2, 1: B401
		Att. i, 2, 2: B302
(letter 2 =) 5		*Att.* i, 5, 8: B2
	8	*Att.* i, 8, 1: B3
	12	*Att.* i, 12, 2: B303
	13	*Att.* i, 13, 6: B201, B304
	14	*Att.* i, 14, 5: B4
		Att. i, 14, 7: B305
	16	*Att.* i, 16, 11: B5
	17	*Att.* i, 17, 11: B6
	1	*Att.* i, 18, 3: B306
I	1	*Att.* i, 1, 3: B301

		Att. i, 1, 5: B1
(letter 44 =)	2	*Att.* i, 2, 1: B401
		Att. i, 2, 2: B302
(letter 2 =)	5	*Att.* i, 5, 8: B2
	8	*Att.* i, 8, 1: B3
	12	*Att.* i, 12, 2: B303
	13	*Att.* i, 13, 6: B201, B304
	14	*Att.* i, 14, 5: B4
		Att. i, 14, 7: B305
	16	*Att.* i, 16, 11: B5
	17	*Att.* i, 17, 11: B6
	18	*Att.* i, 18, 3: B306
II	2	*Att.* ii, 2, 1: B307
	3	*Att.* ii, 3, 2: B7
	5	*Att.* ii, 5, 2: B308
	7	*Att.* ii, 7, 4: B202
		Att. ii, 7, 5: B8
	8	*Att.* ii, 8, 1: B9
	9	*Att.* ii, 9, 4: B309
	14	*Att.* ii, 14, 2: B203
(letter 42 =)	15	*Att.* ii, 15, 3: B402
	19	*Att.* ii, 19, 5: B403
	20	*Att.* ii, 20, 1: B10
		Att. ii, 20, 6: B11
	21	*Att.* ii, 21, 3: B310
III	5	*Att.* iii, 5: B12
	6	*Att.* iii, 6: B13
	7	*Att.* iii, 7, 3: B14
	8	*Att.* iii, 8, 4: B311
	9	*Att.* iii, 9, 3: B15
	13	*Att.* iii, 13, 2: B312
	15	*Att.* iii, 15, 2: B204
		Att. iii, 15, 6: B404
	26	*Att.* iii, 26: B313
IV	2	*Att.* iv, 2, 5: B205, B314
		Att. iv, 2, 7: B16
	3	*Att.* iv, 3, 6: B315
	4a	*Att.* iv, 4a, 1: B17
	8a	*Att.* iv, 8a: B316
	9	*Att.* iv, 9, 1: B18
	11	*Att.* iv, 11, 1: B317
	12	*Att.* iv, 12: B19

	14	*Att.* iv, 14, 2: B318
	15	*Att.* iv, 15, 4: B319
		Att. iv, 15, 7: B320
		Att. iv, 15, 10: B20
	16	*Att.* iv, 16, 2: B405
		Att. iv, 16, 7: B321
	17	*Att.* iv, 17, 5: B206
		Att. iv, 17, 6: B322
	18	*Att.* iv, 18, 3: B323
	19	*Att.* iv, 19, 2: B207, B208
V	1	*Att.* v, 1, 2: B21
	3	*Att.* v, 3, 3: B22
(letter 34 =)	6	*Att.* v, 6, 2: B23
	8	*Att.* v, 8, 3: B24, B324
	10	*Att.* v, 10, 3: B406
		Att. v, 10, 5: B209
	11	*Att.* v, 11, 4: B407
		Att. v, 11, 7: B25
	17	*Att.* v, 17, 2: B26, B27
	18	*Att.* v, 18, 3: B325
	20	*Att.* v, 20, 1: B210
	21	*Att.* v, 21, 7: B326
		Att. v, 21, 14: B28
VI	1	*Att.* vi, 1, 3: B29
		Att. vi, 1, 13: B408
		Att. vi, 1, 25: B30, B327
		Att. vi, 1, 26: B31
	2	*Att.* vi, 2, 2: B32
		Att. vi, 2, 10: B328
	3	*Att.* vi, 3, 3: B33
		Att. vi, 3, 5: B211
		Att. vi, 3, 7: B34
	4	*Att.* vi, 4, 1: B409
	5	*Att.* vi, 5, 1: B35
	6	*Att.* vi, 6, 1: B410
		Att. vi, 6, 2: B212
		Att. vi, 6, 4: B329
	7	*Att.* vi, 7, 1: B36
	9	*Att.* vi, 9, 5: B213
VII	1	*Att.* vii, 1, 2: B330, B411
		Att. vii, 1, 4: B214
		Att. vii, 1, 5: B37
		Att. vii, 1, 8: B38
	2	*Att.* vii, 2, 3: B39

	3	*Att.* vii, 3, 11: B331
		Att. vii, 3, 12: B215
	4	*Att.* vii, 4, 2: B40
		Att. vii, 4, 3: B216
	5	*Att.* vii, 5, 2: B332
		Att. vii, 5, 4: B41
		Att. vii, 5, 5: B333
	7	*Att.* vii, 7, 7: B334
	9	*Att.* vii, 9, 3: B217
		Att. vii, 9, 4: B42, B335
	11	*Att.* vii, 11, 1: B218, B412
		Att. vii, 11, 3: B413
		Att. vii, 11, 4: B336
	13a	*Att.* vii, 13a, 1: B43
	17	*Att.* vii, 17, 1: B219
	18	*Att.* vii, 18, 2: B414
	21	*Att.* vii, 21, 1: B44, B415
(letter 40 =)	22	*Att.* vii, 22, 1: B416
		Att. vii, 22, 2: B220
	23	*Att.* vii, 23, 1: B45, B221, B417
VIII	2	*Att.* viii, 2, 4: B222, B418
	3	*Att.* viii, 3, 6: B223
	4	*Att.* viii, 4, 3: B46
	5	*Att.* viii, 5, 1: B419
	7	*Att.* viii, 7, 1: B47
	8	*Att.* viii, 8, 1: B420
		Att. viii, 8, 2: B421
	9	*Att.* viii, 9, 2: B422
(letter 46 =)	13	*Att.* viii, 13, 2: B337
	14	*Att.* viii, 14, 2: B48
	15	*Att.* viii, 15, 3: B49
IX	2a	*Att.* ix, 2a, 1: B224, B423, B424
	9	*Att.* ix, 9, 1: B50
		Att. ix, 9, 2: B51
	10	*Att.* ix, 10, 2: B52, B225
	12	*Att.* ix, 12, 1: B425
	13	*Att.* ix, 13, 8: B53
	14	*Att.* ix, 14, 2: B226
	15	*Att.* ix, 15, 4: B54
	17	*Att.* ix, 17, 1: B426
		Att. ix, 17, 2: B338
	18	*Att.* ix, 18, 2: B55, B427, B428, B429
	19	*Att.* ix, 19, 2: B227

X	2	*Att.* x, 2, 2: B56, B57
(letter 47 =)	3a	*Att.* x, 3a, 2: B430
	4	*Att.* x, 4, 8: B431
		Att. x, 4, 11: B58
'	8	*Att.* x, 8, 4: B228
	10	*Att.* x, 10, 3: B59
		Att. x, 10, 6: B432
	11	*Att.* x, 11, 2: B60
		Att. x, 11, 4: B229, B433
	12	*Att.* x, 12, 1: B230
		Att. x, 12, 2: B61, B434
		Att. x, 12, 3: B435
		Att. x, 12, 4: B62
	12a	*Att.* x, 12a, 1: B231
	13	*Att.* x, 13, 1: B339
		Att. x, 13, 2: B63, B64
	15	*Att.* x, 15, 3: B65
		Att. x, 15, 4: B436
	16	*Att.* x, 16, 3: B66, B437
	17	*Att.* x, 17, 4: B67
XI	2	*Att.* xi, 2, 3: B68, B340
(letter 15 =)	3	*Att.* xi, 3, 3: B69, B341
	7	*Att.* xi, 7, 3: B70, B438
		Att. xi, 7, 6: B232, B342
	11	*Att.* xi, 11, 2: B71
	12	*Att.* xi, 12, 3: B439
	15	*Att.* xi, 15, 1: B72, B233
		Att. xi, 15, 2: B234
	23	*Att.* xi, 23, 2: B73
XII	1	*Att.* xii, 1, 2: B74, B235
	2	*Att.* xii, 2, 2: B75, B440
	4	*Att.* xii, 4, 1: B441
	5c	*Att.* xii, 5c: B76
	6	*Att.* xii, 6, 1: B77
		Att. xii, 6, 2: B236
	7	*Att.* xii, 7, 1: B237
	8	*Att.* xii, 8: B78
	11	*Att.* xii, 11: B79, B80
	12	*Att.* xii, 12, 1: B343
	14	*Att.* xii, 14, 4: B344
	15	*Att.* xii, 15: B81
	16	*Att.* xii, 16: B82
	17	*Att.* xii, 17: B238

18	*Att.* xii, 18, 2: B345	
19	*Att.* xii, 19, 2: B83	
21	*Att.* xii, 21, 2: B84	
22	*Att.* xii, 22, 1: B346	
	Att. xii, 22, 3: B347	
24	*Att.* xii, 24, 1: B348	
	Att. xii, 24, 3: B85	
27	*Att.* xii, 27, 1: B86	
29	*Att.* xii, 29, 2: B87, B349	
32	*Att.* xii, 32, 1: B350	
37	*Att.* xii, 37, 3: B88	
37a	*Att.* XII, 37a, 4: B351	
38	*Att.* xii, 38, 2: B239, B442	
38a	*Att.* xii, 38a, 2: B89	
40	*Att.* xii, 40, 2: B90, B240	
	Att. xii, 40, 5: B91	
41	*Att.* xii, 41, 1: B92	
42	*Att.* xii, 42, 1: B241	
44	*Att.* xii, 44, 2: B352	
	Att. xii, 44, 3: B242	
48	*Att.* xii, 48: B93	
	Att. xii, 48, 3: B353	
49	*Att.* xii, 49, 2: B443	
51	*Att.* xii, 51, 2: B94	
52	*Att.* xii, 52, 3: B354	
XIII	2	*Att.* xiii, 2: B243
	5	*Att.* xiii, 5, 1: B95
	8	*Att.* xiii, 8: B96
	9	*Att.* xiii, 9, 2: B97
	10	*Att.* xiii, 10, 3: B98
	12	*Att.* xiii, 12, 4: B99
	13	*Att.* xiii, 13, 1: B444
		Att. xiii, 13, 3: B244
		Att. xiii, 13, 4 [olim 14, 1]: B100
	16	*Att.* xiii, 16, 2: B245
	20	*Att.* xiii, 20, 1: B101
		Att. xiii, 20, 4: B102
	21a	*Att.* xiii, 21a, 2: B445
		Att. xiii, 21a, 3: B103
	22	*Att.* xiii, 22, 3: B446
	23	*Att.* xiii, 23, 3: B355
	24	*Att.* xiii, 24, 1: B104, B246
	26	*Att.* xiii, 26, 1: B105
		Att. xiii, 26, 2: B106

28	*Att.* xiii, 28, 4: B107	
29	*Att.* xiii, 29, 2: B108, B247	
31	*Att.* xiii, 31, 4: B109, B110, B356, B447	
33	*Att.* xiii, 33, 1: B448	
33	*Att.* XIII, 52, 1: B119	
	Att. xiii, 52, 2: B120	
33a	*Att.* xiii, 55a, 1: B248	
34	*Att.* xiii, 34: B111	
35	*Att.* xiii, 35, 1: B449	
38	*Att.* xiii, 38, 2: B112, B357	
39	*Att.* xiii, 39, 1: B450	
40	*Att.* xiii, 40, 1: B249	
	Att. xiii, 40, 2: B250	
41	*Att.* xiii, 41, 2: B113	
42	*Att.* xiii, 42, 1: B114	
43	*Att.* xiii, 43, 3: B115	
44	*Att.* xiii, 44, 1: B451	
	Att. xiii, 44, 2: B452	
45	*Att.* xiii, 45, 3: B251	
46	*Att.* xiii, 46, 2: B116	
	Att. xiii, 46, 3: B358	
	Att. xiii, 46, 4: B117	
47	*Att.* xiii, 47: B453	
47a	*Att.* xiii, 47a, 2: B118	
48	*Att.* xiii, 48, 1: B454	
52	*Att.* xiii, 52, 1: B119	
	Att. xiii, 52, 2: B120	
XIV	1	*Att.* xiv, 1, 1: B455
		Att. xiv, 1, 2: B121
	2	*Att.* xiv, 2, 1: B122
	3	*Att.* xiv, 3, 1: B123, B456
		Att. xiv, 3, 2: B252
	4	*Att.* xiv, 4, 1: B124
	5	*Att.* xiv, 5, 2: B457
	6	*Att.* xiv, 6, 2: B125
	7	*Att.* xiv, 7, 1: B126, B253
	9	*Att.* xiv, 9, 1: B458
		Att. xiv, 9, 2: B459, B460
		Att. xiv, 9, 3: B127
	10	*Att.* xiv, 10, 1: B128, B254
		Att. xiv, 10, 2: B255
		Att. xiv, 10, 4: B129
	11	*Att.* xiv, 11, 1: B256
	12	*Att.* xiv, 12, 1: B461, B462
	13	*Att.* xiv, 13, 5: B130

14   *Att.* xiv, 14, 1: B131
      Att. xiv, 14, 3: B359

15   *Att.* xiv, 15, 1: B463
      Att. xiv, 15, 2: B132
      Att. xiv, 15, 7: B360

17   *Att.* xiv, 17, 2: B133

18   *Att.* xiv, 18, 1: B464

19   *Att.* xiv, 19, 6: B134

20   *Att.* xiv, 20, 2: B361
      Att. xiv, 20, 3: B135, B465
      Att. xiv, 20, 4: B136

21   *Att.* xiv, 21, 3: B137, B257

22   *Att.* xiv, 22, 2: B138

xv   1   *Att.* xv, 1, 1: B466
           Att. xv, 1, 2: B139
           Att. xv, 1, 5: B140

      2   *Att.* xv, 2, 3: B141

      3   *Att.* xv, 3, 2: B142

      4   *Att.* xv, 4, 2: B143
           Att. xv, 4, 5: B467

      5   *Att.* xv, 5, 1: B144, B258

      6   *Att.* xv, 6, 4: B145

      9   *Att.* xv, 9, 1: B259
           Att. xv, 9, 2: B468

      10   *Att.* xv, 10: B146, B260, B469

      11   *Att.* xv, 11, 1: B261
           Att. xv, 11, 4: B147, B470

      12   *Att.* xv, 12, 1: B148, B262
           Att. xv, 12, 2: B471

      13   *Att.* xv, 13, 2: B149
           Att. xv, 13, 3: B263, B472
           Att. xv, 13, 7: B473

      15   *Att.* xv, 15, 2: B150, B151

      17   *Att.* xv, 17, 1: B152
           Att. xv, 17, 2: B362

      18   *Att.* xv, 18, 2: B153

      19   *Att.* xv, 19, 1: B363
           Att. xv, 19, 2: B154

      20   *Att.* xv, 20, 3: B155

      21   *Att.* xv, 21, 3: B156

      22   *Att.* xv, 22: B264, B265

      25   *Att.* xv, 25: B157

      27   *Att.* xv, 27, 3: B474

      29   *Att.* xv, 29, 1: B158, B266, B475
           Att. xv, 29, 2: B159
           Att. xv, 29, 3: B267, B476

XVI	1	*Att.* xvi, 1, 1: B477
		Att. xvi, 1, 3: B160
	2	*Att.* xvi, 2, 2: B268
		Att. xvi, 2, 3: B161
		Att. xvi, 2, 4: B162
	3	*Att.* xvi, 3, 6: B163
	4	*Att.* xvi, 4, 1: B164, B478
(letter 51 =)	5	*Att.* xvi, 5, 3: B269
		Att. xvi, 5, 4: B479
	6	*Att.* xvi, 6, 2: B270
		Att. xvi, 6, 3: B271, B364
		Att. xvi, 6, 4: B365
	7	*Att.* xvi, 7, 3: B272
		Att. xvi, 7, 6: B165
		Att. xvi, 7, 7: B273
	8	*Att.* xvi, 8, 1: B166
		Att. xvi, 8, 2: B274
	9	*Att.* xvi, 9: B167, B366
	11	*Att.* xvi, 11, 1: B481
		Att. xvi, 11, 3: B168, B367
		Att. xvi, 11, 5: B480, B482
		Att. xvi, 11, 6: B275
	13	*Att.* xvi, 13, 1: B169, B483
	13a	*Att.* xvi, 13a, 1: B170
	13b	*Att.* xvi, 13b, 2: B276
	14	*Att.* xvi, 14, 2: B484
		Att. xvi, 14, 4: B171, B368
	15	*Att.* xvi, 15, 3: B485
	16	*Att.* xvi, 16, 1: B172
	16a	*Att.* xvi, 16a, 7: B369
	16c	*Att.* xvi, 16c, 10: B370

AD FAMILIARES

III	11	*Fam.* III, 11, 2: B285
		Fam. III, 11, 3: B491, B492
VII	30	*Fam.* VII, 30, 1: B375
	32	*Fam.* VII, 32, 1: B286, B287
IX	3	*Fam.* IX, 3: B288
	16	*Fam.* IX, 16, 9: B289
XI	24	*Fam.* XI, 24, 1: B493
	25	*Fam.* XI, 25, 2: B494
XIII	47	*Fam.* XIII, 47: B376

XIV   1   *Fam.* XIV, 1, 1: B290
                                Fam. XIV, 1, 4: B495
                                Fam. XIV, 1, 5: B291
                                Fam. XIV, 1, 6: B377

                           2   *Fam.* XIV, 2, 3: B187
                                Fam. XIV, 2, 4: B378

                           4   *Fam.* XIV, 4, 1: B496
                                Fam. XIV, 4, 3: B292, B293, B294, B295, B497
                                Fam. XIV, 4, 4: B188
                                Fam. XIV, 4, 5: B296, B297

(LETTER 25 =) 7   *Fam.* XIV, 7, 2: B189

(LETTER 14 =) 8   *Fam.* XIV, 8: B190, B379

                          11   *Fam.* XIV, 11: B380

(LETTER 5 =) 12   *Fam.* XIV, 12: B381

                          14   *Fam.* XIV, 14, 1: B191

                          15   *Fam.* XIV, 15: B192

                          24   *Fam.* XIV, 24: B382

XVI   1   *Fam.* XVI, 1, 3: B193, B383

(LETTER 3 =) 4   *Fam.* XVI, 4, 2: B498
                                Fam. XVI, 4, 3: B384, B385

                           5   *Fam.* XVI, 5, 1: B386
                                Fam. XVI, 5, 2: B387

                           7   *Fam.* XVI, 7: B388

                           8   *Fam.* XVI, 8, 2: B389

                           9   *Fam.* XVI, 9, 3: B194, B195
                                Fam. XVI, 9, 4: B390

                          10   *Fam.* XVI, 10, 2: B196, B391

                          11   *Fam.* XVI, 11, 3: B197

                          14   *Fam.* XVI, 14, 2: B392

                          15   *Fam.* XVI, 15, 2: B393

                          17   *Fam.* XVI, 17, 1: B198

                          18   *Fam.* XVI, 18, 1: B298, B499, B500
                                Fam. XVI, 18, 2: B299
                                Fam. XVI, 18, 3: B300, B394, B395, B396

                          19   *Fam.* XVI, 19: B397

                          20   *Fam.* XVI, 20: B398

                          21   *Fam.* XVI, 21, 8: B199

                          22   *Fam.* XVI, 22, 1: B200, B399

                          27   *Fam.* XVI, 27, 2: B400

AD QUINTUM FRATREM
I   2   *Q. Fr.* I, 2, 2 §6: B486
                                Q. Fr. I, 2, 3 §8: B173

                           3   *Q. Fr.* I, 3, 1: B277, B278, B279
                                Q. Fr. I, 3, 3: B280
                                Q. Fr. I, 3, 9: B487

II	1	*Q. Fr.* II, 1, 3: B174
	2	*Q. Fr.* II, 2, 1: B175
		Q. Fr. II, 2, 4: B176
	3	*Q. Fr.* II, 3, 5: B177
	5	*Q. Fr.* II, 5, 2: B178
		Q. Fr. II, 5, 5: B371
(LETTER 26 =) 6		*Q. Fr.* II, 6, 1: B179
		Q. Fr. II, 6, 2: B488
(LETTER 1 =) 9		*Q. Fr.* II, 9, 1: B281
		Q. Fr. II, 9, 4: B180
	14	*Q. Fr.* II, 14, 2: B282
	16	*Q. Fr.* II, 16, 5: B181
III	1	*Q. Fr.* III, 1, 5 §17: B182, B489
		Q. Fr. III, 1, 6 §24: B283
	2	*Q. Fr.* III, 2, 2: B490
		Q. Fr. III, 2, 3: B183
	4	*Q. Fr.* III, 4, 1: B284
		Q. Fr. III, 4, 2: B184
		Q. Fr. III, 4, 4: B185
	5	*Q. Fr.* III, 5, 9: B186, B372
	6	*Q. Fr.* III, 6, 6: B373
	7	*Q. Fr.* III, 7, 9: B374

❧

INDEX NOMINVM RECENTIORVM

index of modern names

Albers, James R., 746

Benedictine Institute, Ealing, London, England, 744

Benedictine Study and Arts Centre, Ealing, London, England, 744

Benning, J. D., 747

Biblioteca Medicea Laurenziana, Florence, xv–xvi (images), xlii, xlvii, 747

Burns, Peter, 747

Butler, Shane, xxiv, 745

Davis, Sally, xxvi, 745

Day, Jonathan, 747

Ealing Abbey, London, England, 747

Foster, Reginaldus Thomas, xvii–xix, xx–xxii, xxiv, xxvi, xxxvii, xxxix–xli, 190, 743, 745, 746

Gawronski, Rita, 746

Institutum Liturgicum, 743

Kalvesmaki, Joel, 747

Krieger, Barbara, 746

Leachman, James G., 742, 747
Liturgy Institute London, 743
Lynch, Teresa, 747
McCarthy, Daniel Patrick, xix, xxii, xli
McCarthy, Eleanor, 746
McCarthy, Michael, 746
McKillip, Rita J., 746
Milwaukee, Wisconsin, 743, 746
Olathe, Kansas, 746
Parish of St. Rita, West Allis, Wisconsin, 746
Pontifical Institute of Liturgy, Rome, 743
Pooley, Laura, 747
St. Benedict's Abbey, Atchison, Kansas, 747, 746
St. Michael's Abbey Press, Farnborough, England
Salvi, Antonio, xix, xxii
Shipperlee, Martin, 746
The Tablet, 743
Taylor, Dominic, 746
Teresianum, Rome, xl, 746
Vowles, Daniel, 653, 662, 744, 747
Walker, Theresa
Zabler, Charlie, 746

DE SCRIPTORIBVS

about the authors

FR. REGINALDUS THOMAS FOSTER OCD is a Discalced Carmelite priest from Milwaukee, Wisconsin. For forty years a papal Latinist and professor of the Latin language, he is renowned for his unique pedagogical method and presentation of the living Latin language. His long experience of the Latin language and dedication to teaching have made his clear presentation of Latin the standard method of teaching the language directly and without jargon or confusing terminology. In 2010 the University of Notre Dame in Indiana recognized *Reginaldus Legum Doctor honoris causa* for his contribution to the field of Latin studies. Reginald continues to teach Latin for free in Milwaukee throughout the year and during summer school every June and July.

FR. DANIEL PATRICK MCCARTHY OSB is a monk of St. Benedict's Abbey, Atchison, Kansas. His study of the Latin language, concurrent with his doctoral study of liturgy in Rome, led to his collaboration as assistant and eventual colleague of Reginald. With Dom James Leachman he is cofounder of the project *Appreciating the Liturgy* and of the teaching and research *Institutum Liturgicum*, London, England, where he teaches the Latin language and liturgy; they serve as editors of the publication project *Documenta rerum ecclesiasticarum instaurata*, which includes the series *Liturgiam Aestimare: Appreciating the Liturgy*. His publications are on teaching the Latin language, *Ossa Latinitatis Sola*; church architecture, *Come into the Light*; analysis of Latin liturgical texts and rites, *Appreciating the Collect*; *Transition in the Easter Vigil*; *Listen to the Word*; and hundreds of commentaries on liturgical prayers in *The Tablet* of London, England, 2006–2011. He serves as a guest professor of the Katholieke Universiteit, Leuven, Belgium, and on the editorial board of *Questions Liturgiques/Studies in Liturgy*. He is a lecturer on the faculty of the Pontifical Institute of Liturgy, Rome, where he offers courses on Latin liturgical prayers, liturgical ritual, art, and architecture. There he also teaches Latin to translators of Latin liturgical texts for the Congregation for Divine Worship and the Discipline of the Sacraments, at whose request he also served as an advisor to the *Vox clara* committee.

ADIVTORES

helpers

DANIEL VOWLES has been using a draft edition of the first volume in this series, *Ossa Latinitatis Sola: The Mere Bones of Latin*, to teach the First and Third Experiences during the *Experientiae Latinitatis aestivae*, "Latin Summer Experiences" 2009–2018 and during academic terms 2011–2019 at the Benedictine Study and Arts Centre, now the Benedictine Institute, Ealing, London. Thereafter Daniel began teaching the *Reading Cicero* course using the materials from a draft of this volume. Because of a thorough knowledge and experience teaching from this material, Daniel provided the extensive cross-references for this volume. It is hoped that this careful and patient notation will provide quick and easy access for teachers and students to the Latin expression of Cicero.

ANTONIUS SALVI: in pago quodam a. d. IV Kal. Oct. anno MCMXL natus sum qui inde ab antiquorum Romanorum temporibus *Vicus ad Aquas* vocatur (in ipso enim calidae scatent aquae) prope Asculum Picena in regione. Puer Ordinem Fratrum Minorum Capuccinorum sum igressus, in quo sueta curricula persolvi. Anno MCMLXVI presbyterali ordinatione recepta, Romae apud Urbanianum Institutum theologicae disciplinae dedi operam ac posthac in Studiorum Universitate Maceratensi humanioribus litteris me impendi ibique lauream sum assecutus. Anno MCMLXXXV apud Secretariam Status Latina documenta tractare coepi et Litterarum Latinarum anno MMVII Officio moderari. Anno MMVIII sum destinatus Praeses Operis Fundati *Latinitas*, quod, me antistite, anno MMXII miserrime est extinctum. Eius loco Academia *Latinitas* constituta est, cuius ego quoque ipse sum factus sodalis. De inscriptionibus mediaevalibus tria scripsi volumina et quaedam alia id genus breviora.

SALLY DAVIS has degrees in Latin and Pedagogy from Bryn Mawr College, the University of Alaska, and Catholic University of America. She spent her career teaching Latin in the Arlington Virginia Public Schools and teaching aspiring Latin teachers at the University of Virginia. She served as writer and consultant for the National Latin Exam, the College Board Advanced

Placement Exam, and the ACTFL/ACL committee on National Standards for the Teaching of Latin. She also served as President of the Washington Classical Society and the Classical Association of Virginia. During her teaching career, she was awarded the APA Award for Excellence in Teaching at the Pre-collegiate Level and the ACL Merita Award. Her publications include: *Cicero's Somnium Scipionis* (1989 with Gil Lawall); *Latin in American Schools* (1991); *Review for the Intermediate Latin Student* (1995); and numerous articles on Latin pedagogy. Her most exciting educational experience was the time she spent *really* learning Latin under Reginald Foster.

SHANE BUTLER is Nancy H. and Robert E. Hall Professor in the Humanities and Professor and Chair of Classics at Johns Hopkins University. He is the author of *The Hand of Cicero* (2002), *The Matter of the Page: Essays in Search of Ancient and Medieval Authors* (2011), and *The Ancient Phonograph* (2015), as well as the editor or coeditor of *Synaesthesia and the Ancient Senses* (2013), *Deep Classics: Rethinking Classical Reception* (2016), and *Sound and the Ancient Senses* (2019). He is also the ongoing editor and translator of the Latin letters of Angelo Poliziano (vol. 1, 2006) for the I Tatti Renaissance Library, a series he has long served as associate editor. Back in 1991, as an undergraduate abroad in Rome, he stumbled upon Reginald Foster's summer Latin experience. And the rest is ancient history.

We the authors and helpers trust that this volume will prove to be a perennial reference point and source of inspiration for those who come to appreciate the Latin language and its many authors and wish to share that inspiration and appreciation with as many people as possible.

AGNOSCENDA MERITA

acknowledgments

The fifty-fourth anniversary of Reginald's presbyteral ordination at the Teresianum in Rome on 17 April 1966, provides on this day as I write the cause of celebration and the opportunity for expressing our gratitude to so many who have contributed to this volume, which could not have been realized without our reliance upon the generosity and hospitality of others.

We the authors are grateful to the Drs. Michael and Eleanor McCarthy, of Olathe, Kansas, especially for their familial hospitality but also for their help in communicating these ideas more widely by providing constant support and technical assistance in managing numerous web pages. These include:

> www.thelatinlanguage.org
> www.liturgyinstitute.org
> www.benedictine-institute.org
> www.londonspring.org
> www.architectureforliturgy.com
> www.liturgyhome.org
> www.danielmccarthyosb.com

We wish to thank Rita J. McKillip, OCDS, a Secular Discalced Carmelite of Milwaukee, Wisconsin, who helped to facilitate communication between us by printing, scanning and delivering texts, both in person and electronically across the globe, so we could continually and collaboratively work on this project as needed throughout the years.

For providing lodging, a quiet study in the rectory, and warm hospitality, we are grateful to the Parish of St. Rita, West Allis, Wisconsin; and to their pastor, Fr. Charlie Zabler; Pastoral Associate, Barbara Krieger; and Office Manager, Rita Gawronski.

For the monastic leisure and the resources necessary to bring this project to completion, we are grateful to Abbot James R. Albers, OSB, and the monks of St. Benedict's Abbey, Atchison, Kansas. To Abbot Martin Shipperlee, OSB and to his successor Abbot Dominic Taylor, OSB elected on this day as we write this expression of gratitude to them along with the monks of Ealing Abbey, London, England for their hospitality and encouragement, including that of Fr. James Leachman OSB, director of the Benedictine Institute, where we and our colleagues Daniel Vowles and Laura Pooley and Jonathan Day have taught from the preliminary notes to this volume. We are grateful for our students' enthusiasm for reading the letters of Cicero, which inspired our progress and improved this contribution.

In keeping with the tradition established in the *Ossa* volume, for which the Vatican calligrapher wrote out the dedication and provided its image, we are grateful to Fr. Peter Burns OSB also of Ealing Abbey for the image of the dedication of this volume beautifully written in his own hand. Our continuity with scribes of the ninth and fourteenth centuries is further enhanced by the reproductions of their manuscripts now housed in the Biblioteca Medicea Laurenziana, Florence, whose generosity in providing the images which enrich this volume was matched by the technical ability and artistic vision of J.D. Benning, Director of Communications at St. Benedict's Abbey, Atchison, Kansas, whose work is featured on the web-site www.benninggraphics.com. He collaborated closely with Teresa Lynch, Marketing Intern, also at St. Benedict's Abbey, whose technical skill and dedication brought to fruition this presentation of the manuscript words of Cicero copied perhaps by interns and communication officers at abbeys centuries ago.

We admire the professional dedication to the preparation of this volume provided by Catholic University of America Press in the persons of its Director, Trevor Lipscombe, Managing Editor Theresa Walker, and associates proof-reader Kerri Cox Sullivan and book designer Anne Kachergis. We end this volume with a special mention and sympathy for the copyists, but the "Scribe Happily" finishing will have the last words.

～

ATQUI "moriamur..."

—inquimus auctores ipsi nos—si quam laudis cuiusdam commilitonis etiam particulam dempserimus, si quo merita illius cantu minore praeteriverimus, si quis rerum Latinarum studiosus hunc sodalem negligere ausus erit

IOELEM DOUGLASS KALVESMAKI

artis magistrum et librorum perfectorem linguarum peritissimum sua-vissimumque moribus quippe qui mirum quantum subtilitatis illustra-tionis emendationis ex suae Latinitatis sapientiae acuminis thesauris iam nostris paginulis et paragraphis affatim contulerit, quapropter eius prae-sidiis nitentes atque consiliis nitentes quem pio atque memore animo hic potissimum commemoraverimus dum valetudinis ei firmitatem et domus alacritatem augurati sumus precati prosperitatem inceptorum diesque beatissimas - agite ideo!—

"...et in media arma ruamus."   (VERGILIUS, *Aeneis* II, 353)

BUT "may we die..."

—so say we the authors ourselves—if we will have omitted even any bit of praise of a certain buddy-in-arms, if we will have passed over his merits by any lesser song, if any scholar of Latin things will have dared to ignore this companion

JOEL DOUGLASS KALVESMAKI

master of art and perfecter of books, language expert and most gentle in character inasmuch as who has abundantly contributed a marvelous amount of subtlety illumination correction from the treasures of his Latini-tity wisdom acumen indeed to these our simple pages and paragraphs, for which reason, pushing ahead with his assistance and shining forth with the counsels of him, whom we will have mentioned with a dutiful and mindful spirit here most especially, while we have foretold for him strength of health and happiness of home, having prayed for the prosperity of his undertak-ings and most blessed days of life—come on therefore!—

"...and let us charge into the midst of battle."

EXPLICIT VOLVMEN ALTERVM

FELICITER Scriba